Italy Reborn

MARK GILBERT

Italy Reborn

From Fascism to Democracy

W. W. NORTON & COMPANY

Independent Publishers Since 1923

First published in 2024 in Great Britain by Allen Lane.

Copyright © 2024 by Mark Gilbert

For information about permission to reproduce selections from this book, write to
Permissions, W. W. Norton & Company, Inc., 500 Fifth Avenue, New York, NY 10110

For information about special discounts for bulk purchases, please contact
W. W. Norton Special Sales at specialsales@wwnorton.com or 800-233-4830

Manufacturing by Lakeside Book Company

ISBN 978-0-393-86708-4

W. W. Norton & Company, Inc., 500 Fifth Avenue, New York, N.Y. 10110
www.wwnorton.com

W. W. Norton & Company Ltd., 15 Carlisle Street, London W1D 3BS

10 9 8 7 6 5 4 3 2 1

Ai miei amici italiani,
che tanto mi hanno dato

Contents

List of Maps and Illustrations

Photographic acknowledgements are given in parentheses.

Acknowledgements

This book is dedicated to my Italian friends – I am not going to list them, there would be too many. I have lived in Italy for many years now, and even though I've never become an Italian citizen (for reasons I don't quite understand myself), I have never regretted moving to Italy, learning the language, seeing the world through an Italian lens. In large part, this is due to the friends I have made. Italians have a gift for friendship, and it is one I treasure.

Some of my friends are also fellow historians: over the years Lucia Bonfreschi, Gustavo Corni, Mario Del Pero, Rosario Forlenza, Andrea Guiso, Daniele Pasquinucci have all discussed their ideas with me in seminar rooms, conferences, and, more important, informally over lunch or dinner. While writing this book I interviewed and befriended Elena Aga Rossi, whose uncompromising scholarship has been a major influence on me. My post at SAIS Europe, the Bologna Centre of the Johns Hopkins University, has meant that I have had the privilege of working with David Ellwood, Justin Frosini, John Harper, Gianfranco Pasquino, and Vera Negri Zamagni: five of the most knowledgeable scholars of contemporary Italy you can imagine. I have been associate editor of the *Journal of Modern Italian Studies* since 2015; its editor, John Davis, took an early interest in this project and has given me much good advice throughout my career.

Over the years, some of my students have become friends. One of them, Tommaso Milani, took time off from his highly original work on the concept of planning in interwar Europe to read this book in manuscript. He did so with remarkable speed and saved me from some mostly minor, but still embarrassing, inaccuracies, as well as making several useful interpretative suggestions. My research assistants, Irene Quadrelli and Sophia Schmidt, were terrific. Irene found rare pamphlets, created online databases, and, supremely organized herself, very nearly organized me. Sophia stayed calm throughout the production process (I didn't) and was a highly creative problem-solver.

This book was mostly researched during the pandemic, which made the usual process of visiting libraries and archives more complicated, although in Italy public services performed miracles and libraries stayed open in all but the worst months. Enrico Pontieri, a historian himself and a librarian at the Istituto Gramsci in Bologna, was exceptionally encouraging, as were the staff of the Istituto Luigi Sturzo in Rome, the Istituto storico toscano per la resistenza in Florence, the Istituto Ferruccio Parri in Bologna, the Museo Storico and Biblioteca Comunale in Trento, and the Istituto Gramsci in Rome. SAIS's own librarians, especially Gail Martin and Ludovica Barozzi, were friendly and helpful: they always are.

Marco Odorizzi, the president of the Fondazione Alcide De Gasperi in Trento, could not have been more supportive. I particularly wish to thank him for explaining the circumstances of De Gasperi's death and the construction of the monument to De Gasperi. Caterina Tomasi of the Museo Storico in Trento pointed me to several of the photographs that illustrate this volume.

My agent, Zoe Pagnamenta, advised me with skill and sympathy. I was fortunate to be edited by Stuart Proffitt, whose courtesy and interest in this project were inspirational. I shall long remember the final edit of the manuscript. It was a three-hour Zoom masterclass. Alane Mason of W.W. Norton showed great interest in the project from its outset and made several stimulating suggestions.

As always, my thanks go to my mother and father, who were young adults when Alcide De Gasperi died, and to Luciana and Francisco, who put up with me when I was immersed in the 1940s. I can be maddeningly detached from everyday life when I am writing a book, but if I am not engrossed in my material, then the reader will not be. Or so I think.

List of Abbreviations

ACC	Allied Control Commission
ADN	Alleanza Democratica Nazionale (National Democratic Alliance)
AMG	Allied Military Government
APC	Archivio Partito Comunista (Communist Party Archive)
ASAR	Associazione Studi Autonomistici Regionali (Association of Regional Autonomist Studies)
BNL	Blocco Nazionale della Libertà (National Freedom Bloc)
CGIL	Confederazione Generale Italiana del Lavoro (Italian General Confederation of Labour)
CISL	Confederazione Italiana Sindacati Lavoratori (Italian Confederation of Unionized Workers)
CLN	Comitato di Liberazione Nazionale (Committee for National Liberation)
CLNAI	Comitato di Liberazione Nazionale Alta Italia (Committee for National Liberation Upper Italy)
CVL	Corpo Volontari della Libertà (Volunteer Freedom Corps)
DC	Democrazia Cristiana (Christian Democracy)
DL	Democrazia e Lavoro (Democracy and Labour)
ECA	Economic Cooperation Administration
ECSC	European Coal and Steel Community
EDC	European Defence Community
EEC	European Economic Community
EPU	European Payments Union
ERP	European Recovery Plan

EU	European Union
FdI	Fratelli d'Italia (Brothers of Italy)
FDP	Fronte Democratico Popolare (Italian Democratic Front)
FRUS	Foreign Relations of the United States.
FUCI	Federazione Universitaria Cattolica Italiana (Italian Catholic University Federation)
GAP	Gruppo di Azione Patriottica (Patriotic Action Group)
GDP	Gross Domestic Product
GDR	German Democratic Republic
GL	Giustizia e Libertà (Justice and Liberty)
ILS	Istituto Luigi Sturzo (Luigi Sturzo Institute)
IMI	Internati Militari Italiani (Italian Military Internees)
KŠC	Komunistická strana Československa (Czechoslovakian Communist Party)
MRD	Movimento Repubblicano Democratico (Democratic Republican Movement)
MSI	Movimento Sociale Italiano (Italian Social Movement)
NATO	North Atlantic Treaty Organization
NSC	National Security Council
OEEC	Organization for European Economic Cooperation
OSS	Office for Strategic Services
PCdI	Partito Comunista d'Italia (Communist Party of Italy)
PCI	Partito Comunista Italiano (Italian Communist Party)
PdA	Partito d'Azione (Action Party)
PFR	Partito Fascista Repubblicano (Republican Fascist Party)
PLI	Partito Liberale Italiano (Italian Liberal Party)
PNF	Partito Nazionale Fascista (National Fascist Party)
PNM	Partito Nazionale Monarchista (National Monarchist Party)
PPI	Partito Popolare Italiano (Italian Popular Party)
PRI	Partito Repubblicano Italiano (Italian Republican Party)
PSDI	Partito Socialista Democratico Italiano (Italian Democratic Socialist Party)
PSI	Partito Socialista Italiano (Italian Socialist Party)

PSIUP	Partito Socialista Italiano di Unità Proletaria (Italian Socialist Party of Proletarian Unity)
PSLI	Partito Socialista dei Lavoratori Italiani (Italian Socialist Workers' Party)
PSU	Partito Socialista Unitario (Unitary Socialist Party)
RSI	Repubblica Sociale Italiana (Italian Social Republic)
RSS	Regione a Statuto Speciale (Special Statute Region)
UDI	Unione Donne Italiane (Italian Women's Union)
UDN	Unione Democratica Nazionale (National Democratic Union)
UNRRA	United Nations Relief and Rehabilitation Administration
UP	Unità Popolare (Popular Unity)
UQ	Uomo Qualunque (The Common Man)
USI	Unione Socialista Indipendente (Independent Socialist Union)

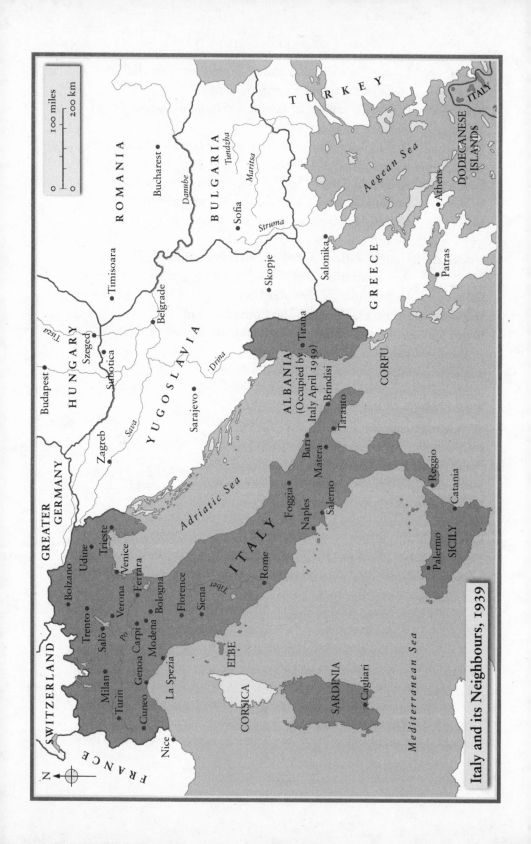

Italy and its Neighbours, 1939

Introduction

In the English-speaking world, Italy's democracy does not have a good reputation. It is associated with corruption, governments that rise and fall with disconcerting ease, and periods of turbulence caused by ideological passion or populism. Italians are considered to have a weakness for mountebanks such as Benito Mussolini or Silvio Berlusconi, and, perhaps, a lingering desire for a strongman's rule in the place of democracy. While this book was being completed, the British and American media had an anxiety attack about the election of a right-wing nationalist party, the 'Brothers of Italy' (FdI), to power in Rome. Its leader, Giorgia Meloni, a woman who few people outside Italy would have recognized until recently, was suddenly on the front pages of the world's newspapers, and commentators worried that her victory represented 'a breakthrough for Europe's hard right'.[1]

Italian democracy has survived graver challenges than Giorgia Meloni. In the 1970s, it overcame a decade of domestic terrorism, which culminated in the spring of 1978 with the kidnapping and murder by 'Red Brigade' terrorists of Aldo Moro, a five-time prime minister who was the éminence grise of the ruling Christian Democracy Party (DC) and an advocate of power-sharing with the principal opposition party, the Italian Communist Party (PCI). In the early 1990s, Italian democracy survived corruption scandals on a grand scale. Thousands of elected officials were investigated and eventually condemned, though most plea-bargained their way out of time behind bars. Christian Democracy's long hold over the political system was broken, and all the political parties were tainted by scandal and swept away. The so-called First Republic had come to an end.[2]

Since the eleventh post-war legislature began in June 1992, the

Italian republic has survived thirteen different prime ministers heading twenty administrations that have been characterized by disconcerting levels of acrimony, scandal, and social tension. The symbol of these tensions was the ineffable Silvio Berlusconi, who stepped down as prime minister in November 2011 when it became clear that his continuance in office might create a run on Italian government debt. He was replaced by Mario Monti, an academic who had been a senior figure in the European Commission. It was the third occasion since 1992 that Italy had had to resort to 'technocratic' government: that is to say, governments of non-party experts formed because the principal political parties of the moment were unable or unwilling to agree on painful reforms. This book was mostly written during the premiership of a *fourth* such technocrat, Mario Draghi, a former central banker, who took office in February 2021 and governed until Meloni's victory in the general election of September 2022.

What have the travails of Italy's democracy in the last forty years got to do with a book about Italy's transition from 'Fascism to Democracy' in the 1940s and the first half of the 1950s? The answer is that they have everything to do with it. The house of Italy's democracy must and would have crumbled during the upheaval of the past three decades, had it not been built on solid foundations. Although nobody can dispute that Italy's society, politics, and culture have been turbulent, its institutions have remained largely the same since 1948. The choices that post-war premier Alcide De Gasperi made in the sphere of foreign policy – Atlanticism and Europeanism – remain crucial for Italy's geopolitical strategy today, while the values of the post-war constitution command assent across the political spectrum. It goes against ingrained habits of thought to regard Italy as being, along with West Germany, the most striking example of a successful transition to democracy during the so-called second wave of democratization after 1945, but I believe that is how we should think about it.

Since 1994, Italy's political parties have tried no fewer than three times to amend the constitutional framework established between June 1946, when Italians elected a Constituent Assembly, and January 1948, when the text negotiated and approved by the Assembly came into force. Yet none of these attempted reforms dared to touch the twelve 'fundamental principles' upon which the constitution is based, or to amend the rest of the first half of the document, which deals with the 'rights and duties of the citizen'. Would-be reformers concentrated rather on reforming the 'institutional framework' that comprises the constitution's larger second half. This has led to some tinkering: regional governments were given more powers in 2001, and in September 2020 a national referendum ratified an amendment that reduced the number of elected representatives in the Chamber of Deputies and the Senate. On the other hand, two substantial reorganizations of the constitution's second half, in 2006 by a centre-right government headed by Berlusconi, and in 2016, by a centre-left coalition, were rejected at the polls, in both cases by approximately 60 per cent of those who voted.

This book had its genesis during the 2016 referendum campaign. The referendum debate illustrated that millions of Italians were profoundly concerned about the organization and purpose of their state. It was a vibrant exercise in civic patriotism, and although both sides were convinced that their opponents were fools and knaves, beneath the surface acrimony there was mutual respect for the contending views. Italians were aware that their nation was stagnant and in decline; they had to decide whether their circumstances merited overhauling the institutional structure put in place by the Republic's founding fathers. They decided not to, by an unambiguous majority, but they thought about it hard. It was an impressive example of democratic maturity. One, moreover, that suggested that to grasp fully the complexities of Italy's present and future, one simply had to go back to the origins of its democracy and study the republic constructed after the fall of Fascism.

So I did, and this book is the outcome. Its argument, put simply, is that the resilience of Italian democracy was forged by the completeness of Fascism's failure and by the democratic culture that was painstakingly acquired after 1945. Italy sank into an abyss of moral, military, and political humiliation between 1940 and 1945, but experienced a democratic apotheosis in the following ten years. Its democratic miracle preceded the better-known economic miracle; indeed, the country's economic transformation in the late 1950s and 1960s simply would not have been possible had democratic transition not already taken place.

The use of the word 'miracle' might seem to suggest that Italy was the beneficiary of divine providence, or certainly much good luck. Good luck was certainly necessary. Italy's post-war leaders faced the task of rebuilding a war-torn nation that was as divided, geographically, politically, and ideologically, as any nation of its size could be. Many Italians longed for a socialist millennium; others wanted a crackdown on modern ideas. Some looked to the United States for assistance, millions of others gave their allegiance to Moscow and regarded the Soviet Union – or their idealized conception of Soviet life – as a model to be implemented in Italy. Families and villages were split on doctrinal grounds: everybody, even the unlettered, knew which political party he or she supported. Almost all Italians had become nominally anti-fascist, though millions harboured a guilty conscience about their zeal on behalf of the fascist cause in the previous two decades.

The causes of division were not only ideological. In 1945, Italy was bankrupt, its money was worthless, many of its people were jobless or wastefully employed, and illiteracy and malnutrition were rife. Italy's reputation in the international arena was nil. Although Italians depicted themselves as the first victims of Fascism, and many had redeemed themselves by fighting a partisan war against the German invaders, the victims of Mussolini's wars of aggression regarded the Italians as Nazi collaborators. Mussolini had been hailed by too many 'oceanic crowds' for the rest of Europe to regard the Italian people as anything other than mostly complicit in his crimes. Italy was a pauper utterly lacking in political credit.

Yet by December 1955, when Italy was admitted to the United Nations, the nation had contested three acrimonious but peaceful general elections in 1946, 1948, and 1953, had joined NATO as a founder member, was a founder of the Council of Europe and the European Coal and Steel Community, had a flourishing press, was enjoying a cultural and intellectual renaissance in film, literature, and the visual arts, could boast a rising standard of living, and was taking its first, tentative steps towards modernity in social mores and towards greater opportunity – if not yet equality – for the rural poor, for women, and for the industrial working class. Italy had become a genuine democracy, albeit one where hundreds of thousands mourned the demise in March 1953 of Joseph Stalin.

Italy, in short, provides an instructive case study in how democracies are born. Two Harvard professors warned recently that democracies die if their politicians break the unwritten rules of the game. If our elected officials don't display respect for their adversaries' rights and tolerance of their views, and if they abuse the powers of the state to rig politics in their favour, then democracies can degenerate into demagoguery and hence to disarray. This is another way of saying that the moral fibre, restraint and good sense of the political elites is the key variable for a healthy democracy. Democracy needs good leaders, in both senses of the word good: they need to be both principled and competent. Otherwise, breakdown can be close around the corner.[3]

When one studies the birth of Italian democracy in detail, one sees that it, too, owed a great deal to the virtues of forbearance towards adversaries and the willingness to respect both written and unwritten rules. Italy's leaders were conscious that they were rebuilding their nation and deciding its future. Alcide De Gasperi, the leader of Christian Democracy, a political party of Catholic inspiration that emerged as the largest popular force in the country after May 1945, knew full well that Palmiro Togliatti, the leader of the PCI, and Pietro Nenni, the pro-Moscow leader of the Socialist Party (PSI), represented constituencies with real power, notably among the industrial workers. They, in their turn, recognized that De Gasperi represented a 'social bloc' among the peasants and the urban middle class. If they were not to plunge their country back into the violence and class conflict that had encouraged the rise of Fascism after the First World War, Italy's politicians understood that they had to establish a *modus vivendi* that all the principal forces could adhere to. By and large, despite frequent deviations that caused considerable tension, they did.

This is not to suggest that Italy was a model of consensus. An exiled Hungarian humourist, George Mikes, once quipped that post-war British politics was 'a huge and non-compromising fight between compromising Conservatives and compromising Socialists'.[4] Nobody would have made the same remark about Italian politics. De Gasperi would never have trusted Togliatti with power, in the way that Winston Churchill trusted, sometimes grudgingly, Labour Prime Minister Clement Attlee. The wider narrative of the emerging Cold War introduced, moreover, many twists to the domestic plot. The Marshall Plan, the construction of NATO, the Show Trials in the 'People's Democracies' of Central and Eastern Europe, all spilled over into Italian politics and caused moments of high drama and great peril: they could not have done otherwise, given the nature of the contest being played out in Italy itself.

This book, in short, depicts a people making a qualitative leap in their form of social and political organization. There were elements of continuity from the fascist state to the democratic one, and many hold-overs from the fascist period who made a successful career in Italy's democracy. Nevertheless, to borrow Norberto Bobbio's pointed meta-phor, such individuals were mostly 'corks' able to stay afloat because they weighed almost nothing.[5] Overall, the scales of continuity and change tipped towards change. The political culture of Italy in the mid-1950s was unrecognizably different from that of the nation that sided with Hitler in June 1940. In between there was war, invasion, civil war, deportations, the entry into politics, for the first time, of the masses as an active force, a new constitutional order, and the ceaseless toil of a political class that had survived Fascism to remake the nation's political order.

The book that follows is a two-part drama. Part One deals with the downfall of Fascism, resistance to German occupation, and the birth of the Republic in June 1946. It concludes with the terms of the Peace Treaty with the Allies. Part Two is concerned with the consolidation of Italian democracy. It begins with the extraordinary events of the 'hinge year' of 1947, which concluded with the elaboration of the constitution. It proceeds to the landmark elections of April 1948 which were won, after one of the most hard-fought contests in modern European history, by Christian Democracy. The book then turns to the impact of the Cold War on Italy's democracy, and to the efforts of De Gasperi's several governments to fulfil the constitution's generous promises of social justice.

For most of the post-war years, as one perceptive scholar recently noted, De Gasperi's governments were essentially judged by their unavoidable failure to deliver on the utopian aspirations of the left-wing parties that led the struggle against Fascism, rather than by their concrete achievements. Post-war Italy's prevailing intellectual culture – certainly in the historical and social sciences, and in the literary world – was dominated by writers who were progressive in their political sympathies, or by members of the PCI. De Gasperi's 'centrism' was accordingly 'long judged by the defeated, by those who endured it and paid the consequences of it', not by its record in overcoming the immense difficulties of post-war reconstruction or in introducing socially beneficial reforms.[6]

By this standard, this book is a revisionist work, although I hope it is not a polemical one: certainly, I have worked hard to avoid making it so. It paints a positive picture of De Gasperi. He was, I think, every bit the equal of his close German friend and Christian Democratic counterpart Konrad Adenauer. Like Adenauer, he shepherded a defeated, reviled country into the political mainstream of the West, and into Europe. He did so even though he had two large, pro-Moscow parties, one of them well-financed and organized, striving to undermine him most of the time (though not *all* the time, and he and his party owed much to the moderation and genuine patriotism of the left at certain junctures).

I say he: of course, De Gasperi was not the only architect of Italy's passage to democracy, nor does it make sense to think that any one individual could have been. Still, he deserves a larger role than he has generally been accorded in the history of our times. As Richard J. Samuels – a political scientist with an unusual grasp of the importance of agency in human affairs – has written, De Gasperi 'recombined shards of the past into a novel, functional and resilient present'.[7] Like his Japanese counterpart, Yoshida Shigeru, De Gasperi was an 'exemplary bricoleur'.

The metaphor of recomposing shards is a good one. The vase of Italian politics seemed broken beyond repair in 1945 and the Italian masses, by themselves, would not and could not have put it back together again, still less have made it more serviceable than before. There were no inexorable forces propelling Italy in the direction of democracy, nor towards participation in the institutions of European cooperation, which required Italy to implement free-trading rules that ran contrary to the protectionism of pre-fascist Italy and the autarchy imposed by Fascism. Nor would the masses have chosen spontaneously to side with the United States in the Cold War. There were powerful forces in Italy, and even within Christian Democracy, that would have preferred Cold War neutrality: if there was one thing that united Italians of all political stripes after the catastrophe of the Second World War, it was opposition to war.

The Italian masses wanted better lives, greater dignity, work, land. They had had enough of being neglected or manipulated. (The savagery shown by the crowds in Milan's Piazzale Loreto on 29 April 1945, when they desecrated the corpses of Mussolini, his mistress, and leading Fascists, was the rage of a people who knew they had been duped.) The question was which political movement would best channel the surging energies that national defeat and humiliation had unleashed.

This is ultimately why Italy became a 'republic of the parties'.[8] The parties, especially the PCI and DC, were sophisticated sub-cultures that shaped minds, directed activity, and mobilized the masses on an astounding scale, especially at elections, when entire streets were papered over with vivid electoral posters and when tens of thousands of earnest, angry, elated, passionate citizens squeezed into town squares to cheer or heckle their leaders, whose dedication to their respective causes verged on the superhuman. In the June 1953 elections nearly 94 per cent of the electorate voted.

When one is faced with this level of involvement in the sphere of politics, to write political history is also to write social history (and intellectual history). It is hard to imagine what a history of post-war Italy with the politics 'left out' would look like. Such a history would deprive the Italian people of a large part of their identity. The people were not mere 'voices off' in the political struggle, nor did they appear only in crowd scenes as extras. They were the raw material of politics, the clay that enabled the vase to be recast. If the vase has never since broken irreparably, despite some very hard usage, it is because the clay is good and the craftsmanship of the original potters was outstanding.

PART ONE

Humiliation

I

Undemocratic Italy

Italy became a nation state between 1859 and 1871, but it did not become a democracy until after the Second World War. In this regard, it was hardly exceptional. We easily forget how recently democratic institutions developed in Europe. Most West European nations experimented with authoritarianism before 1939 and even those states that did not, such as Belgium, France, Great Britain, and the Netherlands, were imperial powers that ruled over hundreds of millions of Asians and Africans. Racialism – the view that some races or peoples were inherently inferior to others – was all but ubiquitous; for the most part, the working classes of Europe acquired social rights only after they had fought and died in huge numbers for their respective countries during the First World War. In most countries, women acquired partial voting rights only after 1918.

Even by the standards of its peers, however, Italy's path towards democracy was a troubled one. The central question all European nations faced in the first four decades of the twentieth century was how to integrate the masses into political life while preserving (or establishing) liberal institutions; some succeeded, but most did not. When the new century dawned, the Italian state found itself dealing with accelerating economic modernity, the spread of socialism, the politicization of Catholics, and a widespread yearning for national greatness.

Unsurprisingly, its elites struggled to cope. The First World War was the tipping point. Like a cyclist on a steep climb, Liberal Italy buckled at the knees after 1918: the strain of the conflict was too great for such sinews as it possessed. It was replaced by Fascism, a regime whose contempt for the ideals and institutions of representative democracy – its

3

'deserted temples', in Mussolini's contemptuous phrase – was accompanied by a spurious claim to represent the will of the people as a whole.

DIVIDED NATION

Italy's sheer complexity – territorial, cultural, and social – made the job of forging a nation, let alone a democracy, extremely challenging. Three main fractures divided the new nation in the 1860s. First, Italian unification strengthened one part of the peninsula relative to the rest. Second, it exacerbated relations with the Catholic Church. Third, Italian society was, like others in Europe, divided into *two* nations, the rich and the poor, between whom there was no intercourse and little sympathy.

Italy was unified politically between 1859 and 1871 by shrewd diplomacy that enabled the Kingdom of Sardinia, whose capital was the Piedmontese city of Turin, in the north-west of the peninsula, to profit from wars between Europe's great powers. Habsburg rule over Lombardy, Emilia, and Tuscany was ended by the Franco-Piedmontese victory over Austria at the battle of Solferino in June 1859 and the subsequent Peace of Villafranca. Sicily and the southern regions were brought into the new state by the exploits of Giuseppe Garibaldi, whose red-shirted volunteer army, with the assistance of the British fleet, aided a revolt in Palermo against Bourbon rule, and then invaded the mainland, entering Naples in September 1860. Piedmont's army, which had occupied the Papal States, blocked the road to Rome, so Garibaldi relinquished his conquests to King Victor Emmanuel II at the village of Teano on 26 October 1860. Victor Emmanuel was crowned king of Italy in March 1861, although, symbolically, he did not rename himself 'the first'. His allegiance was to his dynasty, the House of Savoy, not the nation. His successors were no different.

The king's new realm stretched from Ragusa in Sicily, which is on the same degree of longitude as Tunis, to the border with Switzerland and France in the Alps. The fastest way of travelling between Turin and Naples in March 1861 was by sea, while large tracts of the interior of the Mezzogiorno, or South, were simply *terra incognita* to the men who now governed the peninsula. The Piedmontese regarded the Mezzogiorno as an exotic, backward territory. The South needed, its new rulers believed, laissez-faire and a strong state, if it were to join the European mainstream. It is a refrain that one still hears today. In fairness, nationhood did bring genuine progress, and the South was by no means left out. It is instructive to compare a map of the rail network in 1861 with the more extensive one just a decade later.

Piedmont nevertheless acquired hegemony over the Italian peninsula. Its constitution became the supreme law of the land. All Victor Emmanuel's prime ministers from 1861 until his death in 1878 came from the North, except one from Tuscany.[1] The public debt that had financed Piedmont's military adventures was nationalized and paid for by higher taxation on all Italians. This transfer of power to northerners was naturally resented. A revolt in Palermo against the new regime was crushed with the loss of hundreds of lives in September 1866. Martial law was introduced across Sicily. In the mountains of the Abruzzi and Basilicata, troops suppressed resistance from so-called brigands in a manner that recalls the way in which the Scottish Highlands were 'cleared' after the battle of Culloden in 1745 (there are more parallels between British and Italian history than one might think). In both cases, forcible unification was justified, not least by historians, as a way of bringing enlightenment to backward regions and recalcitrant clans.

In 1866, Italy gained Venetia in the north-east by siding with Prussia in Bismarck's war against Austria. Its contribution to Berlin's victory was nil. Italian forces were defeated on both land and sea, but the Prussians routed the Austrians at the battle of Sadowa (July 1866), and Italy gained Verona, Vicenza, Padua and, above all, Venice, *la Serenissima*, when peace was made. In 1870, the Italian state resolved the question of Rome, where Pope Pius IX was guarded by French troops, in its favour. French forces withdrew from Rome after Napoleon III's defeat by the Prussians at the battle at Sedan (September 1870). The Pope was left defenceless. Italian troops breached Rome's city wall and marched in all but unopposed. By a gigantic margin, Romans voted in a plebiscite to join Italy, and Rome became the capital.

On 2 July 1871, when Victor Emmanuel and his retinue entered

Rome, to take residence in the Quirinale Palace, Italy's capital was a middling city of 200,000 people. The ruins of imperial Rome must have reminded the new ruler of the glory that Italy had once possessed, while the city's baroque splendours, incremented by the sculptures and buildings of Gian Lorenzo Bernini in the seventeenth century, surely seemed extravagant to a court used to the sobriety of Turin.[2] Certainly, Victor Emmanuel, who spoke French for preference and had only halting Italian, would have been able to converse with few of the subjects who lined the streets to greet him. Like the inhabitants of every other city in Italy, Romans spoke an earthy Italianate dialect of their own.

Rome was just the most prominent of the dozens of proud cities with glorious histories and distinctive cultures that had been amalgamated into the new state: Italy had 'many regional traditions, but few national ones', one British historian reminds us.[3] It would be even more accurate to say that it had a wealth of *communal* traditions (Siena and Pisa are both Tuscan, but it is unwise to equate the *Pisani* or *Senesi* with the *Fiorentini*). Italy was not Poland. It was not a land whose people's consciousness of national identity had survived intact under oppression and conquest. It was, rather, a collection of peoples whose incorporation into a single state was desirable for pragmatic reasons, but whose natural form of political organization was arguably, as a Lombard polymath and political thinker, Carlo Cattaneo, contended, some form of federalism.

Instead, after 1871 unified Italy would seek to 'make Italians' by the elaboration of a nationalist myth about the Risorgimento in history books and public artworks, through the cults of Victor Emmanuel and of Garibaldi, and by the patriotic agitation of those who believed that Italy would be *irridenta* (unredeemed) if it did not encompass Trento and Trieste, the two main cities still languishing under Austrian rule.

One institution that might have united the Italians behind the new state was the Church. Practically all Italians were Catholics. Yet the state's relations with the Vatican remained fraught long after Rome was occupied. Pius IX had fled to Naples during the revolutionary upheaval of 1849, when a republic had been created in Rome.[4] Scarred by the experience of revolution, he had recoiled from the mild liberalism of the earliest years of his reign. He refused to accept Piedmont's usurpation of authority in the former Papal States and declined to have any direct relationship with the Italian government, which nevertheless unilaterally acknowledged papal sovereignty over the Vatican and certain other religious sites in Rome. In 1868, Pius furthermore intimated to the faithful that participation in national elections was 'inexpedient'.[5]

Outright papal disapproval of political activity by Catholics would endure until the first decade of the twentieth century, when the rise of socialism persuaded Pope Pius X that Catholic engagement in politics was now desirable (the ban was officially retracted only in 1919 by Benedict XV). The Italian state was thus deprived of the moral imprimatur for its actions that, say, the Anglican Church bestowed upon Westminster and the British Crown. No priest beseeched his flock to pray for the well-being of Victor Emmanuel, or his successors Umberto I and Victor Emmanuel III, on Sunday mornings. 'Italy may have been a Catholic nation, but the leader of the Catholic Church refused to recognize it.'[6]

The third great fracture in Italian society was between the rich and the poor. In 1861, Italy was a largely agricultural economy whose GDP per head was below average European standards (it was about half of Britain's, where the industrial revolution had been under way for more than half a century, and about 80 per cent of that of Germany, Ireland, or Denmark).[7] Within Italy, differences in development between North and South were less striking than one might expect, if only because subsistence farming was everywhere the main source of economic activity. Some economic historians have estimated that the Mezzogiorno's income per head was almost identical to the North's at unification and its standard of living may even have been higher since the cost of living was probably lower.

In the first decades after unification, in fact, the biggest disparities in income came *within* regions: Campania and Apulia were more prosperous than Calabria in the South, and Lombardy was wealthier than Venetia in the North.[8] Indicators of social and economic development such as average lifespan were not notably different, though southerners were less tall on average.

In one respect, the North did have a marked advantage. Educational attainment was low everywhere in Italy, when compared to northern

Europe, but illiteracy rates in the North were much lower than in the Mezzogiorno, where only a small percentage of the population could read and write. In no fewer than twenty-two out of the South's twenty-five provinces, illiteracy rates surpassed 90 per cent in 1871.[9] This figure was gradually improved by the introduction of compulsory primary education in 1877, but education provision remained much patchier in the South than the North. In 1901, the centre-north illiteracy average had fallen to about 40 per cent, with Piedmont having the lowest level at 18 per cent and the Marche, at 62.5 per cent, doing worst. In the Mezzogiorno, Campania was the *best* performer with 65 per cent. Illiteracy in Calabria was still approximately 80 per cent. The average across the South was 70 per cent.[10]

Between the last decade of the nineteenth century and the First World War, 'economic dualism' emerged. The South thereafter grew steadily poorer relative to the North. The principal cause of this phenomenon is obvious: industrialization. The textiles industry burgeoned in Milan from the 1890s onwards, and in the early twentieth century, manufacturing attracted job seekers from the countryside, which stimulated agricultural productivity and urbanization, and helped the services sector to grow.

As the century came to an end, the slum dwellers of Naples and Palermo, and the shepherds subsisting on the barren hills of Basilicata or Calabria, sought a better life in the United States, a place that took on mythical status. Millions of Italians, mostly from south of Rome, took ship and sailed to North and South America. The numbers are overwhelming: between 1900 and 1914, 619,000 *calabresi*, 203,000 *lucani*, 332,000 *pugliesi*, 672,000 *abruzzesi*, and 991,000 *campani* left Italy. To put these numbers in perspective, the population of the continental Mezzogiorno (i.e. not counting Sicily and Sardinia, from which there was also a wave of migration) was, according to the 1911 census, 8,895,000. In two regions, Basilicata and Abruzzo-Molise, the population outright diminished between the censuses of 1901 and 1911. One historian has rightly described the first decade and a half of the twentieth century in Italy as one of 'social breakdown and mass exodus'.[11] Entire communities lost the flower of their menfolk, for often young men departed alone in the hope of being able to return to their loved ones with hard-earned cash to buy land.

Of course, very often they did not return, but made new lives in the new world.

Migration acted like the valve on a pressure cooker. In the absence of industrialization to provide rising incomes, migration enabled the social system of the Mezzogiorno to survive by reducing competition for work and for land. There was just enough of both for those who stayed behind to eke out a living. Like modern-day North Africa or Central America, and for essentially the same reasons, the principal export of Italy at the end of the nineteenth century was its people.

In northern Italy, meanwhile, greater literacy generated critical thinking, which in turn generated political pluralism. The Italian Socialist Party (PSI) emerged as a political force in the 1890s largely because by then most working people in the cities of the North could read and write.[12] The PSI at first sought to improve working conditions and higher wages by peaceful means, but its efforts were thwarted by state violence. Protests over the price of bread were suppressed with severity in Milan in 1898 with the loss of eighty lives. Thousands of demonstrators, including the PSI's leader, Filippo Turati, an elected parliamentary deputy, were arrested. Radical ideas accordingly began to prevail within the PSI. So-called 'maximalists' denounced the party's 'reformist' wing for its willingness to collaborate with the bourgeois Italian state. In 1912, a firebrand advocate of social revolution, Benito Mussolini, became editor of *Avanti!*, the PSI's newspaper.

The 'political class', to use a term invented by an Italian political thinker, Gaetano Mosca, showed few signs of understanding the intensity of the social challenges facing Italy. Parliament was elected by the well-off and well-educated and was almost entirely composed of *latifondisti* (big, usually absentee, landowners), lawyers, and university professors.[13] Many of these *notabili* cynically treated the state as an instrument for the pursuit of their private or class interests, not the improvement of the condition of the people. They also switched sides in the legislature with cynical ease (for there were no formal political parties to restrain them). Italians even have a word – *trasformismo* – to describe this practice.[14]

The political class was also obsessed with the idea of national greatness. Francesco Crispi, prime minister of Italy from 1887 to 1891, and again between 1893 and 1896, sought a colonial empire in East Africa (Eritrea, Somalia, Abyssinia), which was destined to become Italy's 'lung', where her impoverished masses could go to breathe. An ill-led Italian expeditionary force was, however, humiliated in battle by Abyssinia on 1–2 March 1896 at Adowa. The disaster brought Crispi's career to an ignominious end: he might indeed have done better to concentrate upon an 'intelligent and rational colonization' of his native Sicily, and to provide it with water, roads, sewers, and schools, rather than seek futile glory abroad.[15] Such utilitarianism would have conflicted with the spirit of the times. At the turn of the century, upper-class Italy seethed with colonial deprivation. Like Germany, Italy's intellectuals and politicians regarded their country as one that had been robbed of its rightful place in the sun. The more extreme openly longed for war, supposedly the 'world's sole form of hygiene'.[16]

Pre-1914 Italy, in short, was under-developed but over-proud. The stream of history was propelling it towards shipwreck unless good fortune and skilled leadership intervened. The most significant political figure of the time, Giovanni Giolitti (a four-time prime minister between 1892 and 1914), was a master coalition builder. He steered the country by deftly appealing to both the nationalist right and the moderate left. Under Giolitti, Italy waged colonial war in Libya in 1911–12, but also introduced reforms attractive to the moderate socialists, of which universal (male) suffrage was the most important.

The outbreak of war in August 1914 rendered Giolitti's parliamentary prowess irrelevant. Italy was in a defensive alliance with Austria and Germany, and Giolitti's first thought was to obtain territorial concessions from Austria in return for staying neutral. Vienna offered generous concessions, but Italy discovered that France and Britain would offer an even better bargain. In April 1915, the secret Treaty of London offered Italy vast territorial gains at Austrian expense. Giolittian doubters in parliament were swept aside by enthusiastic nationalists, headed by the poet and pioneer aviator Gabriele D'Annunzio, who wanted to join the war at any price. Massive pro-war demonstrations were held in Rome. Italy entered the war on the side of the Entente Cordiale against its erstwhile allies in May 1915.[17]

The First World War was a catastrophe for Italy. By the summer of 1917, eleven huge battles had been fought in the country's north-east, as Italy's generals inched towards Trieste. As on the Western Front, lions were led by donkeys. An army of ill-equipped peasants captained by idealistic young intellectuals was mown down by the troops of the Central Powers as they tried to storm well-defended positions in the Julian Alps and the Asiago Plateau. Tens of thousands perished from cold and disease. G. M. Trevelyan, a British historian serving in a hospital unit on the Italian front, remarked that 'in the war of 1915–17 the Italian staff-work and commissariat was not worthy of the courage of the "povero fante", often left for weeks at a time unrelieved in the trenches and fed on chestnuts'.[18]

At the end of October 1917, morale cracked.[19] At the battle of Caporetto, a small village in modern-day Slovenia, the line broke and the Italian army was thrown back almost to Venice. More than 30,000 Italian troops were killed, and 350,000 prisoners were taken. To this day, when some project has failed miserably, Italians say it has been 'a Caporetto'. The Caporetto disaster was followed in November 1918 by the battle of Vittorio Veneto when Italian troops turned the tables on the Central Powers and inflicted a victory of their own, but by then the damage to the national psyche had been done.

The costs of war outweighed any possible territorial gains. Approximately 650,000 Italian troops had died by Armistice Day, along with 600,000 civilians who succumbed to malnutrition or the Spanish flu, although many civilian lives were also lost to shelling. Some 3.48 per cent of Italy's pre-1914 population of 35.6 million perished during the conflict.[20] Approximately 850,000 people were made refugees. Our collective memory of the First World War is dominated by the Western Front, with the muddy fields of northern France reduced to moonscapes from artillery barrages, but the mountainsides of the Italian Front were a killing field, too.

The economic consequences were less tragic, but equally serious. Italy was bankrupted by the war. Putting an army of 5.5 million men in the field was a crippling effort for a still agricultural nation that lacked heavy industry. Public expenditure surged from 2.5 billion Italian lire in 1914 to almost 31 billion in 1918–19. Taxes were raised but did not keep pace with spending: the annual deficit, 214 million lire in 1914, had risen to 23 billion by war's end. Governments financed the conflict by borrowing from Britain and from the middle class – 30 per cent of national wealth was 'invested' in war spending between 1916 and 1918 – and by printing money. The lira accordingly devalued sharply against the pound and the dollar: between 1914 and 1923 it lost over 75 per cent of its value against both. [21] For a resource-poor nation that imported raw materials, this was a disaster since it launched an inflationary spiral which, while it never reached Weimar levels, impoverished the salaried middle class. The wages of the industrial workers, a class that had benefited from the wartime boom in manufacturing, were cut sharply in real terms.[22]

The poorest of the poor, the agricultural labourers, found themselves without work or income as their landlords slashed costs. Even before the Armistice, rebellious peasants were demanding land redistribution, and once the conflict had concluded, agricultural labourers' 'leagues', marching behind the red flag of socialism (or the Cross; Catholic workers were militant, too), occupied unutilized land on the great estates or even land that was actively being tilled.

THE MARCH ON ROME

Italy's exorbitant losses in blood and treasure during the war explain the petulance of its politicians during the 1919 Paris Peace Conference. Premier Vittorio Emanuele Orlando demanded that the Entente keep the promises made to Italy in the Treaty of London and then, when they didn't, flounced out in a huff. He was eventually recalled to the table and secured a settlement that satisfied the decades-old longing for possession of Trento and Trieste and for good measure added the Brenner frontier, and hence the incorporation of South Tyrol, most of whose population were ethnic German.[23]

There were still Italian minorities left outside the motherland, however. The town of Fiume (Rijeka) on the Dalmatian coast was not awarded to Rome. The nationalist press bayed hysterically against a 'mutilated peace'. In September 1919, Fiume was seized by a 'legion' of adventurers, including many soldiers who had deserted their regiments, led by the dandyish figure of D'Annunzio, *Il Vate* ('The Bard'), as he grandiosely styled himself. The town was occupied by this dissolute band of freebooters until the so-called bloody Christmas of 1920, when Italian troops enforced the Treaty of Rapallo, which had assigned the town to Yugoslavia. D'Annunzio surrendered Fiume on 31 December 1920.[24]

The First World War and the 'mutilated peace' that followed broke the political system that had governed the Kingdom of Italy since 1861. The traditional elites lost authority over society. New political forces rose to supplant them. Under the leadership of an independent-minded Sicilian priest, Luigi Sturzo, Catholics entered mass politics by forming the Popular Party (PPI), an avowedly non-confessional movement, though its symbol, the *scudo crociato* (a shield with a superimposed Cross), gave voters a clue. The PPI's advocacy of greater social equality, but without the abolition of private property as the PSI promised, won adherents, especially among peasants.[25] In the November 1919 general elections, for which a complex form of proportional representation was adopted, the PPI took 20.5 per cent of the votes and 100 deputies in the fragmented parliament.

Don Luigi Sturzo in 1919.
The 'priest from Caltagirone' made Catholicism a mass political force.

The clear winners of the 1919 elections, however, were the PSI, which obtained 32 per cent and over 150 deputies, three times as many as in 1913.[26] Nearly two million votes were cast for the PSI, whose party programme was unapologetic for the party's neutralism during the war.[27] *L'Unità*, a political weekly edited by the historian Gaetano Salvemini, made no bones about the significance of the election:

> The general election of 16 November tells us that we just can't go on as we have done so far; it tells us that the political class, which waged war badly and is making a mess of the peace, has been condemned by the country as unfit to govern.[28]

In November 1919 the PSI felt itself to be on the cusp of power. *Avanti!* warned comrades that they now had to win over 'individualistic' workers who were 'unconscious enemies' of the working class. Workers and peasants enrolled in so-called 'white' (i.e. Catholic) cooperatives, and abstainers at the polls (only 56 per cent of those entitled to vote had cast a ballot) had to be brought into the fold.[29] Despite the PSI's electoral success, the years 1919–20, the so-called *biennio rosso*, were dominated by bloody confrontations between protesters and the police.

The PSI was split over how to use its new-found centrality in politics. Many of its key figures, notably the party's founder Filippo Turati, favoured cooperation with Giolitti and the more enlightened members of the old regime. Another faction, dazzled by the genius of Lenin and the triumph of the Bolshevik Revolution, advocated moulding the masses into an *Ordine nuovo* (New Order), to evoke the title of a Turin journal of culture and politics.

The founding editor of *L'Ordine nuovo* was a hunchbacked Sardinian, barely out of university, called Antonio Gramsci. In June 1919, an ecstatic Gramsci wrote that the 'Russian Revolution has so far overcome all the obstacles posed for it by history'. Russia was led by 'an aristocracy of statesmen that no other nation possesses; a couple of thousand men who have dedicated their lives to the study of the political and economic sciences', who during their years in exile from their homeland had 'acquired a precise and exact awareness of their task, an awareness as cold and sharp as the swords of the conquerors of empires'. The achievement of this intellectual aristocracy was to have galvanized the 'immense Russian people', which had been cast into misery by its humiliating defeat in war, and impressed 'shape and dynamism onto the disintegration and chaos'. The Bolsheviks, inspired by Lenin's 'clear and undeviating will', had convinced the Russians that 'the new State was their state, their life, their spirit, their tradition, their most precious patrimony'.[30]

The majority faction of the PSI, the maximalists, applauded all such eulogies to Soviet Russia. They were nevertheless 'revolutionaries in word, not deed'.[31] They shrank from the sectarian logic of Leninism. In October 1919, the PSI party congress adopted the hammer and sickle symbol and applied to join the Third International of Communist Parties. When Moscow insisted that all members should abide by a 21-point ideological catechism, the PSI balked. Point 7 asserted that member parties should be intransigent towards social democratic reformism. Filippo Turati, whose journal *Critica sociale* had denounced the reign of terror prevailing in Bolshevik Russia, was singled out by name for purging.[32] Both for tactical reasons (Turati was a popular figure in Milan) and out of sentiment towards the party's grand old man, the PSI leadership refused to adhere to this condition.

The result of this stance was that in January 1921, at a tumultuous party congress in Leghorn, the Leninist wing of the party left the PSI to form the Communist Party of Italy (PCdI). It was a divorce whose wounds never healed. It is not much of an exaggeration to say that the Italian Marxist left would be divided for the next four decades over whether loyalty to the USSR should be conditional or absolute.

Gramsci sided with the splitters, along with two former law students who were fellow founders of *L'Ordine nuovo*, Palmiro Togliatti and Umberto Terracini; both would become protagonists in the building of Italian democracy after the Second World War. Togliatti, short in stature and slight of build, became chief editor of the PCdI's new daily newspaper, *Il Comunista*. The paper's typesetters playfully nicknamed him Ercole (Hercules). With a minor revision to the spelling (to Ercoli), it would be his cover name as an official of the Communist International for more than twenty years.[33]

When the Leghorn Congress took place, the PSI was under siege from the *Fasci italiani di combattimento*, a new movement founded in March 1919 by Mussolini, whose support for the war had caused him to break with the PSI. Street clashes between socialist militants and the aggrieved veterans enrolled in Mussolini's *fasci* were a commonplace throughout 1920. Squads of paramilitary toughs, commanded by local *Ras* (an Ethiopian word meaning 'warlords'), launched bloody punitive expeditions against their political rivals across Piedmont, Lombardy, and Emilia.[34] Membership of the *fasci* grew rapidly, and Giovanni Giolitti, hoping to coopt Mussolini, included them in the 'National Bloc' coalition that he formed to contest new elections in April 1921. They took just thirty-five seats, although Mussolini himself was the third most-voted member of the new parliament.

The PSI's candidates needed courage to stand for office in the April 1921 elections. One individual who possessed courage in abundance was Giuseppe Di Vittorio, a trade unionist from Cerignola in Apulia. Aged twenty-eight in 1921, Di Vittorio had started work in the fields at the age of seven, when his father died, as a *cacciacorvi*, a boy paid pennies to scare crows away from the crops. He had been involved in the struggles of the *braccianti* – farm labourers – of his region since his early teens and had won a reputation as a subversive. He had been imprisoned on more than one occasion. His bravery as a soldier during the war, where he was wounded in action, did not, in the eyes of the landowners, compensate for his radicalism.

In April 1921, Di Vittorio stood as PSI candidate in Apulia. His candidacy infuriated a local landowner who commanded the fascist squad in Cerignola and was himself a candidate in the elections. Several citizens were killed during a campaign of intimidation to prevent working-class electors from voting for the local war hero. Di Vittorio nevertheless attracted thousands of votes elsewhere and was elected.

When the election was over, Di Vittorio was warned to stay away from his home town. He took no notice. On his return, he found a gang of thugs waiting for him at the railway station. Calmly, Di Vittorio waited for the other passengers to move away from danger and then advanced to the station exit with a pistol in one hand and a heavy stick in the other. Most of the waiting Fascists were 'petrified' by his bravery, but a handful did move aggressively towards him. Di Vittorio pointed the pistol and said, 'step forward anybody who wants to die'. The squad backed off and Di Vittorio was soon surrounded by fellow citizens who carried him in triumph to the town square. Hundreds of labourers surrounded his mother's house that night to ensure his safety.[35] The 'Garibaldi of the farmhands' would go on to become an influential figure in the PCdI and, after the Second World War, leader of the Italian General Confederation of Workers (CGIL), the largest trade union.

In general, the 1921 results affirmed the centrality of the PSI and the PPI, which between them continued to command half of the electorate. Mussolini transformed the *fasci* into the National Fascist Party (PNF) in November 1921 and jettisoned his long-time anti-clericalism to broaden the party's appeal to Catholic voters. There was, however, only a brief pause in his campaign of intimidation against rival parties, trade unions, and workers' associations. In 1922, it revived and intensified.

The democratic political parties wavered in the face of the assault. By the summer of 1922, Italy desperately needed a 'Popular Front' of Catholics, Liberals, and Socialists to defend its infant democracy. But the opposition could not bury its differences. The Popular Party 'did not have the support of the Church hierarchy' for an anti-fascist alliance. It was forced to work 'in a state of almost humiliating abandonment'.[36] The PSI's parliamentary contingent, led by Turati, wanted to form a broad anti-fascist government. The maximalist faction insisted that the party would not be true to its identity as the party of the proletariat if it allied with the bourgeoisie. In the autumn of 1922, the reformists were expelled. They formed the Unitary Socialist Party (PSU), with Giacomo Matteotti, a principled young lawyer from Rovigo on the Adriatic coast, as party secretary. The new party's journal was called *Giustizia*; the party emblem pictured the sun of socialism emitting potent rays of *Libertà*.

Just days after the PSU was founded, Mussolini staged a bold coup. On 27 and 28 October 1922, Fascist squads seized strategic buildings, telephone exchanges, and railway stations, meeting little resistance from the police. Some 30,000 Fascists, led by the leading *Ras*, converged in 'columns' upon the capital: the so-called 'March on Rome'. As one sympathizer wrote: 'Mussolini's revolutionary army was not the Salvation Army, and his blackshirts were not armed with daggers and grenades for the sake of philanthropy, but to fight a civil war.'[37] They were also not trained troops: it is doubtful that they would have withstood a whiff of grapeshot. Yet the government could not summon up the will to give Mussolini the same medicine that Giolitti had administered to D'Annunzio in Fiume, even though 'a forthright order to the army could still have saved everything'.[38] King Victor Emmanuel III, who had succeeded to the throne in 1900, shrank from proclaiming a state of emergency and thus condemned Italy's nascent democracy to a premature demise.

On 29 October 1922, Mussolini set off for Rome from Milan by train. At every station the train was delayed by crowds that gathered to hail the chief. He arrived in Rome on the morning of 30 October and was given an audience at the Quirinale Palace. The king conferred the premiership on Mussolini, who formed a ministry that contained only three Fascists and included ministers from the PPI, although the decision to participate in the government split the party between 'collaborationists' and anti-Fascists, notably Don Sturzo.[39] Summoned by Mussolini, exultant Fascists celebrated in the streets of Rome, to the delight of the proprietors of wine shops and the *case di tolleranza*, but few others.

Mussolini in Naples on the eve of the March on Rome, October 1922. The future Duce (*centre*) is flanked by the 'quadrumvirate' of Fascist squad leaders: (*left to right*) Michele Bianchi, Italo Balbo, Cesare Maria de Vecchi and Emilio de Bono.

THE SEIZURE OF POWER

Italy's elites soon discovered that they were riding on the back of a tiger with a ravenous appetite. In his first speech to the Chamber of Deputies, Mussolini told legislators that he could have turned 'this deaf and grey chamber' into a 'bivouac' for his legionaries, but he had chosen not to – at any rate for the moment. His words provoked indignation among the opposition deputies and cries of 'Long Live Parliament'.[40]

Over the next year and a half, club-wielding blackshirts, acting with impunity, turned Italy into a prime example of 'competitive authoritarianism'.[41] The political opposition was systematically intimidated, although Italy nominally remained a parliamentary democracy and the PNF remained a minority in the government. Hundreds were killed; many more were humiliated by being compelled to drink doses of castor oil at gunpoint. Parliamentary elections in May 1924, held under a gerrymandered electoral law, were marred by fraud and widespread violence. Mussolini's list of Fascists and fellow travellers took 65 per cent of the vote, though a tenacious opposition remained unliquidated.

On 10 June 1924, Mussolini overreached himself. On his orders, a squad kidnapped Giacomo Matteotti, his most outspoken critic.[42] The crime was too blatant for Italy's elites to ignore. An influential Turin newspaper, *La Stampa* – the mouthpiece of the FIAT industrial group – warned on 19 June that only a 'new Fascism' could survive the crisis provoked by Matteotti's disappearance: Fascism, the paper opined, had 'lost in an hour, a day, almost all the ground gained in 22 months of government'. *La Stampa* was equally lukewarm about Mussolini's future: certainly, it would have to be 'a Mussolini greatly different from the past'.[43] The opposition parties demanded an inquiry into the kidnapping and, when it became clear that a cover-up was taking place, walked out of parliament in protest: the so-called 'Aventino'.[44]

Matteotti's corpse was discovered on 16 August. Yet the opposition, or so one contemporary protagonist claimed, merely 'awaited in trepidation' Mussolini's arrest and 'ingenuously' trusted that Victor

Emmanuel would act.[45] Neither the Crown nor the Church were prepared to break with Fascism. The recently elected Pope, Pius XI, who was more doctrinaire than his predecessor, Benedict XV, stated in September that the Church believed in avoiding the 'greater evil', which was godless socialism, not Fascism.[46]

Mussolini took heart from the pusillanimity of the king, the Church, and the democratic parties. Speaking in the Chamber of Deputies on 3 January 1925, he defined the opposition's boycott as 'unconstitutional, blatantly revolutionary', and he evoked a utilitarian justification for the violence that had been unleashed in the country:

> If Fascism just boils down to castor oil and truncheons and is not the sublime passion of the finest Italian youth, well, blame me! [applause] If Fascism is no more than a criminal gang, well, I'm the gang's leader! [enthusiastic and prolonged applause] ... If violence has been caused by a particular historical, political, and moral climate, well, I take full responsibility since I created this climate ... I would never have had recourse to such methods if the national interest hadn't been at stake. But no government that allows itself to be slandered is respected by the people. The people want to see their dignity mirrored in the dignity of the Government, and the people, long before I said a word, had already said that's enough! The measure is full![47]

Mussolini was mobbed by sycophantic deputies celebrating this repudiation of constitutional government. Pietro Nenni, a passionate republican, sometime friend of Mussolini, brilliant journalist, and veteran who would lead the PSI for most of the next fifty years, would subsequently bracket off the Fascist era as the period between 'the murder of Matteotti and the murder of the nation', and he – in common with the rest of the left, for whom the lawyer from Rovigo became a martyr figure – regarded all of Italy's elites, not just Mussolini, as sharing the moral responsibility for both crimes.[48]

'Fascism is the autobiography of the nation,' said Piero Gobetti, an intellectual from Turin who, like Matteotti, would be beaten by Fascists for his effrontery in 1925 and die of the blows he received the following year.[49] Gobetti's analysis of the circumstances that had enabled Mussolini – someone lacking the 'exquisitely modern virtue of irony,' he thought – to take power was unsparing towards the Italians themselves. 'The Italians surely have the soul of slaves,' he commented in frustration.[50] Gobetti thought that the Italian people, certainly their political representatives, had shrunk since the First World War from the 'terrible duties' inherent in building a state.[51] All the parties, including the supposedly revolutionary PSI, had backed away from fighting for their beliefs.

Only one political leader was spared Gobetti's scorn. Gobetti was impressed by the man who had taken on the impossible job of leading the PPI after Don Sturzo had yielded to a papal order to desist from political activity. In July 1925, observing the last party conference before the PPI was outlawed, Gobetti commented that the new leader was:

> . . . tall, thin, straight-backed . . . his eyes don't miss a trick. From the podium he watches over tactics, he listens to every speaker, he shrugs with approval or disapproval at even the humblest speakers who are boring the assembly . . . He is irritated by adulation, by compliments, by fine words. There is no false bonhomie, he has no need of noisy popularity, but much prefers consensus, opinions mediated by others. All the same, he is a decision-maker, and has no taste for debate for its own sake . . . even when he is reading a speech, he is cold and incisive; he does not sway the crowd so much with his intensity, but with his precision, emphasizing points by modulating his tone to sound more attentive, calmer, slower, less loud . . .

This personality also possessed, according to Gobetti, a 'capacity for political sacrifice', which meant he knew how to fight for a cause, and 'a sense of self-esteem'.[52]

The intimidating figure thus described was Alcide De Gasperi, a devout Catholic from the Trentino who had been an Austrian citizen until 1919 and a member of the imperial parliament in Vienna. The bilingual De Gasperi had never been an Italian nationalist, intent on the territorial incorporation of the Trentino into Italy, but had rather represented the Italian minority within the Habsburg Empire. His detractors, on both the fascist right and communist left, subsequently would not hesitate to call him a German.[53]

Gobetti would have liked there to be more astringent, calm men of integrity like De Gasperi. In Gobetti's interpretation, the real attraction of Fascism was that it allowed the Italian political class to take refuge in a wholly spurious unity.

A more prosaic way of looking at the crisis that had brought Fascism to power, one that avoids generalizations about the Italian national character, would be to say that, between 1921 and 1924, the centre did not hold. Committed democrats were too few to prevail. This would prove to be the crucial difference between the two postwar epochs. After liberation in 1945, there was a broad-based will to construct a democracy, both among Catholics and the Marxist left. Democracy was not just the goal of exceptionally brave men like Matteotti: it was a project that found widespread support among workers by hand and brain, among women, and in the *canoniche* (parsonages) of Italy's towns and villages.

THE REGIME

Gobetti was nevertheless right to say that Fascism exercised broad appeal. Italy's upper classes saw the Fascist state as a way of protecting their interests and maintaining the social order. Italy's poor were looking for a saviour who would provide them with land and bread. Many intellectuals were looking for someone to create a modern nation worthy of Italy's incomparable artistic and cultural achievements and restore the glory of Rome. Mussolini was the man upon whom they projected their desires: a man of destiny who would bind the nation into one. The fascist symbol was the *fascio littorio*, a bundle of wooden rods containing an axe. It signified that, while the individual rods could easily be snapped, together they were unbreakable.

The Fascist state built after 1926, when Mussolini took the title of *Duce*, was accordingly the deliberate opposite of parliamentary democracy. On principle, it condemned egalitarianism, pluralism, and freedom of thought in favour of a doctrine that exalted the superiority of warriors and philosophers over other men, of men over women, of Europeans over other civilizations, and of the white races over other peoples. The Fascist state, Mussolini wrote, was an 'ethical'

Mussolini strikes a pose. The Duce in Trento, 31 August 1935.

entity; a 'spiritual and moral fact' that orchestrated its citizens, and gave them not only security, but meaning and indeed greatness.[54]

The PNF was an intrinsic part of the state and, in effect, its agent. As one fascist apologist wrote in 1931, 'the Fascist Party is not a party, but the Party: the Party of the State, the Party of the Italians.'[55] All other political formations were banned, their party organizations disintegrated and their leaders imprisoned, driven into exile or murdered. Dissident intellectuals were chased from their university chairs, or out of their editorial offices. The secret police, the OVRA, monitored social dissent meticulously. Ordinary citizens who despised the regime were reduced to scribbling on the walls.[56]

The advent of Fascism caused a substantial new wave of emigration from Italy in the first half-decade after the March on Rome. The number of people departing for other European countries was 155,554 in 1922; 205,273 in 1923; 239,088 in 1924; 177,558 in 1925; and 139,900 in 1926. France took the lion's share: more than half a million Italians moved to France in these years. Many of them were economic migrants, but most were political refugees.[57]

The Party's decision-making apparatus took precedence over that of the state; parliament was turned into a mere rubber stamp assembly which was 'elected' by plebiscites where one voted for a *listone* (long list) of approved candidates. On 26 May 1928, when introducing the legislation that enabled this electoral 'reform', Mussolini proudly stated that Fascism was 'solemnly burying the sham of universal democratic suffrage'.[58]

In 1939, the Chamber of Deputies was substituted by the *Camera dei fasci e delle corporazioni*. This body united the top officials of the PNF with the representatives of the twenty-two 'corporations', regulating commercial agriculture, industrial production and services, that managed the principal sectors of the economic and cultural life of the nation. Corporativism, or so a contemporary school textbook explained, was an attempt to find a middle way between the unbridled individualism of laissez-faire liberalism and Marxism's imposition of the dictatorial rule of a single class. Both workers and entrepreneurs should acknowledge that they shared a 'common duty' to work for social justice, which the Duce had often indicated as 'a noble and necessary objective' for the Fascist state. Since the 'corporatist consciousness' was not something human beings were born with, the institutions of corporativism, alongside the parallel Party institutions, existed to socialize Italians into becoming more selfless human beings. The state's role was ultimately moral. Its objective was to mould 'a new Italian' – men and women fit for the new fascist age in Italian history.[59]

The author of this paean of praise for the beehive state, which in real life soon became a vast edifice of sinecures providing employment for political favourites, was called Amintore Fanfani, a professor of economic history at the Catholic University of Milan. Between 1954 and 1987, he would hold the office of prime minister six times, and would become one of the architects of Italian democracy.

Mussolini did not abolish the second chamber of parliament, the Senate, whose members were nominated by royal decree, not elected. In the Senate, a handful of liberals, such as the philosopher and historian Benedetto Croce, criticized the regime, although they were denigrated for their pains and subjected to occasional house arrest. The regime's cabinet was the Fascist Grand Council, which united the party 'hierarchs'. Even this institution was a mere echo chamber for the Duce's strident voice. The main Fascist leaders – many of whom were intelligent men – did not distinguish themselves by their willingness to stand up to the Duce, whom they called, with sickening servility, *Capo* (boss).

The only institution granted space by the Fascist state was the Catholic Church. The 1929 Lateran Pacts allowed the Church to teach religion in the public schools and allowed Catholic Action, the umbrella body coordinating the activities of youth, social, student and professional movements, to retain a substantial degree of freedom. This crack in the façade of the supposedly totalitarian state rankled. In May 1931, Mussolini issued a decree dissolving Catholic Action, provoking a major crisis between Church and State. Pope Pius XI responded to Mussolini's démarche with an outspoken encyclical, *Non abbiamo bisogno* ('There is no need'), that protested against treating Catholic Action as 'a vast and perilous conspiracy', objected to the 'depressing profile of irreverence and violence' that accompanied the actions taken by Fascist squads towards Catholic activities, and condemned Fascism's efforts to 'monopolize youth, from earliest childhood, to adulthood' as 'an authentic act of pagan state worship' that infringed the rights of families just as much as the 'supranatural rights of the Church'.[60]

After the Pope's intervention, a compromise was reached. Catholic Action's statute was altered to define it as 'apolitical' and power was devolved from the national level to the dioceses of Italy's bishops, who were given a bigger supervisory role. The Church appeased the regime in order to protect its autonomy. This choice was timid, but it did enable certain Catholic associations, notably FUCI, the Catholic university students' association, to preserve independence from Party control, no small concession in a regime that popularized the word 'totalitarian'.

Many individual priests were sincere opponents of the idolatry of the Fascist state, and of the unchristian maxims of Fascist doctrine, with its exaltation of violence and rejection of meekness and humility. 'Better one day as a lion than a hundred years as a sheep' was not a slogan that an honest priest could recommend to his flock, though dishonest ones did. Many parish priests continued to teach young people the Gospels, not the Fascist catechism 'credere, obbedire, combattere' ('Believe, Obey, Fight').

It is also true that the 'Vatican played a central role both in making the Fascist regime possible and in keeping it in power'.[61] The Church was conscious that the Party State could crush it and hence collaborated with Mussolini, blessed his wars, and turned a blind eye to his vilest policies, notably the racial laws that in 1938 banned Jews from membership of the Fascist Party, the army, professions such as the law or university teaching, from land ownership and the ownership of all but small businesses. The Church did protest against this Nazism by imitation, but on juridical, not moral grounds. As a prominent public intellectual pointed out, the Pope 'never said a word in support of the thousands of Jews who, through no fault of their own, had been excluded from civil society'.[62]

It should be added that some beneficiaries of the racial laws showed scant sympathy for their former colleagues. In the universities, for instance, Renzo De Felice has commented that the racial laws provided an opportunity for professors to 'show off, boost their careers, make money, or vent their spleen and envy against one colleague or another'.[63] A hundred Jewish professors lost their jobs, including some of Europe's most distinguished scholars; the rush to sit on their chairs was embarrassing.

The periodical *La Difesa della Razza* (Defence of the Race), launched to promote the new racial policy, became a symbol of the Fascist regime's racial turn. Its first number published a 'Manifesto of Racial Scientists', signed by both biological and social scientists, which asserted that Italy and its civilization was largely 'Aryan', that the 'time had come for Italians frankly to declare themselves to be racists', and that Jews did not 'belong' to the Italian race, which was defined as 'pure'. In fairness, some of the signatories of the Manifesto added their names only when they were informed that the Duce expected their adherence.[64]

Public opinion was perplexed by Fascism's embrace of racism. Many Italians had no idea what the word 'Aryan' meant and took it to refer to the 'Arian' heresy in the late Roman Empire. Racism nevertheless became a key component of the Fascist state's ideological apparatus: many of the regime's intellectuals proved adept at assimilating it. Amintore Fanfani's textbook on corporativism helpfully explained, for instance, that the 'problem of the Defence of the Race' had arisen from the need to 'destroy the phenomenon of Hebrewization that spread throughout the fields of culture, economics and politics after Italy was unified'.[65]

The guiding principle of representative democracy is, of course, that of institutional checks and balances. Fascist Italy had no such checks. 'Mussolini is always right,' children chanted in meetings of the Balilla, the Fascist youth organization. Mussolini was the subject of a cult of personality that would have made Caligula blanch. He was the leader and could do no wrong, but he was also depicted as a *man* of superhuman political and intellectual gifts. Hagiographical studies of Mussolini abounded. His admirers called him 'a spirit of steel at the service of a formidable will', a 'corrective to the half-hearted', a 'whole, open, flexible, picturesque, acute, temperamental energy', a 'genuinely great actor in the company of hams'. He was said to be 'Taciturn. Hardworking. Courageous. Tenacious. Coherent in his apparent incoherence. A mesmeriser of crowds' and a 'force launched within the body of Italy', a man 'completely without bonds', with 'a solid head, but with ultra-dynamic eyes that race as fast as cars on the plains of Lombardy', someone who preferred to be 'Zarathustra rather than a caricature of Jesus'. He was, one writer concluded with sober understatement, 'the driving force of the century'.[66]

The 'mesmeriser of crowds'. Trento, 31 August 1935.
Photograph: Enrico Unterveger.

It will be seen that the Duce, whatever else he was, was also a fantasy created by intellectuals with a servile soul. But their fantasies, instead of being a private indecency, were in the public domain and posted on the walls. A myth was constructed around the figure of Mussolini that had no connection with the reality of Fascism as it was experienced by Italy's masses.

Fascism's rhetoric was often revolutionary, but this was a sham. In fact, Fascism perpetuated the power of the traditional ruling classes: the *padroni*. In the urban conurbations of the North, the official Fascist trade union collaborated with the management of large industrial concerns and ensured that working-class militancy was kept in check. Italy weathered the Great Depression better than many European states, thanks to the regime's willingness to protect domestic producers and to engage in public works, but Mussolini's movement did not so much repair the cracks in the social structure as shore the old edifice up and slap on an expensive and weighty façade of Fascist ornamentation.

In the South, indeed, the cracks still gaped wide. The gap between rich and poor was wider in the South from the outset of the unified state, but in the South the bourgeoisie never fully developed as a class independent from the landowning aristocracy, which retained considerable political power, and which extracted considerable rent from the land it owned. Nor did a politically conscious class of entrepreneurial property-owning peasants emerge.

Fascism broadly acquiesced in the perpetuation of the exploitation of people in the South by their traditional ruling elites. True, the Fascist state famously drained the Pontine marshes and undertook other works of land improvement. It also waged a war of attrition against the Mafia in Sicily, 'using methods that would have caused the Jesuits of the Holy Inquisition to turn pale'.[67] Mass arrests, the indiscriminate use of appalling tortures, and summary trials were the norm, and the campaign only lost steam when it touched the upper reaches of society. So much can be said in Fascism's defence. But little effort was made to boost industrial production, to modernize agriculture, or to achieve an equitable distribution of land. The last thing southern rentiers wanted was increased competition for labour. When the Italian Republic was born in 1946, almost 60 per cent of men in southern

Italy still worked, hand-to-mouth, in the agricultural sector, mostly as day-labourers or as sharecroppers. They were as poor as their peers a hundred, or even two hundred, years before.

Ignazio Silone's novel *Fontamara*, set in the Abruzzo, east of Rome on the Adriatic, at the height of Fascism, is an acute depiction of the social and institutional origins of economic backwardness of the Mezzogiorno – and a biting description of the consequences. Silone described the fictional village of Fontamara as:

> About one hundred ragged, shapeless, one-floor hovels, blackened by time, worn by wind and rain, imperfectly roofed with tiles and slates of every kind, surround a dilapidated church on a stony hill-top. Most of these unpaved hovels have but one opening for door, window, and chimney. Inside them, men, women, and children, donkeys, goats, and hens live, sleep, eat, and procreate their kind.

The draining of nearby Lake Fucino had changed Fontamara's climate and made it hotter, which had destroyed the local olive groves, while the vines 'produced a sharp, acid wine, like lemon juice' that was useless for commercial purposes: the 'same wretched peasants that produced it were doomed to drink it'. The peasants' 'meagre soil' was 'divided and subdivided, racked with mortgages. No peasant possessed more than a few acres.' The drained land, by contrast, was fertile, 'among the richest in Italy', but no compensation in land had been given to the inhabitants of Fontamara, who had been 'reduced practically to serfdom'. The wealth produced by the reclaimed land 'emigrated to the capital'. Prince Torlonia, a Roman aristocrat, owned 8,000 acres, together with other estates in Tuscany and Lazio. About 10,000 peasants worked on his land. The prince let his land to 'barristers, doctors, solicitors, professors and the wealthy farmers of the neighbourhood', who cultivated the land by hiring the poorest peasants as 'day-labourers' or else sub-let it further. The prince obtained '40,000 tons of sugar beet, 15,000 tons of corn, 2,000 tons of vegetables' from the land he rented out, but sugar remained 'a rare luxury' for the peasants who cultivated the beet fields. The peasants ate 'maize bread for the better part of the year' since they only earned 'starvation wages'.[68]

Fontamara, in fact, is depicted by Silone essentially as a colonial society, and the benighted inhabitants of the barren hill towns are the colonized. Lake Fucino has been drained, but the product of the locals' labour is leeched away to Italy's cities, just as the resources of Congo or Indonesia or Burma benefited white people in the metropole. Anticipating a debate that would explode among writers in the newly freed countries of Africa in the 1960s, over whether they should write in French or English rather than their native tongues, Silone asks rhetorically 'in what language ought I to tell this story?' since 'Italian is like a foreign language, a dead language, a language the vocabulary and grammar of which developed without any connexion with us or our mode of thinking or expressing ourselves ... Italian civilization is a foreign civilization for us.'[69]

Silone was a communist apostate who became a social democrat and a central figure in Europe's post-war intellectual and political life. But the picture he leaves of the social structure and political climate of the Mezzogiorno in *Fontamara* and his other great novel from the 1930s, *Bread and Wine,* is perhaps his most lasting achievement. It is a picture of a conflictual world where every peasant strives for the protection of someone educated, preferably a lawyer, who can intervene on his behalf with people in authority in the state. The only difference Fascism had made was that 'the old state, with its rival competing conspiracies, had come to an end. A new state, with one conspiracy only, had come in its place.'[70]

EMPIRE AND HUBRIS

The colonialism of the Fascist state within Italy was not limited to the Mezzogiorno. It also encompassed the peoples who came under Italian rule after the Treaties of Paris (1919–20). Over 200,000 Germans became Italian citizens in 1919, whereas, before, 300,000 Italians had been ruled from Vienna. Italian nationalism's pretensions to Fiume were thwarted by Giolitti, but the award of Gorizia and Trieste to Italy still meant that nearly a third of all Slovenes were placed under Italian rule, along with 100,000 Croats, not under the rule of the new Kingdom of Yugoslavia.[71] Under Fascism, the newly acquired linguistic minorities in Italy's north-east were treated abominably. 'Alto Adige', as

South Tyrol was dubbed, was 'Italianized' by the regime after 1922, with place and family names being changed, and with justice and public administration being carried out exclusively in Italian by officials, often from southern Italy, brought in to administer an occupied territory. The education reform introduced by the philosopher Giovanni Gentile in 1923 banned instruction in any language other than Italian. German-language newspapers were forbidden. Workers were moved from southern Italy to staff an industrial hub built in Bozen, or Bolzano, as the city was now officially known, which permanently changed the ethnic balance of the city. The Germans of the South Tyrol were turned into second-class citizens in their own homeland.

The process of Italianization was symbolized by the construction of a 'monument to victory' in Bolzano designed by a great rationalist architect, Marcello Piacentini. It was originally intended to be a memorial to Cesare Battisti and Fabio Filzi, two socialists and nationalists hanged in Trento in July 1916 by the Austrians for the crime of fighting for Italy, but Battisti's widow objected to her husband's memory being politicized. The first stone of the monument was nevertheless laid on the tenth anniversary of the death of the two martyrs, with great pomp and ceremony, by Victor Emmanuel. The Italian state's continuing discrimination towards the German minority naturally did not go unnoticed in Austria and Germany during the monument's construction, and in February 1928 Austrian Chancellor Ignaz Seipel publicly denounced the Italian regime's policies towards the German minority.[72] The monument, the physical symbol of those policies, was inaugurated on 12 July 1928, again in the presence of the king, in a city draped in fascist banners. It stands to this day.

Italianization took place with equal vigour in the provinces of Gorizia and Trieste. The culture and traditions of the *allogeni* ('other races'), which had thrived under Austrian rule, were persecuted by the zealous functionaries who administered the territory.[73] As in Bolzano, surnames were Italianized in an attempt at 'forcible acculturation'.[74]

After the outbreak of war, Italian imperialism only worsened. When Germany invaded Yugoslavia on 6 April 1941, Italy, Hungary, and Bulgaria cleared up after the Nazi wolf like jackals. In the ensuing carve-up of Yugoslav territory, Italy gained the whole of Slovenia, including Ljubljana, as well as Montenegro and substantial parts of Dalmatia.

Triumph set in stone. The Monument to Victory in Bolzano was the
epitome of Fascist architecture. Photograph: Sergio Perdomi.

Imperial ambitions ultimately led Mussolini into the arms of Hitler.
In the 1930s, Mussolini became more and more headstrong. He was
not content to have absolute dominion within the narrow confines of
the Italian peninsula, and to rule over a few hundred thousand Germans and Slovenes and a similar number of Libyans. His aim was to
emulate the glory of the Caesars. In the iconography of the regime,
Mussolini was 'more and more frequently portrayed as a Roman condottiere' or even as a reincarnation of Emperor Augustus.[75]

Romanità was expressed in the regime's grandiose architecture, in evocations of the martial values, but above all in the pursuit of Empire. Mussolini's originally prudent foreign policy, of keeping close links with Great Britain in order to balance both France and Germany, was discarded in the 1930s as the Duce sought to build a 'Greater Italy' that would have included the entire Dalmatian coast, Albania, and Corsica, as well as the habitable parts of Italy's colony, Libya, and 'Italian East Africa'.

Everyday objects are sometimes more revealing than the speeches of leaders or the treatises of ideologues. A school textbook for elementary students, *L'Impero d'Italia*, published in Year 17 of the Fascist state (i.e. 1939), began with four maps showing the expanse of the Roman Empire when Rome was founded (the city alone); after the Punic Wars against Carthage (from 146 BC); at the death of Emperor Augustus (AD 14); and in the time of Emperor Trajan (AD 98–117). The message was clear. A new age of imperial power had begun. The lavishly illustrated book was a model of hagiographical colonial literature. It depicted the exploits of heroic explorers and missionaries, explained the geography, resources, and peoples of Italy's long-standing colonial possessions: Eritrea, Somalia, Libya, the islands of the Aegean Sea. Italy was portrayed as a benevolent power intent on bringing civilization, education, and peace to the peoples it ruled. The book concluded with a detailed account of the conquest of Abyssinia in the spring of 1936, with a delirious speech on Italy's mission from the Duce and a judgement upon the historical significance of Mussolini's foreign policy: 'Italy, thanks to the actions of Fascism, is reasserting, *after a pause of fifteen centuries*, its imperial role in the Mediterranean and the world.'[76] Irony, as Gobetti said, was not a fascist virtue.

The war against Abyssinia – as Ethiopia was then known – aroused enthusiasm, even hysteria. On 18 December 1935, 'as if they were taking part in a great plebiscite', the Italians surrendered their wedding rings to provide the state with bullion. Over 35 tons of gold and 114 tons of silver were collected to replenish the state's coffers. The gold alone was worth 437 million lire.[77] A popular song, 'Faccetta nera' ('Little Black Face'), had been written in April 1935. It promised a 'bell'Abissina', a beautiful young Ethiopian girl, that the Italians would bring liberation from her backward society. She would become Italian and 'march in front of the Duce and the King'. In fact, women were raped or taken as concubines without regard to age or propriety: the brutal colonial war removed many of the taboos imposed by the rigid Catholicism of Italian society, and African women paid a steep price. Indro Montanelli, a war correspondent who became one of post-war Italy's most prominent journalists and an acclaimed popular historian, 'married' a fourteen-year-old girl called Destà, whom he bought from her father for 1,253 lire plus a mule and a straw-roofed hut.[78] Such transactions were eventually banned, though they persisted throughout the duration of the new East African Empire, of which Mussolini was styled the 'Founder'.

Mussolini's pilot sons, Bruno and Vittorio, fought in the war and delighted in machine-gunning civilians from the air. The use of poison gas was authorized by Mussolini and used abundantly on the orders of Rodolfo Graziani, the Italian general who became the viceroy of the new colony. Many Italians still cling to the idea that they were 'brava gente' – good guys – by comparison with other colonizers, but this self-serving myth does not stand even cursory examination. The conquest of Ethiopia was one of the most savage conflicts in all colonial history: many tens of thousands of Africans, including huge numbers of civilians, died during the conflict.

The subsequent consolidation of Italian rule was also ferocious. A failed attempt to kill Graziani in February 1937 was 'punished' by reprisals on the civilian population of Addis Ababa. Squads of Italian settlers roamed the city, beating and killing civilians.[79] The oppression continued until May of that year, when Italian troops massacred the entire religious community of the thirteenth-century Copt monastery at Debrà Libanòs: over 1,400 monks and nuns were murdered in cold blood on Graziani's direct orders. Never before in African history had any 'religious community experienced slaughter on such a scale'.[80] Up to 1937, Hitler, despite his elimination of his political opponents and his introduction of the Nuremberg laws against Jews, had not done anything remotely as brutal as the conquest of Ethiopia and the atrocities against its civilian population.

Contemporaneously, Mussolini threw Italian men and resources into the Civil War in Spain on the side of Francisco Franco: thousands of Fascist 'legionaries' died in Spain. At the battle of Guadalajara in March 1937, there was a civil war within the Civil War as the

'Garibaldi Brigade', composed of Italian anti-fascist volunteers – some 4,000 in all, about half of whom were communists – fought for the Spanish Republic against Mussolini's militia. Six hundred Italian anti-Fascists were killed in Spain; some 2,000 were wounded. Bologna alone contributed 132 volunteers, including two women, to the front in Spain; no fewer than thirty-four were killed.[81]

When the Fascist legionaries returned home from Spain and paraded in triumph through Italy's cities, the private reactions of the country's intellectuals were disdainful. One eminent jurist, who is celebrated to this day for the elegance of his prose, confided to his diary that it was 'hard to know whether pity or disgust should prevail' when one saw Mussolini's *milites gloriosi*. Fascism, he fumed, had clearly 'caused a kind of chemical reaction among the people' that had 'made all the shit precipitate' in the militia units.[82]

In October 1936, Mussolini signed a treaty of mutual understanding

Hailing the Axis. Mussolini, Hitler, and Victor Emmanuel during Hitler's visit to Italy, May 1938. Elena of Montenegro, the Queen consort, is in full ostrich feathers on the right; Josef Goebbels stands behind the king.

with the Third Reich that was dubbed the Rome–Berlin 'Axis'. Rome, hitherto sensitive to developments in neighbouring Austria, stayed silent when the Nazis carried out the *Anschluss* in March 1938. Less than two months later, on 3 May, Hitler was received with great pageantry in Rome. The Führer's visit persuaded Galeazzo Ciano, Mussolini's son-in-law and foreign minister, that an alliance with the Nazis would be disastrous: Ciano listened to Hitler's plans for future wars against the USSR, the British Empire, and even the United States, with well-concealed horror.

The Duce, by contrast, was captivated. By 9 May 1938, when the two dictators said an emotional goodbye at the railway station in Florence, Mussolini had been converted to the Nazi cause: 'now no force can ever come between us,' he told the Führer, whose eyes glistened with tears.[83] The days of Hitler's visit had been 'special days' indeed.[84] Italy subsequently backed Germany's annexation of Czechoslovakia in March 1939 – Mussolini had played an important role in brokering the October 1938 Munich Agreement that ceded the German-speaking parts of Czechoslovakia to the Reich – and annexed Albania in April 1939.

On 22 May 1939, in Berlin, Ciano signed the so-called Pact of Steel with Germany on behalf of Italy. He returned to Rome to a hero's welcome from the Fascist hierarchy, but not from the royal family. King Victor Emmanuel III told Ciano on 25 May that 'so long as the Germans need us, they will be courteous and perhaps even servile. But the first chance they get, they'll show themselves for the scoundrels that they are.' On the same day, Ciano recorded a frustrated Mussolini saying that he 'envied Hitler' because he didn't have to 'drag empty wagons' behind him.[85] The Duce meant the king, the court, and the aristocratic upper reaches of the military.

The mood of mutual admiration between the two dictators permitted a solution to the thorny problem of Italy's treatment of the German population of South Tyrol. To ease tensions, on 22 June 1939, Italy and Nazi Germany signed a pact that gave German speakers the opportunity to opt for German citizenship and to migrate to the Third Reich or stay in Italy, as Italian citizens, without tutelage of their linguistic heritage. To Mussolini's dismay, over 200,000 *optanti* from the provinces of Bolzano, Trento, and Belluno took up the offer to become Germans, whereas a mere 34,000 chose Fascist Italy.[86] In the end, only some 75,000 people packed their bags and left in 1940, but the whole of South Tyrol, including Trento, which was anyway governed from Innsbruck from October 1943, was throughout the war starkly divided between Italians and Germans, between Fascists and anti-Fascists, and between returned *optanti* and those who had betrayed the *Heimat* by accepting Italian nationality.[87]

Emilio Gentile, a distinguished Italian historian, has suggested that Fascism was a political religion which 'clearly rivalled traditional religion in claiming its own prerogative over the ultimate aim of life'. It was 'the first totalitarian nationalist movement of this century which used the power of a modern state in an attempt to bring up millions of men and women in the cult of the nation and the state as being supreme and absolute values'.[88]

As such, Fascism was a form of government that could appear as a model for Europe during the half-time break between Europe's two great wars, when the values and efficacy of liberal democracy were in doubt almost everywhere. Even in the United States, the state and society constructed by Mussolini was lionized for most of the 1930s as a kind of New Deal for the Italian people.

Gentile's depiction of Fascism also clarifies what it was not. Whatever it was, Fascism was not democratic. It required one party, not a plurality of parties; one leader, not many; one set of unquestioned beliefs, not lots of competing ones; social hierarchy, not fluidity; plebiscites, not elections; one race and one cultural identity that was to be imposed on all others. Ordinary men and women were supposed to applaud the Duce's speeches frantically, not discuss or pick holes in them.

Democracy also requires a measure of equality between citizens. Fascism left the yawning social inequalities of so-called Liberal Italy largely unaltered. It kept millions mired in pre-industrial poverty and ignorance. The masses were mobilized and manipulated by the regime's skilful propaganda, but their well-being was ultimately of secondary concern. Under Fascism, the people were supposed to work for the state, not the other way around. Fascism brought about a partial change of guard in the country's elite, but it left the traditional structures of social hierarchy substantially intact. The key social forces of that hierarchy – the monarchy, the Church, the landowners, the professions, the industrialists of Milan and Turin – had preferred to cede power to Mussolini rather than embark on long-neglected social reforms. They had also connived, for the most part, with Fascism's chauvinism, racism, antisemitism, and imperialism.

Fascism needed victory in war to legitimize its democratic failings. It measured success in glory and conquest, and the construction of imposing architecture, not in the provision of schools and hospitals, or a rising standard of living. Mussolini loved to pose as a warrior. 'War alone brings up to their highest tension all human energies and puts the stamp of nobility upon the peoples who have the courage to meet it,' he wrote melodramatically in 'La Dottrina del Fascismo', the regime's textbook statement of ideological purpose, but his words were hollow.[89] War would reveal the chronic economic, military, and political weakness propping up Fascism's monumental façade. Just as the First World War smashed the political system constructed in Italy after unification in 1871, so the Second World War, and alliance with a real revolutionary, Adolf Hitler, would expose Mussolini's regime as a bluff. The *fascio littorio* would prove to be loosely bundled together, and its axe was blunt.

2

Into the Abyss

When war broke out in September 1939, Mussolini was, in addition to being the country's supreme leader, also the minister of aeronautics, the minister of Italian Africa, the minister of war, the minister of internal affairs, and the minister of the navy. Every major decision concerning war preparations or domestic security had to pass through his office. He rarely called meetings of the Fascist Grand Council, preferring bilateral colloquia where he could give orders to his subordinates. It would have been an impossible burden even for somebody of genuine executive ability, but Mussolini, in the last resort, was a demagogue who 'ran the State as if it were a great journalistic enterprise'.[1] To make matters worse, everybody with an eye to advancement told Mussolini what he wanted to hear, not the truth.

The truth was that Italy was unprepared for war in September 1939. The wars in Ethiopia and Spain had pushed Fascism to the limits of its strength. Several key figures in the regime, notably Foreign Minister Ciano, were fearful of siding with Germany, as were King Victor Emmanuel III and Marshal Pietro Badoglio, the head of the armed forces. But how could Italy back out of the Pact of Steel? The solution was to state that, since Germany had anticipated the timetable of war by almost three years (in the previous spring Hitler had envisaged going to war in 1942), Italy could only stand by the Third Reich if Germany provided vast amounts of basic war materials. This device enabled Italy to avoid declaring war on France and Great Britain on 3 September 1939 without too much dishonour, although, as one Italian intellectual recorded in the privacy of his diary, it was 'truly humiliating' that Italy was 'standing out' when its leader, a 'sawdust Caesar', had 'for years been rolling his eyes at the world and making threats'.[2]

THE TEST OF WAR

Non-belligerency left Italy a bystander as Hitler's armies rapidly overran Poland, Denmark, Norway, Belgium, the Netherlands, Luxembourg, and France. The Duce blamed his own people for the regime's impotence. According to Ciano, Mussolini fumed 'what I lack is raw material. Even Michelangelo needed marble to make his statues. If he had had only clay, he would have been a mere pot-maker.'[3] On 10 June 1940, when France was on its knees, Italy declared war on the Allies. The regime tried hard to make this manoeuvre seem like a work of a warrior. The front cover of an illustrated magazine, *Tempo*, depicted an ungainly Duce seated on a parade horse striking a martial pose, with sword held high: 'WAR!' bellowed the headline.[4]

Entry into the war was announced to an oceanic crowd in Piazza Venezia in Rome. It was the 'hour of destiny', Mussolini intoned, reaching into his quiver of clichés; a moment for 'irrevocable decisions'. Italy was 'taking the field against the reactionary plutocratic democracies of the West', which, Mussolini asserted, had 'throughout the ages obstructed the forward march and often threatened the very existence of the Italian people'.[5] *Tempo*, echoing the Duce, asserted that Italy's 'supreme task' was to 'strike a deadly blow' against the British Empire in order to ensure that its 'civilization of slavedrivers and plutocrats' disappeared from Europe.[6]

Entry into the conflict was 'a huge collective act of dishonesty', according to one thoughtful Italian historian. Mussolini was trying to 'con the Germans into the conviction that the Italians would fight by their side', while deluding himself and the Italian people with 'the presumption that the Germans had all but won'.[7] On 21 June 1940, the Italians launched a limited offensive along the Franco-Italian border in the Alps and advanced about thirty kilometres while taking heavy losses. Mussolini was staking a claim to a place at the peace conference table.

When the British did not sue for peace, the notion that Italy was waging war against reactionary capitalism became the regime's main justification for its intervention. In July 1940, *Gerarchia*, the 'monthly review of the Fascist revolution', portrayed Italy's entry into war as an act of social justice. The journal argued that the world's so-called democracies propagated the 'nauseating' myth that they defended the 'rights of peoples', whereas they really desired to preserve the 'right of the rich to suffocate for eternity the rights of the poor'. Hitler and Mussolini by contrast sought to 'redistribute the wealth of the earth' between nations, so that the poorer nations (i.e. the Axis powers) could 'reduce the disparities' of wealth within their own societies and replace 'hierarchies of money' with 'hierarchies of the spirit'. The 'demo-plutocracies' had responded ruthlessly when their interests were at stake and had declared war. So be it, the magazine asserted. The 'sacrifice in human lives necessary to reach this higher justice' had not been desired by Italy or Germany, but by the 'modern Midases' of capitalist democracy.[8]

Such arguments might suggest that the Red Queen in *Alice in Wonderland* was justifying Fascism's foreign policy, but that would be to fail to look at the logic of the war from Rome's standpoint. *Gerarchia*'s argument was reasonable if you regarded the goal of world politics to be the exploitation of the world's undeveloped territories. Britain, France, even the United States, were 'have' powers by that standard. Germany, Italy, and Japan objectively were 'have-nots'. Of course, the moral issue was whether *anybody* should be ruling over the masses of Asia, Africa, and Latin America for their own profit or prestige, but this was a question that none of the major powers asked themselves in 1940.

The regime's justifications for the war were disparaged by anti-Fascists. They were 'sophistries', said Pietro Nenni, a socialist who knew Mussolini well, from exile in Paris.[9] Mussolini's opponents grasped that Germany, not Britain, was the real danger for the Italian nation. If Italy had any common sense left, Piero Calamandrei fulminated in April 1940, its entire people, 'fascists and anti-fascists alike', would be working 'day and night' to 'resist this *flagellum dei*'. Some time in the 'murky future' he foresaw 'a German governor in Florence and our departure for concentration camps being organized on a serious scale'.[10] It was a grimly accurate forecast of what the alliance with the Third Reich would lead to.

In the meantime, Britain fought on. In 1941, a propaganda pamphlet warned Britain that it would finish 'like Carthage' at the hands of the 'young peoples' of Italy and Germany, who were fighting 'like lions' in a 'war of liberation' against the British 'hyena', which the Italians had 'driven from its den'.[11] Alas for Mussolini, the hyena had the last laugh. On 9 February 1941, Genoa was awoken by a dawn bombardment from a British naval squadron that arrived unopposed and departed without taking losses. By the end of 1941, British forces had overrun Ethiopia and Somaliland. Italian forces were repulsed as they sought to advance on the Egyptian capital of Cairo from Libya.

Such defeats were compounded by humiliations in the Balkans. On 28 October 1940, Italy declared war against Greece without alerting its German ally. This action, 'every bit as morally repugnant as the attack on already beaten France', was Mussolini's hasty response to Hitler's occupation of the Romanian oilfields.[12] The invasion 'destroyed the prestige and the morale of the Italian army'.[13] The Greeks checked the Italian army's advance and threw the invaders back into Albania in December 1940, though the regime's propaganda machine suggested that Italy had acted to pre-empt a Greek assault and that the war was being won by skilful tactics against overwhelming odds.[14] In the spring of 1941, after a grisly winter campaign, the Duce begged Berlin for help and then watched, acutely embarrassed, as German troops conquered Greece in less than a month. The first year of war demonstrated that Italy had inadequate tanks, aircraft, and transport, and preening, careerist generals.

Mussolini was wounded by these military failures and by a personal tragedy. His son Bruno died in an air crash in August 1941. The dictator dashed off a memoir called *Parlo con Bruno* ('I Speak with Bruno').[15] Intended as propaganda, the book's 'mingling of Fascist rigour and maudlin family sentiment' makes for curious reading.[16] Many must have struggled to reconcile the book's pathos – Mussolini's pride in his son is evident, as is his sense of loss – with the regime's appeals for unflinching commitment to the cause of the state. Mussolini was asking Italians to sacrifice their sons on the altar of national greatness, but *Parlo con Bruno* was a mawkish reminder that such sacrifices pained even the Duce. Nevertheless, crowds roared approval on 11 December 1941 when Mussolini declared war against the United States, four days after the Japanese attack on Pearl Harbor. The Duce's harangue was interrupted by chants of 'Ja–pan! Ja–pan!'

In 1942, nearly a quarter of a million men and the nation's best tanks, trucks, and artillery were committed to the Russian Front. The Italian forces took appalling casualties. Yet they counted for little in the existential struggle taking place between Nazism and Stalinism. Had the same troops and equipment been used in North Africa, where Italian forces were outgunned and chronically lacking in motorized transport, they might have tipped the balance.[17] Instead, further disasters followed in Libya, culminating in a decisive defeat of Italian and German forces at the battle of El Alamein in Egypt in November 1942.

After El Alamein, all remaining illusions were dispelled. War came to the Home Front, initially from the air. Against Italy, the bomber always got through. Italy possessed only scant means – few fighters, limited anti-aircraft guns, insufficient bomb shelters – to protect its people from the Allied incursions. In November 1942, a clandestine broadsheet protested that 'Mussolini is now leaving our people undefended and without aid. The bombers of the RAF are cruising undisturbed in the skies over Genoa, Milan, and Turin.'[18]

In a histrionic speech to the Chamber of Fasces and Corporations on 2 December 1942, Mussolini took stock of the progress – or lack thereof – of the war and subjected Winston Churchill to a string of puerile insults. His speech, though punctuated by prolonged applause from the sycophants in the audience, contained a sobering admission. It was necessary, Mussolini acknowledged, to 'evacuate the towns, above all of women and children'. Those 'able to find lodging far from the urban and industrial centres should do so'.[19] In the winter of 1942–3, hundreds of thousands of Italians sought refuge in the countryside.

PRELUDE TO THE FALL

Many Italians were also starving, as Mussolini acknowledged to Heinrich Himmler, when the head of the SS visited Rome in mid-October 1942.[20] There was little food to go round for much of the population – though senior members of the PNF lacked for nothing. Back in 1940, a propaganda poster had shown a gentleman devouring a large dinner, while behind him stood a war hero in military uniform. The poster was captioned, 'If you eat too much you are robbing the fatherland.' By the winter of 1942–3, such posters were a sour memory. The official ration was just over a kilogram of bread per person per week; 100 grams a week of meat were doled out. Butter, pasta, cheese, were distributed in derisory quantities, though they were available on the black market at prohibitive prices. Many workers had lost 10 or 15 kilograms in weight and 'cases of fainting in the workplace, or in the streets, as a result of under-nourishment' had become common, as had 'cases of deaths by poisoning from eating adulterated food'.[21] Statistical data confirm such statements. Between 1921 and 1930, the average calorie intake was 2,834 per day; in the following decade, it was 2,641 per day (2,657 in 1939, the last year of peace). In 1943, the number dropped to 2,112 calories (and plunged to under 1,900 in 1944). It was debilitating to do long hours of factory work, or to till the fields, on so exiguous a diet.[22]

The *sfollati*, those who had abandoned their place of residence, had been given a bonus: industrial workers wanted it, too. Women workers were especially resentful. Their piece-work rates were 30 per cent less than their menfolk's, no matter how much they produced. The injustice rankled. Increasingly, the factory workers of the big industrial cities, especially Milan and Turin, began to voice their discontent.

The PCdI (Communist Party of Italy) was the only pre-regime political party to maintain a clandestine network of cells inside the country. Inspired by the heroes of Stalingrad, communists were 'longing to take action' and fanned the flames of working-class discontent.[23] The party paper was distributed by the thousand, with copies passing from hand to hand in the workshops until they were unreadable.[24] On 20 February 1943, an article entitled 'How to Use *l'Unità*' advised:

When *l'Unità* arrives in your hands, first read and study it attentively yourself. In second place, choose among your acquaintances and decide whom you can trust to pass the paper on to, so they can read it too. Keep in mind that the reading, study, and distribution of the paper is important, but is not everything. Always remember that reading and study ... enable you to absorb advice and orders for action that you and your fellows must implement.[25]

The wartime editions of *l'Unità*, with their dense type and amateurish layout, give a striking insight into the political consciousness that the PCdI wished to diffuse among the proletariat of the industrial cities. First and foremost, the paper sought to demonize Mussolini and the clique around him. A sharp distinction was made between the Duce and 'honest fascists'. There was an 'overwhelming duty to approach these fellow citizens' and urge them to 'link arms with us to bring back peace to our land'.[26]

This appeal for a popular, anti-fascist front was a tactical manoeuvre; by December 1942, it was an open secret that the Crown was losing faith in the Duce. Communists were hoping for a coup against the dictator, which would also deliver a body blow to the Nazi cause and assist the Soviet Union: in December 1942 the battle of Stalingrad still hung in the balance and the USSR was still being defiled by the 'Hitlerite animals'.[27]

Indeed, the second dominant theme of *l'Unità*'s message to the working class was the correctness of the foreign and domestic policies of the Soviet state. The 7 November 1942 edition celebrated the twenty-fifth anniversary of the Bolshevik Revolution with an evocation of the show trials in the 1930s against the 'Trotskyite and Bukharinite monsters' who had plotted to 'restore capitalist slavery in the USSR'. The same article also explained helpfully that:

> In August 1939 the Soviet Union concluded a Pact of Non-Aggression with Germany (this pact was a pact of peace between two states. The Soviet government, in line with its commitment to peace, could not reject any such agreement).[28]

A third theme emphasized by *l'Unità* was the need for Italians to commit acts of sabotage, and to organize 'armed and disciplined squads', able to seize foodstuffs and distribute them to the people. If Italy were to 'erupt in an insurgency, in pursuit of an immediate separate peace, the Anglo-Russo-Americans would come rushing to our aid', the paper contended, though the writer must have known that this comment was false.[29]

The PCdI's clandestine activities radicalized the workshops of northern Italy: communists were not numerous, but they were zealous. A wave of strikes slowed war production in March–April 1943. There were 187 work stoppages in Piedmont between 5 March and 8 April: eighty-one in Turin alone. Factories important for the war effort, such as the FIAT plant in Turin, were shut down. Strikes broke out in Milan on 16 March: more than sixty plants were involved over the next two weeks.

> On the morning of 8 March 1943, the word went round that we would down tools at 10 o'clock ... at 10, I stopped my lathe, turned round, and stared at everybody who met my eye: after a few seconds every machine in the workshop was still. Not long after, the Fascists arrived with the police, and the first person to be arrested was me. The March 1943 strikes were such a shock because [they showed] people were at the end of their tether. We were living like dogs: cold and hunger.[30]

In his indispensable book *Italy 1943–1945*, David W. Ellwood notes that it was 'the March strikes that sounded the death knell for Fascism'.[31] They sent a clear message that frustration with the privations imposed by the war had reached boiling point. One socialist activist commented as the strike wave ended: 'In the last few days the struggle has ... become overtly political. Cries of "Down with Fascism" and "Long Live Peace" have predominated at every public protest.'[32]

Mussolini was uncomfortably aware that the strikes illustrated the weakness of the regime in Rome: the working classes of Nazi-occupied Europe were too afraid of the Gestapo to down tools. He replaced the secretary of the PNF, Aldo Vidussoni, with the more energetic Carlo Scorza, and upbraided the local party authorities in Turin and Milan for having been too circumspect in the means they had used to cow the workers.

It was too little, too late. By the spring of 1943, the reputation of the PNF was too compromised to be saved. No small part of the anger motivating the strikes was generated by the ostentation and corruption of the regime's chief officials. Galeazzo Ciano, whom Mussolini removed as foreign minister in February 1943, was a particular target. Radio Milano Libertà, a Moscow-based propaganda station, which purported to be a clandestine operation within Italy, had called the foreign minister 'the most scandalous example of the nepotism inflicted on us by Fascism', and 'a clod willing to sell himself to anybody and everybody', in a January 1942 radio broadcast.[33]

The Ciano family was a sitting duck for shotgun rhetoric. It was the epitome of the degeneration of the regime. Ciano and Mussolini's daughter, Edda, were a dissolute couple whose sexual experimentation would be considered shocking today, let alone in wartime Italy. Both abused drugs and alcohol. Ciano's father, Costanzo, was despised as a war profiteer. The Ciano clan were not alone, moreover. Many of the *Ras*, the former revolutionaries, had become millionaires. They lived in luxury, conducted high-profile affairs with film stars, and abused their position shamelessly. Edmondo Rossoni, who became head of the official trade union in the 1920s and subsequently undersecretary to Mussolini himself, was described as the 'most avid eater' of the regime, i.e. the most corrupt figure. Selling 'Aryanization' certificates to Jews was a lucrative line of business for the functionaries of 'Demorazza', the Office of Demography and Race, whose director general, Antonio Le Pera, and responsible minister, Guido Buffarini Guidi, 'ate with four jaws', according to Ciano, no saint himself. Buffarini Guidi paid Claretta Petacci, Mussolini's mistress, 200,000 lire every month because 'to be in the good graces of Claretta meant being in the good graces of the Duce'.[34]

In May 1943, Axis troops were driven back into Tunisia by an Allied pincer movement and eventually surrendered with honour: in this last battle, Italian troops distinguished themselves. On 10 July 1943, the Allies landed in Sicily where Mussolini had promised that they would not get beyond the *bagnasciuga*, or tideline. Instead, resistance was nominal: entire units melted away rather than fight. The 'Assietta' division recorded 9,110 desertions by the beginning of August 1943. Over fifty officers and 2,635 soldiers from other ranks deserted from the 'Aosta' division.[35] Mussolini himself described the Italian troops' resistance as 'sporadic and half-hearted'.[36]

Almost 200,000 Italian servicemen had been killed or had gone missing since 1940. Every one of them was somebody's son, husband, or *fidanzato*. Nearly 30,000 civilians had been killed, mostly in air raids.[37] The country was sick of sacrifice. On 17 July 1943, Allied planes dropped leaflets urging Romans not to 'die for Mussolini and Hitler but live for Italy and for civilization'. Two days later, the bombing of defenceless Rome began, although the Allied planes flew low, in daylight, and avoided sacred or historical monuments. Thousands of casualties were recorded, and entire quarters of the town were badly damaged: Victor Emmanuel met with sullen hostility when he toured the ruins. Mussolini, meanwhile, encountered Hitler in the Alpine town of Feltre, where the Führer refused to commit more troops and aircraft (there were eight German divisions in Italy already), but urged the Italian high command to move troops south and fight harder. Mussolini rejected his own advisers' recommendation to threaten withdrawal from the war: the Duce understood that Hitler would not give the Italians such freedom to act.[38] If Italy surrendered, Germany would overrun north and central Italy and incorporate it into the Reich.

As the Duce piloted himself back to the capital, he and his flight crew saw Rome, in his words, 'wrapped in a vast black cloud'. When he made his way to Villa Torlonia, his imposing private residence, he saw a 'human river' of people fleeing for the countryside carrying their possessions on their backs and in carts.[39] Three days later, the Sicilian capital, Palermo, fell to the Allies. As President Franklin D. Roosevelt asserted in a newsreel film distributed in the United States after the bombing raid, 'the jig was up' for Mussolini's regime.[40]

25 JULY 1943

On 24 July, Mussolini called a meeting of the Fascist Grand Council, the first meeting of the regime's cabinet since December 1939. All its members were to present themselves at Palazzo Venezia, the Duce's official residence, wearing party uniform, at 5 p.m. At the appointed hour Mussolini strode into the Sala del Papagallo (the 'Parrot's Chamber') and received the Roman salute from the twenty-eight gathered hierarchs, many of whom had confessed before the meeting. They were fearful, for they were about to express frank dissent.

Mussolini's chief opponent was Dino Grandi, who had been plotting with other members of the Council for over a week. For a long time ambassador to the United Kingdom, Grandi had once been one of Mussolini's more obsequious followers. But he was no fool and knew which way the wind was blowing.

At the Council meeting, Grandi presented a motion proclaiming it was the duty of all Italians to defend at all costs the 'unity, independence and liberty of the Fatherland' and asserting that it was necessary, to this end, to restore the constitutional order, with all the institutions of the state being reinstated with their proper function. The head of government (Mussolini) should ask the king, according to article 5 of the constitution, to 'assume' supreme command of the armed forces. Beneath the fine words, the Duce was being given a vote of no confidence. In no uncertain terms, moreover: according to Mussolini, Grandi's speech was 'a violent philippic', the speech of a man 'finally able to vent long-concealed spleen'.[41]

Grandi's motion was countered by a second motion, put forward by Roberto Farinacci, the most pro-Nazi member of the Fascist hierarchy, which similarly asked the head of government to request that the king take over 'effective command' of the armed forces, in order to show the whole world that the Italian people were fighting for the 'salvation and dignity of Italy' under his orders, but which also referred to the 'unchanged loyalty to the regime' of Italian Fascists. A heated debate followed. At 2 a.m. on 25 July, the Duce put Grandi's motion to the vote. It received nineteen votes in favour, eight (including Farinacci) against, and one abstained. By his own account, Mussolini concluded the meeting with the words, 'you have provoked the crisis of the regime!'[42]

A morning of plotting followed. At 5 p.m. on 25 July, Mussolini was called to an audience with an 'exceptionally agitated' king, during which he was told that the morale of the army was shattered and that he, the Duce, was 'the most hated man in Italy'.[43] He was deprived of office and Pietro Badoglio was appointed in his place. As he left the royal residence, Mussolini was arrested and escorted to the local police barracks in an ambulance. Subsequently, he was transported to Ponza, an island off the coast of Latium that had served as a prison for numerous opponents of the regime, then to the Maddalena, a naval base in north-east Sardinia, before being moved to the resort hotel in Campo Imperatore in the Abruzzo, which served as his prison.

The *coup d'état* on 25 July did not come out of the blue. Victor Emmanuel had consulted with Grandi and with long-time opponents of the regime. The king had hesitated to act, however, so long as the PNF's chief figures backed the Duce.[44] In the late evening that day, the radio broadcast the news that the king had 'accepted the resignation' of Mussolini. Badoglio issued a proclamation stating that he had been commanded to take over the 'military government' of the nation. The war would go on, with Italy still on Germany's side. Any disturber of public order would be 'inexorably struck down'.

Such admonitions were disregarded by the people. Several days of iconoclasm ensued. Monuments were pulled down, portraits of Mussolini were burned, and other symbols of Fascism were destroyed. The smashing of icons had its vulgar side. Piero Calamandrei recorded in his diary how in the outskirts of Rome 'an old gaffer', followed by various 'hangers-on', had arrived in a square carrying a plaster bust of Mussolini and an axe. Putting the bust on the ground, he 'proceeded to the execution' and with a few blows smashed it to bits. But the show wasn't over. The 'murderer' next 'imperturbably' unbuttoned his trousers, 'stood athwart the shards', and 'from on high sent his regards in a gurgling stream'. The 'ladies present ran for it', Calamandrei added gleefully.[45]

Such anecdotes were, of course, pure hearsay, but the fact that a man of Calamandrei's stature took pleasure in them was significant. As Sergio Luzzatto has argued in a brilliant book, *Il Corpo di Mussolini*, though the downfall of the Duce was applauded by those who 'had for years blistered their hands' clapping Mussolini's orations in Piazza Venezia, the people who committed symbolic acts of violence on Mussolini's 'body', and who called for his execution, were the 'visceral anti-fascists'.[46]

Pietro Ingrao, an intellectual producing the underground edition of *l'Unità* in Milan, watched, fascinated, as the mob 'shouted, smashed, exulted' at the news of Mussolini's downfall.[47] On 26 July, Ingrao addressed a mass meeting in Piazza Duomo to illustrate an improvised twelve-point programme for a new regime. It called for a provisional government of anti-fascist parties; the end of the alliance with Germany and the disarming of German troops in Italy; an armistice with the Allies; the withdrawal of Italian troops from the front; the disbanding of the PNF and the Fascist militia; immediate elections; and the trial of Mussolini and all others 'responsible for the national catastrophe'. Every point was greeted with 'enthusiastic cheering'.[48]

Radio Milano Libertà underlined these same themes. Mussolini was the 'cause of all Italy's ills', it asserted on 26 July 1943. But 'chasing the bloody buffoon from Palazzo Venezia' was insufficient: 'The Fascist bosses responsible for the defeat and ruin of Italy . . . should face a court martial and be shot.' At the same time, it was necessary to distinguish between the upper ranks of the PNF and its millions of card-carrying members. 'We hold out the hand of friendship to all Fascists, good Italians and good citizens, who today are ready to acknowledge that they have been fooled. We won't harm a hair of their heads. Indeed, we will welcome them as brothers.'[49]

In the meantime, sensible Fascists took off their uniforms and mingled with the crowds. Some fled to Germany. Roberto Farinacci, for instance, took refuge in the German Embassy in Rome on the night of 26 July; dressed in Nazi uniform, he was flown to Berlin the following day. There, Farinacci had a brief interview with the Führer, who contemptuously told him that he should have remained loyal to Mussolini. Farinacci's misjudged meeting with Hitler ended whatever plans he – and Goebbels, his main backer in the Nazi hierarchy – might have had of persuading the Nazis to make him the new Duce.[50]

VOICES FROM THE UNDERGROUND

The end of July 1943, in addition to being an anti-regime bacchanal, was a liberating moment of proclamations, pamphlets, and appeals to the Italian people. In a sop to public opinion, Badoglio's new regime freed political prisoners and allowed the resumption of political activity. Political forces suppressed for twenty years emerged into the open. They would be the protagonists of democratic Italian politics for the next five decades.

The Italian Communist Party or PCI, as the PCdI was renamed in

May 1943, the smallest of the pre-regime parties, was the only one with a significant clandestine organization. After 25 July, the party leadership was assumed by a group of militants in their forties who had sacrificed their youth to the cause of anti-Fascism. Without exception, they had served sentences in Mussolini's jails, or had been interned on the island prisons of Ponza and Ventotene, off the coast of Latium. Some had fought in the Spanish Civil War or had been political commissars. They had often lived as exiles in France, or had been interned there, and though they were by no means all intellectuals by education they were all active journalists and propagandists. Some (Giuseppe Di Vittorio, Luigi Longo, Pietro Secchia) were of peasant or working-class origin; others were from upper middle-class backgrounds. Giorgio Amendola's father had been a prominent Liberal MP who had died from a beating by a Fascist squad; Emilio Sereni's father had been doctor to the royal family; Eugenio Reale was a doctor by training and born into an aristocratic family from Naples.

First among equals in July 1943 was Mauro Scoccimarro, a trained political economist from Udine in Italy's north-east. He had given proof of his loyalty to the PCI through nearly two decades in jail, including four years of solitary confinement, in 1928. He was locked up in brutal prisons with common criminals for many years before being transferred to Ventotene. Upon his release in August 1943, the prestige derived from the 'courage of his convictions' he had shown while in jail established him as the 'most authoritative figure' of the PCI within Italy.[51]

The commitment to the cause of these individuals – and others like them – was formidable. Their faith in the proletarian revolution and the historical mission of the Soviet Union had given them the resilience to risk their lives in the trenches of Madrid, to live as exiles in flea-pit hotels in Paris, to eat slops as prisoners behind barbed wire. It had also bred in them intolerance for dissent. *They* had remained faithful to the party line during their years of exile and prison. They were pitiless towards those who had not.

The history of the PCI had been punctuated by polemics with, as the phrase went, 'erring comrades'. The party had been born, at the Leghorn conference of the PSI in 1921, from a split caused by Moscow's intransigence towards the PSI. Subsequently, many senior party members had been expelled because they objected to one reversal or another in Moscow's line. Expressing qualms about Soviet policies made one a heretic.

One critic of the party's dogmatism subsequently recalled that even the Great Terror in the Soviet Union had only strengthened the Italian communists' commitment to Stalin and his policies:

> The purges obviously had a major impact on party comrades . . . but . . . in that moment they contributed, in a way that is difficult to grasp today, to reinforcing the positive judgement bestowed upon Stalin . . . the purges not only did not cause Stalin's star to wane, but if anything caused it to shine more brightly. In other words, even the facts [of the purges] raised no doubts or rethinking. Rather than stimulate debate, [the purges] if anything damped [dissent] down still further, by conferring respectability upon heretic hunting, and ensuring that every dissenter was treated with distrust.[52]

The writer of these words, Umberto Terracini, had been Gramsci's collaborator on *L'Ordine nuovo*, a founder of the PCdI, and a parliamentary deputy. Terracini spent eleven years in jail before he was transferred in July 1937 to Ponza and subsequently Ventotene. He and the party's most prominent woman activist, Camilla Ravera, who was serving a fifteen-year sentence for anti-fascist agitation, broke with the party line over the Nazi–Soviet Pact in August 1939. They were ostracized by their fellow prisoners on Ventotene for their pains and expelled from the party in 1941.

After 25 July, when Terracini was released from internment, the ostracism continued. As he recalled in the 1970s:

> It is sad for me to remember it, but one of the first things that the leadership cadres on Ventotene did, as soon as they reached Rome, was circulate the organizational network of the party warning members to have no dealings with me, and to reject any step I might take to contact them.[53]

The PCI leadership's deference to Moscow is important because so many of the party's actions after July 1943 were conditioned by it, as we shall see. At the same time, Moscow understood that communists would have to operate in national political contexts after the war and could not afford to be seen as agents of a foreign power. The Communist International (Comintern), the transnational organization coordinating the activities of national parties around the world, was formally abolished in April 1943, which is why the Italian party changed its name from the *Communist* Party of Italy to the *Italian* Communist Party.

The PCI's leader was based in Moscow when Mussolini fell: Ercoli, Palmiro Togliatti, who had taken over the direction of the party after Antonio Gramsci's arrest and imprisonment in 1926. From 1927 to the summer of 1934, Togliatti ran the party's Paris headquarters and was its representative in the Comintern. He was handpicked by Georgi Dimitrov, the Bulgarian head of the Comintern, to be deputy-secretary and spent the years until 1939, at the height of the Great Purges, at the top of an organization that Stalin described, in February 1937, as a 'den of spies'.[54]

Togliatti was an indefatigable worker. He must have written, edited, or chaired thousands of flat ephemeral pamphlets or boring meetings. While he was head of the party and senior official in the Comintern, many Italian emigrés living in the USSR – people who had fled arrest in Italy and moved to the Socialist fatherland out of idealism – were condemned, 'with the explicit assent of Togliatti and the other party leaders operating in Moscow', to disappear into the 'vortex' of Stalin's Terror.[55]

During the Spanish Civil War, under the code name of 'Alfredo', Togliatti was chief commissar in Spain, charged with enforcing ideological orthodoxy upon the left-wing republican government of Juan Negrin. He was an éminence grise until the Republic's fall and 'played an active role in the anti-Trotskyist witch-hunt' that took place throughout its last two years.[56]

Togliatti escaped from Spain on the last plane out in May 1939, literally minutes ahead of Fascist troops sent to arrest him. He was under a cloud in the USSR: a 'thick and menacing dossier of accusations and suspicions' had accumulated against him.[57] The wreck of the Spanish Republic required a scapegoat: Togliatti was blamed. He compounded his position by getting himself arrested in Paris in

September 1939 while on a mission to recompose an Italian party leadership disoriented by the Nazi–Soviet Pact: he was only freed in March 1940. In December of that year, Antonio Gramsci's widow wrote to Stalin to accuse Togliatti of having done little to liberate her husband and of being a traitor.

Togliatti survived all these storms. In wartime Russia he made himself useful. He broadcast to Italy on Radio Moscow and Radio Milano Libertà and worked tirelessly and without complaint. He stuck religiously to the party line. The subsequent ascendancy of Togliatti over the party in Italy ultimately derived from two complementary facts: Moscow regarded him as able, and the party cadres deferred to Moscow's judgement.

The Italian Socialist Party, along with a handful of clandestine groups, reconstituted itself as the Italian Socialist Party of Proletarian Unity (PSIUP) on 22 August 1943, in the house of Oreste Lizzadri, a wine merchant, in Rome's Via Parioli. There was a distinct taste of old wine in new bottles about the PSIUP. Its founding 'Political Declaration' averred, in mechanical prose, that the PSIUP intended 'to promote by all means the political struggle of the oppressed against the oppressors and the class struggle of the exploited against the exploiters, in order to lead the proletariat to the conquest of power'. The PSIUP's immediate demands were: (1) An immediate armistice with the Allies and a repudiation of the alliance with Germany and Japan; (2) the 'liquidation' of Fascism, the monarchy, and the capitalist groups that had 'laid hands' on the 'nerve centres' of the economy; (3) the re-establishment of all civil and political liberties and the creation of a 'provisional government of public safety' in which all 'popular and progressive parties' would be represented.[58]

The language and tone of the 'Political Declaration' was that of the old PSI's 'maximalist' faction: the usual revolutionary platitudes. More interesting was the declaration's statement that there was a 'fundamental community of doctrine and ends' between the PSIUP and the PCI and that their 'fusion' into a single party was the PSIUP's aim. This objective reflected the influence of Pietro Nenni, who was elected party secretary and editor of the party newspaper, *Avanti!*

Nenni was the PSI's most charismatic personality from the mid-1920s to the mid-1970s, a period that was characterized by the party's complex, mostly subaltern relationship with the PCI. Born in Faenza (Romagna) in 1891, Nenni was the son of a sharecropper. He lost his father when he was five and received only an elementary education. He nevertheless became a prolific radical journalist at an early age. He wrote for the *Lotta di classe* ('Class Struggle'), a weekly edited by Mussolini in the Romagna town of Forlì, and the two men became friends (and cellmates) after they took part in protests against the war in Libya in 1911. Nenni, like Mussolini, supported Italian entry into the war against Austria-Hungary, though he was a much better soldier: he was twice promoted and was decorated for bravery. After the war, he briefly became a member of Mussolini's *Fasci di combattimento*. The experience would be thrown in his face for decades to come. By an 'irony of fate', Nenni was an internee on Ponza in July 1943 when Mussolini, escorted by a detachment of military police, arrived. Nenni, however, was amnestied a few days later.

Despite his working-class background, and lack of formal education, Nenni was a fluent writer, witty speaker, and an able sloganizer. He also believed that ideas and personal commitment were the key determinants of politics: Fascism would not collapse of its own accord, and socialism would not arrive through historical necessity, but only through the action of working people and the parties that represented them.[59] There was nothing mechanical about Nenni's world view.

It was this trait that drove him to conclude that unity between the non-communist left and the PCI was the only strategy likely to defeat Fascism and to build socialism in Italy. This conclusion came to Nenni somewhat late. He emerged as a major figure in the PSI before its dissolution by Mussolini in 1926 because he was an *opponent* of fusion with the PCdI. In exile in France in the late 1920s, Nenni polemicized hard with the Italian communists for the crudeness of their slurs against the 'social-Fascism' of the democratic left. Nenni, who became leader of the exiled PSI in 1930, also worked closely with Carlo Rosselli, a charismatic liberal-socialist from a wealthy Jewish family steeped, on both his mother's and his father's sides, in the traditions of the Risorgimento. In 1929, Rosselli founded a political movement, Justice and Liberty (GL), critical of both the maximalist socialism of the old PSI and, above all, of Stalinism. Justice and Liberty attracted adherents among the educated

young: many of post-war democratic Italy's most revered public intellectuals began their political education in the 1930s by reading clandestine
copies of the movement's newspaper.

Rosselli was subsequently murdered on Mussolini's orders, along
with his brother Nello, at the French spa town of Bagnoles-de-l'Orne
in June 1937. Tens of thousands attended the brothers' funeral in
Paris: 'only the murder of Matteotti in 1924 had caused such a sense
of bereavement among Italian anti-fascists'.[60]

In the early 1930s, Nenni nevertheless made a choice that would
have huge implications for Italy's democracy after 1945. Under his
guidance, the PSI moved towards a rapprochement with the PCdI,
signing a pact of 'unity of action' with the communists in August
1934. The rise of Hitler had convinced Nenni that Europe's Marxist
parties had to work together to fight Fascism and establish democracy. Across Europe, the Spanish Civil War became a symbol for those
who took this line. Nenni became one of the Republic's best-known
supporters, though he turned a blind eye to the Comintern's undemocratic role in Spain's domestic politics.

Inevitably, the Nazi–soviet Pact brought unity of action between
the two parties to an end. Nenni attacked the pact but continued to
argue wishfully that cooperation with the PCdI remained a valid
strategy. The other most prominent PSI exiles thought rather that the
USSR had lost all claim 'to be a model for socialism'.[61] Nenni was
forced out of the party leadership as a result. Only the heroic resistance of the Red Army at Stalingrad made the notion of a 'pact of
unity' with the PCI a feasible proposition again. By the time Nenni
had made his way back to Rome from Ponza in August 1943 (in
anguish for the fate of his daughter, Vivà [Vittoria], who had been
arrested in France and transported to Auschwitz, where she would
later die), the socialists emerging from the shadows within Italy were
ready for his leadership once more.[62]

The legacy of Carlo Rosselli and Justice and Liberty was represented
after 25 July by the Action Party (PdA), although other currents of
liberal opinion – liberal socialists, members of the nascent European
federalist movement, Republicans, advocates of a mixed economy, and
southern Italian radicals – all found a home in the new party. The fact
that the Action Party was an intellectuals' party helped its diffusion in

Italy's university towns. Its first members were people of social position who could travel for work and with less risk of being stopped by the police. They could hold meetings relatively freely.[63]

The PdA was founded in June 1942 at meetings in Rome and Milan. Its initial political standpoint was expressed in a programme published in the first (January 1943) edition of *l'Italia Libera*, the party's clandestine broadsheet. The programme announced the 'unpostponable need' for a republican form of government in which the executive was 'assiduously and permanently controlled' by parliamentary institutions and by an independent judiciary. The monarchy should go. The PdA's economic policy was radical: the party wanted to nationalize the largest financial, industrial and insurance companies and give land to the peasants by breaking up the estates of the big landowners. The Action Party also expressed the hope that the end of the war would give birth to a 'unitary European conscience', which it regarded as an 'indispensable premise' for the creation of a European federation of democratic nations and the superseding of the principle of national sovereignty.[64]

The programme was accompanied by an article entitled '*Chi siamo*' ('Who We Are') written by Adolfo Tino, a lawyer originally from southern Italy working in Milan, and an able young political economist from Palermo who would become one of democratic Italy's most important politicians, Ugo La Malfa. This article asserted that the new party was not the 'continuation' of Justice and Liberty, or any of the other movements that had struggled against Fascism for the previous two decades, but rather 'encompassed and superseded them all into a political plan of action that is at once broader, more decisive and more radical'. Tino and La Malfa's article also underlined that the Partito d'Azione regarded itself as an agent of renewal for the Italian *nation*:

> It is necessary to restore to Italy and to the Italian people, who have been battered by so many misadventures, their faith in the tradition of the Risorgimento, which Fascism has spurned, and in the future of the liberal institutions that the Risorgimento bequeathed us ... Italians should remember that the Action Party ... was born in a dark moment of our national renewal to bring about the completion of the great

work of unification and national independence. The present moment is darker still, and everything is still to play for. But the spirit that must unify and drive the Italians is the same.[65]

This evocation of Giuseppe Mazzini's original Action Party, founded in 1853 with the participation of such heroes of the Risorgimento as Giuseppe Garibaldi and Carlo Pisacane, an aristocratic soldier of fortune turned utopian socialist, is why the PdA seemed the most *Italian* of the political parties that emerged from clandestine existence in August 1943 – at any rate it did to the English, whose imagination has always been captivated by the romanticism of the Risorgimento, that greatest of victories for a seemingly lost cause. In reality, of course, all the new parties potentially reflected the aspirations of significant sections of the Italian people, though none of them knew how strong their position was or might become. Superficially, they were clandestine networks of intellectuals and politically conscious workers, but they were not rootless.

The most important political formation to take the stage after 25 July emerged from the part of society that had remained freest during the regime: Catholicism. Christian Democracy took early form in the autumn of 1942 during meetings in the small pre-Alpine town of Borgo Valsugana and at the Milan home of Giorgio Enrico Falck, a Catholic businessman, attended by a number of intellectuals, clergymen, and professionals. The new party was given this name because the founders wanted 'to appeal to the young who had not lived through the battles of the popularist movement (i.e. the PPI) and therefore to promote the fusion of two generations'.[66] Meetings of FUCI, the students' association, and of the Catholic graduates' association were places where critical discussions of the regime were widespread. Such discussions increased after Pope Pius XII's Christmas 1942 broadcast (Pius XI had died in 1939), which was interpreted as an 'incitement' to the revival of political activity by Catholics.[67]

The acknowledged leader among Catholics was Alcide De Gasperi, the last leader of the defunct PPI. After its dissolution, De Gasperi had been imprisoned after a farcical trial in 1927. He spent more than a year in Rome's notorious Regina Coeli prison. Upon his release in July 1928, living with his family almost in destitution, he found sanctuary in the Vatican library and spent the intervening years until 1943 cataloguing manuscripts and writing occasional articles for Vatican newspapers.[68]

In the spring of 1943, in meetings in Rome at the house of Giuseppe Spataro, a lawyer who had worked tirelessly to maintain contacts between democratic Catholics under the regime, De Gasperi led discussions which produced a pamphlet-manifesto called *Le idee ricostruttive della Democrazia Cristiana* ('The Ideas of Christian Democracy for Reconstruction'), which was distributed widely on 31 July 1943, under the pseudonym of 'Demofilo'. It was a thoughtful piece of work, not an attack on the regime or even a statement of Christian Democracy's promises for the future; the document's opening lines, in fact, confessed that it was not 'the right moment to launch partisan programmes, which would be unworthy of this solemn moment that requires the unity of all Italians'. De Gasperi hoped, however, that the pamphlet's main themes might become 'guiding principles' for the postwar reconstruction. 'Demofilo' called for political liberty expressed through a representative democracy in which all citizens had both equal rights and equal duties. An elected parliament, not an all-powerful leader, would be the highest institution of the land and would alone have the power to declare war. A Supreme Court would protect fundamental rights from the 'abuses of the public authorities and the attacks of political parties'. Italy would become a federal state divided into autonomous regions with substantive administrative responsibilities.

Together with these 'liberal' positions, *Democrazia Cristiana* took a confessional line on the question of the state's role as moral arbiter: a democratic regime would only be safe, 'Demofilo' averred, if the state 'kept morality in its tutelage, protected the integrity of the family, and gave parents its full support to educate the new generations in a Christian fashion'. The pamphlet stated that it was crucial for the 'yeast' of Christianity to 'ferment' in society and that the 'spiritual mission' of the Church should be allowed to flourish. Demofilo's economic ideas also recalled Catholic doctrine, specifically Pope Leo XIII's encyclical *Rerum Novarum* (1891). The goal for social policy, the pamphlet proposed, should be the 'suppression of the proletariat'. This was not a call for repressive measures, but an appeal for the social inclusion of the poor. Italy should aspire to build a society in which inequality was diminished and class differences were less antagonistic.[69]

De Gasperi was concerned above all to avoid 'the anti-libertarian mentality of dictatorship, be it the dictatorship of the bourgeois republic, or the military-monarchist, or proletarian-communist'. He might have added to this list 'clerical-military' since, despite his deep faith, he was no apologist for the authoritarian regimes preferred by the Church in Spain and Portugal. De Gasperi was suspicious of 'the revolutionary passion of the committee for public safety' or of any 'Jacobin ambition' to impose blueprints on unwilling subjects.[70] At the same time, he knew that it was not a conservative moment: the masses were entering politics and their demands for social justice would require the transformation of the Italian state.

THE KING RUNS AWAY

Badoglio's government dissolved the PNF, and amnestied political prisoners, but it showed no sign of regarding the political formations described in the previous section as legitimate interlocutors. It was composed exclusively of military men and courtiers; even moderates sympathetic to the monarchist cause were excluded, as were liberal critics of Fascism such as the philosopher Benedetto Croce. Public protests against the war were suppressed bloodily. In the last few days of July, eighty-three citizens were killed and over 300 were wounded as troops crushed demonstrations organized by the leftist parties. Provincial governments, the judiciary, and the police remained firmly in the hands of people appointed by the regime. The Fascist militia, though disbanded, was absorbed into the regular army, which strengthened the position of the many army officers who did not want, either for ideological reasons or reasons of professional honour, to desert the German ally with whom they had waged war.

The Badoglio government's reluctance to break with the Reich, as Togliatti pointed out in a volley of radio broadcasts from Moscow, was giving the Germans time to reinforce their military presence in Italy and would make liberation bloodier. The king and Badoglio needed to 'make up their minds' to end the war, Togliatti warned on

31 July 1943, or else they should make way for a 'provisional peace government' composed of the anti-fascist parties. He returned to the point on 3 August, insisting that 'no distinction is possible between Fascism and the war'.[71] On the same day, a delegation of the anti-fascist parties urged Badoglio to end the war at once, with a unilateral declaration that it would no longer fight the Allies. Beneath a banner headline demanding 'Peace', l'Unità warned on 4 August that the longer Italy's 'subjugation' to the Nazis continued, the more it would share the blame for Germany's atrocities and the tougher would be the peace imposed by the victorious Allies.[72]

Badoglio rejected outright this strategy, whose obvious concomitant was war with Nazi Germany. In the words of Elena Aga Rossi, 'every initiative of the [Badoglio] government was entirely conditioned by fear of the reaction of the German armed forces'.[73] They feared the 'return of the Fascists who had fled to Germany' as quisling rulers.[74] The Italian army would have had to cut off the retreat of the Germans fighting the Allies in the south and engage in battle the Nazi troops present near Rome. There were also numbers of well-armed Nazi police and officials within Rome itself. The eight German divisions deployed in Italy in July 1943 were far better trained, armed, and equipped than the demoralized Italian army; in August further German divisions under the command of Field Marshal Erwin Rommel were deployed into northern Italy from Austria.

The fate of Italy's substantial army in the Balkans also entered the government's calculations: if Italy found itself at war with Germany, those forces were bound to be attacked by the Germans. There were also 300,000 Italians working in the Third Reich: they would be interned as slave labourers if Italy switched sides. One can see why Badoglio and the king shrank from such a step. They were small men faced with fraught consequences for any action that they might take.

One can see also why Togliatti and the PCI wanted them to take the leap: had Badoglio stabbed his erstwhile allies in the back, it would have damaged the Nazi war effort and might have compelled the German high command to divert resources from the life and death struggle on the Russian Front. The PCI now began calling for popular insurrection against the Germans – recognition that an armistice could only bring an intensification of the fighting, not peace. Togliatti condemned Badoglio and the king as 'enemies of the nation' in a 24 August 1943 broadcast.[75]

Nenni's *Avanti!* was equally hostile to the king and to Badoglio but seemed blissfully unaware of the military realities. On 3 September, the newspaper of the PSIUP declared that 'Either Badoglio makes peace, or Badoglio must go.' It acknowledged there was a risk that the Germans would overrun part of the country and install 'someone like Farinacci' as head of a 'ghost government' but complacently affirmed that there were 'forces in Italy well able to cope with any German provocation'. The people should 'stand up to' the 'German peril' with 'masculine vigour'. It was wrong to let oneself be 'blackmailed' by fear of German retribution, *Avanti!* commented; what Italy now needed was a 'government of public safety', rooted in the popular masses, that would recall Italian troops from France and the Balkans, make an armistice with the Allies, and 'tell Hitler to withdraw his troops beyond the Brenner frontier'.[76]

What such a government should do if Hitler balked was not stated: 'masculine vigour' was all very well, but if Italian soldiers were to fight the Germans, the army needed sufficient firepower, and officers willing to die at the head of their troops. The Sicilian campaign had exposed the feebleness of military morale. Badoglio and the king were not prepared either, because of who they were, to call for an insurrection against the Germans. They were afraid of the Nazis, yet equally scared of a mob stirred by agitators such as Nenni.

The king's and Badoglio's doubts were comprehensible but the policy they followed in August 1943 was dishonourable. In effect, they double-crossed their former Nazi comrades-in-arms, by conducting a secret negotiation with the Allies; the British and Americans, by not keeping their word to mobilize Italian troops to help Allied landings; the Italian army, by leaving it leaderless and without orders; and the Italian people, by surrendering Rome to the Nazis.

Secret talks began between Italy and the Allies in August. At the Quebec Conference (11–24 August 1943), one of the main items of business discussed by the Allies was what became known as the 'Long Armistice', i.e. the full statement of conditions that would be imposed upon Italy, in exchange for which the Allies were willing to recognize

Badoglio as the rightful head of the Italian government, as they had previously recognized General Darlan, a Vichy official, in Algiers.

On 3 September, at Cassibile, near Syracuse in Sicily, Brigadier General Giuseppe Castellano signed the 'Short Armistice', or act of surrender, on behalf of the Italian government. US General Walter Bedell Smith signed for the Allies. The armistice was composed of twelve conditions. The first obliged Italy to cease 'all hostile activity': Allied prisoners were to be handed over; the Italian fleet was to surrender; French Corsica and all Italian territories were to be used as operational bases as the Allies saw fit; Italian troops in other theatres of war, in other words southern France, or the Balkans, were to be withdrawn to the homeland. Crucially, the Italian government committed itself to denying the Germans the use of 'facilities that might be used against the United Nations' (Point 2); protecting airfields and naval ports in Italian territory (Point 7); and 'employing all its available armed forces to ensure prompt and exact compliance with all the provisions of this armistice' (Point 9). The Badoglio government explicitly committed itself, therefore, to defending key military assets from the Nazis, even if it did not pledge itself to take the offensive against German units on Italian soil. General Eisenhower, the Supreme Allied Commander, would communicate news of the armistice the day before the invasion began.

While these negotiations were taking place, Badoglio privately assured the Nazis that Italy would continue to fight at their side. The German ambassador, Rudolf Rahn, met Badoglio on 3 September. At the end of their interview, the old soldier grasped Rahn's hand and stated, 'with an air of pathos', that he had 'given his word and would keep it'. Rahn found Badoglio's manner a little 'theatrical', but would never have guessed that the armistice had been 'signed and sealed' three hours before their conversation. The 'old marshal had known how to act his part to perfection'.[77]

Throughout the armistice negotiations, Castellano pressed for information about where and when landings would take place, but the Allies sensibly did not trust the Italian government or military to keep the secret. In fact, the Italians correctly guessed that troops would come ashore around Salerno (which was the furthest north that air cover could be given by fighters based in Sicily), but thought landings would take place on 12 September. Badoglio and his ministers made no preparations for the clashes with German units that were bound to take place at airfields, barracks, ports, munition dumps, refineries and so on once the surrender was announced; nor did they make plans to seize airfields under German control near Rome where Castellano had assured the Allies that they could land troops, as American General Maxwell Taylor discovered on 7 September when he conducted a secret mission to Rome. In compensation, the Italian military had prepared Taylor and his comrade, William T. Gardner, 'a generous lunch'. Taylor insisted on meeting Badoglio, who was having a nap.[78] The Italian premier urged the Allies to call off the landings: a ridiculous request so late in the day, but one entirely in keeping with Badoglio's conception of honour.

The Italian royalists were thus compelled, finally, to choose sides. An emergency meeting in the late afternoon of 8 September between the king and his chief ministers, at which several voices were raised in favour of reneging on the armistice, was interrupted by the news that Eisenhower had announced the Italian surrender. In response, Badoglio made an equivocal radio broadcast in which he acknowledged that Italy, faced with the prospect of continuing 'an unequal struggle' against 'the overwhelming power of its adversaries', had requested an armistice, which had been granted. All hostile acts against the Allies should cease at once, but Italian forces should 'react' to 'eventual attacks from any other source'. This last ambiguous phrase was the only guidance given by the prime minister to the Italian army as to its conduct towards the German forces based in Italy.

Early the next morning, on 9 September, the royal family, and its chief courtiers, headed for Pescara, where a boat would take them to Brindisi in Apulia. They were terrified at the thought of falling into the hands of the Germans and this led to 'somewhat undignified jostling' to escape. Most government ministers were not even informed of the king's flight.[79] The convoy of vehicles was in fact stopped at a roadblock by German troops but was waved through. Many believe that a deal was struck with Albert Kesselring, the German commander in central Italy, to ensure the royals' free passage in return for the peaceful cooperation of the Italian armed forces in the occupation of Rome.[80] On 10 September, indeed, Italian troops capitulated after posing only sporadic resistance and Rome was declared an 'open city', under de facto German control.

Bereft of orders, the Italian army surrendered almost everywhere without firing a shot: 'a substantial portion of the generals and senior officers ... took to their heels and ran.'[81] Though *l'Italia Libera* was surely exaggerating when it said entire regiments had 'surrendered to a single German kitchen orderly', the military collapse was total.[82] In northern Italy, Rommel's troops took 13,000 officers and 402,600 other ranks prisoner in a few days, though many escaped: there were simply too many to guard. The most fortunate troops were those ordered to desert with their arms by junior officers: tens of thousands obeyed and took to the hills or sought refuge in their home cities. They became the backbone of the resistance.

The armies in the Balkans and the Aegean were less accommodating. Although most divisions surrendered passively, and some diehard Fascists joined the Germans, the Aqui division on the island of Kefalonia fought rather than surrender after 8 September. In two weeks of battle its troops inflicted heavy casualties on the Germans: an uncertain, but certainly very large, number of prisoners of war was massacred in revenge.[83] In all nearly 400,000 Italian troops were taken prisoner in the Balkans. At least 13,000 of these men drowned when the ships transporting them sank after hitting mines. By October, nearly 500,000 former Italian soldiers had been transported to Germany to work as slave labour. The dissolution of the Italian army liberated more than 150,000 Germans for military service.[84]

There was little civilian resistance to the German takeover. Pietro Nenni, walking around Rome on 9 September, was struck by the fact that 'groups of German soldiers' could pass through the crowd 'without provoking the slightest reaction'. He could not but compare it to the 'long and heroic battle of Madrid'.[85] One city that did erupt into an insurrection was Naples. Outraged by the 'scorched-earth' policies implemented by the retreating German army, and by atrocities against civilians, especially rape, the city's revolutionary spirit was unleashed. Between 27 and 30 September, the *scugnizzi* from Naples' teeming popular quarters harried the Germans mercilessly.[86] Some 300 patriots were killed, but when Allied troops arrived on 2 October they were met by jubilant crowds – and a social catastrophe that would endure for the rest of the decade.

The German forces, reinforced by troops from the North, positioned themselves in a provisional defensive line stretching from Termoli on the Adriatic coast to just north of Naples. Behind this temporary line, preparations began on more permanent defensive fortifications centred upon Montecassino (to give its Italian spelling), an imposing mountain, topped by one of the oldest abbeys in Christendom, some sixty miles north of Naples. Kesselring counted on Italy's rugged topography to slow down the Allied advance and convinced the Führer that it was wise to defend as much of Italy as possible.

The northernmost provinces of Bolzano, Trento and Belluno, the so-called Voralpenland, were absorbed into the Reich and administered from Innsbruck, though quislings were found to act as proxy rulers: in Trento, for instance, it was a prominent pro-Austrian romantic called Adolfo De Bertolini.[87] Udine, Gorizia, Trieste, Pola, and Fiume were administered from the Austrian province of Styria. Italy was once again 'unredeemed', and Germans were once again ruling over Italians. Hitler further decided upon a tripartite system of governance for Italy: front-line areas would be subject to the commander of the army; the rest of German-occupied Italy would be administered by a German military government, while an SS command would act as the police force for Germany's new colony, whose principal task would be to feed war production for Germany. But the Nazis needed an Italian figurehead for their hegemony.

On 12 September, Mussolini was rescued by German parachute troops. Hitler was exultant and even broke the news to Mussolini's son Vittorio in Italian, the only time anybody had ever heard him speak the language.[88] The Duce was taken to Berlin on 14 September. He was a sadly shrunken figure. He looked pale and ill, was poorly shaven, wore crumpled clothes, and his tie was awry. One onlooker snidely remarked that 'he looked like a bricklayer wearing his father's best suit at a party'.[89]

Mussolini, who was still demoralized by his rejection on 25 July, now came under immense pressure from the Nazis to restore Fascism in Italy. Plenty of important Nazis had wanted to find a more ruthless leader than Mussolini, but Hitler, although he had 'acquired a sad scepticism in regard to his friend and one-time political mentor', decided that the Duce would still pass.[90] A browbeaten Duce capitulated. On 18 September, Mussolini broadcast from Munich that he would establish a republic that would go back to the Fascist regime's nationalist and socialist origins.

By the end of September 1943, therefore, Fascism's alliance with Hitler had turned the Italian mainland north of Naples into a colony ruled by German occupiers whose racial contempt for Italians was no longer disguised. The cities of the north were being pounded by Allied bombs. Much of the Italian army was being transported to Germany to work as slaves. Sicily and the deep South were under the control of the Allies. Hundreds of thousands of people, especially young men, had died to achieve this catastrophic outcome: it was obvious, moreover, that many more were about to die as the Allied armies clawed their way up the peninsula. In early September, *l'Unità* had poetically warned that if the Germans occupied Italy:

> Every telegraph pole would have a corpse dangling from it, every vineyard, every field would have a mass grave. The Fascists and the Germans are planning a vendetta against the workers, against soldiers, against the people as a whole; their brutality will be rendered more savage by their desperation. Our country is the land of the swallows. It would become the land of carrion crows.[91]

The grim prediction of the PCI's newspaper was about to be proved right and Italy's would-be leaders could do nothing about it. Mussolini was scrambling to put together a collaborationist government from the Fascists who had betrayed their country and fled to Germany. Badoglio, the general who ran away, was trying to preserve a façade of political legitimacy from a hotel room in Brindisi. The new political formations that had emerged after 25 July had sunk back into clandestine activity in Rome and Milan, waiting in fear for the Gestapo to kick in their door. In the weeks since Mussolini had been deposed, Italy had 'touched the bottom of the abyss', Piero Calamandrei wrote in his splendid Pepysian diary. The Florentine jurist remained confident, however, that this period of 'atrocious suffering' would be a 'cauterization' of the wounds left by Fascism.[92] The people hated Fascism, hated the Germans, and wanted to take their country back, Calamandrei was sure. He was right. Italy was about to be reborn.

3

The Emergence of the Parties

After 8 September 1943, Italy became a battlefield. The United Nations' forces – which included Polish, Brazilian, Indian, Kiwi, South African, and Canadian units, as well as British, French, and American troops – inched their way up the peninsula under the command of a British General, Harold Alexander. Italy entered the war on the side of the Allies in mid-October 1943, but only as 'enemies on parole', not as anti-Nazis in good standing.[1] To the chagrin of Badoglio and his successors, Italian troops were used only sparingly. The air force and navy were more deeply integrated into the war effort, and the navy, especially, performed a valuable support role.

Progress was slow for three main reasons. Italy's mountainous terrain lent itself to defensive warfare; German commander Albert Kesselring was a competent battlefield general; the Italian front was deprived of men and materiel by the Allied High Command. At the Tehran Conference between 28 November and 1 December, the 'Big Three' (Roosevelt, Churchill, Stalin) took a strategic decision, on Stalin's insistence, to open a 'second front' across the channel in Normandy in the spring of 1944. The Italian Front subsequently became a strategic sideshow, albeit a bloody one. Rome did not fall until 4 June 1944, nine long months after troops had come ashore at Salerno.

The war took a huge toll on a country that was already grievously hurt by Mussolini's military adventurism. Italians who had been intoxicated by his war of conquest in Abyssinia now learned what it was like to be colonized by Europeans. They experienced colonialism with the gloves off, not the benign fantasy world depicted in the Fascist regime's propaganda. Being a Nazi colony meant being treated as

71

racial inferiors; it meant a reign of terror; it meant deportation and slavery for hundreds of thousands of Italian men. It meant, for the politically minded and others, making an existential choice between collaboration with the colonizers and resistance to them.

The Allies, by contrast, ruled their part of the peninsula more like a trusteeship, or mandated territory. They did not rule alone, however. Until June 1944, the fugitive royalist government of Marshal Badoglio was shored up, at the insistence of the British, as the recognized government of Italy, even though practically all anti-fascist Italians regarded Badoglio and the king's court as traitors or accomplices with the deposed regime, or both. The Allies accordingly became embroiled in the internal politics of Italy: in heated constitutional debates whose historical roots and contemporary vehemence they never fully grasped. The anti-fascist parties were adamant that sovereign power resided in and flowed from them, as representatives of the Italian people, and not in and from a discredited monarchy.

In the end, they carried their point. The anti-fascist parties became the interlocutors with whom the Allies had to deal. By the summer of 1944, having established their right to govern, the most important Italian politicians were already sketching out their aspirations for the future form of democracy that the state would embody.

THE POLITICS OF CO-BELLIGERENCY

In the eyes of anti-fascists, the catastrophe of 8–9 September 1943 disqualified the government of Pietro Badoglio of any moral right to continue in office. The House of Savoy had lost all authority. As if appointing Mussolini to power, closing a blind eye to the killing of Matteotti, approving the racial laws, and acquiescing in the stab in the back of France in 1940 had not been enough, now the king, by his flight, had facilitated the dissolution and enslavement of the Italian army, the occupation of most of the Italian peninsula by the Nazis, and the absorption of Trento and Trieste into the Third Reich.

On 9 September, as the Nazis occupied Rome, the four political parties introduced in the previous chapter, the Action Party (PdA), the PCI, the PSIUP, and Christian Democracy (DC), formed the Committee of

National Liberation (CLN). They did this along with the Democracy and Labour Party (DL), a party of reformist socialists founded by Ivanoe Bonomi in 1943, and the reconstituted Liberal Party (PLI), the heirs to the tradition of pre-1922 parliamentarianism.

The new CLN's steering committee was chaired by Bonomi, a relic of pre-Fascist Italy who had been expelled from the PSI in 1912 because of his willingness to cooperate with Giolitti. Bonomi, from Mantua, had been elected to parliament in Giolitti's National Bloc in 1921 and briefly held the premiership between July 1921 and February 1922. He had not compromised himself during the regime. In the weeks after Mussolini's downfall, as the most socially acceptable opponent of the regime, he had been the point of contact between the anti-fascist parties and the king. The DC was represented by De Gasperi, the PSIUP by Nenni, the PCI by Scoccimarro (or Giorgio Amendola), the PdA by La Malfa. Bartolomeo Ruini, a lawyer from Modena who had been a valiant soldier during the First World War and an active anti-fascist after the March on Rome, represented Democracy and Labour.[2] During the regime, Ruini had been deprived of his right to practise professionally and had been forced to live a penurious life as a known but semi-tolerated opponent of Mussolini. The last member of the CLN was Alessandro Casati, a Milanese aristocrat who had briefly served under Mussolini as minister of education, but who had followed his friend and mentor Benedetto Croce into dignified opposition against the regime. Casati represented the Liberal Party (PLI), which Croce had revived after Mussolini's downfall in July. The PLI was essentially a party of *notabili*, of the few distinguished relics of Giolittian Italy who had not compromised themselves during two decades of Fascism.

The creation of the CLN gave anti-Fascists hope in a very dark moment. On 25 September 1943, an acute editorial in *l'Italia Libera* boldly predicted that 'Italy will reclaim its place among the free democracies' through its conduct during the remainder of the war. The clandestine newspaper forecast that the struggle against the Nazis would provide Italy with a means both of redeeming itself in the eyes of the world and of repaying the moral debt the nation owed to the 'most noble part of us': the heroes who had already perished in the twenty-year struggle against Fascism.[3] But the struggle had to be led by the CLN, since this body 'derived its authority' from the fact that its members had never compromised with the regime and had remained in Rome when others had fled. The CLN alone possessed the moral right to 'unify all the spiritual and political forces of the nation', while Badoglio and the king had forfeited their right to rule.[4]

The Allied high command paid no heed to such arguments, in so far as they were aware of them. The British regarded the defeated Italians with distrust and were determined both to punish them for siding with the Nazis and to ensure that Italy presented no future threat in the Mediterranean: as the phrase went, they wanted to 'keep Italy down'. On 29 September 1943, on HMS *Nelson* in Valletta harbour, the Allies imposed a 44-article supplement to the original armistice signed by the Badoglio government's emissary on 3 September. Colloquially known as 'the long armistice', the document made clear that occupied Italy would be a de facto mandated territory administered by a newly constituted Allied Control Commission (ACC) that would possess unconditional power to run the economy, requisition and produce war materials, control ports and airfields, purge Fascists from public office, and supervise the press and broadcasting. The Italian government's own writ would apply only in such territories as the Control Commission designated and even there, as Article 22 specified, the Italian government and people were to 'abstain from all action detrimental to the interests of the United Nations' and to 'carry out promptly and efficiently all orders given by the United Nations'.[5] As David Ellwood has underlined, 'the victorious powers had little doubt that the terms were cruel.'[6] They carefully ensured that the full surrender terms remained a secret restricted to the king and his principal ministers until after the conclusion of the war. Badoglio signed: he had no alternative. The Italian delegation was not even invited for lunch afterwards.[7]

In Malta, General Eisenhower, the then Supreme Allied Commander in the Mediterranean, also pressed Badoglio to declare war on Nazi Germany, a request that the Marshal insisted could only be taken by the king, who was concerned that his authority extended over too little territory for any such declaration to be credible. The Allies pointed out that numerous governments-in-exile (Poland, France, the Czechs) controlled no territory at all. In the meantime, without a declaration of war, the Germans would treat captured Italian troops as *francs-tireurs*, liable to summary execution, rather than as prisoners of war.[8]

On 13 October, the Italians yielded to the Allies' pressure and formally declared war on Germany. This action was insufficient to make Italy a member of the United Nations, however. It was unthinkable, especially for the Free French government of General Charles de Gaulle and for the British, that the Italians should be an ally: the French foreign minister, René Massigli, pugnaciously described Italian entry into the war as a 'farce'.[9] Italy was accordingly deemed a 'co-belligerent', a term invented by the resident British minister in the Mediterranean theatre, the future premier, Harold Macmillan. The French government in Algiers complained even about this compromise term: the fact that Italy continued to be governed by the same men (notably the king and Badoglio) who had led the aggression against France in June 1940 was, as Italians say, 'too large a toad to swallow' for de Gaulle.[10] The use of the term 'co-belligerent' incidentally had damaging consequences for Italy's 'enforced diaspora', the 600,000 men taken prisoner by the Allies since Italy's entry into the war in June 1940.[11] It meant that they remained as prisoners of war, often being used for forced labour, rather than being returned to their homeland. Italian labour was too useful to the Allies to set these men free, as a strict interpretation of the Geneva Convention required.

The main advantage of the Malta conference for Badoglio was that his presence meant that Washington and London at least had recognized his 'government of under-secretaries', so-called because most of the ministers had been left in the lurch in Rome, as the sovereign authority of the Italian state. Harold Macmillan's first impression of Badoglio was to call him 'honest, broad-minded, humorous. I should judge of peasant origin, with the horse common sense and natural shrewdness of the peasant . . . A loyal servant of his king and country, without ambitions . . .' He soon realized that this patronizing description underestimated the wily old Marshal. At the end of March 1944, Macmillan commented that Badoglio, 'who looks a stupid old man . . . is in fact an extremely clever and intelligent diplomatist. He seems to twist our people around his little finger.'[12]

Dealing with the royal government was far more convenient for the Allies than assembling and cooperating with a genuinely anti-fascist body. As Bonomi noted in his fascinating diary, any anti-fascist government would have wanted to 'review' the instruments of surrender 'in the light of a higher justice'.[13] In the five months following the 'long armistice', Badoglio's government exercised nominal authority only over the provinces of Apulia (the heel of the Italian 'boot') and even there the ACC shadowed its activities closely. The rest of the territory occupied by the Allies was administered by AMGOT (Allied Military Government Occupied Territories), soon shortened to AMG, which grew into a sprawling bureaucracy that drained resources from the areas under its jurisdiction. The Bourbon palace at Caserta, near Naples, which is bigger than Versailles, was requisitioned to house the thousands of desk officers engaged in what we would today describe as 'nation building'.

The men in Caserta made many errors as they administered a country about which they mostly knew nothing. In fairness, the task they faced was anything but easy. In a 1944 speech at Chatham House in London, Lord Rennell of Rodd, a British major general and experienced colonial administrator, gave a vivid contemporary account of the difficulties that the AMG faced:

Let me give an idea of what happens when any town over which the 8th Army is fighting is taken over and administered by my officers. The town will be a heap of ruins; the municipal government will probably have gone . . . most of the inhabitants are scattered over the countryside living in farms, caves, or shelters in the hills. Houses and whole streets are abandoned, there is no water supply . . . there is no electric light . . . especially after the Germans have paid particular attention to the destruction of power lines by blowing them up. You do not come by pylons, or even insulators for 40,000 volt lines . . . at the local ironmonger. It may take weeks before you can restore the current. It is almost certain that the local flour mills are driven by electricity . . . and are therefore without power; you have no flour, even if you have the wheat . . . The town is covered with debris, with a large number of bodies buried under it; the Sicilians and southern Italians will not touch a corpse if they can help it, so you have to get troops to bury the civilian dead after digging them out ... In the large towns there has never been any local government in being when we got there and that goes for Naples, too ... The principal notables of the large towns, on their return, for the most part display only one feature in common, willingness to give advice and unwillingness to do any job which involves responsibility.[14]

One colossal error was monetary policy. The lira was given a fixed parity of 450 lire to the pound, 100 lire to the dollar, and the occupation forces could exchange their pay into 'Am-lire' to purchase goods and services. This exchange rate moved the entire Allied armed forces, especially the US troops, into the upper middle class: the well-paid officers of the bureaucracy in Caserta could (and often did) live like millionaires. As one of Alcide De Gasperi's most trusted advisers commented in frustration:

Fixing the basic [monthly] pay for ordinary soldiers already fed, clothed, and transported for free at 6,000 lire (I repeat, six thousand), to spend on whatever little luxuries they feel like, is an unheard-of thing to do when, with the same sum, at least four schoolteachers and their families must make ends meet.[15]

Black Market prices prevailed for scarce commodities, yet most commodities were scarce since the war had played havoc with supply chains and production. Prices spiralled out of control, hitting, as always, the poor hardest. One service industry that thrived as a result was prostitution, as Italian women sold their bodies to Allied soldiers with fistfuls of cash. What else were they to do? The family breadwinner was often away in a camp, or had been killed or disabled. Or simply had no work. There was no welfare system in place for starving children. A barter economy sprang up among the agricultural labourers of the rural south; large parts of the population in the towns were living in a state of absolute destitution. They could not even complain about it democratically: the Allies, wary of the perceived extremism of the left-wing parties, restricted political rights throughout the Mezzogiorno.

OF COFFEE POTS AND KINGS

From a military point of view, having a deferential government was useful. From the political point of view, it meant that the Allies became embroiled in a prolonged debate about Italy's democratic future and were gradually compelled to acknowledge the superior claims of the CLN to act as the representative of the Italian people. From the outset, the men in the steering committee of the CLN deemed the Allies' recognition of Badoglio's cabinet to be a moral and constitutional abomination. Their parties, not the king's courtiers, were the expression of the 'healthy and progressive forces of the country'. In words that are worth quoting at length, for reasons that will become apparent, the PCI's leadership in Italy stated on 21 October 1943:

> The adversarial political relationship between the CLN and the Badoglio government is clear and well-delineated, and it must remain so in order that all Italians can be sure of the correct political line that they need to take. Equivocating and deal-making [with Badoglio] would be deleterious for the national interest and would amount to a deception of the popular masses.[16]

The PCI was nevertheless more measured than the PSIUP, which, reflecting Nenni's ardent, lifelong republicanism, raised the rhetorical ante in their attacks on the 'faithless king', or the 'Badoglio fudge':

> The monarchist-bourgeois fudge of which Badoglio is the exponent might meet with the complacent approval of Anglo-American generals, but it will never strike a chord in the conscience of Italians intent on the conquest of their destiny. The Badoglio government, which is a transformation into monarchist guise of the policies that dragged us into the abyss, must go. The Risorgimento will regain its course. The Italian revolution will find its own solutions.[17]

On 16 October 1943, the steering committee of the PSIUP issued an unambiguous proclamation entitled 'No National Union with the king', who was variously described as a 'runaway' and 'felonious'. The PSIUP categorically refused to have dealings with the 'royalist clique'.[18]

On the same day, the CLN itself formally proclaimed that 'national renewal' could not possibly be carried out under the auspices of the king and Badoglio. It was necessary to create an 'extraordinary anti-fascist government' from the ranks of those who had 'struggled without cease against the Fascist dictatorship'. Such a government should 'assume all the constitutional powers of the state', while avoiding any 'stance' that might 'compromise national harmony'; 'conduct the war of liberation alongside the United Nations'; and, upon the cessation of hostilities, 'summon the people' to decide upon the future 'institutional form of the state'.[19]

The 16 October declaration was important since it came as a four-power conference of foreign ministers (China was represented, in addition to the Soviet Union, the United States, and the British Empire) was getting under way in Moscow. During the conference, the USSR pressed for a purge of former Fascists in Italy and for a government that included the anti-fascist parties. The final communiqué contained a joint declaration by the three Allies fighting Germany that stated they were 'in complete agreement' that Allied policy towards Italy should be based 'upon the fundamental principle that Fascism and all its evil influence and configuration (sic) shall be completely destroyed'. Somewhat defensively, Britain and the United States insisted that their actions had been 'based upon this policy' from the 'inception' of the war on Italian soil. The three powers acknowledged that it was 'essential' that the Italian government should be made 'more democratic' by 'inclusion of representatives of those sections of the Italian people who have always opposed Fascism', and promised that all 'Fascist or pro-Fascist elements shall be removed from the administration and from institutions and organizations of a public character'. A final caveat restricted the implementation of these principles to the discretion of the Commander-in-Chief of Allied forces in Italy so long as 'active military operations' continued. An Advisory Committee, to be composed of representatives from France, Yugoslavia, and Greece, as well as from Britain, the Soviet Union, and the United States, was created to monitor Italy's political problems. In his diary, Bonomi fumed that Italy was being placed under tutelage 'as if she were a minor, or morally unfit' to decide her own future.[20]

The Moscow Conference sent a powerful signal that the Badoglio government was not democratic enough: it did not include the CLN and it manifestly did contain 'Fascist or pro-Fascist elements', trying to restore their virginity, as Italians say. Badoglio for instance burnished his anti-fascist credentials after the conference by drafting a law establishing general principles by which Fascists would be purged from the public administration and a second law ending racial discrimination against Jews. In the meantime, the *carabinieri* of the territories under the king's control were largely led by policemen who had risen under the previous regime.

Badoglio also gave a bravura performance in front of the Advisory Committee on Italy when it met in Naples on 10 January 1944. The meeting – which included, representing the USSR, the intimidating Andrey Vyshinsky, the prosecutor during the Moscow Show Trials of the 1930s – was a success for the Marshal. He defended the actions of the government, promised to employ 'every resource in his power' to bring Italy back to the 'road of liberty, democracy and international cooperation', and stood up well to Vyshinsky's pointed questioning about inclusion of the CLN in the government, an issue that Badoglio promised to resolve when the Allies reached Rome. The Committee need not worry, Badoglio declared: 'the problem of broadening the basis of the government was more important for him, Badoglio, than for the Allies'.[21]

At the end of his visit to Italy, Vyshinsky told Macmillan that Badoglio was, along with Count Carlo Sforza, a veteran Italian diplomat who had opposed Fascism from its inception and spent two decades in exile, the only person he had met who counted: the others were 'provincial men of small stature'.[22] Certainly, Badoglio's protestations that he was merely 'an old soldier, who had lived far from politics for too many years to begin now, as a novice' smack of false modesty.[23] Badoglio was in fact much abler at politics than military strategy.

After the Moscow Conference, in a bid to widen the government, Badoglio had already made overtures to Bonomi (who punctiliously informed the rest of the CLN) and to prominent intellectuals in Naples, notably Croce, to a former president of the Chamber of

Deputies, Enrico De Nicola, and to Count Sforza. The British government hoped that an infusion of liberal grandees would provide a fig leaf of respectability to the Badoglio cabinet. Sforza, the most radical and anti-monarchist of the three, had been required to pledge his support to Badoglio before the British would consent to his re-entry into Italy from the United States.[24]

Badoglio's problem was that these dignitaries had clear memories of his twenty years of collusion with the regime. They snubbed the Marshal. Indeed, they raised the stakes by suggesting that Victor Emmanuel's abdication was a precondition for participation by anti-fascist groups in government. Sovereignty in Italy, Croce explained, lay with a monarch who respected the constitution. For twenty years the monarchy had permitted the excesses of the Fascist state. To 'regain sovereign legitimacy' while 'preserving the constitutional monarchy', it was necessary for a regent, or 'Lieutenant of the Realm', to be appointed until such time as the Italians could freely decide how their state would be organized.[25] Even monarchists, Bonomi noted with satisfaction, wanted a 'clean' monarchy, 'not a dirty rag like the current sovereign'.[26]

Meanwhile, Christian Democracy tended to see the demand for abdication as a diversion. Abdication could wait, the DC reasoned, until after the liberation of the nation, although they comprehended the motives of the people who were asking for it. For the DC, the 'essential need' was to 'create the conditions' for an extraordinary government that could 'maximize all available energies for the national war, launch the process of reconstructing the country, and prepare the necessary institutional reforms and new social-economic order'.[27]

The clamour for abdication nevertheless grew stronger, especially after the Allies relaxed the ban on political activity in liberated Italy. At the end of January 1944, in the Apulian city of Bari, 'the first important national political assembly to be held in Italy by anti-fascist parties since 1926' was held.[28] The Bari Congress was lively and chaotic, and the 150 delegates from across the Mezzogiorno disagreed on many things: in other words, it was democratic. The CLN in Rome sent a message via a member of the PSIUP's Central Committee, Oreste Lizzadri (under the *nom de guerre* of Longobardi), which set the tone for the Congress as a whole:

This government must disappear. The position that both you and the central Committee have taken, for the constitution of an extraordinary government of national liberation that assumes all the constitutional powers of the State, without compromising the harmony of the nation, and without prejudice to the free expression of popular will on the institutional question, represents the indispensable condition that will allow Italy to conduct the war vigorously until victory and assure its own future.[29]

The Congress added abdication to the CLN's core demands that there should be an 'Extraordinary Government' and a Constituent Assembly. Condemnation of the House of Savoy was unanimous. Sforza roused the delegates with a closing speech sprinkled with *ad hominen* remarks about Victor Emmanuel:

Many ask me: Was the King always like this? And they mean, so false, so disloyal, so selfish? No, he wasn't . . . When he was surrounded by the most representative men of Liberal and democratic Italy, from Saracco to Giolitti, or Bonomi . . . he strove to imitate them and did his best to be worthy of them. This wretch's tragedy began with his encounter with Mussolini, and his twenty years of contact with him. He found a maestro in Mussolini, and he believed, since he had no love for Italy (few hereditary monarchs love their country), that he had found a marvellous helpmeet to keep the Italians down, to thwart them, to disparage them . . . Mark my words. When we with all our devotion for Italy arrive at the table of the peace conference intent on defending the sacred borders of our fatherland and preserving our oldest and most venerated colonies (which should not be confused with the senseless and un-Italian adventures in Ethiopia and Albania), there will be more than one important statesman who will say to us: don't you come telling us what to do – you who could not get rid of the king of Italy.[30]

Sforza's rhetoric was regarded as a poor substitute for action by the left-wing parties. Rather than demand the king's abdication (a solution regarded as 'too simple, too easy, too accommodating'), at Bari the left-wing parties proposed a three-point motion that indicted the king of all the constitutional transgressions he had committed during the Fascist era; opted to transform the Congress itself into a representative assembly until such time as a Constituent Assembly could be elected; and further proposed that an 'executive committee' should be elected by the assembly and be entrusted with the task of harrying the Badoglio government for its failings.[31] In the end, as a result of the reluctance of the DC delegates, the Congress stopped short of endorsing the first two of these demands, but the PdA and the PSIUP sought in the wake of the Congress to re-open the accord reached on 16 October 1943, causing a harassed Bonomi briefly to offer his resignation as head of the CLN.[32]

The anti-monarchist mood in liberated Italy, which made headlines in both Britain and America, only stiffened Winston Churchill's determination to stand by the royal government. In February 1944, the British war leader dismissed the Bari Congress's demands in a speech to the House of Commons. In Churchill's view, Britain had signed the armistice with Badoglio and the king; the Italian navy, which was 'discharging useful services' on behalf of the Allies in the Mediterranean, had surrendered on the king's order; Italian troops had joined the front line, suffered heavy casualties on one occasion, but continued to 'fight alongside our men'. Churchill was unconvinced that any other Italian government 'would command the same loyalty from the Italian Armed Forces', much though the politicians that had gathered at Bari were eager to form one. Churchill made it clear that he would regret political changes in Italy. In a passage that became famous, he said:

> When you have to hold a hot coffee-pot, it is better not to break the handle off until you are sure that you will get another equally convenient and serviceable or, at any rate, until there is a dishcloth handy.[33]

By the time Churchill gave the 'coffee-pot' speech, he knew that other important actors had concluded that the king had to step down. The CLN had adopted an idea, first proposed by Enrico De Nicola, that the king should abdicate in favour of his son, Prince Umberto, who would himself confer the monarchy's executive prerogatives upon an 'individual or collective Lieutenancy' that could 'proceed to the immediate constitution of an anti-Fascist government'.[34] Churchill knew, too, that Eisenhower's successor as commander-in-chief in the Mediterranean, Sir Henry Maitland Wilson, regarded the CLN's position as constructive. He also knew that these developments had shifted the position of the United States: President Roosevelt, who had hitherto played second fiddle to the British in Italian affairs, was now pressing for immediate democratic enlargement of Badoglio's cabinet.[35] Churchill was more monarchist even than the king. Victor Emmanuel had reluctantly decided that, once Rome had fallen to the Allies, he should make his son 'Lieutenant of the Realm', with full constitutional powers.

Churchill's justification for the intransigence of his position was spelled out in a note to Roosevelt on 13 March 1944. He claimed that 'timing is all I plead for' and emphasized that he favoured a 'broadly-based government' once Allied forces had reached Rome. But his disdain for the 'ambitious windbags, now agitating behind our front that they themselves may become the government of Italy', was evident: his real objection was to the men, not the measure. Churchill plainly had Sforza in mind when he dictated those words, and he was right to think that neither the count, nor Croce, nor any other southern Italian grandee had a 'representative footing' among the people.[36]

But that was not true of the Rome CLN, though the British did not yet know it. Its members had been in hiding since 8 September, dwelling in courageous friends' houses, at permanent risk of recognition by a nark every time they left seclusion to meet collectively or to conduct the affairs of their parties. Bonomi, De Gasperi, Nenni were well-known public figures. The Vatican gave the CLN's steering committee sanctuary for weeks at a time in the Lateran Palace, though Nenni's habit of playing a radio to drown out the sounds of mass ruffled De Gasperi's feathers.[37] On one occasion, practically the entire committee had to be rushed into a secret chamber to sit in pitch darkness when a German patrol parked itself in front of the gates and seemed likely to conduct an illegal search. To expect men who were running such risks to bow the knee to a king they regarded as a traitor was, as we say nowadays, a big ask. The constitutional issue, whether Churchill liked it or not, was a critical question of principle for all anti-fascist Italians. But by March 1944 it had led to an impasse that was jeopardizing Italy's political stability.

MOSCOW RULES

Help for the royalist government – and Churchill – came from an unexpected quarter. On 14 March 1944, the Soviet Union, which had been astutely courted by the Italian foreign ministry, recognized the Badoglio government and, a few days later, reiterated its demand that the government should encompass the democratic forces.[38] On 27 March 1944, a 'knight of great portent', a 'resurrected Lohengrin', 'miraculously' arrived from 'distant shores' in Naples, after a voyage via Baku, Cairo, and Algiers, to take charge of the PCI and re-orient its political line.[39] Togliatti had returned from the USSR.

On 1 April, Togliatti held a press conference attended by 'numerous renowned Allied journalists' to publicize a new policy that a hastily summoned meeting of the PCI's National Council had approved that day. Premising his remarks with the statement that the PCI was in favour of 'everything that reinforces our country in the war against Germany and against everything that weakens it', Togliatti recommended a three-point policy: (1) unity of the anti-fascist forces; (2) a guarantee that a constitutional assembly, elected by universal suffrage and by secret ballot, would decide the form of the state as soon as the war was over; (3) the establishment of a war government, with a clear programme for the conduct of the war. When asked by journalists whether this meant he was willing to collaborate with Badoglio, Togliatti replied that the PCI had 'no objection in principle' to doing so.[40]

L'Unità, blithely forgetting its strictures against collaboration with the royalist government, boasted that Ercoli (as Togliatti was initially named, even in the minutes of the PCI's *direzione*, or steering committee) had 'exposed the blind alley into which the free political parties had gradually entered' and presented them with 'a way out'. Entry into a cabinet led by Badoglio was suddenly presented as the 'road to salvation'.[41] It would have been regarded as collusion with the enemy before Togliatti's démarche – which is why the DC, intent on maintaining anti-fascist unity, had never proposed it.

Togliatti's initiative was dubbed the '*svolta di Salerno*' (the 'Salerno pivot') since the royal court and the government had moved in February to that town. It masterfully 'served to insert the party into the mainstream of legality and political power'.[42] The PCI had become the agenda-setter for Italian politics – no small feat for a party that in Italy's pre-fascist democracy had been a breakaway splinter from the PSI.

It is an intriguing matter of historical fact that Togliatti and the PCI adopted the new 'patriotic' line on Stalin's orders. In the mid-1990s, scholars working in the newly opened Soviet archives established that Togliatti left the USSR a few days after a 45-minute meeting with Stalin and Molotov on the night of 3–4 March 1944 (Togliatti claimed to have left Moscow on 26 February and this date had hitherto been accepted by historians). There is no available stenographic record of what Stalin said, but the diaries of Georgi Dimitrov

Pietro Badoglio (*right*) and Palmiro Togliatti
(*left*) were united by the necessities of Soviet foreign policy.

report conversations about the meeting with both Molotov and Togliatti. Stalin seemingly instructed Togliatti that the existence of two camps (Badoglio-king and the anti-fascist parties) was weakening the Italian people to 'the advantage of the English'. The PCI should join the government to intensify the war against the Germans and to democratize and unify the Italian people, although the Soviet paternity of the shift in policy should be publicly denied. Even though Dimitrov and Togliatti had recently proposed that the PCI should intensify the policy of intransigent opposition to Badoglio, they adjusted to the line traced by Stalin.[43] Anybody with Togliatti's well-honed instinct for survival would hardly do anything else.[44]

On 11 April 1944, the PCI leader spoke in Naples to the first mass meeting of the party cadres since his return from Moscow. It was a set-piece opportunity to explain the new party line. For this reason, grandees such as Croce and Sforza were in the audience to hear what Ercoli had to say. Togliatti grasped the opportunity with a subtle speech that cast the PCI, thanks to its uncompromising resistance to Fascism, as the party not only of the working class, but of the Nation (with a capital 'N'), too. With a nod to Lenin and Stalin's teachings on the subject, Togliatti affirmed that it was sound Marxist doctrine to be patriotic:

> The flag of the national interest, which Fascism has dragged into the mire and betrayed, we will pick up and make our own . . . we will give to the life of the Nation a new sense of purpose that corresponds to the needs, to the interests, and to the aspirations of the mass of the people.[45]

In pursuit of this objective, Togliatti was adamant that the PCI could not be 'an association of propagandists who curse the past, dream of a distant future, but do not know what to advise or to do in the present'.[46] The party had to be the avant-garde of a mass popular movement; one capable of guiding a desperate people out of the 'abyss' into which Italy had fallen during the years of Fascism:

> Our political strategy is a strategy for the masses: it is and wants to remain the strategy of ordinary people. The means [i.e. the party] by which we implement the strategy must also be characterized by popular mass support.[47]

In the following weeks, the PCI acted upon these words. A party that had been a byword for sectarianism transformed itself into a mass movement. Notorious Fascists apart, everybody could suddenly obtain a PCI membership card. Even before Togliatti spoke on 11 April, in fact, an alarmed Count Sforza had warned the Americans that every day there was a 'long line of applicants for membership in the party including every type of citizen: businessmen, professional men and artisans' outside the PCI's headquarters in Naples. Sforza regarded Togliatti's new party line as a ruse to ensure that Italy fell 'under the complete domination of the Soviet Union'.[48]

The PCI's sudden change of direction dumbfounded the other parties of the CLN, especially the PSIUP, which had not been given prior notice, despite the party's pact of 'unity of action' with the PCI. 'Ercoli's bomb has exploded!' the Socialist leader Pietro Nenni wrote in his diary after Togliatti gave his press conference. Over the issue of joining the government, Nenni found himself in a bind: his anti-monarchism and commitment to cooperation, even fusion, with the PCI were in irreconcilable conflict. In private, he fulminated against the 'characteristic ruthlessness of Bolsheviks' and reflected, ruefully, on the similarities with the Communists' behaviour in August 1939.[49]

Nenni nevertheless swallowed his pride and followed the PCI's lead. In his diary, he made no bones about the frustration that 'going into power with Victor Emmanuel' cost him. He thought that the deal might 'prejudice the struggle for the Republic', but saw no way of staying out of the government.[50] Nenni recognized that 'behind Ercoli' stood Stalin, 'with the immense prestige brought by the Red Army's victories'. It was pointless to condemn oneself to 'sterile isolation' by taking a stand on principle.[51]

The other parties of CLN reasoned along similar lines. On 22 April 1944, they joined 'an emergency government of national necessity', as the DC defined it, headed by Badoglio.[52] Seven months of opposition to any idea of national union with the king vanished like breath off a razor blade, to use Orwell's marvellous simile. Togliatti became minister without portfolio and another Communist, Fausto Gullo, became minister of agriculture. Croce and Sforza, who together with Togliatti had made the government possible, also became ministers.

The PdA alone dissented over joining the Badoglio–Togliatti government, even when two prominent *azionisti* from the Mezzogiorno joined the Council of Ministers.[53] The steering committee of the party deplored the whole train of events set in motion by Togliatti's actions. The government was 'a false and perilous departure', according to the Rome edition of *l'Italia Libera*. The PdA pointed out that no other government in Nazi-occupied Europe retained individuals whose anti-Fascism was so ambiguous: not Yugoslavia, not France, not Czechoslovakia. Only Italy, the party warned, remained 'suspended' between 'defeat and resurrection, between Fascism and anti-Fascism, between the past and the future'.[54]

The Free French government echoed the PdA's sentiments and logic. The Algiers government had facilitated Togliatti's passage to Rome on the assumption that the PCI leader would strengthen opposition to Badoglio, not shore him up. On 14 April, de Gaulle firmly stated that it would be possible to have 'relations of trust and collaboration' only with a 'new Italy', one in which all trace of Fascism had been 'thoroughly repudiated'.[55] As would so often be the case during the rest of his career as a statesman, the General remained politically isolated, but obdurate.

COMING INTO THEIR OWN

In the event, the PdA was reconciled with the other anti-fascist parties when the Allies liberated Rome on 4 June 1944. Prince Umberto assumed the Lieutenancy of the Realm and – to the consternation of Churchill – Badoglio was promptly dumped as premier on 8 June during a meeting between the Salerno government and the CLN at the Grand Hotel in Rome, with Bonomi being proposed in his stead. Both Ruini and Nenni, who had still not digested Togliatti's April *démarche*, spoke out strongly for a government headed by an anti-fascist; the other party leaders quietly agreed. Sensing the prevailing mood, Togliatti, who had arrived at the meeting 'arm in arm' with Badoglio and Benedetto Croce, 'chucked Badoglio overboard' rather than break with the PSIUP.[56] The Marshal had served his historical purpose.

The only representative of the Allies at the talks was the head of the ACC, General Mason-McFarlane, who told London that Badoglio had faced 'strong and very active and vocal' opposition. He had judged it best to acquiesce in the parties' decision. Churchill was so annoyed by Mason-McFarlane's willingness to placate 'an extremely untrustworthy band of non-elected political comebacks', presenting Britain with a *fait accompli,* that he terminated his career. Mason-McFarlane was replaced at the ACC by a US naval officer, Ellery Stone, and was 'retired' in disgrace.[57] Churchill grudgingly recognized Bonomi's government only after it had accepted the 'long armistice' *in toto* and promised not to re-open the institutional question, but the imposition of these conditions was mere 'face-saving', as Macmillan acknowledged.[58] The Italian parties had carried their point, namely that the head of government should be a proven anti-fascist, and somebody *they* regarded as suitable, and so accepted Churchill's terms. This did not mean that learning about the armistice terms did not rankle. De Gasperi subsequently commented that reading the terms was 'like a rough hand that passes over a wound that has not yet healed'.[59]

The all-party government chaired by Bonomi included several members of the CLN (De Gasperi and Ruini as ministers without portfolio; Casati as minister of war). Togliatti and Croce also served as ministers without portfolio. The premier also held the office of foreign minister: the British did successfully exclude Sforza from this key post. Each of the six parties contributed three ministers to the cabinet. Time would prove that it was an administration of heavyweights, not the has-beens of Churchill's fulminations. Several members of the government would play crucial roles in the consolidation of democracy in Italy over the next decade, and two of them, the progressive Christian Democrat Giovanni Gronchi and the Socialist intellectual Giuseppe Saragat, subsequently became presidents of the Italian Republic.

Above all, there was Togliatti, who had impressed everybody since his arrival on the scene. The skill with which he had made the PCI indispensable aroused widespread admiration. Within weeks, the Togliatti myth, the notion that he was 'il migliore', the shrewdest politician around, had taken root. Young intellectuals, whom Togliatti actively courted, were particularly starstruck:

When we saw Togliatti for the first time, we felt like we were in the presence of a kind of repository that preserved the historical memory of the party and its political wisdom. It seemed to us that this man's speeches gave meaning and order to the experience that we had lived through in a chaotic and piecemeal manner. In person, Togliatti looked just right for the role of 'intellectual organizer', too. Small, wearing a blue suit with a herring-bone pattern, high-heeled black boots, dandruff on his collar, little round spectacles, a voice with a slight drawl and the accent of somebody who had lived abroad for a long time, he was the portrait of a Cominform official. He was what we needed. Very affable and yet inscrutable, occasionally sarcastic, he expressed himself with the humour of a veteran professor talking to a pupil. He emitted a cold fascination, like the motor of an electronic machine: you could hear the clicking sound of an intelligence at work . . . [60]

Unlike Togliatti, Nenni did not take office. He was immersed in publishing *Avanti!*, which under his editorship was emerging as the most widely read party paper in Italy, selling 300,000 copies a day. He also harboured doubts about Bonomi's ability to hold a government together. Nenni thought that Bonomi was 'a good man, but we need a strong man'.[61]

Eight decades on, it is hard to dissent from the judgements of contemporaries, but Bonomi's first actions as premier did not convey weakness. Quite the contrary. To take just one instance, on 22 July 1944, he sent a memorandum to US Secretary of State Cordell Hull that summed up the Italian government's priorities for its relationship with the Allies. Bonomi argued that it would be an act of 'justice and political wisdom' to adjust the 'de jure situation imposed on Italy' by the 'long armistice' to the 'de facto situation existing today'. Italy had evolved, Bonomi argued, and the Allies' refusal to recognize this fact was 'detrimental for us and for everybody'. Bonomi urged the Allies to 'arm and feed' more Italian troops so that they could take part in the liberation of the country. He pointed out that the 'Italian people still feel themselves quarantined, shut off . . . in hermetic isolation' and instanced the way that the government's request to adhere to the Atlantic Charter and to the forthcoming monetary conference at Bretton Woods, New Hampshire, had been denied. Bonomi made the practical suggestion that

'Italian experts and technicians' should be authorized to go to the United States to discuss questions of economic development with their American counterparts. Italy was being 'bled white' by the existing occupation regime and the inflation it had engendered, Bonomi (correctly) asserted.

Bonomi believed the root of the trouble was that no country could be long administered by 'two governments'. In his view, the AMG needed to be relieved of 'at least three-fourths of its duties'. It was wrong for 'a highly civilized people like the Italians' to be kept indefinitely in 'a state of tutelage', Bonomi protested. He also vigorously condemned the fate of the prisoners of war held by the French government in North Africa, whose condition had 'reached the limit of all physical and moral endurance'.[62] The memorandum concluded with a statement of the resolve of the 'new democratic Italy' to 'represent a factor for stability and order' in post-war European reconstruction. Bonomi appealed to the Americans to take the lead in beginning a 'truly reconstructive policy' for Italy.[63]

Cordell Hull replied on 19 August with a bland letter that expressed interest in the idea of allowing technical experts to visit the United States. He could hardly say more, for fear of British and French reaction. Still, though it had little impact, the *tone* of Bonomi's memorandum was strikingly different from the unctuous missives sent by Badoglio to the Allies, or from the bombast of Mussolini. It was a frank letter written by one statesman of substance to another, as equals. It was the analysis of a man who understood that Italy's reconstruction was part of a wider European problem of moral and economic renewal that would need imaginative leadership by the United States. It was an Italian voice of a kind the world had not heard for over twenty years: a democratic voice.

Perhaps for this reason, Churchill, when he visited Rome in late August 1944, swiftly became reconciled to Bonomi being premier, although Badoglio continued to intrigue behind the scenes. Bonomi may not have been a political leader of great charisma, but he was the opposite of a windbag. He was principled, shrewd, and quietly brave; De Gasperi described him as 'a man of impeccable political probity and great administrative experience', in a speech shortly after the formation of the government.[64]

On 25 June 1944, eleven months to the day after the fall of Mussolini, Prince Umberto, in his capacity as Lieutenant of the Realm, signed into law a short decree approved by the new government that stated:

> After the liberation of Italian soil, the institutional forms of the state will be chosen by the Italian people who to this end will elect, by universal suffrage and a secret ballot, a Constituent Assembly to decide upon the new Constitution of the State.[65]

It was the formalization of a principle that, despite their many disagreements, had bound the six parties together during the anxious months of clandestine activity. At war's end, the Italian people would pass judgement on the king's conduct and would be permitted to free themselves from the ties of monarchy if they chose to.

TWO CONCEPTS OF DEMOCRACY

The concept of a Constituent Assembly presupposed that the CLN parties would be willing to compromise on the construction, from zero, of a new state. In the first flush of the Bonomi government, this did not seem improbable. By the late summer of 1944, the parties – as we shall see in the next chapter – were conducting, with harmony of purpose, a large-scale partisan struggle against the German invaders and Mussolini's puppet regime. Trade unionists from the PCI, the PSI, and the DC had also worked together in the spring of 1944 to reach an accord on the creation of a single trade union, the General Confederation of Italian Workers (CGIL), whose goal was to remedy the exploitation of the workers institutionalized by the corporatist system, by giving the working class an effective organized voice in post-war Italy.

The accord was careful to privilege no single party. The CGIL was to be governed by the 'fullest internal democracy' at all levels, but also, with respect for minority rights, there was to be 'maximum freedom of expression' for members and for all political or religious views. It would be governed by a steering committee of fifteen members, five from each party, while executive power would be entrusted to a triumvirate of secretary-generals, one from each party. Yet, though the accord was between trade unionists from the three parties, it also carefully stated that the union would be 'independent of all political parties'.

The PSI's and DC's nominees as secretary-general were anti-fascist stalwarts. The PCI's nominee was Giuseppe Di Vittorio, the pugnacious MP from Cerignola in Apulia. Di Vittorio's biography since the 1920s had followed the same pattern of the other top cadres in the PCI. Since the mid-1920s he had been a Comintern official in Moscow, had fought at the front in Spain and been badly wounded in the battle of Guadalajara in 1937, and had edited the daily newspaper of Italian anti-fascists in Paris, *La voce degli italiani*. After the Nazis conquered France in the summer of 1940, he and his family had 'changed abode every week' in order to stay one step ahead of the Vichy police.[66] He was arrested in February 1941 and expelled to Italy, where he finished up, via several prisons, in the island jail of Ventotene. He was amnestied in August 1943. When he became the PCI's nominee as secretary-general of the CGIL, Di Vittorio was a relatively independent-minded man of immense energy, at the peak of his mental and physical powers. He had bowed to Stalinist orthodoxy over the Nazi–Soviet Pact, but not without dissent and personal turmoil. The CGIL gave him a vehicle that would make him, Togliatti apart, the most influential communist in Italy.

In the summer of 1944, Togliatti sought to forge a common *political* bond between the same three parties of the workers. Togliatti's suggestion was founded on pragmatic considerations. Queues of would-be members might be forming outside the party's headquarters in Rome (party membership in the city and wider province of Rome multiplied almost *tenfold* between liberation on 4 June and the beginning of September), but that did not mean the PCI would become the party of choice for all Italy's workers by hand and by brain.[67] The PSIUP could call upon the residual loyalty of the factory workers of the North, while the DC commanded broad support among the rural masses and Catholic artisans and labourers. All three parties were the expressions of significant 'social blocs' within the Italian people.

Togliatti argued that the leaders of the three 'popular' parties should find out what they could agree on and what divided them. Italy's future democracy would be stronger if they could work in unison.

A lengthy article entitled 'Communists and Catholics' published in *Rinascita*, an intellectual monthly started by the indefatigable PCI leader in June 1944, insisted in its peroration that 'the collaboration of Catholics with Communists and all other popular forces might be especially fertile right now. Communists know from personal experience how heavily and for how long the divide between Catholics and non-Catholics has weighed in the recent history of Italy.'[68]

At first sight, the notion of cooperation between the PCI and the DC may seem outlandish, not pragmatic. The PCI and the PSIUP were both avowedly Marxist parties; cooperation between them, despite their many quarrels and different traditions, was intellectually coherent. But what did the PCI have in common with the DC? How could there be any common ground between godless Communists and fervent Catholics? Yet a careful reading of two set-piece speeches delivered to huge audiences first by Togliatti then by De Gasperi at Rome's Brancaccio Theatre, on 9 and 23 July 1944 respectively, indicate that the PCI leader's intuitions were not entirely astray.

The two speeches were clearly intended as *botta e risposta*: Togliatti launched his blow first, De Gasperi parried. But the mutual respect of the two statesmen, as they circled each other warily, was unmistakable. A 'cautious exchange of views' had begun.[69]

Togliatti's speech was delivered with verve – the PCI leader's ability to speak the language of Marxist theology in some gatherings and colloquial Italian in others was one of his greatest gifts – and it was interjected frequently with ringing applause, cries of '*Evviva!*', '*Benissimo!*' and occasional standing ovations from the new, enthusiastic party members in the audience. A brief aside on the monarchy was greeted with 'angry shouts, whistling' and a noisy demonstration that apparently continued for some minutes.[70] If one has any imagination at all, one's mind is seized, upon reading this speech, by an image of an audience of thousands of dark-haired Romans, vehement and vociferous, of all ages and social classes, mostly men wearing their Sunday best, but with many women present, *being political*. It must have been a day of great meaning for the crowd gathered in the Brancaccio Theatre: after all, they had not been able to speak their minds publicly for twenty years. As well as venting their anger against a social order that had condemned them to terror, hunger, and penury, they were, whether they knew it or not, by their applause and shouts, signalling to Togliatti what their priorities were.

Playing to the gallery, Togliatti threatened retribution on those who had enriched themselves under Fascism or had colluded in the regime's crimes, while wisely underlining (given that he was in Rome) that the PCI would never 'persecute' the small fry 'who had bought a party card and worn the black shirt for the sake of a crust of bread'.[71] But the speech was mostly concerned to argue for 'wide-ranging democratic renewal', 'unity of the working class' (the audience roared approval when Togliatti named 'our comrade and friend' Pietro Nenni), and 'unity of action with the Catholic working masses' and with their representative, the DC. The aim of the three main parties should be the construction of a 'progressive democracy'. What did that mean? Togliatti sketched it out in detail:

> Progressive democracy is that which looks to the future, not back to the past. Progressive democracy is that which gives no quarter to Fascism but destroys any possibility of its revival. Progressive democracy will be, in Italy, that which eliminates all residues of feudalism and resolves the agricultural question by giving the land to those who work it; it will be that which will take away from the plutocratic elites any possibility of return ... Progressive democracy is that which will liquidate the economic and political backwardness of the Mezzogiorno ... [and which] ... will recognize the rights of Sicily and Sardinia to enjoy self-government in a free and united Italy. Progressive democracy is that which will organize a government of the people and for the people, and in which all the healthy forces of the country will have their rightful place, will be able to make their voice heard, and advance towards the satisfaction of all their aspirations.[72]

There was much here with which De Gasperi agreed. Certainly, he wanted land reform, was passionate about the decentralization of government, and was no less anti-fascist than Togliatti: Mussolini had thrown him in prison, after all. All Italian parties, of all political colours, recognized that the calamitous condition of the Mezzogiorno was a looming issue that would inevitably dominate the post-war period.

Moreover, when De Gasperi took to the stage at the Brancaccio

Theatre, he was prepared to acknowledge merits in the communist faith, just as Togliatti had approved the sincerity of Catholics. True, he referred to the PCI's habit of depicting the USSR as a terrestrial paradise with an ironic 'so be it'.[73] Yet he did admit that there was 'something truly admirable, something extraordinarily evocative in the universalist tendency of Russian communism'. De Gasperi explained that he found the USSR's success in merging the 'races' of Europe and Asia to be 'universalist in the same way as Christianity is'. Equally, the USSR's efforts to 'lessen the distance between social classes' and 'dignify manual work' was also Christian in inspiration, in De Gasperi's view. Everybody worked for a living in Russia. De Gasperi commented – it is a remark worth remembering when we reach the debates that produced the Italian constitution of 1948 – that 'this is a principle towards which we are moving, and which must also be applied in Italy'.[74]

Some young intellectuals in the DC welcomed these words and openly embraced the cause of building a 'progressive democracy'.[75] De Gasperi would not go so far. He shrank from the *intensity* of the Soviet regime. Making a striking parallel, he said in his speech at the Brancaccio Theatre that to build communism you need a 'high moral temperature'; the same kind of absolute faith that monks, who live communistically, sometimes achieve but which is alien to ordinary people. Terror was intrinsic to the Soviet system because people were compelled to live by a creed. De Gasperi preferred to let people run their own lives, through traditional political institutions such as the *comune*, or local government, without a coercive, norm-setting, interfering central state. The state, rather, ought to be seen in negative terms as 'a protective wall around the garden in which the flowers and fruits of humankind are born and mature'.[76]

One can see why some Italian scholars have depicted De Gasperi as a Catholic apologist, intent on keeping the state out of the private lives of its citizens; of believing, in short, that the state should render to the Church that which belonged to the Church. Also – and more deeply – one sees why the acutest interpreters of his political ideas, such as the Catholic historian Pietro Scoppola, have depicted De Gasperi as a Tocquevillian liberal, intent on the dispersal of power and on winning an illiberal Church over to the merits of what we would today call political pluralism.[77] Democracy – a multi-party system, institutional checks and balances, a free press, dispersal of power – was more an end for De Gasperi than a means to a greater good. Moreover, it was vital that the new democracy should emerge with the people's participation and approval:

> This time we want to create something lasting. Enough with pseudo-democratic experiments. The New State must be the definitive Italian state in which the people can govern themselves. It must be based upon the consenting support of the broad masses and the formula chosen should not reflect the preferences of a sect or party, but of the people.[78]

Togliatti judged that De Gasperi had not rejected outright his proposals of unity of action. In September 1944, the PCI leader wrote to De Gasperi, in the latter's capacity as political secretary of Christian Democracy, to express the Communists' 'desire for fraternal collaboration'. Specifically, the PCI 'hoped' that there would be:

> ... a precise political accord with your party ... with the purpose of creating ... on the basis of a programme of wide-ranging social and political renewal, a bloc of popular forces able to guarantee the triumph and stability of a progressive democratic regime, which is what the workers of this country aspire to achieve.[79]

De Gasperi replied with a letter stating that the DC favoured cooperation with the PCI, albeit within the structures of government, and provided Togliatti with a policy document that expressed Christian Democracy's positions on key questions such as land reform. Yet he drew back from a formal agreement on 'unity of action'. Too many acts of intimidation by PCI militants had been reported by DC members working on the ground in southern Italy and Rome.[80]

More generally, De Gasperi was suspicious of Greeks bearing gifts. In January 1944, not so long before, *l'Unità* had written:

> There will be no place in the Italy of tomorrow for a soft-reactionary regime, nor for a democracy that is fettered. The new political, social, and economic system must be a democracy that is uncompromising and effective.[81]

De Gasperi wanted a fettered democracy, with serious checks and balances; he wanted compromise – even, perhaps, at the price of some ineffectiveness. He was aware that there were many in the PCI who regarded him as a soft reactionary, for all Togliatti's soft soap. De Gasperi was obviously also aware of how abruptly the PCI's line could reverse course whenever Stalin willed it.[82]

Nevertheless, it was important for the future of Italian democracy that Togliatti and De Gasperi intuited that the two parties could, despite their differences, be collaborators in the great work of reconstruction that faced the nation. Catholics and Communists were not, in July 1944, separated by an unbridgeable ideological gulf. Indeed, the year that elapsed after 8 September 1943 had illustrated that all Italy's parties were willing to work together, though they squabbled constantly and differed on much. Out of deep adversity, a political culture of democratic cooperation was emerging. The struggle of the Italian resistance against Mussolini's puppet regime, the so-called Italian Social Republic, and the Nazis, underlined this point. The CLN parties had conducted the clandestine war against the invaders and by so doing both established their right to lead Italy's post-war democracy and revived Italy's sense of self-respect.

4

Resistance and Liberation

The Duce's new puppet state, the Italian Social Republic (RSI), was based in Salò, a resort town at the southern end of Lake Garda in the province of Brescia. Mussolini himself dwelt in Villa Feltrinelli, an imposing lakeside mansion in the adjacent village of Gargnano, where he held cabinet meetings in the library of a nearby house.

Between the autumn of 1943 and the spring of 1945, the Salò Republic, as the RSI is familiarly called, was complicit in the Nazis' pitiless exploitation of their Italian colony. Its complicity compelled Italians living under its jurisdiction to confront an existential choice: resist or collaborate. Evading the duty to resist meant that racial persecution, slave labour, and national humiliation would continue until others liberated Italian territory. For many Italian patriots, of all political hues, resistance was the only acceptable choice. In Norberto Bobbio's words: 'At history's turning points, there aren't many alternative roads to choose from. As in a difficult climb, the right path is one alone: all the others lead inexorably into the abyss.'[1]

That so many Italians did choose the right path, and that so many of them displayed extraordinary courage in the process, remains a source of national pride and an endless font of historical research. One could fill a library with interpretations of the resistance's meaning or microhistories of the principal partisan brigades. There are, by contrast, few works of scholarship in Italian on the military campaign conducted by the Allies, which is what ultimately liberated Italy.[2] The reason why the resistance looms so large in the Italian psyche is that it was vital for restoring national self-respect and it conferred lasting legitimacy upon the political parties that directed it. The post-war democratic republic was rooted in the resistance.

BLACK RECORD

The RSI was a parasite regime that depended upon the colonizers for its survival: if the Germans had withdrawn to the Alps in the wake of the Italian surrender, Italian Fascism could never have been reconstituted. One PCI propagandist derided Mussolini's regime as 'a decaying corpse that remains on its feet merely because it is propped up by German bayonets'.[3] Mussolini exercised nominal control of the Salò puppet state but was powerless to thwart Germany's systematic despoilation of northern Italy's people and economy.

The most ardent *republicchini* strove to prove that they were good Nazis.[4] They believed Fascism should be a cleansing force in Italian society and were as ferocious in their denunciations of the corruption of the pre-war Fascist leadership, Mussolini publicly excepted, as the anti-fascist parties. In the autumn of 1943, such people wanted to begin the new regime by washing their spears in the blood of their enemies. The RSI was envisaged as a state purged of upper-class traitors and fainthearts. On 27 October 1943, Mussolini's government proclaimed that revolutionary tribunals would be set up in every province under the RSI's control to judge former PNF members who had betrayed their oath of loyalty to 'the Ideal and its Chief', or those who had 'denigrated' Fascism after 25 July.[5]

At the turbulent first Congress of Mussolini's new Republican Fascist Party (PFR), held in Verona between 14 and 16 November 1943, the delegates approved a party manifesto, personally drafted by the Duce, that proclaimed the abolition of the monarchy, condemned King Victor Emmanuel as a 'traitor and runaway', announced that a Constituent Assembly would be held, and promised that the head of state would be re-elected every five years. It proposed that Catholicism should be the official religion of the state, though other Christian faiths were to be tolerated. In foreign policy, the RSI's goal was to be the construction of a 'European Community' of all states that 'rejected centuries-old British intrigues' and were disposed to participate in the struggle against 'international plutocracy'. The natural resources of Africa were to be 'productively employed' for the benefit of Europeans but also of the peoples of Africa. How Nazi Germany and Italy were going to re-conquer Italy's colonies was wisely left unexplained.

The manifesto had a marked socialist component. The basis of the Social Republic was to be 'work, manual, technical, or intellectual, in all its manifestations'. Private property was to be guaranteed by the state so long as it did not 'degrade the physical and moral personality of other human beings'. The manifesto asserted, furthermore, that the right to own land ended when it was uncultivated: the redistribution of the land to individual peasants, or agricultural cooperatives, should take place in such cases. Workers would be represented on the boards of capitalist enterprises and the state would launch a housing programme to enable workers to buy their own homes through the payment of rent. There would be a single trade union representing all workers, but the manifesto concluded unambiguously that the PFR was 'on the side of the people', not of capital. During the *ventennio*, the party's trade unionists had mostly acted as instruments of social control in the workplace.

The Manifesto's socialism was a sham. Mussolini's Republic had neither the power nor the will to implement the social reforms advocated by the Verona Congress. Nevertheless, despite its repugnant features, the Manifesto was a shrewd assessment of what was politically necessary. Wider land ownership, homes fit to live in and raise families, the centrality of work as a source of dignity for the citizen, a shift towards workers' rights at the expense of the privileges of capital, and the abolition of the monarchy were, objectively, prerequisites for a lasting regime of any kind in Italy.

The issue was whether Fascism could credibly claim it might realize such goals. The Manifesto of Verona naturally expressed no doubts: it stated that to 'one body alone belongs the task of educating the people in politics'. The 'party', defined as an organization of 'combatants and believers', was charged with the historical mission of leading the Italian people. For anybody with critical intelligence, or a house in ruins, or a son missing in Russia or Greece, it was nonsense. One had to be inebriated with doctrine to believe it.[6]

The Verona Congress also demanded that a special tribunal be created to decide the fate of six members of the Fascist Grand Council who had voted against Mussolini on 25 July and who had since fallen into the RSI's hands. The most high-profile figure awaiting his fate was the Duce's son-in-law, Galeazzo Ciano (at Verona, delegates openly shouted, 'Death to Ciano!'), but the others were hardly unknowns: they included Emilio De Bono, one of the *quadrumviri*, the four captains who had led the 'March on Rome', and Tullio Cianetti, the former minister of the corporations. The other three prisoners, Luciano Gottardi, Giovanni Marinelli, and Carlo Pareschi, had all held prestigious roles in the PNF and the state.

The show trial of the so-called traitors began on 8 January 1944 in Verona in front of a nine-man jury of party officials. A huge black flag decorated with a silver *fascio littorale* hung portentously behind the panel of judges as they listened to the charges levelled against the hierarchs. After a farcical three-day hearing, death sentences were pronounced on all but Cianetti, who had written to the Duce on 26 July 1943 retracting his previous day's vote. Even he was sentenced to thirty years in jail. Death sentences *in absentia* were passed on the thirteen other members of the Council who had shown no confidence in Mussolini. They were all by now well hidden: Dino Grandi, the chief conspirator, had fled to Lisbon.

After the trial was over, the condemned men were taken to Verona's Forte Procolo, where they were tied to chairs and shot in the back, as a sign of dishonour, by a firing squad at 9.20 a.m. on the morning of 11 January 1944. Ciano, dressed in a fashionable greatcoat, was finished off with a pistol shot by the officer in charge of the execution, which was filmed for propaganda purposes.[7] At 10 a.m., an 'extremely pale' Duce presided at the Council of Ministers, where he promised that now that heads had rolled, and those 'perhaps the least guilty', many others would follow. The Council conducted its business rapidly in 'pitiful silence'.[8]

There is an apocryphal story that Churchill, who was no admirer of his daughter Sarah's first husband, remarked that Mussolini had at least had the consolation of shooting his son-in-law. In fact, Ciano died because the Duce could not show clemency. The count symbolized the worst excesses of the defunct regime's degeneration, and he was detested both by the Nazis, who rightly regarded him as anti-Hitler, and by the rank and file of the PFR. Mussolini could not have commuted the death sentences without confirming his inadequacy as a revolutionary leader to the many top Nazis who doubted he had the guts to be frontman for National Socialism in Italy.

Indeed, Mussolini told the minister of corporations, Angelo Tarchi, that 'Hitler would say that my pardon was a sign of weakness towards a relative, who, like anybody else, or more than anybody else, ought to be sacrificed to the national interest and to the war effort.'[9] Having chosen the path leading 'inexorably into the abyss', the Duce had to go right to the bottom, though it cost him the love of his daughter, Edda, whom Mussolini adored. She never spoke to him again. It was the price of 'acting like a head of state in the face of history'.[10]

The RSI followed its leader's existential choice. First, it collaborated actively with the antisemitism of the Nazis and shared in the crimes committed against Italy's Jews. The Manifesto of the PFR explicitly stated that Jews were enemy aliens.[11] All Italian Jews – men, women, and children – were subsequently treated as such, without mercy. The Racial Laws had already transformed Italy's Jewish community into a persecuted minority (Jews constituted less than 0.1 per cent of the Italian population), but, after the creation of the RSI, Jews lost all remaining rights. Approximately a quarter of Italy's Jews were deported and murdered after 8 September 1943.

The Nazis began their reign of terror by 'liquidating' the Jewish quarter of Rome. Major Herbert Kappler, head of the Gestapo in the city, summoned the leaders of Rome's Jewish community to his office in the German Embassy on 26 September 1943. Kappler told them that as Italians and Jews they were doubly enemies of the Third Reich. He proceeded to blackmail them. If the community collected 50 kilograms of gold by 11 a.m. on Thursday 28 September, he would countermand orders to deport 200 Roman Jews to Germany. After enormous efforts – helped by non-Jewish citizens, who anonymously entered the Synagogue, 'not knowing whether to remove their hats or not', and 'almost humbly asked whether they too ... whether their contribution would be appreciated ... ' – the enormous sum was raised, just a few hours after the deadline. On 29 September, despite the ransom payment, the SS raided the Jewish quarter and, apparently under the command of an officer who was a scholar of Hebrew philology, sequestered the contents of the rabbinical college library and the temple, and with them the historical memory of Rome's Jewish community; documents of inestimable cultural value dating back to the times of the Roman Empire were looted by the Nazis.

On 16 October 1943, the Nazis escalated the terror. Troops erupted into the historically Jewish part of central Rome, the former ghetto, and detained hundreds of men, women, and children officially registered as Jewish. In other parts of the city, smaller-scale operations were carried out. Those rounded up were taken to the Termini Station where cattle trucks were waiting. After a lengthy wait in a shunting yard, until the trucks were full, they set off north. The heart-rending cries of those trapped inside the train sounded like pleadings from Purgatory, according to one eyewitness.[12] It was a scene being repeated all over Nazi-occupied Europe in the autumn of 1943. In all, 1,022 Jews, including 276 children, were captured during the *rastrellamento* ('rake-through') of 16 October 1943 in Rome: sixteen survived the war, none of them children.[13]

Mussolini could not have stopped the deportation of Italian Jewry, even if he had wanted to, but after the Verona Congress determined that Jews were enemy aliens, the state bureaucracy assisted the Nazis' plans. On 30 November 1943, the arrest of Jews and their detention in local holding camps was made an official duty of the police. The *carabinieri*, aided by the party militia, rounded up known Jews in the territory under their jurisdiction and interned them. 'Enticing bounties' – as much as 40,000 lire – were paid to informers who betrayed the whereabouts of Jews.[14] The *Corriere della Sera* – to cite just one major newspaper – suggested that the arrest of every person with the 'perverse lineage' of being Jewish would reduce cases of espionage and terrorism.[15] In January 1944, the Duce ordered the expropriation of all property owned by Jews.

By mid-February 1944, Fossoli, a concentration camp outside Carpi in the province of Modena, had become an SS-run hub to which Jews and political prisoners were brought and from which train convoys of deportees – about 5,000 in all – were taken to Auschwitz-Birkenau, Mauthausen, Belsen, and elsewhere.[16] What awaited Italy's Jews in Auschwitz was described by a young industrial chemist from Turin who had been captured after joining a partisan band in the Piedmont mountains, Primo Levi. *Se questo è un uomo* (*If This Is a Man*), Levi's memoir of Auschwitz, through its sparseness, matter-of-factness, indeed pitilessness of observation, is perhaps the most powerful portrayal ever published of the Nazis' experiment in treating millions of human beings as things.

Even today, some minimize the extent to which antisemitism became an intrinsic part of Fascist ideology. It is a mistake to do so, even if it is true that antisemitism did not occupy the same all-consuming place as it did for the Nazis. After the foundation of the RSI, racialism was propagated with 'even greater virulence and ruthlessness' than in 1938. The 'plutocratic-Masonic-Jewish conspiracy' became a 'cornerstone' of the regime's propaganda, alongside the myth that Fascism had been defeated from within by traitors like Ciano, Grandi, and Badoglio, not by its own weakness, or the errors of the 'Capo'.[17] Antisemitism became part of the curriculum in the training given to the officers of the Republican National Guard. Officer cadets had to read 'theoretical' works by the Fascist ideologue Julius Evola; *Gog*, a novel, tinged with antisemitism, by the Catholic convert Giovanni Papini; and the *Protocols of the Elders of Zion* in an edition published by Giovanni Preziosi, a former priest whose anti-semitism was so hallucinatory and fanatical that it earned the admiration of the top Nazi echelons, Hitler included.[18]

Preziosi, ironically, had espoused Italian intervention on the side of the Entente in 1915. He had insinuated, then, that there was a pervasive conspiracy within Italy in the Germans' favour. The Jews, naturally, were behind it. In 1942 his contribution to a propaganda volume by various apologists for the regime was entitled 'The Jews Wanted the War'. It fantasized that a transnational conspiracy led by President Roosevelt, 'the guiltiest party in this global war desired by Judaism', had caused the conflict.[19] When one reflects that this 'essay' was broadcast to millions over the state radio, one grasps why Hannah Arendt regarded the essence of totalitarianism as being not violence or repression, which are common to many regimes, but the telling of huge lies and the use of state power to construct a parallel world in which such lies are consolidated as the truth.

Preziosi returned to Italy from Germany in March 1944 and was made Inspector General for Race Affairs, running a small de facto department of government in Desenzano, near Salò. Preziosi achieved nothing of substance in this post, but his mere presence in the upper ranks of the RSI illustrates an important fact about Mussolini's regime: the paranoid style in Italian politics was in power and longing for Nazi approval.[20]

The desire to be in good standing with the Nazi hierarchy also conditioned the RSI's acquiescent approach to the Germans' use (or abuse) of Italian forced labour, which occurred on an enormous scale. After September 1943, some Italians voluntarily left for Germany to work in the factories and fields: the conditions of such volunteers were harsh, but not much worse than they would have been had they stayed in the factories at home. Such volunteers were, however, a small minority. They were supplemented by the hundreds of thousands of soldiers interned and transported to Germany after Badoglio surrendered, the so-called IMI (Italian Military Internees), and by large numbers of young men who were arrested for evading military service after the formation of the RSI.

The case of the IMI illustrated the inability of Mussolini's regime to protect its nationals from the Nazis' systematic cruelty. The Italian troops – there were some 716,000 of them scattered across 250 camps in Russia, Poland, France, and Yugoslavia, as well as Germany itself – were denied all rights laid down in the Geneva Convention, even access to the Red Cross. The camps that housed them were inhumane: the interned conscripts were often given no new clothing, slept on straw mattresses in the cold, and received only basic rations. A typical day's food was herb tea or watery ersatz coffee; a litre of what the internees called *sbobba* ('slop'), i.e. vegetable soup of a dire kind, usually turnip-based, about 300 grams of black rye bread with a smear of margarine, and two or three potatoes per head. The bread ration was reduced in 1944 to as little as 150 grams. In the poignant words of an interned Italian officer: 'I have been starving for eighteen months now: yet every day it seems like something new.'[21]

On this diet – which entirely lacked protein and fats – the Italian internees were made to do hard labour, although officers were mostly exempted. Typically, soldiers were forced to work in fields, factories, steelworks, construction sites, or in clearing rubble caused by Allied bombing. The working day was a twelve-hour shift. Many prisoners became too debilitated to work within weeks. Claudio Sommaruga, an internee, lost 14 kilograms in twenty-five days (down from 73 to 59 kilograms) between 4 and 29 August 1944, burning 27,000 calories from his bodily reserves of muscle. Only hospitalization saved his life, though in many cases, given the rudimentary medical facilities available in the camps, it was a death sentence.[22]

Sometimes, hunger drove the internees to extremes:

> Once the head, feet and tail were cut off, it was quite easy to skin rats. They had a fat, pinkish meat, a bit like rabbit. There was no way to roast them: there was neither time nor space, not to mention the unmistakeable smell that roasting would have given off. It was quicker to cook them in boiling water and then chop them up into small pieces to disguise the rodent's shape from your mind's eye.[23]

The Italians were treated with contempt by the German population and by prisoners of war from other defeated nations, especially the French. It is the settled opinion of IMI memorialists that, excluding Jews and political prisoners singled out for extermination, only Russians and Poles were treated worse than the Italians by the Nazis. A fascinating post-war collection of short memorial articles, reflections, and drawings by IMI prisoners carries the significant title of *Men and Germans*.[24] The author of the title piece says that the Italians' guards were 'brutal thugs' for whom the 'life of a prisoner had no importance'. While it was rare for a British prisoner to be 'clubbed', the beating of Italian or Russian prisoners was a 'fact of no concern' to the camp authorities.[25]

In July 1944, Mussolini, with the help of the German Foreign Ministry's 'civil plenipotentiary' for Italy in Salò, Ambassador Rudolf Rahn, got the IMI reclassified as 'free civil workers'. The change of nomenclature improved the Italians' legal status, but conditions remained as bleak as ever for those labouring in the foundries or mines. Overwork, workplace accidents, hunger, Allied bombs, and arbitrary German disciplinary measures took the lives of 35,000–40,000 interned soldiers by April 1945: in the last weeks of the war, as the Reich crumbled and camp administration broke down, many Italian internees literally starved to death.

Italian prisoners nevertheless showed notable psychological resilience. Discussions, improvised theatre groups, and lectures flourished among the officers: the camps became a place for reflection on the causes of the plight in which Italy found itself. In one camp, a group of engineers assembled a functioning radio, affectionately nicknamed 'Caterina', out of ordinary camp debris.[26] The prisoners took pride in not being dehumanized. The humourist Giovanni Guareschi, whose *Diario clandestino* was one of the first memoirs of an Italian internee to appear, famously wrote:

> Together with a lot of other officers like me, I found myself one day in a concentration camp in Poland, then I changed camp, but nothing much really changed, all camps are pretty much alike ... The only interesting thing, from the point of view of the story I'm telling you, is that even in prison I kept the typical stubbornness of an Emiliano from the Bassa. I gritted my teeth and said: I'm not going to die even if they kill me! And I didn't die. Probably that's because they didn't kill me, but the fact remains that I didn't die. I stayed alive in both body and soul and kept working ... We didn't live like brutes. We didn't become prisoners of our own selfishness. Hunger, dirt, cold, illness, pangs of terrible nostalgia for our mothers and our children, sheer despair for the unhappiness of our homeland, didn't defeat us. We didn't forget to be civilized human beings, men with a past and a future.[27]

At bottom, this sense of self is why the IMI, or most of them, also participated in an extraordinary act of principled resistance. Mussolini hoped that the IMI would provide recruits for a new army that could fight alongside the Germans to restore Fascism throughout the peninsula. Some RSI troops had joined the Germans in the front line: the X Mas, a specialist force of marines, commanded by Prince Junio Valerio Borghese, were the most notorious of these soldiers. Rodolfo Graziani, the butcher of Addis Ababa, who was now Mussolini's minister of war, committed the RSI to raising four divisions of volunteers to fight at the side of the German forces. Such a corps, had it ever been constituted as a well-equipped unit and stiffened by German officers, might even have made a material difference to the Italian campaign, since General Alexander's Allied forces were overstretched as they tried to penetrate Italy's unfriendly mountainous terrain.

To the Duce's embarrassment, the IMI snubbed the Salò regime.

Hard labour and turnip *sbobba* were regarded as a more honourable option than serving the RSI. Despite the offer of generous pay and conditions, and the prospect of returning to Italy and their families, only about 14 per cent of the IMI chose to take Mussolini's bribe. The others rejected the RSI because they were anti-fascists, or because they had sworn an oath to serve the king, not Fascism, or because they were anti-German and wanted the Nazis to lose the war.[28] Graziani did eventually assemble four divisions, supplementing the *optanti* (as they were called) with press-ganged men, but they did little to improve the sorry record of fascist troops during Mussolini's wars and suffered greatly from desertion.

SEVENTH CIRCLE

In the *Divine Comedy*, Dante consigned those who committed sins of violence to the seventh circle of hell, where they simmered for eternity in a river of boiling blood. One of the greatest crimes of Salò, and of the Nazi colonizers of Italy, was that their savagery compelled ordinary Italian citizens who had never fired a gun, and who would never normally have settled a political issue through bloodshed, to kill and even murder for the cause of national liberation. As for the RSI's militia, and the SS battalions dedicated to suppressing resistance behind the lines, their violence was not just sickening, but nihilistic. For them, Norberto Bobbio's 'abyss' exercised a macabre attraction.

In the first weeks after 8 September 1943, Italian partisans, in addition to printing and distributing propaganda and performing acts of sabotage, carried out numerous terrorist attacks and assassinations against German troops or prominent Fascists. The two most significant of these took place in Rome and Florence in the spring of 1944. On 23 March, a Patriotic Action Group (GAP) – a partisan cell committed to carrying out assassinations – ambushed troops from the XI company of the Bolzano Police Regiment (in popular accounts they are often referred to as SS troops but were in fact recruits from the German-speaking valleys of Alto Adige). As the company passed down Via Rasella, a street only eight paces wide in central Rome, it was blasted by a rudimentary roadside bomb composed of 12 kilograms of

TNT and 6 kilograms of other explosives and chunks of metal, hidden in a streetcleaner's cart. The cart had been placed there by Rosario Bentivegna, a twenty-one-year-old medical student, who lit the fuse on the signal of Franco Calamandrei, a young literary critic, whose father Piero Calamandrei, the eminent jurist and insightful diarist encountered in Chapter Two, had rebuked him in the past for his lack of anti-fascist commitment.

The explosion was terrifying; the heat and the flying metal generated by the explosion even ignited the hand grenades carried by the German troops. Other GAP members added to the slaughter by shooting at the panic-stricken soldiers from the rooftops. Thirty-three German soldiers died; many others were wounded. Two children in the wrong place at the wrong time were also killed; one was literally blown to pieces. In the gun battle that followed the attack, numerous civilians were wounded and five killed.[29] The commander of the SS in Rome, Eugen Dollmann, described the scene as 'gruesome' when he arrived there; 'severed human limbs were scattered around, large pools of blood had formed all over the place, the wounded were lying in agony, the air was filled with cries and whimpers of pain'.[30]

The Germans began a *rastrellamento* of the area, making random arrests of citizens. An enraged Hitler demanded that fifty Roman citizens should be shot in reprisal for every fallen soldier; he later apparently changed this number to ten.[31] The Nazi commanders in Rome obediently drew up a list for execution. All those under arrest for political crimes were put on the list, as were the people arrested near the scene of the attack. Nearly sixty Jews (plus ten more added when the thirty-third German soldier died of his wounds) were scheduled to be executed. The numbers still did not reach the required 330, so the chief of the Rome police, Pietro Caruso, consigned fifty unfortunates from Regina Coeli prison.[32]

On the afternoon of 24 March 1944, 335 prisoners, none of whom bore any responsibility for the attack in Via Rasella, were escorted to the Ardeatine caves and murdered. Herbert Kappler, the persecutor of Rome's Jews, and other senior Nazi officers personally supervised the killings to set an example to the common soldiers. The site of the massacre was then sealed off by explosives.

Except for the fact that they were all men, the victims represented a cross section of Roman society. Professionals of all kinds were represented, but so too were manual workers: butchers, waiters, bricklayers, salesmen, market traders, mechanics. The *podestà* (the fascist equivalent of mayor) of Nespolo in the province of Rieti, Loreto Finamonti, had been arrested by the SS for hiding Allied airmen. Several policemen and army officers, including Colonel Giuseppe Cordero Lanza di Montezemolo, who was a member of the resistance, were taken to their deaths. The youngest victims were Duilio Cibei, a carpenter aged fourteen, Franco di Consiglio, a butcher aged seventeen, and Ilario Canacci, a hotel waiter, also aged seventeen. Two non-Italian citizens, a German Jew called Paul Pesach Wald and a Hungarian, Sandor Kereszti, perished.[33] Many of those murdered had only been arrested after the authorities received *delazioni*, anonymous letters, or reports from spies. The 'Open City' of Rome was a place of deep ambiguity, where the best and the worst sides of human nature were struggling for dominance.[34]

On 25 March, the German High Command issued a statement saying that to punish the 'vile ambush' carried out by 'Comunisti-Badogliani', ten criminals 'will be shot' for every German life lost. Despite the use of the future tense, it concluded brusquely, 'the sentence has already been carried out'. The goal of the Nazis had not been to 'punish the guilty, but to terrorize the city'.[35] In response, the CLN issued a 'solemn incitation' to 'Italian men and Italian women' to strive to liberate the country from the 'Nazi invader' and 'rebuild an Italy worthy of her fallen sons'.[36]

Not long after the ambush in Rome, another high-profile GAP attack took place, this time in Florence. Giovanni Gentile, co-author of Mussolini's textbook *La dottrina del fascismo*, a renowned philosopher and former minister of education, was assassinated by partisans on 15 April 1944. Gentile was president of the Accademia d'Italia, the institution that honoured the regime's academic and literary acolytes, which had moved to Florence from Rome the previous month. A burly, white-bearded sage, Gentile was an ardent exponent of the mystical notion that Fascism was the latest manifestation of Italy's civilizing mission in the world. 'Barbarians' elsewhere had been educated first by the Romans, then by Catholicism, then by the scholars and artists of the Renaissance, and then, last but not least, by the

Risorgimento, which Gentile regarded as the most sublime expression of European liberalism.[37] Fascism, whatever its mistakes, had restored the greatness of the Italian spirit when the country had degenerated into the inglorious parliamentarianism of the Giolittian age. True liberals, he argued, were the first to rejoice when Mussolini 'demolished' the 'hovel' of parliamentary democracy.[38]

For this reason, Gentile appealed to all Italians to collaborate, on behalf of *la Patria*, with the RSI rather than subvert it by force, or by remaining unengaged. As one historian has remarked, Gentile's writings were 'a last-ditch attempt to rouse traditional patriotism, by placing the fatherland over and above the Fascist Party, yet without calling the party's political prerogatives into question'.[39] The core of his message was to cooperate with Mussolini's government and trust in its historical mission. Such sentiments made him anathema to the PCI in its new guise, in the wake of the *svolta di Salerno*, as the party of national unity, leading a patriotic war. Did Gentile – a man of vast learning and culture – truly believe that Mussolini, a *condottiere* who had given ample proof of his inadequacy as a leader, would guide Italy to a new renaissance arm in arm with the SS? He must have known that the Nazis were in command even in Mussolini's own home: Rudolf Rahn monitored the Duce's decisions and gave Germany's assent or placed its veto.[40]

Gentile's pleas for national unity can also only be described as squalid apologetics when one considers what was happening in the city where he lived. Florence was the fiefdom of Alessandro Pavolini, the secretary of the PFR, who, after Mussolini himself, was the most powerful figure in the RSI. He was also an admirer of Hitler. A 'Centre for the Study of the Jewish Problem' had been established in Florence and was inundating the city with propaganda. The city's main newspaper, *La Nazione*, was openly philo-Nazi: its editor described Jews as a 'hereditary disease of humanity' in an article published in February 1944.[41]

By the spring of 1944, the authorities in Florence had taken over from the Germans the task of hunting down and deporting Jews. Only the willingness of many citizens to hide their friends and neighbours, and the fact that many Tuscan Jews took to the hills and joined the resistance, saved Florence's 2,000-strong Jewish community from destruction (though in Florence, too, *delazioni* occurred). Over 600 Jews were deported to Auschwitz from Tuscany, 311 of whom were from Florence itself.[42]

Opponents of the regime were also rounded up in large numbers. On 8 March 1944, a few days before Gentile gave an inaugural lecture to the Accademia, a train carrying 597 prisoners left Florence's Santa Maria Novella station bound for Mauthausen concentration camp. Some 338 of the detainees on the train came from Tuscany. Most were workers who had taken part in strikes in local factories a few days earlier. Only sixty-four of the Tuscans (19 per cent) survived the war and returned home.[43] The regime to which Gentile added a gloss of intellectual respectability was engaged in terrorism against the people under its rule.

The attack in Via Rasella and the liquidation of Gentile were terrorist actions, too. Italians were fighting terror with terror of their own. In Rome, GAP squads had been carrying out two or three attacks a week. By the time the capital was liberated on 4 June 1944, PCI partisans had killed or wounded 200 Germans and gunned down nine prominent Fascists. The PCI also had 1,000 'effectives' under arms, a quarter of its membership in Rome.[44] The Via Rasella attack was part of a campaign; it was not an isolated event.

Such feats were celebrated by the anti-fascist press, which published lists of the 'spies', members of the Fascist militia, or open collaborators with the Germans, who had been *giustiziati* ('brought to justice'), the euphemism employed to describe assassinations. As early as October 1943, *l'Unità* had proclaimed:

We must fight strenuously, with virile courage, without hesitation or weakness. We are not a cowardly people, or poltroons, nor do we have a serf mentality. The Germans in their arrogance assume they can reduce us to subjection with violence and terror: it is up to us to strike back with violence and terror ourselves.[45]

The bomb attack in Via Rasella and the assassination of Giovanni Gentile ratcheted up the resistance's use of terrorism to a new level. The ambush against the Bolzano Police Regiment was a just act of war, in so far as its targets were soldiers, but the action's mercilessness made some squeamish at the time and has aroused disquiet ever since.

Perhaps the GAP should have skirmished in the streets using rifles and pistols? Or attacked a harder target of greater military value? Instead, the GAP inflicted the maximum damage possible on a relatively soft target and accepted the risk that innocent lives would be lost in reprisals. What the *attentato* in Via Rasella indicated, in short, was that the GAP would fight like revolutionaries, for whom the political end justifies the means employed.

The case of Gentile aroused even more disquiet. Gentile was a distinguished figure in European letters. He was unmistakably a civilian, albeit one identified with the regime. The PCI's action was criticized by the PdA, which argued that Gentile should have been spared until he could be tried after the war. 'Violence,' the PdA contended, 'though it might be justified in response to the violence of others', had 'a limit' which, if transgressed, 'rebounds on its perpetrators'. The 'brutal elimination' of Gentile had overstepped this mark.[46] Piero Calamandrei, in hiding in Umbria, reflected thoughtfully that history had 'paid [Gentile] back in his own coin'. He was guilty of encouraging 'high culture' to kowtow to a 'regime of legalized brigandage', and, most seriously of all, he had 'justified power politics philosophically'. His murder, paradoxically, could be justified only in terms of the Machiavellian ethics he himself had preached.[47]

The PCI had no such qualms: the philosopher had got what he deserved. The fullest response of the PCI to critics of Gentile's killing came in the July 1944 edition of *Rinascita*, where Togliatti reprinted a ferocious attack on Gentile's appeals for national unity originally published in March 1944 in a clandestine PCI journal, *La nostra lotta*. It is worth quoting the article's peroration at length:

Those who today appeal for harmony are accomplices of the Nazi and Fascist murderers; those who suggest a truce want to disarm the patriots and give the Nazi and Fascist murderers time to recoup and to renew their criminal activities undisturbed . . . The sword should not be sheathed until the last Nazi has gone back over the Alps, and the last Fascist traitor has been exterminated. Senator Gentile, the People's Justice has already announced its verdict on the Nazi invaders' lickspittles and their Fascist fellow travellers: Death![48]

An unsigned coda was added to this harangue stating that Gentile was 'a philosophical monstrosity, an Idealist, Fascist, and traitor to Italy'. It added that a group of 'generous' youth had since freed Italy of 'one of the vilest authors of its degeneration'.[49]

What the PCI demanded from everybody was commitment to the cause. Relentlessly, the PCI's clandestine press campaigned against all 'temporizing' (*attesismo*). Luigi Longo wrote, in one of the first post-war explanations of the historical meaning of the resistance, that the PCI had grasped by 1944 that 'only struggle, only open conflict without quarter, delay or compromise, could bring about the revival of Italy'.[50] For the PCI the immediate goal of the struggle was to 'crush the Germans and exterminate the Fascists'.[51]

The PCI's position was a harbinger of one that national liberation movements in the post-war world would soon face: how can one fight against the militarily superior forces of a colonial power if one shrinks from being ruthless? In the *Wretched of the Earth*, Frantz Fanon's implacable essay on the use of violence in wars of colonial liberation, the answer is that one cannot; indeed, one *should* not. In such circumstances, the use of terror, even against civilians, is both inevitable and *right*. Nothing strengthens national consciousness so much as killing on its behalf. The same logic was at work in Italy, in 1944. For the PCI, there was no such thing as a Fascist civilian or a good German, and it was simply liberal sentimentality to think that there might be.

In practice, on the ground, distinctions were made by the men (and women) who pulled the trigger. The GAP groups mostly carried out *targeted* assassinations. They did not carry out attacks that were bound to cause 'collateral damage' among citizens. Relatively few Germans captured by Italian partisans were killed out of hand, though the practice was not unknown; Fascist officials were generally not marked down for elimination unless their behaviour had been egregious. But the PCI wanted them to fear that they might be. The murder of Gentile, by this token, sent a powerful message to RSI officials of all ranks: you might be next.

Above all, the PCI thoroughly understood that the Italians could not in all conscience allow the Allies to fight for them and then wait passively for liberation:

If we wait for others to bring us national independence and freedom, can we truly call ourselves a free people? *A people that wants to have the right to call itself free has the duty to fight with every means in its power to conquer its freedom.*[52]

It was the Italians' patriotic duty to do everything they could to disrupt, damage, and destroy the German war effort and to spread fear among all those who worked for the Germans or did their bidding. Workers should strike, or sabotage, or hold up production in the factories. Young men called up for military service, or to work for the German war machine, should take to the hills or join the clandestine struggle in the towns. Peasants should provide food and lodging for anti-fascists and hide their harvests from the Germans. There were several women in the GAP group that launched the attack in Via Rasella: women were urged to become politically conscious and active in the anti-fascist resistance. As *La nostra lotta* urged in March 1944:

> Working women have become part of the economy of the nation: well then, let them sabotage production intended for the Germans; during mass meetings let women be the most ardent critics, the most outspoken at putting forward demands and in raising issues. Let women be the inciters of their menfolk, be their advisers, let them revive and stimulate the men's willingness to fight, and support them in the struggle.[53]

Everybody, henceforth, would be judged by their actions – but temporizers and fence-sitters would face the people's wrath when the war was won.[54] More than any other party, the PCI, even before Togliatti returned from Russia with Stalin's injunction to intensify the military struggle against the Nazis, was the Italian party that organized resistance most effectively in occupied Italy. Its underground press was tireless – the variety and quality of its pamphlet literature is astonishing – and its militants were most active in carrying out acts of sabotage and assassination. From March–April 1944 onwards, such activities escalated sharply.

Mussolini's regime responded to the partisans' attacks by waging a dirty war alongside the Gestapo and the SS against their own flesh and blood. No fewer than three intermingled conflicts were fought on Italian soil in the last two years of the Second World War. There was a conventional war between the Allies and the Germans, a war of liberation being fought by Italian partisans against Nazi occupation, and last, but certainly not least, a civil war between Italians.[55] The last of these conflicts was probably the most ruthless of the three. The war between the RSI's array of militias, which included privateer 'bands' commanded by pro-Nazi delinquents, and the 'bandits', as the fascists called them, that constituted the resistance, was fought on the fascist side without even lip service for due process.[56]

Just as the colonial settlers of Kenya and Algeria would subsequently unshackle their most unspeakable, most sadistic fantasies under the pretext of fighting rebellion, so the RSI and the German occupation forces committed rape, torture and wanton murder as they struggled to retain control of the territory under their command. Captured partisans were tortured as a matter of course. Methods used included flogging with bull whips, electric shocks, anal rape with metallic or wooden objects, boiling-pitch baths, cranial crushing by iron bands, ripping off fingernails, and beatings with nail-studded belts or staves in which prisoners often lost an eye or received multiple bone fractures. Simulated executions where prisoners were hooded and kept waiting for hours in the imminent expectation of death were another, more sophisticated, torture technique. Astonishingly, many partisans resisted such maltreatment and kept their secrets to themselves, at least until they could be sure that their contacts had escaped. Such heroes – and there were dozens – were usually murdered out of hand and then dumped in the squares of occupied Italy's cities so the town folk could see what happened to those who joined the 'rebels'. Corpses were often left to rot for days.[57]

The treatment of captured women partisans was particularly vile: rape was the norm; it was accompanied by depravities such as stubbing out burning cigarettes on the women's nipples or sprinkling their pudenda with salt so the torturers' dogs would lick them. Torture sessions were sometimes part of the 'entertainment' during orgies frequented by prostitutes or the wives and mistresses of the *aguzzini* (torturers) involved; cocaine abuse was frequent and extreme.

The popular historian Mimmo Franzinelli has rightly underlined that Pier Paolo Pasolini's notorious 1975 film *Salò o le 120 giornate di Sodoma* – in which four libertines, symbolic of the class, ecclesiastic, legal and economic powers within the state, take a group of young victims to a villa in Salò and have them subjected to a hysterical cycle of indignities, concluding with mass murder, the mutilation of corpses, and necrophilia – is scarcely a parody of the worst abuses committed by the RSI's most dissolute bands during the later stages of the civil war. Pasolini himself said that 'never had power been more lawless than during the Republic of Salò.'[58]

In the Piero Calamandrei archive in the Tuscan Historical Institute of the Resistance in Florence, there is a file that mostly contains the stories of women partisans captured during the occupation by the Nazis or by RSI paramilitaries. Some cases are supported by letters sent by private citizens to Calamandrei, who became a legislator in Rome after the end of the war. Reading the file, one becomes numbed by the stories of individuals such as Irma Bandiera, who was posthumously awarded the gold medal of the Italian Republic for her courage (one of nineteen women to be so honoured so far): Bandiera was captured by the SS, tortured, blinded, and murdered in a public execution in Bologna in August 1944, but never revealed any of her many contacts. Gabriella Degli Espositi, also awarded a posthumous gold medal, was a valiant combatant who, during interrogation, had her breasts slashed off and eyes gouged out, but who 'resisted stoically without uttering a word'. She was shot by firing squad in February 1944. Bruna and Matilda Zebri were two young communist partisans murdered during the Marzabotto (Bologna) massacre in October 1944; German troops bayoneted the pregnant Bruna and ripped her unborn child from her womb.[59]

The list of atrocities against women is endless. In all, about 35,000 women took part in the resistance; of these, 4,653 were arrested and tortured, over 2,800 were hanged or shot, while 1,070 died in combat. Hundreds more were transported to concentration camps in Germany.[60] Luigi Longo once wrote: 'An old Italian adage says that, when the skirts espouse a cause, you can be sure it's as good as won.'[61] The cause of recognition for the democratic rights of women was greatly helped by the actions and heroism of female partisans during the resistance.

A note to Calamandrei from Angelo A. Sabatini of Forlì in the Romagna recalled how 'one hot day' in August 1944 the citizens of the town had been shocked to see the 'macabre spectacle' of four dangling corpses in the town square, one of whom was the 'legendary hero' of the resistance Silvio Corbari, along with two of his men. The fourth corpse was a woman, Iris Versari, 'a woman of the people, a hero of the resistance'. Mr Sabatini pointed out that the three men had rightly been awarded medals for valour, but Iris Versari so far had not. He added, however, 'If in Rome, in the high, cold offices, Iris has been forgotten, that is not the case in Romagna, where women and where men have good memories.'[62]

Whether he knew it or not, Sabatini was a poet. Calamandrei was a scholar, jurist, and liberal. The whole experience of the RSI and the Nazi occupation made men like Calamandrei passionately determined to ensure that the sacrifices of the partisans tortured and left for dead, or the Jews of Rome, or the common soldiers interned in Germany, would not be forgotten; at any rate, that those sacrifices would never happen again. During the RSI, the Italians learned, through thousands of episodes of atrocious suffering, what happens when the rule of law is swatted aside by political power.

THE WAR OF LIBERATION

The resistance was considerable in size and represented a painful thorn in the Nazis' side. Approximately 200,000 Italians fought in the resistance and tens of thousands of patriots assisted in non-combatant roles, although these figures are swollen by those who joined the partisan movement in the last weeks of the war, the so-called *partigiani dell'ultima ora*. Many of those who took to the hills in September 1943 did not survive to see Mussolini's final defeat: combat deaths and the torture chambers of the RSI accounted for between 30,000 and 40,000 lives among partisans.

The original partisans were mostly soldiers who spontaneously took up arms after the flight of Badoglio and the king. Until the spring of 1944, they were only a few thousand in number. They were gradually mobilized by the political parties into military formations known as 'brigades' of approximately 300 men and women, which were sub-divided into smaller 'detachments'. The PCI ensured that its 'Garibaldi' brigades had a political commissar, on the model of the Red Army, and placed a high premium on the political education of its front-line sol-diers, as did the PdA. The PdA's troops were named the 'Justice and Liberty' brigades, while PSI units were named in memory of Giacomo Matteotti, although the PSIUP played a relatively minor role in the armed struggle. Many units had no official political leaning but were simply composed of patriots: many members of these forces were Catholics or monarchists. Christian Democrat brigades also took an active role in the military resistance, especially in Emilia.[63] Priests served with the Catholic partisans, and not purely as spiritual advisers, either. Many were killed, either in combat or after capture.[64]

The partisans armed themselves by carrying out raids on the bar-racks of the carabinieri or the Fascist militia, by taking the weapons of captured or killed enemies, or using weapons and munitions parachuted in by the Allies. Their numbers were replenished by young men evading conscription into the RSI's armed forces, Jews escaping *rastrellamenti*, deserters from the police, or workers avoid-ing forced labour in Germany. Mussolini made draft dodging a capital offence in February 1944, but that did not deter many young Italians from slipping away during leave or from joining the rebels after capture.

The partisans fought ferociously: they knew what awaited them if they were captured. Vital support was provided for the partisan bri-gades by the peasant communities of the Apennines and the Alps: 'The guerrilla movement could never have nourished itself and sur-vived without the support of the people of the countryside.'[65] Partisans dwelling in *baite* (mountain huts), barns, and caves counted on the local farmers and their families for both provisions and intelligence about the movements of the enemy. Communication between the local community and the partisan forces, or between different parti-san bands, or, in the city, GAP groups, was the main function performed by women *staffette* (relays), who transported messages, medicines, and weapons to and fro, often using bicycles, at permanent risk of being stopped by patrols. The humble bicycle, in fact, is an emblem of the Italian resistance.[66]

The resistance was organized politically by the CLN. In every province, the parties formed clandestine committees mirroring the composition of the central committee in Rome that decided on the priorities of the armed struggle, produced and distributed propaganda, decided on assassinations by the GAP squads, and dispensed funds. Only Democracy and Labour, Bonomi's party, was unrepresented since it had no presence on the ground in the north. In February 1944, the Milan CLN was recognized by Rome as the coordinating body for the whole of the North. It became known as the Committee for National Liberation – Upper Italy (CLNAI). Relations between the CLNAI and the Bonomi government in Rome were often less than idyllic, but there is no doubt that the tenacity the political parties showed in conducting the resistance reinforced their legitimacy: the parties 'enriched the resistance with political content' and ensured that it did not become mere banditry.[67] Certainly, by directing the partisan struggle the CLN parties made themselves indispensable for the political process after the war. The Italian people became accustomed to politics being refracted through them.

Military operations were initially decided upon by the sub-committee of the CLNAI, but on 19 June 1944 the direction of the partisan war was placed in the hands of a new body, the General Command of the Volunteers for Freedom Corps (CVL), which was given the task of disciplining, formalizing, and intensifying partisan actions. Its key figures were an *azionista*, Ferruccio Parri, or 'Maurizio', to give him his *nom de guerre*, and the Communist Luigi Longo, who had held a similar military/political role as commissar of the Garibaldi Brigade during the Spanish Civil War. Longo was among the most doctrinaire of the PCI's top cadres, but he was an implacable fighter and a tireless worker. To them was added a serving officer, General Raffaele Cadorna, who was parachuted into occupied Italy by the Allies to take command of operations.

Parri, a Piedmontese schoolteacher and writer, was an upright, heroic figure. He had served with distinction as an officer in the First World War, winning no fewer than three Italian medals for valour and the French *croix de guerre*. Invalided out of the front line with frostbite, Parri became a senior officer on the general staff that rallied the army after the disastrous battle of Caporetto in 1917. His military experience was therefore considerable. Parri was a courageous opponent of the regime. He had served several years in jail and internal exile because of his political views. A close friend of Carlo Rosselli, with whom he organized the escape from internment on the Isle of Lipari of the historian Gaetano Salvemini, Parri was a member of Justice and Liberty (GL) and a founder in 1942 of the PdA.

The General Command of the CVL spurred insurrection behind the German lines. An edition of *l'Unità* in July 1944 listed the attacks carried out by the Garibaldi Brigades of Ravenna, Bologna, Modena, Forlì and Reggio Emilia in the single month of June. Nine bridges had been destroyed, four military trains had been derailed; two railway lines had been interrupted; power plants had been sabotaged across the provinces; and there had been no fewer than 282 cases of cutting phone and telegraph wires. In the same provinces, the paper claimed that 343 Germans and 397 Fascists had been killed in ambushes, that attacks had been launched on forty military checkpoints or barracks, and that thirty-five machine guns had been captured along with 700 rifles and two tons of ammunition.[68] These figures were doubtless inflated, but by July 1944, large swathes of the northern and central provinces were de facto war zones: some 50,000 partisans by then were under arms, and the number was increasing by the day.[69]

Florence was liberated by partisans in August 1944. As the Allies advanced from north of Rome in July, German troops prepared to evacuate the city. General Alexander was anxious that Florence – given its inestimable value to human civilization – should not be turned into a battlefield. His caution opened a door for the Tuscan CLN. On 21 July, the political parties decided not to negotiate an orderly withdrawal with the Nazis, to spare the city from damage, but to attack the German army. The Germans' retreat was harried by partisan units, which also hunted down the remaining local Fascists prepared to die for an ignoble cause. The bridges over the river Arno were destroyed, with the sole exception of the Ponte Vecchio, and considerable damage ensued. But the skirmishes in the city enabled the CLN to make a political point. When the Allies arrived on 16 August, they encountered something they had not experienced in the South or in Rome: a city whose public administration was functioning under the guidance of a government composed of representatives of political parties confident that they had the authority to act in the people's name.[70]

The Tuscan CLN's ideological viewpoint was expressed via a newspaper, *La Nazione del Popolo*, which replaced the collaborationist daily newspaper, *La Nazione*, and was written by the flower of the city's intelligentsia: Piero Calamandrei, who became Rector of the University of Florence, was a regular contributor. It was soon selling 50,000 copies a day. On 12 August the paper's leading article was significantly entitled 'A New Nation'.

> Without freedom and without a State we lost our unity and our independence . . . But the Italian people . . . are rediscovering its worth. Its worst vices, which date back to long before Fascism, although they reached their most extreme form under the Fascist regime, must end with Fascism . . . Today, despite the bloodshed, the destruction, the total dissolution of all civilian life . . . [the Italian population] . . . is resurgent, and in its most tragic hour has begun, under the leadership of its National Government, for the first time in its history to create political institutions and values that reflect its peculiar form of life; to give birth, at long last, to a State.[71]

The newspaper recognized that national rebirth would not be painless: indeed, it considered that political renewal would be incomplete if it were unaccompanied by an energetic cleansing of Fascism from the body politic. On 6–7 September, an article entitled 'Epurazione' (Purge) underlined this point with a wealth of rhetorical devices:

> The ruling class that created Fascism, tolerated Fascism, cut deals with Fascism; the ruling class that has brought Italy to its present state of ruin; must be, totally, destroyed . . . Just as the work of reconstruction must be total, so must the purge be complete. It can't just be limited to the functionaries and hierarchs [of the Fascist state], but it must include all those, irrespective of rank, in the worlds of the economy, finance, work, culture, and the military, who were part of that ruling class.[72]

This verged on Jacobinism. Certainly, it was very far from the instrumentalist reasoning that had enabled Togliatti to cut a deal with

Badoglio or tell an audience at the Brancaccio Theatre that those who had worn the black shirt for purely economic reasons had nothing to fear from progressive democracy. It was even further from the political culture of the Mezzogiorno, where a propensity to let bygones be bygones was already pervasive and where the traditional elites intended to preserve their power even if, like the character of the general in Leonardo Sciascia's marvellous satire *Candido*, this meant that they had to transform themselves from ardent fascists into communists. Yet the notion that the war must end in the eradication of Fascism and the political and intellectual structures that had given birth to it and sustained it in power was the moral fuel powering the partisan military machine.

The number of partisans in the field would reach 80,000–100,000 in September 1944, the high point of the resistance until April 1945. By then, partisan brigades were fighting what amounted to small battles involving thousands of guerrillas at a time. In December 1944, the Emilia-Romagna edition of *Il Combattente*, another PCI news-sheet, claimed that partisans had killed over 6,000 Germans in the region and wounded more than 4,700 since June. Nearly 1,300 'militiamen, spies and fascist traitors' had been killed. Four trains had been blown up, with the destruction of fifty wagons, and nineteen had been derailed. Forty-seven bridges had been destroyed, as had 676 lorries and thirty-one tanks. Thousands of rifles, bombs and machine guns had been captured.[73] Again, these figures were probably exaggerated. But the 'bandits', as the Nazis called them, were indisputably causing havoc. The German army had discovered that the despised Italians were tough opponents when they were well-armed and believed in their cause.

Emilia-Romagna was by no means exceptional: large parts of Val D'Aosta, Piedmont, Lombardy, and the upper Apennines were under partisan control during the summer and early autumn of 1944: so-called free zones. The most famous cases were the 'republics' of Montefiorino (Modenese Apennines), Carnia (Friuli), and Val d'Ossola (a part of Piedmont bordering on Switzerland), where the partisans governed unchallenged for several weeks.[74] The Val d'Ossola briefly became a commune on the model of the Mazzinian Republic of Rome during the 1849 revolution against papal rule, or of working-class Paris in the spring of 1871.[75]

The strength of the resistance, however, was illustrated best by its ability to survive adverse circumstances. In the autumn of 1944 these were the norm. After the conquest of Florence, the Allied advance bogged down as the Germans defended the Gothic Line, defensive emplacements spanning the Apennines from Pesaro on the Adriatic coast to the Ligurian Sea near La Spezia. A pincer movement in September–October 1944 to break through along the Adriatic coast towards Rimini, and through the Apennines towards Imola and Bologna, encountered fierce opposition and caused heavy casualties for both sides. General Alexander hunkered down for a winter campaign of attrition. On 13 November, he warned the partisans in a radio message that now rain and mud were bound to obstruct the Allied advance, and the number of flights to drop war materials to the resistance would inevitably be reduced, it was necessary for the 'patriots' to 'cease large-scale operations', to avoid excessive risks, but nevertheless to take every 'favourable opportunity' to harass the Nazi–Fascist forces. Alexander concluded his message by expressing his admiration for the contribution that the partisans had made to the summer campaign.[76]

What Alexander's words implied for the partisan brigades in the hills was clarified by *l'Unità* in its next edition after the proclamation: 'a dead German means a gun, clothes, a pair of shoes for a Partisan'.[77] In the absence of British aid, the partisans would have to clothe and arm themselves from the dead bodies of their enemies. In December 1944, a delegation from the CLNAI made a clandestine voyage to Rome, where they negotiated a deal with the Allies by which, in exchange for a promise to disband their forces and to consign their arms at war's end, they received a cash subsidy of 160 million lire to keep the partisan brigades in the field.

Some Italian historiography has interpreted General Alexander's proclamation as an attempt to rein in the revolutionary impulses unleashed during the summer, but this explanation finds no support within the British archives. Italy was a marginal front, the Allied troops were too few and exhausted, material constraints were real, Tito's army in Yugoslavia had a greater claim on such resources as were available, and the partisans, on their own, could not raise a full insurrection capable of challenging the German army. The British government was impressed by the contribution made by the Italian brigades, which had been far more effective than expected. Lord Selborne, the minister responsible for the Special Operations Executive, which coordinated operations with guerrilla forces in occupied Europe, had written to Churchill on 24 October that the Italian resistance had done 'a magnificent job' and worried that it would be morally wrong to leave them in the lurch over the winter without adequate supplies. Indeed, though supplies dipped to 149 tons in November, they were quickly restored to over 350 tons the following month. By then, however, the 'damage had been done' and Alexander's proclamation, which one Italian historian sympathetic to the British has described as 'a glaring and dangerous gaffe from the psychological standpoint', would influence relations with the partisans (and Italian historiography) thereafter.[78]

The failure of the Allies to break through the Gothic Line exposed the partisans to a Nazi–Fascist counter-offensive intended to restore control over the territory. From September 1944 to March 1945, life in 'upper Italy' was a bloody chronicle of reprisals carried out by the SS, the Black Brigades, and the X Mas in revenge for partisan activity. Villages were burned, peasants were shot in large numbers for providing partisan bands with food and shelter, GAP assassinations in the towns were punished by the random murder of political prisoners. There were literally hundreds of *stragi*, massacres where multiple civilians or partisan prisoners were killed to intimidate the local population, or simply to sate the bloodlust of the troops involved.

Luigi Longo claimed, after the war, that 'Italy's massacres were reminiscent, in both the methods adopted, and their scale, of the slaughter in Poland and Russia.'[79] This was an exaggeration – the Italian historian Elisabetta Tonizzi has estimated that, in all, about 15,000 civilians were victims of over 400 *stragi* during the Nazi occupation – but the methods employed were indeed similar.[80]

The worst massacre of all – though it is almost invidious to single one out – was the case of Casaglia, Grizzana, Marzabotto, and Monzuno, villages south and west of Bologna, where a partisan brigade was weakening the German defence against the Allied advance through the Apennines. Between 29 September and 5 October 1944, SS troops who had already slaughtered hundreds of civilians in

Tuscany, wiped out these villages in cold blood: about 800 people were murdered in a few days.[81] Adults and children alike were machine-gunned without pity. It was the worst act of terror carried out against a civilian population in western Europe by the Nazis during the Second World War, although even greater horrors were committed in Yugoslavia.[82]

Yet the mounting death toll did not daunt the CLN. Massacre was followed by reprisal, assassination, and terror by the GAP squads and by hit-and-run attacks by armed partisans in the provinces. A good example is provided by the Commander of the Garibaldi Brigade of Genoa, who communicated to the PCI's party bulletin that, in reprisal for the killing of three patriots, the Genoa partisans had decided to launch an 'energetic operation for the suppression of spies' starting on 30 November 1944. A lengthy list of fascist office holders (in one case with his fiancée, who was also allegedly an 'enemy spy'), members of the militia, German soldiers, and informers who had been *giustiziati* followed. A 'republican fascist', the personal secretary of the local PFR leader, was 'taken off a tram, disarmed, marched to a nearby square and executed'.[83] Early December 1944 was a bad moment to identify publicly with the RSI in Genoa.

THE END OF THE REGIME

The last few months of the RSI must have been an unbearable wait for an inevitable end. The regime whistled energetically in the dark to keep its spirits up and vaunted the German army's 'new weapons', such as the V2 missile, as evidence that the Third Reich would soon regain the military initiative. The Duce grandiloquently promised that, though the Allies had reached the Apennines, the Po River valley would remain untouched by foreign invaders:

> We intend to defend, by tooth and nail, the valley of the Po; we want to ensure that the Po valley stays republican until such time as all Italy is republican. Were the Po valley to be contaminated by the enemy, the destiny of the nation would be compromised; but I sense, I glimpse, that in that case an irresistible new form of armed organization would

soon burst out, one which would make life impossible for the invader. We would make all the valley of the Po into an Athens![84]

These words, which were delivered to an audience of 1,600 diehards at Milan's Lirico Theatre on 16 December 1944, were greeted by ecstatic applause, with the Duce being called back to the stage six times, like an ageing tenor who had treated his audience to a selection of greatest hits. But the speech, read today, rings more like Lear's ravings on the heath. Like King Lear, Mussolini was howling at the moon, though the comparison should not be strained: the Duce was not a man 'more sinn'd against than sinning', but a political gangster about to meet his end.

The end came in April 1945, when Allied troops smashed through the last German defences and invaded the supposedly inviolable Po valley, where they were greeted by joyous crowds and partisans carrying the rifles of dead Germans. On 24 and 25 April, as Allied tanks overran the flat plains west and north of Bologna, partisan formations attacked the garrisons of the North's big cities, whose populations broke into spontaneous insurrections in their support, seizing factories and workplaces and capturing collaborators of the regime. As in Florence, when Allied troops arrived in Milan, Turin, and Genoa, the public buildings, squares, principal industrial undertakings, and transport hubs were in the hands of the local CLN. The Nazi–Fascist units meanwhile sought frantically to escape. They pillaged and killed as they fled: hundreds of Italian civilians died in massacres committed by German columns in the last days of April 1945.

There was no mercy for Fascists who had not heeded warnings issued by the CLN to desert their posts. In March, l'Unità had ratcheted up the intensity of the struggle:

Disarming the captured is not enough! We need to mow down pitilessly every fascist and every German that gets in our way. We need to hunt them down in their lairs and dispense summary justice! Only mass action and patriotic terror can overcome Nazi–Fascist terror.[85]

On 19 April, the eve of the insurrection, the CLNAI issued a proclamation whose title was unambiguous: 'Surrender or Perish!' The

Women partisans march through liberated Bologna. April, 1945

proclamation added: 'let nobody say, at his graveside, that he was not warned, or that he was not offered one last way out.'[86]

Thousands did indeed perish in the next few days as popular justice was dispensed by 'People's Tribunals' that listened to citizens' denunciations of collaborators, spies, and profiteers, and then expeditiously put on the black cap. The party newspapers for the week after 25 April are dotted with brief reports recording the fates of Fascists and collaborators shot in batches.[87] Even after the purge, hundreds of thousands of people implicated in the crimes of Mussolini's regime remained. What to do with them would be a political conundrum in the coming months. Giovanni Preziosi, a man whom many would have volunteered to shoot, flung himself from a fourth-storey window, one of many suicides. He was doubtless convinced to the last that the ruination all around him was due to the machinations of the Jews.

There was no escape either for Mussolini. On 18 April, the Duce left Lake Garda, against the advice of Ambassador Rahn, for Milan. The last days of the regime were spent with his ministers discussing febrile plans for a last stand in the Valtellina, in northern Lombardy, and, more pragmatically, on negotiations with the CLNAI. Mussolini was unwilling to surrender unconditionally and at 8 p.m. on 25 April, when an impatient CLNAI ordered the insurrection to begin in Milan, he fled to Lake Como, which was still in fascist hands. He was joined the following day by the Secretary of the PFR, Pavolini. On 27 April, Mussolini and Pavolini, together with an entourage of fascist hierarchs and the Duce's mistress Clara Petacci, united with a German military convoy retreating towards Merano in the South Tyrol. They were stopped

Piazzale Loreto, 29 April 1945. Mussolini (*centre*) hangs between Clara Petacci (*right*) and Giuseppe Gelormini.

by a communist partisan band and arrested, although Mussolini, who was wearing a German coat and helmet, remarkably wasn't recognized immediately. Mussolini and his lover were separated from the others and shot on 28 April in Giulino, a small village on the western shore of the lake. Their entourage was shot in Dongo, their place of capture.

The bodies were transported to Milan in the early morning of 29 April and symbolically dumped in Piazzale Loreto, where a notorious massacre of fifteen partisans had taken place in 1944. Early-morning passers-by identified them and soon thousands of people had gathered. In a collective paroxysm of rage, the crowd subjected the corpses to vilification for several hours: the bodies were spat and urinated upon and stomped until they were all but unrecognizable. One woman fired five pistol shots into Mussolini's corpse; one for each of the sons she had lost during the war. The bodies of Mussolini, Petacci, Pavolini, three prominent hierarchs, and Petacci's brother were then strung up by their heels from the cantilever roof of a petrol station. As a gesture of decency, since her underwear had been torn off, Petacci's skirt was fastened to her legs. During the day, another prominent Fascist who had just fallen into the partisans' hands, Achille Starace, was brought to Piazzale Loreto and *giustiziato*. He was hoisted up, too.[88] What happened in Piazzale Loreto was

> an emancipatory spectacle: by stomping on the idol, one symbolically stomped on idolatry, and one was absolved for having been idolatrous. For this reason, Piazzale Loreto can be characterized as a ferocious act of ritual dismemberment through which a people ... destroyed the myth of the regime, but also its own silences and acts of complicity.[89]

Italy thus embarked on its experiment with democracy in a climate of hatred and pervasive national catastrophe. What the country did possess, however, were political parties that had become the interlocutors of the Allies, had led the resistance, had mostly put their ideological differences aside to work together patriotically, and, most important of all, had a shared conviction of the need for a political system based on greater social justice. The country also had a people that had given ample proof of their extraordinary resilience. Italy was riven with hatred, but there were grounds for hope.

5
The Republic

The insurrection of April 1945 ended Ivanoe Bonomi's premiership.
For all his skill as a mediator, Bonomi was the embodiment of old-
fashioned parliamentarianism: part of his charm was that he 'gave
off a whiff of mothballs'.[1] His personality was too old-fashioned
for the spirit of the times. The industrial cities of the North were
draped in red flags, or else with tricolour flags with a torn hole in
the centre where the emblem of the House of Savoy had been. Decades of neglect, culminating in the devastation and dislocation
produced by the war, had turned the Mezzogiorno into a powder-
keg. A 'forgotten revolution' had taken place in 'dozens of villages
and small towns' of the South. Communes had been formed to
redistribute the land, provide an equitable distribution of food, and
establish people's courts: 'Red flags fluttered over town halls; pictures of the king were banned, crucifixes removed, and individuals
urged to create a perfect communitarian society.'[2] These experi-
ments in popular socialism were sometimes accompanied by the
frenzied murder of hated local officials, or by 'trials' in which the
lives of landowners or Fascists were spared so long as they kissed
the feet of peasants, or performed humiliating tasks such as walking barefoot through mud for miles, carrying heavy loads, or
digging deep ditches: in other words, the *signori* were transformed
into peasants for a few hours.[3] The revolts were typically crushed,
after a few days, by the landowners' hired thugs, or *mafiosi*. They
were still a portent of social breakdown.

The desire for radical political change was real. In such a moment,
Bonomi was a man of the past. He was governing, furthermore, without the backing of the whole CLN. Bonomi had survived a crisis of

his government in November 1944 only because De Gasperi and Togliatti had supported him. The crisis had been provoked by an overt intervention in politics by Crown Prince Umberto, the Lieutenant of the Realm. On 1 November 1944, Umberto floated, to a sympathetic American journalist, the idea that the constitutional question might be resolved by a referendum on the monarchy.[4] The PSIUP and PdA were irate, since they regarded the question of the monarchy's future as one that would be settled by an elected Constituent Assembly. The two parties refused to serve in a reshuffled cabinet headed by Bonomi, who made the further gaffe, in their view, of submitting his resignation to Umberto, not the central committee of the CLN.

The PCI stayed in the government in order to avoid a 'stage of acute struggle between a right-wing bloc and one of the left . . . bound to diminish the already feeble independent authority of the Italian government'.[5] Togliatti was frustrated by the intransigence of the PdA, in particular, and by the PSIUP's failure to coordinate its political line with the PCI.[6] The decisive meeting of the party leaders, which took place in the headquarters of the PCI in Rome's Via Nazionale on 7 December 1944, was characterized by Togliatti and De Gasperi tersely telling Nenni and the PdA's representative, the writer Emilio Lussu, that a majority for Bonomi existed and that they should 'draw their own conclusions'. De Gasperi concluded that a government representing 'three great streams of opinion' – the liberal, the communist, and the democratic Catholic – provided a 'better balance' than a six-party government.[7]

Bonomi therefore limped on, but he spent the first months of 1945 surviving rather than governing, although his reshuffled government did achieve one landmark piece of legislation: female suffrage. From February 1945, women could vote on the same terms as men, although Article 3 piously excluded prostitutes who plied their trade in the streets.[8] The decree also did not implement full democratic rights: women were still denied the opportunity to be candidates and to stand for election.

Togliatti voiced his discontent with the progress of the Bonomi government in a speech to the National Council of the PCI on 8 April 1945:

Italy has not found a de Gaulle within the ranks of its political class, but naturally these same men have barred the path to make sure the people did not find a Tito of their own ... In essence, these men always rely on old-fashioned parliamentarianism with its methods of greater or lesser intrigue, and of evading difficult decisions by boiling them down to striking bargains and making deals ... If one adds that today we are faced with parliamentarianism without a parliament, without any kind of public debate or possibility of popular accountability ... we cannot but be struck by [the political class's] inability to adapt to the nation's real needs.[9]

It was Nenni, free from the constraints of government, who articulated the desire for rapid social change best. He famously contended in *Avanti!* that a 'north wind' was blowing, and prophesied that its gusts would sweep away any government that ignored the aspirations of Fascism's opponents and victims:

The men who have worked clandestinely in the cities for the last eighteen months, who have slept in the mountains for two long

Leaders of the left. Pietro Nenni and Palmiro Togliatti, spring 1945.

winters with a rifle clutched in their hands, who are being released from prison or returning from concentration camps, these men are proclaiming, and if they must, are ready to impose, a revolution of actions, not words.[10]

On 10 May 1945, Nenni spoke at a rally at Rome's Brancaccio Theatre, like Togliatti and De Gasperi before him. The galleries were packed, and he was overwhelmed with applause at the end of his speech. One can see why: the speech was a firework display of invective that accused Bonomi of working to restore the pre-fascist Italian state rather than start afresh with the spontaneous 'new forces' in society thrown up by the war. Bonomi, Nenni jeered, had become the 'servant of a tainted bureaucracy'.[11]

Nenni's speech was not only invective. It went to the heart of the dilemma that Italy's democratic politicians were facing. They could not pretend that they had superseded Fascism, unless they had ended the social injustices that Liberal Italy had bequeathed to Fascism, and that Mussolini had done nothing to remedy. The establishment of a democratic republic was a necessary condition for democracy, but not a sufficient one. As Nenni passionately demanded:

What does the Republic mean for the farm labourers depicted in the novels of my comrade, Silone, who are waiting as they sweat at their work on the scorched mountains of the Majella? What does the Republic mean to the factory workers, or to the Sardinian and Sicilian miners who work 700 metres underground, but who have no shoes and when they go home often don't have bread? For the labourers, the miners, the Republic is just a word. For it to have meaning, we need to add social justice to political reform; for it to have meaning, sharecroppers in the Majella need to know that the choice between republic or monarchy will decide whether they will continue to be exploited tillers of land that is not theirs. The Sardinian and Sicilian miners, and assembly-line workers in Milan or Turin, should know that the choice between monarchy and republic will decide their fate on the factory floor, will decide whether they are to be free workers in a socialized industry, or whether they are to be slaves.[12]

Not long after Nenni's fiery speech, an amused De Gasperi told the Socialist leader that somebody had scrawled 'De Gasperi in the vestry; Nenni in Power' on the wall of his house in Rome.

De Gasperi liked Nenni, but he did not want the Socialist leader's popularity to be translated into political authority. On 24 May, at a stormy meeting in Milan of the six party leaders and the CLNAI, Nenni and De Gasperi crafted a motion stating the priorities for the new government that would replace Bonomi's administration. The document asserted that the government should, in cooperation with the Allies, regain full sovereignty over Italian territory in the 'shortest possible period of time', and call elections for a Constituent Assembly as quickly as possible. It should carry out an *epurazione* of Fascists in the state bureaucracy as rapidly as possible while ensuring a 'complete and effective' disarmament of all civilians. Above all, the motion concluded, the people had the right to expect that the parties of the CLN would lead the country along the road of 'moral and material revival' by ensuring that all citizens would enjoy the 'protection of justice' as Italy proceeded to construct 'a new popular democratic State'.[13]

Backed by the PCI, Nenni put forward his own name for the premiership.[14] De Gasperi demurred. At any rate until the people's will had been ascertained via free elections, De Gasperi averred that it was 'not permissible' that a 'wholly Catholic country' should have as head of government somebody who was the representative of a party with a 'materialist ideology'.[15] A letter sent by De Gasperi on 7 June 1945 to the steering committee of the PSIUP sweetened the pill by proposing that Nenni should be made deputy premier and should be responsible for the key tasks of preparing for the Constituent Assembly and supervising the removal of Fascists from the public administration.[16]

This solution was in fact eventually adopted, though without a Christian Democrat as premier (De Gasperi was confirmed in his role as foreign minister). After further discussions between the parties, on 17 June 1945 they settled on Ferruccio Parri, the vice-president of the CVL, as head of the new government. Some in the PSIUP's leadership objected to this choice, despite Parri's exemplary resistance record. In February 1945, he had been captured by the Germans and was freed only because the American secret service, the OSS, the forerunner of the CIA, secured his release as part of the deal it struck with SS

General Karl Wolff for the surrender of German forces in Italy: so-called 'Operation Sunrise'.[17] The PSI's representative in the CLNAI, the future president of the Republic Sandro Pertini, who had been one of the organizers of the insurrection in Milan, was adamant that the PSIUP should claim the premiership, but failing that, it should not participate in the government at all. 'The committee in the North is unanimously against Bonomi and Parri,' Pertini told the party's steering committee.[18]

The 'Roman' politicians were more cautious than Pertini, who was a notorious hothead. Nenni was worried that violence would be the outcome, if the PSIUP refused to join the new government. It might be 'like 1920, only worse', he told a joint meeting of the PCI and PSI steering committees on 15 June, referring to the land occupations and strikes of the *biennio rosso* after 1919. Togliatti worried that the Allies would intervene if there was serious unrest: 'we'll finish up in Egypt in a concentration camp,' the PCI leader commented dryly.[19]

Parri's personal integrity weighed in his favour. Pietro Nenni was struck by his 'droiture' when he first met him and described him as a 'Jansenist in politics'.[20] There is a famous photograph of the leaders of the CVL heading a parade along Corso Matteotti in liberated Milan. The bespectacled Parri, with his thick white hair, looks every inch a soldier as he strides alongside General Cadorna, the PCI leader Luigi Longo, and the Christian Democrat Enrico Mattei. One can see from the set of his shoulders why Nenni remarked that 'with him [Parri] we will face a battle, one we may win or lose, but at least we will not waste time in backstairs intrigues'.[21] The new premier certainly set an example of commitment to the job: Parri worked long hours and slept on a camp bed in his office.[22]

The British admired Parri's uprightness of character, too. Upon his appointment, the British ambassador, Sir Noel Charles, telegraphed a eulogy to the Foreign Office lauding 'the sincere democratic spirit of this remarkable man', his 'strong sense of responsibility' and 'lack of personal ambition'. Charles was less enthused by Nenni's portfolio of key jobs but acknowledged that no one political force held too many key posts.[23] Parri headed the Interior Ministry himself and hence supervised the police.

The United States' representatives in Italy were more sceptical about

Marching towards democracy. Ferruccio Parri third from left,
to his left General Raffaele Cadorna, then Luigi Longo (PCI);
Enrico Mattei (DC) to Longo's left.

the new government. The Truman Administration (Roosevelt had
died on 12 April 1945) was alarmed by the leftism of the government.
The US pressed the government to demonstrate its democratic credentials by holding local elections in the areas under its control before
holding national elections for a Constituent Assembly. Acting Secretary of State Dean Acheson argued that 'the important thing in the US
view is that Italians at last begin to prove rather than argue that they
are a democratic nation.'[24] The PCI considered that it had no need to
prove its commitment to democratic principles to anybody. The fifty
PCI members of the *Consulta Nazionale*, an advisory assembly serving until the Constituent Assembly could be elected, had collectively
served 464 years in fascist jails.[25]

The other powerful voice dubious about the new government was,
in fact, the PCI. Togliatti regarded the PdA as an anomaly, and as a divisive source of left-wing ideas. They were members of the old bourgeois
regime yet advocates of progressive social ideas. They accordingly complicated Italy's passage to a government based upon the mass parties

that could count on support among the masses. Writing in *Rinascita*, Togliatti tepidly welcomed the new government as 'a step forward that might even turn out to be a worthwhile one', but did not mention Parri by name.[26]

THE AMBIGUITY OF THE PCI

Togliatti's ambiguity towards the new government was prompted by the fact that its power was in the ascendant. By November 1945, it had enrolled almost 1.8 million people: at liberation card-carrying party members had numbered no more than 400,000.[27] The party's high profile in the resistance partly explained the surge, but a relaxation in the rules governing membership helped. The PCI declared that anybody who accepted the party's political line and discipline could join, including people with religious convictions, or even former members of the PNF. Satirists had a field day: Guglielmo Giannini, the founder of *L'Uomo Qualunque* (The Common Man), a populist party that would enjoy electoral success in Rome and the South in the autumn of 1945, printed a cartoon of a soap-box agitator with a megaphone outside a PCI branch office bawling, to a crowd of officers in uniform, that 'only with us can fascists become anti-fascists!'[28] In truth, enrolling former Fascists was not hypocrisy. In a country where millions of people had worn the black shirt as a matter of course, it was necessary to reclaim them for democratic politics. Christian Democracy did the same.

Greater openness was supplemented by a less disciplined political style. During the latter stages of the war, the PCI lambasted comrades for their sectarian mentality.[29] It encouraged the emergence of 'militants and leaders of a new type'. PCI leaders were to be those who had grasped that it was necessary to 'break with old habits'. The new class of party militants and functionaries should be people with 'an intimate knowledge of the most vital problems facing the popular masses'.[30] They were to be organic intellectuals, to use a term coined by Antonio Gramsci, able to win over voters with practical arguments, without relying on rote learning of Marxist theory to provide stock answers.[31] The PCI's political strategy, in other words, was to act as an educator within Italian society and, over time, win the trust of the citizens and persuade them to interpret the world in a progressive way.

Nevertheless, for several months after liberation, former partisans connected to the PCI used more direct methods against 'enemies of the people', rather than wait for the Allies, or for the justice system of the future Italian state, to deal with former militiamen, or industrialists, priests or landowners who had collaborated with the RSI. Hundreds of such people were murdered, sometimes after torture, in the late spring and early summer of 1945. This campaign of terror was incited by some members of the party's leadership: several days after liberation, Giorgio Amendola wrote in *l'Unità* that 'Pity has died', and stated that it would be 'treason' to 'give way to leniency' while the corpses of the partisans' fallen comrades were still unburied.[32]

In Emilia, the 'red triangle', the territory comprised between the three points of Ferrara, Bologna, and Reggio Emilia, was the site of numerous assassinations. Genoa and Piedmont experienced similar or even higher levels of clandestine terror by the PCI's militants.[33] In the Veneto, too, several massacres were committed by Communist partisans. At Codevigo, in the province of Padua, an estimated 136 former RSI militiamen were killed at various locations by partisans between the end of April and mid-June 1945. At Schio, in the province of Vicenza, more than fifty prisoners awaiting trial were machine-gunned on 6 July 1945 by partisans after the local Allied administration warned that they could not be held in prison without specific charges being levelled against them. There is still disagreement over how many of those killed were guilty of atrocities. It seems clear, however, that many bore no responsibility at all.[34]

The post-war campaign of extra-judicial killings by PCI supporters must be depicted in the context of the times. Passions were running high. At Schio, for example, local Fascists and the Germans had tortured prisoners barbarically in the last weeks of the conflict. It is certainly an error to sensationalize the murders committed by the PCI's militants.[35] Nevertheless, it is also an error to attribute the activities of the PCI's squads solely to the desire for reprisal. A study by a political scientist, replete with the quantitative paraphernalia of that discipline, has concluded that the motive for the campaign of killings was essentially political: 'the violence was a local, bottom-up tactic to consolidate power, rather than a systematic, top-down strategy to gain it. The organizational and ideological legacy of the resistance sustained the capacity of the partisans to kill through collective action and territorial coverage and led to the selection of the victims.'[36]

The campaign of violence stirred the indignation of the other CLN parties. On 29 May 1945, the party secretary of the PLI, Leone Cattani, thundered that it was 'no longer permissible' to neglect the 'widespread campaign of intimidation taking place in many regions against some political parties and classes of people'.[37] Cattani demanded an urgent summit meeting of the central committee of the CLN.

On 1 June 1945, the six parties concurred on the need to act to ensure that political activity did not degenerate into 'abuses and violence' and that everybody would be 'guaranteed' the right of 'freedom of speech' and the right 'to propagate their own ideas'.[38] The PCI leadership subsequently told its members that they should 'conduct the purge in an orderly and legal manner', although it minimized the 'handful of violent episodes' that had taken place and decried the lack of zeal shown by the justice system towards the prosecution of 'fascist delinquents', and 'collaborators with the Germans'. Indignantly, the party protested that 'we communists were the first to put down our weapons and to pick back up the peaceful and constructive tools of our jobs. They have always been the instruments we hold most dear.'[39]

They protested too much. The Schio massacre took place after the publication of this reprimand to the base membership. In January 1946, *Risorgimento Liberale*, the daily broadsheet of the PLI, exposed the state of terror in which the bourgeoisie of Emilia were living, caught as they were between the twin perils of *banditismo* – criminal gangs that were targeting the well-off and making travel within the region unsafe – and the violent tactics used by the PCI against the propertied, or other political forces, which the article claimed had 'cost hundreds of lives'.[40] Sporadic murders of political opponents – by no means just former Fascists, but members of the PLI, Christian Democrats, priests, outspoken critics of the PCI from civil society – continued for the next two years. Condemnation of such killings would be a staple in the DC's propaganda against the PCI for years to come.[41]

There had been a harbinger of communist violence against other political formations even before the war ended. At Porzûs, a mountain village in the province of Udine, PCI partisans had liquidated seventeen partisans from the 'Osoppo' Brigade in cold blood on 7 February 1945. The victims' alleged crime was collusion with the enemy, and one of the *giustiziati*, a woman named Elda Turchetti, had been publicly accused of being a spy. Subsequent historical research has proved that the underlying motive for the murders was the Osoppo Brigade's refusal to acquiesce in the absorption of eastern Friuli into Yugoslavia.[42] This territorial transfer had been authorized by PCI leader Togliatti. Following a meeting in Bari with Edvard Kardelj, the leader of the Slovene Communist Party, in October 1944, Togliatti had instructed communists in Udine to favour 'the occupation of the Julian region by the troops commanded by Marshal Tito'. Togliatti added that it was necessary to 'position' the PCI against all 'Italian elements' who persisted in 'acting in favour of imperialism and Italian nationalism'.[43]

At war's end, the PCI sided with Yugoslavia over control of the Julian region. The 'race for Trieste' was won by the Yugoslavs, who beat the Eighth Army to the gates of the Adriatic city. Togliatti urged the citizens of Trieste to greet Tito's partisans as liberators on 1 May.[44] The Yugoslavs in fact snuffed out the insurrection against the German occupiers begun by the CLN of the city on 28 April: Italian patriots, who were poorly armed, posed no resistance to the Yugoslav troops. Allied troops arrived on 2 May and accepted the surrender of the remaining German and Fascist forces (who had unsurprisingly been afraid to surrender to the Yugoslavs).

For the next forty days, when negotiations led to the withdrawal of Yugoslav troops to the so-called 'Morgan line' outside the city, and the installation of an Allied military government, Trieste and its Istrian hinterland were in the hands of Yugoslav partisans. In this brief period, 'terror and insecurity reigned'.[45] The secret police (the 'Ozna') accompanying the Yugoslav army hunted down and murdered opponents of rule from Belgrade. The bodies of the victims were *infoibati*, that is thrown into the *foibe*, natural geological rock fissures common in

Istria.[46] The exact number of people killed is unknown (indeed, is still the source of intense polemic), but it certainly numbered in the thousands. Many of the individuals killed were indeed Fascists: Trieste had been a hotbed of so-called 'frontier Fascism' after its incorporation into Italy and anti-Slav extremism was a commonplace. Others were simply Italians. The Yugoslav forces were less inclined than the Italian partisans to make fine distinctions between those who had merely worn the black shirt and subscribed to fascist ideology and those who had committed political or war crimes.[47]

Togliatti and the PCI maintained a deafening silence about these events. The reason, of course, was that Stalin favoured a major revision of Italy's borders in Yugoslavia's favour. In the early summer of 1945, the Yugoslavs, the only people to have defeated the German Army by their own efforts, enjoyed higher favour in the Kremlin than the PCI. Togliatti's influence in Moscow was real, but Tito's standing as a war leader was greater.

The PCI's intimidatory tactics, the long queues of people clamouring to join it, its ties to Moscow, and the ideological fervour of its leaders made the party a looming presence in Italian politics by the summer of 1945. Whether or not the wolf was serious in wanting to lie down with the lambs, its teeth and its muscular presence could not but disquiet Christian Democracy and the PLI (and awe the PSIUP).[48] Italy's propertied classes feared that they were destined to be liquidated should the PCI ever come to power.

THE PARRI INTERLUDE

The situation that faced the new government in June 1945 was thus dramatic. It is true, as two professors remind us, that the 'destruction, bombardment, and upheaval' that Italy had undergone had not been 'remotely comparable' to that of Germany and Japan, or to Poland, Russia, and Yugoslavia. It is also true that Italy never experienced outright famine, as the Greeks and Dutch did in the winter of 1944–5, and that Italy's cultural heritage escaped mostly intact.[49] But Italy remained a grievously wounded nation. The insurrection had prevented the destruction of most of the nation's northern manufacturing base, but the factories no longer had orders: industrial production plunged to 29 per cent of 1938 levels by the end of 1945, though it rebounded in 1946. Electricity generation was a fraction of pre-war levels. A fifth of the country's housing stock had been damaged or destroyed by bombs or shells. Hundreds of thousands of refugees had fled to the country-side and many had no homes to go back to.

Transport and communications were a nightmare: thousands of bridges were in ruins; the railway network had been disrupted by bombing and there was a chronic shortage of rolling stock. The first post-war direct passenger train service from Milan to Rome, inaugurated in August 1945, was scheduled to take seventeen hours, and often took longer. Lorries, cars, and tractors were few and far between; tyres and petrol were sought-after commodities. A third of the road network was anyway unusable, though jeeps driven by Allied soldiers sped recklessly along rutted roads and were responsible for dozens of fatal accidents every month.[50]

The nation's stock of farm animals had been drastically reduced during the war, thanks to requisitions by the contending armies, and the peasants' need to avoid starvation. There was a shortage of horses to plough the fields. The daily ration of citizens in the southern and central provinces run by the Italian government barely kept body and soul together: less than 1,000 calories a day, which meant that citizens spent time and money on transactions on the black market. Spivs got rich quick by buying or stealing goods from the Allied forces and re-selling them at handsome profits. To put food in the larder, people were transferring the acquired assets of a lifetime to corrupt foreign soldiers and entrepreneurial middlemen. Yet without the black market, and deliveries of grain from the Allies, the Italians would have ached from malnutrition and shivered with cold.[51]

Last, but not least, the state was bankrupt. Its income from taxes was a fraction of what it needed to spend on salaries, upkeep of buildings, pensions, and ordinary administration, let alone the public investment required to rebuild Italy's shattered infrastructure. The first meeting of the Parri cabinet on 26 June 1945 was drenched with an ice-cold shower of facts about the state of the public finances. The government expected to spend 113.6 billion lire in 1945 in the provinces under its control. Incomings were expected to be a mere 29,900 billion lire. Treasury Minister Marcello Soleri estimated that, if one added the costs of the state in the northern provinces and the costs of rebuilding key infrastructure, the Italian state was bound to spend at least 250 billion lire, and would have a deficit of 150 billion.[52]

Soleri dropped dead from stress and overwork the following month. His replacement succinctly described the state of public finances as 'tragic' in a cabinet meeting on 3 August. The Italian state was in deficit to the tune of 15 billion lire per month and, if the Allies were to suspend free delivery of grain and coal, it would have to find a further 150 billion to purchase such commodities.[53] Transport Minister Ugo La Malfa estimated that fully rebuilding the rail network would alone cost 480 billion lire at current prices.[54]

In the second half of 1945, Italy was on economic life support, dependent on the Allies for food aid and for the economic stimulus provided by the armies present on the territory. As Parri told the first session of the Consulta Nazionale on 26 September 1945: 'We need, urgently need, Allied aid. It alone can provide us with bread, coal and fuel, raw materials, financial credits; in a word, the opportunity to live and work.'[55]

What economic strategy was the government to follow? Balance the books by sacking state employees by the hundreds of thousands? The social implications of such a course of action were obvious, and, in fact, it was never contemplated. On the other hand, the consequences of paying for the state and for reconstruction by merely printing more money were equally obvious: it meant pouring petrol on the inflationary flames caused by the American troops' spending power and by supply shortages. Too much cash was chasing too few products as it was. In the absence of large-scale foreign investment, or even with it, the only plausible solutions were either a policy of wealth taxes and state direction of investment, or an anti-inflation strategy of holding public spending in check, keeping incomes down, and boosting production at the expense of consumption. Or some combination of the two.

The CLN parties could not postpone for ever a decision on what kind of surgery they would perform on the economy. They could, however, find palliatives to ease the worst of the immediate problems. Hence, the Parri government imposed a modest wealth tax in a bid to claw back funds from individuals who had profited from the war. It also approved spending to subsidize northern industrial workers who had been laid off and a 'special indemnity' of 3,000 lire for state officials, whose living conditions were recognized to be 'miserable'. These new expenditures brought the total cost of salaries and pensions for state employees to 85 billion lire – more, literally, than the Italian state was raising in revenues, but politics trumped good housekeeping.[56]

The Italian state could not afford to alienate the industrial working class because of the state of public order in northern Italy. It could not antagonize the state administrative machine, either. State officials were already disgruntled by the government's efforts to identify and remove Fascists. The process of *epurazione* was extremely bureaucratic: one historian of public law has described the legislation regulating the purge as 'flood-like, fragmentary and contradictory'.[57]

During the Parri government, Nenni, in his new role as political referent of the purge, sought to accelerate the process by limiting the sanction of 'destitution from post' to those officials of grade 8 or above on the civil-service scale (or of comparable rank in the judiciary or the universities). Such officials were to be removed if they had been active in the PNF, had shown signs of 'fascist character' or 'partisanship for Fascism' in their official duties, or if they had been nominated to their position purely for their ideological allegiance (this was the case, for instance, of professors of Fascist Doctrine). A further seven tests, automatically disqualifying people who had served the RSI as officers, or who had been collaborators or informers, were added.

This was all reasonable, but it ran into the twin problems of sheer numbers – tens of thousands of officials would have had to be removed if the criteria had been applied rigorously – and the fact that the guilty were largely judged by their peers. By the end of 1945, the *epurazione* was bogged down in a morass of appeals, with a huge backlog of cases, and many questionable decisions that aroused angry comment.[58] The purge of the public sector rankled in Rome and the South, where huge numbers of people had worked for the Fascist state and carried out its policies. Such people did not think, for the most part, that they had done anything wrong.

FROM PARRI TO DE GASPERI

The Parri government's demise was brought about by the PLI. Parri had antagonized the grandees of Italian liberalism from the outset. In his address to the first plenary meeting of the *Consulta*, at the end of September 1945, he had said, in a passage that became notorious:

> Be clear about one thing: democracy is at its inception in our society. I don't think, don't consider that we can regard the pre-fascist regimes as democratic ... I'm sorry if this definition of mine offends anybody. I simply wanted to say this: the word 'democratic' has a precise, even technical meaning. We can define and characterize those [pre-fascist] regimes as liberal.[59]

The first of these sentences was greeted with interruptions and jeering. In hindsight, it is hard to understand why. Pre-Fascist Italy was imperialist; its social structure was shaped like a wine decanter, with an elite class of landowners, industrialists, and professionals tapering down to a wide base of sharecroppers, industrial workers, and labourers at the bottom. The people at the bottom lived precarious lives, had little access to education, to decent housing, or to health care when they were sick. The largest Italian cities, especially the big southern ones – Palermo, Catania, Bari, Naples, Rome – were, outside their sublime historical cores, largely squalid slums rife with crime. The rural areas of the Mezzogiorno, but also much of the rest of the country, were mired in secular poverty, superstition, and ignorance. The condition of women mirrored the position of their menfolk but was worse since they had to labour under the structural inequality of being tied to the home and to bringing up large broods of children. Some of these social inequalities had worsened during the *ventennio*, but that did not alter the fact that they had existed before Mussolini came to power.

Parri, like the Labour government of Clement Attlee in Britain, believed that a state that gave the opportunities of modern civilization only to a few gave democracy to none. Democracy was not just about voting, or the sound and fury of parliamentary debate. It was about state-mandated action to deliver social and economic justice. And, just as many British Conservatives quibbled at measures that provided the workers who had fought for their country with elementary social rights, so many Italian conservatives trembled at the prospect of a strong state delivering reforms to the masses.

Parri's radicalism, combined with alarm about the condition of both public finances and public order, caused a government crisis to break out on 17 November 1945, when the PLI demanded a smaller government, stiffened with non-party technocrats. Parri had also lost the support of De Gasperi. At a meeting of the cabinet on 23 November, Parri sought to defend his position by arguing for the inclusion of technocrats sympathetic to the PLI in the party's stead. De Gasperi was implacable. He argued – turning what he had said during the December 1944 crisis of the Bonomi government completely on its head – that the six CLN parties had to stick together and if Parri had lost the support even of one of them, then he should step down.[60]

Parri resigned on the morning of 24 November, a 'rainy autumn day'.[61] His mood was as bad as the weather. At a press conference that afternoon, he made an unstatesmanlike attack on the DC: he had, he claimed, been forced out by a conspiracy between the PLI and the DC that had amounted to a coup.[62] De Gasperi, alive, as foreign minister, to the damage such injudicious words might cause to Italy's shaky diplomatic position, protested that Parri's strictures were not to be taken literally.[63]

De Gasperi protested too much. He had made up his mind that the DC should hold the reins of government. On 29 November 1945, De Gasperi, who had been struck down by influenza, was urged by the steering committee of the DC, fifteen of whom clustered around his bedside, to allow his name to go forward as premier.[64] History does not record what Mrs De Gasperi thought about this impromptu caucus in her bedroom, but her husband rose like Lazarus from his sickbed and went, looking 'pale and tired', to the Quirinale Palace at midnight on 30 November to receive the *incarico* (literally, the 'task') of forming an administration from Prince Umberto.[65] For the first time since the unification of Italy, the leader of a party of religious inspiration took over the leadership of the government. The first nine days of December were occupied with the usual tensions over how the parties would divide the ministerial offices.

De Gasperi took over as President of the Council of Ministers in order to increase his party's political leverage. He kept the job of foreign minister, which meant negotiating the peace treaty with the Allies, in his own hands and entrusted the job of treasury minister to a technocrat, Epicarmo Corbino, a Sicilian economist who was a staunch advocate of sound money. The government still 'tilted to the left'.[66] The PCI retained the three ministries they had held under Parri: Justice (Togliatti), Finance (Scoccimarro), and Agriculture (Fausto Gullo, the Calabrian 'minister of the peasants'). Nenni remained deputy premier and minister for the Constituent Assembly, while another Socialist, Giuseppe Romita, became minister of the interior, and hence oversaw the police and the organizing and supervising of elections. It was the first time that a Socialist had held this sensitive position, but the PSIUP had been determined to ensure that the ministry 'was in safe Republican hands'.[67]

If possible, Romita, a Piedmontese engineer who had endured multiple imprisonments during the *ventennio*, was an even more visceral republican than Nenni. He publicly resolved, however, not to be a partisan figure, and worked tirelessly over the next six months to restore public order, without which no democracy was possible, and to build the machinery of democracy essentially from scratch, down to the nitty-gritty detail of ensuring that sturdy wooden ballot boxes were available.

In the opening pages of his memoir of his spell as interior minister, Romita gives us a sardonic picture of how the De Gasperi cabinet was the last government in Italian history to swear the oath of office to the House of Savoy – to Prince Umberto whom 'had he been a clerk in public office, rather than the heir to the throne, would have been purged outright'.[68] On 10 December 1945, the electric light had failed at the Quirinale so the ministers had to process into the royal presence behind flunkies wearing red tailcoats and carrying lighted candles. The ceremony, carried out in the flickering light of the candelabras, had a funereal mood, the final obsequies paid to a moribund regime that knew it was dying. Or so Romita, the ardent republican, fondly recalled. Like most of Italy's new generation of leaders, however, he had greater respect for Umberto than for his father, Victor Emmanuel III, 'the man who had no friends because ... he was so self-obsessed that it verged on absurdity'.[69]

One reason why the DC and the PSIUP had been concerned to control key ministries was that they were conscious of the growing organizational and social power of the PCI. The Communists were the first party to hold a national congress in the wake of the formation of the De Gasperi administration. Held between 29 December 1945 and 6 January 1946, the PCI's 5th Congress was an impressive display of unity of purpose. An awestruck Pietro Nenni wrote in his diary:

> I was present at the first session of the fifth communist Congress to listen to Togliatti's four-hour speech to the delegates. It is a magnificent, youthful, ardent occasion. There are about 2,000 congress-goers. The party membership has reached one million seven hundred and sixty thousand. Just citing this figure brings home the difficulty the Socialist party and I are facing. How long can we cling on to our position on the left when the Communists have wrenched the leadership of the working class from us?

He added that the delegates listened to Togliatti's speech with 'genuine religious fervour'. Nenni was moved by the ovation he received when he made a speech of fraternal good wishes on behalf of the PSIUP. The PCI truly believed in the unity of the working-class parties, he concluded, while his own party was riddled with 'reformist and petty-bourgeois prejudices' against this necessary 'leap in the dark'.[70] Over the next two years, the determination of the PSIUP's maximalist left wing to pursue unity with the PCI would split the PSIUP, consign it to a subordinate position relative to the PCI, and consign the political centre to the unchallenged hegemony of the DC.

The PCI's congress approved a radical programme at the conclusion of its labours, in addition to a statute that delineated the structure, organization, rights and duties of party members. This latter document described the PCI as 'the political organization of the Italian workers', who were, as a class, working for 'the destruction of all remaining traces of Fascism, for the independence and freedom of the country, for the construction of a democratic and progressive regime, for peace between peoples, and for the socialist renewal of society'.[71]

The party programme appealed for a 'union' of all democratic forces. In particular, the party called for unity of the working class, via the 'thoroughgoing merger of socialists and communists' into a single party. The PCI's priorities were, like those of the PSIUP and PdA, immediate elections for a Constituent Assembly that would abolish the monarchy and establish a Republic, which was to be based upon representative democracy and strong guarantees for the fundamental rights of citizens. 'Let every form of political and juridical discrimination against women be eliminated, let the way be opened to the fulfilment of every citizen through work, repose, education and social security,' the PCI proclaimed. The Italian state should be reorganized to ensure greater autonomy for Sardinia and Sicily, which had been subject to 'semi-colonial exploitation'.

In economic affairs, the PCI recommended the nationalization of industrial monopolies and of the banking and insurance sectors. It demanded an agrarian reform that would 'liquidate' the holdings of big absentee landowners, encourage cooperative farming, and defend small and medium-sized proprietors. The PCI's intended policy for agriculture, in other words, was reminiscent of the 'New Economic Policy' followed by the Bolsheviks in the years preceding Lenin's death in January 1924: in rural areas, land and power should go to the small producers, who would be freed to become entrepreneurs and literally take their surplus to market.[72]

Underpinning this programme was a reading of Italian political history that was akin to Parri's, but more bluntly expressed:

Summing up, Italian society, notwithstanding a pseudo-democratic façade, was substantially anti-democratic because it was extraneous from the common people. There are few countries in which so much of the people's blood, be it the blood of the workers of the North or the peasants of the South, has been shed so freely as in the streets and squares of Italy. There are few countries that in little more than 70 years of national history have known periods of reaction comparable to the bloody decade of Crispi's premiership, or Mussolini's two decades of criminality. To us, it is as if throughout its history the Italian state was shrouded in a reactionary fog that at a certain point condensed into storm clouds and unleashed a bloody tempest which sent us spinning into a vortex of bereavement, ruin, and misery.[73]

Unlike Parri, the speaker of these words (Mauro Scoccimarro) made no apology for dismissing the traditional elites' depiction of pre-fascist times as an epoch where liberty and democracy were gradually prevailing. Scoccimarro considered himself to be the embodiment of a new class on the verge of taking political power. Nor was he alone. Luigi Longo's speech to the Congress, a militant call to action, was reprinted on the front page of *l'Unità* and the partisan leader from the North was elected deputy leader of the party, with a billing hardly inferior to Togliatti's own.[74]

The PCI was following a twofold strategy that was subsequently dubbed *doppiezza* (literally, duplicity): publicly proclaiming its commitment to working through democratic channels, while at the same time hinting broadly to its rank and file that the proletarian revolution was only being postponed until the party had a freer hand. The PCI was a lion in strength and a fox in tactical sophistication; a force able to inspire devotion among its followers and daunt its adversaries. None of the other CLN parties could match its organizational drive, its appeal both to intellectuals and factory workers, its association with the Soviet mythos, its air of historical destiny. Even so, free elections would prove that the PCI was less invincible than it seemed.

DRESS REHEARSAL

In the first half of 1946, Italy finally got a taste of democracy. The Allies relinquished administrative control of the provinces of the North, Udine and Trieste excepted, on 1 January, and the De Gasperi government opted, in keeping with the Allies' wishes, to hold local elections on five successive Sundays (10, 17, 24, 31 March, and 7 April 1946) prior to holding elections to the Constituent Assembly. Women who had reached the age of majority (twenty-one) were allowed to stand as candidates, as well as vote.

By March, the government had also decided that the 'hexarchy' (six-party government) would continue until the Constitution had been drafted and general elections held. The other great institutional question of Republic versus Monarchy was to be decided by a referendum, to take place contemporaneously with elections to the Constituent

Assembly, which would draw up the constitution. All these major decisions, especially the issue of the referendum, were in fact taken only after a good deal of polemic and, in the case of the monarchy, an unsuccessful back-door attempt by De Gasperi to persuade the Allies to impose the referendum.[75]

It is a mistake to dwell overmuch on Italian political theatre. One should focus on the outcomes, which in this case were striking. Only a very bold person would have bet, in December 1945, that Nenni or Togliatti would have agreed to decide the nation's institutional future with a one-off poll of the citizens. The Council of Ministers on 27 February 1946 was an all-day marathon, as the politicians hammered out details, but they stuck to their task with discipline, not to mention the self-irony that is such a large part of the Italian character. Defeated on the question of the referendum, Togliatti irritably suggested that the monarchy could be represented on the ballot paper by the *fascio littorio*; the PLI minister of war, Manlio Brosio, himself a republican, replied that in that case the electoral symbol of the Republic should be a rendition of Mussolini's head in profile![76] The law establishing the Constituent Assembly, for which both men *and* women over the age of twenty-one could vote and be candidates, and regulating the conduct of the referendum (decree law no. 98), was published in the *Official Gazette* of the Italian government on 16 March 1946.

The collaborative mood was helped by the fact that the parties of the CLN were largely republican. The three left-wing parties were overtly so; the DC had a far from negligible monarchist component, but most of its leaders were republican. The PLI was mostly monarchist, but also contained plenty of people, like Brosio, who were against the continuation of the monarchy. When Italians want to say that someone is deeply committed to a cause, they, like the French, say he or she is 'more monarchical than the king'. It would emerge that the parties of the CLN were significantly more republican than the people, especially the people of the Mezzogiorno.

In all, two-thirds of the country's towns and villages voted during the March–April local elections. Some 16.3 million people went to the polls – 82.3 per cent of those entitled – and women voted in comparable numbers to men. In his memoirs, Romita cheerfully acknowledged that he deliberately opted to hold the elections in parts of the country where the parties that supported the Republic were likely to prevail.[77] Only two big cities – Milan and Bologna – voted. A momentum-building victory for the Republic was certain in both.

Romita's dodge worked. In the larger municipalities where the proportional electoral system (PR) was in force, pro-Republic parties (the PCI, PSIUP, PdA, the tiny Republican Party, and left-wing coalitions) obtained nearly 60 per cent of the votes. If one assumed that the DC's electorate would split 50/50 on the question of the monarchy, it seemed probable that there would be a clear majority for the Republic. But this overlooked the weakness of the republican parties in the South and the islands and the strength of the monarchist vote in rural areas. There was a touch of hubris in the exultation of republicans in April 1946.

The elections proved that the three self-styled popular parties genuinely did have widespread support. Christian Democracy won outright in 2,034 municipalities. Coalitions including the DC won in an additional 349 municipalities. The PSIUP won in 146 municipalities, including Milan, the birthplace of the socialist movement in Italy, where it took 36.2 per cent of the vote. The PCI won in 143 municipalities, including Bologna, and was the largest party across what would become known as the 'red belt' (Emilia, Romagna, Umbria, the Marche, and Tuscany). Coalitions of the two left-wing parties also won in nearly 2,000 municipalities. In the cities big enough to vote by PR, the DC obtained 31.5 per cent, the PCI 24.7 per cent, and the Socialists 23.1 per cent, although the vote was much more fragmented in the South and the islands, with votes going to a host of regional lists and personal parties formed by local notables. In all, an astonishing eighty-one parties contested the election: a fact that vividly illustrates the suppressed longing of the Italians for political participation. Unlike the DC and the PCI, the PSIUP was not a national force: its dismal showing in the South and the islands (less than 9 per cent) prevented it from emerging as the biggest party of the left.

The biggest winners were the Italians, three-quarters of whom had never voted before in a free election. Oral histories and memoirs leave no doubt that the Italian people, of both sexes, all ages, educational attainments, and professions regarded the simple act of voting as being a symbolic act of political maturity. The political philosopher Norberto Bobbio expressed the sentiment perfectly:

> When I voted for the first time in the April 1946 local elections, I was almost 37 years old. The action of dropping a ballot paper into the box, with no fear of indiscreet glances, has now become a habit. Indeed, when we are obliged to do it in pointless referendums, it has become repugnant. But the first time that we voted felt like a great conquest for civility. Voting made us, finally, adult citizens. It was symbolic of the start of a new phase of history for us, the citizens, and for our country.[78]

The political parties, especially the left-wing ones, organized lessons to teach citizens the mechanism of voting: the documents that one had to take to the poll, step-by-step guides to the voting procedure, explaining the different symbols on the ballot paper, even how one should fold the ballot paper. At a more cerebral level, Nenni's Ministry for the Constituent Assembly worked hard to explain the fine points of the electoral system and the constitutional choices facing Italy, but they also mixed education with exhortation. The ministerial bulletin instructed citizens, in capital letters and no uncertain terms, to 'VOTE FOR WHOM YOU WANT, BUT VOTE!'[79]

Women were especially targeted for exercises in civic education. *Noi Donne*, the periodical of the *Unione donne italiane* (UDI), a movement that had grown out of the experience of women during the resistance, and whose chief organizers were members of the PSIUP or the PCI, dedicated a four-page special insert to persuade women to vote. The front page, which featured a drawing of Irma Bandiera, the partisan heroine, being hunted down and captured, urged women to vote for those who would defend the jobs of their menfolk, for those who would give bread to their children, and for those who would bring progress to women and freedom to the country.

Inside, there was a comic strip that featured two young women, one blonde, the other dark-haired, talking about politics beneath a sign saying 'women have the right to vote'. The blonde (some stereotypes are universal) exclaims 'We would be better off without this voting business. What a bore!' Her friend responds that 'Not at all. We women should vote.' 'Why should I bother?' The dark-haired woman urges her to take a brief walk around town with her, promising to give her 'seven good reasons' for voting. They stop in front of a shoe shop: 'Good heavens! How expensive these shoes are!' says the blonde. Her friend replies that an 'honest administration' would distribute shoes and cloth, control prices, and keep the black market in check. It would repair schools and get children off the streets. It would rebuild bomb-damaged houses. Walking along, the two women see a woman washing clothes in the river. Good public administration would construct public laundries with roofs, the dark-haired woman states. The two women then meet 'Signor Arturo', a soldier returning from intern-ment in Germany, and ask him how he's doing: he replies 'badly'. He has no job and no prospect of one. The dark-haired woman says the town council should help prison-camp 'survivors' with jobs. Such jobs could be paid for, if only a 'people's administration' levied taxes on those who could afford to pay them, not the poor. The blonde at last exclaims: 'I see you have not seven, but a thousand reasons! I am going to vote, too!' The last frame of the picture board shows the blonde crossing out the word 'right' on the sign and replacing it with the word 'duty'.[80] The cartoon strip was a brilliant and, for a histo-rian, socially revealing piece of propaganda.

All the principal political leaders personally backed women's par-ticipation in politics, often against the prejudice of their members at local level. The most thorough academic study of the subject praises De Gasperi, Nenni, and Togliatti for their commitment to including women in the political process.[81]

FOUNDATION STONES

Once the local elections were over, a new season of electoral cam-paigning immediately opened. The political parties began mobilizing for the vote to the Constituent Assembly and for the referendum on the monarchy. The DC and the PSIUP held their national congresses: as anyone with even a cursory knowledge of the history of Italian social-ism might have predicted, the PSIUP's 24th Congress, held in Florence between 11 and 17 April 1946, was a contentious one dominated by what Nenni called 'the vexed question of our relations with the PCI'.[82]

Pressed by Togliatti, in his fraternal address, to move towards outright fusion of the two proletarian parties, the PSIUP divided between three main strains of opinion that each advanced subtly different approaches to the question.[83] All three factions recognized that both parties were expressions of the Italian working class, but none advocated fusion. Fear of being swallowed up by the Communists was a powerful deterrent. All factions in the party knew, moreover, that open support for fusion would lead to an immediate split. Seven weeks before the most important elections in Italian history, which gave the left the historic opportunity to rid the nation of the monarchy, the PSIUP could not risk such a fate – for all factions were utterly committed to the democratic Republic. Instead of communicating to the voters – to the women who wanted public laundries and the returnees from camps who wanted a job – a clear idea of what democratic socialism in Italy would mean in practical terms, Italian socialists might seem to have wasted a week on ideological navelgazing. But first impressions are usually wrong, and were certainly wrong in this case.

The conflict in the PSIUP was ultimately between Nenni and Giuseppe Saragat, an intellectual and former editor of the clandestine edition of *Avanti!* in Rome, who had led the rebellion against Nenni's leadership of the PSI when he equivocated over the Nazi–Soviet Pact. Saragat had been imprisoned by the Nazis in October 1943 and was only saved from the firing squad in January 1944 by a partisan cell who forged papers to get him transferred first to an Italian jail and then released. Saragat had just returned from Paris, where he had served as ambassador since April 1945.

Nenni and Saragat clashed on two fundamental points: what the PSI stood for and what its end goal should be. In his speech to the Congress, on 11 April 1946, Nenni contended that the essence of socialism was that it was a proletarian movement. He was against 'bourgeois socialism' because the socialism of the middle classes was invariably tinged with nationalism and too easily became 'Bonapartism' or Fascism.[84] Socialists should reason in class terms (and be workers, or intellectuals who had accepted the logic of Marxist theory). From this analysis, Nenni drew the conclusion that the working class should be politically united and that could only mean, ultimately, the creation of a common party with the PCI. Fusion should take place spontaneously through the experience of working together to obtain goals that both parties held dear. The time for fusion was not ripe, but it would, Nenni hoped, become so soon. 'Let the day dawn when the working class will stand compact, in the complete unity of all its forces, in defence of the democratic state that we are about to create,' he orated.[85]

Saragat, by contrast, argued that it was a mistake to 'mechanically dissolve all social reality in terms of class'. Like the Labour Party in Britain, the PSIUP should be a reformist force able to appeal beyond the ranks of the industrial workers. It should become a people's party, intent on realizing social and political rights and extending social justice. It should avoid unification with the PCI at all costs.

Saragat regarded Clement Attlee's Britain as a much more progressive society than Soviet Russia. Echoing Arthur Koestler's *Darkness at Noon*, which had become a *cause célèbre* in France in 1945, Saragat warned that the Soviet Union had become a totalitarian state because Russia was an essentially backward society in which the urban elites ruled over an inert mass of peasants: 'even today in Russia, the five million adherents to the only legal party control the state's powers almost entirely; the other 180 million inhabitants are politically passive bystanders in a gigantic experiment.' Dictatorship of the minority, and an 'enormous expansion of an omnipotent bureaucracy', had been an inevitable concomitant of the Bolshevik revolution, not least because the Soviet government had found itself in a state of siege, in perennial fear of invasion.

Saragat, who had recently returned from France, knew full well that men such as Jacques Duclos and Maurice Thorez, the leaders of the French Communist Party, were as Stalinist as Stalin. They saw themselves as an elite destined to mould society. Such men did not want the unity of the working class, but control over it, Saragat argued. It was 'misrepresenting facts', he suggested, 'to present communism as being converted to democracy when everything about its organization, its politics and its mentality, proclaims the opposite'.[86] He did not say so outright, but the implication of his speech was that Togliatti, Longo, and Scoccimarro were cut from the same cloth as their French and Russian counterparts.

The threatened split in the PSIUP over the character of communism might seem arcane stuff of interest only to intellectual historians.
It was not. The debate within the PSIUP conditioned the birth of Italian democracy profoundly. Saragat's conviction that democracy was
essentially a vital means to the end of social reforms was far closer to
De Gasperi's outlook than to Nenni's.

Saragat's motion to the congress got less than 12 per cent of the
vote. The motion most favourable to fusion with the PCI received 46
per cent. The third motion, advanced by the resistance hero Sandro
Pertini and Ignazio Silone, got 40 per cent. The PSIUP made Nenni
president and elected Ivan Matteo Lombardo, a moderate, party secretary. But the outcome was a truce, not a lasting peace. Saragat's
speech was both a harbinger of a split to come and a rationale for
what would eventually become known as *centrismo*, the politics of
the centre ground uniting progressive Catholics, republican liberals,
and democratic socialists.

A second development that would eventually be important for the
construction of the centre ground in Italian politics had taken place
two months earlier, in February 1946, when the PdA had split. Since
April 1945, the PdA had been divided between the northerners who
had conducted the resistance and fought in the hills and streets, and
the more 'political' wing who had led the party in the regions of Italy
liberated by the Allies. There was also a great deal of friction between
personalities. The PdA was not short of big egos and contained a lot
of professors (the overlap between the two categories was considerable).[87] Some of the PdA's members were also discontented over the
leadership's decision to stay in De Gasperi's cabinet after Parri's
removal from office. The party's fundamental identity was also a bone
of contention. Some *azionisti* saw the party in doctrinaire socialist
terms; others, above all Ugo La Malfa, wanted the PdA to emerge as
a movement capable of appealing to small entrepreneurs, artisans and
shopkeepers, as well as professionals and intellectuals. La Malfa also
argued persuasively that the PdA could not avoid cooperating with
the DC. He insisted that the future of democracy in Italy would
depend on whether the DC evolved in a reformist, democratic direction, or whether it became a force of reaction buttressing the Church,
the landowners, and traditional forces in general.[88]

La Malfa's perceptive speech was to no avail. Defeated, he resigned ministerial office and founded the Democratic Republican Movement (MDR), along with Ferrucio Parri and a string of distinguished scholars and writers. Had the men (there was only one woman) who signed MDR's manifesto been members of a humanities faculty, it would have been among the strongest in Europe.[89]

The birth of the MDR was hardly an earth-shaking event. The PdA, despite its valiant contribution to the resistance, was in numerical terms, as Italians say, 'four cats'. The split simply produced two mini-parties with two cats in each. Within months, the new movement had dissolved, with its members migrating into other political forces (or concentrating on their scholarship as universities reopened and revived). La Malfa himself, along with many other members of the MDR, joined the venerable but tiny Republican Party (PRI) in September 1946.

But he took his ideas with him and swiftly became the PRI's principal thinker, though its leader, Rodolfo Pacciardi, a war hero in Spain, kept a tight grip on the party organization. Like Saragat's principled rejection of totalitarian communism, La Malfa's departure from the PdA, and his openness to (and recognition of) the potentially progressive character of Christian Democracy's programme was a second foundation stone of *centrismo*. La Malfa made the case for the democratization of Italy, and for what would today be called social inclusion, eloquently. He contended that the adoption and *practice* of democracy was bound to work fundamental changes upon Italian society. If the people were not actively obstructed, they would find their way to progressive policies on their own, via the ballot box, if they informed themselves, participated politically, and took citizenship seriously. De Gasperi believed the same. The two men would be drawn even closer over the next four years by their Europeanism.

The third foundation stone of centrism laid during the spring of 1946 was the DC's decision to support the Republic. De Gasperi feared that a right-wing 'Nationalist' party, capable of taking votes from the DC, might emerge to champion the monarchy and traditional values. This was why he had supported the idea of a referendum: he wanted to avoid a vote in the Constituent Assembly that would coalesce right-wing political sentiment behind the monarchy.[90] The

Church was opposed to the party taking an explicit position on the issue: Pope Pius XII refused Luigi Sturzo, De Gasperi's mentor, permission to return to Italy from the United States until the referendum was over because of the priest's open sympathy for the Republic.

The DC's congress, which met in Rome between 24 and 27 April, nevertheless voted by a substantial margin in favour of the Republic, though there was a strong monarchist minority.[91] The DC stated, however, that it would 'unconditionally accept' whatever result emerged from the ballot box. The motion favourable to the Republic was not made binding on the mass membership, who were told to vote according to their conscience. During the electoral campaign itself, the DC persistently argued against conflating the votes for the Constituent Assembly and the so-called institutional question: voters were told that one could vote for the DC and also be a monarchist. Moreover, if enough people voted for the DC in the Constituent Assembly, the Republic would not be a 'leap in the dark', but a way of consolidating Christian values.[92]

Supporting the Republic ensured that the DC could cooperate subsequently with liberal progressives like La Malfa and reformist socialists like Saragat. Had the DC equivocated on this issue, cooperation would have been impossible. Yet had the DC been intransigently pro-Republic, conservative voters would have deserted the party and swollen the National Freedom Bloc (BNL), which was the monarchists' electoral vehicle. De Gasperi steered the middle course deftly throughout the election campaign. So well, indeed, that it was falsely alleged he was a secret monarchist himself.[93]

BIRTH PANGS

The date set for the referendum on the monarchy and the election to the Constituent Assembly was 2 June 1946. As the date neared, the parties intensified their propaganda efforts for both polls. The PCI threw resources at the elections. Posters were printed by the hundred thousand, pamphlets with print runs of 300,000 copies or more were distributed, 500,000 copies of the manifesto were provided to cells and sections round the country. The PCI even distributed three short propaganda films called *From the People, For the People*, which was about the 5th Party Congress, *The People Will Judge*, which was the case against the monarchy, and *A Woman Like Any Other*, which was about the everyday situation of Italian women.[94]

The DC parried blow for blow. De Gasperi proved to be a tough campaigner, who emphasized the socially progressive aspects of the DC's policies, straddled the institutional question carefully, and lost no opportunity to kindle the party's Catholic sentiments. He also stressed the *italianità* of Trieste, which Yugoslavia wanted as war reparations. The DC's militants were as committed as the PCI's. The party's training materials for candidates, canvassers, and local organizers portrayed them as missionaries, whose job it was to diffuse the party's programme in society, without faction or intrigue, and whose personal life should exemplify the doctrines of social justice and individual moral rigour that the DC espoused: 'a genuine apostolic spirit must imbue the propagandist's every activity'. The propagandist was 'a living standard bearer', carrying the flag of the party into political battle. The recommended reading for these Christian soldiers was not a technical manual of political organization, but two works of theology: Dom Jean-Baptiste Chautard's *L'anima di ogni apostolato* and *La via di Cristo*, by the future Pope Paul VI, Giovanni Battista Montini.[95]

Like the PCI, Christian Democracy wanted its active members to spread gospel by word and deed. The religious language is chosen deliberately. The DC and the PCI were two *churches*, not just two political formations taking part in a polite contest. Time would prove that their theological standpoints were incompatible.

The Church itself mobilized parish priests and Catholic Action, its network of voluntary confessional organizations, in the DC's support. The DC had fewer members than the PCI, but Catholic Action had more. On 20 April 1946, Pope Pius XII stoked Catholic activists by telling them that the religious tradition of Italy was at risk from an insidious enemy (socialism) that had been working for a century to abolish the Church and that now judged the moment was ripe for the 'final assault'. Catholic Action should persuade citizens one by one of their duties towards the faith – which meant, of course, voting the right way.[96] On the eve of the poll, the Pope intervened by making a plea for the status quo in both Italy and France, which held a general election on 1 June. Pius said the day had come in which these two 'Latin sisters', who could boast an 'ultra-millennial Christian civilization', would decide whether to stand firm on the rock of Christianity' or 'pin their hopes for the future on the inscrutable omnipotence of a materialistic state, without religion and without God'.[97]

The enemy was certainly doing its best to seduce good Catholics from the path of righteousness. The PSIUP disseminated a marvellous poster of a bare-footed, long-haired Christ, arms open in welcome, that recalled the Gospel according to Saint Matthew: 'Truly, I say to you it is hard for a rich man to enter the kingdom of heaven.' The poster urged Italians to 'Vote for socialism which redeems the poor from the exploitation of the rich.'

In addition to the PSIUP, which naturally conducted a passionate campaign for the Republic, the other principal parties to contest the election were the PdA, the Republican Party (PRI), the monarchist BNL, *L'Uomo Qualunque*, and the National Democratic Union (UDN), an electoral cartel that united the PLI with Bonomi's Democratic Labour and various relics from Giolittian Italy, notably Benedetto Croce, Meuccio Ruini, and former premiers Vittorio Emmanuele Orlando and Francesco Saverio Nitti.

The Monarchy fought for its survival. Remarkably, given its record, it remained an institution with popular support. Crown Prince Umberto was also more popular than his father. Recognizing this, on 9 May 1946, Victor Emmanuel III abdicated, leaving the throne with 'deep trepidation' for the future of the country.[98] As a final gesture he generously left his collection of coins to the nation.[99] On 10 May, Umberto II issued a proclamation, line edited by De Gasperi, which assured the Italians that he would rule in a 'renewed constitutional monarchy'. A huge crowd of cheering royalists gathered outside the Quirinale Palace. Wounded veterans enthusiastically waved their crutches in support of the king and his photogenic family.[100]

Victor Emmanuel's abdication caused a fierce clash in the Council of Ministers between the republican ministers, especially Togliatti, who regarded it as a breach of the Crown's duty to stay out of politics, and the PLI, which threatened to leave the government if monarchist demonstrations were suppressed (the unexpected size and enthusiasm of the royalist crowds had touched a nerve). The new king campaigned actively, and royalist crowds grew bigger and bigger: 200,000 people greeted Umberto II in Naples on 20 May.[101]

Election Day, 2 June 1946, was thus a momentous one for Italy. Would the PCI emerge as the largest party of the left, or even as the largest party overall? Would disorder follow the defeat of the monarchy (for none of the CLN parties doubted that the Republic would win). Would the Constituent Assembly be able to begin its work in a mood of national reconciliation, or in one of partisanship and rancour?

Italy voted peacefully for the most part, to the relief of Giuseppe

Redeeming the poor: PSI electoral poster, spring 1946.

Romita, whose hard work as interior minister reaped its reward. Voters gathered outside the polling stations clutching their documents in a mood of high excitement, especially those for whom it was the first opportunity to vote. Twenty-eight million people were entitled to vote, of whom 25 million (89.1 per cent) did cast a ballot. There were, however, many blank or spoiled ballots, a fact that proved politically significant. Women and men voted in virtually identical numbers: 89.2 per cent of men voted, 89 per cent of women.[102] There is no question that Italians regarded 2 June 1946 as a day of liberation, and of both popular and national self-affirmation.

The elections to the Constituent Assembly registered some surprises. The DC was the largest party. It attracted 8.1 million votes (35.2 per cent) and was awarded 207 seats in the Constituent Assembly. The DC's victory was not a surprise, but its margin of victory over the second party was: the PSIUP took 4.76 million votes (20.7 per cent) and secured 115 deputies. The PSIUP had supporters outside the ranks of the proletariat: Maria José, the wife of Umberto II, allegedly voted for the Socialists and cast a personal vote of preference for Giuseppe Saragat.[103] The PCI, despite its propaganda blitz, took only 4.36 million votes (18.9 per cent). No matter how it tried to 'spin' the result, the election was a setback.[104] The two left-wing parties together did not achieve 40 per cent and the northern proletariat had preferred their old allegiances to the new. The PdA obtained only 335,000 votes (1.4 per cent): its pretensions to represent the masses were shown to be overblown. Three mass parties represented three-quarters of the people and the DC ranked first among them.

L'Uomo Qualunque mobilized disenchantment in the slums of Naples and Rome, taking 1.2 million votes (5.3 per cent). This result would presage a surge in its support in local elections later in the autumn. At the other end of the social scale, the UDN's 1.57 million votes (6.8 per cent) disappointed Italy's *alta borghesia* but enabled a handful of eminent gentlemen to retain their *scranno* (desk) in parliament. Irony aside, the Liberal Age was over. The concerns of the new democracy could not be articulated by the mellifluous prose of Croce or Orlando, who were as out of date as a frock coat. Even so, in the Mezzogiorno, the sum of the votes of UQ, the UDN, and the monarchist BNL matched the DC and in some areas was ahead of the combined vote of the parties of the left.[105] In the South, moreover, the DC was a much less progressive force than in the North and Centre. Italy's political North/South divide was stark.

The same gap between North and South was even more evident in the referendum on the monarchy. To the horror of Romita, the monarchy briefly pulled ahead in the count. 'Would I, a lifelong Republican, be compelled to tell the workers that the last relic of the most incompetent royal house in Europe would stay in his place and be enormously reinforced by having a popular mandate?' Romita was momentarily 'heartbroken'.[106]

Umberto II polled better than predicted in the North and in parts of the Mezzogiorno he won by a landslide. Nevertheless, as the tally of votes mounted, it became evident that the Republic had won a clear, though underwhelming, victory. The slowness with which the votes were counted, however, caused fervid speculation about ballot fraud. Romita was alleged to have a 'million votes in his drawer' in case the Republic needed them.[107] At 5.30 p.m. on 5 June 1946, with results from about 1,000 polling stations still unreported, but with pressure for an announcement mounting, Romita appeared before a scrum of reporters and announced that the Republic had so far obtained 12,182,855 votes and the monarchy 10,362,709. The Republic was winning by a 54 to 46 per cent margin. The royal household was plunged into 'great depression'.[108]

Mussolini famously said that Italy was a land of 'saints, poets, and navigators'. He forgot lawyers. Faced with defeat, monarchists resorted to legal casuistry to annul the referendum result. Professors from the University of Padua, supported by the monarchists in the cabinet, contended that the majority required by the 16 March decree was 'constituted not by a comparison of the votes obtained by the republic and the monarchy, but by the relationship between the sum of the two with respect to a third number, namely the number of all those who voted'.[109] In plainer language: for the Republic to win it had to obtain not just more votes than the number of ballots cast for the monarchy, but an absolute majority of the ballots cast, including spoiled ballots and ballots left blank. These had still not been quantified but were known to be very numerous. At 6 p.m. on 10 June, the Court of Cassation (High Court of Appeal), which had been given the task of ascertaining the definitive results, pronounced that the Republic had obtained 12,672,767 valid votes, the monarchy 10,688,905.[110] The Court announced that it would at a subsequent date update these figures (a handful of polling booths *still* had not reported a week after the poll had closed) and decide on the merits of the monarchists' appeals. Despite the Court's verdict, the king told De Gasperi that he would wait until the Court's definitive pronouncement before abdicating.

When De Gasperi reported this decision to the Council of Ministers, the left-wing parties insisted that the legal conditions had been met to declare the Republic. Liberal Party leader Leone Cattani objected. Togliatti heard him out and then said bluntly:

> All this juridical hair-splitting is not relevant. What we are talking about is the transformation of the State which will happen either by revolutionary action or through legal means. It has happened legally, and we should shorten the period of uncertainty. In this situation we should have the courage to give a sensation of closure.

This came very close to saying 'the Republic, or insurrection'. Nenni backed the PCI leader, by saying that if the Council of Ministers waited upon the king to step down, and did not at once declare the Republic, it would 'throw the country into anarchy'.[111]

De Gasperi departed for the Quirinale at 9.45 p.m. and, once there, insisted that even though the Court of Cassation had not definitively proclaimed the Republic, the spirit of Article 2 of the 16 March decree, which made the prime minister temporary head of state until the Constituent Assembly could elect a provisional head of state, should be respected. Umberto's advisers responded angrily to this suggestion. De Gasperi, at the end of his tether, told them that his ability to converse in Latin (i.e. in euphemistic language) had run out. Did the royalists want to resolve the question through force? So be it, the prime minister stated: 'It means that either I will come and visit you in Regina Coeli prison, or you will come and visit me!'[112]

The government declared 11 June 1946 a public holiday. Hundreds of thousands of people celebrated the victory of the Republic in the squares of the major cities: the crowds were truly 'oceanic', although

Long live the Republic: Italian voters celebrate
the Republic's victory on 11 June 1946.

the people were now celebrating democracy, not war and imperialism.[113] Yet still the king refused to back down. On 12 June, monarchist mobs rioted in Naples, showing the king that he had popular backing, but the ex-partisans of the North would have taken up arms if Umberto had tried to impose his will on the government. Togliatti's veiled threat was not a bluff.

On the evening of 12 June, at the end of a turbulent day, the Council of Ministers formally affirmed that a 'transitory regime' had begun during which the 'functions' (not powers) of head of state would be exercised by the prime minister. On the night of 12–13 June, neither ministers nor members of the royal household slept in their own beds: both sides were afraid that the stand-off would be resolved by a coup.

Umberto, the 'May King', was therefore at a fork in the road. He could divide the nation, risking bloodshed, or leave the country. To his credit, he decided on the second alternative. But he did so on his own terms. He departed from Ciampino Airport near Rome without formal ceremony on 13 June. In a last proclamation, Umberto stated that it had been his duty to wait until the Court of Cassation concluded its deliberations but that the government had carried out a *coup d'état*. He could not acquiesce with the government's decision without 'becoming an accomplice' to illegality. He therefore had no choice but to leave the country. He did not formally abdicate as king or cede his powers to De Gasperi.

The prime minister thus found himself the temporary head of state of a country that was divided in two by the narrow victory for the Republic. The South had voted 67–33 per cent for the monarchy, the North 65–35 for the Republic. The centre regions had tipped the balance. The most republican towns in Italy (Ravenna, Forlì, Grosseto, Livorno, Reggio Emilia, De Gasperi's own Trento) were without exception in the Centre-North. In the principal towns of Sicily, by contrast, less than 20 per cent of the people had voted for the Republic. Naples was the same.[114] Italy was already divided ideologically between moderates and the radical left and facing economic collapse, especially in the South. The referendum, for all the triumphalism of the republican parties, had exposed the extent of Italy's geographical divides.

At 5 p.m. on 13 June, Guido Gonella, the then editor of the DC newspaper, *Il Popolo*, entered De Gasperi's office and found the exhausted premier sprawled in an armchair behind his desk smoking a cigarette – the otherwise austere De Gasperi had a weakness for tobacco and in the previous week he had amply earned whatever relief nicotine could give him.[115] But the prime minister now had to address the questions of signing a Peace Treaty with the Allies that did not provoke nationalist outrage, drawing up a constitution with Togliatti and Nenni that did not inflame Catholics, pacifying the South, and reconstructing the economy without causing inflation to surge. His efforts had just begun.

6

Faltering Steps

The transition to Republican government was carried out on 28 June 1946, when the newly elected Constituent Assembly met to choose an interim president. The man selected, with 396 of the 501 votes cast, was Enrico De Nicola, the Neapolitan jurist who had devised the formula of the 'Lieutenant of the Realm' in 1944 and thus helped to facilitate the formation of a CLN government when the Allies reached Rome.

De Gasperi was ill-disposed towards the new president, who had not been his first choice. Pietro Nenni told the steering committee of the PSI on 22 June that the premier thought De Nicola possessed a 'quitter's mentality' because he had 'failed to live up to his responsibilities for the last 50 years'.[1] This is hearsay, but believable hearsay: the new president was something of a prima donna, and De Gasperi was anything but. De Nicola had been a weak president of the Chamber of Deputies after the March on Rome and had also, in 1929, been nominated life senator of the realm by Victor Emmanuel III not long after De Gasperi had been released from prison and when he was still being actively persecuted.

De Gasperi's second government took the oath of office in front of De Nicola on 13 July 1946. In addition to the premiership, De Gasperi held the *dicastero* (portfolio) of foreign affairs until the end of the Paris Peace Conference, which began on 29 July, two weeks after the formation of the government, and ended on 15 October. He was also minister of the interior and minister for Italian Africa (as well, of course, as de facto party leader). This proliferation of roles prompted an eminent Liberal intellectual and former prime minister, Francesco Saverio Nitti, to remark that, while De Gasperi was undoubtedly gifted, Cavour, assisted by Talleyrand, Sir Robert Peel, and Bismarck could not have done the job the premier had set himself. Even if De Gasperi had a brain 'as big as the dome of Saint Peter's', Nitti ironized, subtly insinuating that the Vatican would provide the premier's advisers, it would not be enough for such an immense task.[2]

The new government was based on the three popular parties, with the PRI in a minor role. According to Nenni, again, this arrangement was not to De Gasperi's liking. The DC was divided on the issue of whether to cooperate with the PCI and Nenni noted that there was 'an evident anti-communist tone' in De Gasperi's conversation. Nenni did not think the leader of Christian Democracy would be able to cooperate with the PCI for more than 'three or four months', and De Gasperi made overtures to the PSI leader, hoping to persuade the Socialists to form a government with the DC alone. Nenni, staying loyal to the PSI's pact of unity with the PCI, told him this was 'unacceptable'.[3] It would not be the last time De Gasperi made such overtures.

Christian Democracy provided ten cabinet ministers in addition to the premier: agriculture, education, and foreign trade, among others, were assigned to the DC. The PCI and PSIUP held eight ministries between them. Nenni was made minister without portfolio, but took over as foreign minister in mid-October, while Togliatti opted not to be bound by collective ministerial responsibility and stayed out of office. The Treasury Ministry remained in the hands of Epicarmo Corbino, though he did not last long. There were no women ministers.

De Gasperi had not wanted De Nicola as interim president of the republic, but he had wanted a southerner. He himself was from the Trentino. The President of the Constituent Assembly, Giuseppe Saragat, hailed from Turin. He would be replaced in February 1947 by Umberto Terracini, another politician from Piedmont. The newly appointed governor of the Bank of Italy, the distinguished economist Luigi Einaudi, from Carrù in the province of Cuneo, was by character a Swiss Calvinist. President De Nicola was the only Neapolitan – Naples was Italy's third city by population – to hold high public office as the new republic began its odyssey.[4]

The DC was the most 'national' of the three main parties in its

leadership (the PSIUP was almost entirely northern). Its general secretary, Attilio Piccioni, an 'intelligent, lazy, and taciturn' man, came
from the province of Rieti, near Rome (though he had cut his political teeth in Turin as leader of the PPI in the early 1920s),[5] and the
DC's team of ministers included two Romans, the Sardinian agriculture minister, Antonio Segni, and De Gasperi's most able lieutenant,
Mario Scelba, a lawyer from Caltagirone in Sicily who had started
his career, when he was an undergraduate in Rome, as an aide to
Luigi Sturzo and as a party worker for the PPI. Scelba was somebody that De Gasperi had literally trusted with his life during the
Nazi occupation of Rome. He had organized clandestine meetings,
acted as a courier of secret documents, and maintained links between
De Gasperi and the other party leaders. Fittingly, he became minister
for post and communications in the new government. Scelba, at
forty-five the second-youngest minister in the cabinet, was a formidable organizer with a ferocious work ethic, a streak of nationalism,
antipathy for the monarchy – and, like De Gasperi, little sympathy
for the PCI.

De Gasperi's pass for the Constituent Assembly

The presence of southerners at the highest levels of the state was important. The referendum on the monarchy had shown the gulf between political opinion in the Mezzogiorno and the North. To start a demonstration in Naples, all you needed to do was wave a flag and shout 'Long live the king!', grumbled one future president of the republic, himself a *settentrionale* from Savona, a coastal town near the border with France.[6] Underlying the discontent of the South was a narrative of disempowerment and exploitation among the poor. Italy needed leaders who could understand its deep-seated problems and make their remedy a national priority. But most northerners still had little knowledge of the South.

THE NEW NATION

De Gasperi's new government, in so far as it was based upon the three parties that had won the elections, enjoyed broad support among the electorate. There were, however, deep ideological fissures between the three parties and between the victorious parties of the resistance and former Fascists and Monarchists. In a bid to reconcile this latter divide, one of the last acts of De Gasperi's first government was to pass the so-called Togliatti amnesty of 22 June 1946. Most of the perpetrators of atrocities during the regime – the officials of the RSI who had organized the regime's bloodiest crimes – had already met rough justice after liberation or had been shot by partisan bands. Others had been hanged or sentenced to long prison sentences by the justice system. Remaining Fascists, even those of high rank, were mostly people who had administered the state and prospered under it, not ideologues or murderers. It was possible, even desirable, Togliatti argued, to show clemency to such people.

There were pragmatic considerations for the amnesty, too. Professionals – lawyers, professors, high-ranking officials, policemen, diplomats, the managers of state enterprises and privately owned businesses – wanted to draw a line under the past and move on. The political parties needed such people to run the state – and all of them, especially the DC and the PCI, had absorbed individuals who had made successful careers before July 1943. The success in the South of the monarchy in the 2 June referendum was also a flashing light indicating that fascist sentiment could be rekindled if the Republic was perceived as being the state of the anti-fascists only, not of the entire people.

The decree proposed by Togliatti was an *ad hoc* measure. It gave a generalized amnesty for all those convicted of crimes carrying a sentence of under five years (Article 1). It also (Article 2) amnestied people guilty of 'political crimes' in the areas administered by the Allies, even if these offences had merited prison sentences of longer than five years. This clause opened the gates for imprisoned PCI partisans who had 'executed' collaborators of the RSI or the Germans (but also political rivals) in the tumultuous weeks after 25 April 1945. Article 3 of the decree crucially extended the amnesty even to those who had committed offences on behalf of the regime so long as they had not held high public office or committed 'heinous acts' such as massacre, murder, or looting.[7]

Although the intention of Togliatti's amnesty was to create a mood of national reconciliation, instead it created a surge of bitterness – not least within the PCI itself. For the first and perhaps only time, Togliatti was publicly criticized by the party grassroots for the measure. Militants and former partisans couldn't understand why the very people they had been fighting until a year before should not be held accountable for the disaster that had been inflicted on the country.

The amnesty was predictably interpreted in an elastic way by judges. Giorgio Bocca, one of Togliatti's less forgiving biographers, fumed that 'the conservative and fascist judicial profession interpreted the phrase "heinous acts" in such a loose way that all the Salò Republic's worst hangmen and torturers were set free'.[8]

There certainly were some scandalous cases, the most egregious of which is probably that of Rodolfo Graziani, Mussolini's minister of war, of whom it can fairly be said that, had he been German, he would have been tried at Nuremberg for crimes against humanity during Italy's colonial wars. Graziani, instead, was only tried by the Italian state for his offences during the RSI. He was interned on the Isle of Procida in February 1946, where he wrote, before he came to trial, an autobiography, dedicated to 'the Italian people, the supreme judge', entitled 'I defended my country'.[9] The title summarizes his defence when he was accused of collaborationism in October 1948: he claimed he had acted out of patriotism and had not materially assisted the Germans. After four months, the civil court imitated Pontius Pilate and decided that it did not have jurisdiction in his case. Graziani was accordingly tried by a military tribunal that in May 1950 proceeded to sentence him to nineteen years imprisonment for the crime of collaborationism but suspended thirteen years and eight months of the sentence. A few months later, Graziani was released from jail – where he promptly became a hero and honorary president of the neo-fascist Italian Social Movement (MSI).

The biggest impact of the amnesty derived from the fact that state bureaucrats were now largely exonerated for their collusion with the regime, or else were allowed to appeal against previous convictions and get their jobs back. The Italian state accordingly remained manned by officials who, whether from conviction or opportunism, had made their careers under the regime. Intellectuals who had enjoyed prebends in the gargantuan bureaucracy of the Ministry of Popular Culture created by Mussolini, and businessmen who had been worthies in the corporate state, were also able to start afresh. Claudio Pavone, a celebrated historian of the Italian resistance, has argued powerfully that the failure of Italy to have a thorough-going purge of the bureaucracy and professions enabled the 'continuity of the state' and ensured that 'innovative political leaps forward' were 'enfeebled', and that the path towards democracy was compromised.[10]

The three parties not only agreed on the amnesty, they also nominally agreed on the broad thrust of economic policy. In his first speech to the Constituent Assembly, on 15 July, De Gasperi outlined a bold economic strategy on behalf of the government which emphasized that the development of the Mezzogiorno would become a central concern, and he even rashly promised that 'every effort' would be made to bring the 'social conditions' of the South and the islands to 'the same levels as the most advanced parts of Italy'. In general, the government needed, among other things, to raise production, slim down the state bureaucracy, preserve the value of the lira, find the financial resources to launch a 'large-scale programme of public works', and take particular care that small and medium-sized businesses prospered. To pay for reconstruction, the government needed to float a domestic loan, impose a wealth tax, and 'appeal' for foreign credits, since Italy did not possess the wherewithal to rebuild on its own.

As a sop to public opinion, which was hard hit by inflation, the premier raised the daily bread ration to 250 grams and announced that a one-off bonus of 3,000 lire would be paid to all heads of families earning less than 30,000 lire per annum. De Gasperi also promised to bring about a more 'equitable distribution' of land ownership. He carefully warned, however, that this could not happen immediately. Land redistribution had to be preceded by measures to make the designated land suitable for commercial farming: 'chopping up untransformed land' into small subsistence plots would simply condemn the peasants to 'succumb'. The principles of the land reform would also be decided, as a constitutional matter, by the Constituent Assembly. In the meantime, the premier proposed measures to compel landowners to draw up plans to make uncultivated land suitable for farming and announced a commitment of 10 billion lire to finance land improvement.[11]

The reason the DC, PSIUP, and PCI could find common ground on the main principles of economic policy was that all three broadly agreed Italy's new democracy had to be a 'progressive' one. A return to liberal parliamentarianism would be inadequate. The social order urgently needed to become more equal, as did the geographic divide between North and South.

This shared conviction had been strengthened by the publication of Carlo Levi's *Cristo si è fermato a Eboli* (*Christ Stopped at Eboli*). The book first appeared in 1945, in instalments in *Il Ponte*, a journal edited by Piero Calamandrei, and then in book form by Giulio Einaudi, a progressive publisher in Turin. It met with critical acclaim. In the months when the Italian republic was being born, Levi's depiction of the lives of the people of 'Gagliano', the fictional name for the small town of Aliano in Basilicata, where Levi, a doctor from a Jewish family in Turin, had been exiled between August 1935 and the spring of 1936, became the most widely discussed book of the day.

The book gave a 'thick description', as we would say today, seen through the narrator's own eyes, of the customs, sexual mores, social relations, and material and spiritual poverty of the malaria-ridden town. An English comparison might be the first half of *The Road to Wigan Pier*, George Orwell's examination of poverty in Britain's mining towns during the Great Depression.

The reason the book made such an impact was its unsparing portrayal of the condition of the peasants: the *cafoni* of Silone's novels. Levi showed that they were not mere beasts of burden, but warmhearted, shrewd human beings. They had made him welcome. They knew he was being persecuted by someone in Rome, and that was enough to make him an object of sympathy – especially when he cured their children of sickness. Conversation with the peasants quickly slid towards the guerrilla war fought by the brigands against the Italian state after unification in the 1860s. The brigands were still folk heroes and their resistance to rule from Rome was a source of pride.

A visit by Levi's sister, who had been in Matera, the provincial capital, gave Levi an opportunity to describe, through her, the living conditions of the 20,000 troglodytes living in that town, in caves cut out of the hillside. In Matera, Levi reported, 'men, women, children, and animals', even pigs, sleep together and an 'infinite number' of nude children, or children in rags, sit in the hot sun covered in flies, their faces 'wizened', their stomachs bloated from the effects of malaria, or else they are 'reduced to skin and bones' by dysentery.[12]

In Gagliano itself, the peasants lived in three layers in their hovels. The animals lay under the bed covering much of the floor area. The humans huddled promiscuously on the bed, newborn and small children slept in woven baskets hanging by cords from the ceiling. In every home there were pictures of two 'inseparable tutelary deities'. These were the black Madonna of Viggiano, the sainted protector of Basilicata, and President Franklin Delano Roosevelt, the symbol of American optimism, 'a kind of Zeus, a benevolent and smiling God, the commander of the other world'.[13]

This was how the peasants of Basilicata were still living when De Gasperi's second government was formed. But poverty was just as bad, or worse, in the big cities of the South. Naples, especially, was a giant war-damaged slum, in which hundreds of thousands of people lived without access to latrines, let alone mains sewage, and where the *scugnizzi* roamed the streets, living by expedients, because there were so few schools.[14]

Levi's book was important because it vividly illustrated the scale of Italy's historic state failure, just as Orwell's book had laid bare Britain's. Anybody reading *Cristo si è fermato a Eboli* would conclude that Gagliano needed, as a bare democratic minimum, a modern elementary school with trained teachers, a clinic with a competent doctor and nurses, a campaign to eliminate malaria, public housing to replace insanitary hovels, mains drains, and sources of income other than subsistence farming to keep more young men at home. The town, in short, needed public investment to give it the rudiments of contemporary civilization – just as in Orwell's England, post-war governments, both Labour and Conservative, needed to clear the pit villages and industrial towns of northern England and the Midlands of their slums and build modern 'council houses'. In both countries, democracy was impossible if the poorest citizens lived in squalor and ignorance. Democracy could not merely signify voting for one party rather than another in periodic elections. It meant that citizens should possess equal dignity and opportunity.

Christian Democrats would have added that Christ really did need to come over the mountains to Eboli. The town needed a dynamic priest able to minister to his flock and restore Christian morality. Certainly, spiritual renewal of some kind, be it Catholic or secular, was something the town required. It needed a faith to believe in, rather than be resigned to the impossibility of change.

The PCI were confident that they could provide this spiritual dimension. The party had been working hard to establish a presence on the ground in the South and Sicily, and not without success. Even though the Mezzogiorno had voted overwhelmingly for the monarchy on 2 June, and even though the PCI and the PSIUP combined had finished a distant second in the South behind the DC, the electoral results had been encouraging for the social-communist left.[15] Even though the traditional elites had mobilized against the two working-class parties everything 'backward, uneducated, and conservative' that southern society could offer, the popular parties (including the DC) had broken the traditional political mould whereby downtrodden peasants simply voted for the landlord. Every ballot cast for the

PCI or the PSIUP was a vote against passive subjugation to the 'surviving old champions of southern *trasformismo*'. In even the most remote villages of the South, wrote Giorgio Amendola, the head of the party in Campania and Basilicata, it was possible to find branch offices of the PCI in a 'single room with whitewashed walls, a portrait of Togliatti, a few books, and our flag'.[16] De Gasperi, a reformist conservative, knew that he could not allow the PCI to steal a march on the DC in the South.

All three parties agreed that reviving production and creating jobs was a matter of priority. National income, measured in constant 1938 lire, leapt from 83 billion in 1945 (a level comparable to 1900, to give some idea of the war's impact on the economy) to over 127 billion in 1946. Nevertheless, life remained grim for those who lived on wages or pensions or had no fixed employment. Millions of people were surviving, but not thriving. Average calorie intake reached a low point in 1945 (1,747 calories per day), but a year on it was still all but unchanged (1,760 calories). Almost all these calories came from vegetables or grain. Most Italians were eating little butter, cheese, and meat.[17] The prices of staples, moreover, were shooting up: a litre of olive oil, for instance, had cost 15 lire in 1943. By September 1946, it cost 680 lire, up from 400 lire in July.[18] Wages could not begin to keep up. In the weeks after the government took office, there were 'energetic agitations' for pay increases in many factories of the North, while illegal seizures of fallow land multiplied across the Mezzogiorno.[19]

On 9 October 1946, tens of thousands of building workers protesting against layoffs marched on the Viminale Palace, the then seat of the government, being joined on the way by discontented citizens from Rome's popular quarters. An attempt by Nenni to dissuade the unruly crowd was brushed aside: the proletariat were in no mood for mere words. Once at the Viminale, the protest became a riot. The doors of the building were forced, and the windows smashed by a hail of stones. A second attempt by Nenni at a parlay ended in insults and threats of personal violence. In the meantime, mounted police had charged the rioters and skirmishes had broken out on the squares and streets of central Rome. Some rioters possessed firearms; hundreds had makeshift clubs. Miraculously, only one person was killed, but more than

140 were injured, including nearly sixty policemen, some with gunshot wounds or shrapnel injuries sustained from grenades.[20] *L'Unità* deftly blamed the riot on property speculators who had whipped up a mob to subvert the government's efforts to control their excessive profits, but in truth it was a sign of frustrations boiling over.[21]

The PSIUP had foreseen this situation, which in hindsight was indeed inevitable. When De Gasperi had been forming his government, the party steering committee had openly discussed whether the party should insist that the Interior Ministry should remain in its hands, with the continuation of Romita as minister, or perhaps with Nenni in charge. It had concluded that it should not. Romita worried that 'from now on the minister with that portfolio will have a difficult life'. Party secretary Ivan Matteo Lombardo concurred. There would be 'protests by the war-wounded, by the unemployed, by southern beggars etc . . . [the minister] . . . will have a heck of a lot of issues to handle and might be compelled to resort to bloodshed by the police.'[22]

The social tensions of September–October 1946 threw into relief the fact that the three popular parties' broad agreement on the *ends* of economic policy masked a fundamental disagreement over the *means* that macroeconomic policy should adopt. Inflation, according to the PCI, was primarily being driven by the shortfall in production. Too much paper money was chasing too few goods. If the economy produced more, prices would fall. The PCI's 'new course' in economic policy, unveiled in September 1946, urged De Gasperi to take a dirigiste approach towards the economy by imposing an 'energetic fiscal policy' that would 'hit the better-off', by giving greater power to the 'workers' councils' that had spontaneously been established in many factories, and by controlling prices more effectively. Rations and wages should be raised for the poorest. Monopolies should be nationalized, and an immediate start should be made on land redistribution to the poorest peasants.[23]

Epicarmo Corbino, staunchly supported by Luigi Einaudi, was by contrast a proponent of austerity. Inflation should be countered by keeping wages and public spending down. The PCI attacked 'Corbinismo' and accused the hapless treasury minister of being the stooge of powerful lobbies in industry and finance.[24] Corbino resigned on 2 September, in open polemic with the PCI's campaign of denigration against him.[25] He was replaced by a northern Christian Democrat, Giovanni Battista Bertone, who took emergency measures to refill the state's coffers by issuing tax-free reconstruction bonds in October. The 230 billion lire attracted by this measure enabled the Italian state to keep the lights on and to pay public servants' salaries: at the end of September, the state had been down to its last 5 billion lire in cash reserves.[26]

The danger of the 'new course' in economic policy advocated by the PCI was that it risked dilapidating a national asset: the savings of the wealthy. On the other hand, the risk of austerity was that frustration at the privations of daily life would cause social upheaval long before private enterprise began to provide jobs and products in sufficient numbers – not least because Italy did not have enough hard currency to buy the raw materials that it needed to boost production. To alleviate hunger and poverty, Italy needed dollars – lots of them – to buy coal, timber, wheat, machinery: the United States was 'the only nation capable of supplying enough currency to enable the Italians to make purchases abroad'.[27] In the autumn of 1946 Italy was only kept going by the drip-feed of dollars from the United Nations Relief and Rehabilitation Administration (UNRRA), an American-financed initiative to blunt the worst consequences of economic collapse in Europe's war-struck nations. But such palliatives were scheduled to end in 1947. De Gasperi bluntly warned in September that Italy would need $4 billion in outside aid by 1950.[28] Would such aid materialize? And if not, how would the resources be found?

Industrial relations were soothed after the CGIL and the employers' confederation signed a 'wages truce' on 27 October 1946 in which, in exchange for a notable increase in minimum wages, inflation indexing, and a 'thirteenth month' Christmas bonus, unionized workers agreed on a six-month renewable pause in wage increases.[29] Such *concertazione*, or harmonious cooperation, between the employers and the employees ensured that production continued apace through 1947, despite a million difficulties caused by broken supply chains, transport inefficiencies, and shortages of imported raw materials. But the underlying issue of economic strategy remained. In Giuseppe Di Vittorio's words: 'Who should pay for the cost of the war and the national catastrophe? Big capital or the workers?'[30] Should the poor pay by working harder for less pay, perhaps for years, or should the rich, most of whom had colluded with Mussolini, pay via the nationalization of privately held assets and the imposition of stringent wealth taxes? Or both? In the absence of a fairy godmother, money had to come from somewhere, or else peasants in 'Gagliano' would continue to live in hovels without clinics for their children.

Although they did not proclaim it in public, the principal leaders of the PCI and the PSIUP knew that reconstruction of Italy's economy and society along socialist lines would mean sacrifices for everybody, not just the rich. But that was why it was *their* duty, not the duty of the bourgeois parties, including the DC, to impose the proverbial hair shirt. Emilio Sereni, minister for reconstruction in De Gasperi's government, was probably the most doctrinaire of the PCI's leading cadres. He confided to his diary on 14 December 1946, on the eve of a protest by veterans wounded in the war, that the premier had told him he was so anguished about the state of the public finances that he had a 'dirty conscience' and 'felt he ought to be in jail' whenever he approved extra spending even on 'sacrosanct' causes. Sereni commented:

> Increasing a pension or a wage, is for [De Gasperi] a painful ethical question. I am certain that he would like to send the police against the wounded veterans who tomorrow will protest in front of the Viminale: if he did that, he'd have a much cleaner conscience . . . I don't like glad-handed policies either at this moment . . . but the condition for resisting lax public spending would be . . . the dictatorship of the proletariat, or at least a democracy that is a good deal more progressive than this one. Only we (I say we in the broadest sense: the sons of need and of struggle) can say no, would be able to say no, would have the strength to say no with justice.[31]

TRIESTE AND BOLZANO

The most pressing immediate issue facing De Gasperi's government when it took office was the peace conference set to begin on 29 July 1946 in Paris to finalize the progress made in negotiations between the four principal wartime Allies – Great Britain, the United States, the

USSR, and France – with Nazi Germany's allies: Bulgaria, Finland, Hungary, Romania, and, of course, Italy. The territorial claims of neighbouring nations, above all Yugoslavia, and the scale of the punishment that would be inflicted upon Italy by the victorious powers, seemed likely to be large. Italy risked losing territories and peoples that most Italians regarded as intrinsic to national identity, above all Trieste.

There was a glaring disconnect between the mood of the legislators gathered in the Constituent Assembly and the 1,500 delegates from seventeen countries, plus the two Soviet Republics of Belorussia and Ukraine, scheduled to attend the conference in Paris.[32] The latter, especially the French and Yugoslavs, saw Italy as a defeated aggressor and made no distinction between the Fascist regime and the Italian people. The Constituent Assembly saw itself as the agent of national rebirth. Even those who interpreted history since the Risorgimento as a story of failed attempts, first by the Liberal state, then by Mussolini, to 'make Italians', thought that their task was to reconstruct the state, and this time build it on the rock of democratic principles, not sand. One British writer recently published a thoughtful general history of Italy that concluded by suggesting that:

> Geography and the vicissitudes of history made certain countries, including France and Britain, more important than the sum of their parts might have indicated. In Italy the opposite was true. The parts are so stupendous that a single region – either Tuscany or the Veneto – would rival every other country in the world in the quality of its art and the civilization of its past. But the parts have not added up to a coherent or identifiable whole. United Italy never became the nation its makers had hoped for because its making had been flawed both in conception and in execution, because it had been truly . . . a 'sin against history and geography'.[33]

Such doubts would have outraged the *costituenti* in 1946, although nobody would have denied the complexity of Italy's component parts, and everybody would have boasted of the richness of Italian culture. Denying the fundamental unity of Italy would have been regarded as an insult even by those, like Pietro Nenni, whose entire life until 1944 had been dedicated to fighting the Italian state (except for the

1915–18 war, when he fought heroically for it). The Mazzinian notion that *Italianità* was based upon a shared language and culture ran deep. Italy was where the Italian language (or versions thereof) was spoken, where Dante was revered, where the tricolour flew (for many, this included Libya, where some 150,000 Italians had made their home during the dictatorship). Italy was regarded as a triumph *over* history and geography, not a sin against them, whatever the short-comings of its human instruments in Rome.

The reception (and content) of President De Nicola's first commu-nication to the Constituent Assembly illustrates the point. Read out by Giuseppe Saragat, an able orator, the first mention of the word 'Nation' (with a capital 'N') was greeted by a standing ovation from the deputies, the ministers, and the public galleries, by repeated cries of 'Viva la Repubblica!' and 'enthusiastic, prolonged, reiterated applause'. De Nicola told the Assembly that a new period of 'decisive historical importance' was beginning for Italy, but 'regenerated by anguish and fortified by sacrifice', Italy would resume the 'path of well-ordered progress in the world' because its 'genius' was 'immor-tal'. Pointing a finger at the powers gathering in Paris to discuss Italy's future, De Nicola added that 'each humiliation inflicted upon [Italy's] honour, independence, and unity' would provoke not just 'the col-lapse of a Nation' but the 'downfall of a civilization'. He enjoined those who were the 'arbiters of Italy's destiny' to remember that fact. Though Italy had participated in the war on the German side, war had been imposed on her 'against her sentiments, aspirations, and interests' and Italian forces had given an 'efficacious contribution to the final victory'.

De Nicola's message ended with the exhortation, 'may God Almighty hasten and protect the resurrection of Italy!'[34] Catholics, socialists, monarchists, republicans, liberals, communists, and repentant fascists of all parties, many of them atheists, cheered lustily. Fraternal salutes to the Assembly from the peoples of the *italianissime terre* that risked cession to Yugoslavia followed the president's message. They were greeted with cries of 'Long live Venezia Giulia!'[35]

In his first speech to the Constituent Assembly, De Gasperi expressed the hope that Italy would keep Gorizia, Trieste, and southern and western Istria, since those territories were largely inhabited by Italian speakers. He was willing to accept minor territorial revisions to the border with France, and to treat South Tyrol as a 'bridge between the two nations' (Italy and Austria) while retaining the Brenner frontier. On the thorny question of whether Italy should pay reparations to the nations that Mussolini had attacked, De Gasperi took the position that Italy 'cannot and must not pay them'. The damage inflicted by the war on Italy made payment impossible, but, more important, Italy had become a co-belligerent and had fought alongside the Allies. The new Italy born of the resistance and the CLN should not have to pay for the crimes of the Duce, especially when Italy had already paid such a heavy price in blood and treasure.

When the Conference began, De Gasperi knew that *italianissime terre* were at genuine risk. With the powerful backing of the Soviet Union, the Yugoslav government was pressing for a territorial settlement that would push Italy back beyond the former border with the Austrian Empire (see map). Gorizia, Pola, and, above all, Trieste, the symbol of Italian national unity, would be lost.

Hundreds of thousands of Italians would be ruled from Belgrade, or else forced to give up their land and homes and flee to safety, if the borderline either of the Yugoslavs or the Soviets prevailed. The memory of the campaign of terror by Tito's partisans in May 1945 was fresh in Italian minds. Since Yugoslav troops controlled much of the contested territory, its position was a strong one: possession, especially when one is armed to the teeth, is nine points of the law. Great Britain, the United States, and France accordingly all proposed territorial settlements that redrew the pre-war border considerably in favour of Yugoslavia, with all three proposals restricting Italian territory far more than President Woodrow Wilson had contemplated during the Versailles peace conference in 1919 (which was De Gasperi's preferred option).

The French borderline was the most favourable to Tito's regime: France, which had its own memories of Italian treachery from June 1940, was Italy's most tenacious foe throughout the conference. But even France placed Trieste in Italian hands. The Yugoslavs themselves did not dispute that the city's population was overwhelmingly Italian. At the beginning of July 1946, under Russian pressure, the three Western foreign ministers compromised on a frontier based on the French

Proposed changes to Italy's
North-eastern border, July 1946

line (although Yugoslavia remained dissatisfied). It gave all Istria to Yugoslavia, but Gorizia would remain in Italian hands. The city and province of Trieste would become a 'free territory' under the sovereignty of neither Italy nor Yugoslavia. It was these twin decisions that had sparked the patriotic fervour of the Constituent Assembly.

By August, Italy also knew it would have to pay substantial reparations; would in effect cease to be a colonial power; and would have irksome limitations placed on its sovereign right to maintain armed forces and defend itself.

On 10 August 1946 at 4 p.m., De Gasperi, accompanied by Saragat and Bonomi, was ushered into a plenary session of the Conference and invited to speak. From the memorable first line ('I feel that everything – except your personal courtesy – is against me: above all, my indictment as a former enemy which places me here as it were, in the dock') onwards, he proceeded to deliver an unflinching speech that made no apology for Italy's past – for which many have criticized him. Yet it would have undermined the theme of the speech had he done so. De Gasperi addressed the Conference delegates as an equal, not as the representative of a defeated power: 'It is my duty to defend the life of my people, but I also feel the responsibility, and have the right to speak as an anti-fascist and a democrat.' De Gasperi, in short, did not hesitate to take the moral high ground. The speech soon became a cutting rebuke, delivered in places more in cold anger than sorrow, of the draft treaty's vindictiveness. He said frankly that the draft treaty was 'a hard treaty indeed'. The preamble, especially, systematically minimized the contribution that Italy had made to its own liberation; indeed, the 'extent of the Italian people's participation in the war had to be toned down in order that the Preamble might somehow fit the articles which follow it'. Not one article of the draft treaty, De Gasperi cried, 'recalls Italy's war effort as a co-belligerent'.

On Trieste, De Gasperi was scathing. The French line left 180,000 Italians in Yugoslavia and 59,000 Slavs in Italy. It was not a rational ethnic line, and the loss of Pola was an 'unbearable wound on the Italian national conscience'. But at least the French line was a frontier between Italy and Yugoslavia. The proposed creation of the 'free territory . . . maims our national unity and bites into our very flesh'. The 'free territory', for a series of economic and ethnic reasons, would be an 'unstable experiment' and was, in effect, an act of appeasement to Yugoslavia that would leave nearly 650,000 Italians 'severed from their country'. In a moment of emotional appeal, De Gasperi asked:

> Gentlemen, what good will come of clinging to a solution which only asks for trouble? Why shut your ears to the cry for help of the Italians in Istria – remember the appeal of nearly 50,000 of the people of Pola – who at this very moment are preparing to abandon hearth and home rather than submit to the new regime?

De Gasperi concluded by referring to Bonomi and Saragat, pointing out that they had both resisted Fascism courageously and were 'authoritative spokesmen' in 'that Assembly whose task it will be to decide whether it can assume the responsibility of signing the Treaty you are about to issue without jeopardizing the freedom and democratic evolution of the Italian people'. This veiled threat that Italy would not ratify an unjust treaty was followed by an appeal to the Conference not to 'linger on the steps of transient expediency', but to grant 'respite and moral credit' to Italy, a 'nation of toilers, 47 million strong', so it could participate in building a lasting peace consistent with the Allies' stated war aims.[36]

There was no applause. De Gasperi was greeted with a deafening (or perhaps stunned) silence. He got up and the Italian delegation left the room. He had been forthright, dignified, and principled. The American Secretary of State, James Byrnes, for one, was impressed – something that would have important consequences over the next few months. Even after De Gasperi's speech, of course, the peace conference's delegates continued to believe that the Italians had overwhelmingly supported Mussolini's imperial wars and that it was right to punish them for Fascism's misdeeds. That was a state of mind that could not be altered.

Nevertheless, by not apologizing for the crimes of the regime, De Gasperi communicated an important message. Italy was a nation whose modern history had culminated in the Duce's megalomaniacal attempts to reconstruct the Roman Empire and to imitate the Third Reich, but that did not mean Italian history should be *reduced* to Fascism. The Risorgimento had given birth to a nation whose politics blended the 'humanity of Giuseppe Mazzini's vision' with the 'universal aims of Christianity' and the 'international hopes of the working class', De Gasperi told the conference delegates in a significant passage of his speech. Italy was a nation that possessed a rich intellectual heritage, which meant it could genuinely aspire to political pluralism.

Over the next month, De Gasperi proceeded to demonstrate that he and his government practised what he preached. In the South Tyrol, Italy showed that it could make amends for Fascism's totalitarian disregard for diversity and could resolve ethnic conflict by negotiation and tolerance, not through violence and the diktat of the great powers.

When the war ended, the issue of what to do with the German-speaking upper half of the South Tyrol had come to a head. Many of the 75,000 people who had packed their bags and left for Germany after Mussolini's June 1939 deal with Hitler began to return to their former homes. These people in many cases had been fanatical Nazis.

One solution that was widely mooted was incorporation of the province of Bolzano into Austria. Especially after November 1945, when Austria held free elections in which the Communist Party was crushed by the Social and Christian Democrats, Vienna pressed hard for a plebiscite in Bolzano as a way of solving the ethnic problem democratically. There is no doubt that a large majority for Austria would have been the outcome of any such poll.

The weakness in Austria's position was that it was Austrian. Italy had an international credibility problem in the summer of 1946, but Vienna's reputation was still more tarnished. De Gasperi deftly countered appeals for a plebiscite by arguing that there was no need to reward Austria, or the pro-Nazi Tyrolese who had opted for German nationality, at Italy's expense, while promising to guarantee democratic and linguistic rights and local autonomy for the population involved. There would be no return to Mussolini's policy of ethnic discrimination.[37]

His position was also influenced by the public mood in Trento, where the end of the war was a catalyst for a plethora of autonomist initiatives from across the political spectrum. The Association of Regional Autonomist Studies (ASAR), despite its scholarly-sounding name, quickly became a force to be reckoned with. Founded in August 1945 at a packed meeting in Trento's eighteenth-century communal theatre, the ASAR soon enjoyed 'overwhelming success'.[38] It could boast tens of thousands of adherents by the spring of 1946, when it held its first congress. It was particularly strong in the Val di Fassa, the heart of the Dolomites, which has a strong *ladino* community, and the Valsugana, a narrow valley that connects Trento with Bassano del Grappa in the province of Vicenza.[39]

The movement's goal was simple: to unite the whole of the South Tyrol, from Ala, a small town on the border of the province of Verona, to the Brenner Pass, into a single autonomous region within the democratic Italian state. The movement's argument was that the territory was defined precisely by the fact that its identity was *both* German and Latinate and had enjoyed a long pre-fascist tradition of relative autonomy.

The ASAR was traditionalist, conservative with a small 'c', and exceptionally conscious of the need to preserve local customs and languages. Many of Trento's intellectuals – the town's lawyers, schoolteachers, and officials – regarded the ASAR, which was hostile to the mainstream political parties, as provincial and boorish. Be that as it may (middle-class intellectuals are always wary of spontaneous popular protests), the ASAR certainly could not be ignored by De Gasperi, who was a proud native of the Valsugana. The DC had been easily the biggest party in the Trentino on 2 June.

De Gasperi took an important first step to trying to solve the problems of Trento and Bolzano in the late summer of 1946. Together with the foreign minister of Austria, Karl Gruber, De Gasperi reached a bilateral accord on 5 September that guaranteed 'complete equality of rights' to the German-speakers of Bolzano and the German minority in Trento. Specifically, German-speakers would be able to complete both primary and secondary school in German, all public business would be conducted in both languages on a basis of equality, place names would be identified in both languages, not just Italian, and Italianized German family names would be restored if the families wished it. What we would today call 'affirmative action' would be exercised to increase the number of German-speakers in the public administration.

The accord further promised that the populations of Trento and Bolzano would be granted legislative and executive autonomy from Rome. Last, but not least, the Italian government committed itself to holding talks with Vienna to revise the Mussolini–Hitler agreement of June 1939, to ensure free trade between the two halves of the Tyrol, and to permit the reciprocal recognition of professional and university qualifications: graduates from Bolzano trained in Innsbruck or Vienna would be able to practise freely in Italy.[40]

The De Gasperi–Gruber accord was an act of statesmanship that settled a question that had looked intractable. Italy simultaneously demonstrated its anti-Fascism by making amends for the discrimination towards Germans of the pre-war period; signalled its willingness to begin a policy of cooperation with Vienna, ending the legacy of enmity between the two countries; heeded popular sentiment among the Italian-speakers of Trento; and wrote into an international treaty a guarantee that the reborn Italian state would be decentralized and not just administered from Rome. Decentralizing government went to the heart of what De Gasperi thought democracy was all about. Government should take place at the nearest possible level to the citizenry, and with their active participation.

The PCI had no qualms about accepting De Gasperi's agreement with Austria over the South Tyrol, but the Soviet Union's role in demanding a harsh settlement over Trieste and the north-east had placed the party's divided national loyalties in sharp relief. Public discontent over Trieste only grew in the autumn. The PCI squawked in protest when the DC accused it of being pro-Yugoslav and ambiguous on the question of Trieste, but the attacks hurt because they were substantially true. *Vie nuove* (*New Paths*), a PCI magazine aimed at popular audiences and first published in September 1946, singled out Yugoslavia for unstinting praise in November of that year: the article was accompanied by a socialist-realist portrait of Tito looking suitably heroic.[41]

Vie nuove's article appeared immediately after an act of personal diplomacy by Togliatti, who, unasked, travelled to Belgrade to negotiate with the Yugoslav leadership over the question of Trieste. On 7 November 1946, Togliatti gave an interview to *l'Unità* in which he announced that Tito was willing to return Italian prisoners of war and concede sovereignty over the city of Trieste to Italy if Rome agreed to Belgrade's territorial claims to Gorizia and Monfalcone. Togliatti insisted that he had acted solely 'for Italy and for Peace'.[42] There was no question of party advantage. To underline the point, *Vie nuove* published a cartoon of a repellent-looking rodent, labelled 'anti-communist calumnies', caught in the mousetrap of the 'Togliatti–Tito Talks'.[43]

Pietro Nenni, who had taken over from De Gasperi as foreign minister in October, on this occasion was not to be bulldozed by his PCI counterpart. On his recommendation, the government thanked Tito for his positive gesture, but rejected the proposed deal, which would have meant, as Nenni noted ironically in his diary, that Tito would 'give up that which he has not got and ask us for what we have'.[44] Apart from the government's natural reluctance to cede more territory, Trieste would have been transformed into 'an enclave within Yugoslavia', cut off by land from the rest of Italy, had Gorizia and Monfalcone been ceded.[45] Trieste would have become an Adriatic twin of West Berlin. Togliatti's mission to Belgrade confirmed the suspicion that the PCI lacked national feeling and placed the interests of international communism first.

SHARPENING CONTRADICTIONS

Togliatti's personal mission to Belgrade had been an electoral stunt, despite his protestations of lofty moral purpose. In the first week of November 1946, local elections were in full swing in the towns and cities that had not voted in April. Indeed, Togliatti's announcement of Tito's offer came as a 'bombshell' during the electoral campaign.[46]

By November, the PCI, despite its underwhelming showing in the 2 June elections, was emerging as the heir apparent for power. A regular party with less discipline might have relapsed into a period of soul-searching about its policies and recriminations about its leadership after its June setback. The PCI was not that kind of party. Its goal was clear, its leader was anointed by Moscow, its organization, especially in the Centre-North, was capillary, its victory was believed by its members to be historically ordained. It just had to intensify its tactics.

The PCI had done this by following a populist strategy. Populism is often associated with the political right, even the extreme right, but left-wing parties can be populist, too. Populist rhetoric juxtaposes elites (unscrupulous, self-serving) and the people (pure, deserving) in its political message. In the months after the formation of De Gasperi's second government, with Togliatti freed of ministerial responsibilities, the PCI did just this. On the one hand, it took the side of the workers whenever they rebelled against social conditions and for better wages. On the other hand, it depicted Italy's woes as essentially the responsibility of the capitalist, landowning classes: of corrupt, venal elites.

Vie nuove was an important addition to the PCI's propaganda effort for this reason. It was intended as an instrument of political education whose core task was to underline the centrality of class struggle in simple (indeed caricatural) terms and to explain the issues of the day in language that the mass membership of the party could grasp. Capitalists and landowners were parodied in cartoons: invariably, they were fat, smug, and often had a blonde hanging on their arm, wearing a mink stole. They lived off the labour of the *operai* and worked hand in glove with the Church and with thugs with stubbly jowls willing to do their dirty work. Workers, by contrast, wore patched trousers and flat caps and were depicted looking courageous and/or exhausted. Articles, apart from one on the front page by a prominent member of the party steering committee (Togliatti, Emilio Sereni, Luigi Longo, Pietro Secchia and Umberto Terracini all wrote such articles for the earliest editions), were short, pithy, and emphasized working-class grievances: inflation, unemployment, landlessness. As the first edition of *Vie nuove* asserted powerfully, 'the Republic is defended, not by arguments, but by giving work, land, and bread to those who haven't got any'.[47]

In adopting this populist approach, the PCI was being astute. It was common sense to stress the policies that most directly concerned the party's membership and could mobilize political action at the grassroots. At the end of September 1946, the PCI had 2,068,000 members, organized in ninety-one provincial federations, more than 8,500 sections, and nearly 36,000 cells.[48] Some 53 per cent of party members were *operai* (industrial workers); 11.9 per cent were *braccianti* (farm labourers). 'Sharecroppers' (*mezzadri, fittavoli*) amounted to 16 per cent of party members. Peasants and artisans comprised some 8 per cent. Office workers accounted for less than 4 per cent; intellectuals (0.8 per cent), and students (0.6 per cent) contributed minuscule numbers. More than 200,000 *casalinghe* (housewives) possessed a party card.[49] Ninety per cent or more of the party membership were thus workers by hand rather than brain, to use the patronizing expression common at the time. The PCI was a party of proletarians, though it was led by intellectuals steeped in the intricacies of Marxist theory, who could read, in *Rinascita*, the execrable poetry of a French communist writer, Louis Aragon, and who thrilled to the 'battle of ideas' in that paper's literary section and to the excommunications that took place there.[50] It accordingly made sense to recast Marxist social analysis as a morality play of goodies versus baddies. The baddies, in truth, often had very murky pasts.

An excellent example of the PCI's propaganda in this period is the pamphlet *No alla fame!* (*No to Hunger!*). Published sometime in the winter of 1946–7, this was propaganda for the masses as Togliatti liked it: full of striking images and punchy slogans. Jargon was kept to a minimum. The back page consisted of a photograph of a worker who had frozen to death while sleeping rough in Milan. The front page was a graphic masterpiece. The foreground was dominated by a suicide hanging from a rope called 'De Gasperi government', while in the background faceless workers marched in unison carrying red flags with the hammer-and-sickle emblem.

The text of the pamphlet hammered home the party's 'new direction' in economic policy, in openly populist tones (the capital letters were bright red in the original):

> It would be enough for the government to tax, according to the same inflexible criteria with which it punishes the artisans and small shop-owners, every member of the 60 families who have the Italian economy in their grasp, TO FIND THE MONEY THAT IS NECESSARY TO SAVE MILLIONS OF MEN, WOMEN, AND CHILDREN FROM HUNGER.[51]

The device of blaming the 'sixty families', or the idle, parasitical rich, for stealing bread from the mouths of the good Italian people, was excellent propaganda. It contained an undeniable element of truth, and yet at the same time it enabled the PCI to evade its share of responsibility, as a member of the government, for the hardship being inflicted on the Italian people.

On 25 October 1946, the eve of the local elections, the PCI and the PSIUP renewed their 'Pact of Unity of Action', with the agreement of all the factions within the PSIUP, including the minority headed by Giuseppe Saragat. The two parties' common programme accentuated

the thrust of the PCI's 'new course' in economic policy by demanding the implementation of concrete measures to improve democracy
in the workplace, the 'wholesale development' (*sviluppo organico*) of
a planned economy, and measures to guarantee the workers' 'human
dignity' via sweeping social legislation to be financed by taxes on
the rich.

The PCI believed that the rich could well afford it: 'Only the poor
pay taxes', proclaimed *Vie nuove* on the eve of the local elections, in
an article imaginatively illustrated by a cartoon of an industrial
worker and an office clerk carrying a huge steel girder, symbolizing
their tax burdens, on their shoulders.[52] The idea of a wealth tax found
an audience within the DC, too, but the Pact of Unity's programme
was in the last analysis incompatible with the long-term continuation
of the De Gasperi government. As De Gasperi himself said, in a set-
piece speech at Rome's Brancaccio Theatre, the 'Marxist bloc' was
proposing policies that were 'fatally destined' to lead to 'collectivism'.
Collectivism, De Gasperi warned, led ineluctably to dictatorship and
hence to the 'negation of democracy', an outcome that he had no
choice but to combat.[53]

The local elections, held in many big cities in November 1946, were
the first test of the Pact of Unity's programme. The PCI and PSIUP
fought many cities in a united 'People's Bloc', occasionally in conjunction with the tiny PdA. The DC, meanwhile, suffered a collapse in
support, as the citizens of the South blew a loud raspberry at the
beleaguered figure of De Gasperi.[54]

The November 1946 elections were a dual populist victory. Industrial cities such as Genoa, Turin, and, in the South, Taranto, voted by
substantial margins for the 'People's Bloc'. The other big winner was
L'Uomo Qualunque (UQ), which built upon its success, in June, in the
less salubrious quarters of Rome and Naples. The 'Common Man', to
give UQ an approximate English translation, played shamelessly on
lower middle-class fears that the PCI–PSIUP alliance was planning to
expropriate their hard-earned property. Many of its voters were
former fascists.

The DC was manoeuvred into the uncomfortable position of
being the party of harsh choices. It came third or worse behind
UQ and the 'People's Bloc' across the South; in Naples, where the

left-wing parties won ahead of UQ, De Gasperi's party finished a dismal fifth, behind even the Liberals and Monarchists. It received only a third as many votes (28,650 to 89,850) as on 2 June. UQ was the biggest party in Palermo. The DC was thumped in Rome, where, compared to 2 June, its vote more than halved, and where the 'People's Bloc' obtained 37 per cent of the votes cast. UQ shaded the DC by 2,000 votes for second place, with both parties getting approximately 20 per cent. Perhaps most significant of all, turnout plummeted compared to both the spring local elections and the 2 June poll. Only 65 per cent of the electorate went to the ballot box. Disenchantment with the democratic process was already starting to spread.[55]

The newly enfranchised electorate was signalling that conditions of life had to improve fast. The parallel with the turbulent years after the First World War was apparent to everybody. Italy in November 1946 was not a consolidated democracy with a tradition of political moderation and unwritten rules of fair play in governance. It did not even have written rules – work on the constitution was only in the preliminary stages. For this reason, despite the DC's thrashing at the polls, De Gasperi rebuffed overtures from UQ to make an anti-communist pact.[56] The premier refused to go down the road of cooperation with the anti-party populist right, just because he had lost an election. Democracy would never be consolidated if it deteriorated into squalid deals with undemocratic forces. The memory of 1921 loomed large: De Gasperi did not want to imitate Giovanni Giolitti by including UQ in a national bloc against Bolshevism.

In the meantime, Togliatti could proudly report to Moscow that the party had made huge gains even in towns that had previously been 'citadels' of reaction.[57] The PCI superseded the PSIUP as the largest party on the left. This fact inevitably reopened the question of the relationship between the two left-wing parties: if the PSIUP was being eclipsed by the PCI, perhaps it should merge with it? The PSIUP scheduled an extraordinary congress to discuss the issue of relations with the PCI in January 1947. The motion proposed by the party's 'fusionists', as well as recommending enhanced cooperation with the PCI, asserted that there was an 'imperative necessity' for greater party discipline that would 'render impossible' the 'displays of flagrant egoism' that had 'poisoned the life of the party' since the Florence congress in April 1946. 'Permanent factions' should be banned, the motion averred.[58] These strictures were designed to paint Saragat's faction into a corner, and perhaps even drive him out of the party, although Pietro Nenni disputed this interpretation well into old age.[59]

A STILL DIVIDED NATION

The year 1946 ended with a final blow for the Italian people, and for the De Gasperi government. The peace treaty was agreed at a plenary meeting in New York in December, and the full scale of the sacrifices imposed on Italy became clear. Its army, navy, and air force were reduced in size and banned from possessing capital ships, submarines, and bombers. It was allowed (Article 54) to possess only 200 tanks. Its borders were to be demilitarized, as were the island of Pantelleria, off the shore of Libya, some small islands off the Yugoslav shore and, *carabinieri* barracks excepted, Sicily and Sardinia. Over seven years, Italy was to pay reparations to the Soviet Union ($100 million), Albania ($5 million), Ethiopia ($25 million), Greece ($105 million), and Yugoslavia ($125 million): colossal sums for a bankrupt nation that was begging for hard currency to buy wheat and coal for its own citizens. It was to renounce all title over the territories of Libya, Eritrea, and Italian Somaliland, although they were to remain under Italian administration until their future had been ascertained.

Italy's borders were redrawn. France obtained some 770 square kilometres in the north-west, along with the villages of Brig and Tenda.[60] Yugoslavia absorbed over 8,000 square kilometres, and more than 400,000 ethnic Italians, in the north-east. Greece regained the Dodecanese islands, notably Rhodes and Kos. Within a year of the treaty entering into force, Italians living in ceded territories were entitled to opt for Italian citizenship (Article 19), but the nations that had benefited from the cession of Italian territory were entitled to demand that such individuals should leave their territory within a year. Italians opting to remain were to be guaranteed their fundamental human rights.

In the case of Stalinist Yugoslavia, Italians knew that such promises were unlikely to be respected. An exodus of Italians from

Dalmatia and Istria had already begun by December 1946. Pola's Italian community had voted overwhelmingly in July 1946 to leave Yugoslavia should the territory be ceded to Belgrade. In December, some 30,000 packed their bags and departed. The city was left half-empty. Still more Istrians would leave the ceded territories once the Treaty of Peace had been signed on 10 February 1947. They were by no means all Italian mother-tongue speakers: many Croats and Slovenes who feared for their futures under Tito's rule left with them.

Above all, Trieste was to become a 'Free Territory'. In the interim, it was to be divided into two zones: Zone A was the city itself and its suburbs; Zone B was composed of Trieste's provincial hinterland. In the city, an Allied military government was in control; in Zone B, Yugoslavia was. The 'Free Territory', which was supposed to have an elected assembly that would nominate a civil governor, was never actually formally established because the British and Americans feared, with some justice, that its institutions would be dominated by communists. As a result, the city remained under Allied military rule until 1954. A symbol of Italian unity, the loss of territorial sovereignty over Trieste was perceived in much the same way as Germans greeted the loss of Danzig in 1919. It was a huge psychological blow for patriots, of whatever party. For partisans of the Risorgimento, especially Benedetto Croce, for whom the creation of Italy was the greatest glory of the nineteenth century, the Treaty of Peace was an amputation whose scars would never heal: a limb had been lopped off, disfiguring the nation. The following summer, Croce cast a symbolic vote against ratification of the treaty.

In the long run, Italian democracy would benefit from the harsh peace inflicted upon it between July and December 1946. Italy – unlike France, the United Kingdom, Belgium, or Portugal – was compelled to accept its own insignificance in the post-war world order as a poor, medium-sized Mediterranean state, and to relinquish century-long dreams of cutting a bold figure on the world stage. Rather like West Germany, henceforth Italy concentrated its efforts in the sphere of foreign policy on the building of inter-governmental European institutions of economic cooperation. The Treaty of Peace, in short, served a useful humbling function. This exercise in hindsight would not, however, have consoled the peasants of Istria loading their worldly belongings onto a cart.

By December 1946, the euphoria that had caused millions of people to celebrate the advent of the Republic in the streets and squares had dissipated. The harsh reality that Italy was a poor country, with no natural resources, little money, and few friends, was sinking in. It was also a flagrantly unjust country. The social structure of the nation still resembled a wine decanter with a wide base and a tapering neck. The rural masses remained mired in grinding poverty and ignorance; the urban masses, whose labour drove the machine of production, were increasingly aware of their collective social power, but were exhausted by decades of thankless toil.

The PCI, with the still untarnished allure of the Soviet Union on its side, appealed to the masses' resentment of Italy's social and economic stagnation. At the end of 1946, Italy was in a fluid state, politically, and large parts of the PCI's programme, above all land distribution, struck a chord with millions of voters, some of whom were untraditional, even improbable, supporters of a communist party. The PCI–PSIUP alliance could unite the underprivileged in a campaign *for* a progressive democracy and *against* the upper classes, who – the two parties could plausibly contend – had brought calamity upon the common people. 'Liberal and democratic Italy was never really either liberal or democratic but rather was pregnant – to the point of bursting – with Fascism,' sneered one leading PCI intellectual, savagely.[61]

The left-wing parties accordingly offered hope in a country where hope was in short supply, by pointing the finger of blame at a class of people who were hardly innocent and offering an alternative model – state socialism – that seemed to be successful. Italian sharecroppers or factory hands, huddled in overcrowded, cold, ill-lit rooms, feeding their children polenta and beans, were less worried than De Gasperi about the threat that collectivism theoretically posed for democracy. They would take fairness over freedom if that was the choice. As E. H. Carr, a British scholar of international relations, argued at the time, the world was entering into a phase in which the test of a regime's claim to sovereign authority would be its success in providing welfare to its people. Carr thought the Soviet Union would meet that test better than any other – that it had the future on its side – and would act as a pole of attraction for the masses of Europe.[62] Millions of Italians far less sophisticated than he were moving towards the same conclusion on the basis of their lived experience.

From the perspective of the Vatican, the advance of the two left-wing parties in the autumn of 1946 represented a potential catastrophe. Pius XI had preferred Mussolini, despite the regime's blatant idolatry, to Italian liberalism, let alone socialism. The Church's integral place in Italian society had been recognized by a supposedly totalitarian state with a readiness that the state constructed after the Risorgimento had never displayed. The Lateran Pacts had been a great gain. Pius XII now faced the horrifying prospect of Togliatti and Nenni shaping the constitution and potentially winning a general election in the New Year. The religious question, which had always bubbled fitfully beneath the surface of Italian political life, seemed ready to spill over. Anticlericals, rubbing their hands with glee, considered that the Lateran Pacts had been 'negotiated between a Pope and a dictator and had been approved by a parliament that represented nobody and was not entitled to discuss seriously about anything'. Therefore, they were 'politically a dead letter'.[63] In a homily to the faithful on 22 December 1946, Pius sounded the alarm, telling the Romans that their native city was now the 'theatre' of 'incessant efforts' to 'rekindle' strife 'for Christ or against Christ, for His Church or against His Church'. He urged the Romans to wake from their lethargy and to 'act with vigour'.[64]

As 1946 concluded, the traditional social order seemed to be at risk, at any rate to religious conservatives and the wealthy (and to increasingly perturbed Italy watchers in the United States). It did not seem possible for Italy to revive its economic fortunes without collectivism – to use De Gasperi's word – but collectivism was not compatible with religious values, or so most Catholics believed. In fact, the political mood was less dire than it appeared. One distinguished Italian historian even described the political scene as 'comforting', at any rate by comparison with the tumult of previous pivotal moments in Italian history. The post-war transition, he believed, illustrated the 'high degree of civility, meekness, and Christian spirit of our people'.[65] This may be too charitable, but it is true that the Catholic community contained political thinkers who saw the Constituent Assembly as being an opportunity to bridge the gulf between the Church and socialism, in all its forms. The most important of these, a distinguished jurist (and lay monk) from Reggio Emilia called Giuseppe Dossetti, believed that the DC should strive to achieve a new type of civilization based on greater political, economic, and moral equality. Dossetti, who had chaired the CLN of his native city and had fought alongside the communists in the mountains as a 'partisan without a gun', was the voice of the more open-minded clergymen of Italy's North. In September 1946, he was among the founders of a Catholic ginger group called *Civitas Humana*, which was pledged to working for a radical renewal of Italian society.[66] The New Year would show that the parties of the left were also conscious that a constitutional democracy based upon progressive values should be respectful of civil rights, and acknowledge the unique place occupied by the Church in Italy's spiritual life and society.

Last, but not least, developments in international affairs would also revive the DC and enable it to meet the challenge from the PCI. In 1947, the onset of the Cold War meant that domestic Italian politics became a matter of tremendous concern to both the superpowers. De Gasperi would throw in his lot unequivocally with the Americans. The PCI's singular lack of independence from the shifts and geopolitical manoeuvres of Moscow would also become painfully clear. The social and political polarization of December 1946 had become an overt ideological divide by the end of 1947. But Italy's leaders had nevertheless worked together to draft a progressive constitution that bridged the divide.

PART TWO

Renewal

7

Hinge Year

In 2005, Giulio Andreotti published his 1947 diary.[1] Although a senator
for life of the Republic, Andreotti was for many the personification of
Italian democracy's malaise. Only the year before, in 2004, he had
been acquitted in high-profile criminal proceedings. His hunched
figure (one of his nicknames was 'il gobbo', the hunchback), bat ears,
and large, heavy-rimmed glasses made him an irresistible figure for
Italy's unforgiving cartoonists.

At the start of 1947, Andreotti was De Gasperi's newly married,
twenty-eight-year-old adjutant and the national secretary of the DC's
youth movement. He wrote subtle articles for *Il Popolo* and other DC
publications. He had been elected to the Constituent Assembly with
over 25,000 preference votes and at De Gasperi's insistence had become
secretary of the parliamentary group, acting as liaison between the
DC's legislators and the leader. Contemporary wits slyly remarked that
when he and De Gasperi went to church together, Andreotti spoke to
the priest while De Gasperi spoke to God.[2]

Andreotti subtitled his diary a 'year of great turning points'. Italian
politics was defined for decades to come by the stances taken in 1947
by the two superpowers, and by the realignment of the political parties
within Italy that ensued. The onset of the Cold War was decisive in
terminating the fraught but genuine commitment of the three popular
parties to cooperate in government with each other and to find mutual
compromises. In 1947, Italian politics became polarized in two camps:
Christian Democracy aligned with the United States; the PCI, obviously, sided with Moscow and Stalinism. The Resistance coalition that
had fought the Germans and defeated the monarchy was not strong
enough to withstand a conflict between America and the Proletariat.

Yet the great irony of 1947 was that the three parties managed, despite the ideological strains that divided them, to hammer out a constitutional settlement that has endured to the present day. The Italian constitution laboriously agreed by the Constituent Assembly in the course of 1947 is one of the great documents of post-war democratization in Europe. Astonishingly progressive by the standards of pre-fascist Italian liberalism, it safeguarded the Church from the State, and secular liberties from encroachment by the Church. It established an institutional structure that made any future Duce (or Commissar) impossible, so long as the three major parties were content to work within the confines of the fundamental principles of the constitution and were prepared to accept their potential nemeses as legitimate political actors.

MR DE GASPERI GOES TO WASHINGTON

The DC's poor showing in the November 1946 local elections underlined the precariousness of De Gasperi's government to Washington. Unless living conditions improved fast, then the likelihood was that public opinion would shift decisively leftwards.

Inside the Truman administration, official opinion saw De Gasperi as the best hope of keeping Italy out of the grasp of the PCI. His dignified speech to the peace conference in August 1946 had raised his profile. James Byrnes, the Secretary of State, was among De Gasperi's admirers, although Byrnes' relationship with President Harry S. Truman had deteriorated by the end of 1946 and he was on the point of resignation. Italian American groups – a big constituency – were vocal in their support for their home country in its moment of travail. The Italian ambassador to Washington, Alberto Tarchiani, who had served briefly as minister of education under Badoglio, had spent most of the dictatorship in exile in the United States. An anti-fascist journalist, he had numerous contacts in political circles, and he used them assiduously to press Italy's case. Tarchiani, an 'able deus ex machina', was conducting what amounted to an independent foreign policy by the end of 1946.[3]

Still, many Americans were wary of involvement in Europe. In November 1946, there were mid-term elections in the United States that resulted in a swing to the Republicans, whose leader in the Senate, Robert Taft, was an isolationist. Policymakers wanting to fund Italy, or other European countries in the same boat, now had to contend with Congressional opposition. America was rich, it possessed the atomic bomb, its economic prowess had been enhanced, not destroyed, by the war. Europe's troubles still seemed far away and anti-communism had not yet become a crusade.

The Southern Europe desk of the State Department, prompted by Tarchiani, nevertheless persuaded the administration to shore up De Gasperi. Walter 'Red' Dowling, the staffer dealing with Italy, was convinced that the United States had to be generous. Italy, he wrote in November 1946, needed a 'judicious mixture of flattery, moral encouragement, and considerable material aid'. He added:

> This policy would of course require a sustained program for a considerable period. It would not be a one-shot cure, but should consist of a kind word, a loaf of bread, a public tribute to Italian civilization, then another kind word, and so on, with an occasional plug from the sponsors advertising the virtues of democracy American style. Naturally it would not be anti-communist, nor would it need to be, just pro-Italian. Also, it would cost a lot of money and mean a lot of bother, but if I know anything about Italians, it would pay off handsomely.[4]

This was patronizing, but excellent psychology. It was astute of Dowling to grasp that pride in the glories of Italian civilization could be nurtured to bolster the Italians' commitment to democracy. Dowling advocated inviting De Gasperi to the United States for an official visit and committing the American government to granting Italy, with the maximum of publicity, a package of relief aid. The alternative, he contended, was a government crisis and a PCI triumph by the spring.

Dowling's reasoning convinced his superiors of the need to make De Gasperi better known in the American foreign-policy circles. This new consensus 'paved the way' for an invitation by Henry Luce, the proprietor of the Time Life newspaper empire, to De Gasperi to address the 'Cleveland Forum', a forthcoming conference on world affairs.[5] Several prominent US leaders would participate, including Arthur Vandenberg, the Republican chairman of the Senate's foreign-relations sub-committee and a possible presidential candidate. Tarchiani and the State Department organized a punishing programme of speeches, meetings, lunches, and gala dinners with the political elite and with the Italian communities of several of America's largest cities. Tarchiani also drew up a detailed document on Italy's emergency needs: wheat shipments and a $100 million credit from the Import–Export Bank (the official credit agency of the United States) were at the top of the list, along with a request for a $200 million gift to replace the funds contributed by UNRRA.

The official announcement of the visit was made on 21 December 1946. It would begin on 3 January 1947 and De Gasperi would arrive in Washington DC on 5 January. He would stay until 15 January, arriving back in Italy two days later. De Gasperi was pessimistic about the outcome. On the eve of his departure, he told Andreotti that 'only the saints' could make the voyage a success.[6] The American visit nevertheless injected optimism into public opinion. De Gasperi was seen off by a guard of honour and a cheering crowd, while President De Nicola made an unheralded trip to Ciampino Airport to shake the prime minister's hand before his departure.[7] The only sour note was sounded by the PCI, which grumbled that De Gasperi should not 'sell our independence for a plate of lentils'.[8]

De Gasperi was accompanied by a minuscule retinue. The Italian delegation was composed of the director general of the Bank of Italy, Donato Menichella, the head of the Bank's foreign-exchange division, Guido Carli, and the minister for foreign trade, Pietro Campilli, along with the director general of the Foreign Ministry and De Gasperi's private secretary for foreign affairs. De Gasperi's twenty-three-year-old daughter, Maria Romana, kept him company. The outward journey was marred by frightening turbulence, and the plane was twice forced to land in the Azores. De Gasperi maliciously told his daughter, as the plane was buffeted by a storm, that he was worried for the safety of the corpulent Menichella, who had been unable to fasten the buckle on his parachute when they had practised before the flight.[9]

The saints were obviously watching over the Italian statesman because he not only survived the flight but enjoyed a personal triumph with American public opinion. This was even though the visit began under troubled circumstances. On the very day the Italian party arrived, Senator Taft called for foreign aid to be limited to 'reasonable assistance' only, rather than 'huge loans'. [10] De Gasperi had arrived in Washington at the start of a wrangle over the administration's budget proposals, which the Republicans wanted to slash. The Italian leader was given only a low-key greeting at the airport and did not see Secretary of State Byrnes until midday on 6 January. Byrnes, moreover, seemed 'preoccupied' at their meeting and evaded substantive issues. [11] A bemused De Gasperi told Tarchiani that the Americans had surely not invited him over for such an interview: there had to be 'some other factor' at work. [12] This factor became clear the following day when Byrnes's resignation was announced.

The visit soon picked up steam. De Gasperi met a cordial Harry Truman on 7 January and held talks with Dean Acheson and the portentous Senator Taft, who lectured the Italian delegation on the ideological orientation of Italy's government, which must have tried even De Gasperi's patience. He then left his aides behind in Washington to iron out the details of the economic assistance package. He himself visited Chicago, Cleveland, where he addressed the Time Life conference on the subject of 'What the World Expects from America' on 10 January, and New York. He returned to Washington DC on 14 January. It was, or so he told listeners at home in a radio talk squeezed into his schedule on 13 January, a visit conducted at 'dizzying' pace. Crowds of Italian Americans greeted him wherever he went and, although De Gasperi always spoke some of the time in English, 'whenever our maternal tongue issued from my lips, it was as if there was a rush of blood to the head and the crowds gave way to a deeply moving, nostalgic show of support for Italy'. [13]

The Italian premier met not only Italian Americans, but 'countless' Americans of all ethnic backgrounds. [14] De Gasperi was fêted in Chicago and New York by the Irish American political establishment, and twice encountered Senator Vandenberg. The eminent columnist Walter Lippmann advocated a policy of generosity for

Broadway parade: New York welcomes the
Prime Minister of Italy, January 1947.

Italy in the *Herald Tribune*, as did the influential *Saturday Evening Post*.[15] De Gasperi was even given a parade down Broadway. His progress around the country was a reminder that Catholic voters in the United States were sympathetic to the plight of Italy's fledgling democracy.

De Gasperi's Cleveland speech was the set-piece address of the tour. It was a simple description of Italy's economic plight, and a dignified plea for American aid. It evoked the moral responsibility of the world's rich to help the poor to rebuild their lives, praised the 'mighty spirits' who had founded the United States and bequeathed it a lasting constitution, and, more subtly, lauded the quest for social justice that had underpinned Roosevelt's New Deal. De Gasperi emphasized that he did not doubt the United States would begin to 'pull its weight' in the world. He had 'faith' both in the 'international role' of the United States but also – and this was a telling phrase – in 'the America in us'. The implication was that resolute action by the United States might liberate the free, democratic spirit of the Italians (and of other European peoples). De Gasperi's peroration was 'May God Almighty bless and guide these nations [the ones facing the challenges of the postwar world] as it once blessed and guided your country.'[16]

The speech pressed every American button imaginable. In a radio broadcast after the speech concluded, Clare Booth Luce, Henry Luce's wife and a future US ambassador to Rome, immediately enquired about the strength of Italian communism. De Gasperi responded diplomatically, but throughout the tour the role of the pro-Soviet left in Italy had been a frequent topic, and he 'had not missed the opportunity to underline' that there was an 'incipient and perilous' communist threat. He needed American aid to stave off the growing power of the PCI and frankly told the Americans so.[17]

Nevertheless, it would be wrong to read the Cleveland speech, especially the comment about the 'America in us', as a rhetorical ploy for a susceptible audience. De Gasperi was impressed during his visit by American political culture, especially the willingness of politicians to invoke God. On his first days in the United States, he visited the Jefferson Memorial, George Washington's house at Mount Vernon, and the Lincoln Memorial. He was particularly moved by the Christian charity of Lincoln's second inaugural speech, 'with malice towards none . . . ', which is inscribed in full on the Memorial's walls. De Gasperi commented thoughtfully:

These men did not share the reluctance of so many Europeans to call upon their Maker. This people are not afraid, as so often happens with us, to evoke the Divine Being. Perhaps this is the secret of the enduring blend of pragmatism and idealism that dominates American life and that we struggle to comprehend.[18]

The visitors' book at Mount Vernon:
Ambassador Tarchiani looks on as De Gasperi signs.

De Gasperi returned from the United States on 17 January bearing a credit for \$100 million from the Import–Export Bank, plus other financial concessions. This did not solve Italy's economic problems, but he had avoided the ignominy of coming home with, as Italians say, 'a fistful of flies'. His entire cabinet, including the PCI's ministers, assembled at Ciampino Airport, south of Rome, to greet him, although the PCI's propagandists depicted the returning premier as an oriental merchant, selling the pure beauty of the Republic to lascivious foreigners.[19]

The principal outcomes of De Gasperi's American visit, however, were political, not pecuniary. At what would turn out to be a critical juncture, on the eve of the onset of the Cold War, 'the American democracy had recognized the Italian democracy'.[20] It had done so, moreover, in the *person* of De Gasperi. Henceforth, he was equated with democracy in the eyes of the American government and public opinion.

SOCIALIST SCHISM

De Gasperi's return from Washington coincided with dramatic developments in domestic politics. On 9 January, the extraordinary Congress of the PSIUP began in the Aula Magna of La Sapienza University in Rome. By the time the premier reached home on 17 January, the PSIUP – the second-largest party in the Constituent Assembly – had split. The simmering debate between those favouring closer cooperation, or even fusion, with the PCI and those, like Giuseppe Saragat, who regarded communism as a totalitarian form of socialism, boiled over irretrievably.

On the Congress's second day, the party's reformists strode to the podium and standing in front of the party's emblem – a hammer and sickle superimposed on an open book with a rising sun in the background – defended the party's autonomy. A speech by an icon of the early history of Italian socialism, Angelica Balabanoff (Anzhelika Isaakovna Balabanova), a Russian-Jewish woman by origin, caused 'pandemonium' to erupt.[21] Balabanoff had been an important figure in the international socialist movement and a prominent member of the maximalist wing of the PSI.[22] Fascism had condemned her to a life of exile since 1922, most recently in the United States, from which she had returned to attend the Congress. The seventy-year-old Balabanoff was greeted by an ovation when she rose to speak, but her outspokenness about the Soviet Union, and her pointed criticism of Nenni, roused delegates against her. At 10.30 on 11 January, a 'pale, tight-lipped' Saragat took to the podium to announce his decision to leave the party. At an impromptu gathering in Rome's Palazzo Barberini on 12 January, Saragat was elected leader of a new Italian Socialist Workers' Party (PSLI). The PSIUP, meanwhile, reverted to the party's traditional name and once more became the PSI.

The split led to mutual condemnation. Saragat's vision of socialism, *Avanti!* commented disdainfully, ignored the centrality of class forces. 'Liberty, democracy, dignity, and human personality' were mere words, the paper commented, if they were detached from the priority of obtaining 'social justice' for the working class.[23] Saragat argued, by contrast, that 'democrats' (in ironic inverted commas) like Lelio Basso, the new secretary general of the PSI, 'liquidate liberty in the illusion of achieving socialism, while we intend to construct socialism to ensure liberty'.[24] The PSLI nevertheless continued to characterize itself as a Marxist party.[25]

Lelio Basso was a stocky intellectual in his mid-forties from Genoa, of bourgeois origins, who sported a Lenin-like goatee beard. He had gone to *liceo*, had studied political philosophy and law at university, and had been a prolific contributor to the underground press. A courageous man, who had risked his life daily as a pamphleteer in Nazi-occupied Milan and twice served time in Fascist jails, he was nevertheless the epitome of the university-trained intellectual, not a man of the people.[26] He and the self-taught orphan Nenni now dominated the PSI. Both men were betting that the PCI's sectarianism – which they did not dispute – would be attenuated by cooperation with the PSI. In his concluding speech to the Congress, Nenni insisted that the PSI need not collaborate with the PCI 'from inferiority', but as partners striving to find 'the synthesis of our and their fundamental needs via a political strategy that is simultaneously one of political liberty, of national independence, and the bold transformation of class relations'.[27]

In hindsight, this assumption of parity with the PCI was naïve. Giuseppe Romita, who nevertheless stayed in the PSI in February 1947, wrote retrospectively that 'Nenni didn't grasp that we had to detach ourselves from the PCI.' In Romita's judgement, the PCI had ceased after the referendum on the monarchy to be a party of the CLN and had become one 'closely tied' to Soviet policy that was 'striving for hegemony'. The PSI, in this context, were 'competitors, not allies' of the PCI, 'satellites' to be 'used or consumed' according to political need.[28]

Romita's retrospective analysis was spot on: hindsight is always easier. The PCI's leadership privately welcomed the schism as an opportunity for the PCI to consolidate its growing hegemony on the left at the expense of the reborn PSI. The party's steering committee agreed that if the PSLI were to emerge as the stronger of the two socialist parties, it would be necessary to fuse with the PSI and 'push Saragat's party to the right'. In the meantime, PSI members were to be allowed to join the PCI, even if they retained their PSI party cards. The objective, obviously, was to convert such individuals into proselytizers for the PCI's positions within the PSI.[29]

GROWING PAINS

The ructions within the PSI made a cabinet reshuffle inevitable.[30] De Gasperi was presented with a dilemma. Should he persevere with the 'tripartite' formula and continue in government with the PSI and the PCI? Or should he try to form a coalition with Saragat's reformists, the PRI, and the PLI, perhaps even with external support in the Constituent Assembly from UQ?[31] Or try to find a middle way?

De Gasperi blandly called the crisis a case of 'growing pains' at a 20 January press conference he called before going to see President De Nicola. He insisted that all parties in the government had to show 'sincere commitment' to its policies, or the government would neither be efficient nor 'enjoy domestic or foreign confidence'.[32]

It remains unclear whether De Gasperi ever thought seriously about governing without the PCI and PSI, but the question was moot in any case since both the PRI and the PSLI declined to join the government. After the usual skirmishes, De Gasperi formed a smaller cabinet, with fifteen ministers instead of twenty-one. Compared to its predecessor, it tilted away from the left. Both the DC and the two Marxist parties were allotted six cabinet places, but the DC took the Ministry of the Interior (Scelba) and a new combined Finance-Treasury Ministry, which went to Pietro Campilli, De Gasperi's *compagno di viaggio* to the United States. Mauro Scoccimarro was removed as finance minister and, in general, the PCI and PSI were given second-tier positions. Nenni was replaced as foreign minister by Carlo Sforza, a name that caused hearts to sink in London, but who was better regarded in Washington DC. Togliatti did not obstruct the choice of Sforza: he had already informed the Soviet ambassador to Rome, Mikhail Kostylev, that Sforza was 'a stupid and unstable man, but no reactionary, who is loyal to the left and can be influenced'.[33]

The new government took the oath of office on 3 February 1947. On 6 February, Saragat stepped down as President of the Constituent Assembly. He was replaced by Umberto Terracini: the PCI insisted that this position belonged to a communist since it was now the second-biggest party in the Constituent Assembly. Nearly thirty of the

PSI's 115 deputies in the Constituent Assembly had adhered to the PSLI at Palazzo Barberini, and others joined them subsequently.

The PCI was oddly complacent about the composition of the new government, with its kernel of hard-nosed, able DC ministers. At the height of the crisis, Togliatti had published an admonitory leading article in *l'Unità* that attacked De Gasperi personally for concentrating too much power in his own hands. The DC, the PCI leader warned, needed to 'share with others' the responsibilities of government rather more than hitherto. In a striking metaphor, Togliatti stated that the PCI was not in government to be a 'tambourine', while the DC acted as the 'drum'. Nobody should think the PCI would play a merely 'decorative' role. If the DC gave up its pretensions to hegemony, the PCI would provide a 'worthwhile contribution to the reconstruction of Italy and the consolidation of the Republic'.[34]

De Gasperi responded in a statesmanlike way, by meeting with Togliatti at once and healing the breach. Togliatti complacently concluded that the main lesson of the government crisis was that 'nobody can govern without us'. He assumed that the government would now last until the autumn, when the Constituent Assembly in theory would have concluded its work, and that the new administration would be 'electoral' in character.[35] The fact that the PCI no longer controlled the Finance Ministry did not seem to him to be 'a matter of any great substance'.[36] Not for the first time (nor the last), *il migliore* was underestimating his opponent.

The new government would prove to be, in fact, the last gasp of the CLN coalition. The circumstances of post-war life were making the unnatural alliance between Marxists and Catholics (and Marxists and reformists) unworkable. Contemporaneously with the formation of De Gasperi's new cabinet, the Polish communists, united in an egregiously misnamed 'Democratic Bloc' with the pro-Moscow wing of the Socialist Party, had used widespread ballot fraud and overt violence against opposing parties to win elections in the European country whose political and social structure was arguably the most akin to Italy's. It was impossible for Catholics and moderates in Italy not to draw parallels. Even the PCI seemed embarrassed. Poland had been hailed as a model in party publications. The electoral triumph of Poland's communists was passed over almost in silence by the PCI press.[37]

The Polish elections were only a prelude to other developments. At the end of February 1947, London dumped the problem of Greece, where the British were aiding a deeply unsavoury regime in Athens to defend itself against a communist insurgency, in America's lap. Cash-strapped Britain could not afford to act as a neo-imperial power in the eastern Mediterranean. On 12 March 1947, President Truman told Congress that the United States would help the Greek and Turkish governments resist the encroachment of 'totalitarian regimes' – the so-called Truman Doctrine. Talks between the 'big three' over the future of Germany collapsed in April 1947 at Moscow. In early May, the Communist Party was excluded from the government in France.

These developments had a direct impact on domestic Italian politics. They made the tripartite coalition untenable. Both the DC and the two parties of the left, to some extent against their will, were compelled to pick sides in the international conflict. Timing matters, however. Counterfactuals are always to be treated with caution, but if the breakdown of the tripartite coalition had occurred in February 1947, then contemporary Italian history would have been very different. Had De Gasperi broken decisively with the PCI and PSI after his return from Washington DC, then the final terms of the peace treaty with the wartime Allies would have been blamed on him alone: the two left-wing parties would have made hay out of public discontent against the harshness of the terms. More important, the three parties would also never have agreed on the core principles of the new Italian Constitution, which they did in the spring of 1947 during De Gasperi's brief government. Had they failed to do that, Italy would have had no safety net when Cold War tensions heightened in the second half of 1947. Had De Gasperi been an impulsive Cold Warrior – and had Togliatti not been committed to consolidating the Republic – then the infant of Italian democracy might have died prematurely.

HISTORIC COMPROMISES

Italy signed the Treaty of Peace with the 'Allied Powers and their Associates' on 10 February 1947, a week after the formation of the government, in the Clock Room of the French Foreign Ministry, the

Quai d'Orsay.[38] To the last, there were some who wanted the Italian government to refuse to sign. The treaty was regarded as a Versailles-style 'diktat': one that had been 'imposed not negotiated'.[39] The government decided that it was its duty to sign, though one important minister, Mario Scelba, came close to resigning over the issue.[40]

The signature was greeted by national mourning. At 11 a.m. sirens sounded, and the nation came to a standstill. Vigils were held at war memorials and other sites of national memory. The Constituent Assembly suspended its work for thirty minutes. On the radio, Sforza stated that Italy's signature demonstrated that the country was willing to suffer for the sins of its former regime if it would 'hasten the creation of an enduring peace in the world', but stated that the 'struggle of the Italian people against Fascism' had been insufficiently recognized by the peacemakers.[41]

The Constituent Assembly was Italy's opportunity to demonstrate that it had turned the page on Fascism. On 1 February, just a week before the signing of the peace treaty, the so-called 'Commission of Seventy-Five', a committee of the Assembly presided over by Meuccio Ruini and drawn from all the parties with seats in the parliamentary hemisphere, had presented a first draft of Italy's new basic law.[42] Even though the Commission was packed with academic jurists, an argumentative sub-set of humanity, the Commission had drafted a compromise text that met certain sensible standards. It was written in a way that was comprehensible – if not to the masses, at any rate to people with some education; it contained clauses guaranteeing social and economic rights, not just legal-political freedoms; and it concentrated upon principles, rather than concerning itself with the detail of how such principles should be enacted. One Sicilian jurist had voiced a preference for a constitution that was 'simple, skeletal, and brief'.[43] Such pleas found a hearing and the draft constitution, while far from being bare bones, did not sprawl and was logical in construction.

Historians have generally concurred that the Commission of 75's work provided a useful starting point, although that did not prevent grandees such as the eighty-six-year-old V. E. Orlando or Benedetto Croce from pillorying its work during the three-day debate between 10 and 12 March 1947 that began the phase of debating and voting, article by article, on the final text. Just as the three Allied powers had presented Italy with a diktat in international affairs, Croce lamented theatrically, so the leaders of the big three parties were presenting the Assembly with a *fait accompli* of their own.[44]

Togliatti, in fact, was openly critical of some aspects of the draft produced by the Commission. He emphasized the need for the constitution to be committed to the achievement of social progress for the working class. Togliatti thought that the constitution might 'illuminate and guide the Italian people for a long period of their history', if the rights of workers were made central to the text.[45]

The Commission of Seventy-Five had proposed that Article 1 should read: 'Italy is a democratic republic. The Italian Republic is based upon labour and the effective participation of all workers in the social, economic, and political organization of the country. Sovereignty derives from the people and is exercised in the forms and within the limits set by the law.' On 22 March 1947, the PCI proposed an amendment insisting that the Article 1 should state 'Italy is a democratic workers' republic.' Moreover, for the PCI, sovereignty should *belong* to the people, not derive from them. The PCI's amendment was only narrowly defeated: by 239 votes to 227. The PSLI and PRI voted with the PCI and the PSI.

This was not just a quibble over words. It was a guarantee that the new Italian state would be progressive, as Togliatti had envisaged at the Brancaccio Theatre in July 1944, not merely liberal, or parliamentary. On the other hand, the PCI's preferred form of words evoked increasingly dictatorial Poland and Hungary to nervous moderates. Rather than stand pat, which would have created a political crisis of the first order, the DC responded creatively. Its leaders in the chamber accepted the second part of the PCI's motion *in toto*. For the first sentence, the DC proposed, simply, 'Italy is a democratic republic founded upon labour.'

The new formulation was approved overwhelmingly. It remains the touchstone phrase of the Italian constitution, as well known to Italians as the first lines of the Bill of Rights are to Americans. To understand why, one must realize that the word labour (*lavoro*) in this context implied not jobs for everybody, though the right to a job would indeed become an aspiration of the constitution, but that the millions of anonymous Italians who worked by the sweat of their brow – *operai* in the windowless factories of Milan and Turin, *casalinghe* rolling pasta by hand in the slums of Rome or Naples, *contadini* tilling the soil, *portuali* unloading grain from America in Genoa's docks, or *mezzadri* ploughing dry soil under the scorching suns of the Mezzogiorno – would, for the first time in the nation's history, have a state that was *theirs*. This principle was as important for progressive Catholics in the DC as it was for the parties of the left. The cross-party approval of Article 1 was a signal that the DC was open to dialogue and collaboration with the Marxist left. There was a basis for cooperation if only the PCI did not exclude themselves by imitating the rhetoric and actions of the people's democracies too slavishly.

The PCI returned the favour when the debate turned, a few days later, to the thorny question of relations between Church and State. It will be remembered that Mussolini had signed the Lateran Pacts with the Church in 1929 and acknowledged the Church's supremacy in spiritual questions and its right to maintain Catholic social and educational associations independent of the state. There were many DC deputies to the Constituent Assembly for whom the Church had acted as a safe haven during the 1930s and some, De Gasperi of course included, who had been protected from discovery and death by the Church during the Nazi occupation. Such individuals did not want the Church's prerogatives to be touched.

Such ideas were, of course, a red rag to anticlerical opinion. The one thing that could unite most members of the PCI, PSI, PRI, PSLI, and even the PLI, was anticlericalism. The DC nevertheless insisted that the Lateran Pacts should be given constitutional status. Its speakers argued *quieta non movere*. The article drafted by the Commission of Seventy-Five succinctly reflected the DC's views in three short clauses. Clause 1 stated that the State and the Catholic Church were each 'independent and sovereign' within their own ambits. Clause 2 said that relations between the two were to be regulated by the Lateran Pacts and that any reform of the pacts would not require the constitution to be reformed. Clause 3 said that other religious faiths were free to organize themselves according to their own rules, provided that these rules did not conflict with the constitution.

Even Nenni recognized the utility of avoiding an outright battle over the respective rights of Church and State. A party that wanted to carry out an agrarian reform and nationalize industry did not 'go looking for butterflies under the Arch of Titus' and did not resuscitate the 'old ghosts' of anticlericalism, he said, elegiacally.[46] At the same time, acquiescing in the second clause meant agreeing, among other distasteful things, to Catholic priests teaching religion in state schools or to divorce remaining the prerogative of the Church. On 25 March 1947, when the Constituent Assembly debated the question, the PSI proposed that the first two clauses should read 'The Catholic Church, within its own ambit, is free and independent. Relations between the State and the Church shall be regulated by mutually agreed terms [*termini concordatari*].' This formula opened the door for a revision of the Lateran Pacts. Other speakers from the lay parties went further: they wanted all Italy's religious confessions to be granted equal religious status. The Catholic Church would have been put on a par with the tiny Protestant or Jewish communities and the Lateran Pacts would have been moot.

De Gasperi made clear that such formulae would not be acceptable to the DC. Speaking on 25 March, he pointed out, first, that 99 per cent of Italy's citizens, in the 1931 census, had defined themselves as Catholic. Jews, Protestants, and declared atheists were negligible in number. In De Gasperi's view, the Republic should respond with 'good faith' to the constructive attitude hitherto displayed by the Church. The Lateran Pacts, he argued, were 'elastic' and open to gradual mutual reform. They reflected 'historical reality' but did not limit the freedoms of any other faith. Suddenly repudiating them would end the current peace over the religious question and would inevitably re-open the question of Rome's status. De Gasperi warned anticlericals: 'you will open a new wound in the flayed body of Italy, and I do not know when it will heal.' The speech, which was a formidable statement of a deep conviction, was greeted with a standing ovation by the DC's parliamentarians.[47]

Togliatti, who followed shortly afterwards in the debate, regretted allusions to the spectre of religious unrest, denied that the DC had a monopoly of the Catholic vote, and criticized the premier for speaking with a partisan voice. Still, he acknowledged that 'we need religious peace, and we can't permit it to be disturbed in any way'.[48] Togliatti had sent an emissary to the DC to give them advance warning of his latest shift of position, but the secret had otherwise been well kept. Many of his own party's deputies did not know, and the PSI had naturally been kept in the dark.[49] Togliatti was ironically congratulated upon his 'conversion' by various socialist and liberal speakers in the rest of the debate, but the PCI voted compactly with the DC. Article 7 of the new constitution reproduced the first two clauses approved by the Commission of Seventy-Five (clause 3 eventually became Article 8) and was approved by 350 votes to 149 at 2 a.m. in the morning of 26 March 1947.

The PCI's discipline prevented the Republic from being split in two on a fundamental question for the identity of Italy's new democracy. It was an act of statesmanship that evoked 'a sense of relief' throughout the country.[50] The rest of the left nevertheless found it indigestible. In his diary, Nenni fumed that Togliatti's move was 'cynicism applied to politics'. Togliatti had acted towards the Church as he had previously acted towards the monarchy in April 1944, with the *svolta di Salerno*. He added shrewdly, 'Togliatti is calculating that he is safeguarding 15 or 20 years of collaboration with the DC. I think this calculation is wrong from A to Z.'[51] He was right: the two parties would not collaborate for even fifteen weeks more. What Nenni did not acknowledge was that Saragat's worst fears about the one-sidedness of the PSI's relationship with the PCI had been confirmed within weeks of the schism in the Socialist Party.

Further evidence that the PCI was counting on long-term cooperation with the DC in the spring of 1947 can be derived from a meeting of the party's steering committee between 16 and 18 April 1947. This three-day summit involved all the top officials of the party debating what the PCI should do if the United States, in the wake of the Truman Doctrine, were to offer Italy soft loans or cash grants. By April, there was a widespread debate on both sides of the Atlantic about the need for a 'New Deal' for Europe months before Secretary of State George C. Marshall made his Harvard speech on 5 June 1947. Everybody knew that a transfusion of American wealth was needed if Europe were to produce more and rebuild without harmful inflation. Europe already was rebuilding extremely quickly, on both sides of the Iron Curtain, but it needed hard currency that only the United States could provide.

During the 16–18 April meeting of its steering committee, the PCI decided that the need for dollars was paramount and that it would support an American loan if one were offered. Luigi Longo presented a document that argued that US loans were necessary for Italy's economic welfare, since they were the only way of purchasing 'raw materials, products and tools that we can't obtain in the domestic market'. He added that the PCI could only gain by not acting as 'an obstacle' to eventual loans, even if they came with conditions attached. Longo further advocated rowing back from the commitment to a programme of state-driven economic reconstruction agreed with the PSI. Nationalizations, while they should be pursued energetically, should only concern firms that had a 'leading role' in the economy, while it was vital to 'unhitch the harness bequeathed by Fascism' and 'give free rein to private enterprise'. Scarce raw materials should be directed towards artisans and small businesses, who were likely to make good use of them and boost economic activity.

Longo contended that such an economic strategy would pay a political dividend. It would appeal to the more progressive elements within the DC who might succeed in imposing a policy of long-term collaboration with the PCI on the party leadership. There would be no 'complete peace', between the two parties, Longo thought, but the struggle between them could be transferred onto 'another plane' whereby the two mass parties competed to convince the electorate whether the 'burden of policy' should on balance favour the wealthy or the popular classes. Longo's speech, in short, was characterized by pragmatism rather than Stalinist dogmatism. Like Lenin in war-torn 1921 Russia, it advocated a New Economic Policy; one that recognized the centrality for the Italian economy of small businesses and craftsmen.

In addition, Longo was suggesting that the policy was a method of consolidating political pluralism.[52] It was the economic complement to the vote on Article 7 of the constitution: it represented a second plank for a platform of cooperation with the DC and with political forces such as the PSLI.

Longo's speech unsurprisingly evoked a mixed reaction. Many of the PCI's top bosses were critical of the thrust of his argument. Togliatti patiently waited until everybody had spoken and then produced a summing-up (twenty-two typed pages long) that laid down the party line. In essence, he backed Longo's position in more sophisticated language: his speech was a masterclass in how Marxist concepts could be used to smooth the edges of a policy with jagged implications for party unity. Togliatti nevertheless made clear that he agreed with the broad shift in economic policy that Longo had suggested. Although he was sceptical that Uncle Sam would write big cheques any time soon, Togliatti had no doubt that the PCI should accept them if he did:

> We must say, as communists, that we want the loans, that we are prepared to participate in any negotiation along with the members of the government to get credits conceded to us.[53]

The public outcome of the debate in the PCI's steering committee was a leading article in *Rinascita* which asked for 'American loans and Italian guarantees'. The article acknowledged that it was reasonable for the 'would-be American creditor' to require guarantees of economic stability as a condition of disbursing money. Italy, however, had the equal right to expect that the Americans would keep their nose out of Italian politics, and would not insist on the Italian government being 'composed in one particular way or another, with this or that party being excluded from membership'.[54]

By the time the article was published, a political crisis, which would end with the exclusion of the PCI and the PSI from the government, had begun. Post-war Italy has endured hundreds of government crises since May 1947: Italians typically treat them in the same way as the Japanese react to earth tremors, namely by getting on with their lives and waiting for them to pass. The May 1947 crisis, however, was an earthquake, not a mere tremor.

ORANGE BLOSSOM OR CHRYSANTHEMUMS

De Gasperi had become increasingly dismayed by what he considered the bad faith of his coalition partners. From his perspective, they claimed to support the government and acquiesced in its policies in the Council of Ministers, but relentlessly depicted him as the man who was starving the people and acting as the tool of reaction. The PCI and PSI, by contrast, regarded De Gasperi as a moaner who couldn't take criticism. De Gasperi, wrote a future president of the Republic, had 'wanted the cooperation of the parties of the left, only to work with them grudgingly and with hostility'. He had agreed programmes of government with the parties of the left, but always with a 'mental note not to put them into practice'.[55] Like Signor Laudisi, the voice of reason in Pirandello's play *Così è se vi pare* (*Right You Are*), one can only resolve this dispute with an ironic laugh.

By April 1947, the economic crisis was sharpening. Inflation was making life impossible for low earners. If one takes 1913 prices as a base, equal to 1, then retail prices for ordinary consumers had been 4.5 in 1938, 11.9 in 1943, 52.8 in 1944, 104 in 1945, 122.7 in 1946, and would arrive at almost 200 by the end of 1947.[56] Prices, in other words, had increased twentyfold during the war and had all but doubled since it ended. Within the government, the PSI was pressing hard for radical measures for a state-directed economy, with public ownership and redistribution of wealth, to boost output and to increase supply in the economy. So far as De Gasperi was concerned, this programme was too socially divisive. On 28 April, De Gasperi, like FDR during his 'fireside chats', spoke directly to the people over the politicians' heads. The premier made an appeal over the radio for the construction of a government of national unity, one that would embrace all the principal economic interests: capital and labour. He argued that such a government was needed if Italians were to regain confidence in their future, and were to persuade foreign lenders to risk their money. The most striking soundbite in the broadcast was 'if we can agree among ourselves, then we won't be alone!'[57]

On the same day, De Gasperi sent, via a 'Vatican intermediary', a private letter to President Truman in which he said, with absolute frankness, that he intended to 'broaden' the composition of the government to ensure a greater 'influence' from those parties that wanted 'the stability and freedom of a democratic regime'. Italy's own strength was insufficient, however: 'we need help', De Gasperi asserted nakedly. He promised Truman that he and his government would 'defend' with 'all the power at their command' the 'principles of our common Christian civilization'.[58]

A letter of this kind, coming just six weeks after the enunciation of the Truman Doctrine, was tantamount to a plea for its extension to Italy. Even though the letter was nominally written in the name and on behalf of his government, it was in reality a signal of personal and party commitment. De Gasperi was coming as close as he decently could to pleading for American intervention in Italian affairs.

The 'social-communists', as De Gasperi called them, divining that the premier wanted to bring the PSLI and Liberal technocrats such as the governor of the Bank of Italy, Luigi Einaudi, into the government, dismissed the suggestion of a broader-based government. When De Gasperi made his broadcast, the PCI and PSI were rejoicing over an important electoral victory. Their joint electoral list had emerged as the largest single force in Sicily in regional elections, with nearly 31 per cent of the vote, 10 per cent more than the DC, which was forced to cobble together a ragbag regional government with the PLI, the UQ, and the Monarchists. The two Marxist parties felt they were in a position of strength. As in January, they reasoned that De Gasperi could not govern without them.

The left's victory celebrations in Sicily were truncated when gunmen opened fire on a communist crowd during May Day celebrations in Portella della Ginestra, a small town near Palermo. Eleven people were killed, twenty-seven wounded. Traditional Sicilian elites, via the mafia, were sending an unequivocal message that the PCI would not be permitted to radicalize the peasantry further.

Sicilian elites were not the only powerful forces to watch the growing popularity of the PCI and the PSI with alarm. The American Embassy was, by the beginning of May, deeply concerned about Italy's future, a concern that De Gasperi's letter to Truman alimented. On 1 May 1947, Secretary of State Marshall wrote to Ambassador James C. Dunn, asking for his advice on three points: (1) the likelihood of further PCI gains when national elections were held; (2) the utility of De Gasperi's relinquishing the premiership, or stiffening the government with technocrats; (3) what political and economic measures should be taken by the US government in order to 'strengthen' pro-US democratic forces, given the importance of Italy for US

Mediterranean policy.[59] Dunn replied on 3 May with an impassioned, dictated-but-not-edited response that is worth quoting at length:

> [T]he lack of confidence in the Govt as present formed of Christian-Democrats, Communists, and Communist inclined Socialist groups has progressed to a point which results in a psychological impediment to effective action by the Govt to correct present economic and financial conditions. I am convinced that no improvement in conditions here can take place under Govt as at present composed. Communists who are represented in Cabinet by second-string team are doing everything possible outside and within the Govt to bring about inflation and chaotic economic conditions. Population generally and particularly more responsible banking and industrial leaders have lost confidence entirely in the Govt and are afraid to venture upon new or expanded enterprises. A flight from the lira is beginning; rise in spiral inflation is unchecked. The pity is that there exists all over Italy a real will to work and there could easily be a general confidence in the future if it were not for the political agitation of the Communists and I doubt if there can be any real effective measures taken to improve the situation as long as the Communists participate in the Government. The Communist Party would, of course, fight hard against any effort to form a Govt without its participation but I do not believe it is too late for a govt to be formed without their participation and there appears to be a growing realization that the Communist Party is not really trying to bring about the restoration of economic stability.[60]

Ambassador Dunn's advice, in short, was to encourage De Gasperi to move against the PCI before it was too late. He argued that there was a 'growing belief' among Italians that the 'Italian Communist bandwagon is not seriously opposed by the US, and it is the one to board'. The American Embassy was 'constantly receiving letters from individuals begging the US to take a stand in Italy against this drive towards a totalitarian Communist Italy'. Dunn urged Marshall or the president to say that they were 'ready to lend our assistance to the development of an economic life based upon the liberty of the individual and the protection of his individual rights', and were 'confident that the Italian people will not desire a totalitarian regime which would inevitably break down the close ties that bind together the Italian and American people'.[61]

It did not occur to Dunn to stroll down to the Via delle Botteghe Oscure, where the PCI had its headquarters, and ask for a brief exchange of ideas on economic policy with Luigi Longo and Togliatti. Of course, if he had, they would have regarded his visit as a ruse to co-opt them. Our concepts and categories define our perception of reality. Dunn was a Cold Warrior. For him, communism was a threat to freedom and American values (the two were coterminous in his mind) and the PCI was an integral part of that threat. It was impossible to cooperate with them. Longo and Togliatti were convinced, by contrast, that the Truman Doctrine presaged American imperialism in the Mediterranean and was part of a plot to encircle (or 'contain') Soviet Russia.[62] The irony is, of course, that they were both right (or not wrong). De Gasperi's problem was that he was walking a tightrope between these two irreconcilable positions, and both his coalition partners and the Americans were jerking the rope. By early May 1947, he was steeling himself to jump off.

The PSI's national steering committee applied the 'holy oils' to De Gasperi's government on 12 May when it disowned the strategy that the prime minister had outlined on 28 April.[63] He resigned the following day. In the evening, De Gasperi went over the heads of the politicians again by making a broadcast that defended the government's record in increasing taxes and reducing government expenditure, including whittling down the enormous number of civil servants ('one for every 42 inhabitants!' he exclaimed, with genuine outrage). But this was not enough. What was necessary was:

> discipline to win the battle of prices, discipline to rein in consumption and expenses, discipline to combat speculation and unemployment, discipline to match the political timetable with that of the economy.

De Gasperi evoked recent history: the struggle for economic stability was, he said, 'a new civil resistance in which it is our sacred duty to participate and to make sacrifices'.[64] He knew that he was asking a lot. In the absence of American loans, social discipline would be necessary for years to come. But De Gasperi also suspected that, unless he acted against the PCI, then American aid might not be forthcoming. As a fascinating letter sent to De Gasperi by Tarchiani from Washington on 14 May illustrated, the presence of the two left-wing parties in the government was becoming a touchstone issue for the Americans.

In the letter, Tarchiani accurately reported that there were many individuals in American foreign-policy circles thinking of committing 'billions of dollars' for a new system of 'lend-lease for European reconstruction'. Tarchiani asserted, however, that the United States was 'by now resolved only to "help their friends"'. Truman had told Tarchiani that, while the United States had 'complete trust' in the Italian premier, the president considered, in light of the experience of France – where the French Communists had been expelled from the government on 5 May, on explicit American orders – that a 'government without Communists or pro-Communists' would be the most 'convenient' for Italy; though he was 'ready to understand' if De Gasperi judged that a broader-based government that 'diluted' the PCI's presence was politically necessary. Truman had stressed, however, that the stronger the PCI's representation in government was, the harder it would be to get 'any measure favourable to Italy' through Congress, though the president promised to make a 'warm declaration of friendship' in Italy's support. Tarchiani, in response, had underlined De Gasperi's willingness to do whatever was necessary to 'demonstrate the loyalty of our country for the supreme norms of domestic and international freedom'. Using the informal 'tu' habitual between close friends, Tarchiani concluded his letter to De Gasperi by saying that 'I am writing these things only for you, in the most absolute confidence.'[65] The ambassador did not report them to his nominal boss, Foreign Minister Sforza.

The May 1947 government crisis was an authentic drama. In a speech on 18 May, De Gasperi said – with uncustomary vehemence – that he would no longer accept the two left-wing parties working with him in the Council of Ministers and then 'hanging him in effigy' during 'public meetings'. They had to stop presenting him with 'orange blossom', the bridal flower, and then boasting that they had given him a 'bunch of chrysanthemums for his funeral'. They had to choose: 'orange blossom or chrysanthemums!'[66] De Gasperi vetoed attempts by President De Nicola to find a compromise premier who could recompose the tripartite government.

Squeezing in three generations: from the left, Vittorio Emanuele
Orlando in a voluminous overcoat, Ivanoe Bonomi, De Gasperi,
Giuseppe Saragat, Rodolfo Pacciardi. Orlando was proposed as
De Gasperi's replacement during the May 1947 crisis.

Togliatti strengthened De Gasperi's hand by publishing an ill-timed
anti-American article on 20 May. Offensively titled 'What Cretins
They Are!', the article argued that Americans 'in their soul' remained
'slave traders' who now wanted to deal in entire countries and peoples, treating them as if they were 'batches of cotton on sale cheap'.
For good measure, he added that Americans were 'unintelligent',
because they lacked 'cultural and historical background', 'subtlety of
thought', and 'empathy'. Hollywood films were indicative: despite the
resources poured into them, their technical prowess, and the beauty
of the actresses, one couldn't watch them without an 'infinite sensa-
tion of irritation and boredom'. They were just too 'mechanical' and
lacking in real human sensations.[67]

Togliatti's outburst had been provoked by a prominent American
New Dealer, Sumner Welles, who had publicly accused the PCI of

being in the pay of Moscow. His target was the American establishment, not Americans per se. The last line of Togliatti's article, indeed, asked 'don't you think this type of *anti-communist* American is a cretin?' (italics added).

Yet the article was wildly impolitic, for two reasons. First, people like Welles controlled the US government. Second, the PCI *was* taking large sums of money from Moscow (magazines like *Vie nuove* did not come cheap), although until 1948 'Soviet financial aid to the PCI did not amount to a regular and structured flow.'[68] As De Gasperi's most authoritative biographer says, in Italy, Welles' indiscretions were 'things everybody knew about, though they were kept quiet in order to avoid political fall-out'.[69]

Togliatti's sneering article was widely reported in the American press. Tarchiani warned De Gasperi that it had stirred up 'animosity and intransigence'.[70] The Italian trade envoy in Washington DC, Ivan Matteo Lombardo, who had been secretary of the PSIUP between April 1946 and January 1947, telegraphed the Council of Ministers to say the Truman administration had taken the article as proof positive of Soviet influence over the PCI.[71]

Yet Togliatti did not withdraw or apologize. He replied to Lombardo by declaring that his strictures could only be explained by the 'influence upon you of American anti-communist pogromist circles'. The PCI leader also wrote to De Gasperi asking him to declare that Welles had made a mistake, based on 'false and misleading' evidence from discreditable Italian sources. In effect, he asked De Gasperi to lie on his behalf, and to risk his credibility with the Americans. De Gasperi refused: it is hard to understand why Togliatti thought he would do otherwise.[72]

The Togliatti–Welles episode was the last straw for De Gasperi. The optimal solution from his perspective, a significant dilution of the influence wielded by the social-communists in the government, and a more collaborative attitude on their part, was always an unlikely outcome. Togliatti's article showed that it was a pipedream. De Gasperi had to choose between working with the two left-wing parties or turning his back on them. De Gasperi was formally given the 'burden' of forming a new government by De Nicola on 24 May and opted to jettison the PCI and PSI.

He had to exercise all his authority with the top echelons of the DC to get his way: Giulio Andreotti recounts in his 1947 diary that 'many faces paled' when De Gasperi announced his intention to govern without the left-wing parties at a meeting of the party's steering committee on 26–27 May. Many feared the nation would become ungovernable. De Gasperi flatly told the doubters that Nenni was 'unreliable', and that Togliatti's links 'internationally' meant that he did not have 'free hands'.[73] He won a clear but not unanimous majority in support of his position, and many who voted for him were doubtful.[74] The party secretary, Attilio Piccioni, was among the doubters: when he asked De Gasperi whether the government could resist the inevitable backlash from the PCI, the premier simply replied 'we either do it now, or we'll never do it. This is the right moment.'[75] De Gasperi would subsequently tell Tarchiani that he had spent 'mortally perilous hours' in which he had been 'abandoned' by 'many friends'.[76]

De Gasperi broke cover with an article in *Il Popolo* headlined 'No to the Tripartite Coalition'.[77] He formed a new government on 1 June 1947, on the eve of the Republic's first anniversary. Its chief novelty was the presence – or omnipresence – of Luigi Einaudi. One of the most accomplished orthodox academic economists in Europe, Einaudi had spent most of the war in exile, in Switzerland. Einaudi became deputy premier and super-minister for the economy, in charge, simultaneously, of the Treasury Ministry, the Finance Ministry, and a newly created Budget Ministry. De Gasperi could now be certain that his appeals for fiscal discipline would be heeded. Giuseppe Grassi (PLI), an aristocrat from Apulia, became minister for justice. Carlo Sforza remained as foreign minister. Otherwise, the DC provided all the members of the Council of Ministers.

The new government's parliamentary majority was wafer thin. The PSLI and PRI were still not ready to take office. Their recalcitrance dismayed the State Department. As Tarchiani wrote to De Gasperi, the 'so-called experts on Italian questions (the Italian desk) all fear that without Saragat's support, you might not pull off a vote of confidence'. He added, 'I can't deny . . . that they might be right.'[78]

In the absence of the PSLI, the government was dependent upon the Monarchists and UQ for a parliamentary majority. There was some truth in Togliatti's gibe that De Gasperi had started the crisis with the intention of presenting the 'most inclusive government of national unity possible', but had ended up deprived of the 263 votes of the PCI–PSI bloc and reliant on the 67 votes of the extreme right.[79] The Soviet ambassador, Mikhail Kostylev, reported to Moscow that the DC had 'found itself isolated' by its move against the PCI.[80] This judgement was correct only in narrow political terms. Italy had a centrist, pro-American government in place when, on 5 June 1947, General Marshall made his famous speech at Harvard University promising that the United States would do whatever it could to 'assist in the return of normal economic health in the world'. That was what mattered.

The outcome of the May 1947 government crisis placed Italy at the front of the queue for the American aid promised in Marshall's speech. In hindsight, the exclusion of the PCI and PSI 'represented a decisive pro-western turn in Italian political life and the beginning of Christian Democrat hegemony', although the DC's leaders, faced as they were with coping with public discontent and overcoming rampant inflation, could have been forgiven for not realizing it.[81]

It had been a close-run thing. Had De Gasperi heeded the anxious voices in his own party's top leadership, then he would have lost the regard of the Truman administration. Instead, his personal standing in Washington soared and sympathy for Italy increased. By the end of June, Tarchiani could write to inform De Gasperi that the 'overwhelming merit' for Italy's strengthening position in Washington lay with the premier because 'you managed to form the government that they desired and to get it approved by the Chamber when few at the Department of State believed it was possible . . . So far as Italy is concerned, you're the man they trust.'[82] For the third time since the end of the war (the first two occasions being the government crisis of December 1945 and the dramatic events that followed the 2 June referendum), the Italian premier had shown that he knew when to be bold. He would reap political rewards in the coming year.

ABOUT TURN, COMRADES!

The Marshall Plan speech and the Soviet reaction to it marked the definitive beginning of the Cold War in Europe, and the division of the

continent into two opposed blocs. The hastily organized Paris Conference in late June to discuss the European response to Marshall's offer
was attended by a sizeable delegation from the USSR and from the
Central European countries soon to be known as 'Soviet satellite
states'. Some of these states, especially Czechoslovakia, were as keen
as any West European nation to secure American financial assistance
for economic regeneration. When the USSR learned, however, that
American largesse would depend upon the construction of a European organization that would have the task of administering the
distribution of aid and supervising the economic modernization plans
that each country would draw up for approval by its peers, Stalin's
representative at the talks, Foreign Minister Vyacheslav Molotov,
announced on 2 July 1947 that Soviet Russia would not itself be
asking for American aid.

Czechoslovakia remained favourable to the putative European
organization, in any case. The Czechs' enthusiasm disquieted the
more dogmatic Yugoslavs, who were in favour in Moscow. The USSR
instructed all the countries in its sphere of influence to desist from
participation in the Paris talks. Before long, the Soviet press was
denouncing Marshall's initiative as a plot to subordinate the countries
of Europe to dollar imperialism. On 31 August 1947, a Socialist-
Communist coalition took power in Hungary, despite obtaining less
than 40 per cent of the vote, while the Peasants' Party, whose leader
Ferenc Nagy had had to flee for his life after winning elections in May,
plummeted to 14 per cent. The election was far from free and fair.
Contemporaneously, smallholders' parties were banned in Bulgaria
and Romania. The PCI was placed in a delicate position by these
developments and by its earlier exclusion from the government. How
should it react to De Gasperi's move against them? Its whole strategy
had been based upon Soviet encouragement for Togliatti's attempt to
build a progressive democracy together with the other parties, including the DC, that commanded mass support. Now, De Gasperi had
thrust the PCI into opposition, and the USSR was circling socialist
wagons against the West. The PCI leaders knew how badly Italy
needed American dollars and knew, too, that the DC would make
electoral hay if the PCI opposed Italian participation in an American-
financed organization of European democracies.

During the summer of 1947, the PCI doused the ardour of militants who wanted insurrectionary tactics in response to the party's exclusion from power. The party leadership agreed that it should 'prevent the party and the masses that follow us from slipping into positions that lead to combat and to armed insurrection'. 'Any possibility of violent action is to be excluded,' Togliatti stated.[83] The party issued a public statement to this effect. As Togliatti argued in a short article on 27 July 1947, the PCI's biggest contribution to the Republic, hitherto, had been its refusal to yield to 'the reactionary challenge of civil war'. The PCI's sound judgement had saved Italy's democracy from the fate of Greece, with parts of the country perhaps controlled by the PCI, but with most of it 'prey to black reaction'.[84] This article, while ostensibly blaming reactionaries for the threat of civil war, was clearly sending a message to the party's would-be insurrectionists.

Togliatti believed that the party had to keep its head and ensure that progressive ideas were incorporated into the constitution, even if the PCI was no longer part of the government. When the Constituent Assembly finished its labours there would be elections, and, when they occurred, Togliatti was confident that the PCI and its allies would emerge victorious or, at any rate, hold the balance of power. For Togliatti, who was supervising an edition of the *Prison Notebooks* of the PCI's former leader Antonio Gramsci in these months, the PCI was waging what Gramsci called a 'war of position', a long-term conflict that would take time and patience (and a hegemonic role in society) to win. It could not expect to win via a 'frontal assault'.[85]

This policy of restraint was tested to breaking point in the autumn of 1947. Einaudi tightened the anti-inflation vice relentlessly. Interest rates were raised, a wealth tax was implemented, and private credit was slashed by compelling banks to invest heavily in government bonds. By December 1947, such restrictive monetary policies were working as Einaudi intended. Retail prices were lower in December 1947 than in September, and a bubble in stock prices was deflated. The amount of money raised by the state in taxes surged. In the first meeting of the Council of Ministers in January 1948, Einaudi revealed that the treasury was estimating that '8/850' billion lire would be raised in taxes during the year June 1947–June 1948, far more than the forecast 520 billion. If one added in local government taxes and compulsory insurance contributions, the state was raising 1,100–1,200 billion lire in taxes, about a quarter of a national income estimated at 4,500 billion lire.[86] On the other hand, industrial production, which had been increasing rapidly, was squeezed by the higher cost of credit and hundreds of thousands of jobs were lost.

Einaudi's shock therapy for the economy was 'hard, bitter, and inflexible', and it dismayed both entrepreneurs and the workers. Industrial agitation spread across the manufacturing cities of northern Italy, while unrest among the agricultural workers of the Po River valley was comparable in scale to the disturbances after the First World War.[87] On the other hand, Einaudi's measures interrupted the inflationary spiral. Consumer retail prices, again taking 1913 as a base year equal to 1, were 199 at the end of 1947, 210.6 in 1948, 213.6 in 1949, and 210.8 in 1950.[88] Price stability was established, and with it the possibility that savings would be invested productively instead of in financial speculation.

The PCI was naturally to the forefront in organizing protests against Einaudi's credit squeeze, not least because it had received a humiliating admonition from the world communism movement to take a less passive line in domestic Italian politics. On 22–23 September 1947, a special meeting of delegates from the communist parties of Bulgaria, Czechoslovakia, France, Hungary, Italy, Poland, Romania, and Yugoslavia was held with two of Stalin's closest henchmen, Andrei Zhdanov and Georgij Malenkov, in the Polish town of Szklarska Poręba. All the parties sent top-ranking officials. Togliatti was invited to attend but demurred, sending instead the deputy leader, Luigi Longo, and Eugenio Reale, who was married to a Pole. Reale had served as ambassador to Poland during the first De Gasperi government and as junior minister for foreign affairs under Bonomi, Parri and, most recently, during the De Gasperi government that had ended in May. He was, in short, one of the PCI's leading experts on matters of foreign policy.

Togliatti, a survivor of the great purges in the 1930s, guessed that the meeting would turn into a denunciation of the PCI and warned Longo and Reale to underline in the party's defence that it had been in the interests neither of Italy nor of the Soviet Union for Italy to be transformed into a second Greece.[89] By this he meant that they should insist that armed insurrection would have been a mistaken policy.

Togliatti guessed right. The summit was dominated by a lecture from Zhdanov on the need to resist the American imperialist aggression, and on the failure of 'parliamentarianism' as a strategy. His harangue was complemented by venomous attacks by the Central European parties on the lack of revolutionary zeal shown by the PCF and, above all, the PCI during the political crises in May. Once again, the Yugoslav delegation, which was headed by Edvard Kardelj, a Slovene, was more zealous even than the Soviets: Kardelj openly said that insurrection would have been advisable in France and Italy and that the parliamentarianism of the Western parties had caused an opportunity to be missed.

A shaken Longo replied with dignity to the insults and accepted much of Zhdanov's critique, but distanced himself from Kardelj's extremism. Longo and Reale were nevertheless left in no doubt that the PCI had put itself on the wrong side of history by its strategy of working within democratic institutions.[90] The fact that Togliatti's strategy had originally been imposed by Stalin was, of course, unmentionable, in public at any rate. Stalin had changed his mind. The summit decided to create a new body, the Communist Information Bureau, or Cominform, to organize the common struggle against American imperialism. It was to be based in Belgrade.

Longo and Reale reported back to the steering committee on 7 October and explained that the PCI had been found to be in grave error. Since July 1944, Togliatti had based the party's strategy upon the concept of progressive democracy, a concept that acknowledged that, in Italy, there were powerful social forces, including a substantial part of the working class, that looked to the DC for political representation. The PCI's leaders had prided themselves on their realism in adapting to local conditions. Their *tactics* had nevertheless frustrated De Gasperi to breaking point and had led to their exclusion from office. Kardelj and Zhdanov were now instructing them that their *strategy* had also been mistaken. Togliatti must have listened to Longo's report and speculated whether the men sitting around him would not soon be denouncing him as a class enemy, as he himself had denounced others in Spain and the USSR.

Ritual required the party leadership to bow in deference to the greater wisdom of Moscow. Umberto Terracini, president of the Constituent Assembly, caused consternation by failing to recite the right lines. Terracini, as we have seen, had had an uneasy relationship with Moscow's policies ever since his deviation over the Nazi–Soviet Pact in 1939. He now intervened early in the debate and stated, full knowing what the harvest would be, that he saw no need for the party line 'to undergo significant modification'. A more radical anti-parliamentary strategy could only lose the party votes with the middle classes, even though it might temporarily reinforce the party's position with the workers and peasants. Terracini added that the method adopted by the conference in Poland had been an error: the PCI should have been given an opportunity to defend its policies properly. For good measure, he objected to Belgrade being made the seat of the new institution.

Terracini was supported by an old enemy, Mauro Scoccimarro, but nobody else. To read the minutes of the meeting, nearly eighty years later, is to be transported into a dystopian novel by Arthur Koestler or George Orwell. One can easily visualize the tense, bespectacled faces seething with indignation as they rebuked the heretic in their midst. One by one, the party officials expressed their 'profound amazement' that there was among them one who 'did not recognize the guiding role of the Bolshevik Party of the Soviet Union'. One party boss theatrically urged the leadership to send a letter to Zhdanov to thank him for pointing out the error of their ways.[91]

Pietro Secchia, the head of the party organization, sided with the most strident critics of Terracini and stated, ominously for Togliatti, that the post-war strategy had been wrong from the outset. There was no chance of carrying out a 'fully fledged critique of our actions' in that meeting, Secchia said, but such was 'the road to follow'.[92] All present would have known that an insurrection, if it were to happen, had to occur soon. Italy had ratified the Treaty of Peace over the summer, and it came into effect on 15 September. Remaining United Nations forces were being redeployed out of Italy, in accordance with Article 73 of the treaty, when the steering committee met. Secchia was no match, intellectually, for Togliatti or Terracini, just as Stalin was less intellectually sophisticated than Trotsky and Bukharin. But Secchia did represent the party militants who had been edged out when the 'New Party' had been created.

These true believers in the need for revolution had risked their lives and liberty in the struggle against Fascism and had never fully digested Togliatti's parliamentarianism.

Terracini's intervention was beneficial for Togliatti, who rounded off the debate with a patronizing rebuttal of Terracini's arguments and hence sided with the majority. Togliatti gave an interview to *Corriere della Sera* on 9 October, affirming (mendaciously) that the PCI would not lose autonomy as a result of the Cominform and half-promised that it would remain committed to democratic methods.[93] This became the new party line.

Terracini was not to be silenced so easily. The following week he gave an interview to an American news agency in which he staked out a neutral position in the Cold War, stating that if war were to break out then the 45 million Italian people would oppose it, *whoever the aggressor was* – an astonishing thing for a prominent communist to say in October 1947. Under duress, Terracini made a partial retraction, but he was not purged. He retained his place on the steering committee of the party and remained president of the Constituent Assembly.[94] Over the next three years the principal leaders of the Central European parties would be arrested, tortured, shot, or hanged after the ritual humiliation of a show trial for harbouring similar convictions. Terracini was fortunate to live in Italy, where the worst sanction he faced was ostracism by the more dogmatic members of the party hierarchy.

To purge Terracini, or to mimic Kardelj, would have been to throw Togliatti's entire strategy since 1944 under the bus, at the very moment that the constitution was receiving its finishing touches. The PCI nevertheless had to do *something*. In the wake of Zhdanov's strictures, the PCI went on the offensive: there was a 'radicalization' of the party's propaganda and an intensification of political conflict on the ground.[95] The De Gasperi government was routinely accused of being the creature of the reactionary classes at home and of Wall Street in foreign affairs.[96] The official communiqué published by the Central Committee of the PCI after its meeting in mid-November 1947 was a diatribe that accused the government of turning Italy into a 'vassal' of the United States, and of 'putting at risk' all the liberties that Italians had won in the struggle against Fascism and the German invader.[97] De Gasperi described it as a 'manifesto for war' in his speech to the second party congress of the DC, which was held in Naples between 15 and 20 November.[98] In all honesty, one can see why he interpreted it in that way.

Political intimidation by the PCI became rife. In mid-October, a DC party worker was murdered by a squad of PCI members while he was putting up electoral posters in Rome: the entire Council of Ministers ostentatiously attended the funeral, along with a gigantic crowd of citizens.[99] Attacks on local headquarters of the DC became so frequent that the party's National Council urged militants in December 1947 to form paramilitary groups in self-defence.[100]

The violence was by no means all one way. Illegal neo-fascist squads attacked PCI buildings and militants. On 13 November 1947, the PCI organized a huge demonstration in Milan against neo-fascist terrorism. When, two weeks later, the government decided to remove the prefect of Milan, a former partisan, and replace him with a career policeman, chaos erupted. The PSI mayor resigned, along with dozens of his colleagues across the province. Uniform-wearing PCI militants flooded into the city from all over the North. A general strike was declared, roadblocks were set up, and lorries full of gun-toting partisans rushed through the streets. The prefecture, the radio station, and the telephone exchange were taken over by militants commanded by the party secretary in Milan, Gian Carlo Pajetta, who was seething with revolutionary zeal. Supposedly, in the thrill of moment, Pajetta telephoned both Interior Minister Scelba, to inform him that he now had 'one fewer prefecture, that of Milan', and Togliatti, to whom he said, 'we have the prefecture of Milan'. Togliatti, at his most frosty, allegedly replied, 'Well done. What are you going to do with it?'[101]

Days before, Scelba had received a standing ovation after his speech to the national congress of the DC. He had frankly warned that there was a public order crisis. Scelba stated that he would put law and order first: the law could not be subject to 'the whims of a party'. Nothing would lead to the return of Fascism sooner than disrespect for the law. To 'thunderous applause', Scelba asserted that, if a 'supreme moment' occurred 'in which freedom in our country was being put at risk', he would not hesitate to use the full power of the state.[102]

In Milan, such a 'supreme moment' presented itself. Public buildings in Italy's second-largest city were in the hands of the illegally armed militia of a political party that was openly defying a decision taken by the legally constituted government. Using troops to restore order was arguably justified. Instead, the government sent a junior minister, Achille Marazza, to negotiate. Marazza was a good choice: he had been a partisan leader of some renown in Lombardy. Showing exceptional courage, he went to the prefecture alone in a jeep and, 'pale but dignified', walked, unarmed, between 'two human hedges' of PCI militants along the corridor to the prefect's Office, where Pajetta, the prefect, and local PCI leaders were waiting for him.[103] After hours of talks Marazza brokered a compromise whereby the prefect of nearby Pavia would act as a substitute for two months, whereupon the government's original choice (the prefect of Turin) would take office. Nobody would be arrested. On these terms, the occupation ended, almost without bloodshed. Pajetta told the insurgents to go home. The occupation had ultimately been street theatre, not a seizure of power.

Kardelj was in a way right. The PCI was not fundamentally a revolutionary party, just as the DC was not reactionary, as the PCI's propaganda maintained, still less fascist. *Per fortuna*. The contending parties shrank from using violence in pursuit of their political goals. Indeed, throughout the upheaval provoked by the creation of the Cominform, the Constituent Assembly had continued the work of crafting a constitutional settlement. By December 1947, they were close to concluding their task.

THE CONSTITUTION

On 22 December 1947, the Constituent Assembly voted by 423 votes to 62 (the Monarchists, who had taken an active role in the Assembly's debates, remained loyal to their faith) for the final text of a new republican constitution. There were a few last-minute hiccups. On 15 December, De Gasperi brought the PSLI and PRI into his majority. Christian Democracy no longer needed to rely on the right-wing parties in parliament. It was free to be a party of the centre, with left-wing allies, acting as a bulwark against the challenge of the social-communists. De Gasperi pulled off this manoeuvre without resort to all-party consultations with the president. Speaking in the Assembly on 20 December, Togliatti denounced De Gasperi for effecting an improper 'change of the guard', and mounted a scathing personal attack on Saragat and the PSLI, who were accused of having lost all support among the working class, and on the PRI, whom he accused of dragging the tricolour flag of Giuseppe Mazzini through the mud.[104] The debate finished in tumult, and had to be suspended for thirty minutes after PRI and PCI deputies engaged in a shouting match and scuffles broke out.

At a more cerebral level, a devout Catholic, Giorgio La Pira, who had played an active and important role in the Constituent Assembly's proceedings, and who had often acted as a mediator between the left-wing parties and the DC, concluded at the last moment that the constitution needed a preamble. Hours before the final vote, the saintly La Pira proposed that the text of the constitution should be preceded with the words, 'In the name of God, the People give themselves this constitution.' In September 1946, La Pira had advocated a much lengthier preamble that had sought to identify Italy as a Christian civilization. On that occasion, he was wittily reminded 'not to name God in vain'. On this second occasion, after a short debate, Terracini, in his role as president of the Assembly, persuaded him to withdraw his motion. The Constitution could not evoke God, just as it could not begin, as many constitutions do, with a brief statement of the historical circumstances that had led to the constitution's creation. There simply was not the necessary consensus within the Assembly either on religious principle, or on the country's modern history.

There was, however, consensus on three main points. First, Italy should be a republic with progressive aspirations in social policy. Social justice was to be the rock upon which the Republic was founded. Second, Italy must never go down the road of Fascism again. Political rights should be firmly protected, men and women should be equal, war was to be abhorred, and political power was to be exercised only with caution and in the context of a web of institutional checks and balances. Third, in principle at least, it was recognized that Italy was a variegated nation whose unique regional and local diversity should be reflected politically.

The first of these three points was strongly asserted in the 'Fundamental Principles' of the constitution (which are a kind of preliminary 'Bill of Rights' to the rest of the document) and in 'Part I' of the document, which deals with the 'rights and duties of the citizen' and which is sub-divided into four *titoli* or sub-parts. Starting with Article 1, with its famous proclamation that Italy is a 'democratic republic, founded upon labour', the document underlined the centrality of the principle of greater social equality and opportunity. Article 3 stated that every citizen possessed 'equal social dignity', without distinction of 'sex, race, language, political opinion, or social status', and was equal before the law. It added that it is the 'task' of the Republic to 'remove the economic and social obstacles' that 'impede the full development of the human personality' and 'the effective participation of the workers' in the organization and affairs of the state. Article 4 asserted that there was a 'right to work' and committed the Republic to 'promote the conditions' that made such a right meaningful.

The second and third *titoli* of Part I ('Ethical-Social Relations' and 'Economic Relations') added substance to the constitution's socially progressive stance. The rights of the family, which was to be based on the 'moral and juridical equality of the partners', were protected (Article 29). Large families (there were many, of course, thanks to Mussolini's drive for a larger population) were to be helped by the state (Article 31). Healthcare was defined as a 'fundamental right of the individual and interest of society' (Article 32), school was to be 'open to all' and free of charge, at least for the first eight years. 'Able and meritorious' students lacking financial means would be assisted by grants to enable them to study beyond the age of fourteen (Article 34).

Workers were to be guaranteed an income that guaranteed a 'free and dignified existence.' Paid holidays were a right (Article 36). Women workers were to have the same rights and pay as male workers, so long as they were doing comparable work, and their working conditions should allow them to fulfil their 'essential function in the family' (Article 37). Social assistance was guaranteed for those unable to work (Article 38). Private enterprise was free, so long as it did not conflict with 'social utility', or cause damage to 'security, freedom, and human dignity' (Article 41). Article 44 made clear that land ownership was to be regulated by law to promote wider distribution of land and more productive use of the soil.

The rejection of Fascism as a system of government (and political ideology) was even more pronounced. Mindful of the forced Italianization of the German and Slav minorities under Fascism, the 'Fundamental Principles', affirmed that 'linguistic minorities' would have their rights protected (Article 6). Equally mindful of the 1938 Racial laws, Article 8 confirmed that all religious faiths were equal before the law and were free to organize themselves according to their own rules, so long as they were in conformity with Italian law. The new republic, conscious of the hundreds of thousands of Italians who had had to flee to France to escape Fascism, permitted foreigners from countries that did not enjoy similar liberties to Italy to request asylum and banned the extradition of foreign citizens for political offences (Article 10). Above all:

> Italy repudiates war as an instrument against the freedom of other peoples and as a way of resolving international controversies; it will allow, on equal terms with other states, the limitation of sovereignty necessary for an international order that ensures peace and justice between nations: it will promote and favour international organizations that pursue this goal. (Article 11)

The new Italian republic, in short, was to be all but pacifist. The contrast with Fascism could not have been more stark. Title 1 of the 'Rights and Duties of the Citizens' (Articles 13–28) emphasized the breach between the new regime and the old in clear terms by defending individual rights with determination. Personal liberty, homes, and correspondence were 'inviolable', unless judicially motivated. Freedom of movement, association, dwelling place, (unarmed) gatherings of citizens were all guaranteed. Freedom of speech was the object of one of the longest articles in the whole constitution (Article 21). It stated that people were free to express their opinions by word, print, or any other means. There was to be no censure of the press except in certain carefully prescribed cases. On the other hand, publications and shows that contravened 'common decency' were banned. What exactly 'common decency' meant was not specified, but it was safe to assume the clergy would have an opinion.

Political rights were the subject of Articles 48–54. Again, in contrast with Fascism, they emphasized that citizens were active participants in the political life of the nation, not clay to be moulded by the regime. Voting – which was to be free, equal, and secret – was a 'civic duty', not simply a right (Article 48). Citizens were free to join parties in order to 'contribute to determining national politics' (Article 49). All citizens (Article 52) had a 'sacred duty' to defend the country – and not allow it to be occupied by a foreign power like Nazi Germany. Article 53 stated that all citizens should contribute to public spending according to their ability to pay. Taxation would be 'progressive' in character. It is fair to say that this article was respected more in the breach than the observance in future decades.

Above all, the institutions of the state were structured in such a way that no Duce could ever emerge. First, a proportional electoral system was retained, though no article of the constitution specified that the electoral system had to be proportional, a point that would become very important in 1953. This decision made multi-party coalition government more likely. Second, the two chambers of parliament enjoyed what constitutional lawyers have called 'perfect bicameralism'. The Senate (elected by citizens over twenty-five years of age) and the Chamber of Deputies (elected by men and women over twenty-one) had equal powers over legislation. The Senate, however, was elected for a six-year, not a five-year, term. As in the United States, no law could be passed unless it had been approved by both chambers. Both chambers also had to approve the government in a vote of confidence. The loss of a confidence vote in one chamber, at any time during the legislature, thus brought the government down. The two chambers (Article 78) had absolute power over declaring a state of war. Anything less like the Caesarism extolled by Fascism – the idea of a Man of Destiny commanding the nation by announcing sweeping, bold decrees – is hard to imagine. In fact, not by chance, the use of decree legislation by the government was minutely regulated (Article 77).

To avoid any taint of charismatic rule, the president of the republic was indirectly elected for a seven-year term (Article 85), by the two chambers of parliament in a common session (Article 83), not directly elected by the people. From the outset, the president was intended to be someone able to command a broad consensus among the political parties – the *organized* citizenry – rather than the whims and moods of the populace, whose fickleness Italians knew all too well. As well as ratifying treaties and performing the ceremonial offices of the state, he (there has still never been a woman)[105] could dissolve the chambers (or just one of them) and call elections; nominate the president of the Council of Ministers; and approve, or disapprove, of his choice of ministers (Article 87). The president would also chair the 'Supreme Council of the Magistrates', the body responsible for the administration of the state's prosecutors.

The President of the Council of Ministers, too, was defined by the constitution as a mediator between ministers and with the president, not as a leader. He (or since October 2022, she) strove to 'maintain the broad political and administrative unity of the government, by promoting and coordinating the actions of the government' (Article 95). The premier's role was to act as a chairman, not be chief executive.

The constitution's final dispositions, appended to the rest of the document, explicitly dealt with the legacy of both Fascism and the House of Savoy. Number XII banned the Fascist Party 'in any form' and forbade former PNF chiefs from voting for five years. Number XIII specified that the members and descendants of the House of Savoy could not vote and could not serve in the public administration. Kings Victor Emmanuel and Umberto, and their male heirs, were banned even from setting foot in Italy again.

Last, but not least, the constitution recognized the nation's diversity. One of the 'Founding Principles' was that the Republic, despite being 'one and indivisible', was bound to 'recognize and promote' local autonomy, and to 'implement' the 'widest decentralization' of state services possible. To this end, the constitution dedicated no fewer than twenty-six articles (Articles 114–139) to the role of local government. The constitution promised regional government, alongside existing provincial and municipal government (Article 114) and indicated the sphere of their exclusive powers (Article 117). Nineteen regions were identified (Article 131), of which five (Val d'Aosta, Trentino-Alto Adige, Friuli Venezia Giulia, Sardinia, and Sicily) were to be 'special statute regions' (RSS) and possess a wide range of powers, notably over funding and taxation.

Four of the special regions were instituted in quick order by a series of constitutional laws passed on 26 February 1948 (Friuli Venezia Giulia became an RSS only in 1964). The other 'ordinary' regions had to wait until 1970 for parliament to pass the necessary enabling legislation. Moving away from the centralized state, however incrementally, was a big step for Italy. Unity in a single state had been a principle of the Risorgimento. Under Fascism, of course, the 'State' had possessed a capital letter and all power, in theory at least, was meant to be centralized. The new constitution did at least signal the first step away from enforced uniformity in this most heterogeneous of nations.

Article 138 of the constitution dealt with the process of revision: it was deliberately made extremely difficult.[106] This is one reason why the Italian constitution has subsequently been so little changed. The main reason, however, is that the drafters of the constitution got it right. They produced a blueprint for a 'progressive' constitution that commanded (and still commands) widespread public consensus and that encapsulated a vision that the Italian people could aspire to create (few believed, in 1947, that the constitution's social principles could be realized any time soon). Articles 1–54 have never been significantly revised for the good reason that they are what most Italians continue to believe that their country stands for.

That a document with such staying power and emotional charge should have emerged from a country whose politics were those described in this chapter was nothing short of miraculous. Or, more likely, a testament to the ability of political leaders to impose their will on even the most unpromising circumstances. On 27 December 1947, in Palazzo San Giuliani in Rome, the constitution was signed by Terracini, as President of the Constituent Assembly, by 'De Gasperi, Alcide', by Justice Minister Giuseppe Grassi, who was 'Keeper of the Seals', and, with a flamboyant flourish of the E in his first name, by Enrico De Nicola, the provisional head of state.

The constitution came into effect on 1 January 1948. De Gasperi

A Republic founded on labour: from the left, De Gasperi, a civil servant,
President De Nicola, Justice Minister Giuseppe Grassi,
Umberto Terracini, President of the Constituent Assembly.

worked until almost midnight on 31 December. When he left the office
he said to Andreotti, who was still at his desk, 'this year has been
decisive, but next year will be even more so.'[107] Certainly, 1947 had
been a transitional year of immense significance. The unity of the parties that had resisted Nazism had been definitively ruptured, but the
same parties now had a robust set of rules to regulate the political
struggle.

8

Moment of Truth

The elections of 18 April 1948 in Italy have some claim to be the most tense democratic elections in post-1945 European history. Both the DC and the PCI–PSI 'Democratic Popular Front' (FDP) fought with bare knuckles. Both sides acted as if victory for their opponents would be the precursor to the imposition of an authoritarian regime and the abolition of democracy. Less than four months after the constitution of the Italian Republic became law, its political parties fought a battle for its soul.

The April 1948 elections were so raw because the stakes were so high. So long as the campaign endured, nobody pretended that the process was somehow more important than the outcome. The parties stopped short – mostly – at outright physical intimidation, but 'fake news' and shameful smears were the hard currency of electoral propaganda throughout the campaign. No blow was low enough and millions of citizens – literally – were engaged in delivering the blows. The PCI and PSI mobilized their three million *tesserati* (approximately one adult in ten belonged to one or the other of the two parties). The DC, which itself was a mass party with hundreds of thousands of members, was also backed by every parish priest and by 'civic committees' of Catholic activists. As a result, Italy was plastered with posters during the campaign. The sides of houses, even blocks of flats, were often covered from ground to roof with competing political material.

A QUESTION OF PROPORTION

The 18 April date was set on 8 February after the Constituent Assembly had finished drawing up an electoral law for the Senate. The

Senate, which was being elected for the first time (senators had previously been appointed by the king), required a law that respected the constitutional provisions that the chamber should be elected on a regional basis by citizens over twenty-five years of age. The law that was adopted divided Italy into 232 British-style constituencies. To be directly elected, however, a candidate had to obtain 65 per cent of the vote, not a mere majority. Accordingly, most senators were subsequently chosen in nineteen regional electoral districts that awarded the seats according to a proportional system designed to reward the largest parties.[1]

Some 107 'senators by right' were also entitled to serve for the first legislature. These were veterans who had been elected at least twice to parliament before 1926 or condemned to prison terms of more than five years for anti-fascist activity. The PCI had no fewer than thirty-one such individuals, the PSI eleven, the PSLI thirteen. The DC had eighteen and hence started the elections at a disadvantage compared to its rivals, a fact that deeply worried De Gasperi.[2]

For the Chamber of Deputies, it was decided to persevere with the law that had been used for the election of the Constituent Assembly.[3] The electoral law for the Chamber was a proportional system that was based upon four cardinal features: (1) The country was divided into electoral districts that elected large numbers of deputies (usually about twenty, but in the cases of Rome and Milan over fifty). The votes cast in each district were divided by the number of seats available to provide a quota necessary to elect a deputy; (2) The elector voted for party lists but could indicate preferences for three or four candidates; (3) The only parties excluded from representation were those that had not obtained 300,000 votes nationally, or elected one candidate directly in an electoral district; (4) The party's surplus votes (i.e. those 'left over' in each district that had not contributed to the election of a deputy) were amassed separately in a 'single national constituency' and then divided proportionately among the parties that had elected deputies to parliament.[4]

The reader must forgive these arcane details about electoral law. Anybody who studies modern Italian political history cannot avoid them. The carefully calculated proportionality of the Italian electoral law is one reason why, when the campaign started, an inconclusive result seemed probable. Majoritarian systems, such as the British, tend to exaggerate the margin of victory of whichever party gets a majority of the votes nationally (or of parties that are dominant in a particular geographical area). Even some proportional systems reward the biggest parties, or else have high minimum requirements for representation (such as the 5 per cent threshold adopted in West Germany) that are implemented to exclude minor parties and to give voters an incentive not to spread their vote too thin.

Italy's law had none of these features. Roughly speaking, to get 50 per cent plus one of the seats in the Chamber, a party would need about 47 per cent of the popular vote; in the Senate the percentage was lower but still high. It will be remembered that in June 1946 the DC had been the largest party with only 35 per cent of the vote. The PCI–PSI combination had obtained almost 40 per cent, but that was before the split that created the PSLI: the question of how many votes Saragat's party would subtract from the PSI was therefore a vital one.

When the campaign began, the key issue was not whether any single party would emerge with an overall majority, but whether the FDP, whose electoral symbol was an image of Giuseppe Garibaldi set within a red star, would match the total of votes cast for the DC's shield-and-cross symbol and hence be able to demand their return to government. The election was, in the final analysis, a referendum on De Gasperi's conduct since May 1947. The electors would pass judgement on his openly pro-American stance and his decision to terminate the resistance coalition. According to one historian of the PCI, when the campaign started, communists still regarded De Gasperi's decision to dissolve the CLN coalition as an 'unbearable affront' or even 'a kind of betrayal'.[5] They were determined to overthrow him at the ballot box – and many were ready to overthrow him in the streets.

In 1948, Italy had an untried political and constitutional system designed for cooperation, if not consensus, between the principal political parties. But the political climate made cooperation, still less consensus, impossible. As a Catholic intellectual prophetically wrote in early 1948, Italy had reached the moment when its people had to 'decide the destiny of the nation for a lengthy period of time, perhaps even for several decades'.[6]

RED FRONT

The 'Democratic Popular Front for Work, Peace, and Freedom', to give the FDP its full title, was originally proposed by the PSI, although the PCI made the idea its own in December 1947. Theoretically, the Front was not just an electoral pact between the PSI and the PCI, but an assemblage of progressive movements that included Christian Socialists opposed to De Gasperi's alleged reactionary turn, disaffected Republicans, a breakaway faction from the PSLI, and numerous civil society organizations, some of which were artificial creations of the PCI. Many intellectuals publicly lined up with the Front, though some later retracted.[7] It was launched on 28 December in Rome and then endorsed at the PCI's 6th Congress, which took place in Milan's Lirico Theatre between 4 and 10 January 1948.

The FDP's manifesto, reflecting its nominally ecumenical composition, was strikingly moderate in spirit. It made no mention of class war, but rather stressed that its purpose was to unite all those who 'crave peace, freedom, and work'. It had three objectives: (1) *Structural reforms* to agriculture, industry, and the South; (2) *Democratization* and decentralization of the state bureaucracy, of the schools and culture, of scientific and intellectual life. Democracy for women, through the establishment of equal rights, but also through policies that ensured a 'solid defence of the traditional home'; (3) *Peace*. Foreign policy was to be based upon a 'policy of cooperation and friendship with every country that loves peace and freedom'. To obtain these goals, the Front proposed to mobilize the energies of 'all thinking Italians' to 'shatter the selfish resistance of sections of the population and interest groups that are organized to preserve their privileges'. This sentence was the only one in the entire document that even hinted at Marxist doctrine.[8]

The Front's propaganda subsequently confirmed the moderate language and tone of the manifesto. A pamphlet called 'Save our Industry' was aimed at skilled workers, craftsmen and white-collar workers, not at assembly-line workers. It made the argument that the DC's economic policy was working for 'Confindustria and the big American trusts'. A PSI pamphlet urging the same class of people to vote for the FDP asked voters whether they wanted to be a 'donkey or a man'. Only an *asino*, it was alleged, could vote for a government that favoured the big capitalist concerns so blatantly. Inside, the pamphlet showed a small businessman tied up by the constraints imposed by banks and monopolies, and another, wearing a sharp suit, who had been freed of restraints by a socialist administration. Officials in the public administration were urged to set up branches of the FDP in their workplaces; a long list of people who had done so was appended. A PCI-produced pamphlet underlined that the action of the PCI ministers, when they had been in government, had aimed at 'alleviating the sufferings of the people'. Togliatti, during his time as minister, had apparently worked for 'national pacification' by ensuring an amnesty for 'all those who, either because they were compelled to or in good faith, followed or served Mussolini's regime'.[9]

The moderation of the FDP's manifesto contrasted sharply with the mood of the PCI's Congress. It was 'the Congress of obedience to the Cominform'.[10] The Congress was an imposing event, with delegations from the Communist parties of France, Yugoslavia, and the Soviet Union in attendance. Behind the banners and slogans proclaiming proletarian unity, the party leadership was divided over the course to follow. Togliatti's leadership was no longer uncontested. Pietro Secchia was striving to undermine him. In mid-December 1947, Secchia had been sent as emissary to Moscow, where he met Zhdanov and had an audience with Stalin. In the meeting with Zhdanov, Secchia disparaged Togliatti's preference for parliamentary tactics. The conflict with the forces of reaction was 'just over the horizon', Secchia believed, so why wait to fight at a time of their enemies' choosing?[11]

When Secchia met Stalin, on 14 December, the Soviet leader sided with Togliatti. 'Comrade Togliatti's evaluation of the situation and the tactics he is following are correct,' Stalin stated unambiguously.[12] The remainder of Secchia's audience with the Soviet dictator was taken up with sorting out the logistics of transporting $600,000 in cash from the Soviet Union to Italy, to help finance the electoral campaign, and with some paternal advice from Stalin about the importance of looking after Togliatti's health. 'Was he eating and sleeping well?' the dictator asked solicitously. The Central Committee of the PCI should vote a resolution to take extra good care of Togliatti, Stalin ordered. He should eat well three or four times a day. The Italian leader mustn't give 'the impression of being an ascetic'. Given that the Soviet leader must have known about Togliatti's extramarital affair with the twenty-seven-year-old PCI deputy Nilde Iotti, this last remark smacks of irony.

Secchia sensibly expressed agreement with Stalin's judgement of the Italian situation. Nevertheless, before leaving Moscow for Belgrade, he made a speech to party cadres in which he condemned the 'illusions of parliamentarianism'. Secchia returned to Italy bearing the money bags and with his reputation as a 'high-ranking international functionary' enhanced.[13] At Soviet insistence, he was promoted to the role of deputy leader of the party, on a par with Luigi Longo. The suggestion was rubber-stamped by the party's steering committee on 21 January 1948. Rather than wait for the next meeting of the Central Committee, the body charged with making such appointments, Togliatti hastily wrote to Central Committee members asking them to confirm the decision. This they did with varying degrees of enthusiasm and formality.[14]

An Italian Bolshevik: Pietro Secchia addressing a party rally in Bologna.

Togliatti was doubtless delighted to discover that he was one of the few human beings whose health Stalin cared about and relieved that the dictator supported his 'line'. Togliatti had known – Secchia had not – that in November Stalin had told the French Communist Party (PCF) leader, Maurice Thorez, that the PCF should follow an insurrectionist policy only if it was attacked.[15] He had gambled that Stalin would give the same advice to his ambitious rival. In December 1947, the PCI leader nevertheless must have been wondering whether his position in the party was on the wane. Even Togliatti was not immune to nerves.

With Stalin's backing, Togliatti was free in his marathon Congress speech to underline the peculiarity of the Italian case. He eulogized the Soviet Union and hailed the revolutionary advances made by the countries in the Soviet bloc, but he contended that in Italy it was still necessary to pursue a policy of alliances with other parties, 'constructed according to the principles of Leninism', and participate in the democratic process, rather than attempt a seizure of power.

This did not mean that the party should relax its vigilance. 'We are following a line of democratic action, but we will not allow ourselves to be caught out by any provocation, by any reactionary plot,' Togliatti warned. He warned that the PCI had 'tens of thousands' of militants well versed in the use of weapons. If a situation were created where freedom had to be 'reconquered by arms', they would defend democracy and their homeland.[16] This was a striking public admission that the party had illegal hidden arsenals that it was prepared to use in pursuit of its objectives.

Three things stood out from the 6th Congress. First, the PCI was aligned with Moscow. The internal debate was between those, like Secchia, who hankered after Belgrade's intransigent line, and Togliatti's adherence to Stalin's tactical preferences. Second, all knew that the PCI's respect for the constitutional niceties was malleable. If Moscow thought it stood to gain from causing upheaval in Italy, the PCI's commitment to working democratically would be reversed as a matter of course. Third, the *mood* of the party was intransigent, even if party discipline kept insurrectionary impulses in check. Many speeches from the floor gave the impression that a 'violent settling of scores' was imminent. One of the Soviet delegates noted that every mention of Saragat or De Gasperi was greeted by cries of 'Piazzale Loreto!'[17]

When the PSI met for a four-day congress in Rome on 19 January 1948, the twenty-sixth in the party's history, the motion supporting the Front was passed by a landslide: only a handful of dissidents, headed by Ivan Matteo Lombardo, the former party secretary and trade envoy to Washington, voted against. Lombardo, together with Ignazio Silone, would shortly leave the party for good.

There was more opposition to the idea of having shared electoral lists with the PCI, which many senior party members believed – accurately, as it turned out – would lead to the PCI getting the lion's share of elected candidates. The party secretary, Lelio Basso, gave a labyrinthine opening speech to the congress that sat on the fence on this issue. Other Socialist leaders were strongly opposed, although a 'cult of unity' kept them in the party.[18] Sandro Pertini, for example, stated that it was necessary to be 'fanatics of the Front', but not to forget to be socialists, 'just as the communists won't forget that they are communists'.[19] Pertini's pointed reminder of the PCI's powerful sense of identity went unheeded. By a 66 per cent margin, the vote favoured common lists.

The vote was a triumph for Nenni, the most committed supporter of the FDP. His speech was a firework display that equated the bourgeoisie of Italy in 1948 with the French middle classes in 1940, who had accepted the Nazis and Marshal Pétain, rather than be led by a Popular Front. The DC, the Church, Saragat, and the PRI all came in for biting criticism over their various 'skeletons in the cupboard'. The speech was reheated soup, but it nourished the congress delegates one more time: misgivings over shared lists with the PCI were swept away by Nenni's verbal élan.[20]

The speech was, however, constructed upon an untruth. 'We don't intend to be part of a western bloc, any more than we intend to part of an eastern bloc,' Nenni asserted. *Avanti!* highlighted this phrase in large letters in its report of the speech.[21] In hindsight, remaining neutral in the East–West conflict was an absurdity if the PSI intended to govern with the PCI. It is nevertheless true that the illusion of neutralism was widespread in Italy at the time: the PSLI also supported it and even within the DC there were many who did not wish to be embroiled in the conflict between Moscow and Washington.

Moreover, when Nenni delivered the speech, he knew that he had made a compromising choice of his own. On 24 November 1947, he had flown to Czechoslovakia for a clandestine meeting in Karlovy Vary, 120 kilometres west of Prague, with none other than Georgij Malenkov, the rising star of Stalin's politburo and secretary to the Central Committee of the Soviet Party.[22] Malenkov would eventually emerge as Stalin's successor after the dictator's death in March 1953. He had also accompanied Zhdanov to Szklarska Poręba in September 1947.

Without time for rest, Nenni was plunged into an eight-hour discussion with Malenkov; a further conversation took place at the dead of night on 25–26 November. Nenni's diary was for long the only account of these discussions. It was also a selective one. The Soviet archives, when they were opened in the 1990s, included a twenty-four-page memorandum on the conversations with Nenni, plus a four-page summary written by Malenkov for the politburo. The Soviet leader had prepared himself from a dossier that included talking points, a psychological profile of Nenni provided by the Soviet Embassy in Rome, and an untitled document indicating what the USSR wanted Nenni to do immediately: obstruct the refoundation of the Socialist International at a meeting of Europe's Socialist parties in Antwerp in Belgium at the end of the month.

The conversation was frank. Nenni gave Malenkov an overview of events in Italy that was critical of his own errors but disparaging of the policy followed by the PCI since the *svolta di Salerno*. In particular, he suggested that the exclusion of the two parties of the left from the government in May 1947 had been more Togliatti's fault than his own.[23] When Malenkov pressed Nenni on the failure to form a single unified workers' party, the PSI leader argued that forming a single party of the proletariat was unwise since the PSI's autonomy enabled it to appeal to middle-class voters who would otherwise be lost to the Marxist parties. Nenni accordingly revealed to Malenkov the PSI's compromise plan for a popular front, with shared lists of candidates, with the PCI. Nenni was optimistic, however, for Italy's future. Via the ballot box or via insurrection, Italy would join the progressive camp guided by the USSR.[24]

There was a caveat. The PSI leader pleaded for aid from the USSR to forestall the Marshall Plan: 'if we are unable to propose a serious plan to the people to resolve the economic crisis, we won't be able to stay in power and the people will hang us all, socialists and communists alike.'[25] In their second conversation, Malenkov told Nenni that the USSR would provide grain for Italy in 1948, if the left-wing parties took power, but it could not make coal shipments for at least three years.

Nenni nevertheless agreed to break with the social democratic parties, even British Labour, which had loyally backed the PSI rather than Saragat in January 1947. Beginning at Antwerp on 29 November 1947, where Nenni's hostility to the Truman Doctrine 'evoked scandal', Nenni and his party publicly identified with a pro-Moscow position in foreign policy, at any rate until the dramatic events of 1956.[26] In compensation, the PSI received a share of Moscow's financial largesse, while the PCI in the mid-1950s became the chief European beneficiary of 'Moscow gold'.[27]

Understanding the pro-Soviet positions of the two parties of the left is necessary background if one is to have a clear picture of what was at stake in the first general elections in the history of the Italian Republic. By February 1948, the leaderships of both Italy's parties were working closely with Moscow. The PCI was well-financed and two-million strong. It boasted a clandestine military organization of unknown size. Its grassroots membership would obey orders to the letter, even insurrectionary orders. The PSI was a less formidable force, but its dominant faction, the maximalist left led by Nenni and Basso, was in thrall to the PCI and to the Soviet mythos.

Any portrayal of the 1948 elections in Italy as a kind of Vatican-State Department semi-coup, during which the plucky forces of the democratic left were overwhelmed by American money and threats, and scaremongering propaganda by the Church, is a parody of what happened, though it remains the dominant interpretation in English-language scholarship.[28] The elections were never going to be a cricket match. In the face of the de facto union of the left under the effective direction of the PCI, neither the United States nor the Vatican, let alone De Gasperi, could afford to play by the rules. They knew Togliatti, Longo, and Secchia would not.

If there was any doubt about the threat posed by the PCI, the *coup d'état* carried out by the Communist Party in Czechoslovakia at the end of February 1948 and the uncritical response of both the PCI and the PSI to the events in Prague confirmed the worst fears of those who regarded the moderate language of the Front's manifesto as a smoke-screen for the electorate.[29] The electoral stakes were suddenly even higher.

Italy and Czechoslovakia had much in common. As in Italy, the Czech and Slovak Communist parties had led the resistance to the Nazis and had followed a policy of national unity and parliamentari-anism in the post-war period. In the general election held in May 1946, some three million people had voted Communist in the Czech lands and Slovakia, in percentage terms slightly better than the DC's performance in Italy. The Czech Togliatti, Klement Gottwald, had subsequently been nominated premier by President Edouard Beneš. Gottwald's multi-party government, like the PCI, had favoured accepting American aid and had only been dissuaded by Moscow with difficulty from participating at the Paris conference in July 1947. At Szklarska Poręba, the Czechoslovak Communists were accord-ingly ordered by Zhdanov, like the French and Italians, to intensify the domestic class struggle and adopt a more aggressive policy against American imperialism. Unlike the PCI, they were in power. They began to press for divisive policies such as the collectivization of agri-culture and to extend their control over key government ministries, notably the police. The interior minister, Václav Nosek, stuffed the upper ranks of the police with party members.

Nosek's activities, which would have ensured that the communists had a monopoly over law enforcement in upcoming general elections in May 1948, provoked a cabinet rebellion. Twelve non-communist ministers submitted their resignations to President Beneš on 21 Febru-ary 1948. In response, the Czech Communist Party (KSČ) mobilized the workers and the police. For four days ministries in the capital, Prague, were occupied by party cadres, mass demonstrations were held, protests by opposing parties were violently broken up. A general strike was scheduled. Under intense pressure, Beneš capitulated and on 25 February he let Gottwald form a government dominated by the KSČ and its Social Democrat allies. Only one truly independent min-ister remained in the government, the foreign minister Jan Masaryk. He was found dead beneath the third-floor window of his office two weeks later.

The PCI and the PSI greeted the expulsion of the non-communist parties from government in Prague with enthusiasm, not embarrassment. On 26 February 1948 *l'Unità* published an article by the PCI's expert on the Peoples' Democracies, Ottavio Pastore, who boasted that the response of the Czech Communists had been like a 'bolt of lightning'. The Republic had been saved from a plot and, according to Pastore, the mass of the people had secured the opportunity of greater freedom and prosperity even if the freedom of the 'bosses, exploiters and reactionaries' would be curtailed. Pastore concluded his article with the cry: 'Long live the Czechoslovak People's Republic!'[30] The PSI newspaper *Avanti!* wrote approvingly of the 'Prague confirmation'. To the disappointment of Washington and the domestic reactionaries, *Avanti!* argued, the working masses of Prague were showing that they could 'legitimately aspire to a leading role'.[31]

Another PCI intellectual, Pietro Ingrao, asked, speciously, what the difference was between De Gasperi's government and Gottwald's. Both had excluded rivals, but, if anything, Gottwald's administration had more popular legitimation since the forces of the left were more numerous in Czechoslovakia and represented the mass of the people. This argument, of course, rather ignored the fact that De Gasperi had not mobilized armed party workers and the police to crush protests and shut down dissent to his move.[32]

Pietro Secchia was predictably the most celebratory of all:

The Czech workers have won. The democratic and popular forces of free countries are rejoicing. The wolves whose prey escaped from them are howling rabidly. This time round Truman and company's blow went astray. In Prague, too, there were those who wished to kick the communists and socialists out of government. Just like in Rome and Paris. The reactionary interests wanted to eject the representatives of the workers to grab back from the people the land and the factories that have been nationalized. To oblige Czechoslovakia to break its alliance and friendship with the Soviet Union. To make it join the Marshall Plan. But the coup attempt by the imperialist predators has failed. It proved impossible, ten years on, to bring off a second Munich ... Let the wolves and jackals of Europe and from across the ocean howl with rage. The workers of Czechoslovakia have triumphed. They are marching towards socialism. Moreover, it is not just their victory: the front of peace and democracy has taken a step forward in Europe.[33]

The events in Czechoslovakia in February–March were a heavy blow for the newly formed FDP's pretensions to lead Italy. The Prague coup energized some Italians but repelled far more. 'Prague has taught us how to vote to defend our freedom,' asserted *Nuovo Corriere della Sera*.[34] As the communists tightened their grip over the political system of Czechoslovakia in March and April, this sentiment only grew.

BLACK REACTION

The creation of the FDP and the communist coup in Prague prompted the mobilization of Catholic opinion in the electoral contest. In December 1946, Pius XII had warned that the political conflict in Italy was between those who were 'for Christ or against Christ, for His Church or against it'. At Christmas 1947, the Pope gave, in baroque syntax, an even more explicit hint of the Church's position:

> Deserter and traitor would be he who wished to lend his full collaboration, his personal service, his skills and abilities, his help or his vote to parties and powers that deny God, that replace right with might, freedom with fear and terror, and who likewise make lies, clashes, the mobilization of the masses, into weapons of political struggle, thus denying any hope of peace, whether at home or abroad.[35]

The Church also relied on the talents of Padre Riccardo Lombardi, a Jesuit priest known as the 'Microphone of God', who had spent the previous two years sermonizing against the materialism, atheism, and immorality of communism with what he doubtless regarded as divine inspiration. A true Christian soldier, Lombardi was indefatigable before and during the electoral campaign. Yet as the electoral campaign picked up steam, he was but the captain of tens of thousands of priests who worked tirelessly on behalf of the DC: priests who respected the separation of Church and State were an exception, not the rule. Almost everywhere, the faithful were assiduously reminded from pulpits that they had a moral obligation to vote for a party that was both Christian and democratic.

Aware that many Catholic working men and women might possibly vote for the left, important figures in the religious hierarchy such as Cardinal Ildefonso Schuster of Milan or Cardinal Giuseppe Siri of Genoa produced short guides on voting and sin to orient parish priests. Cardinal Siri summed up the message that parish priests should communicate to their flocks in eight points:

1. It was a grave matter of conscience to vote.
2. Not to vote was to commit a mortal sin.
3. One should only vote for the parties and candidates who gave sufficient grounds for believing that they respect the laws of God, the Church, and Men.
4. The materialistic and atheistic doctrines of communism were not compatible with Christian faith and practice.
5. Anybody who voted without taking points three and four into account would commit a mortal sin.
6. Those who did not vote, or did not vote for a Christian party, not only committed a mortal sin, but bore a share of responsibility for all subsequent offences committed against the laws of God and Men.
7. Confessors should refuse to give absolution to those who sinned in the ways described above.
8. The declarations of respect for religious principles enunciated in Europe and Italy by 'eminent representatives of communist doctrines and methods' were to be regarded as being without value.[36]

Parish priests scaremongered shamelessly. The arrival of *Baffone* ('big moustache', i.e. Stalin), the communist anti-Christ, was portrayed as imminent in hundreds of Sunday sermons. Property would be nationalized and taken away from the peasants, and the Front would introduce the community of women, or so some priests warned. Apparitions of the Virgin Mary abounded among the faithful. As a Canadian historian has written, the 'Virgin was everywhere to be seen in the weeks preceding the 1948 election. She appeared in the most unlikely places: high atop churches, in caves and . . . even several metres underground.' He adds, 'the cult of Mary had moved from fighting secularization . . . to fighting the spread of Soviet communism.'[37]

It is small wonder that the PCI railed against clerical interference in the election. The PCI's own propagandists played dirty themselves – witness the accusations that De Gasperi was a 'starver of the people' only the previous winter – but they now faced an enemy that was fighting them with even less scrupulousness. The language of heaven and hell was more effective, certainly, than the theoretical disquisitions of Lelio Basso in *Avanti!*

Christian Democracy could also count on the assistance of irregulars. One of the single most useful pieces of electoral propaganda was authored by Giovanni Guareschi, the Italian officer who was determined to survive a concentration camp in Germany, even if the Germans killed him. Guareschi had become the editor of *Candido*, a satirical weekly, and the writer of the immensely popular Don Camillo stories, in which an impetuous priest battled with Peppone, the communist mayor of his little village in the Bassa, near Parma. Guareschi himself was no lover of the Church, but he was intensely hostile to the PCI. His simple drawing showed a working man about to cast his vote in the secrecy of an electoral booth. It reminded him to listen to the voice of his conscience, for when he voted, 'God can see you, Stalin can't!'

During the electoral campaign, *Candido* also reserved a space in its pages for the single word 'Cretin' printed in large letters. Readers were invited to cut it out and gum it to their foreheads if they voted for the FDP.

The key irregulars mobilized by the Church, however, were the so-called 'Civic Committees'. Using Catholic Action to flank the DC, as the Church had done in June 1946, would have been a scandalous breach of Article 7 of the constitution. Pope Pius accordingly resorted to subterfuge. At the end of January, he appointed Luigi Gedda, a distinguished medical doctor and scientific researcher who was both a devout Catholic and a leading figure in Catholic Action, to create, in Gedda's words, 'a new initiative that had the purpose of giving life to an enterprise involving all the Catholic institutions of Italy . . . and through them, all thinking Catholics, so that they would know how to take part in the imminent electoral battle'.[38] Gedda threw himself into the task and, starting in mid-February, constructed a network of committees in every parish and diocese in the land. Hundreds of thousands of volunteers participated in the everyday work of the Civic Committees, perhaps especially after the Pope's Easter sermon on 28 March 1948. Pius XII took Matthew 12, verse 30, as his starting point in scripture: 'he that is not with me, is against me'. The choice was between good and evil. Italy was at a *bivio* (fork in the road), Pius proclaimed.

Gedda enjoyed regular access to the Pope (the chapter in his memoirs that deals with the 1948 campaign is narrated via accounts of his multiple audiences with Pius XII), during which the two men prayed together before Gedda handed over a list of the expenses his operation had incurred. The list went into a drawer in the Pope's desk and all bills were settled by the Vatican (the Irish government also contributed to the Committees' costs).[39]

Gedda gave no indication in his memoirs of how much the Committees spent, but it must have been a considerable sum. In addition to printing bills for millions, literally, of posters and leaflets, and the running costs of a fleet of delivery vans and lorries, the Civic Committees produced several short films that were shown to audiences in the church halls of the nation. The best of these films were minor masterpieces of the propagandist's art, not least because, though partisan, they were essentially truthful. Togliatti periodically grumbled about the over-intellectualization of the PCI's propaganda; the FDP would have done well to copy the straightforwardness and imaginativeness of the scripts of the Civic Committees' films.

The slogan *Vota e fai votare* ('Vote and Get Others to Vote') was the common theme of practically all the Committees' films. *Vota per questo vota per quello* ('Vote for One, or Vote for the Other') explained to citizens the mechanics of voting, the purpose of democratic elections, the secrecy of the ballot, and urged people to vote according to their conscience: its last disingenuous line was 'Vote for whom you like'. Women, young and old, were foregrounded in this film as they exercised their democratic rights (even by turning a queue into a scrum as they pushed to get into a polling station). Of course, the higher the turnout, the higher the DC's vote was likely to be. The same film also emphasized the difference in electoral law between the countries beyond the Iron Curtain and Italy. In the communist countries one had a choice: vote for an official list, or publicly express dissent. In *Vota per questo vota per quello* an official-looking hand was seen grabbing the arm of someone who had opted for the latter.

La strategia della menzogna ('The Strategy of Lying') was the most openly anti-communist of the Civic Committees' films. It began with images of magicians beguiling the eye with card tricks and other illusions, and proceeded to show Italian politicians, notably Togliatti and Nenni, allegedly promising *mari e monti* (literally 'seas and mountains') rather than working constructively for the national recovery. The parties of the left were exploiting the 'discontent' of the workers, the film argued, and pursuing power by stealth. The experience of communist rule showed where that led, the narrator explained. The last few minutes of the film showed DC offices that had been ransacked by communist squads (not in 1922 but 1947, the narrator underlined), images of Trieste and Gorizia divided by barbed wire, images of bodies being exhumed from the *foibe*, and scenes of churches being looted, and their bells broken, during the Spanish Civil War. In Trieste, the narrator intoned, 'the possibility of having a fatherland has been abolished'. The film ended, inevitably, with the slogan *vota e fai votare*.

Another, longer, film called *Mondo libero* ('Free World') made the point that our lives are full of conflict: like bulls, we lock horns. We argue, we fight, we shout at one another when we disagree. Democracy has been invented to civilize this innate human tendency to conflict by allowing all to express their views in a measured manner, and by compelling the majority to listen to the views of minorities while requiring minorities to bow to the will of the majority. Behind the Iron Curtain, communism has disregarded this principle. Speaking over images of a parade of workers carrying a banner of Stalin, the narrator says, 'those who can't vote, must march'. Nations who respect democracy receive aid from 'the generous American people', the narrator adds, as the film shows images of stevedores unloading grain from a ship. The film ended with an idyllic pastoral scene and a slogan that was a slight variation on the usual refrain: *Vota, vota bene, fai votare*.[40]

The United States was as worried as the Vatican about the consequences of a PCI victory. The Truman administration's newly established National Security Council (NSC) dedicated its earliest meetings to the Italian situation and, incited by some eminent figures, notably George Kennan, the architect of 'containment', even contemplated military intervention in Italy if the PCI won, or even dominated, a post-elections government.[41]

Although plans for military intervention remained paper projects only, the Truman administration did engage in what the *New York Times* called 'roughhouse diplomacy'. The United States supported the DC and Saragat's PSLI with covert aid, although the figure of $10 million, much cited in the literature in Italian, is seemingly a substantial exaggeration: a likelier figure would be one-tenth of that sum. This did not stop various CIA agents from claiming in their memoirs that American covert operations had 'saved' Italy from communism. The perception of 'success' for political warfare methods in Italy served to legitimize the use of political warfare by the Truman administration, and to set it up for some future disappointments with De Gasperi when the United States urged him to take repressive measures against the PCI.[42]

Overt US intervention came in several forms: Italy was the focus of information films and propaganda disseminated by the American Embassy and by the 'Voice of America' radio service; Ambassador Dunn meanwhile toured the country tirelessly to extol the virtues of the Marshall Plan. Dunn also celebrated the sheer scale of the aid already given by the United States to Italy. When the 500th shipment of American raw materials since 1945 docked two weeks before the election, Dunn was in the port to watch the cargo's unloading and to draw the appropriate conclusions for propaganda purposes.

Last, but not least, US intervention came from the Italian American community which inundated the peninsula with millions of form letters and postcards urging relatives to side with the United States, not with godless communism. What these letters had in common was Manichean language and a blatant appeal to Italian self-interest. If Italy ended up on the wrong side of the Iron Curtain, it was destined to slavery, repression, and foreign rule. If it voted for De Gasperi and his allies, it would enjoy the fruits of American democratic prosperity. 'Slavery, terrors, tears, misery and hunger would be your daily heritage, because America would abandon Italy to her destiny without sending aid, nor would she permit the shipment of packages to you, our dear ones', said one letter distributed from New Jersey.[43]

Ending US aid was the real threat in America's arsenal. It is widely agreed that the most decisive intervention by Washington in the Italian electoral campaign was the pointed announcement, in mid-March 1948, that aid from the European Recovery Plan would not be extended to any country with a communist government. The DC could ask perfectly legitimately what the FDP would replace American aid with. There was no convincing answer.

THE 'CHANCELLOR' AT WAR

Italians say that 'success has many fathers'. The DC's success in the April 1948 elections was no exception to this maxim. American Embassy officials were convinced that they had tipped the balance. Luigi Gedda, with more justification, stated in his memoirs that the 'DC did not obtain its "stable majority" by its own efforts. The Civic Committees won it for them.'[44] Gedda thought that some of the DC's leaders had been over-reluctant to acknowledge their debt to the work of his committees. Perhaps, but the DC's own efforts to achieve victory, especially the almost super-human campaigning of Alcide De Gasperi, were also indisputable. The DC's propaganda appealed shrewdly to the anti-communist instincts of peasants and women, to patriotic sentiment, and sometimes had a touch of the macabre.

The DC won the battle to capture the public's attention. The propaganda of the DC's press office impressively identified the weak points of their enemy's position and attacked them mercilessly.[45] The DC's posters and leaflets hammered home simple points. 'We must win. Or we'll never vote again in Italy.' 'The War destroyed. The De Gasperi government has rebuilt.' Posters underlined the risk of agricultural collectivization, Soviet style, and of peasants being turned into slaves working under armed guard. A poster called 'Our Prisoners' showed an Italian soldier sitting at a table with his loved ones. From the United Kingdom and its dominions, from France and its colonies, from the United States, Italian prisoners had 'all returned'. The bottom half of a poster asked, 'What has happened to our brothers in Russia?' According to the poster, 80,000 men had been taken prisoner, 12,540 had returned. 'Why don't they return?' A Soviet concentration camp was pictured to give readers a clue.

The fate of Czechoslovakia was a gift for the DC's propagandists: one rather cluttered poster was a mock newspaper called the *Prague Daily News*. It compared the Munich agreement of 1938 ('the Nazis take hold of power') with 1948 and the PCI's seizure of power. Asiatic-looking Russian soldiers marched, red arrows were drawn emerging from Asia to clutch the heart of Europe. A sidebar headed 'Latest News' listed various acts of repression committed since February, including the death of Jan Masaryk. The condemnation of the Prague coup by the Labour Party was compared to the PSI's congratulations to the Czech Social Democrats who had supported Gottwald. The poster concluded with a quotation from De Gasperi: 'We have no desire to finish like Czechoslovakia, we want to maintain and defend our freedom.'

The DC also relentlessly emphasized traditional values, above all the family, as the bedrock of a stable society. Marxism was inimical to the traditional family's continuance, the DC warned. As Rosario Forlenza has pointed out, the DC's posters deliberately recalled Christian iconography by depicting the PCI and the ideas of the left as dragons, serpents, or bears devouring (i.e. raping) young women, while 'Catholic forces were represented pictorially as angels, knights, and other idiosyncratically pure beings exuding the aroma of sanctity.'[46]

The missing prisoners, the collectivization of agriculture, the subordination of Togliatti and Nenni to Moscow, the PCI's progressivism over family matters objectively were damaging issues for the FDP's leadership. The DC's propaganda played on these themes relentlessly. Its campaign was ultimately more ruthless than the FDP's. The DC went 'negative' early and stayed negative until 18 April.

The campaign was spearheaded by De Gasperi in person. To read his private papers from the end of February 1948 onwards is to follow a man on a crusade. As he criss-crosses the country giving speeches, he is combative, responsive to every slight (and there were many), and is above all determined to paint the PCI as an enemy of democracy.

Onward Christian soldiers: DC propaganda promised that the family
would be protected from promiscuity and divorce.

There are no shades of grey, no hints of future compromise, few traces
of De Gasperi's habitual courtesy.

A speech he gave in Bologna on 18 March 1948 is typical. De Gasperi began by taking issue with Luigi Longo, who had accused him of
being the creature of the Catholic Movement, the Vatican and America. To the first charge, he pleaded guilty. He was indeed, like almost
every Italian, a servant of the Church. If the light of the Church ever
went out, De Gasperi added, men would become 'wolves among

wolves'. The Vatican had been a 'bulwark of human dignity' during Fascism, De Gasperi argued. It had protected him and many other opponents of the regime, including communists. Why now did the PCI deny that he, too, was a democrat? De Gasperi asked. After all:

> For democracy I fought against Fascism; for democracy I withdrew to the Aventine hill, for democracy I made a common front, after the murder of Matteotti, with socialists, freemasons, and liberals; for democracy I struggled to survive; I finished in prison, I was marginalized from national life. Moreover, for democracy I suffered and took risks, during the occupation, by organizing the resistance with the other parties, communists included. Why is all this, which even my adversaries have always acknowledged, now being called into question?[47]

De Gasperi pointed out how much Italy owed the United States. It had given Italy $1,800 million since 1945. It had spent $400 billion during the war and had given $14 billion in aid to Russia. For all Russia's great contribution to defeating Hitler, 'without America the war would not have been won'.[48] Unlike the USSR, Washington had been willing to make a fair compromise over Trieste.

The PCI, by contrast, was indeed the servant of a foreign power. De Gasperi gave his audience a detailed (and largely accurate) account of the creation of the Cominform and accused the PCI and the PCF of being given the task of sabotaging the Marshall Plan in the West. 'That's it in a nutshell, Mr. Longo!' De Gasperi cried.[49] After the 'tragic case' of Czechoslovakia, De Gasperi warned, the elections were no longer merely about who would govern. They were about 'whether we will proceed according to democratic criteria or finish in the sort of dictatorship we've already experienced for 20 years'. Unlike the DC, the PCI was ashamed of its ideology. It was hiding behind Giuseppe Garibaldi.

De Gasperi blasted the 'Peoples' Democracies' for not permitting workers' rights, such as the right to strike, and attacked the FDP, with a metaphor he would use gleefully until the end of the campaign, as a 'soup'. He joked that he did not know who the 'beans and potatoes' were, although there were 'a few chunks of bourgeois lard', but he was certain that 'Togliatti has the ladle firmly in his hand'.[50]

A peroration urging the crowd to vote could not be neglected:

FRO. DE POP
W il fronte democratico?

The two faces of Garibaldi: turn the book upside down to see another face.

> Bolognesi! I am telling you; I repeat the commandment: not to vote is a
> craven thing to do. To vote is a duty. To vote the wrong way is treason! ...
> We are talking about saving a regime of freedom ... about fighting for
> freedom and the fatherland![51]

De Gasperi gave variations of this speech over the next month in
every corner of Italy. As Italians say, 'he kept hammering at the nail'.
He attacked the PCI as agents of Moscow, urged the Marxist parties
to fight under their true colours, condemned the PCI's pro-Yugoslav

role in the Trieste crisis, warned that Czechoslovakia might be a harbinger, lauded the Marshall Plan and American aid as 'an insurance policy against a third world war', and described the members of the Cominform as 'little puppies facing a Siberian wolfhound'.[52] Few listening to his speeches would have learned what a DC government's policy priorities would be. If anybody took the 'gloves off' it was De Gasperi, not the Americans or even the Church.[53] His tour of the nation was an exercise in verbal pugilism, with more than a few low punches in every round. De Gasperi had clearly decided that there was no alternative but to fight his former partners in the resistance movement as ferociously as he could.

He was, in fairness, only giving as good as he got. During the campaign, the PCI tried to destroy the premier's credibility in its electoral propaganda. The Front's positive propaganda stressed working class themes: better homes, women's equality, fairer distribution of land. As the campaign went on, however, its campaigning became increasingly negative and focussed on the DC's leader. The PCI depicted De Gasperi as an Austrian, with Prussian authoritarian tendencies, who couldn't even speak Italian properly and who had been in the pay of foreign masters throughout his career: the Americans, the Vatican, and the Austrians. Cartoonists portrayed him as a goblin-like figure, frothing at the mouth with bile, as he smeared the PCI and the Soviet Union with lies and false accusations.

The PCI's hostility to De Gasperi was not merely simulated for electoral purposes. It was personal. While the premier's relations with the warm-hearted Nenni remained cordial after May 1947 – when the two men met at the bar at the Chamber of Deputies the two leaders would chat affably about their daughters – Togliatti, by contrast, always snubbed the premier whenever they met.[54]

Some idea of the depth of Togliatti's animosity can be gathered from a letter addressed by *Il migliore* to the PCI mayor of Turin, Celeste Negarville, on 12 March 1948. A few days before, Negarville had greeted the premier at the airport when De Gasperi arrived to address a rally of local DC and Catholic Action activists. He had even offered De Gasperi's daughter a lift in his car. The DC newspaper, *Il Popolo*, described him (in English) as a 'gentleman' for these courtesies. Togliatti was somewhat less charitable towards his erring subordinate:

Which Fatherland? The cartoonist Michele Majorana depicts De Gasperi dressed as Uncle Sam and with a Prussian spiked helmet and Austrian, Vatican and American citizenship papers in his pockets.

De Gasperi did not come to Turin on an official visit but for a propaganda event on behalf of his party, one of those events where, to make matters more serious, he delivers speeches that are totally unbecoming for a prime minister and in contradiction to all the agreements concluded between the parties about correct behaviour during the electoral campaign. Why, therefore, did you have to go to greet him and fawn all over him in your capacity as mayor? Do you think that DC mayors behave remotely as chivalrously towards our elected officials, propagandists,

273

orators, and candidates? Sure, they do! Every chance they get they treat our people like scum. In Calabria and Sicily, they are having our candidates bumped off. In Apulia they are mounting terror campaigns against us . . . Seemingly, you have not yet grasped that De Gasperi is a man who is employing the most vile, dirty, and low-down methods against us, methods that morally speaking are worse even than those adopted by Mussolini; in him [De Gasperi], there's not a crumb, I won't say of good faith, but of the basic honesty that even most common criminals possess!

Togliatti concluded that he doubted the electoral campaign could possibly be going well in a workers' city like Turin, if it were in the hands of a mayor capable of such 'maudlin' behaviour.[55] Accusing Negarville of sentimentalism came close to anathema; only the deadly word 'Trotskyist' carried more stigma in the communist lexicon. The episode wrecked Negarville's career in the party.

As campaigners, Togliatti, Nenni, Longo and company were almost as indefatigable as De Gasperi himself. They, too, toured the peninsula, sometimes addressing several rallies in a day. The crowds packing the *piazze* to listen to them were larger, more vocal, and more buoyed with conviction, or so they believed. In the final days of the campaign, the FDP sensed that it had wind in its sails, that victory was near. This mood of confidence bred contempt for the enemy.

Attacks on De Gasperi became more and more unscrupulous, culminating in an article published by *l'Unità* on 15 April, just three days before the poll. An entire page of the PCI's daily was dedicated to a comparison between De Gasperi and Cesare Battisti, the Italian patriot from the Trentino who was captured by the Austrians and executed as a traitor in July 1916. Headlined 'The River Piave Murmured', the article said that 'while Battisti died by hanging and Italian soldiers fell on the Piave Front, De Gasperi was refurnishing the Austrian army with arms'. A list of De Gasperi's – or von Gaspern, as Battisti was quoted calling him – wartime committee appointments in the Austrian parliament flanked a picture of the premier stained with rivulets of blood. At the bottom of the page was the slogan 'Against the Austrian chancellor, the serf of the dollar, the lifelong enemy of Italy'. Readers were urged to cut out the page and distribute it, or else affix it to walls.[56]

This attack recycled accusations made by the press in the 1920s to justify the Fascist state's persecution of the then leader of the Popular Party. De Gasperi's pre-1919 conviction that the South Tyrol should remain part of the Austrian Empire, albeit with autonomy from Innsbruck and Vienna, had come back to haunt him at a delicate moment. Like the DC's negative campaigning against the communization of Czechoslovakia and the deference of the PCI to Moscow, attacks on De Gasperi as an anti-patriot who had once preferred Vienna to Rome, while slanderous, were effective because they contained a kernel of truth. De Gasperi had not been an Italian irredentist, like Battisti. He was above all a Catholic and a democrat. Not by chance, he would become one of the founding fathers of European integration in the five years following the election. Virulent nationalism was alien to his creed, but, in the turbulent days before the April 1948 poll, his lack of it became an electoral liability.

The hostility and unscrupulousness of the PCI's attacks on De Gasperi derived from the fear that he might not respect the electoral result if he lost. During the campaign, Togliatti repeatedly asked the premier whether he would allow the FDP to govern if it won, and De Gasperi adroitly avoided answering him. (It was a clever question: if De Gasperi had said 'no', then the PCI press would have sounded the alarm of a fascist coup; if he had said 'yes', it would have been blazoned to the skies as proof that the FDP could be trusted with power.) Togliatti and the other communist leaders were genuinely afraid, however, that, if the Front did win outright or won a plurality of votes, then the DC might seek to annul the elections and claim that it was saving democracy from a PCI coup by carrying out a coup of its own.

On 23 March 1948, Togliatti held a clandestine meeting in a wood on the outskirts of Rome with Ambassador Kostylev and in 'a moderate and thoughtful tone' asked the ambassador to sound out Moscow over whether the FDP should 'seize power by force of arms' if the DC ignored the electoral results. Togliatti stressed that the masses of northern Italy were being prepared for such an eventuality by the PCI's officials, though recourse to armed insurrection would only occur in case of extreme need. Togliatti, aware of Stalin's caution on this matter, added that he was aware civil war in Italy might spread to the rest of Europe. Kostylev, for his own part, suggested that, while the PCI might succeed in an insùrrection in northern Italy, it would require 'immediate outside military aid, from the Yugoslavs first of all' if the United States or other countries interfered. Neither man, presumably, knew that Stalin was about to break with Belgrade.

Kostylev telegraphed his conversation with Togliatti to Moscow and asked for guidance. Soviet Foreign Minister Molotov told him on 26 March that the PCI should only use armed force in self-defence if directly attacked and that 'so far as seizing power by armed force is concerned, we consider that the PCI in this moment cannot implement it in any way'. This was unambiguous advice. But it is obviously worth wondering what Togliatti would have done had the answer been different. As Elena Aga Rossi and Victor Zaslavsky have pointed out, until the close links between the Soviet leadership and the leaders of the PCI had been demonstrated by research in the Soviet archives in the 1990s, 'the refusal to have recourse to armed insurrection was seen as a purely Italian choice for which Togliatti could take the credit.' Instead, the decision had lain in Moscow's hands.[57]

High officials in the Ministry of the Interior were afraid that insurrection was a possible outcome of the elections. On the eve of the poll, the office of the director general for public security sent to all prefects and to the general command of the *carabinieri* a document supposedly obtained from a 'trustworthy source' that illustrated a 'Plan K' to seize power in the event of a Front victory. The plan foresaw demonstrations, roadblocks, and the cutting of communications as a prelude to attacks on the local offices of the DC, Catholic Action and the PSLI, and the establishment of 'People's Tribunals' to deal with 'fascists or traitors to the people'.[58] Was this document a fake? A 'Zinoviev letter' *all'italiana*? Nobody can know. The fact that it was distributed to the police two days before the election does unquestionably show the 'high state of alarm and the climate of tension and of uncertainty reigning in Italy in the days preceding the elections'.[59]

OUTCOMES

After the emotions generated by the FDP's giant electoral rallies in the last week of the campaign, which culminated in Rome's Piazza San

Giovanni on 16 April, when 250,000 people packed the square to cheer Togliatti, the actual results came as a shock to the leaderships of the FDP.[60] They were not just beaten but thrashed. The DC took almost half of the popular vote in elections to the Chamber of Deputies (48.51 per cent), whereas the FDP barely achieved 31 per cent, more than 8 percentage points less than the combined PCI–PSI total on 2 June 1946. The DC obtained 4.6 million more votes than the FDP (12.7 million to 8.14 million) and acquired a working majority of the seats in the Chamber (305 of 574). Party secretary Attilio Piccioni memorably said that it hadn't so much rained votes as it had been a flood. *Il Popolo* proclaimed a 'staggering' victory for the DC.[61]

The PSLI, which fought the elections together with Lombardo and Silone under the banner of 'Socialist Unity', took nearly 1.9 million votes, slightly more than 7 per cent of the vote. They were disappointed with the outcome. They had been well financed by American trade union sources during the campaign and had expected to hold the balance of power. Still, when the PRI's 2.5 per cent was added, De Gasperi's centrist allies were a far from negligible force in parliament.

The largest of the smaller parties was the so-called National Bloc, an electoral cartel composed of the PLI, the UQ and a mini party headed by the veteran Francesco Saverio Nitti: the Bloc garnered a million votes. The Monarchists and the Italian Social Movement (MSI), a recently formed neo-fascist party, together obtained less than 5 per cent of the vote. The least voted political movement was the Existentialist Party, which, presumably to the angst of its leadership, took only 816 votes nationally and officially received zero per cent. The idea that political parties should present a cash deposit prior to the vote, to be returned only upon their superseding a minimum threshold of votes, has never taken root in Italy.

Elections to the Senate, despite its older electorate, was almost identical to the Chamber poll, although the National Bloc did better in both percentage and absolute terms. The DC beat the FDP by almost 17 percentage points and by nearly four million votes. The DC obtained almost twice as many seats in the Senate as the FDP, and well over half of the 237 elected senators (131), although the PCI and PSI's bloc of 'senators by right' meant that the DC, despite its triumphant showing, still needed allies to pass legislation in the Senate.

Three further observations should be made about the results. The first is that efforts to boost electoral participation bore fruit. Turnout was exceptionally high – indeed, it was one of the highest in a free election in European history. Some 26.3 million people voted in the elections to the Chamber of Deputies (92.23 per cent); 92 per cent of eligible voters cast a ballot for the Senate, too.[62] The Church's injunction that failure to vote was a mortal sin, and the tireless work of the Civic Committees, did contribute to the *size* of DC's victory: had 'only' 80 per cent of the electorate voted, the DC's winning percentage share would certainly have been lower. The DC was the biggest beneficiary of the stratospheric turnout.

More women voted than men, but even though Article 3 of the new constitution recognized gender parity, there were only forty-nine women representatives in parliament (four senators and forty-five deputies): 5 per cent of the 982 legislators in both chambers.[63]

The second observation about the elections is that they marked the ascendency of the PCI on the left. As one electoral analysis put it, the FDP, relative to 1946, had lost 350,000 votes to the DC and over 1.8 million to Saragat's breakaway from the PSI. This was a crude way of totting up the numbers, but it was true that the Front's weakness had derived from the PSI's failure to take votes from Saragat.[64]

The PCI nevertheless took comfort from the fact that the Front's electorate had mostly given their preferences to the PCI's candidates, while PSI votes had been dispersed. As a result, an overwhelming majority of the Front's elected representatives were Communists: in the Chamber of Deputies, 141 PCI members were elected, up from 109 in June 1946. The PCI exited the second general election to be held in Italy since Liberation with less of a bloody nose than from the first. The big loser was the PSI. The practical result of Nenni's obtuse alliance with the PCI was a meagre contingent of just over forty deputies in the Chamber, down dramatically from 114 in June 1946. Socialist Unity elected thirty-three deputies.[65]

History is not written in might-have-beens, but it is impossible not to speculate what Italy's democracy would have looked like had the PSI followed the Atlanticist lead of the social democratic parties of northern Europe, as Saragat had wanted. Had the PSI retained its autonomy, identified itself with the domestic agenda of Britain's

Labour Party under Clement Attlee, and welcomed the Marshall Plan, it could still have salved its conscience by attacking American policy towards Greece and Spain, by pressing for domestic social reforms, by sniping at the Church, and by making itself the natural home for free-thinking progressive intellectuals. Such a PSI would have drawn the ire of the PCI, indeed, it would certainly have been denounced as 'social fascist', but it would have been able to treat with the DC on terms of greater parity, which the PSLI by itself was not strong enough to do.

The third point to be noticed was that the DC had become a true national party. It won in both the North and in the Mezzogiorno by ample margins, while in the Red Belt it came a respectable second. In Emilia (Bologna, Ferrara, Ravenna), the DC got around 30 per cent, and in the electoral district for the western part of Tuscany (Pisa, Lucca, Massa Carrara), it narrowly beat the FDP. Togliatti had been right to worry about Negarville's campaign in Turin, since, in the electoral district containing the city, the DC beat the FDP by almost 140,000 votes, though the gentleman mayor was far from alone in delivering poor results.[66] In Bergamo and Brescia, the heartland of the North, the DC took an astonishing 67 per cent of the vote. In the South, the DC scored around 50 per cent of the vote almost everywhere. In Naples, it took over half the vote and was by far the largest party.

Becoming a national party was both good and bad. On the one hand, it conferred legitimacy on the party. On the other hand, victory meant that the DC became the party of reference for the mass of the citizenry, and the natural home for opportunists in search of a political career, or a sinecure in the bureaucracy of the state or the publicly owned industries. In the South, especially (but not only), clientelism would soon become a way of life for the DC's small army of elected officials in all tiers of the state administration.

The downside was for the future. In the here and now, the parliament had to elect a President of the Republic and De Gasperi had to form a government once that had been done. De Gasperi had said on the eve of the elections that he regarded the DC as a 'party of the centre, that is marching leftwards . . . the objective (*meta*) is an Italian labourism'.[67] It was a promise of pragmatic social reform. Despite the role played by the Church in his victory, De Gasperi opted to keep the anticlerical PRI and PSLI in his government after the poll. This guaranteed him a majority in both chambers and signalled that the government would not pander to the Vatican.

As another sign of his willingness to engage with the liberal left, De Gasperi backed Foreign Minister Carlo Sforza as his preference for the presidency, rather than persevere with President De Nicola, who was coy to the point of exasperation. De Nicola liked to be wooed and would often turn down positions of authority, protesting his unfitness for the office, before 'reluctantly' acquiescing. In the case of the presidency, when De Nicola prevaricated De Gasperi immediately took him at his word.

Sforza was the wrong choice. To become president, the new constitution provided that a candidate had to win a secret ballot of the 982 members of parliament by a two-thirds majority in one of the first three ballots, or by a simple majority thereafter. The secrecy of the poll placed a premium on party discipline. In the case of Sforza, discipline immediately broke down. De Gasperi was not able to deliver the DC's votes. When the voting began on 10 May 1948, DC 'sharpshooters' limited Sforza's vote to 535, over a hundred votes short of the two-thirds majority needed.[68]

Sforza was vain and had made enemies in all the parties, including the PSLI, which ought to have been a bastion of support for him. The seventy-five-year-old also enjoyed the reputation of being an active, not even decently retired, 'skirt-chaser'.[69] This was more than many devout deputies could swallow. Italy in 1948 was almost as moralistic on the question of monogamy among politicians as the United States is today. On the evening of 10 May, a DC delegation headed by Giulio Andreotti shamefacedly trooped to the count's villa to tell him they did not have the numbers to elect him. Sforza had his acceptance speech written and ready on his desk, but he took his defeat with good grace.[70]

De Gasperi accordingly put forward the name of Luigi Einaudi, who had the advantage of being a 'model husband'.[71] After an inconclusive third ballot, Einaudi obtained 518 votes on the fourth ballot, far more than the FDP's candidate, who was none other than Vittorio Emanuele Orlando, a week short of eighty-eight years of age, the ardent nationalist of 1919 and the most distinguished living representative of the

Prime Minister and President:
De Gasperi is received by President Luigi Einaudi.

traditional Sicilian upper classes that the PCI excoriated in the columns of *Vie nuove*.

Once Einaudi had ascended to the Quirinale Palace, De Gasperi could reshuffle his government. He formed a carefully constructed administration in which the key ministries, except for foreign affairs, where Sforza continued in post (but where De Gasperi himself directed policy), were in the hands of the DC. Agriculture, education, work and pensions, public works, the three economic ministries (finance, treasury, budget), and, of course, the Ministry of the Interior, where the indispensable Mario Scelba was confirmed, were all conferred upon DC ministers of proven competence. The PLI, the PRI, and the PSLI were given prestigious portfolios, but not ones that enabled them to direct domestic policy. The electoral battle had been a triumph for the DC, but the party's leaders knew that their victory would evaporate if social reforms were not rolled out, and under the stewardship of the DC.

The PCI greeted the new government with invective. It was 'born in blood', said Pietro Secchia, in an article whose abundance of pejorative adjectives almost choked its meaning. The American and British *padroni* had inserted their 'trusties' in the centrist parties, to ensure their bidding was done. The task of the government headed by 'Chancellor Von Gasperi' would be to 'squeeze more profits from the workers' hide' and compel the Italian people 'to shoulder the yoke of foreign imperialism'.[72] Secchia concluded with a peroration that implied the PCI would not accept the electoral outcome:

> We must prevent this foreigners' government from forcing Italians to kill other Italians ... There is no time to lose. The FDP must mobilize the Italian people against the peril looming over them. It is a question of saving their freedom and peace.[73]

THE SHOOTING OF TOGLIATTI

Secchia's inflammatory article was indicative of the PCI's wider reaction to electoral defeat. The election had become 'a plebiscite on the issue of "do you want communism or not?"' One PCI leader glumly admitted that it was obvious the PCI would 'never get a legal majority' if it were 'forced to fight on this terrain'.[74] The party's hierarchy accordingly constructed a theft narrative around the 18 April defeat and demonized the DC government as an enemy of the Italian people and the Republic.[75] The FDP was the authentic voice of the Italian people, even though it had lost, because millions of electors had been bamboozled by clerical propaganda or bought by the 'American Empire' whose 'gauleiter' were killing a hundred people every day in Greece.[76]

At the end of May 1948 the party leadership outlined a detailed plan, to 'denounce and unmask foreign intervention and religious terrorism' and the 'continuing enslavement of Italian foreign policy to hysterical American warmongering and provocations'. The party should campaign against the Marshall Plan, by underlining that it would provide for the return to power of the capitalist elites responsible for the fascist dictatorship and to a 'full-scale offensive' against working-class rights. It should also condemn the actions of the DC, which was accused of aiming to create 'a confessional and police State' and to exercise a 'monopoly over the direction of public life'. Ideological training and indoctrination were to be intensified and the 'socialist conquests' of the USSR, especially in the realm of culture, were to be given (even) more space in the party press.[77]

The FDP was to be the main agent of the resistance to the incumbent DC threat, both in parliament and outside. Luigi Longo spoke of the need to 'maintain the popularization of the Front's symbol as an element of unity and as a symbol of democratic struggle'.[78] This was in spite of the fact that senior figures in the PCI knew full well that the Front's 'artificial character' had not persuaded the 'shopkeeper, the carpenter, or the shoemaker' to vote for the PCI.[79]

The problem with this strategy was that the PSI itself no longer backed the Front. At the end of June 1948, in Genoa, the rank and file of the PSI turned on the party leadership that had led it to humiliating defeat. The 27th Congress of the PSI, the fourth since April 1946, renounced Pietro Nenni's 'frontism'. On 11 August, the PSI left the Front, which was thus revealed as the sham that De Gasperi had always declared it to be. The PCI, its strategy in ruins, began, at the behest of Secchia, a clandestine campaign to infiltrate activists into the PSI to subvert the party's new leadership and to restore Nenni and Basso's control.[80]

Before the Front could be dissolved, however, Italy lived through its most dramatic three days since Liberation. At approximately 11.40 in the morning of 14 July 1948, Palmiro Togliatti sauntered out of the Chamber of Deputies by a side door arm in arm with Nilde Iotti. The couple were seemingly intent on enjoying a late-morning ice cream. Ever since the affair had begun, Togliatti had behaved more like a love-struck middle-aged man and less like a high-level official. His legendary self-discipline had eroded, and he tended to disappear and reappear without warning, to the despair of his party minders.[81] He had refused police bodyguards.

Togliatti and Iotti were being stalked by a law student from the Sicilian town of Catania, called Antonio Pallante, who had spotted the PCI leader's preference for the side exit. Pallante, who held right-wing nationalist political views, was determined to kill the man he regarded as a traitor to the nation. He approached the communist leader from behind and fired four shots from a 38-calibre pistol from three yards away. Three bullets were subsequently extracted from Togliatti in hospital; one glanced off him and left only a flesh wound. Iotti screamed 'they've killed Togliatti, they've killed Togliatti' and, showing great courage, shielded his fallen body from further shots.

Pallante, however, did not deliver *a coup de grâce*. He remained standing there, smoking pistol in hand, stunned by the immensity of what he had done, until police officers who had come rushing to the scene in a jeep (according to Pallante's account; other witnesses said they arrived on foot) arrested him without a struggle. He was taken to a nearby *carabinieri* barracks and signed, after a lengthy stand-off with a panicky police official sweating profusely from every pore, a confession that he had carried out an act of revenge on behalf of all the patriotic Italians assassinated by the PCI.[82]

Pallante nearly became Italy's Gavrilo Princip (the assassin of Archduke Franz Ferdinand in June 1914), though unlike Princip he always insisted that he acted alone and was not part of a conspiracy. His pistol shots unleashed the 'impossible revolution'.[83] The working class erupted in fury at the murder attempt on the PCI leader. Simmering anger caused by the interference of the Church and the American government in the election campaign, stoked by the PCI's post-election campaign to tar the DC election as stealers and subverters of democracy, boiled over in a two-day explosion of violence and popular protest against the government. A general strike was called by the CGIL, which denounced the 'tense climate' caused by the government's policies, and the threat of a 'return to Fascism and the suppression of all liberties'.[84] All over Italy, but especially in the big industrial cities of the North, the PCI's hidden arms were brought out and distributed by its militants. Police units were fired on and disarmed and several barracks were occupied. Dozens of local offices belonging to the DC, or its allies, especially the PSLI, were smashed up or torched. In all, fourteen people, including seven police officers, were killed and more than 200, including 120 policemen, injured during the disturbances. To moderates, the scenes in Turin or Genoa, where tens of thousands of workers, many armed, thronged the streets, seemed reminiscent of Prague.

In Turin, the managing director of the FIAT car company was held hostage in his office, while armed workers patrolled the factory. He won kudos by offering to fly Togliatti's wife, Rita Montagnana, to Rome in the firm's aeroplane, though there was tension when she arrived and found her rival Nilde Iotti by Togliatti's bedside.[85] When Montagnana entered the room, Togliatti's surgeon, unaware of the circumstances, innocently asked him if he recognized her. Togliatti replied, 'Yes, it is Mrs Montagnana,' not 'It is my wife.' They formally separated not long afterwards. Togliatti had chosen Iotti instead.[86]

Special editions of *l'Unità* and *Avanti!* were rushed out on the afternoon of 14 July. The headline in *l'Unità* was 'In the nefarious climate created by De Gasperi and Scelba ... CRIMINAL ASSAULT ON TOGLIATTI'. In only slightly smaller letters, the paper said, 'civil war government out now!'[87] The 'government of disharmony' should resign at once, the paper declared. The special edition variously spelled Pallante's name 'Polante' and 'Ballante': there had plainly been little time for proofreading.

Avanti! was, if anything, even more outspoken in its snap judgement. Its front page shrieked, 'THE GOVERNMENT IS RESPONSI-BLE!' in gigantic type and insinuated that Pallante was connected to the DC. A powerful accompanying leading article stated that the blame lay with those who had 'taken on themselves the task of driving a wedge, almost of establishing two categories of citizenship, between those who side with a government that has degenerated into a regime, and those who are with the opposition'.[88]

The Soviet Union's reaction, next day on 15 July, was to issue a communiqué that picturesquely expressed its indignation for the 'brigand-like' murder attempt on Togliatti by a 'being who is removed from the category of human beings'. The Kremlin added, pointedly, that it was 'saddened by the fact that the friends of comrade Togliatti had not succeeded in defending him from the vile act of treachery'.[89] This form of words implied that the PCI's cadres might be accused of having 'objectively' betrayed the party leader themselves by their failure to take adequate safety precautions. As they all knew, the punishment

Workers read of the attack on Togliatti.

for such errors was to be purged from the party, if the Kremlin decided the 'crime' was serious enough. The Kremlin's veiled message caused a palpable sense of panic among the party leadership.

The attempted murder of Togliatti provoked dramatic scenes in parliament for the next five days. The PCI's speakers sought, in some cases somewhat hysterically, to pin the blame for what had occurred on the government. The PCI's case was made most subtly by Umberto Terracini. Speaking in the Senate during an emergency debate on the afternoon of the murder attempt, 14 July, Terracini underlined the fact that Pallante had been a member of the PLI and that he had been given a parliamentary pass by a Christian Democrat deputy with whom he had an acquaintance. Terracini also persuasively expressed the view, uttered more stridently by *l'Unità* on the same afternoon, that Pallante's gesture was not 'the isolated act of a madman'. Nor, although Fascism, war, and national defeat were the 'primary causes' of the political climate that had made Pallante possible, was contemporary social upheaval to blame for 'awakening in this young man ... the impulse for bloody violence to sate everything fermenting in his soul'. What had tipped Pallante over the edge was the climate of terror fomented by the Church and the DC during the recent electoral campaign. Terracini compared Togliatti to progressive martyrs like the French Socialist leader Jean Jaurès, and the Italian anti-fascists Giovanni Amendola and Giacomo Matteotti, all of whom had been victims of 'planned campaigns of provocation'. All three had been 'identified as the enemy of the people, as a traitor to the fatherland'. Alas, there had always existed disturbed, violent people 'predisposed to turn a willing ear to the dissemination of hatred' and whose reaction to such propaganda could bring tragedy. For this reason, Terracini, on behalf of the PCI, moved a motion that stated:

> The Senate affirms that the ignoble act of violence carried out on the steps of parliament against the hon. Palmiro Togliatti, one of the truest and bravest combatants of the cause of anti-Fascism and republican democracy, represents the coronation of the policy of popular disunity and fanatical exacerbation of passions that has increasingly inspired the action of the government. The political and moral responsibility for this criminal act therefore falls upon the government. The Senate further affirms that this government ... cannot carry out the political actions necessary to re-establish the harmonious unity of spirit and action under whose auspices the people founded the Republic.[90]

Terracini's speech was greeted with 'vigorous applause' by the deputies seated on the left of the parliament. There was indeed much to be said for his argument. The PCI had unquestionably been demonized by Italy's right-wing and centrist political forces, and by the Church. The day before the attempted murder on Togliatti, the editor of *l'Umanità*, the newspaper of the *saragattiani*, had suggested in an inflammatory article that 'the Russian Togliatti', along with his 'accomplices', aspired to the 'miserable power of Quislings', and asserted that the time was coming for the Italian government to 'nail' the PCI 'to the wall of their treason' – and 'to nail them not just metaphorically'.[91]

The reader, however, will already have seen the flaw in the argument put forward by Terracini and the PCI. For if anybody had been smeared as an enemy of the people during the electoral campaign, it was De Gasperi. And the PCI had done the smearing, just as they habitually denounced Saragat as a 'social-traitor', rather than as a progressive who distrusted the Soviet Union. If one wanted to be harsh, one could define Terracini's speech to parliament as cant. Perhaps, however, it is simply the case that in politics, especially in moments of high tension, trespasses committed against us invariably loom larger than trespasses that we ourselves commit.

For all the real rage (and some posing) in parliament, it seems clear the leaderships of the two parties realized that civil war might break out. The leaders of the PCI, who were apparently told by the Soviet Embassy that the USSR would not intervene in support of an insurrection, opted for a wait-and-see approach: if the general strike gathered strength, they would let it escalate, but if it petered out, they would block it.[92] They gave no orders that would intensify confrontation.

Togliatti, who supposedly whispered 'don't do anything stupid' before he was put in the ambulance outside parliament, gave his lieutenants clear instructions not to turn the unrest into an uprising, and from his sickbed made a reassuring broadcast promising his party comrades that he would soon be back at his post. His self-command and lucidity during the broadcast were, in the circumstances, quite remarkable: nobody listening to him would ever have guessed that he had been shot multiple times and operated upon only hours before.[93]

De Gasperi and the government meanwhile did not escalate the conflict by outlawing the PCI (though thousands of people were arrested for public-order offences, many for serious crimes, above all the possession of arms). He believed that what was happening was a spontaneous popular expression of anger, not a deliberate manoeuvre by the PCI to seize power, and the premier limited himself to appealing against the use of violence and respect for the outcome of the vote on 18 April. De Gasperi and other DC leaders ostentatiously visited Togliatti in hospital to offer their sympathies.

De Gasperi's caution should not be mistaken for appeasement, or weakness. He took a strong line with the CGIL. On 15 July, De Gasperi encountered Giuseppe Di Vittorio at the Viminale Palace, the seat of the government, where the premier and Scelba informed the trade union leader that they would use all necessary means to restore law and order unless the strike was called off. The prospect of large-scale bloodshed loomed. At midnight on 15 July, after consulting with the union's other leaders, Di Vittorio made a radio broadcast in which he urged workers to return to work.[94] His appeal was effective. The protests lost momentum on 16 July and fizzled out over the next few days. One consequence of the CGIL's strike was that it was the final straw that broke the unity of the trade union movement. On 16 July, the Christian Democratic faction of the union published an open letter denouncing the union's politicization by the PCI and, on 15 September 1948, established a 'free CGIL'. Subsequently, in April 1950, this became the Italian Confederation of Unionized Workers (CISL).

Meanwhile, the exploits of a great Italian cyclist, Gino Bartali, may also have helped restore calm. Following a phone call from the premier, Bartali, a devout Catholic and a friend of De Gasperi's, won two mountain stages of the Tour de France on 15 and 16 July, to regain the yellow jersey worn by the leader. The Italian recovered more than twenty minutes on the previous leader in these two stages and won a further stage on 18 July. He eventually won the overall race, an unprecedented ten years after his first triumph in the *grande boucle*. In the event, Bartali's victory was probably not critical, but it did serve to provide an alternative focus for public debate and discussion.

Once calm had been restored, the PCI was disarmed. Scelba had been enforcing Italy's laws on the possession of arms with vigour since he became minister of the interior in February 1947. In that year, the police had sequestered 797 machine guns. In the first five months of 1948, a further 2,100 had been confiscated. In the same period, some 36,000 hand grenades had been impounded. Scelba asked for the legislation outlawing the private possession of arms to be extended in June 1948. After the disturbances in mid-July, which vividly illustrated how many guns remained in the PCI's hands, the law was indeed renewed. By the end of 1948, 28 artillery pieces, 202 mortars or grenade launchers, 995 machine guns, 6,200 automatic rifles, 27,123 breach-loaded rifles, 9,445 pistols and revolvers, 49,640 grenades, 564 tons of explosives, 81 radio transmitters, and 5.5 million rounds of ammunition had been sequestered.[95] Hundreds of PCI militants who had hidden caches of arms were arrested after the events of July 1948. Scelba became a hate-figure for the PCI, not least because he made no bones about declaring his conviction that the PCI was Moscow's agent within the country and asserting that the attack on Togliatti had served as a pretext to put 'Plan K' into operation.

Scelba's energy and competence as minister of the interior ruled out insurrection as a strategy for the PCI. It was just as well. In 1949–50, De Gasperi's administration would proceed with its legislative agenda and launch a series of transformative foreign and domestic policy initiatives, above all membership of NATO, that met with the PCI's implacable opposition. The tensions intrinsic to Italy's status as a Cold War democracy were about to tighten further.

9
Cold War Nation

The most insightful American commentator on post-war Italy, the Harvard historian H. Stuart Hughes, who had headed the European Research Division of the State Department and served as a political analyst in the OSS, the forerunner of the CIA, predicted in January 1949 that Italy would sooner or later become Portugal writ large:

Slowly, by almost imperceptible stages, Italy is moving to the Right. De Gasperi himself, one presumes, is resisting the trend, but the forces of conservatism are gradually overwhelming him. His peculiar political construction – Bismarckian in its deft combination of apparently contradictory elements – may, like Bismarck's, scarcely outlast his lifetime. And De Gasperi is no longer young . . . If so, what is the next stage? A return to full-bloom Fascism, with all the trappings of national pride and expansion, appears most unlikely. Present signs point, rather, to the clerical-corporative type of state that existed in Austria under Dolfuss [sic] and Schuschnigg and is represented today by Salazar's Portugal – a sleepy, traditionalist regime and an indigenous outgrowth of the Mediterranean tradition. In such a state, liberty would disappear more by police practice than by fiat, and administrative corruption and inefficiency would provide loopholes for a certain tolerated opposition. To the outside world, its ostensible mildness would mask the regime's true character. But within Italy it would be quite obvious that Fascism, in its essentials, had returned.[1]

Ten years after the publication of Hughes' article, Italy was one of the fastest-growing economies in the world. Its intellectual life was the acme of pluralism: seldom in human history can there have been a society where so many magazines and reviews provided so many forums for literary Don Quixotes to tilt at each other – or where there was such a ferment of ideas. Federico Fellini was hard at work shooting *La Dolce Vita*, a film that can be accused of many things but not, certainly, of being sleepy and traditionalist, and Rome was preparing to host – with laudable efficiency but after a good deal of corruption – the Olympic Games. Italians were leaving the land and flocking to jobs in the factories, workshops, and department stores (a recent invention) of the 'golden triangle' (Milan-Turin-Genoa). Far from being a Mediterranean backwater, Italy was embracing unprecedented prosperity. Even the austere PCI was having to adjust to a society where the proletariat zipped to cell meetings on scooters, or even in FIAT mini-cars.

Historians do better to stick to retro-casting, where they are more likely to be proved right. Yet it is important to grasp that Hughes' pessimism might easily have turned out to be accurate. Salazarism *was* a possible future for Italy in the immediate period after the landmark 1948 elections. If it did not come to pass, it was largely because De Gasperi's government committed Italy to following the democratic path in the five years that followed his victory at the polls: the years of so-called *centrismo* (centrism).

In foreign policy, the Italian government ably inserted Italy into the Western camp. Italy benefited from Marshall Plan aid, signed the North Atlantic Treaty, and took a significant role in launching the fledgling institutions of European unity. Mussolini's bluster, autarchy, and militarism was replaced by a growing conviction that Italy could thrive only if the wider European political milieu improved. In hindsight, the choice for full, active engagement with the nascent institutions of European economic and cultural cooperation was an inspired one. Becoming 'European' was decisive for fragile Italy's modernization and democratic consolidation.

The years of *centrismo* were also crucial for the two parties of the left, especially the PCI. The period between the 1948 elections and the repulsive, antisemitic trial of Rudolf Slánský, the former general secretary of the Czech Communist Party, in November 1952, was comparable to the late 1930s in the world communist movement. Heroes of the proletarian revolution became enemies of the people overnight as Stalin purged the parties of Central Europe of comrades lacking ideological zeal (or who had simply lost internal power struggles). The PCI weathered this storm with its leadership intact, though not without sullying its reputation. It organized opposition on a major scale to De Gasperi's foreign-policy choices and made inroads into middle-class opinion by championing, on the Soviet Union's behalf, the cause of world peace. It resisted Italy's shift from post-fascist purdah and into the Western camp with tenacity but for the most part constitutionally and democratically.

THE MARSHALL PLAN

The European Recovery Plan (ERP), to use the formal name that its proponent greatly preferred, kickstarted Italy's democratization by enabling the government to *accelerate* the post-war reconstruction. It is important to understand this point. The United States, via UNRRA and various post-war soft loans and credits, gave Italy more cash between 1943 and 1948 than it did between June 1948, when the Marshall Plan was launched, and June 1952, when the programme terminated.[2] US charity had already helped Italy to *survive*: to warm and feed enough of its people to preserve social order. By June 1948, Italy, thanks to the parsimony of the De Gasperi governments, which had diverted resources to reconstruction by squeezing consumption, had begun to reach pre-war levels of output in many sectors of the economy and had repaired much of the damage to its national infrastructure (the rail network, for instance, had reached 80 per cent of its pre-war dimensions). Italy was straining at the leash.

To leap to a higher level of economic development than had existed before the war, Italy (like other European countries) needed to *invest* more in housing, machinery, ports, and transport. Further years of austerity beckoned – and that meant taking a large political risk in a country where the pro-Moscow left, despite its defeat in the April 1948 elections, still represented an angry third of the population. The Marshall Plan ensured that European countries improved living standards quickly, by enabling them to import raw materials, machinery and foodstuffs, to *sell* such imports to domestic consumers, and to employ the cash so raised in local currency for investment purposes. In Italy a 'lire fund' was created to finance infrastructure projects and social reforms with the proceeds deriving from imports from the United States.

In effect, the Plan solved the problem of the so-called dollar gap. To grow, Europeans needed American raw materials and machinery. But they had no dollars to buy them and could not earn them through exports since they were not making products that Americans wanted to buy (and their European neighbours were hoarding the dollars that they had). It took a lot of Scotch whisky, handmade Italian shoes, or Dutch porcelain to buy a locomotive. The Plan accordingly empowered European nations to finance a further surge in national development by spending in their *own* currencies with resorting to deficit spending.

The Truman administration's motivation was not altruistic. Quite aside from the political benefits that a thriving Western Europe contributed to America's strategic position, the Marshall Plan gave domestic American producers a stimulus that reduced, by the judicious use of an affordable amount of public money, the severity of the inevitable post-war decline in national output. Not by chance, businessmen and bankers were the Plan's biggest supporters.

One such businessman, Paul Hoffman, the chief executive of the Studebaker car company, became head of the Washington-based Economic Cooperation Administration (ECA). The ECA coordinated the Marshall Plan with European governments and with the Organization for European Economic Cooperation (OEEC), an intergovernmental institution that was established in June 1948 to slice the ERP cake and to promote European integration, especially the creation of a single borderless and barrierless European market on the American model. Ambassador Pietro Quaroni, in Paris, described European integration as an American *pallino* (obsession) in May 1948, but advised De Gasperi that it was one that European nations should indulge, while making constructive criticism.[3] Italy, along with France, became Western Europe's leading proponent of greater integration – to its lasting benefit.

The Marshall Plan was front-loaded: the first year saw the biggest

US aid contribution. No fewer than 370 ships carrying American raw materials and goods had docked in Italy by 30 September 1948.[4] The United States suddenly became Italy's largest source of imports, with ERP-funded trade accounting for nearly 40 per cent of all Italian imports in the Plan's first six months, and almost a third in its second semester.[5] Italy was the third-biggest recipient of direct aid in the first year of the Plan's operation: it received grants of just over $600 million in 1948–9, approximately half of the amount given to the UK. France obtained nearly $1,000 million, while the far smaller Netherlands received just under $500 million and was the biggest beneficiary per capita.[6] A contemporary pamphlet that explained the rationale for the ERP underscored that the scale of US aid was such that the average American family was providing Europe with 75,000 lire per year. Italy had received '1,000 dollars a minute' in 1948–9: the equivalent of almost 700 billion lire.[7]

Over the whole four-year period, Italy received just under $1.35 billion in aid, 10.9 per cent of the $12.4 billion total aid package dispensed by the Plan to the member states of the OEEC. In Italy's case, most of this money took the form of grants to buy imports of raw materials and machinery ($1.19 billion), though some money was disbursed as soft loans.[8] Italy bought raw materials to propel production: cotton for the large textile industry, petrol to fuel tractors, coal to keep the trains running, wheat for bakers. Italy had suffered significant war damage, but its principal factories in the north-west had fortunately mostly been left in functioning condition. The Marshall Plan set their chimneys belching smoke. Nobody in Italy in 1949 worried too much about environmental concerns. Production and jobs were all. Italy was, after all, a 'Republic founded on labour'.

The Italian government's report on the Plan's first semester was at pains to underline that 'ERP aid' would be an 'indispensable foundation' for the 'invigoration' of the nation's productive capacities so long as American money was not 'absorbed into the consumer economy', as a 'simple form of welfare', but used for a politics of productivity that would bring long-term 'economic progress'.[9]

De Gasperi outlined the theory underpinning the government's economic strategy on 29 November 1949. Speaking in parliament, he said:

There have been three phases in our economic strategy. The first: the struggle against hunger and national paralysis ... The second phase was the struggle to guarantee the value of money and ensure a certain stability in price increases ... We managed to save the lira from losing all value and now prices have stabilized in a way that will permit the development of productive activity ... The third phase will be one in which we will strive to give the economy enduring growth across the board. This means reducing costs, producing on a large and competitive scale, while providing for an adequate development of exports.[10]

Investment in infrastructure was an essential part of this strategy for the third phase, and in 1950–51 it intensified. Italy invested primarily in transport and communications (railways, building bridges), in land reclamation for agriculture, in industrial modernization, especially power plants, and in the reconstruction of houses. Investment from the 'lire fund' was spread equitably across the country, with war-hit and/or poor regions (Emilia-Romagna, Campania, Sicily) particularly benefiting. The economic historian Francesca Fauri has published a breakdown of how 'lire fund' money was spent in Emilia Romagna and Piedmont. Emilia-Romagna had received nearly 23 billion lire in investment by 1952 (nearly $37 million). Thirty-seven per cent of this money was spent on rebuilding the rail network and its stations, 16 per cent was spent on public works, 15 per cent on rebuilding damaged houses, 13 per cent on land reclamation, but just 2.15 per cent on workers' housing. In Piedmont, nearly 31 per cent was spent on railways, but 34.8 per cent of the 8.5 billion lire budget went on housing, while agriculture received nothing.[11]

The impact of this investment on ordinary people's lives was of course immense. Millions of people in rural Italy saw their villages being connected to national life, in some cases for the first time. Waterlogged fields were drained, bombed houses made habitable, bridges and viaducts rebuilt, roads repaired, telephone wires installed. Hitherto unemployed men dug ditches and plastered walls, while the construction of new houses gave young couples the chance to marry and move out of the family home. Soft loans to electricity providers enabled them to upgrade their technology, generate more power, broaden the grid, and bring electric light to even the most remote stretches of the countryside.

The ERP's Mission to Italy – the ECA's Rome office – ran an energetic propaganda campaign pointing out the moral dimension to Marshall Plan investments. A 1951 leaflet produced for a touring exhibition about the benefits of the Marshall Plan left no doubt as to what Italy had achieved with the help of American money in the previous three years:

TOGETHER WE HAVE WORKED
TOGETHER WE HAVE REBUILT
TOGETHER WE DEFEND FREEDOM AND PEACE.[12]

The pamphlet reminded its readers that Italy had imported nearly seven million tons of coal thanks to the ERP by 1951. The United States had shipped over two million tons of grain, nearly four million tons of crude oil, and almost 300,000 tons of cotton to Italy since the Plan began to function. Large quantities of vital medicines such as penicillin, insulin, and streptomycin had been furnished by American taxpayers.[13]

The ERP's propagandists contrasted the benefits of the Plan with the grim realities of the immediate post-war period. 'Do you remember 1945?' asked another pamphlet that combined expressive line drawings with a didactic text. Five years before, there had been long queues for rationed goods. There had been little food to put on the table. Women had 'dragged themselves around, along with their frail children'. Many children had died for lack of basic medicines.

Now, in 1950, there were 'plenty of foodstuffs', and the cost of living had dropped. Black marketeers had vanished. Ordinary commercial life was resuming and smiling citizens and their children could sit down to 'a plate of pasta and a nice glass of wine'. Thousands of lives were being saved every day by American medicines. Children were now 'steady on their legs'. Whereas in 1945 it had taken thirty-six hours to travel by train from Rome to Milan, and passengers had often had to cling to the roof of the carriages, thanks to the ERP smartly dressed men and women could make the journey in comfort in a mere seven hours.[14]

The improvement was not merely material. Right after the war, a 'dangerous moral decline had set in' (a shapely young woman wearing a ragged dress was pictured from behind, arm in arm with an American soldier, while a young child was portrayed picking up a cigarette butt from the ground). A mere five years later, the traditional family had regained its role in society – thanks to the ERP. Men were working, children were studying, young women could 'live without being humiliated'.[15]

But more needed to be done. The pamphlet suggested that the regeneration of Italian civilization, along with those of the other free European peoples, in a common European federation, was the greatest wish of the Senate of the United States. The point was helpfully illustrated by a full-page drawing of the Senate deliberating soberly and three pages of sketches of European nationals (a Dutchman wearing clogs, a luxuriously bearded Norwegian, an Englishman with a pipe, large teeth, and plus fours, a Turk in a fez, a Zorbaesque Greek, a paunchy Belgian wearing a trilby, a bulky German with a frothing beer in his hand, an Austrian in *lederhosen* and Tyrolian hat). The point of this ponderous exercise in national stereotyping was that these visibly diverse peoples, and others, had been united by the opportunity to build a new life with the assistance of the United States, unlike the peoples 'subject to a tyranny that does not permit them to decide their own fate' behind the Iron Curtain. But after 1952, when US aid ceased, the pamphlet warned that Europe would have to 'go it alone'. Europeans should make sure that the ERP, which was defined as a 'great intercontinental act of solidarity,' was not a 'wasted effort'.[16]

As a leading British scholar of both post-war Italy and the ERP has remarked, the PCI was placed at a hopeless propaganda disadvantage by the Marshall Plan:

Here was a scheme which, whatever its strings, promised immediate relief on a mass scale, a promise of industrial revival, and a long-term future of inclusion in a prosperous international community. The Soviets had nothing of the sort to offer . . . In this situation it was an uphill struggle for the party to proclaim convincingly that the whole ERP

scheme was a plot to colonize Europe, escalate the Cold War and transform the national economy into a market for rapacious American
corporations and Wall Street.[17]

The PCI nevertheless strove to do precisely this: *Vie nuove* was full
after the summer of 1948 with cartoons showing the capitalist octo-
pus enfolding the globe, or top-hatted Wall Street bankers clutching
bags of money earned by building tanks and warships. Such propaganda must have seemed formulaic even at the time.

One DC poster ironically replied to the PCI's rather hackneyed
attacks on the ERP by depicting scenes from Palmiro Togliatti's daily
life. The PCI leader was shown devouring a plate of spaghetti made
from wheat imported from America, driving a car powered by American petrol, being cured of a cold by American medicine, holding a
public meeting on an ERP-financed viaduct, and greeting his formidable wife at the station, where she had arrived on a train fuelled by
American coal. In the final picture, Togliatti is seen in the offices of
l'Unità writing a leading article that starts 'The Marshall Plan is a
fake. American aid encourages the enslavement and starvation of the
Italian people ... '[18] The political conflict in early Italian democracy
produced some inspired propaganda posters on both sides of the ideological divide; for sheer cleverness, 'Togliatti's Day' was among the
most amusing of them all.

All such propaganda, be it by the ERP Mission or by the DC,
underlined the inevitable political consequence of accepting Marshall
Plan money: Italy had chosen sides in the Cold War. The American
government did its best to persuade Italian public opinion that the De
Gasperi government had chosen the *stronger* side. The United States
was portrayed as a nation organized to harness power on an unprecedented scale in service of the inalienable rights of mankind: 'life,
liberty, and the *pursuit of prosperity*'.[19]

Like the Soviet Union, whose propaganda emphasized steelworks,
immense dams, and combine harvesters cutting a swathe through the
wheatfields of the Ukraine, much American propaganda in Italy
emphasized the technical prowess of the United States – its mines,
skyscrapers, turbines, and highways. The quality of life enjoyed by its

citizens, who were all white and lived in neatly painted mass-produced houses with picket fences, was the other main selling point. Americans had cars, radios, telephones, and even television. They shopped in supermarkets, which had abundant supplies of food. Women worked: domestic drudgery was facilitated by household appliances. The free peoples of the world were enjoined to share in the United States' struggle to achieve social/material progress. The 'implied message' of the Marshall Plan's propagandists was that 'You too can be like us' – so long as the peoples of Europe followed American prescriptions for growth and merged their economies into an integrated whole.[20]

De Gasperi's Italy became an enthusiastic supporter of the project for greater integration of Western European economies. As Vera Zamagni has argued, the Marshall Plan years were *foundational* for Italy's future prosperity, not simply a period of *reconstruction*. They created a prosperity that was not built on sand. Thanks to the De Gasperi government's emphasis on keeping inflation down and modernizing the country's industrial base, Italy managed:

> [Not only] to tie itself to Europe, but even to be a protagonist of the formidable European effort to catch up with the United States. An enormous leap in [Italy's] productive capacity occurred, and it proved able to expand its share of the world's exports while preserving greater exchange rate stability than countries like France and Great Britain were able to maintain. After 1949 Italy never devalued the lira until the gold standard was abandoned.[21]

Participation in the construction of the first institutions of European unity was essential for this economic success. If there is one thing scholars of the Italian economy agree on (and they do not agree on much), it is that opening the Italian economy to the world – above all, to its democratizing European neighbours – was vital. The self-referential Italy constructed by Mussolini's corporate state, and by the Liberal state before it, which had stunted growth and confined entrepreneurship, was superseded as Italy stood on its own two feet and searched for markets.

A MYTH TO LIVE BY

Italy's most noted scholar of the history of European integration talks of the 'glories and ambiguities' of Italy's approach to the project of greater economic and political cooperation between Europe's democracies in the late 1940s and early 1950s.[22] Italian thinkers played a significant role in diffusing the conviction that pre-war conceptions of nation sovereignty were now outdated. It was necessary for democratic Europe to coordinate its economy, establish transnational institutions of governance, achieve higher standards of living. Such convictions were an inspiration for Italian politicians in all the parties of government and acted as a glue that bound the parties of the centre together. Ugo La Malfa fervently believed that 'without Europe, you will have a desert'.[23] There were hundreds of politicians and intellectuals in Italy who shared this deep-seated 'European patriotism', certainly within the DC.[24] The European Movement, of which De Gasperi, along with Winston Churchill, the French socialist Léon Blum, and the Belgian socialist Paul-Henri Spaak, was honorary president, boasted a strong presence among all the parties of government. Italian intellectuals and party politicians exercised 'significant influence' on the 'galaxy' of Europeanist pressure groups elsewhere.[25]

The post-war project of European unity is perhaps best seen as a reaction to the bellicosity and state worship of Fascism, which was regarded in the late 1940s as the highest stage of European imperialism.[26] Building Europe was also depicted as a *moral* project that could stand in opposition to the cynicism and terror of the Soviet regime. Alcide De Gasperi famously defined European unity as a benign 'myth' in a November 1950 speech in the Senate. It was a political ideal that, unlike the other ideologies that had competed for European minds in recent decades, promised only good:

It has been said that European federation is a myth. It's true. It is a myth in the Sorelian meaning of the word. Though if you want people to believe in something, you tell me what better myth we can give young people concerning the relationship between states, the future of our Europe, the future of the world, security, peace, if not this effort to create a Union? Do you want the myth of dictatorship, the myth that might makes right, the myth of the national flag, despite the acts of heroism that accompany this last? In that case, we will once more create the climate of conflict that leads to war. I am telling you that this myth brings peace.[27]

At the same time, Italy's support for greater European unity was not the mere pursuit of an ideal. It was grounded in the nation's self-interest, as well as a broader notion of the continent's greater good. Despite the doubts of many interest groups within Italian society, Italy's shrewdest leaders understood that the country would gain more than most from lower barriers to trade in Europe, and from more relaxed attitudes to the free movement of peoples. De Gasperi stated unambiguously in 1949 that for him, and for Italy, greater 'European collaboration' meant in the first instance greater economic cooperation.[28] Moreover, to quote the prescient La Malfa again, Italy's leaders grasped that Germany, France, and Italy needed to exercise 'reciprocal control' over one another, via joint institutions, and by so doing they would 'fulfil a new civilizing function'. In the absence of such cooperation, which, La Malfa argued, would give Western Europe substance and a degree of autonomy, Europe was bound to become a 'battlefield' for two 'formidable groups of powers' to fight over.[29]

Italy's engagement with the European project should be seen, in other words, not simply as an episode in the nation's foreign policy, nor as part and parcel of its domestic economic strategy. It was rather an essential part of its consolidation as a democracy. To prosper, democracy needed the right *milieu*.[30] Without European unity – or, at any rate, without much closer cooperation between the states of Western Europe – Italian leaders believed that its democracy (and European democracy more generally) would be fragile, and perhaps destined to fail. The choice facing democratic Europe's politicians, or so Italian leaders believed, was 'more Europe' or a new *déluge*.

To secure a better milieu, Italy became one of the ten founder members of the Council of Europe (May 1949), a body whose parliamentary assembly was regarded at the time as a kind of constituent assembly for a federal European state.[31] The Council failed to live up to such lofty expectations (although it did, early on in its existence, draw up the European Charter of Human Rights, of which Italy was a signatory). Italy

Europe's founding fathers: the Belgian Foreign Minister Paul Van Zeeland
(*left*), De Gasperi and the French Foreign Minister Robert Schuman (*right*)
at a meeting of the Atlantic Council, Ottawa, September 1951.

took an active role in the measures of economic liberalization being
proposed by the OEEC: an Italian banker, Guido Carli, who had been
one of De Gasperi's party to Washington DC in January 1947, became
president of the European Payments Union (EPU) when it was established in August 1950. The EPU successfully acted as a kind of
import–export bank to facilitate trade between the OEEC's member
states.[32]

When Ugo La Malfa, fresh from his experience as vice-president of
the International Monetary Fund, became minister for foreign trade in
April 1951, he deliberately placed Italy at the forefront of the OEEC's
efforts to deregulate, liberalize, and stimulate economic growth.[33] La
Malfa slashed tariffs in November 1951 and facilitated competition in
the domestic market by eliminating quotas on imported goods.[34] His
policy was an 'open challenge' to the 'protectionist temptations' rife in

Italian business circles, but it worked.[35] Total trade (imports plus exports) was estimated at $3.7 billion in 1951, a 60 per cent increase on the 1938 figure: a fine performance, even allowing for American aid. In 1952, the total trade figure was higher still. Italy was surging into the global market.

La Malfa explained the rationale for the Italian government's policy in an October 1952 article that began by stating that 'foreign trade is of vital importance for Italy'. Italy suffered from a paucity of natural resources, which meant that it needed to import raw materials and foodstuffs and pay for them in dollars, and a high 'demographic potential', which meant incomes tended to be low. It largely exported to the rest of Europe, which, notwithstanding the EPU, did not have enough dollars to fund imports, and which had mostly not lowered trade barriers as swiftly or as fully as Italy. This had meant that Italy's quickness to open its market had been rewarded with a substantial and growing trade deficit (over $700 million in 1952).

La Malfa's solution to this dilemma was not the crony capitalism of Giolittian times, still less Mussolini's pernicious autarchy, but even more extensive liberalization of trade. The Italian leader argued that Western Europe's nations should move rapidly to 'well-nigh complete liberalization of imports', i.e. mutual free trade.[36] La Malfa was, in other words, one of the most important voices arguing for the concept of a European Economic Community (EEC). Such a solution was politically progressive, in La Malfa's view. It was a necessary step beyond the economic nationalism that had been a primary cause of the rise of Fascism. It is precisely this combination of self-interest and idealism that characterized most Italian thinking on European unity.

Italian pragmatism was also on show during negotiations to construct the European Coal and Steel Community (ECSC). Italy responded positively to the Schuman Plan, the 9 May 1950 declaration by French Foreign Minister Robert Schuman pleading with European nations to place the economic planning of their coal and steel industries under the guidance of a 'High Authority'. Unlike Britain, whose Labour government rejected participation out of hand, the Italian government committed itself to the project with conviction.[37] Its chief negotiator, Paolo Emilio Taviani, was a close associate of De Gasperi's. Crucially, Taviani was backed by the head of the nationalized Italian steel industry

(FINSIDER), Oscar Sinigaglia, who realized that the Italian steel industry, which was using Marshall Plan money to modernize its principal
plants, would soon be highly competitive in an open European market.[38]
No Italian minister is recorded as having said anything remotely like 'we
can't do it. The Durham miners won't wear it,' which is what Herbert
Morrison, one of the Attlee government's key ministers, is reputed to
have said when the Schuman Plan was presented to the UK cabinet.

Italy's first representative on the High Authority, when it began
work in August 1952, was another close associate of De Gasperi's,
Enzo Giacchero, an engineer and former partisan from Turin who
was a prominent member of both the DC and of the European Movement. Italy did not get freer movement of labour, one of its key goals
during the negotiation. The countries of northern Europe were keen
to hire skilled, qualified Italian workers, but these were the ones the
Italian economy could least afford to lose.[39]

Participation in the movement for greater European unity was both
an inevitable choice for Italy and the right one. It pleased the State
Department and the Vatican, opened the prospect of export-driven
growth, and appealed to the instincts of all the political formations that
had opposed Fascism, but were equally opposed to the threat posed by
Communism. For the common people, in so far as they knew anything
about European unity, it represented the prospect of an end to war.

Aside from a handful of economic interest groups that feared greater
competition, the only opponent of European economic and political
unity was the PCI. The Schuman Plan came in for savage criticism in
its press. On 10 May 1950, the day after Schuman's historic démarche,
l'Unità headlined its report on the scheme as 'the arsenals of the Ruhr
and the Saar merged in a gigantic cartel'.[40] A month later, Mauro Scoccimarro described the adherence of Italy to the 'French-German steel
cartel' as a 'display of servility'. In his view, European economic cooperation was a mere 'ruse': the Schuman Plan was to be interpreted as 'a
response to the needs of American war planning'.[41]

Two years of negotiations to clarify the scope and purpose of the
ECSC did not modify such snap judgements one jot. A 1952 PCI
pamphlet, *La Minaccia del Piano Schuman*, explained that Italian
elites had rushed into the plan for a coal and steel community through
'idyllic faith in the birth of a European federation'. The author of the

pamphlet repeated that the Community was at bottom a deal to 'control production and keep prices high'. It fitted into a broader American strategy, initiated by the Marshall Plan, 'that aims to organize the economies of Europe's capitalist states and the colonial and semi-colonial states into economies complementing that of the United States'. The pamphlet's introductory essay concluded:

> The coal and steel pool ... is a means of removing any pretence of being able to conduct independent policy from the ruling classes of these nations [i.e. Western European states]. It is a way of obliging the satellite states to choose rearmament as the only solution for the crisis that is overcoming outdated national structures.[42]

The PCI's opposition to the Schuman Plan, and subsequently to the ECSC, paled by comparison with the furore created by the next initiative in European cooperation, namely the European Defence Community (EDC), which was proposed by French premier René Pleven in October 1950, in the wake of the outbreak of the conflict in Korea, as a way of evading American demands for German rearmament. The EDC swiftly became another of the Americans' *pallini*. European cooperation in defence matters, under American leadership and guidance, was presented as a vital adjunct to the wider construction of an American security umbrella for the democratic nations of Europe. The EDC, signed on 27 May 1952 in Paris, with the same members as the ECSC, added fuel to an already burning controversy over membership of what the Italians called the 'Atlantic Pact', in other words the North Atlantic Treaty, and subsequently NATO.

LOOKING WEST

By taking Marshall Plan aid, and by opening the domestic market with zest, the De Gasperi government cast itself as anxious to accede to the United States' 'empire by invitation'.[43] Membership of the North Atlantic Treaty, which was signed in Washington on 4 April 1949, was the keystone of this policy. It was one thing to receive Marshall Plan aid, quite another for a former fascist state to count as a member of the 'West' in good standing. West Germany would not achieve the same status until 1955.

Italy pursued its goal via intelligent diplomacy. If by the early 1950s Italy was not yet the 'most important of the small nations' in Europe – this was De Gasperi's pragmatic assessment of the role to which Rome might one day aspire – it was getting there. They would not have succeeded, however, without the backing of France, hitherto post-war Italy's bitterest foe. Relations with France, glacial during the Peace Treaty negotiations, improved steadily between 1947 and 1949. Even though both countries were traditionally protectionist, the two governments painstakingly negotiated a customs union that was signed in Paris on 26 March 1949. It was promptly rejected by France's Economic Council, an advisory body of economic interest groups, but the ice had been broken.[44]

The climate of cooperation inculcated by the trade talks was one reason why France supported Italian adhesion to the North Atlantic Treaty, despite the obvious geographical incongruity involved in Italian membership. A further, more important reason, was that Paris considered another 'Latin' state was needed to dilute the hegemony of the 'Anglo-Saxons' and to provide France with a 'useful junior partner'.[45]

Such ethnic/cultural reasoning makes one smile (or grimace) today, but the underlying sentiments were real enough at the time: in Italy, as well as France. From the party's foundation, Christian Democracy's intellectuals had made great play of the salience of Latin civilization as a reason for rehabilitating Italy diplomatically after the war.[46] How could Italy, the home of both Catholicism and the glories of Rome, of spiritual *and* temporal greatness, be excluded from any post-war project of European reconstruction or renewal? The struggle against communism was seen through the same lens. Indeed, as the concept of the 'West' increasingly became the ideological rationale for the policies of the United States, Christian Democracy's publicists portrayed Italian civilization as being coterminous with it.[47] Italy's destiny, the DC proclaimed in March 1949, was 'bound to Western civilization, of which our people are one of the most illustrious progenitors, just as the future and progress of our economy directly depend upon the prosperity of the Western world'.[48]

After Harry S. Truman was confirmed in office in the November 1948 presidential election, negotiations for a security pact between the

Holding back the red flood: the DC evokes NATO and European unity.

United States and selected European countries accelerated. De Gasperi and Sforza were circumspect at first. Ambassador Tarchiani, on the ball as ever, grasped that Italy would risk being marginalized if it were not part of an alliance that was bound to become the 'fulcrum' of the West's broader political and military organization.[49] In January 1949, De Gasperi instructed Tarchiani to signal Rome's interest in the venture. Italian involvement was resisted by the British, who considered Italy to be of negligible military value and feared that Rome would interfere with Britain's own plans in the Mediterranean, notably in Libya.[50] In the face of pressure from both France and the State Department, which raised the spectre of communist subversion, London was forced to back down.[51] It was better to have a fragile democracy like Italy's inside the tent, however many problems it might cause.

Britain did succeed in excluding Italy from the final negotiations, forcing Rome to sign the treaty as a *fait accompli*. This snub no doubt grated with Sforza and De Gasperi, but they turned the other cheek: the prize at stake made putting up with British pettiness worthwhile. Membership of the 'Atlantic Pact' ensured that Italy became a fully fledged member of the Western bloc and that its 'involvement in future projects concerning European unity was all but automatic'.[52]

So recounted, the government's foreign policy seems like a 'realistic policy of peace', which is what De Gasperi dubbed it in March 1949.[53] At the time, the Atlanticist turn provoked turmoil. The debate over the merits of the North Atlantic Treaty between 12 and 18 March 1949 was one of the great parliamentary battles of Italian history. The two parties of the left opposed the Atlantic Pact fervently: Pietro Nenni's speech in the debate, in which he accused the government of colluding in a plan that would sow both internal and international division, was hailed as one of his most forensic performances, not least by himself.[54] The grandees of the Giolittian era – Bonomi, De Nicola, Orlando, Nitti – distanced themselves from the policy on constitutional grounds: Article 11 of the constitution outlawed war as an instrument of national policy and they were not convinced that the pact was intended to be defensive only. The PSLI was divided on the question. There was a current of opinion within the DC itself that sympathized with the constitutionality argument and was also averse to an excessively close identification with the United States.

Government speakers rebutted these arguments by stating that Italian participation in the North Atlantic Treaty by no means implied acquiescence in a war of aggression. Democracies did not start wars. Second, as De Gasperi lectured the parliamentary group of the DC on the eve of the great debate, the pact was being proposed by the United States, a country that had intervened in the last two world wars only after being attacked, because it was 'truly and sincerely a lover of peace'.[55] Third, as Ugo La Malfa contended during the debate, the North Atlantic Pact was part of the process of building Europe.

The PCI rejected all these arguments outright. The party leadership, notably Togliatti, who returned to the political fray in October 1948, averred that the United States was not only not a peace-loving nation, but was a warmonger. Togliatti argued that the only thing to do was to 'reject adhesion to any alliance or bloc, or whatever else they might be called, that is concluded in the sphere of interest of the United States or other imperialist power'.[56]

Togliatti was convinced that the root cause of American aggressiveness was its fear and envy of the 'incredible rapidity' with which the USSR was reconstructing after the war and at the extent of the Soviet Union's appeal, as a model, to the peoples of what would soon be called the 'Third World'. China, Indochina, India, 'even the negroes of Africa' were demanding justice.[57] It was important for Italy to be on the correct side in this gigantic struggle between oppressors and oppressed. If it shirked the task, it would, yet again, 'tread the tragic path of vassalage to foreigners, to the ruin of our interests, and to the humiliation of our ideals'.[58]

When Togliatti spoke in the Chamber of Deputies against the North Atlantic Treaty on 15 March 1949, he emphasized all these points and more. His intervention was a genuine debating speech, with parts of it improvised in response to previous speakers. It still makes for entertaining reading: clumsily interrupted by Matteo Tonengo, a Christian Democrat former partisan from Piedmont, Togliatti ironically told him that he should hope that the treaty contained no secret clauses compelling *persino lei* (even you) to drink Coca Cola instead of wine from the 'hillsides of Asti'.[59]

In his speech, the PCI leader pointed to the Americans' network of bases around the world, even in the most remote places where the United States could have no possible security interest.[60] He demolished the notion that democracies did not make wars by pointing to the crusade launched against the Bolshevik revolution and to the wars then being fought against colonial peoples. With another shaft of irony, Togliatti remarked that even the Netherlands, 'the country of cheese and fat queens', was currently fighting a savage war against the people of Indonesia.[61]

As for the story that the Americans were a peace-loving people, Togliatti suggested that the government's speakers should tell it to the

Indians, whose tribes the government of the United States had all but eliminated by one of history's first 'crimes of genocide', or to the Greeks, who were then being brutally repressed by their fascist rulers with advice and material help from Washington.[62]

Togliatti proceeded to equate the United States of Harry S. Truman with Hitlerism. Just like Nazi Germany, the Truman administration was striving to dominate the world. Moreover, this doctrine was not merely limited to 'leading echelons', but was being diffused via the press to the people 'exactly as the Hitlerites spread . . . the doctrine of German national superiority over all other peoples'.[63] Numerous intellectuals (Togliatti quoted the former Trotskyist turned conservative social theorist James Burnham) were advocating 'putting all peoples under the yoke of a single power'. That had been Hitler's objective, and the same thing was now being 'preached on the other side of the ocean'.[64] Why was the De Gasperi government helping the Americans in this endeavour? Its own ministers – and here, with heavy irony, Togliatti read out a long quotation from a speech in 1920 by Sforza – had once believed that the USSR was peaceful in its intentions.

La Malfa's argument that the North Atlantic Treaty would reinforce the construction of Europe was given short shrift. Togliatti accused La Malfa of succumbing to a displaced romantic nationalism. Political 'catastrophes' in Italy, Togliatti argued, had always begun with people 'muddying the waters' of political analysis by shouting 'Viva l'Italia!' La Malfa had shouted 'Viva l'Europa!' but the 'method was just the same'.[65] Later in his speech, Togliatti added that the construction of European institutions, be they the 'gimmicks' of the OEEC or blueprints for a federal Europe, had weakened the centrality of the United Nations, and of the cooperation of the great powers under its aegis. To that extent, 'all the so-called unifying initiatives that you are praising to the skies are initiatives . . . that have broken the unity of Europe'.[66] They had divided the continent and split the socialist East from the West at the behest of the United States. This was a tendentious interpretation, to use no stronger word, of the Soviet bloc's withdrawal from the Marshall Plan negotiations during the summer of 1947, but it was also a skilful rhetorical device to rob plans for European unity of their allure.

Much of the remainder of the speech was dedicated to a somewhat strained defence of the Soviet Union's exemplary behaviour in international negotiations since the defeat of Nazi Germany and to the liberation of the peoples of Central and Eastern Europe that had taken place under the USSR's guidance. The Stalinist regime in Moscow had, or so the PCI leader asserted, brought only good to its own peoples and to its neighbours since 1945. Ergo, Togliatti reasoned, it was the supreme task of the working class to defend the Soviet state: 'war will not be made against the Soviet Union because the people will stop you from waging it.'[67]

The PCI leader concluded his speech by announcing that left-wing parties everywhere in Europe would mobilize not just their supporters, but entire peoples, into a common front against the warmongering policy of the Atlantic Pact. Ordinary citizens from all walks of life and all political beliefs would be transformed into 'warriors for peace' willing to combat their governments' policy of war were the left-wing parties 'intrepid' enough to seek them out and mobilize them. The greater good of achieving peace meant eschewing sectarianism.[68] Not for the first time, Togliatti was seeking to broaden the PCI's appeal and find a cause able to make the party the vanguard of a mass movement.

The days following Togliatti's intervention in the debate over the North Atlantic Treaty were marked by a PCI filibuster in parliament and clashes between the police and protesters outside the building. The PCI placed a motion on the order paper proposing that Italy should instead sign a 'pact of permanent peace with all other countries' rather than belong to an alliance that 'can have no other purpose than unleashing a new and worse world war' and that would 'drag the Nation into an aggressive imperialist and class war conducted by American grand capitalism against the Soviet Union'.[69] A more moderately worded motion urged the Chamber to reject the Pact because it meant reducing national independence and agreeing to provisions that the government had hitherto not specified. Italy should not buy a pig in a poke.

The tone of the subsequent debate, however, strongly reflected the ideological and partisan character of the first motion. When De Gasperi attempted to make the government's case, he was shouted down and the proceedings became an orchestrated demonstration against the Atlantic Pact. For nearly three days, dozens of mostly PCI deputies, with women deputies to the fore, rose to make impassioned speeches against the government's foreign policy, as the president of the Chamber and his deputies struggled to keep speakers within time limits, and limit their speeches to an explanation of the reasons for their vote. Fierce exchanges took place between exasperated DC deputies and their counterparts in the PCI. At times, the debate degenerated into name-calling. The stenographic record is 324 pages long. It was a marathon.

It was also the prelude – once the North Atlantic Treaty signatories had agreed to a 'Status of Forces' treaty that established the conditions whereby troops from one member state could serve in another – to the return of American troops and support staff to Italy in dedicated military bases between 1951 and 1955.[70] The first of these were Camp Darby, near Pisa, and the headquarters of the American Sixth Fleet in Naples. In 1955, US military personnel who had been administering the American zone in Austria were relocated to Italy after the signing of the Austrian Peace Treaty. Most of these troops were headquartered at Aviano, in Friuli, or in Vicenza.

The PCI did not make 'I Giò' (Joe), as the US troops were known, welcome. The Italian historian Andrea Guiso has unearthed a fifteen-point 'etiquette guide', which was intended to orient party members in their interactions with the American occupiers. Militants were not to 'deign' Americans with a glance, or speak to them, or even give them directions. Party members should always show their 'aversion'. In bars, or shops, Italians should always be served first, to indicate disdain. Women were especially enjoined to avoid all contact with Americans, though they could be polite if they were directly addressed.[71]

PARTISANS OF PEACE

Togliatti's appeal during the March debate for 'warriors of peace' to resist the North Atlantic Treaty was an allusion to the groundswell of opposition to American foreign policy that the Cominform had been orchestrating since Marshall Plan aid began arriving in mid-1948.

Between 20 and 26 April 1949, just days after the signing of the North Atlantic Treaty, the first World Congress of the 'Partisans of Peace' was held in Paris. More than 2,000 official delegates attended, from dozens of different countries around the world (a parallel session was held in Prague, because the French authorities restricted visas to citizens from the Soviet bloc). A communist fellow traveller, the Nobel Prize winner Frédéric Joliot-Curie, presided over the assembly. Pablo Picasso contributed his famous sketch of a dove holding an olive branch in its beak as the Congress's emblem. Italy sent a 300-strong official delegation, headed by Nenni and Emilio Sereni, but hundreds of supporters also travelled to Paris, financed by a fund-raising campaign that accumulated 50 million lire: no small sum in the spring of 1949.[72]

The Paris Congress drew up a manifesto that condemned atomic weapons, which it wanted to ban outright, and appealed for nations to respect the Charter of the United Nations, not 'military alliances that nullify the Charter and lead to war' (a clear reference to the North Atlantic Treaty). The Congress confidently proclaimed itself to be a 'world-wide bulwark of truth and reason' and asserted that accordingly it would oppose:

> ... war hysteria, the preaching of race hatred and hostility between peoples. We urge the denunciation and boycott of newspapers, literary productions and films, individuals and organizations which make propaganda for a new war.[73]

Collaboration in the Peace Partisans' movement healed the breach between the PCI and PSI. The PSI held yet another congress between 11 and 16 May 1949 in Florence, and this time Nenni's faction managed a 51 per cent majority. The veteran agitator became party secretary again, in addition to being editor-in-chief of a new weekly journal, *Mondo operaio*. Nenni's victory caused the amoeba-like PSI to split once more, with the centrist group headed by Giuseppe Romita leaving the party in protest at this latest pro-Stalinist turn. They, Saragat's PSLI and the independent socialists led by Ignazio Silone and Ivan Matteo Lombardo finally, after much futile squabbling, fused into the Italian Democratic Socialist Party (PSDI) in January 1952.

Nenni used his soap box in *Mondo operaio* to mount a tireless campaign against 'the noose' represented by the Atlantic alliance.[74] It is unnecessary to list all his many articles and speeches on behalf of the Partisans of Peace, but they sufficed to win him the Stalin Peace Prize, a red-ribboned medal with Stalin's face in profile, in 1952. The first two years of the 1950s were the period of Nenni's most uncritical adhesion to the Soviet Union. Unfortunately, his usually copious and revealing diary is sketchy in the extreme for 1950–51, with few references to either international or domestic political events, and several long silences.

Nenni was more the movement's public face than its organizer. That role was taken by Sereni. The Italian national committee of Peace Partisans collected seven million signatures for a 'peace petition' to the United Nations in late 1949. Even after the Soviet Union had exploded its first atom bomb at the Semipalatinsk test site (northeast Kazakhstan) on 29 August 1949, the campaign continued – in keeping with the Cominform's instruction to national parties, at its third conference in Bucharest in June 1949, to resist American imperialism with all the resources at their disposal. In March 1950, a second World Peace Congress held in Stockholm passed a famous resolution against atomic weapons:

> We demand the outlawing of atomic weapons as instruments of intimidation and mass murder of peoples. We demand strict international control to enforce this measure.
>
> We believe that any government which first uses atomic weapons against any other country whatsoever will be committing a crime against humanity and should be dealt with as a war criminal. We call on all men and women of good will throughout the world to sign this appeal.[75]

The Stockholm Appeal, as it became known, mobilized tens of millions all over the world. The entire adult population of the USSR allegedly signed it, though only a Soviet citizen anxious to inspect a labour camp from the inside would have refused. In Italy, the appeal fulfilled Togliatti's greatest wish since he had returned from Russia in 1944: it gave the PCI an issue upon which it could mount a cross-party, ecumenical appeal to liberals, progressive Catholics, and socialists, and could raise the party's support among middle-class voters.

In July 1950, the Peace Partisans' bulletin published a supplement that listed the people who had already signed the Stockholm Appeal. In addition to political grandees such as Ivanoe Bonomi, Francesco Nitti, and Vittorio Emanuele Orlando, and an array of left-wing politicians, the Appeal had been backed by half a dozen university rectors, dozens of lawyers and judges, hundreds of doctors and scientists (including Renato Einaudi, a distinguished professor of physics and the son of the President of the Republic), and a lengthy list of scholars, intellectuals, and artists. Two pages were taken up by the list of 'industrialists'. The entire national football team had signed, along with many famous cyclists and athletes. But the Appeal was not just an elite fad. There were pages listing towns, villages, schools, and factory workshops where adhesion had been 100 per cent, or close to it.[76]

The Korean War, which broke out on 25 June 1950, only accentuated the general mood in favour of peace and gave a fillip to the campaign. The PCI's press stated that Washington's decision to back South Korea recalled 'the grievous aggressive actions of the Japanese imperialists, of the Italian fascists and the Hitlerian Nazis in the last ten years of the other post-war period'.[77] The Korean conflict epitomized why citizens should choose to become partisans of peace. In all, 16.7 million signatures in favour of the Stockholm Appeal were collected in Italy (more than a third of the population) and some 20,532 local committees were formed. In cities in the *zone rosse*, especially Emilia, those citizens who had not signed were few indeed.[78]

How had this miracle been achieved? There is an amusing short story by Giovanni Guareschi dating from this period called 'The Petition', in which Peppone, Guareschi's fictional communist mayor, makes collecting signatures against the Atlantic Pact a question of personal prestige. The whole village must sign. He assembles the toughest local party members and instructs them not to take no for an answer as they go from door to door: 'peace must be defended; with blows if necessary!'[79]

In fact, most people signed voluntarily. Italians had been thoroughly inoculated against war. For Italians, war meant national humiliation and destruction, not heroism, loyalty, patriotism, or the Blitz spirit (and still does). Neutralism in the Cold War struggle – Nenni's central message in his speeches – seemed like a better option for many, even those who were thankful for the Americans' economic aid. Others were simply repulsed at the prospect of weapons that could kill a hundred thousand people in a few seconds and did not trust either the Americans or the Russians not to use them.

Hard work and discipline did the rest. Sereni's committee did a masterful job at instructing would-be volunteers on what the key propaganda points were and how to get them across to doubters.[80] A pamphlet entitled *Fai firmare tutti contro l'atomica* ('Get everybody to sign against the atomic bomb'), designed to train volunteers for the petition in support of the Stockholm Appeal, explained that an activist could convince Christian Democrats by pointing out that those who had died at Hiroshima had been killed without distinction of party card. If someone were a fervent supporter of the Atlantic Pact, one should say that if they believed the Pact was essentially defensive, as the government insisted, then they had no reason not to sign. Above all, activists needed to stress the ecumenical nature of the campaign. People of all political credos, not just PCI members, were engaged in the struggle for peace.[81]

Fai firmare tutti contro l'atomica concluded with a detailed discussion of the 'Ten Commandments' that would-be partisans were ordered to follow (I am synthesizing, not quoting):

1. Get in touch with the local 'Peace Committee' to get literature and advice.
2. Distribute the Stockholm Appeal.
3. Organize a plan. Target opinion leaders first: the priest, the doctor, the local expert on agriculture. Keep them involved.
4. Always keep your list of potential signatories with you.
5. In agreement with the local Peace Committee, hold small-scale meetings (no more than 100 people) to explain what the Stockholm Appeal is about.
6. Set up a permanent centre for collecting signatures in every village or town quarter. Make sure that it is 'a genuine electoral booth in the election for peace'.
7. Involve every local association, without distinction of party. Unions, church groups, charities should all be involved.

8. Never lose your temper during discussions and never be afraid to ask the doubtful twice. Never bring politics into the argument: all can sign.
9. Pay particular attention to getting the signatures of women, children, and war-wounded. Get groups of women with children or of the wounded to collect signatures.
10. Once your list is full, get another from the local Committee. Compete to get as many signatures as possible. Check constantly to ensure you are not neglecting one of the commandments.

Above all, the would-be partisan should understand that she (or he) was doing something important that required commitment and dedication:

> The Peace Partisans' army must be an army of disciplined partisans, who grasp why discipline has been imposed, who understand what they are doing. For this reason, we ask you to do what this pamphlet tells you to do, and to understand why you do so, why you should accept the discipline of the Peace Partisans.[82]

Women were given a central role in the campaign against the Atlantic Pact and atomic weapons. The cover of *Noi donne*, the magazine of the Italian Women's Union (UDI), the week before the March 1949 parliamentary debate on the Atlantic Pact, proclaimed 'No to war. No to the Atlantic Pact.'

Inside, the paper declared that, on 8 March, International Woman's, Day, women had 'everywhere protested against Italy's adhesion to the Atlantic Pact'. On page six, the magazine published an appeal from the steering committee of the UDI urging all their provincial branches to organize rallies where women, 'without distinction of religious or political credo', could 'cry out loud' that they 'rejected every military pact', and that they rejected the Atlantic Pact specifically because they did not want 'foreign armies as masters in our homes', and because they did not want to 'cry pointlessly over corpses and destroyed homes'.[83]

The magazine's campaign did not just urge women to act as concerned citizens. It played relentlessly on the maternal instinct. For some weeks in 1949, for instance, the magazine solicited and published

Women demand peace: front cover of *Noi donne*, March 1949.

photographs of babies and toddlers, impeccably dressed in their Sunday best, under the headline 'They are all little angels of peace.'[84] 'Women can no longer permit their husbands, sons, and brothers to be snatched from their arms in the name of so-called "reasons of state" which mask the vilest interests of the ruling class.' underlined one article in March 1950.[85] In July 1950, Emilio Sereni wrote an article in the magazine appealing for a 'Women's Crusade against the atomic bomb'. Progressive women should convince 'millions and millions' of other women to sign the appeal 'before it was too late'. Before long, the 'American aggression against the peoples of Korea and China' might drag the whole world into a new, inhumanely destructive war fought with atomic weapons, Sereni asserted.[86]

Noi donne reached a substantial public. The paper sold 135,000 copies per week and it was distributed widely: for every subscriber, one could be sure that several women would read it (subscribers, indeed, were encouraged to share the magazine with friends). This public, moreover, was clearly a mostly middle-class one. The magazine was certainly not aimed at mill hands or fisherwomen. Its stories, feature articles, and editorials required an advanced educational level and implied a middling income. It was a magazine for aspirational progressive women with spending power: a socialist equivalent of commercial middle-brow magazines such as *Oggi*, and an antidote to frankly reactionary women's magazines of Catholic inspiration (the best known of which was *Famiglia Cristiana*).[87] Such women (and their husbands and boyfriends) were exactly the kind of people that Sereni wanted to join the cause.

The campaigns against the Atlantic Pact and for the Stockholm Appeal did not rely purely on committees of local worthies collecting signatures. They also used large-scale coercion. Industrial workers and dockers obstructed the production of military equipment in Italian factories and the supply of American weapons. In both Italy and France, the grassroots organization to collect signatures was accompanied by a 'mass mobilization of communist forces, involving not only strikes and stoppages, but also the slowing down of arms production, and acts of sabotage against military communications lines and the loading and unloading of American arms'.[88]

The culmination of the PCI's anti-war campaigns came in its coordinated opposition to the EDC, a treaty that objectively did require Italy, and the other European signatories, to make enormous concessions of national sovereignty: not until Maastricht in February 1992 was a treaty of comparable scope signed by West European nations. Under the EDC Treaty's provisions, defence policy was to be in the hands of a collective European Commission answerable to a Council of Ministers, and the Italian Army, except for police formations, was to be under the direct orders of the commander-in-chief of NATO, who was perforce an American. West Germany was to be a member of the EDC and was to contribute divisions to the common army. During the negotiations, De Gasperi leveraged his personal standing to insert an article (Article 38) into the treaty that encouraged the assembly of the Coal and Steel Community to draw up a plan for a 'European Political Community', with genuine representative institutions that would hold the supranational European authorities created since 1950 to account.[89] But this distant prospect of future European union in democratic institutions (which, indeed, subsequently came to nothing) did not prevent Italian public opinion from feeling disquiet in the here and now about the revival of German militarism.

The PCI harped relentlessly on this mood of disquiet. Its policy was motivated by the practical goal of obstructing the construction of stronger European institutions, which could only bolster the influence of the West.[90] Its propaganda featured monstrous caricatures of blood-sodden German soldiers. Its arguments against the

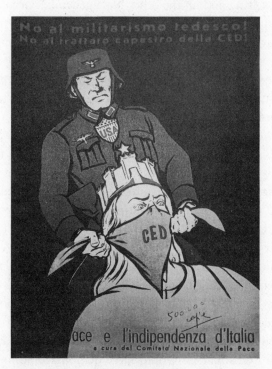

The new Nazis gag Italy: the PCI campaigned relentlessly against the EDC.

EDC can be summed up by a 1953 pamphlet – no fewer than 500,000 copies were distributed – published by the National Committee for Peace called 'No to German Militarism! No to the Gag of the EDC Treaty!'

This masterpiece of the propagandist's art showed a soldier in a German uniform, but with a US military badge, gagging the figure of *L'Italia turrita e stellata* (the emblem of Italy, as Marianne is of France) with a kerchief marked CED (the Italian acronym for the EDC). Inside, the pamphlet quoted Eduard Herriot, a distinguished French statesman, saying 'this treaty can only be approved by those who have not read it'. The treaty would eliminate the Italian army and 'bring foreign soldiers to Italy'. For the next fifty years (the duration of the treaty) the Italian constitution and parliament would be bypassed and 'Italian life would be guided by a foreign high command in Paris'. The pamphlet also warned that the EDC was 'a formula dreamed up by the Americans to re-arm Germany, to give the power of command back to Kesselring and all the other Nazi generals'. German divisions would return to Italy and have a 'position of command'. In third place, the EDC, far from being a pro-European development, was something that would 'divide' Europe and 'destroy the possibility of a European Union'. One small part of Europe would be united against the rest. Last, but not least, the EDC would mean that atomic weapons (and perhaps chemical and bacteriological weapons) would be held on Italian soil. The EDC 'would transform Italy into a 'storehouse for nuclear bombs, poison gas, and bacilli'. Italian citizens should say no to the EDC because Italy should never lower its flag, never allow the Germans to return, prevent the destruction of Italy's 'hundred beautiful cities', and should save 'peace, security, and national dignity'.[91]

The PCI campaigned against the EDC with the same, or greater, energy as it did on behalf of the Stockholm Appeal. A treaty that brought the German Army back into being was a godsend for the PCI's leadership. The EDC did reduce Italian national sovereignty, rehabilitate Germany, and subjugate Italian defence policy to that of the United States. A propagandist's task is always easier when he can plausibly claim to be telling the truth. But if the EDC hadn't existed, the PCI's leaders would have demonized something else – indeed, there were several concurrent campaigns to keep its militants active. They were never allowed to pause, to relax, or to become complacent. There was always a new international threat looming, or an insidious plot or intrigue, that was used to mobilize the party base and keep them in a mood of indignation and fear.[92]

THE APEX OF STALINISM

The late 1940s was an age of political commitment, a time when one made existential choices and stuck to them through thick and thin (or became an apostate, like the former communist Arthur Koestler, who compensated for his initial choice with crusading rhetoric on behalf of the 'Free World').[93] The PCI had made its existential choice in September 1947, with its sycophantic response to Zhdanov and Kardelj at Szkarlska Poręba and with its acceptance of Moscow's edict against participation in the Marshall Plan. As Umberto Terracini retrospectively affirmed, 'we had declared our contrariness to the Marshall Plan and followed the Soviet line in that regard. This was, and remained, the decisive choice in relation to which any and every other choice was no more than an accessory'.[94]

The PCI had doubled its bet on the Soviet Union in June 1948, when a subterranean dispute between Belgrade and Moscow had burst into the open and the top cadres of the Yugoslav Party – the doubleplusgood comrades of Szkarlska Poręba – had officially become unpersons and traitors to the international working-class movement. Tito had become a propaganda hate figure – the Stalin of the Balkans was suddenly its Trotsky – and the Yugoslav leadership had been unmasked as conspirators with the American imperialists and of being in their pay. The Cominform moved its headquarters to Bucharest.

It was not a moment for nuance. As the breach between Moscow and Belgrade widened, the PCI's leadership showed no trace of unorthodoxy, no qualms about the unwisdom of conducting frontal opposition to the North Atlantic Treaty and to De Gasperi's government. They were very conscious that Big Brother was watching them. Even Terracini kept his mouth shut.[95]

Indeed, the PCI strove to ensure that its own mass membership uttered no heretical thoughts. While the PCI was constructing a mass movement of 'partisans for peace' drawn from all strata of Italian society, its leadership was contemporaneously engaged in indoctrinating its mass membership to ensure conformity in its own ranks. In December 1948, the party steering committee had passed a resolution making the Italian translation of Stalin's history of the Communist Party (Bolshevik) of the USSR an object of compulsory study at all levels of the party as part of a concerted effort to 'raise the ideological level' of the mass membership. Some 250,000 copies of the book had already been sold, but the party pressed for an even wider diffusion of Stalin's 'ground-breaking work', whose 'straightforward language' had given communists 'a living and real example of how the science, theory, and culture of the avant-garde ... can become the common patrimony of millions'. Regional federations were to send their most able cadres to special training schools to learn the correct interpretation of the book prior to teaching its insights to the ordinary membership.[96]

Stalin's textbook was one of the most mendacious in human history, one that presented a carefully fabricated version of the achievements of Soviet power since 1917. People like Togliatti, a survivor of the purges, or Emilio Sereni, a stern advocate within the party of ideological discipline, knew perfectly well, with one part of their minds, that the book was a prolonged (and stylistically turgid) exercise in falsehood and omission. Their goal, however, was not to reveal the truth about the USSR, but to increase zealotry among the mass membership. According to the steering committee's resolution, Stalin's book illustrated that:

> The Bolsheviks won because they were able to create a Party in which both criticism and self-criticism are the normal method of educating the party cadres, a Party where every member is a militant intimately linked to the masses and has a precise and concrete job to do among them; a Party armed with revolutionary vigilance, that permitted it to unmask, within and without its ranks, the enemies of the working class, the enemies of the People.[97]

Self-criticism was accordingly promoted vigorously in the party schools (which all cadres singled out for responsibility within the party had to attend). It was obligatory for those frequenting the schools to write short autobiographies which were often meticulously (even maliciously) critiqued to identify personal weaknesses, class origins, reactionary tendencies, and so on. These biographies were then discussed in great detail and comrades were upbraided in public for their faults by their peers (to react angrily to such criticism was regarded as a sign of bourgeois individualism). The comparison with Catholicism is inevitable: the DC's militants naturally attended Mass and took the sacraments, which meant divulging their sins to a priest. But at least they did not have to do so in public and be berated for their failings. The PCI's practice was more like the Inquisition.[98]

The cult of criticism did not extend to the Soviet Union and its policies. A communist militant called Paolo Robotti could write a book entitled *This is How They Live in the Soviet Union* which provided answers to commonly asked questions about the USSR. He notably did not mention the existence of the labour camps, or Gulag, despite being himself a survivor of them.[99]

Stalin, meanwhile, was fêted. He was a father figure for Italy's communists. Paolo Spriano, author of a five-volume history of the PCI among dozens of other works, wrote retrospectively of the PCI's 'great love' for Stalin and of the myth of the USSR, which he said was 'absolute, blind, desirous only of approval by the object loved'.[100] The PCI's membership deluged Stalin with gifts on his seventieth birthday in 1950. Thousands of people sent handicrafts, olive oil, musical instruments, Etruscan vases, binoculars, leather bags (and much else). The parliamentary group of the PCI sent him 'pictures of Rome' dating from 1823. Some PCI militants even sent portraits of the Soviet leader, perhaps thinking that he didn't have enough.[101]

Accounts of visits to the Soviet Union by 'political pilgrims' also instructed the PCI's membership.[102] Some of these must have strained the credulity of even the naivest party members, especially those who knew anything about the USSR. Maria Antonietta Macciocchi, an 'intellectual' who would subsequently have a long career as an apologist for Maoism, wrote in January 1950:

> We walked through the beautiful streets of the [Moscow] city centre staring at the enormous, illuminated shop windows, which emit a sensation of rich abundance. We saw stores for foodstuffs, books, and

clothing, all packed with people . . . In the Soviet Union a great magnificent world is emerging in which men and women live happily . . . Stalin is the great craftsman who has brought all this about and the people love him for it. They love him for all the joy, for all the prosperity that they have received from him.

This mention of Stalin's name inspired Macciocchi to warm to her central theme: the relationship of Stalin with his people, especially the young. During the May Day parade, she reported:

Hundreds of thousands of Soviet citizens pass by the mausoleum to salute Stalin. Parents carry their children, with their heads and arms decorated with flowers, on their shoulders. When they pass in front of Stalin, they raise their children up with their arms and display them joyously. For their own part, the children wave to Stalin, they smile for him, and they call out words of endearment. Each has brought a favourite toy to show to Stalin. Some have brought a doll, others a woolly lambkin, or a train . . . Stalin jokes with the children. He embraces them all with a glowing face . . . Oh, the dialogue of love that exists between Stalin and his people! Oh, the gracious face of Stalin, his limitless simplicity! What tenderness and affection he shows for this people who are his children, who are free, and for whom he, through extraordinary efforts, has ensured a future of incomparable greatness.[103]

Such effusions were the safest way of remaining a party member in good standing. Nobody was going to sanction you for eulogizing Stalin. By contrast, in 1949–50, the surest way to be branded an 'enemy of the people' by the PCI was to be equivocal about the struggle against American imperialism, or to characterize the De Gasperi government as anything other than fascist or reactionary. To use a contemporary phrase (which derives from this period in communist history), one had to be careful to say the 'politically correct' thing. This doubtless required self-censorship for many, but it was, so to speak, physiological: in a political battle, doubters only weaken the cause.

Political correctness was also required, however, of artists, scientists, and scholars in their creative work. In the visual arts, realism was *de rigueur*. Party artists, some of whom, notably the Sicilian painter

Renato Guttuso, were undeniably gifted, painted 'farm labourers, women in the paddy fields, and sulphur miners'. In music, experimentation was out. Shostakovich, for instance, was out of favour in the USSR for the aesthetic deviation of being a 'formalist'. In 1949, Togliatti attacked his Leningrad symphony (no. 7) for being 'over-refined'. In a rare example of dissent, the PCI's most distinguished music critic, Massimo Mila, who had written in praise and defence of the persecuted Russian composer, told the PCI leader, in print, that he didn't know what he was talking about. Even more unusually, Togliatti backed down, though he did ask Mila whether he realized that he was 'working for the enemy'.

This setback aside, Togliatti, under the guise of 'Roderigo di Castiglia', dictated the party line on the humanities from the columns of *Rinascita*, effectively laying down the law on which writers, composers, poets, painters, and philosophers one could approve of, and which one could not.[104]

Ignazio Silone was the target of some of Togliatti's most merciless rhetoric. By 1950, the success of *Fontamara* had made Silone a world-renowned writer, but he had broken with Nenni's PSI and was becoming one of Europe's most prominent critics of Stalinism. The final straw came with the publication of 'Emergency Exit', Silone's autobiographical account of how he became disenchanted with the cynicism of Soviet communism and eventually broke with it in the early 1930s. Published first in Italian, it was translated and reprinted in English as part of a collection of essays by other former communists called *The God that Failed*, which became one of the milestones of the cultural Cold War. *The God that Failed* was savaged by Togliatti (he said that 'Emergency Exit' could only be believed by 'idiotic sheep' and that the six contributors to the book had fallen into an 'abyss of corruption and degeneration'). Thereafter, Silone was a pariah in the PCI-dominated literary world until the 1980s.[105]

In science, Trofim Lysenko's rejection of a century of genetic science was defended by some scientists close to the party. The campaign against those biologists (in Italy, most of them) who regarded Lysenko as a charlatan, or a political hack, and who thought that science and political ideology should not be confounded, was carried on by the ubiquitous Emilio Sereni. One of the scientists most vocal in debunking Lysenkoism recalled that the scientific merits of the arguments simply did not count in this campaign. Truth was of secondary importance. It was simply anti-Soviet to call Lysenko's theories into question. Some of his colleagues accordingly concluded that it was better 'to be wrong with the party, than be right on your own'.[106]

Historical scholarship was obviously not spared. To give one egregious example, *Rassegna sovietica*, a PCI-sponsored journal that brought Soviet scholarship to Italian academics, dedicated its June 1952 edition to the Renaissance and, more specifically, to Leonardo da Vinci. The key article in the collection was by V. Lazarev and was entitled 'Against the Falsification of the History of Renaissance Culture'. This article was an able but scurrilous attack on the decadence of Italian scholarship, which was found guilty of the heinous crime of breaking down periodization by suggesting that many of the innovations and ideas that characterized Renaissance humanism in fact had been developed earlier, within the Catholic scholastic tradition, during the Middle Ages. This notion contradicted both Marx's and Engels' writings on the subject and hence was *a priori* both unscientific and wrong. Lazarev, however, attributed murky motives to the Italian scholars working in this field. Large parts of the article were given over to personal slurs on the reputation and character of one Professor Giuseppe Toffanin, who was defined as 'a consummate obscurantist of science', as a scholar whose work could 'only please the Jesuits', and as being responsible for 'shameless historical falsifications'. Toffanin's writings, dismissed as 'profoundly clerical in spirit', were allegedly what passed for historical science in 'the Italy of Mussolini and the Italy of De Gasperi'.[107]

Lazarev's article was a storm in an academic teacup, perhaps, but it is quoted because it illustrates a broader illiberal state of mind in which intellectual identification with a revealed vision of the world was absolute. When one was faced with an idea that contrasted that vision, or required its modification, one destroyed it, or at least denigrated and smeared its proponents. Had this mentality been limited to art history, music, or even genetics, the mass of the PCI's membership might have remained untouched by the radical intolerance that it implied. But it did not. At the apex of Stalinism, every major political development was subject to the same process: an official historical

interpretation was promulgated by the USSR, obedience to the interpretation was turned into a test of loyalty, dissenters and opponents
lost all rights and were treated as enemies of the people – even if they
had hitherto been heroes of the socialist movement.

The split with Yugoslavia, for example, led to a wave of purges
across the countries behind the Iron Curtain. Hundreds of alleged
'Titoist' traitors and spies at the highest ranks of the party leadership
were 'unmasked' in Albania, Bulgaria, Hungary, Poland, and Czechoslovakia between the autumn of 1949 and November 1952.

The most fortunate of these individuals, such as Ladislaw Gomulka,
the leader of the Polish Socialist Workers' Party, lived to fight another
day. They merely became 'unpersons' for some years before returning to power after Stalin's demise in 1953. Others, such as Lázló
Rajk in Hungary, Traicho Kostov in Bulgaria, and Rudolf Slánský in
Czechoslovakia were tortured and hanged after show trials that
were every bit as bizarre as the great trials of the 1930s in the USSR
and that, in the case of the Slánský Trial especially, also oozed
antisemitism.

During these elaborately staged witchcraft trials, the PCI meticulously maintained the party line, without nuance, and without any
public expression of doubt. Even in the case of Rajk, who had fought
Fascism in Spain alongside Luigi Longo and other leading PCI officials, the PCI expressed no equivocation about the nature of the
charges brought against him and the other leading communists accused
of being his fellow conspirators.

Some of the PCI's descriptions of the trials in the Peoples' Democracies can only be described as Orwellian.[108] They required PCI
members to erase everything they had previously been told from their
minds and, in the blink of an eye, believe the opposite. To give just one
example, Ottavio Pastore, whom we have already met extolling the
Prague coup, wrote in the preface to a pamphlet on the trial of Traicho Kostov in Bulgaria that Yugoslavia had been in Anglo-American
imperialist pay even during the Second World War:

Who permitted Tito's troops to occupy Venezia Giulia and Trieste, who
prevented Italian troops and partisans from arriving [in Trieste] first,
who held back their forces in the Veneto? The Anglo-Americans, Field

Marshal Alexander. We now have the explanation for facts that were previously unknown to us, we now know that the surrender of Venezia-Giulia to Tito was the first reward, at our expense, for his carefully coordinated treachery.[109]

This rewriting of history was shameless. In effect, it outlined the PCI's own former position on the question of Venezia-Giulia, denounced it, and then claimed it was an Anglo-American imperialist plot against Italy on behalf of Tito! Top officials in the PCI, Pastore included, knew perfectly well that the USSR had sided with Tito during the Peace Treaty negotiations, and that Togliatti himself had favoured the absorption of all Venezia Giulia except Trieste into Yugoslavia. Like Winston Smith in Orwell's *1984*, the PCI's leaders had conveniently dropped all their articles, speeches, and eulogies of Tito and the Yugo-slav party into the memory hole.

Equally, they must have known that the trial against Rajk had not 'laid bare the plans of the Hungarian fascist conspirators', and nor had it 'demonstrated that the leaders of the Yugoslav government and their American paymasters were the inspirers of the plot'.[110] Certainly, 'the spy Rajk' had not been sent to Spain by the secret police of pre-war Hungarian leader Admiral Horthy to inform on his comrades and to act as a *provocateur*, and after the fall of France the Gestapo had not arranged for him to be transferred from an internment camp back to Hungary so he could keep up his good work on behalf of Fascism within the clandestine Hungarian Communist Party.[111]

Yet they may genuinely have believed that 'the imperialists were struggling by every means available, including murder, against the peoples' republics and the USSR' and were planning to wage war against them.[112] In such circumstances, they may have believed that it was legitimate to treat the losers of an internal party power struggle as enemies of the people since, if followed, their policies might have weakened the USSR and led to defeat for the world communist move-ment. They may have believed, in short, that a purely *hypothetical* end justified the vilest immediate means. Machiavelli himself might have balked.

Unquestionably, Ottavio Pastore knew that innocent men (or, at any rate, men innocent of the crimes ascribed to them) were being tortured and butchered. One future apostate from Stalinism, Renato Mieli, subsequently reported in his memoir *Deserto rosso* that Pastore returned from reporting on the Slánský Trial in Prague in November 1952 absolutely 'distraught'. He threw himself into an armchair in Mieli's office in the headquarters of the PCI in Rome and exclaimed 'what a bloodbath ... it's unbearable'. Yet Pastore kept writing eulogies to the peoples' republics, and Mieli himself 'remained in my job in the party, as if [Pastore's] anguished outburst had not opened my eyes for good'.[113] One guesses that many functionaries and intellectuals in the upper reaches of the party were suffering the same agonies of conscience. Several of them, notably Umberto Terracini and Emilio Sereni (and Renato Mieli), came from Jewish families. The Slánský trial surely aroused some qualms about the historical mission of the Soviet state among them, although the question is one that has been treated with kid gloves by the PCI's historians.

DANGER AVERTED

The question of the extent to which the PCI's leadership were willing to show blind faith in the judgement of the Soviet Party, and in Stalin himself, was central to the top echelons of the PCI's reaction to an attempt by Stalin, between Christmas 1950 and February 1951, to remove Togliatti from the party leadership.

On 22 August 1950, Togliatti, Nilde Iotti, and their adopted daughter Marisa were involved in a car crash as they drove for a holiday in the Valle d'Aosta. Their party-provided car, which was travelling at high speed, swerved to avoid a lorry that had entered its lane. Togliatti was seriously injured in the crash. He suffered broken ribs and a head injury and, after several weeks of acute headaches, was forced in October to undergo a successful operation on a cranial hematoma.

Togliatti was invited to Moscow to recuperate. Once Togliatti, Iotti, and Marisa, together with Luigi Amadesi, a PCI veteran who was his personal secretary, had crossed into the Russian-occupied zone of Austria on 17 December, they were treated with unaccustomed pomp and ceremony. The Soviet ambassador to Austria held a reception in their honour before they departed for the Soviet Union, via Prague and Warsaw, on a luxurious train. Security guards joined them aboard. When they entered the USSR, their new train was even more well-appointed and as they sped across the flat plains the watchful Amadesi noted 'fur-clad' party functionaries lining freezing platforms at every station on the way. Togliatti had never been accorded such a high-profile reception in his previous visits to the USSR. He was being treated like a senior member of the Politburo. Half the Central Committee of the Soviet Party were waiting to greet him when he arrived in Moscow. It was clear that something major was being planned.[114]

Togliatti was to stay at the Barvinka clinic, a hospital and care home near Moscow reserved for the top officials of the Soviet party. On his arrival, the best Russian neurosurgeons gravely inspected the handiwork of their Italian colleagues. On Togliatti's second night in the USSR, Stalin himself paid an 'affectionate' visit to the PCI's leader, 'behaving like a jovial old friend'.[115] On Christmas Eve, the *vozhd* summoned Togliatti to the Kremlin and in a two-hour conversation expounded his plans. In substance, he wanted Togliatti to direct the efforts of the Cominform to intensify the struggle against American imperialism, especially in Western Europe. He would be based in Prague. Stalin added that he was alarmed for Togliatti's safety: the PCI did not take good enough care of him. He had survived one assassination attempt, and the lorry accident had probably been another. Stalin flattered Togliatti handsomely, telling him that the workers' movement needed his unique international experience in this crucial moment.[116]

Stalin's offer to Togliatti came almost exactly a year after the conclusion of the Kostov Trial in Bulgaria and fourteen months after Lázló Rajk's hanging in October 1949. In both Bulgaria and Hungary the reign of terror against Trotskyists, Zionists, and Titoist spies was continuing apace. The purges amounted to the physical and political elimination of a large part of the post-war leaders who had implemented Stalin's policy of collaborating with other popular forces to establish democracies with progressive characteristics. These people were Togliatti's peers. It had been Togliatti who had carried out the *svolta di Salerno* and had served in government with Badoglio and De Gasperi. It was Togliatti who had been manoeuvred out of the Italian government in May 1947. It was Togliatti who had been denigrated in Moscow by Secchia for his lack of revolutionary zeal. In January 1951, Togliatti's résumé looked less than irreprehensible, while Stalin's lavish praise for his accomplishments meant nothing, as Togliatti well knew. Stalin notoriously played with his victims, like a cat with a mouse.

In these circumstances, to leave Italy and reside in a country where the Soviet security services commanded behind the scenes would have been an extraordinarily dangerous thing to do. This was especially the case if Togliatti was doing a high-profile job where failure could be portrayed as conscious sabotage and betrayal. A man as experienced as Togliatti knew that the Cominform offer might be a poisoned chalice. But it 'wasn't easy to say no to an invitation from Stalin'.[117]

On 4 January 1951, after Stalin had renewed his offer on New Year's Eve, Togliatti wrote a letter to the Soviet leader arguing that there was more need for him in Italy, where the PCI could aspire to extend its influence: 'leaving the country again when great opportunities still exist to work legally with the masses' was a mistake in his opinion. Writing partly in the third person, as if to give greater objectivity, the letter argued that Togliatti was the PCI's best-known figure. Ordering Togliatti to leave his job might cause dissent in the party ranks, especially 'among younger officials and the party's rank and file'. (This remark implied, accurately, that the party's more senior officials might not miss him so much.) Most important of all, a change of leader would catch the party 'unprepared' and would certainly have 'serious consequences'.[118] In addition to the upcoming party congress in the spring, there were important local elections, and the mass campaign against membership of the North Atlantic Treaty to organize. The last thing the party needed in this delicate moment was a campaign by the reactionary press against the party's subordination to Moscow, which his departure would inevitably provoke. As Silvio Pons has written, 'in substance his message to Stalin was that, in Italy at least, the Cold War did not need to plunge into armed conflict', but could still be conducted through mass politics.[119]

Togliatti concluded his letter by suggesting that Pietro Secchia should be invited to Moscow to give his opinion, since he did his work so well that he could afford a 'brief absence from the country'.

Stalin took Togliatti at his word and summoned not only Secchia, but Luigi Longo, too. At a meeting with Stalin and the rest of the Soviet leadership – at which Lavrenti Beria, the head of the secret police, and the second most-feared man in the Soviet Union, contemptuously told the PCI leadership that 'in Russia a man like Togliatti would not be able to drive around as he liked' – Togliatti laboriously persuaded Stalin that at the very least the party steering committee should express an opinion on the matter.[120] He seemingly assumed that the *direzione* would urge him to stay as party leader.

He was wrong. Meeting on 31 January 1951, the steering committee decided by an overwhelming majority to back Stalin's request. Umberto Terracini, showing contrarian courage as usual, backed Togliatti, but he was almost alone: only Teresa Noce, Longo's by then estranged wife, and Giuseppe Di Vittorio joined him. Longo himself, as leader *in pectore*, abstained.[121] What had convinced the PCI's most prominent cadres to disavow their leader?

In the first place, it seems clear that Secchia and Longo deliberately failed to convey the intensity of Togliatti's revulsion to the scheme. Secchia, of course, had long considered Togliatti to be a mere word-spinner, not a real revolutionary. Togliatti subsequently expressed his belief that the whole episode had been 'an authentic plot organized by Secchia' in conjunction with Beria. Togliatti believed that they had proposed his removal to Prague to Stalin, representing it as a suggestion emanating from the leadership of the PCI.[122] According to Silvio Pons, Secchia and Longo feared that Togliatti was turning the PCI into a social democratic party and had taken the opportunity to avert the danger.[123]

Personal feelings did weigh in the steering committee's decision. There were plenty of people on the party steering committee who had no reason to love their leader. Togliatti had made himself unpopular with Longo, especially, by making disparaging remarks about his literary gifts. He also had the bad habits of talking behind people's backs and of scoring off others with his quick wit. Often, Togliatti's barbs were on target, but that, of course, only increased the rancour of those wounded by them.

His private life was also a source of unrest. Nilde Iotti was unpopular with the middle-aged men who ran the PCI. She was suspected of religious leanings (she had been schooled by nuns and her family, though socialist in their political sympathies, had been churchgoers), had not been a partisan, and was alleged to have petit-bourgeois habits (she liked, for instance, decorative clothes). Togliatti's love affair with Iotti was regarded as 'shameful' by many of his senior comrades for these reasons.[124] She was not 'one of us' in the way that his legal wife, Rita Montagnana, emphatically was.

Moreover, while Togliatti and Iotti were sequestered in Moscow, the provincial secretary of the federation of Reggio Emilia, Valdo Magnani, who was a distant cousin and friend of of Iotti, was expelled from the party after presenting a motion to the federation's annual congress that called into question the subservience of the party to the USSR and argued, rather like Terracini in October 1947, that Italians should defend their country from any aggressor, whomever it might be. Magnani had fought as a partisan with the Yugoslav resistance and had been decorated for valour. He was joined in his rebellion by Aldo Cucchi, an elected parliamentary deputy. A doctor by training, Cucchi was a recipient of the gold medal for valour for his courage and skill as a partisan (his *nom de guerre* was Jacopo), and he had been honoured on the front page of *Vie nuove* when he received the award.[125]

The reaction of the PCI press to their criticism of the party line was ruthless: Cucchi and Magnani were denounced as 'two traitors' in an official party communiqué on 30 January 1951. On 1 February, the day after the meeting of the steering committee, a front-page article by Longo in *l'Unità* was entitled 'An Outburst of Abuse'. In this egregious piece, Longo slandered Magnani and Cucchi as 'traitors whom the enemy inserted into our ranks some time ago, with the task of rising as far as possible in our organization so as best to fulfil their base desire to betray and harm us'.[126] They were, in short, the PCI's very own Kostov or Rajk in miniature.

Longo's article was only the beginning of a smear campaign against the two men and their families. Togliatti himself, upon his return from the USSR, sneered that 'even in the mane of a noble thoroughbred, one can always find two or three fleas'.[127] Magnani's wife later said that she and her husband experienced 'Stalinism in a democratic country, Stalinism without Stalin' in the weeks and months that followed the apostasy of the two communist leaders.[128] As one historian critical of the PCI has underlined: 'If you left, or criticized the party, you were an outcast, you lost your home, your soul.'[129] There was no mercy for those who lost their faith, or joined another church.

The 'treachery' of the 'Magnacucchi', as they were dubbed by the PCI press, was bound to compel the steering committee to make an ostentatious show of party discipline: nobody wanted to be the next person whose loyalty was called into doubt (which made the dissenters' opposition even more praiseworthy). It is likely that the violence of the reaction against Cucchi and Magnani's deviation from the party line persuaded any doubters in the steering committee that the best thing to do was play safe and grant Stalin's request.

The steering committee's members were, in any case, collectively reluctant to affront the great revolutionary leader himself. The party was instructing the mass membership in cell meetings that Stalin was an infallible teacher and guide. How could he be gainsaid? Like the Catholic Church, international communism was a transnational organization governed by a hierarchy based in a single nation. Just as bishops or ordinary parish priests across the world had to carry out instructions handed down to them by Rome, so the PCI was supposed to obey the cardinals in the Kremlin, and above all heed Stalin, the supreme leader and interpreter of the sacred texts of Marxism-Leninism. Giorgio Amendola, the party expert on the Mezzogiorno, told the journalist Giorgio Bocca that 'I voted "yes" to the Soviet proposal. I thought it was in the interest of the communist movement and Togliatti's own interest.' He added in a published interview in the 1970s, 'if the Cominform were to be directed by a western communist, it might as well be one of our own . . . we gave our assent, even if it was something that might be disagreeable to Togliatti . . . At the end of the day, we were Stalinists.' Teresa Noce more cynically said 'most people voted out of obedience to Stalin, but there were some who clearly wanted to stab him [Togliatti] in the back'.[130]

Secchia returned to Moscow in the company of Arturo Colombi, a former partisan and party hardliner of working-class origin (he was a bricklayer from near Bologna) to convey the party leadership's decision. When they arrived at the airport, the Soviet official who met them whispered that 'the old man [Stalin] is blowing his top'. Their party leader was livid, too. Togliatti angrily accused them of trying to get rid of him. After wrangling with them for two hours, he prevailed. He persuaded the delegation from Rome to sign a letter urging Stalin at least to allow him to return to Italy for the preparation of the party congress, which was scheduled to take place in the spring. Once the congress had concluded, the Italians guaranteed, Togliatti would take up the post in the Cominform. The letter was sent on 12 February, but for several days they received no reply. Only after they had begged for an interview with the supreme leader, did Stalin grant them a few minutes of his time on 16 February. He acquiesced with cold disapproval to the suggested compromise. Togliatti could leave.[131]

Togliatti and Iotti departed for Italy almost at once, via Prague (where Togliatti briefly met Slánský, who was still general secretary of the Czechoslovak Communist Party, although political infighting was rife within the regime). Throughout the journey Togliatti was fearful for their safety. Iotti remembered that when they crossed into Allied-occupied Austria, Togliatti muttered under his breath, 'finalmente'.[132] So long as Stalin lived, Togliatti never returned to the USSR. As Elena Aga Rossi and Victor Zaslavsky have suggested, the 'deepest and most decisive' reason for Togliatti's refusal of the Cominform job was surely one that 'could not be mentioned', namely, 'fear for his life and for the lives of his family'.[133]

Togliatti, whose intuition had been sharpened during the Great Purges, presumably guessed what the stakes were when Stalin offered him such a high-profile position in the one Central European state that had not yet held a treason trial of their post-war leadership. Once behind the Iron Curtain, it would have been child's play to accuse Togliatti of having facilitated De Gasperi's ascent to power and the entry of Italy into the American bloc, and of being a conspirator who had promoted Belgrade's imperialist ambitions (indeed, this last accusation possessed more than a grain of truth). Far more absurd dossiers had been fabricated in previous years against equally prestigious individuals.

Togliatti was a survivor. His skill at walking the party line was unparalleled. But living through a generational purge required more luck than judgement, as he was acutely aware. The losers in internal power struggles were condemned as spies, fascists, Trotskyists, Titoites and Zionists, and cases were constructed against them from confessions beaten out of other suspects. Anybody could be named as an enemy of the people during interrogations. Stalin and Beria then decided whom to frame. Your life was in their hands. Reading Artur London's *The Confession* (London was one of Slánský's co-defendants), with its descriptions of the Gestapo-like horrors that the Czech 'spies' endured as their interrogators constructed a non-existent plot, or the memoir of Heda Margolius Kovály, the wife of another supposed conspirator, Rudolf Margolius, one realizes that Togliatti escaped from a nightmare by not going to Prague.[134] Unsurprisingly, 'the episode provoked an irreparable breach between Togliatti and Secchia and a serious split in the party's senior ranks.'[135] It would have been astonishing if it had not.

From the point of view of the consolidation of Italian democracy, Togliatti's survival as leader of the PCI was critical. Had Longo or Secchia become party leader in the spring of 1951, conflict in Italian society would have spiralled to greater heights. Italy would have been tipped into outright turmoil. While the dispute over Togliatti was being resolved in Moscow, four people were killed in clashes across the country between the police and PCI demonstrators opposing a visit by General (and future president) Dwight D. Eisenhower to Rome.[136]

In his speech to the 7th Party Congress in April 1951, the congress he so nearly did not attend, Togliatti 'asserted the choice to remain within legal and constitutional boundaries after the war, despite the ratchet effect caused by the Cold War'.[137] Togliatti shared the same goal as Secchia and Longo: state socialism of the kind pioneered by the USSR. There is no evidence that Togliatti disbelieved the myth of Soviet greatness and its so-called democratic triumphs. But the right means to achieve the end, in Italy at least, was via the gradual permeation of the PCI and its doctrines into the institutions of society and the minds of the Italians. The PCI should play a long game, not the short one.[138]

A metaphor to encapsulate the debate between Togliatti and the more dogmatic Secchia might be drawn from chess: Secchia wanted to win in a blitz, even if it meant sacrificing his own most prestigious piece. The more cautious Togliatti was content, over the next decade or more, to grind out a gradual advantage. The risk of his strategy was that it would lead to stalemate, or even long-drawn-out defeat.

At bottom, the distinction between the two communist leaders was

Laying down the party line:
Togliatti evokes Gramsci and reasserts his leadership in 1951.

as old as the Bolshevik movement itself. Secchia (and Longo) never shook off the notion, expounded in Lenin's *What Is to Be Done?* (1902), that a revolutionary party should be a sectarian organization: a committed elite dedicated to bringing down the capitalist system. Great social changes were prompted by disciplined cadres with a will for power. Togliatti, by contrast, by arguing for a mass party, one that anybody could join, one desirous of broadening its social base and open to collaborating with other political forces on given issues, was drawing inspiration from the arguments of Yuli Martov, the leader of the Mensheviks. The Peace campaigns in 1949–50 were a successful way of achieving that goal. It is also true that Togliatti was as adamant as Secchia and Longo in believing that new members of the party should be socialized and disciplined in the ideology and practices of communism and in the historical mission of the Soviet Union. This is why he took such a huge interest in propaganda and the party press.[139] Togliatti returned from Moscow and outlined the party line with conviction at the 7th Party Congress of the PCI, but he must have been conscious that part of the party's steering committee continued to regard it as a tactic at best, as heresy at worst.

De Gasperi's choice to align Italy with the United States and to commit his country to the fledgling institutions of European unity was as important for Italy as Konrad Adenauer's Westpolitik was for West Germany. It was a bold action that faced intense opposition, though the PCI, perhaps because it had been largely disarmed, resisted it for the most part by peaceful means. Millions of Italian citizens believed that the USSR represented humanity's future. The PCI told them that Stalinist state socialism was a model to be imitated. To back his policy, De Gasperi counterposed a narrative of his own, one whereby Italy became an equal partner of a community of Christian nations striving to overcome war and achieve prosperity. Both positions were myths, but Marshall Plan aid and the witchcraft trials taking place behind the Iron Curtain gave De Gasperi's story more credibility with the voters. The PCI's peace campaign could attract signatures by the million, since no Italian wanted war, but the party's intellectual and political subjugation to the USSR placed the PCI at a disadvantage in a democratic competition. Italians had, after all, already lived under one system where the leader was always right – they didn't want to do so again.

10

Precarious Centre

De Gasperi's successful foreign policy was carried out despite continuous instability in his parliamentary majority. The cabinet formed in May 1948 (De Gasperi's fifth government) was racked with internal dissent from the start. Giuseppe Saragat and the PSLI were especially uncomfortable partners. They would leave the government in July 1951. The main cause of dissension was Einaudi's anti-inflationary squeeze, which his successor as treasury minister, Giuseppe Pella, continued zealously. It kept inflation down, but at the cost of continuing unemployment. In the Mezzogiorno, conditions were desperate.

Disquiet pervaded the DC itself. At its national congress in Venice in June 1949, one-third of the delegates identified themselves with the positions taken by the party's left, whose charismatic leader was Giuseppe Dossetti, the lay monk and 'partisan without a gun', who became deputy secretary of the party at the congress. Dossetti stood for a 'new democratic state', for a party that sought to 'free much of the working class from the Communist Party', and for 'a virile approach' to the 'conservative classes', not just the workers. He bowed to the party line over the decision to join NATO, but not without qualms. Dossetti regarded his group within the party as a 'goad' prodding the DC to do more for social justice. De Gasperi dryly replied that the word 'goad' was more suited for oxen but, in any case, he wished that more party members, instead of talking, would join him in pulling the plough.[1]

On New Year's Day 1950, President Einaudi exhorted the government to respect the Eighth Commandment in its conduct of public finance. One of Dossetti's closest collaborators, Minister of Labour Amintore Fanfani, an ambitious Tuscan from Arezzo whose textbook extolling the virtues of fascist corporativism we encountered in

Chapter 1, reminded the president that one should respect *all* the commandments, not just one, especially the injunction to love thy neighbour as thyself.[2]

Fanfani was small of stature and adept at public relations. His colleagues at the Catholic University of Milan, where he had taught economic history, said of him *tantillus homo quantum rumorem facit* ('how much noise he makes, for so small a man').[3] But this was academic malice, one of the few commodities not in short supply in post-war Italy. When not writing eulogies to the corporate state, Fanfani was in fact a serious scholar who was sincere about reducing poverty. He had persuaded De Gasperi to make the 'Fanfani House Plan' (a scheme to construct subsidized public housing) a central plank of the government's programme during the first year of the Marshall Plan. Eighty billion lire (over $120 million) were invested in Fanfani's scheme, which was made law on 1 April 1949, its first year of operation.[4] Fanfani's brains and energy would lead future historians to depict him as a *cavallo di razza* (thoroughbred) among the drayhorses in De Gasperi's cabinet.

Fanfani wanted to go further and faster than De Gasperi or Pella were willing to countenance, by creating a 'ministry for economic development zones' with a mission to invest 250 billion lire a year in the poorest parts of the country, and he argued the point with vehemence (behind the scenes, the Marshall Planners at the ECA mission in Rome largely agreed with him). During a meeting on 10 January 1950 with De Gasperi, Fanfani begged the premier to persuade the ministers in charge of the public finances to understand that 'our problem is first and foremost one of jobs'. People had to be given something socially useful to do. De Gasperi's astonished response was to expostulate, 'but this is the New Deal!'

Fanfani's account was doubtless self-serving, but the exchange illustrates very well what the divide within the DC was about.[5] De Gasperi resigned the day after his discussion with Fanfani and during the ensuing government reshuffle, the *Dossettiani* asked for two key ministries, the Ministry of Labour and the Ministry of Industry. When De Gasperi refused, Fanfani did not serve in what became De Gasperi's sixth government, which took the oath of office on 27 January 1950 and lasted until July 1951.

LAW AND DISORDER

De Gasperi's new government took office at the nadir of the social crisis. On 9 January 1950, two days before De Gasperi resigned, police had repelled an attempted factory occupation by workers locked out of an ironworks in Modena by killing six, all communists, and wounding dozens by methods that recalled the tactics of the former regime. The police fired, seemingly without provocation, on a crowd of workers from the roof of the factory. Togliatti and Nilde Iotti's adopted daughter, Marisa, became an orphan because her natural father, Arturo Malagoli, was one of the workers killed.

On 10 January 1950, the press divided along party lines. 'The government of 18 April is drowning in blood', *Avanti!* protested. *L'Unità* asserted that the government had 'smeared itself with blood'. *Il Popolo*, by contrast, reassured its readers that 'calm has been restored in Modena'. The following day, it insinuated that the assault on the factory was part of a 'preordained plan' by the PCI.[6] Hundreds of thousands of workers nevertheless went on sympathy strike across the North and the funerals of the murdered workers were attended by colossal crowds. Pietro Nenni recorded in his diary that the mood among militants was febrile. Again and again, he heard people say, 'when will they let us shoot back with our machine guns?'[7]

The Modena shootings were merely the worst case of many instances of police violence. Led by the PCI, hundreds of strikes, riots, workplace clashes, and occupations of uncultivated land took place in 1949 and 1950. Such protests often encountered shocking police brutality. The Public Security Guard, a militarized police force controlled by the Ministry of the Interior, used firearms against protesting workers on dozens of occasions. On 29 October 1949, for instance, three unarmed farm labourers, the youngest of whom was just fifteen years old, were killed by the police during an attempted seizure of land left fallow by an absentee owner at Melissa in Calabria. This massacre convinced the PSLI temporarily to leave the government.

The militarization of the police was a political choice. Scelba, fearing subversion, had since 1947 sought to weed out card-carrying PCI members from the police by offering them financial incentives to leave, or transferring them away from their home towns. Together with the effects of Togliatti's amnesty, which meant many once enthusiastic fascists retained or reclaimed their jobs, Italy's forces of law and order were overwhelmingly staffed, especially at officer level, by men who regarded working-class organizations as dangerous for the social order. They were a force for 'inhibiting democracy', as one historian has expressed it.[8] The prevailing culture in the police ranked public order above the principles of democracy and equated protest, even peaceful protest, with subversion. But neither Scelba, nor De Gasperi, showed any sign of making reform of the laws regulating police conduct a priority. The police operated according to regulations imposed during Fascism and, at a time of public austerity, were equipped with expensive weaponry, notably tear gas and automatic weapons. Scelba did not invent the *celere* (motorized police units), but on his watch their numbers were expanded and improved in quality. 'For decades, Italy had the highest ratio of police officers to citizens in Europe.'[9]

Further *stragi* followed in the spring of 1950, the most notorious of which occurred at Celano in the province of Aquila, where armed guards employed by Prince Torlonia shot dead three farm labourers and wounded thirteen others at another protest organized by the PCI. The people of Fontamara, seemingly, were no longer content to be protected by the conspiracies that ran the state. Scelba's reaction to the continued violence was to outlaw demonstrations for three months in any province where public disorder had taken place. In all, during the tumultuous months that followed the assassination attempts on Togliatti in July 1948 and mid-1950, sixty-two demonstrators, forty-eight of whom were members of the PCI, were killed in clashes with the police, or by gunmen hired by landlords to protect their property. More than 3,000, predominantly PCI members, were injured by police batons, or knocked over by the speeding jeeps of the *celere*, or suffered gunshot wounds. Nineteen thousand were imprisoned for public-order offences, though sentences were usually light.[10] De Gasperi backed Scelba throughout, even as the toll of victims mounted.

Left-wing intellectuals such as Lelio Basso described this state of affairs as 'De Gasperi's *coup d'état*' and argued that 'demochristian totalitarianism', while formally different from Mussolini's, was 'substantially a continuation' of Fascist rule. According to Basso, De

Gasperi's administration was deliberately not enacting the constitution: the rights enshrined in the opening articles of the constitution were a dead letter and the *celere* were being used brutally to suppress any attempt by citizens to assert their legitimate claims to land, a job, education, or social benefits. The government was thus a 'usurping power' that the parties of the left should confront both inside and outside parliament.[11]

Basso was one voice among dozens. Renato Zangheri, an intellectual who would become a distinguished historian and mayor of Bologna, in April 1949 described the *celere* units (with the implicit approval of Togliatti, since the article was published in *Rinascita*) as 'squadrismo di Stato'. The DC government, in other words, was, according to the PCI's flagship publication, employing the tactics used by Mussolini's *Ras* in the early 1920s during his seizure of power. The police, Zangheri alleged, were a mere 'party militia' at the service of the 'dominant political class' of which the DC was a prisoner.[12] Zangheri's article was no outlier: in 1949 and 1950 the PCI and PSI repeatedly accused the DC of being a proto-fascist regime and warned loudly against a prospective *coup d'état*. Such accusations inevitably destabilized the government. For obvious reasons, the PSLI was acutely sensitive to any suggestion that it was supporting a government with fascist or rightist tendencies.

In the long run, the 'situation of bitter internal struggle and embryonic civil war', and the large numbers of casualties that the PCI's militants suffered at the hands of the *celere*, promoted the notion that the PCI was the 'most weighty force to act in defence of the constitution' to 'sediment itself' in the party's memory.[13] Giorgio Napolitano, President of Italy from 2006 to 2015, then an upwardly mobile functionary in the PCI, underlined this point in his autobiography as being a key reason for his loyalty to the party during the traumas of the 1950s.[14]

De Gasperi and Scelba thought, by contrast, that they were resisting deliberately incited illegality by a totalitarian enemy – violence designed to subvert the government's programme of moderate social reforms.[15] In their minds, the law was the law and the rights of private property had to be defended, even when they were unjust.

It is certainly true that the PCI incited and exploited the turmoil caused by the government's repressive measures. Men like Secchia and Longo thought it was necessary to unmask the government's true character as a defender of capitalist interests. As Andrea Guiso has shown, Togliatti himself, despite his caution towards illegal action, understood this logic. He told the Central Committee of the PCI in March 1949 that the party's activists had to fight physically:

> There are moments in which it is necessary to take a thousand comrades and send them to fight, knowing full well that a hundred, maybe, will finish in jail. There will be clashes with the police. There will be outrage if this [tactic] is necessary, but the avantgarde has a job to do, and I would say that we are doing these things, especially in some places, far too little. We aren't doing them often enough, in the capital, especially.[16]

He added that although it was not desirable that demonstrations should always end in a 'head-on clash' with the police, it was essential that an element of the party should be 'trained' to participate in demonstrations when they and the police were likely to come to blows. Togliatti's words were interpreted by party leaders in the provinces as an instruction not 'to turn the other cheek'. If demonstrations boiled over – as, of course, they were bound to – then the PCI's militants should not shirk a scrap. To quote Guiso:

> The sternness of the orders to the police to keep public order, the combativeness of the demonstrators, the willingness of the keenest activists to trade blows with the police, the depth of the ideological antagonism transmitted by both sides, nurtured in both demonstrators and the police the 'physical' sensation of being on a battlefield, engaged in a military struggle for command of a strategic territory, namely the streets.[17]

This is right, surely. Italy's democracy was precarious, but its fragility stemmed not from De Gasperi's desire to impose Fascism, a thesis for which there is no evidence except for the theorizing of intellectuals such as Lelio Basso, but in the intensity of the mutual antagonism that divided the two sides. Both sides thought the other would, if it attained hegemony, extinguish their political freedom.

If one puts oneself into the shoes of the political actors of the time, one can grasp why. If one were a communist or a socialist, the lessons of Mussolini's seizure of power, and the dubious past of many police and state officials, was bound to cause one to fear that active measures to reduce the left's political freedom were just a matter of time.

To these domestic causes for leftist alarm should be added the Atlanticist rhetoric of the DC, at a time when American anti-communism was moving into its most hysterical phase, its 'Great Fear'.[18] The PCI worried that it was only a matter of time before the US pressured Italy into suppressing its activities. They were certainly being singled out as dangerous by Washington. One PCI pamphlet, published in 1949, was titled 'Sensational! The 40 Ruthless Men of Italian Communism'. The House of Representatives' Committee for Foreign Affairs had published a list of some 500 'ruthless' international communists. No fewer than forty were Italian. The pamphlet gave brief biographical sketches, one by one, of the forty communists who had 'earned this malign judgement by one of those inquisitorial commissions that in America outlaw scientists, musicians, and film actors guilty of being unenthusiastic about the dropping of atomic bombs'. The sketches emphasized the time spent by the men in fascist jails, their gallantry at the front in Spain, and the many medals for bravery that they had won during the resistance. The back page delivered the most telling thrust. It showed a letter, on White House stationery, bearing the signature of Harry S. Truman, commending Luigi Longo for having given 'meritorious service' to the Allies as deputy commander of the CVL in Nazi-occupied Italy and awarding him the Bronze Star for his bravery. The last words of the pamphlet were: 'once upon a time Luigi Longo was not a ruthless communist for Harry S. Truman, president of the United States'.[19]

On the other hand, how could Scelba and De Gasperi look at what had happened to the Christian Democratic, Agrarian, and Liberal parties of Czechoslovakia, Poland, and Hungary without trepidation for Italy's fate? The top officials and intellectuals of the PCI had publicly supported, in those countries, not only the smashing of all political opposition from 'bourgeois' parties, but the absorption of democratic socialists into workers' parties controlled by the communists, the criminalization and murder of classes of the population, notably prosperous peasants and priests, and even the show trials of their own peers among the communist parties of those countries. Why should they behave differently if they took power in Italy? The nation's politicians, of all parties, were people of incompatible convictions who were deeply afraid of one another. Mutual fear was one source of the precariousness of Italian democracy during centrism – and of the violence that punctuated political life.

REVIVING THE MEZZOGIORNO

The record of De Gasperi's centrist governments towards the poor was not as bad as subsequent historians have painted it. Between 1948 and 1951 they launched several major measures to address the structural problems facing the South. In July 1950, moreover, the premier visited the cave-dwellers in Matera made notorious by Carlo Levi. De Gasperi was deeply moved. He subsequently took a personal interest in ensuring that funds arrived to improve living conditions in the so-called *sassi*, which one newspaper described as 'horrid slums in which 60 per cent of the people live'.[20] By the early 1960s, all the cave-dwellers had been moved out to brand-new public housing built in the outskirts of the town.[21]

After a tedious parliamentary tussle, between May and December 1950 the government also pushed through a 'package' of laws reforming agriculture and land ownership. These laws superseded the so-called Gullo decrees, named after Fausto Gullo, the PCI agriculture minister in the Bonomi governments, which had given peasants the chance to claim the right to grow crops on land, both public and private, that was either 'uncultivated' or 'insufficiently cultivated'. The decrees had been turned into law by Antonio Segni, a future President of the Republic, who was agriculture minister from 1946 until 1951.

The occupations of the land, which led to the deadly clashes with the police, were largely promoted by the PCI on behalf of landless peasants infuriated by the bureaucratic sloth and legalistic obstruction that had made the Gullo–Segni laws a dead letter. Landowners had done everything in their power to prevent their land from being certified as 'uncultivated' even after Article 44 of the constitution had clearly established that greater social equity and more rational exploitation of the soil required the state to impose 'obligations and limits' on private land ownership. The constitution promoted land reclamation for agricultural use, the 'transformation' of the *latifondo*, and the building up of 'productive units'. This meant turning sharecroppers into peasants and encouraging the creation of cooperatives. Although the *latifondo* had not been outright abolished, the constitution clearly implied that the state should intervene to increase the amount of land under cultivation, at the expense of the *latifondo*, and to make land ownership more productive.

The constitution carefully did not say that encouraging greater land ownership was a core principle of the state. The reason for this was simple: in 1950, there were already nearly 9.4 million landowners, far more than the country needed. The problem was that most were less smallholders than smidgeon-holders. Of the 9.4 million, 7.8 million owned less than two hectares of land (5.5 acres). A further 1.47 million owned less than 25 hectares. Together, these two groups possessed about 55 per cent of the land. A small class of prosperous landowners – 89,200 in all – owned between 25 and 100 hectares and a mere 21,000 big landowners possessed more than 100 hectares. This last group (0.09 per cent) by itself held 27.7 per cent of the land, 10 per cent more than the 7.8 million subsistence farmers at the base of the pyramid, most of whom not only tilled their own land, but worked as hired labourers.[22] Italy's distribution of land ownership was similar to that of pre-war Poland, Hungary, or Yugoslavia, but in a democracy one could not simply nationalize the land, dispossess the landlords at gunpoint, and curb their protests by 'liquidating' them as a class, which is what happened behind the Iron Curtain.

Moreover, transferring land to the poorest peasants would not make agriculture more productive – indeed, it would make it less so. In 1948, agriculture minister Segni had proposed that large-scale land reclamation, and a substantial redistribution of land from rich to poor, should be a priority for ERP investment. The ECA's representative in Italy, James David Zellerbach, disagreed, and without ERP funds the reform was impossible. Zellerbach thought that the essence of the reform should be to boost production and that uncertainty over the scale of the law was damaging productivity since landowners were reluctant to invest in land that might be taken away from them. The ensuing stand-off, which pushed Segni to the brink of resignation, was only resolved by De Gasperi's insistence that the US should not meddle in domestic politics, and by the surge in violence that led to incidents like that at Melissa. The United States belatedly realized that the delay in land distribution was fomenting communism.[23]

The question of what to do was also complicated by politics. The PCI had succeeded in organizing the poorest peasants, who had nothing to lose, but Italy's 'kulaks' – especially the huge social bloc owning between 2 and 25 hectares – were solidly Christian Democrat. Their lobby, Coldiretti (*Coltivatori diretti*, i.e. 'direct producers'), was a potent pressure group within the DC. Many of the DC's elected representatives owed their seat in parliament to Coldiretti, whose leader Paolo Bonomi was probably, after De Gasperi and Scelba, the most powerful Christian Democrat in the country, although he was merely a parliamentary backbencher. Any solution to the agrarian question had to guarantee Italy's more prosperous peasants that their smallholdings were safe.

The events at Melissa made procrastination politically impossible. In De Gasperi's sixth government, Segni was ostentatiously confirmed as agriculture minister as a vote of confidence in the need for reform. On 13 March 1950, De Gasperi told the Council of Ministers that they had to 'take their courage in both hands and press on'.[24] With the important concession that the law would apply only to the most backward areas of the country, where the need was most pressing, Segni was given *via libera* to introduce substantial measures of land redistribution.

The land reforms were thus a triumph for Bismarck's dictum that 'politics is the art of the possible'. The first part of the package, the so-called 'Sila Law' (May 1950), not by chance provided for land redistribution in the part of Calabria where Melissa is located. Nearly 90,000 hectares of land were expropriated and redistributed to peasant families. The second part of the package, in October 1950, led to the distribution of some 800,000 hectares to tens of thousands of peasant families in the poorest parts of the country, notably the Po delta, the Maremma (northern Lazio and southern Tuscany), the Fucino, Apulia, Basilicata and elsewhere. The law ensured that land that had been made more productive through investment was exempted from expropriation, an astute measure that placated the more enlightened landlords. The third part of the package, in December 1950, extended land distribution on the same terms as the October law to Sicily.

Land reform did not transform Italian agriculture. As the Marshall Planners had foreseen, the smallholdings created were often too small to provide their owners with prosperous incomes, or to raise productivity. On the other hand, the social steam driving the engine of the PCI's protests was dissipated. Land occupations became uncommon and Scelba's police no longer had to break up demonstrations or confront angry crowds. Social inclusion, to use an anachronism, was enhanced. Peasants with land to till felt themselves finally to be equal citizens of the Republic. Moreover, although De Gasperi subsequently grumbled to Nenni that the land reform had 'caused the landlords to rise up against him, without winning the peasants over', it turned out to be a vote winner in the long-term.[25] In the subsequent 1953 elections the DC gained on average two percentage points from the PCI in territories where land distribution had taken place. This immediate gain consolidated over time and turned many of the areas that benefited from the land reform into DC strongholds.[26]

The second major reform implemented by De Gasperi's sixth government became law on 10 August 1950. This was the creation of the Southern Italian Investment Fund (Cassa per il Mezzogiorno), a body modelled on President Roosevelt's Tennessee Valley Authority that was to channel funds from the ERP (at least initially), the Italian government, and the International Bank of Reconstruction and Development to development projects in the South. The PCI strongly resisted the passage of the legislation in parliament, absurdly accusing the government of wanting to create a Trojan horse for American influence in the Mezzogiorno that would lead to its colonization by American capitalist interests. There were reasons to criticize the *Cassa*, but this was not one of them. There was, alas, little desire on the part of American business to invest in the Mezzogiorno in 1950.

The main criticism of the Fund was that though it was well financed – the Italian government committed itself to investing 100 billion lire a year for twelve years – it was highly politicized and arguably unambitious in its goals. Its very name was chosen (by De Gasperi) to evoke a 'constant and uninterrupted flow of resources' that would be destined for the Mezzogiorno. De Gasperi wanted citizens in the South to see that the Fund would not be occupying itself with 'small works carried out piecemeal, but "big things" that would be brought to a firm conclusion'.[27] The Fund was to be run by a board of directors (*Consiglio d'amministrazione*) composed of a president, two vice-presidents, and ten other officials, all of whom were nominated by the government. It reported, moreover, to a supervisory cabinet committee for Southern Italy, composed of the ministers of agriculture, treasury, transport, trade and industry, and public works.[28] The reader can perhaps guess to which political party all five ministers belonged in August 1950. The *Cassa*, in short, was a potential vehicle for pork-barrel politics unless the party in power possessed genuine qualities of abstinence.

Time would show that the DC did not possess such qualities. In the meantime, though, the *Cassa* did much good. Via the *Cassa*, Italy became Europe's largest borrower from the World Bank, receiving, in all, some $400 million by the 1960s and becoming, in the process, a prestige project for the Bank itself.[29] The Cold War symbolism of bringing prosperity to Western Europe's largest undeveloped region was obvious. To the disappointment of Italy's boldest economists, the law authorized the new fund to invest primarily not in the South's industrialization, but in its pre-industrialization, by constructing dams, aqueducts, and irrigation systems, expropriating and reclaiming land for agricultural use, constructing roads and railways, and developing light engineering for agricultural purposes. Tourism was to be developed by restoring the South's unique patrimony of ancient monuments.

In the early years of the Fund's operation, land reclamation was the dominant chapter of the budget. On balance, the choice to modernize infrastructure and concentrate on existing strengths was a sensible one. There was no point, in the 1950s, in imitating the breakneck race to build a heavy industrial base being carried out, at immense social cost, behind the Iron Curtain.

There were political benefits for the DC. Over time, the *Cassa* became a 'powerful electoral tool' that enabled the DC's leaders 'to free themselves from organizational dependence on the Catholic Church' by in effect becoming the party of an activist state.[30] DC leaders would cut a lot of ribbons on new public works south of

Rome over the next few years, although, as in the case of the agrarian reform, both the political benefits and the social benefits for the poor of the Mezzogiorno were not felt until later in the decade.

HOW THE POOR LIVED

De Gasperi's centrist governments should probably have heeded Fanfani and been even bolder in tackling poverty (they were still more radical than any previous government in Italian history). In fairness, the scale of the problem was immense and beyond the power of immediate measures to remedy. On 12 October 1951, an all-party parliamentary commission into 'misery in Italy and ways to combat it' was launched with the specific task of 'conducting an inquiry into the current level of misery for the purpose of ascertaining the standards of living of the poorest classes and the performance of the institutions of social assistance'.[31] The commission reported to parliament on 25 March 1953, at a moment of great political tension.

The commission provided welcome proof that the Italian political parties could work together for the common good. The commission's chairman was a socialist lawyer from Lecco in the north-west. The deputy chair was another lawyer from the North, a Christian Democrat from Brescia. The other nineteen members of the commission were distributed carefully by region, and party affiliation. Seven of the twenty-one members came from the North, three from the regions of the Centre, eleven from the Mezzogiorno or the two islands. The DC provided eleven members of the commission, the PCI four, the PSI three. The remaining members were a Liberal, a Monarchist, and one without a party affiliation. There were four women, one of whom was Giuliana Nenni, the surviving daughter of the PSI's leader. Almost all the commission's members, irrespective of party affiliation, were professionals.[32]

Basing themselves on data collected in the 1951 census, the commission used certain key indicators to estimate the degrees and extent of poverty. These were: housing, diet, and clothing, specifically shoes. Housing could have been measured in many ways (whether there was running water, mains sewage, electricity, etc.), but the commission kept it simple: how many houses were overcrowded? Crowded was defined as more than one person per room. By that standard, there were 4.637 million families (40 per cent) in Italy who had enough space. A further 4.162 million (35.9 per cent) lived in cramped homes where there were up to two people per room. Some 12 per cent of the population (1.391 million) lived in 'overcrowded' dwellings with as many as three people in a room; a million more (9.3 per cent) lived with three to five people per room. Over 300,000 people lived in 'improper dwellings' such as caves, warehouses, or cellars. In all, 2.8 million families were living in severely overcrowded or unsuitable accommodation.

So far as diet was concerned, the commission monitored the consumption of three basic foodstuffs: meat, sugar, and wine. Some 869,000 families did not consume any of these products (7.5 per cent). A further 1.032 million consumed 'very little', and 1.333 million (11.5 per cent) consumed them 'rarely'. Only 244,000 families (2.1 per cent) ate or drank 'extremely abundant' quantities of these foods. As far as clothing was concerned, more than 40 per cent of families wore shoes ranging from 'wretched' (presumably sandals of one form or another) to 'mediocre'.

The Commission then elaborated on these general data to give a rough and ready classification of Italian poverty, on a scale from 0 to 9. Some 1.357 million families were ranked between 0 and 2 (wretched). In addition, 1.345 million were ranked as '3' (disadvantaged). Combined, this meant that 23.4 per cent of Italy's 11.52 million families could be described as living in abject poverty. These were the people who, *at best*, lived two or more to a room, ate scraps of meat two or three times a week, had wine on Sunday, and wore leaky shoes. They limited expenditure on lighting, heating, and medicines as much as they could. Sixty per cent of their family budgets, or more, went on food. A mere 173,000 families, 1.5 per cent of the population, were given a '9' and hence could reasonably be described as affluent.[33]

The poorest families of Italy lived mostly in the Mezzogiorno. No less than 85 per cent of the families living in 'wretched' conditions, and 70 per cent of the disadvantaged dwelt in the south or the two large islands. The Commission estimated that 28.3 per cent of southern families lived 'wretched' lives and a further 21.9 per cent could be classified as 'disadvantaged'. *Half* of the population of the Mezzo-giorno, in other words, was living – or existing – at the bottom of the poverty scale. In Sicily and Sardinia, the percentages were lower, but not by much. In the North, by contrast, only 89,000 families (1.5 per cent) lived in 'wretched' conditions.[34]

In addition to making a quantitative survey of poverty, the commission visited nine geographical areas that were regarded as possessing particularly grave problems of social cohesion, as we would say today in our more euphemistic times. These were the sub-Alpine zone, the delta of the river Po, the mountainous regions of Abruzzo, Apulia, Basilicata, especially Matera, Calabria, Sicily, Sardinia, and the slum quarters of three major cities (Milan, Rome, and Naples). The Commission's investigations into the nine areas that they had targeted added a qualitative dimension to the overall picture of social deprivation. It is impossible to do more than quote single, by no means especially lurid, passages:

[In Comacchio, in the Po delta] the houses are unhealthy and built according to irrational criteria ... almost all houses are constructed below road level, so when it rains heavily there is flooding ... 95 per cent of houses lack a latrine, so all waste water flows through the yards and gathers in stagnant pools nearby; rubbish is thrown into the canals, which are an open sewer ... farm labourers' families that live in more than a single room are a rarity, and as a result domestic life is carried on amid sheer squalor and scandalous promiscuity ... [35]

[In the working-class suburbs of Rome] the amount of space available per person is approximately 9 cubic metres, with a maximum of 16.68 in San Lorenzo and a minimum of 5.28 in Acquedotto Felice ... we have discovered extreme cases such as a family of six people in Acque-dotto Felice who are living in a room of 17 cubic metres, with one window and two beds ... Overcrowding has reached scarcely believa-ble levels in an apartment in the Ponte district where 11 families, 35 people in all, are currently living! There are 9 rooms and a single lava-tory in the apartment and access to the latter in the morning is decided by *taking a number!* There is a single sink in which both plates and clothes are washed. Each family cooks in its room.[36]

[In Naples] Even a superficial observer ... cannot help but notice that even late in the day an exceptionally high number of people, especially men, even young men of good physical condition, are lounging about in the central and port areas of the city, propping up the walls or sitting on park benches, waiting for who knows what ... in the squares and principal streets ... large gangs of kids of both sexes, some of whom are little more than tots, singly or in groups of two or three swarm around visitors offering them contraband cigarettes, shoelaces, other little objects, or services of all kinds, some of an unspeakable nature ... Everywhere there are ... people keeping the wolf from the door by carrying on the strangest dodges, some legal, some not ... Mayor Lauro declared to the delegation that according to plausible calculations some 80,000 people in Naples wake up every day without knowing how they will feed themselves, but this figure may even be an underestimate ... [37]

[In Bompensiere, in Caltanisetta in central Sicily] the Commission visited the village ... and interviewed the mayor. At Bompensiere, cattle are only slaughtered twice a year ... weekly consumption of sheep meat is 25kg, i.e. one or two lambs for a population of 2400 inhabitants ... the hospital is 37km away, there is no chemist's, only a medicine cupboard. The local GP lives in a nearby village 6km away. The villagers work 110–120 days a year on average: during the rest of the year, they consume wheat, vegetables, and whatever else they have stored away ... The Commission visited numerous dwellings that are both 'house and stable' ... the mayor affirmed that about half of the population lived with their animals. [38]

One could multiply such quotations, but there is no need. Italy's poorest were living in inhuman conditions. Lelio Basso was right to argue that, by the yardstick of the core values of the 1948 constitution, millions of Italians were, in effect, second-class citizens – or not real citizens at all. In the early 1950s, beggars in Naples, or slum-dwellers living five to a room in Rome, were equal citizens of the Italian Republic in much the same way as African Americans were equal citizens of, say, Alabama. With one important difference. Italians could vote.

SIREN VOICES

The poverty of centuries could not be wished away with the flick of a wand. The De Gasperi government's strategy – preserving the value of the lira, keeping inflation down, encouraging integration into the wider European market, boosting exports, rebuilding infrastructure, alleviating the worst poverty, encouraging land ownership and light industry in the South – was in hindsight a far-sighted one because it sowed in the present so future generations could reap. In the meantime, however, millions of people were living very hard lives indeed.

In the Mezzogiorno, where *qualunquismo* and monarchist sentiment had been rife in the first two years after liberation, and whose democratic political culture had not been fortified by resistance to the Germans, the poor and desperate constituted an electoral reservoir for politicians peddling populist remedies. In the early 1950s, De Gasperi's centrist coalition, already under attack from the PCI and PSI, also faced a threat from its right flank: the revitalized monarchists and a neo-fascist party, the Italian Social Movement (MSI).

The MSI had been constituted in Rome on Boxing Day 1946 in the offices of an insurance broker called Arturo Michelini. The Togliatti amnesty of June 1946 had freed large numbers of people compromised by the role they had played in the former regime to resume political activity. Michelini was one such. He had fought in Spain with the militia and during the Second World War had served with distinction in Russia, winning several medals for bravery. He was motivated by a conservative vision of what Fascism had stood for. The avowedly revolutionary doctrines of Salò, or the left-leaning programme that preceded Mussolini's decision to enter Giolitti's anti-socialist National Bloc in 1921, were less to his taste. Michelini was prepared to collaborate actively with the Church and the PLI.

Most of the other founding members of the new party, by contrast, were individuals who should have been in jail. Unlike Michelini, they were inspired by the revolutionary social doctrines of the RSI. The party's *de facto* leader, Giuseppe 'Pino' Romualdi, hailed from Predappio in the Romagna, Mussolini's birthplace. Indeed, he was rumoured to be Mussolini's natural son. His identification with Mussolini's pro-Nazi regime had been absolute: the Duce had appointed him deputy secretary of the PFR in October 1944. In the last desperate months of the RSI, he was certainly among 'the best-known and most high-profile members of the party'.[39]

Romualdi was still living a clandestine life when the MSI was formed. In February 1947, he was condemned to death by a tribunal in Parma for the reprisal killing of seven partisans by the Germans in September 1944. He was arrested during the 1948 electoral campaign and served three years in prison before the killing was downgraded in 1951 to the charge of collaborationism and he was freed. His jail time prevented him from being the figurehead of the new party, so in June 1947 the choice fell on Giorgio Almirante.

Almirante was only in his mid-thirties when he took over the party leadership. He came from a socially prominent family: his father was a film director and several of his uncles were well-known actors. Almirante was an unrepentant defender of the Salò Republic. He had begun his journalistic career with *Il Tevere*, a daily newspaper notorious for its antisemitism.[40] He then became part of the editorial team that produced *La Difesa della Razza*. During Salò he was private secretary to the minister for popular culture. In short, Almirante had been one of the RSI's most effective and influential apologists. As party leader, he made no bones about the MSI's identification with Salò and with the goals of nationalist socialism. Under Almirante's leadership, the MSI elected five deputies and one senator to parliament in April 1948. The MSI obtained 527,000 votes (2 per cent) in the election to the Chamber, though a mere 164,000 (0.72 per cent) voted for the MSI's symbol (a red, white, and green flame) in the Senate election.

In January 1950, Almirante was squeezed out of the leadership and replaced by Augusto De Marsanich, an older man who during the regime had been an official in the fascist trade union and editor – yet another journalist – of a newspaper for workers, *Il Lavoro fascista*. He was a junior minister between 1935 and 1943 and in the last two years of the war acted as the government's representative on the board of directors of a car company, Alfa Romeo. This was the c.v. of a functionary, not an ideologue, still less a rabble-rouser. At the MSI's first party congress in July 1948, De Marsanich coined a phrase that would live on as a motto throughout the history of Italian neo-Fascism when he urged the MSI not to 'renege upon or restore' (*non rinnegare e non restaurare*) the former regime.[41] The MSI's adherents should not be ashamed of Fascism's record but they should not strive to subvert the democratic institutions of the Republic either.

De Marsanich had been close to Giuseppe Bottai, a conspirator against Mussolini in July 1943. De Marsanich's emergence as the Movement's leader potentially signified an opening to right-wingers within what Italians call the 'constitutional arc'. Almirante, let alone those in the MSI even more extremist than he, was beyond the pale for the PLI, right-wing Christian Democrats, and the Vatican, but De Marsanich was not – or not necessarily. The MSI, or so De Marsanich, Michelini and others reasoned, had to position itself as anti-communist and pro-Church, as well as nationalist. If it took such positions, it might make inroads into the support of the DC – especially since the DC was promoting radical land reforms that were anathema to the southern middle and upper classes.

The party's extremists consciously worked against any such strategy of accommodation with the constitutional right. Fringe terrorist groups, the *Fasci di azione rivoluzionaria*, engaged in bomb attacks on public buildings and against the offices of rival parties. The state responded firmly. In the spring of 1951, the police arrested several militants from the MSI's revolutionary wing, including one of the party's founders, Giuseppe 'Pino' Rauti (who would remain an important figure in far-right politics until the 1990s), and a political theorist, Julius Evola.[42] The MSI's national congress, slated to be held in Bari in November 1951, was banned by the government after the MSI's militants had given the straight arm 'Roman' salute at several public meetings. In the meantime, De Gasperi ordered Scelba to head a working group that would draft a law to give teeth to the constitutional provision that forbade the reconstitution of the Fascist Party.

The Monarchists, meanwhile, had been revived by a flamboyant Neapolitan businessman, an *armatore* (shipping magnate) with a taste for high-living, football, and beautiful mistresses. Achille Lauro was a proto-Silvio Berlusconi, an entrepreneur who was able to strike a rapport with a population that was losing faith in politics and wanted quick solutions. Like Berlusconi, Lauro invited the people to trust him. He would get things done, with a businessman's nous (though his own career had owed much to the cultivation of political contacts; in this, too, he anticipated Berlusconi). He was also a fervent anti-communist, who was willing to rehabilitate the far right.

'O Comandante' ('The Skipper') as Lauro was nicknamed in Neapolitan, had built one of Europe's leading cargo shipping lines in the 1930s. He joined the PNF in 1933, for 'purely formal and blatantly opportunistic reasons', and had thrived under the regime, transporting merchandise to and from Italy's colonies in Africa.[43] The war in Ethiopia made him richer still. Italy's entry into Hitler's war, however, took a toll on his fleet, with many ships being sunk or sequestered by the British, and when the dictatorship fell and the Allies reached Naples, Lauro's fortunes reached their nadir. He was categorized as a 'big fascist' by the Allies and as a collaborator of the Germans. He was imprisoned in various prison camps, where he amused himself, but presumably few others, by walking around 'stark naked'.[44] At war's end Lauro was singled out for trial. The anti-fascist parties were baying for a harsh sentence. An able defence by Lauro's man of business, a lawyer named Raffaele Cafiero, nevertheless got the 'Skipper' a favourable judgement, to the astonishment of the naïve British officer prosecuting the case. Cafiero, it goes without saying, was a long-standing friend of the judge.[45]

Lauro now had to rebuild his business empire from scratch in an Italy where his political enemies were now in charge. He accordingly set about establishing links with the DC. In the autumn of 1947, together with a fellow *armatore*, Angelo Costa, the head of Confindustria, the employers' federation, Lauro kept the De Gasperi government on its feet by persuading – the word is a euphemism – the parliamentary contingent of UQ to back Alcide De Gasperi in a vote of confidence on 5 October. The government survived with a thirty-four-seat majority – but thirty-three of those were UQ deputies who had disregarded the party line.

In 1948, Lauro took over the National Monarchist Party (PNM), a small, largely southern party that had joined the National Bloc in the 1946 election to the Constituent Assembly but was chronically lacking funds and organization. Lauro provided both. His newspaper, *Roma*, despite its name a Naples daily, was given a Rome office, a morning edition, and generous resources. In 1952, the editorship was conferred upon Alfredo Signoretti, a 'fervent fascist', who had been editor of *La Stampa* from 1932 to 1943. When Mussolini was deposed in July 1943, crowds in Turin had mobbed *La Stampa*'s headquarters shouting, 'Down with Signoretti!'[46] It was an indictment of Italy's haphazard purge that someone with Signoretti's record should have been able to direct a major newspaper just seven years after the end of the regime.[47] Naturally, he filled the pages of *Roma* with contributions by fascist sympathizers, including Julius Evola and Mussolini's hagiographer and one-time mistress Margherita Sarfatti.

SHOES AND SHOWMANSHIP

The prospect of a right-wing alternative to De Gasperi's centrist coalition thus grew after 1950. The DC occupied the centre of the political spectrum, but if it lost votes to the two rebranded far-right parties, it might, paradoxically, be obliged to turn to them to ensure continuation in office. Provincial and city elections were looming in Rome and the South in May 1952, and the MSI and PNM opted to form an electoral pact. De Gasperi, however, was adamant that the DC, so long as he was leader, would not make any kind of deal with the neo-fascists. They were as much the enemy of democracy as the Stalinist left.

De Gasperi came under considerable pressure from the Vatican to change his stance. On 5 December 1951, shortly after the government's crackdown on the MSI, a papal envoy, monsignor Pietro Pavan, visited De Gasperi at his home in Rome to relay the Pope's 'growing alarm' at the way in which the 'extreme left' was improving its organization and propaganda, and the failure of the government to match its success.

The ensuing conversation was fascinating. De Gasperi acknowledged that the Pope was right to be alarmed but pointed out that the communists possessed 'substantial resources' whereas the DC was poor. It cost 180 million lire a month to run the DC and he didn't know how to find the money, since stealing 'wasn't allowed' and nor could he 'shift' money from the state's (empty) coffers. He pointed out that there was no chance of confronting the PCI 'head-on', since that would mean 'civil war, or perhaps an outright war'. Monsignor Pavan replied that if the government followed an 'uncertain' policy, then the 'healthy forces' of the nation would become 'disoriented' and would 'stray' from the DC's leadership. Whereas, if the DC were decisive, people would rally to it. Pavan made clear that the Vatican considered that the PCI was 'enemy number one', and hinted that one only 'played the communists' game' by 'wasting energy' on 'damaging' 'anticommunist nuclei'. He meant the MSI. De Gasperi, 'both joking and melancholic', assured the Vatican's envoy that his efforts to defeat the PCI were second to none. With mordant humour he reminded his visitor that, if the PCI won, 'the first person to be hanged would be me'.[48]

In March 1952, the Vatican, backed by influential figures such as Luigi Gedda, now the national head of Catholic Action, advanced the idea that Don Luigi Sturzo should run as mayoral candidate for Rome, at the head of a civic list that would have the backing of the MSI and Lauro's Monarchists, as well as the DC. Otherwise, it was argued, there was a strong chance that the PSI and PCI, who were themselves opportunistically backing a citizens' list headed by the geriatric liberal Francesco Saverio Nitti, might win.

Don Sturzo, a lifelong anti-fascist, expressed his 'misgivings' about including the MSI but was initially willing to form a list that included the DC and the centre-left parties that was open to 'extraneous elements'.[49] De Gasperi set his face against any scheme emanating from Gedda, who, he grimly told Fanfani, 'is an enemy of ours; he still has a lurking sympathy for the black shirt'.[50]

If 'Operation Don Sturzo' had been successful, it would have driven a coach and horses through the premier's project to create a 'party of the centre, marching leftwards'. As it was, the PRI threatened to leave the government, while Saragat's PSDI refused future electoral collaboration with the DC if the Sturzo plan went ahead. But it was difficult for the DC publicly to disassociate itself from a proposal cherished by the Vatican and guided by one of the DC's spiritual and political founding fathers. De Gasperi had to exercise all his authority to prevent the success of the scheme.

The crisis was resolved, on 22 April 1952, only when Sturzo declined to put his name forward. The prime minister had prevailed. De

Gasperi's opposition to 'Operation Sturzo' led to a personal breach between the Pope and the premier. Pius XII 'long brooded over the insult done to him'.[51] In June 1953, Pius even denied a request by De Gasperi and his wife for a private audience to receive a blessing upon their thirtieth wedding anniversary and to celebrate the decision of their youngest daughter, Lucia, to take perpetual vows. Popes, apparently, need not forgive those who trespass against them.

Not only was there no pact between the DC and the neo-fascist right, but during the election campaign the premier attacked the MSI with a zest he usually reserved for Togliatti. His speeches, which were published by the DC as a pamphlet with the significant title 'Polemics from the Local Election Campaign of 1952', were full of jabs at all his opponents, with the MSI being singled out for special scorn. De Gasperi's speech in Rome, delivered to an immense crowd in Piazza del Popolo, which concluded the campaign on 23 May 1952, was derisive:

De Marsanich has brazenly stated that if he had been in government, then Italy would have occupied Trieste as early as 1947. But who would he have occupied it with? The fascist militia, maybe? With those gun-toting bravos who ran for their lives the day Mussolini was arrested? . . . The *missini* [i.e. supporters of the MSI] believe themselves to be democrats. But they understand democracy in the same way as Stalin does: use the methods of democracy to conquer power and then impose dictatorship![52]

De Gasperi concluded by urging the women of Rome, especially, to put their trust in the Cross, which 'had weathered many storms and many persecutors without succumbing because dictators and persecutors come and go, but God remains'.[53]

His speech was applauded, but in Rome he was swimming against a strong tide. In the first place, the Cross, in its current earthly manifestation, was ambiguous in its support for Italy's democratic forces. Second, as the prime minister admitted in an open letter published by the weekly magazine *Oggi* on 13 May, the DC lacked solid allies. De Gasperi acknowledged that, difficult though it was to resist 'adversaries' who did not abide by the rules of 'fair play' and who flung themselves on you like 'mastiffs' and sought to bite you until they 'drew blood', the DC's collaborators were not much help in a fight:

> As for one's friends, or those who should be friends. My most curious experience [of his time in office] has been with the so-called minor parties. I have tried time and time again to assemble all the political forces that believe in the democratic system and desire to defend it ... They maintain that the best way of renewing their own political élan is to combat the government and oppose it, but in a measured and calculated way, which means just enough to undermine it, but without taking the responsibility for bringing it down.

De Gasperi admonished his allies that in the face of totalitarian enemies, such an approach was dangerous for democracy:

> The adversary, in well-disciplined ranks, is moving both aggressively and stealthily. Against his fanatical and granite-like coherence ... we are scattered and incoherent ... There have been moments when I have found myself wishing that we might succumb to the iron regime of a totalitarian party and hence complete the civic education of certain gentlemen whose consciences too easily exonerate them from making their rightful contribution to the salvation of all.[54]

In Rome and elsewhere, the forces of right-wing populism fought a no-holds-barred campaign themselves. Lauro threw himself into the fight to become mayor of Naples with gusto. His no-expense-spared campaign became the stuff of folk legend (the correspondent of the *Washington Post* in Italy, Leo Wollemborg, calculated that Lauro had spent more than 500 million lire).[55] Fleets of small cars bearing loudspeakers broadcast his name along the streets; his supporters handed out flour, pasta, sugar, and other foodstuffs from street corners, or bought up small loans owed by voters to the banks for cash in hand. On the day of the vote (but this might really be a legend), Lauro's campaign staff gave would-be voters a single shoe. They were entitled to its pair when they had cast their ballot.[56]

Of course, Lauro had no way of knowing whether the shoeless voted for him in the secrecy of the *cabina elettorale*, but the odds were on his side. The people who needed shoes were likely to vote for him. Also, it was a good way of underlining that many people in Naples indeed had no proper shoes – or proper healthcare, housing, sanitation, schools. The logic that the DC had applied in the 1948 election, of getting as many people as possible to the polls, now worked against it.

Another strategy used by Lauro was a precursor to that used by Silvio Berlusconi in the 1990s. Lauro was the de facto proprietor of Napoli Calcio, the city's football team, which, thanks to his largesse, had been promoted to the highest division, Serie A. Naples was as obsessed with football then as it is today, and in the 1951–2 season the team finished sixth, raising public expectations. During the electoral campaign, which took place as the football season concluded, Lauro swore to spend lavishly to strengthen the team for the following year (a promise he kept by buying a Swedish striker, Hasse Jeppson, from Atalanta of Bergamo for 105 million lire, a gigantic sum for a football player in the early 1950s). He would construct, as a campaign slogan had it, 'a great Naples for a great Naples'. Alas, in this he failed, and the 'trophy cabinet remained empty (apart from two Italian Cups) until the arrival of a small Argentinian genius [Diego Maradona] in 1984'.[57]

Last, but certainly not least, for it would be wrong to give the impression that Lauro's success was merely a triumph of showmanship and wealth, 'O Comandante hit the right populist buttons by blaming the central government for Naples' ills. As one Italian historian has written, Lauro 'missed no opportunity to express his contempt for the political class and parties, [whom he] considered as parasites and enemies of the collective interest'.[58] Like all successful populists, he struck a chord with middle-class conservatives and moderate voters, not just the poor and dispossessed. Why should the third city of Italy be so neglected, he asked, completely legitimately. It was a question to which the DC's local and national representatives could provide no convincing answers.

Anybody with crossover appeal to slum dwellers, football fans, and middle-class conservatives was a certain winner in Naples. Indeed, Lauro won an 'overwhelming victory, one greater than the most optimistic predictions'.[59] The Monarchists' coalition with the MSI took 207,000 votes, 41 per cent, and the 'Skipper' received 117,000 personal preferences and became mayor. The electoral law for city elections gave 60 per cent of the seats in the city council to the coalition with the plurality of the vote, and so the third city of Italy fell into the hands of a far-right coalition, with a showman entrepreneur as its head. Naples was the biggest success for the right-wing insurgency, but the PNM and the MSI attracted votes across the South, notably in Bari. In Rome, the Vatican's fear that Cossacks would bivouac in Saint Peter's Square proved to be exaggerated.[60] The PCI–PSI list was fended off by the DC, whose candidate became mayor, even though the DC took only 31 per cent of the vote and had to rely on its centrist allies for a plurality. The MSI–Monarchist list obtained 200,000 votes and finished a strong third.

The DC nevertheless retained its centrality in the political process after the 1952 municipal elections. The PCI and PSI made little headway. The PNM and MSI's gains were limited geographically. The DC's party secretary, Guido Gonella, pointed out that the DC had obtained more votes than the two left-wing parties put together. More than 8.7 million Italians had voted for the DC (35.1 per cent), and, despite the defeats in Naples and Bari, the party had won in a string of southern cities, including Matera, not to mention Trieste and all of Sicily. Gonella predicted that the DC would get 10.5 million votes (approximately 40 per cent) in a national vote. This was almost exactly the figure that the DC subsequently would obtain in the June 1953 general election.

Indeed, when one reads the minutes of meetings of the DC's leadership (or the PCI's), one realizes that these parties were deeply rooted in Italian society. This is why Gonella was not shaken by Lauro's triumph, nor by the successes of the MSI. He knew they were the product of a specific time and particular places and were not a general threat. The take-away from the May 1952 elections was that they had confirmed, yet again, that the DC was 'the most effective bulwark for democratic institutions' in Italy. Any other interpretation was simply the 'fruit of fantasy', Gonella concluded.[61]

The MSI was nevertheless the target of vigorous DC propaganda in the months after the local elections. A SPES pamphlet simply called *MSI*, published in the late summer of 1952, had a scornful quotation from Mussolini on the cover in lieu of a subtitle: 'There won't be a second Fascism. For when a stone is lifted away, the only thing you see beneath are lice.'[62]

The DC was, moreover, determined to limit the MSI's actions by law. The working group chaired by Scelba had been crafting legislation that would ensure fascist activities in Italy were circumscribed – indeed, the price for the MSI's cooperation in 'Operation Sturzo' had been abandonment of this legislation. The so-called Scelba Law was approved by parliament in June 1952, a month after the local elections, and came into force on 8 July. Article 1 defined an attempt to reconstitute Fascism as:

> Whenever an association or movement pursues the anti-democratic ends characteristic of the Fascist party, by exalting, menacing or using violence as a means of political struggle, by advocating the suppression of the liberties guaranteed by the Constitution, by denigrating democracy, its institutions, and the values of the Resistance, by publishing racist propaganda, or else directs its activities to the exaltation of the chief figures, principles, actions and methods of the aforenamed party [the PNF] or conducts public displays of fascist character.[63]

The law provided for severe penalties for those found guilty of pro-fascist activity. Article 2 prefigured punishments of three to ten years of imprisonment, with an extra two years being added to the sentence if any paramilitary organization or the use of violence was proven at the trial. Freedom of speech was limited for the fascist right. Praising Mussolini and evoking the supposed successes of the former regime in public might get you two years' jail and a fine of 500,000 lire (Article 4). Giving the Roman salute at a rally was punishable by a prison sentence of three months and a 50,000 lire fine (Article 5). Article 8 gave the Ministry of the Interior, in other words the police, the power to sequester fascist propaganda and magazines without judicial authorization, though such actions had to be retrospectively approved by a judge within twenty-four hours.

In essence, the Scelba Law put the MSI on notice that the state could and would dissolve the party if it tried to replicate the practices and symbols of the PNF or PRF during electoral campaigning or conducted any kind of clandestine paramilitary activity. The law had a direct effect on the neofascists' behaviour. The MSI's central bureau swiftly put out a leaflet to all members warning that each one of them,

'Deeply rooted in Italian society':
a PCI election rally, Bologna, 1951.

by their individual behaviour, could cause 'grave damage to the movement as a whole'.[64]

If one reads the MSI's subsequent manifesto for the June 1953 general elections, one is struck by the absence of any mention of Mussolini, any mention of the alleged triumphs of Fascism, even any overt reference to fascist ideology and symbols. One has to deduce that the MSI is a fascist movement from its appeals for a strong state that 'stands guard' for 'moral, patriotic, and military values', from its eulogy to women in their role as mothers, from its bellicose pledge to wage a 'battle without quarter' against communist subversion, and from its boastful nationalism on the topic of Trieste. Italian imperialism (a word that is never mentioned) was transformed in the manifesto into an appeal for Italy to act as a 'natural bridge' between Africa and Europe and to 'plug Africa into Europe'. In keeping with the fascist belief in the unitary nature of the state, the manifesto was adamantly opposed to the project of constructing regional government. It also argued that the President of the Republic should possess stronger powers than the constitution had attributed to the office. The cult of Caesarism lived on, even after the Duce himself had proved to be a broken reed. Crucially, though, the MSI wasn't allowed to say so.[65]

The day that the Scelba Law came into force, De Gasperi signalled the need for a 'strong state' in a lengthy interview with the Rome daily, *Il Messaggero*. He made clear that he was not implying the state should be the dictatorship of a class or party. A strong state was simply one where the law was respected and enforced, and where fundamental democratic freedoms were protected, even if this meant taking precautionary measures against political parties that abused the rules. The interview concluded with a homely metaphor. The democratic state, De Gasperi averred, should not be a mere 'motor bus' which political parties temporarily used for a stretch of road, full knowing that their final destination was a Bolshevik *coup d'état*, or the restoration of the corporate state, or a conservative monarchy, while the government acted as a conductor, passively checking tickets and handing out information about the timetable.[66]

The interview is one of the most revealing insights into De Gasperi's mind in the entire canon of his writings. It shows that, for him, the ultimate purpose of the state – its raison d'être – was to safeguard democratic institutions, not pursue lofty ideological goals. Democracy was both a means and an end. When De Gasperi gave the interview, his chief concern was how to guarantee that the state's role as an enabler of democracy could be preserved in an Italy in which the precarious centre had seen its electoral presence shrink. Others in the DC had no doubts: it was necessary to move away from strict proportional representation.

SUMMER IN TRENTINO

De Gasperi departed for his country cottage in Val di Sella in Trentino at the beginning of August 1952. It is a beautiful spot. The house, which is spartan inside, is surrounded by trees, while Mount Ortigara (2,106 metres) and Cima Dodici (2,336 metres) loom behind it, separating the Valsugana from the Asiago plateau. One looks out upon a view of the Lagorai chain, the foothills to the Dolomites, on the other side of the Valsugana: De Gasperi's native Pieve Tesino lies in their

A home from Rome: De Gasperi's cottage in the Val di Sella.

heart. Even today, the Val di Sella is not the easiest place in Italy to get to. The narrow road that links Borgo Valsugana to the meadows where Casa De Gasperi is located rises in a seemingly endless series of tight bends. In the early 1950s, with the rudimentary, under-powered cars of the time, and flimsy or non-existent guard rails, the journey up must have been nerve-wracking.

If you are a lifelong hiker, climber, and enthusiast for the simple mountain life, as De Gasperi was, the valley is a haven. One can see why the Christian Democrat leader, drained by the tensions of political life, came home every year to recharge his batteries. It is as un-Roman, or un-metropolitan, a place as one can imagine. In 1952, when there was far less tourism, the difference must have been even more stark than it is today.

During the summer of 1952, De Gasperi had an almost playful exchange of vacation letters with Nenni, who had just returned from receiving the Stalin Prize in Moscow and was himself holidaying in the Trentino at San Martino di Castrozza, in the core of the Dolo-mites. With his usual human sympathy, Nenni wrote to the prime minister on 5 August offering his impressions of the current political situation in the USSR.

He had a second reason for writing, however. The letter to De Gas-peri was also a polite shot across the bows. The PSI leader wrote that he thought it would be a 'major political setback' for the country if the DC were to 'succumb to the temptation' of 'fabricating a made-to-measure electoral law' that facilitated its hold on power. The letter was signed, using the informal form common between intimates, 'tuo Pietro Nenni'. De Gasperi replied on 11 August with an amiable note saying he was glad Nenni was enjoying a rest in San Martino, which was part of his former constituency (when he was a deputy in the Austrian parliament).[67] He added:

> I therefore have the duty to desire that my mountain breezes bring good health to you and create that dolomitic sense of harmony which soars high above the murk of politics.[68]

This was an elaborate way of saying, 'I know we've got to think about the electoral law, but let's forget about politics for a moment.' But it is hard to imagine that De Gasperi, as he strode through the woods in Sella (he didn't stroll) or served *polenta e funghi* at the family table at *Ferragosto* (Feast of the Assumption), was able to keep his mind off the topic of electoral reform for any length of time. Indeed, we know he did not, for monsignor Pavan, the papal envoy, visited him on 13 August to press the case for an electoral alliance between the DC and the Monarchists. De Gasperi resisted this appeal, stating that he would strive for an electoral pact with the PLI, the PRI, and the PSDI. This was the approach 'imposed' upon him by the 'current historical situation' of Italy. Any other policy would expose the DC to internal turmoil and would launch the nation on 'extremely dangerous adventures'. What De Gasperi was saying was that, while a pact with the Monarchists might please the Vatican and conservatives in the South, it was bound to antagonize the party's left, not to mention staunch anti-monarchists like Scelba. The DC might split, opening the door for the PCI. Without a solid centre, Italy could not be governed. Preserving the unity and centrality of the DC was crucial.[69]

But how was the centre to be shored up? The arithmetic was against the DC. The local election results suggested that the party would remain the principal force in Italian democracy, but it was unlikely to match its success of 1948. The PRI could provide individuals of talent to the Council of Ministers, but its electoral weight was nil. The PLI was only marginally less negligible. The PSDI were unreliable partners, but even if the democratic socialists joined a government coalition and stayed in it, the DC could hope, with the strictly proportional electoral system in the Chamber of Deputies, for a wafer-thin majority at best, and possibly no majority at all.

The only way to consolidate the centre was to shift to a majoritarian electoral system, one that would effectively provide a prize in seats to the largest party, or a winning coalition of parties. This might mean moving to a single member constituency model, like the one employed in Britain, perhaps with a two-stage ballot to allow a run-off between the two largest parties; alternatively, some jurists proposed extending the core principle of the law in force at municipal level to give the winning national coalition a 'majority prize'. The minor parties naturally preferred the second approach. A British-style system might have wiped them out; certainly, it would have left them as pensioners dependent on the DC's goodwill.

Ever since the summer of 1952, Italians have hunted the snark of a model electoral law, one that combines equity in representation with governability, with a passion that leaves less perfectionist peoples lost in admiration (or simply bemused).[70] In Cold War Italy the question mattered immensely. As Nenni's friendly note to the premier hinted, the left-wing parties were bound to regard a majoritarian law of any kind as an attempt to cheat them out of just representation. That could only stoke tension – of which Italy already had more than enough.

On the other hand, De Gasperi desired to liberate the DC from the temptation of leaning rightwards in search of a stable majority. While the premier was in the arcadia of the Val di Sella, he was, in fact, thinking how he could square this circle – and he could be steely with those whose thinking on the subject he regarded as shallow or in bad faith. Even when they were friends and mentors.[71]

The first public fruit of De Gasperi's thinking came in a speech the premier delivered in the town square of Predazzo in the Val di Fiemme, on 31 August 1952, to celebrate his fiftieth year of active politics. Predazzo is the gateway to the Dolomites and less than twenty miles from San Martino di Castrozza, Nenni's vacation resort; in 1952, before the development of tourism and winter sports, it was a town that depended on the timber industry for such prosperity as it had. De Gasperi had deep personal roots there: his mother, Maria Morandini, was a native of the town.[72]

On the day of De Gasperi's speech, rural Predazzo briefly became the locus of Italian politics. De Gasperi swept away all equivocations about his intentions regarding the electoral law: he was in favour of change to a majoritarian system of election.

The Predazzo speech was a disquisition about Italian democracy's immediate requirements. First, by way of compliment to his host, the first president of the autonomous region of Trentino-Alto Adige, Tullio Odorizzi, De Gasperi contended that Italy needed to take a leaf out of the book of cooperation being authored by Germans and Italians in the new border region. Italy would also do well to copy the autonomous region's parsimony with public funds and impose strict limits on the size of officialdom.[73] Second, Italy needed to give the Constitution time to grow. It was necessary to proceed 'slow but sure', De Gasperi argued, by gradually introducing legislation that would make the constitution's aspirations for social reform real. The constitution was a 'living thing', a delicate plant that had to be nurtured, rather than an edict to be implemented as fast as possible, regardless of cost.

Most important of all, Italy needed to understand that the fundamental principle of democracy was 'control by the minority, decision by the majority'. The minority possessed political rights and could put forward its case by any peaceful means it wished, but, as in any human association, when the time came to decide, one counted heads and the minority had to accept the majority's preference. Italy's fundamental problem was that neither the PCI nor the MSI showed any signs of acknowledging this fundamental principle. Both parties saw democracy as being essentially a means of securing power – which they might then use to abolish democracy. De Gasperi did not trust the PCI to behave better than its peers beyond the Iron Curtain, nor did he trust the MSI to hang their black shirts in the closet for ever.

De Gasperi even believed that the PCI and the MSI might reach a deal if it suited their interests. The German Communists and the Nazis had, after all, conspired against the *Zentrum* in Weimar Germany. When one looks at the Italian premier's attitude to electoral reform in 1953, it is essential to remember that De Gasperi was well acquainted with the contemporary history of the German-speaking lands. He was not a German, but he was Germanic in culture and background. He spoke and wrote German like a native. The historical experience of post-Habsburg Austria and Weimar Germany was burned into his consciousness. He knew better than anybody else in Italian politics how quickly the democratic bourgeois centre-ground could be undermined by the unscrupulousness of totalitarian parties, if it were too accommodating or too irresolute. The lesson of Weimar seemed like an ominous one for Italy in the summer of 1952.[74]

In De Gasperi's mind, the issue hence became how to strengthen the centre against the extremes. There needed, in short, to be what Arthur Schlesinger called, in a 1949 book, a 'vital center' united against totalitarianism.[75] That is to say, a coalition of all anti-fascist and anti-communist forces. Such parties had to sink their differences to pursue a reformist agenda. Probably De Gasperi had never read Schlesinger's book, or possibly never even heard of it, but the gist of his speech at Predazzo in support of electoral reform was identical to that put forward by the great American liberal.

Italy's democracy needed stable governments, De Gasperi affirmed at Predazzo. That didn't mean 'keeping De Gasperi or Gonella, or the Christian Democratic party in power for ever'. There was no need for the 'geese of the Campidoglio to sound the alarm' for the future of Italian democracy if the government did proceed with a revision of the electoral law. Freedom was not in peril from the DC.

But which electoral law? 'How many projects, how many ideas, how much discussion?' De Gasperi exclaimed in rhetorical frustration to the good burghers gathered in Predazzo's town square. In his speech, he refused to commit himself to a particular model, though by then he had decided that the 'majority prize' was indeed the most promising avenue to follow. He did, however, underline that any new electoral law had to meet four criteria. Any new law should serve:

1. Democracy in general, not a single party.
2. The majority principle (i.e. enhance the capacity to decide).

Also, it should:

3. Facilitate collaboration between political parties that sincerely accept the rules of the current democratic regime.
4. Guarantee the powers of the minority to hold the government to account.

Moreover, De Gasperi insisted repeatedly in the speech that he hoped the passage of a new electoral law would *broaden* the centrist coalition. If there were 'conversions' to the democratic camp from either the left or the right, they would be welcome in the new centrist coalition. The 'line-up of the constructive forces' should be as 'ample as possible', the premier underlined.[76]

This appeal must have seemed like the insalubrious tradition of *trasformismo* in a new guise to the many intellectuals on the left who were convinced that De Gasperi represented forces of conservatism. De Gasperi, by contrast, thought he was circling the democratic wagons, not thwarting political change. His intention was to create a heterogeneous coalition stretching from the PLI on the right to, say, the anti-fascist writer Ignazio Silone and the Socialist politician Giuseppe Romita on the left, that would nevertheless be unified by their common attachment to democracy and gradual social reform. Secretly (or perhaps not so secretly), De Gasperi also hoped that Nenni's PSI might be detached from the clutches of the PCI.[77]

By the autumn of 1952, Nenni was beginning, tardily, to express doubts about the way Marxist-Leninist ideas had been applied in the Soviet Union. Alas, De Gasperi's adoption of the majoritarian principle would provide the Socialist leader with a new cause for anti-government intransigence. It would be he who coined the term by which the electoral reform has gone down in history, the *legge truffa* (Swindle Law), although some of the merit for this efficacious slogan ought perhaps to be assigned to Stalin. On 17 July 1952, Nenni, who had been awarded the Stalin Prize a few days before, was received in the Kremlin by the Soviet leader (Nenni's diary dedicates four pages to the encounter and is a very psychologically revealing piece of writing). During his conversation with Stalin, who was attended by Mikhail Suslov, 'the red theologian of this species of church that is communism in its Soviet form', the PSI leader indicated that the DC was attempting to consolidate its hold on power by a 'manipulation' of the electoral system. Stalin, 'smiling beneath his moustaches', said it was a *'makinatzia'* (literally, 'machination'), a word that Nenni remembered and translated, with his unerring instinct for the language of stump politics, as *'truffa'* in Italian.[78]

11

The Centre Holds

The electoral reform was presented to the Chamber of Deputies in mid-October 1952. At a prior meeting of the parliamentary group of the DC, party secretary Guido Gonella quoted the anti-fascist intellectual Gaetano Salvemini, who had recently written that 'a party or a coalition of democratic parties that, despite being in government, permitted a totalitarian opposition to conquer power with the methods of democracy, would be the most perfect collection of idiots that has ever existed.'[1] The rationale for the law, Gonella underlined, with a deferential bow to De Gasperi, was to 'defend democratic institutions from the anti-democracy of the left and right alike and prevent democracy from being killed by the weapons of democracy itself'.

According to Gonella, the law that the DC was proposing introduced a system of 'integrated proportional representation'. PR would remain the basis of the electoral law. But in the 'exceptional case' that one party, or a coalition of 'paired' parties, received 50 per cent +1 of the valid votes cast, then two-thirds of the seats would be assigned to it, or to them. The proportional system would still apply in the division of seats *within* the majority, and it would also be applied to decide the distribution of the remaining seats. Moreover, if nobody achieved the threshold required (or surpassed two-thirds), then votes would be distributed in accordance with existing electoral law.[2]

Gonella claimed that giving a prize in seats to the winning coalition was better than either a system of election via single member constituencies, as in Britain, where all the votes not cast for winning constituency candidates simply counted for nothing, or in elections for towns with more than 10,000 inhabitants in Italy itself, where the largest plurality, not majority, was awarded a majority prize. He did not mention the cases of Rome and Naples in the 1952 local elections, but they illustrated his point perfectly. In Rome, the DC's candidate was now mayor having secured 31 per cent of the vote; in Naples, 41 per cent of the electorate had voted for Lauro's list, and he was widely supposed to have enjoyed a triumph. Setting the quorum at 50 per cent was the 'fundamental moral point of the system'. As he put it:

> [The law] is about reinforcing an absolute majority in order to ensure the better functioning of the chamber and the stability of the government: it is not a device to transform a plurality into a majority; that is to say, a minority into a majority. This is the point in which the system of integrated proportional representation differs drastically from the Acerbo majoritarian system, which did not require the absolute majority [for the awarding of a majority prize] and which did not provide, through the pairing mechanism, for the prospect of a coalition of parties, rather than a single totalitarian party, emerging victorious.[3]

The DC were extremely sensitive to any suggestion that their proposed law was inspired by the electoral law drawn up by Giacomo Acerbo, which fixed the 1924 elections by awarding two-thirds of seats in the Chamber of Deputies to any list obtaining more than a *quarter* of the vote (indeed, to distance its law still further from Acerbo's, the majority's share of seats was amended shortly after its presentation to 65 per cent).[4] They underlined the point that no one party would monopolize power, and that the electoral law would never 'destroy' the rights of minorities to be represented in the Chamber of Deputies. Indeed, minorities were guaranteed a third of the seats even if they didn't get a third of the votes.

Gonella waved away the 'fairy tale' put forward by some jurists that the law would damage the principle of voting equality for all citizens. All voters would still possess an equal right to cast a vote for a party that might potentially have a majority. He was less convincing in contradicting the obvious point that the DC might piggyback off its coalition partners to obtain more than 50 per cent of the seats in the chamber, even if a minority of the electorate voted for it. To that argument, Gonella could only assert that the DC had governed well and had not hitherto abused the dominant position it had enjoyed since April 1948. Gonella concluded by quoting Salvemini, who was no friend of the DC, again:

> The problem to be resolved today is whether Italy would be better served by a democratic regime without so-called 'pure' proportional representation in which it is possible to form a non-fascist or non-communist government or a regime that is one hundred per cent democratic in which nobody can govern.[5]

This argument was a compelling one and it prevailed with the leaderships of the minor parties. On 15 November 1952, the self-styled 'four democratic parties' (DC, PSDI, PLI, PRI) approved a formal pact that bound them to:

1. Support in Parliament, against any attempt at sabotage, the bill introduced by the government to reform the electoral system that would assign 65 per cent of seats, in global terms 380 seats, to the coalition obtaining an absolute majority of votes.
2. Present their party lists to the electorate across the national territory as a single ticket. Any further adherent to the ticket could only join if all four parties agreed.
3. Recognize the constitutional and political need to 'discipline' the press, the trade unions, and the defence of democracy by force of law.

Point three clearly implied that restrictive legislation, akin to that imposed on the MSI, might be imposed upon the activities of the PCI if the DC-led coalition won. It was an open secret that the Americans were pressing, behind the scenes, for repressive measures against the PCI. The four parties concluded the pact by denouncing the seriousness of both the national and international situation which, they concurred, 'required all men of good will to combat against forces inimical to human progress'.[6]

It is interesting to note, however, that the four parties made no promise to *govern* together. The pact allowed the smaller parties to use the DC's popular appeal as a springboard to secure a number of deputies disproportionate to their popular standing, but it did not insist on a written commitment to support a DC-led administration after the vote. At most, the parties were morally bound to remain allied with the DC after an election. In July 1953, this point would turn out to be critical.

The pact also ensured that the DC's different factions would have a larger pie of seats to slice. While the goals of governability and strengthening the democratic centre-ground doubtless were central to the DC's motivation for introducing the law (one should not be cynical), the need to satisfy unreliable followers played a major part, too. De Gasperi, whose governments since 1948 had been bedevilled by the small parties' tantrums, and by the factionalism of the DC itself, was dangling the carrot of safer seats and generous prebends. He himself was immune from worldly temptation, but he knew that the men with whom he had to deal were not.

The central political fact at the end of 1952 was that to avoid governing with the Monarchists, as the Vatican wanted, De Gasperi needed a majority in the chamber. In the absence of support from the PSI, that meant making deals. It also implied a majoritarian electoral reform, although since the reform would not extend to the Senate, which then had a six-year term, the odds were that the reform by itself would not be enough to provide the government with a stable majority in both chambers.[7]

Help from the PSI was not forthcoming. Nenni visited De Gasperi on 11 October 1952 and the discussion soon shifted to the proposed reform. Both men spoke 'passionately', according to Nenni. He records De Gasperi expounding what Nenni describes as a 'curious and contradictory' thesis, namely that he needed the electoral law, not for a 'second five-year term of right-wing policies', but to 'resist growing pressure from the clerical right'. With 'genuine emotion', De Gasperi told Nenni that he felt like he was 'reliving' the clash between the Vatican and the PPI between 1925 and 1926, when Pius XI had backed Mussolini rather than support Catholic democrats like Don Sturzo and De Gasperi himself. Nenni responded that such 'clerical pressure' would become overwhelming in the Chamber of Deputies if the elections were 'fixed' in the way that the DC leader was proposing. In the conditions then prevailing, Nenni told the premier, the electoral law 'would be construed as a minor *coup d'état*'. For Nenni, the only way to get lasting democratic reforms in Italy was through cooperation between the three popular parties that had led the resistance.

Nenni thought De Gasperi saw the force of his argument but had made his choice to go on. In the Socialist leader's opinion, it was a choice that was 'mistaken for him, for his party, for us, for everybody'.[8]

Nenni had spurned an implicit appeal for cooperation from the premier in the name of an imaginary policy of national unity. It was Nenni, not De Gasperi, who had a 'curious and contradictory' position. Italian politics was not unifiable in the autumn of 1952. Nenni was reasoning as if the Cominform had not happened, as if Italy had never received a lira of Marshall Plan aid, as if American opinion on the composition of the Italian government were irrelevant. His policy was a fantasy: he simply did not grasp that the prospect of collaboration between the three main parties had vanished in the summer of 1947.

The PSI subsequently decided at a party congress held in the Lirico Theatre in Milan in January 1953 to fight the next general election alone. There would be no repeat of the Garibaldi Front. Even so, Nenni was still unwilling to cut the ties connecting the PSI to the PCI. To do so meant admitting that he had been wrong (and breaking with the PCI would have terminated the secret subsidies from Moscow: money the PSI urgently needed). The Slánský Trial in November shook Nenni's faith in the system being constructed behind the Iron Curtain. His diary betrayed his disquiet:

> We fail to understand how those who were lauded to the skies yesterday are now being dragged not through the dust, but through mud. Nor do we understand the mixture of delirium and sadism in the accused's self-flagellation, in the way they acknowledge everything, admit that they were always pathetic beings or worse, in the way that they even suggest details and misdemeanours of which the prosecutors themselves were maybe unaware. Some try to explain it all by appealing to the Slav soul. *I am content not to understand.* Above all, what I do not understand is what advantage one hopes to gain from trials that illustrate that you can arrive in the highest positions in the party and the government despite being the lowest of the low.[9]

The phrase I have italicized was a moral evasion. It was necessary for democratic socialists to undertake a revaluation of what the Soviet system represented: one could not pretend that the chamber of horrors in Prague had anything to do with socialism as the PSI had always defined it: as justice and liberty. Nenni, however, did not do this. In March 1953, he dined in Prague with one of the Slánský group's political enemies, Zdeněk Fierlinger, who confided that he had no doubt of the guilt of the condemned men, nor of the accuracy of their confessions.[10] Did Nenni believe him? It is hard to know.

In the meantime, however, the battle against the electoral reform provided an issue in which the PSI and PCI were at one. The electoral reform also roused left-wing liberals to indignation. Piero Calamandrei, now a member of the PSDI and editor of an influential Florentine journal, *Il Ponte*, broke the pact his party leaders had signed rather than vote in favour of an electoral expedient. The united opposition of the left (but also the monarchist-fascist right) to the electoral law's approval meant that it outdid even the parliamentary battle over membership of the Atlantic Treaty for contentiousness.

The debate in the chamber began on 7 December 1952. Opponents of the bill used every procedural method at their disposal (there were many) to block the measure, which they declared to be unconstitutional (although the constitution nowhere said that the electoral law *must* be based upon proportional representation). The DC responded with a hard line. Parliament would sit every day, Sunday included. Between 18 and 21 January, the chamber sat continuously for sixty-nine hours. Finally, on 21 January, a vote of confidence was won by 339 votes out of 364 and a successive vote on the law itself passed by 332 votes out of 349. The bill's opponents left the chamber rather than acknowledge the votes were legitimate parliamentary practice.

The bill still had to pass the Senate. There were only forty days left before the end of the legislature and the DC's majority in the upper chamber was slim. If the DC got the 'artificial majority' that the majoritarian electoral law would deliver, it would restrict political liberties and trade union rights. So said a future President of the Republic, Sandro Pertini, in the Senate on 10 March 1953. Pertini warned the moderate socialists allied to the DC that 'reaction' was taking aim at the working class. Echoing (deliberately?) the anti-Nazi Protestant priest Pastor Niemöller, Pertini said that the 'first blow' would doubtless fall on the PCI, but then it would be the PSI's turn, and then that of 'social democrats and liberals'.[11]

There could be no meeting of minds. Opposition to the Swindle Law was an example of what Chantal Mouffe calls 'agonistic democracy' in its purest form.[12] It had become a struggle that one had to win, even if that meant bending the rules. Recognizing this, De Gasperi asked for a vote of confidence at once. He would skip the formalities of democratic consultation and debate. The president (speaker) of the Senate, Giuseppe Paratore, ruled that the government's request was inadmissible, and urged both De Gasperi and President Einaudi that the only way out of the *impasse* was to dissolve both chambers and hold an election with the old rules.[13]

Paratore resigned on 23 March. He was replaced by Meuccio Ruini, the former leader of the Democracy and Labour Party and member of the CLN. Ruini promised that he would preside with 'the same resoluteness with which I went, though already grey-haired, to the Carso Front'. In other words, with the same sense of duty as when he had served as a frontline soldier during the First World War.[14]

Ruini was certainly going into battle. On 29 March, after interrupting an opposition filibuster on the social conditions of the *mondine* (paddy-field workers), which had been dragging on for three days, he permitted a vote of confidence on the electoral law. Tumultuous scenes ensued. The stenographic account of the debate speaks of the 'throwing of many and various objects towards the President's seat' by the left-wing parties.[15] Pens, folders and even parts of desks were flung at the government benches (in the Italian parliament, the government sits below the seat of the president of the chamber facing the hemisphere where deputies sit). One senior figure in the PCI had to be restrained by the Senate's ushers from hurling a chair at Ruini.

Andreotti was the only member of the government left on its benches. Fearful that he might lose an eye from the flying objects, he grabbed a wastepaper basket and used it as a makeshift helmet. 'Thank goodness there were no photographers,' he wrote in his diary, with the self-irony that was his saving grace throughout his controversial career.

The electoral law was passed with 174 votes in favour and three abstentions, with the opposition not taking part in the vote. The result was greeted with a storm of disapproval that sounded like 'an angry stadium', Andreotti noted (he was an ardent football fan).[16]

The price of bulldozing electoral reform through was that the Senate would be ungovernable for the remaining year of its mandate. Moreover, there was also the risk that Senate elections a year hence would overturn the government's majority. On 30 March, after a fascinating discussion, the Council of Ministers asked President Einaudi to dissolve both chambers of parliament, since 'if the Senate continued to function, it would be in a state of continuous opposition to the chamber and so the reform to the electoral law for the Chamber would lose its usefulness'.[17] Einaudi hesitated since there were genuine constitutional issues raised by the decision. Article 60 of the constitution set the Senate's term at six years, not five, like the Chamber of Deputies'. Article 87 gave him the power to 'call elections to renew both chambers of parliament and to set the date for their first meeting'. The question was whether the president could *anticipate* the end of the legislature for the Senate. Pressed hard by De Gasperi, Einaudi finally decided that the president's powers were not merely formal, and that he was entitled to ask the Senate to face the electors early. On 4 April, Einaudi dissolved both chambers. Elections would take place on 7 June 1953.[18]

De Gasperi took to the airwaves to explain why the government had asked the president to take this step. In a partisan broadcast, he told his audience that the violence in parliament meant that the Senate could not carry on as if nothing had happened. It was necessary for both chambers to vote, albeit with different electoral laws. Echoing his July interview with *Il Messaggero*, De Gasperi argued that the new electoral law would serve to 'constitute a strong regime able to impose necessary discipline on the country without putting liberty in peril'.[19]

Italy's history inhibited its intellectuals from accepting any arguments for a 'strong regime'. One immediate consequence of the passage of the electoral law was the creation of a handful of left-wing or liberal parties opposed to collaboration with the DC. In April 1953, Ferruccio Parri (who had abstained in the Senate vote) and Piero Calamandrei formed a new movement called Popular Unity (UP) in opposition to the law. Epicarmo Corbino, the treasury minister inimical to the PCI in De Gasperi's second government, had already constituted a party called the National Democratic Alliance (ADN) on 10 March 1953 in opposition to the PLI. Aldo Cucchi and Valdo Magnani, the PCI apostates, formed the Independent Socialist Union (UIS) on 30 March 1953. These fringe parties would tip the balance in the election.

HALF A NATION MOURNS

The Senate battle over the electoral reform took place in the aftermath of an event that had the potential to transform Italian politics radically. On 5 March 1953, Stalin died. Before the Italian general election campaign began in earnest, the threat posed by the USSR diminished. *Baffone* was dead, and his successors seemed more open to coexistence with the West than the murderous Georgian. This opened up the prospect of 'détente' (*distensione*).

Official reaction to the dictator's death was respectful. The Italian state newsreel produced a survey of Stalin's life which discreetly omitted the great purges, the Nazi-Soviet Pact, and the Cominform.[20] Both chambers of parliament suspended their labours for an hour in respect. One of the few discordant notes was from De Gasperi. His official message of condolence was lukewarm and bluntly stated that Stalin had been no friend of Italy's during the peace negotiations.

The PCI mourned Stalin without reservation: no observer could doubt that the fundamental loyalty of the PCI was to the transnational movement of which it was an integral part. Ten thousand telegrams were sent to the Soviet Embassy in Rome in the first two days after the dictator's death. Thousands of impromptu work stoppages took place, to allow workers to grieve for the Soviet leader, while portraits of Stalin were exhibited outside party offices and private homes. 'The workers cried openly, unable to check their distress ... no other occasion matched the deep grief, like the panic that overwhelms one upon the death of a father, that the death of Stalin aroused among the party militants, and among the workers who regarded Stalin as the cause of their redemption.'[21] The towns of Leghorn (Tuscany) and

Mourning Stalin: citizens express their grief for the Soviet leader's death.

Cerignola (Apulia), the home town of Giuseppe Di Vittorio, proclaimed a state of bereavement. *Rinascita* boasted that Stalin's death had been greeted with the 'unanimous condolences of the Italian people'.[22]

The PSI mourned Stalin as publicly as its communist ally. *Avanti!* proclaimed that the death of Stalin was a 'bereavement for humanity as a whole'. Nenni's journal *Mondo Operaio* said that his death had evoked a sense of 'stunned emotional disbelief'. It was as if the world was now 'out of tilt'.[23]

In *l'Unità* an article promised 'eternal glory to the man who has done more for the liberation and progress of humanity than anybody else'. *Noi donne* pictured a benign Stalin lighting a pipe on its cover; inside, the journal for progressive women published a three-page biography of Stalin along with extracts of the leader's writings on the *questione femminile*.

The obituary in *Rinascita* was entrusted to Luigi Longo, who produced a screed entitled 'Glory to Stalin!' It was an egregious example of the 'cult of personality' that Stalin's heirs would soon abolish. The article's second paragraph gushed:

His titanic works, his genius, his life, have awed the world for over thirty years and stirred the admiration and infinite love of all peoples for his person. One third of humanity, 800 million citizens, thanks above all to his leadership and example, have definitively liquidated the exploitation of man by man, have freed themselves from slavery and have taken hold of their own destiny with confidence . . . [24]

Longo rode this rhetorical wave for another 3,000 words. There was no hint anywhere that the paragon in the Kremlin was one of the twentieth century's greatest tyrants and murderers.

The same edition of *Rinascita* contained an accolade for Stalin's foreign policy since 1945, and an article by the Soviet leader himself assuring readers that self-criticism was as essential as water and air for a communist.[25] One wonders whether the inclusion of this article was a subtle joke by Togliatti; he perhaps grasped intuitively, or knew through his own channels, that the triumvirate that replaced Stalin – Beria, Malenkov, and Foreign Minister Molotov, with Malenkov nominally first among equals – would soon fall out among themselves over the dictator's legacy.

The PCI certainly noticed that Malenkov, when he formally took over as party secretary, had changed the emphasis of the party line on the crucial issue of relations with the West. Malenkov's first speech as party secretary stated that Stalin had dedicated his 'entire genius' to the cause of maintaining peace. It added that the USSR's foreign policy was based upon the 'Leninist-Stalinist thesis' of there being a 'prolonged coexistence and peaceful competition' between the capitalist and socialist systems.[26] Stalin had articulated the same concept as long ago as February 1951 and had spoken in favour of an international conference to reduce tensions, and solve key problems, notably the question of Germany, but so long as he was in the Kremlin nobody in the West was disposed to test Moscow's sincerity.

With Stalin dead, some were so disposed, notably Churchill, who had become prime minister again in October 1951. The grand old man said there was a 'new breeze blowing in a tormented world' and on 11 May 1953 went so far as to call for a 'new Locarno' to reassure the USSR that there was no danger from German revanchism.[27] The prospect of *distensione* between the communist bloc and the West

was a windfall for the PCI in the domestic political struggle. Churchill's intervention was seen as proof that even the most rigid imperialists,
unlike De Gasperi, were prepared to deal with Moscow as equals.
German Chancellor Konrad Adenauer and, above all, De Gasperi,
though they put a good face on it, were irritated. Churchill's opening
to Malenkov harmed the DC in the general election campaign by
weakening the anti-totalitarian message at the heart of its electoral
propaganda.

7 JUNE 1953

The election of June 1953 was a hard-fought one, though not as dramatic as the one in April 1948. De Gasperi once more criss-crossed the
country, delivering speeches with the same zeal as in 1948, or even
more. By now seventy-two, his physical stamina was astonishing.
Between 26 April, when he opened the campaign at the Lirico Theatre
in Milan, and 5 June, when he spoke in Rome's Piazza del Popolo, De
Gasperi gave campaign speeches to *comizi* in Turin (packing San Carlo
Square with over 30,000 people), Florence, Ascoli-Piceno, Genoa,
Bologna, Matera, Avellino, Vittorio Veneto, Treviso, Trento, Cagliari,
Palermo (another gigantic crowd), Bari, and Naples. Between his
speeches in Genoa and Bologna, De Gasperi also fitted in a meeting in
Paris of the ECSC foreign ministers. His electoral campaign would
have been a *tour de force* even with twenty-first-century transport
links.[28]

As it was, the Italian premier travelled mostly by train, with a
battered suitcase, and lodged in the barracks of the *carabinieri*, or
in the homes of relatives or DC activists. Nenni and Togliatti
matched him rally for rally. Seen from the twenty-first century, the
Italian election of 1953 has a quaint feel about it. Its passion, its
obsession with real, not manufactured, issues, its huge rallies willing to listen to two-hour speeches rather than soundbites, its
obvious importance to people who believed (rightly) that they were
deciding their own future, all seem anachronistic to sceptical, post-
modern minds. Yet turnout was astronomical: 93.84 per cent for
the Chamber of Deputies and 93.78 per cent for the Senate.

'Without gallows or dictatorship': the DC reminds
the electorate of De Gasperi's simplicity and integrity, June 1953.

A population that mostly possessed only rudimentary education
took part in the political process without cynicism and with pride.
There is perhaps a lesson here.

De Gasperi seemed regretful that affairs of state had prevented him
from addressing crowds in other cities. He told an Italian news magazine that the 'face-to face contact' with the electorate had 'invigorated'
him.[29] He was especially enthused by the personal warmth shown to
him by crowds in the Mezzogiorno. In Palermo the peroration of his

speech was interrupted by his audience when he hinted that it might be the last time that he addressed them:

> So, tell your families, tell people in the squares, everywhere you can proclaim this simple injunction: don't waste your vote. Voting for the Monarchists or the neo-fascists means subtracting from the centre parties the votes they need to defeat social communism ... I am old by now, today is the fourth time I've spoken to you; perhaps I won't have another opportunity to see your faces again, gathered in a huge assembly around me [*overwhelming demonstration of affection for the prime minister*] ... It doesn't matter. I am just a name and a symbol ... I represent an idea ... that won't die. Above all, it won't die here.[30]

These comments by De Gasperi also underline the main theme of Christian Democracy's offer to the electorate and explain why the Italian premier – and his lieutenants, whose schedules were almost equally strenuous – worked so hard. (Andreotti's diary entry on 4 June 1953 commented: 'Just about all of us have lost our voices, but we're optimistic. Maybe too optimistic.')[31] The leadership of the DC did not believe that the communist menace had expired with Stalin. Their fear that the political centre might not hold was patent. If the Monarchists and the MSI eroded the DC's position, if a revived PSI chipped away at the electorate of the PSDI and PRI, then the economic achievements of the last five years might be impaired and the consolidation of democracy itself would be imperilled. 'Democracy should not allow itself to be broken in two by the concurrent efforts of Communism and neo-Fascism,' warned De Gasperi during a campaign speech.[32]

One sardonic DC pamphlet imagined what Italy would have been like had the PCI won the 1948 elections. Taking inspiration from actual events in Czechoslovakia and Hungary, the DC's propagandists, with a generous dose of black humour, drew a picture of how Italy would have been put under the thumb of a PCI-dominated government. Portraits of Togliatti, Longo, and Secchia would have immediately been appended across the land, but that would have been the least of it. Mario Scelba, naturally, would have been the first to be arrested, tried, and shot for crimes against the working class, in August 1948. De Gasperi would have been assassinated, Togliatti-style, by a PCI

militant, and mass repression would have followed, with the PCI militia firing on churchgoers as they left masses where the former premier
had been mourned. Pacciardi, the PRI leader, like the Czech foreign
minister Jan Masaryk, would have been thrown out of a fourth-floor
window. Bereft of Marshall Plan aid, the economy would have collapsed and Giuseppe Di Vittorio, the trade union leader, would have
been made the scapegoat and condemned as an anti-revolutionary
saboteur in a show trial. Nenni, the minister of posts and telegraphs,
after 'trying in vain to become foreign minister and deputy prime minister,' would have succumbed to bronchitis, 'perhaps too quickly for
there not to be a suspicion that Togliatti's doctors had meddled'. In the
spring of 1953, finally, Togliatti, by now President of the Republic,
would have abolished the 'superseded institutions of bourgeois democracy', and parliament would have been substituted by a chamber of
PCI functionaries. The pamphlet concluded:

> This story is made-up, it has only ever taken place in the realm of
> imagination. But if you, Italian voters, cast a ballot on 7 June for Nenni
> and Togliatti, this fantasy will become the true story of tomorrow. Take
> care not to put Togliatti in power![33]

The pamphlet was scaremongering, obviously, but it was also something more profound. Italian moderates, Christian Democrat and
democratic socialist alike, regarded Italy's democracy as a fragile
bloom that needed tending with extra care. It could not yet afford to
be exposed to the harsh winds blowing from either the far right or
the far left. The DC's upper echelons were well informed of the more
brutal aspects of life under Stalinism, notably the persecution of
the Church, but also its antisemitism, and were determined to preserve
Italy from the fate of the countries behind the Iron Curtain.[34]

The DC accordingly asked the electorate to vote for more of the
same: continuity rather than the disruptive change that a vote for
the left (or for the PMN and MSI) would signify. Voting for the DC,
the party's propagandists argued, was a matter of simple 'common
sense' when one looked at the grim alternatives available.

According to one pointed DC poster, the PCI stood for dictatorship of a single party, suppression of personal liberties and freedom of

speech, concentration camps, state-determined salaries, the abolition of the right to strike, and the suppression of private property. The PSI was indistinguishable from the PCI. The 'fascists of the MSI', by contrast, stood for much the same things as the PCI, except that instead of concentration camps, there would be *confino* for opponents and the economy would be run according to the principles of 'economic nepotism'. As for the Monarchists, they stood for 'fascist-like' government, social division between aristocrats and 'beggars', and 'state paternalism'. The DC and its allies alone could guarantee order, prosperity, and democracy. If its rivals won, disorder and even civil war might ensue.[35] Amintore Fanfani closed his own campaign tour with a speech in front of a 'huge and passionate crowd' in his native Arezzo in which he attacked both the PCI and the MSI as being 'advocates of discord'.[36] He was on-message.

The DC should perhaps have built its campaign more around what it had achieved, rather than fretting publicly about what its opponents would do if they won. De Gasperi was greeted with enthusiasm in the Mezzogiorno because he was the head of the first administration in Italian history to do something constructive about Southern poverty. The land reform, the housing programme, the Marshall Plan reconstruction projects, and the Southern Italian Development Fund were real gains for the poorest parts of the country. They could not remedy generations of neglect, but they did represent a major step forward. Sicily and Sardinia, along with the frontier regions of the North, had acquired status as special regions. Living standards had risen significantly, albeit from disastrous lows.

The DC's foreign policy, especially towards European unity, had restored Italy's reputation with its neighbours and with the United States. *Time* portrayed a confident-looking De Gasperi on the front page of its 25 May 1953 edition and published a lengthy interview with him inside the magazine. The newly arrived American ambassador, Clare Boothe Luce, the glamorous wife of Henry Luce, *Time*'s publisher, committed the US to $28 million in aid as the election campaign reached its climax; in 1952–3, the first post-ERP year, the Americans invested a further $100 million in Italy.[37] Clare Boothe Luce plunged into the electoral campaign, telling an audience of businessmen in Milan that there would be 'grave consequences' for the

Italian-American relationship if Italy were to 'fall unhappy victim' to the 'wiles of totalitarianism'. This clumsy interference in the electoral process misfired: De Gasperi was annoyed and the ambassador was accused of acting as a 'canvasser' for the DC.[38]

Speaking in Cagliari, towards the end of the election campaign, De Gasperi said:

> Friends, we are builders; builders not only of bridges, of railways, of roads, but also of the democratic system in Italy, which we want to consolidate. We have constructed the autonomous regions and we want to develop them, just as we want to construct Europe along with Italy.[39]

This metaphor was the positive theme advanced by the DC's propaganda, alongside the negative attacks on the dangers of totalitarianism of both the left and right. Emphasizing the positives even more forcefully might have paid electoral dividends. The DC objectively did have a story to tell.

At the very least, it would have contrasted with the PCI's campaign. Togliatti's instructions to his propagandists were to focus on the perceived negatives of the DC's record. Propaganda should be 'as simple and concrete as possible'. It was to bat away at four key points: the DC's servility to foreigners, and its status as a 'government of the rich', which was 'against liberty', and was 'the government of corruption' (it may well have been the least corrupt government in Italian history, admittedly not a high bar). The PCI's programme, by contrast, was generically to emphasize the need for a 'peace government', one that would pursue social reforms, and clean up political wrongdoing. The failures of the De Gasperi regime should be contrasted with the triumphs of the Soviet Union and the Peoples' Democracies in the creation of a more just society. In sum, the PCI should present itself as 'a great popular mass movement able to fix the nations' problems'.[40]

One anti-corruption poster depicted a communist broom briskly sweeping away cockroaches marked with the DC's emblem along with pieces of paper depicting taxes, corruption, the Swindle Law, DC violence, hate, scandals, and *greppie* – troughs. The poster's slogan sensibly did not need voters to take a course in dialectical materialism at a party school to understand: *Basta con la DC!*

The communist broom sweeps away corruption:
note the shield and cross symbols on the cockroaches.

The PCI had also spent the previous two years trying to shake off
their threatening image as a party of revolutionary theorists fighting a
class war. *Vie nuove* had been transformed into a standard news weekly
featuring, as well as political articles, human-interest stories, pieces
about film actors and directors who supported the PCI, and lots of
sports coverage, especially football and cycling. *Vie nuove* even
organized an annual beauty contest for young communist women
that opposed 'Italian' notions of feminine beauty to manufactured

'American' ideals.[41] Leading members of the party were meanwhile pictured at home in photo-essays that showed their human qualities. Admittedly, these pieces (on Terracini and Secchia, among others) showed them as balding middle-aged men with lots of books and a piano, but still, they looked less like the commissars of middle-class imagination, which was a gain. In August 1952, Togliatti wrote a piece on 'Alpinismo' and was pictured hiking at Courmayeur in the French-Italian Alps: in plausibility terms this was literally a step too far.[42] The strategy of celebrity endorsements and equating the PCI with cultural modernization was carried into 1953 and the election campaign. It contributed to making the PCI seem more in tune with the new society that was emerging as more people began to have money in their pockets.

In any event, De Gasperi's electoral gamble did not pay off. The election pact formed by the DC and their centrist allies failed to reach 50 per cent of the total poll by a tiny margin. In all, 13,488,813 people voted for the DC or parties paired with it, but 27,087,701 valid votes were cast.[43] The DC thus fell just over 95,000 votes short of the figure needed (13,583,851) to trigger the majority prize.

There was exultation on the left when the election results were announced by the Ministry of the Interior. In a leading article, *l'Unità* proclaimed a 'Victory for the Italian People'. Piero Calamandrei, whose impromptu list had helped tip the balance, contended that the vote had saved Italy from a kind of sleazy semi-Fascism:

> Had the majority prize been triggered on 7 June, our democracy would have been definitively transformed into an oligarchy, into a kind of confessional corporativism, under the supervision of Catholic Action and Confindustria [the employers' federation]: a paternalistic police state, softened and made more urbane by endemic corruption.[44]

The failure of the electoral pact to reach 50 per cent came as a 'bludgeon-blow' for the DC's leadership.[45] Andreotti commented sourly: 'How much time we wasted. How much bile we swallowed!'[46] Yet, though the 50 per cent threshold was not passed, the DC remained the biggest party by far. In the election to the Chamber of Deputies, it took 10.82 million votes (40.1 per cent), and some 263 seats. In the Senate, 9.67 million people marked the party's *scudocrociato* symbol

(39.8 per cent). The DC elected 112 senators. These figures were a setback, but they were not a disaster. One could even argue that they illustrated the solidity of the DC's appeal for the middle classes. Togliatti certainly thought so.[47] So did Ambassador Luce, who pointed out in a despatch to Washington that the DC had 44 per cent of the Chamber of Deputies and 47 per cent of senators. The centre would hold, thanks to the DC's preponderant position:

> Embassy considers that pessimistic view of situation is not warranted . . . De Gasperi and all other center leaders are faced with necessity of making fundamental political decisions concerning organization and orientation of future government. Center leaders are convinced that full cooperation with U.S. and West is in Italian national interest and that they will honestly try to formulate a policy which U.S. can accept as basis for our future relations.[48]

After five years of Cold War propaganda, campaigns by the partisans for peace, land occupations, *stragi* by the police, and economic growth that had not yet improved the lives of the poorest, the DC still got more votes than the PCI and PSI combined. The PCI took 22.6 per cent of the vote in the race for the chamber (6.12 million votes), while the PSI took 12.7 per cent (3.44 million). The PCI and PSI, while they had gained 1.4 million votes more than the Garibaldi Front had obtained in April 1948, were still over a million votes behind the DC's tally. In the Senate poll, moreover, the two parties' share of the vote was lower. The PCI took 20.2 per cent and the PSI 11.9 per cent. In all, 7.8 million voters cast a ballot for one or the other party, almost 2 million less than for the DC.

Togliatti told the party steering committee that the PCI's election victory consisted in the fact, first and foremost, that the Swindle Law had not passed. This had 'roused popular enthusiasm'. Second, there had been a 'great advance' by the party. Third, the three minor parties paired with the DC had been defeated, though the PSDI maintained a solid bastion of support in the north-west. Overall, the PCI had bounced back to a higher level of support than it had enjoyed in June 1946.[49] These points were true enough, but they could not disguise the fact that the PCI had failed to make a breakthrough.

Togliatti was right to point out that the DC's centrist allies had been the election's biggest flops – and the main cause of De Gasperi's defeat. In its first national electoral test, the PSDI took 600,000 fewer votes than the Socialist Unity coalition in April 1948. One-third of its former electorate chose someone else. Just 1.22 million citizens voted for Saragat's quarrelsome party, 4.5 per cent. Saragat, humiliated by the defeat, was incommunicado for some five days after the results were announced.[50] Pietro Nenni could not resist gloating:

> There's no point in the former majority coalition clutching at straws. It has been beaten, and beaten dramatically, on terrain of its own choosing. What makes the result even more just is the fact that the parties that have paid the highest price are the so-called minor parties ... Their liquidation eliminates a source of confusion, corruption, and downright provocation.[51]

The PLI took 3 per cent of the vote; the PRI a dismal 440,000 votes (1.6 per cent). The two left-wing splinter lists, the UIS and Ferruccio Parri's UP, though they did not elect a single deputy, between them accumulated almost as many votes as the PRI, while over 120,000 citizens voted for treasury minister Corbino's ADN. The votes garnered by these three lists (one could not call them parties) kept the coalition under 50 per cent of valid votes.

The Monarchist and neo-fascist parties also drained off votes from the DC, despite De Gasperi's efforts on the campaign trail. Lauro's Monarchists secured 1.85 million votes, almost 7 per cent, and elected forty deputies. The PNM was the fourth-largest party in the new Chamber of Deputies. The MSI got 1.6 million votes (almost 6 per cent), three times more than in 1948. Right-wing votes came overwhelmingly from south of Rome. The Monarchists flourished in Campania, where they took more than 20 per cent of the vote, and in Apulia (in Emilia they got 0.7 per cent). The MSI's best results came in western Sicily (Palermo-Trapani-Agrigento) and Rome.

That 3.4 million citizens were nostalgic for a 'Skipper' and for former black shirts must have perturbed Italian democrats. The election showed that the DC's vote in the Mezzogiorno had been artificially inflated in 1948 by the middle class's fear of the Garibaldi Front. In 1953, the DC paradoxically paid a heavy price for its 'radicalism' (above all, land redistribution), but also for not having been radical enough. The Mezzogiorno would benefit in the next five years from the sound fiscal foundations constructed by the De Gasperi government, which made the economic boom of the late 1950s sustainable and which also led to the great migration of *meridionali* to factory jobs in the bustling conurbations of the North. But in June 1953, too many people were still waiting for improvements in their lives. For many, the vote for Achille Lauro and for the *fiamma tricolore* was cast against the real misery of their everyday lives.

There was a second protest vote that should be underlined, because it certainly diminished disproportionately the DC's share of the poll. The number of people who went to the polling station, waited patiently in long lines, showed their ID cards, and then cast an invalid ballot, was higher than in 1948. In many cases, ballots were spoiled unwittingly. Many voters simply indicated the candidates that they preferred without putting a cross on the party symbol. Such votes, even though their preference was clear, had to be excluded.[52] There were 1.32 million invalid votes in the election to the Chamber of Deputies and 1.2 million invalid in the Senate poll. More people voted for nobody than voted for the PSDI.

The immediate outcome of the June 1953 elections, in short, was a sag in the share of the vote going to centrist parties. More people voted for the left, more people voted for the right, more people voted for nobody. In the long term, it was the June 1953 election, rather than that of 1948, that set the pattern for Italian democracy. For the next thirty-four years, the DC vote would oscillate between 38 per cent and 43 per cent, and it would need allies to be able to form governments. Since the minor parties of the centre never enhanced their share of the vote significantly, and since there were two 'excluded poles' banned from government (the PCI and the MSI), the PSI acquired a pivotal place in the party system. Nenni, with just over half the votes of Togliatti and less than a third of De Gasperi's, emerged from the June election as potential kingmaker. The fundamental democratic weakness of PR in multi-party systems is that instead of rewarding the biggest party, as majoritarian systems do, it empowers middle-sized or even minor parties that can tip the balance of power. So long as the PSI continued to be hostile to European supranationalism and pro-Moscow, its pivotal role was more theoretical than real, but the election results gave the PSI food for thought. Cooperation with the PCI meant permanent exclusion from office and subordination to its better organized partner. Perhaps progressive gains could be achieved by leveraging the PSI's parliamentary contingent in cooperation with the DC?

Cooperation between the DC and the PSI was a prerequisite for governmental stability (and social progress) in 1950s Italy. To understand this, it is worth posing a counterfactual question: if the centrist parties had done better, and if De Gasperi's coalition had managed to squeeze over the 50 per cent threshold, what would the harvest have been? In all probability, a marginal win for De Gasperi would have been a pyrrhic victory. The DC still would not have controlled parliament since they would have had an exiguous majority in the Senate. Power to make or break the government would have passed to De Gasperi's coalition partners, despite their pathetic showing at the polls. Paolo Pombeni, a prominent scholar of the DC, is right when he says that when the votes were counted it 'became clear that the circumstances did not permit a majoritarian democracy'.[53] One is tempted to add, alas.

The only person swindled by the electoral law, in short, was De Gasperi. On 10 June, Andreotti recorded the premier saying that the electoral law was 'the first time I've been wrong since the war ended'.[54] This sounds arrogant, but the premier's record on the hard decisions of his premiership backs his words: he had ousted the ineffectual Parri as premier, opted for the Republic, compelled the king to step down after 2 June 1946, made peace with Austria, made a dignified protest against the Peace Treaty, wooed the Americans in January 1947, ended governmental cooperation with the PCI in May 1947, backed Einaudi to restore sound money, sought Marshall Plan aid, fought the PCI passionately in April 1948 (but respected the PCI's constitutional rights thereafter), joined the Atlantic alliance in April 1949, implemented land reform, stood firm against Vatican pressure to ally with the undemocratic far right, and had committed Italy to being an integral part of the process of constructing greater West European economic and political cooperation. One need only envision what might have happened in Italy had De Gasperi failed to make even *one* of those calls, to see how much his agency had mattered for Italy's transition to democracy.

This is why the rest of democratic Europe honoured him. De Gasperi had been awarded the Charlemagne Prize in September 1952, the third person to win this prestigious award for services to the construction of Europe. When De Gasperi went to Paris for meetings of the ECSC foreign ministers, or spoke in Strasbourg, or visited Bonn, he was treated with respect, even veneration, as one of the founding fathers of the European project. After the election, on 24 June 1953, the Italian premier visited Britain, dined with the cabinet, and was awarded an honorary degree by Oxford University to mark his achievement in bringing Italy back from the desolation and despair of the former regime. He was an equal partner with Churchill or Anthony Eden in the construction of Western unity.[55] Until De Gasperi stumbled over the rock of electoral reform, he had made a friend of fortune by being bold when he had to take big decisions. Over electoral reform, however, he had gone for broke and lost.

His public comments after the election result were marred by bitterness. In a coruscating interview with *Il Messaggero*, De Gasperi cast Christian charity to one side. All the Monarchists had achieved by their overt opposition to the DC was to strengthen the parliamentary contingent of the 'extreme left' by seventy deputies, he said derisively. He was even less kind to former treasury minister Corbino and Ferruccio Parri of UP, who by 'sacrificing themselves as burnt offerings' to Togliatti had not only stopped the electoral law from working but had deprived themselves of a place in parliament where they could have contributed to national politics. The interview betrayed an old man's impatience towards those who, for whatever reason, did not make the struggle against 'the Bolshevik menace' the absolute national priority. In this interview, at least, De Gasperi was not prepared to say of his political rivals, 'forgive them, for they know not what they do'.[56]

CONFIDENCE LOST

In hindsight, De Gasperi should have stepped down after the election and let the DC's coming generation take the helm. He resigned on 29 June 1953, when he got back from Oxford, but Einaudi, conscious of the premier's standing with the US and the other European nations, insisted that he should attempt to form a government. De Gasperi was given a mandate to start soundings on 3 July.

His most interesting meeting was with Nenni. There was enormous press interest in the encounter, and it was widely speculated that the PSI's leadership was thinking of joining the government. De Gasperi met Nenni and his deputy, Rodolfo Morandi, on 6 July 1953. The premier had already met Togliatti on 4 July: the encounter had lasted over ninety minutes and had amply confirmed both men in their conviction that they were 'on two opposing fronts'.[57]

According to Nenni, his meeting with the premier was a 'debacle'. De Gasperi was 'on the verge of physical collapse' and spoke in a way that was 'more suited to the confessional than politics'. The conversation revolved around what Nenni regarded as De Gasperi's exaggerated fears of communism. Italy was different from Czechoslovakia, or Bulgaria, or Hungary, Nenni told him. In Italy, communism was a popular force representing a large bloc of society. De Gasperi's 'mysticism-religiosity' on this point prevented him from seeing reality, Nenni averred.[58]

After the meeting Nenni told waiting journalists that the PSI had demanded a clear break with the policies followed since April 1948. De Gasperi's 'Atlanticist extremism' had to be replaced by a foreign policy that favoured *distensione*. Policies that would enhance the living standards of the masses, and raise production, should be introduced as a matter of priority. Apart from the last point, where the PSI acknowledged that De Gasperi had some interesting ideas, the PSI's leaders had found the premier to be inflexible. Asked whether the PSI regarded the substitution of De Gasperi with another candidate as a precondition to cooperating in the formation of a government, Nenni diplomatically responded that 'a new politics would greatly benefit from being carried out by men who did not bear the burden of the controversies of the last five years on their shoulders'.[59]

The account by De Gasperi's daughter of the meeting with Nenni and Morandi, based on what her father told her, depicts an intransigent Nenni bent on making no concessions whatever. Above all, the PSI would not break with the PCI. Nenni told the premier that even the return of the PCI into government would not be a 'disaster' for the country and that it would be a 'simple fact' to which he would 'align himself with absolute serenity'. Indeed, the PSI would only join a government if the PCI joined it, too.[60]

Giulio Andreotti's account, in his diary, portrays a 'cordial but cold' meeting that revolved around two questions: (1) the Atlantic alliance; (2) the PSI's pact of unity of action with the PCI. On the first of these two topics, Nenni strongly urged the premier to tone down the rhetoric of Atlanticism, and his strong advocacy of the EDC (which Nenni, accurately, regarded as destined for failure), and to treat the latter as a formal commitment, to which Italy was legally bound, without making it a divisive rallying point. Nenni wanted less aggressive posturing by the premier on the values of the free world and the horrors of Soviet communism, if De Gasperi wanted him to support the government.

On the second topic, Andreotti substantially confirms the account of the premier's daughter, Maria Romana Catti De Gasperi. The pre-mier wanted to know how 'autonomous' the Socialists were. By this, he meant not whether the PSI intended to preserve its electoral inde-pendence from the PCI, but whether they had 'decoupled' themselves psychologically from the ideology of the 'extreme totalitarian left'. According to Andreotti, De Gasperi told Nenni that he didn't want to conclude his political career by 'opening the door to an end of this democracy, be it by gradual, indirect means, or directly'. To this remark, Nenni replied with the words attributed to him by De Gasp-eri's daughter.[61]

The three accounts, though different, clearly share much in common. Nenni was doubtless telling the truth from his perspective when he saw an exhausted old man with an anti-communist bee in his bonnet, but in De Gasperi's defence the historical moment required him to ask hard questions of his Socialist counterpart. The mood of *distensione* had suddenly been reversed.

It was the first week of July 1953. On 16–17 June, just three weeks before, a workers' revolt in the misnamed German Democratic Repub-lic had been suppressed by Soviet tanks. Hundreds of thousands of citizens had protested in the streets against the regime headed by Walter Ulbricht. Factory workers had downed tools. Dozens of citi-zens had been killed in street clashes and the regime's opponents were still being hanged by the secret police when Nenni and De Gasperi met. The clashes were the culmination of growing social resistance to the process of Stalinization that had already caused 84,000 East Germans to flee to the West in the first few months of 1953, on top of an outflow of 136,000 in 1952. On 27 May 1953, the Soviet Politburo discussed the German question frankly, with Lavrenti Beria even contemplating a neutral government in Berlin; the majority opted to urge the GDR's leaders to attenuate its drive to implement Stalinist measures. The uprising and subsequent Soviet intervention paradoxically ended any chance that Berlin's hardliners would be compelled to relax their control over society: 'Giving up on socialism in the GDR seemed expedient, until it no longer was.'[62]

Spontaneous mass protests by manual workers against a communist regime was a singular occurrence that might have been expected to give pause for reflection about the nature of the system created beyond the Iron Curtain. In Italy, it did nothing of the sort, at least in public. Both *l'Unità* and *Avanti!* recycled the East German regime's suggestions that the uprising had been provoked by West Germany and had been directed on the ground by American agitators in uniform.[63] During those same days, President Dwight D. Eisenhower, who had replaced Truman in January 1953, declined to commute the death sentence handed down to Julius and Ethel Rosenberg, two alleged spies for the Soviet Union. The Rosenbergs' case was an international *cause célèbre* and both the PSI and PCI's press gave it the maximum attention. Giant banner headlines condemned 'American Fascism' for the murder of the couple when they were executed by electric chair on 19 June 1953.[64] The events in Berlin were removed from the front page as fast as they decently could be.

The Rosenberg case remains a controversial one even today, though historians now broadly agree that Julius Rosenberg did spy for the USSR (whether that crime merited such an atrocious end is another matter).[65] De Gasperi could not but look at the furore surrounding the Rosenberg case and notice that the same orchestrated indignation had not been on display when Traicho Kostov, László Rajk or Rudolf Slánský had been subjected to show trials. Nenni was telling him not to fear cooperation with the PCI, and relatively independent-minded members of the PCI's leadership, such as Giuseppe Di Vittorio, were publicly calling for a national concordat between the CGIL and the government as a basis for accelerating growth to lift more workers out of poverty, but the party newspapers of both the PCI and PSI were united in condemning American Fascism and glossing over the actions of a communist regime that had used tanks against the workers. De Gasperi surely reflected that the same generosity had not been shown towards him in the aftermath of the Modena events in 1950.

The PSI's uncritical adhesion to the PCI's political line on the question of the popular protests in East Germany was presumably why De Gasperi insisted on asking Nenni whether he and his party had 'decoupled' themselves from the totalitarianism of the PCI. It was not the politics of the confessional. He was pointing out to the Socialist leader, to translate a colourful Italian idiom, that he couldn't have 'a full barrel and a drunken wife'. Or, to use a staider English idiom, that he could not run with both the fox and the hounds.

Had De Gasperi contemplated creating a DC government with external PSI support, he would also have had to convince a hostile American administration that Nenni and the PSI were not a Trojan horse for communist totalitarianism. It would not have been easy, to put it mildly. The new Eisenhower administration was determined to 'transform the Italian political landscape in a much more radical and ambitious way than during the Truman years'.[66] Its representative in Italy, Ambassador Boothe Luce, would soon come to regard 'De Gaspari' as being dangerously soft on the worldwide communist conspiracy and would flirt both socially and politically with the extreme nationalist right. Boothe Luce is today 'remembered mostly for her brash anti-Communist stance, her often clumsy intrusions into Italian labour and industrial disputes, and her strident declarations against the Red Peril', but she was no mere 'ideological zealot and obstreperous plenipotentiary'.[67] She echoed and implemented the policies of John Foster Dulles, the Secretary of State and advocate of 'roll-back', towards Italy. De Gasperi would have been taking a huge political gamble if he had courted Nenni. Indeed, it is interesting that he allowed discussions with the PSI leader to develop as publicly as they did.

In any event, developments in the USSR made the issue of the PSI's links with the PCI moot. Four days after Nenni met De Gasperi, the Soviet Union revealed that Beria, the principal architect of the policy of détente, had been arrested for criminal activities against the state and the people of the USSR (in secret, he was also condemned as a serial rapist).[68] Beria's downfall was fall-out from the events in the

GDR: the Politburo thought that his policies ran the risk of destabilizing the Soviet Union's client regimes in central Europe (and worried that Beria, once he had consolidated his position, would purge them for their former slavish loyalty to Stalin). They knew full well that Beria was as much a psychopath as Stalin had been. They had no desire to return to the nightmare of the 1930s, but this time as victims, not beneficiaries, of show trials and mass murder.

For the PCI and the PSI, Beria's downfall came as a deep shock. The newspapers of both parties mechanically repeated the official line taken by the Soviet party, namely that Beria had been unmasked as an adventurer working for a mysterious conspiracy by unidentified reactionary elements within the capitalist states to derail the process of détente. The unrest in the GDR had been part of this plot by unspecified 'warmongers'.[69] Pietro Secchia said the same, at tedious length, in the July edition of *Rinascita*.[70] There was a performative aspect to such pieces. They were probably not even expected to be believed, certainly not by the sophisticated readers of *Rinascita*. Rather, their function was to signal that discussion of what was happening in Moscow, and of the legacy of Stalin, was politically incorrect. Those who transgressed would be made the target of the PCI's formidable methods of censure, just as Cucchi and Magnani had been.

The article in *Rinascita* emerged only after a frank debate among the party leadership. Secchia, who had been despatched to Moscow to get an authoritative interpretation of the line to follow, reported to the party steering committee on 17 July 1953 that Beria's main sins had been using his control of the security services to expand his power and striving to dismantle Stalin's legacy too fast. Secchia was peppered with questions once he had finished his presentation; some were very outspoken. How did a man like Beria reach the top of the party, Giuseppe Di Vittorio asked simply. It was the right question. How was one to explain to the mass membership of the PCI that a hero of the construction of socialism, and recently the architect of détente, was a spy, a traitor, and an agent of capitalist-imperialism? Di Vittorio worried that Stalin might be tarnished by association if Beria was portrayed too negatively; Togliatti agreed that the party should take care not to 'diminish' the 'great inheritance left to us by Stalin' when it addressed the party membership.[71]

The most interesting contribution to the debate was made by Emilio Sereni, who opined that the party should draw upon the experience of the great trials of the 1930s to explain the true meaning of the current leadership crisis in the USSR. It was necessary to explain that even in the Soviet Union there was an ongoing 'struggle between the old and the new', even though 'there was no longer an old social base' for class conflict inside the USSR. Sereni was heartened by the masses' public denunciations of Beria's crimes: it was 'proof of democratization', he thought.[72]

Sereni knew perfectly well that the popular demonstrations against Beria were choreographed. He also knew that there was no social base capable of generating opposition in the USSR because Stalin, using Beria as his most ruthless instrument, had killed or enslaved millions of peasants, intellectuals, members of national minorities, and former Bolsheviks. Seemingly, he thought this was a progressive outcome that had led to democratic results. If one wanted an illustration of what De Gasperi was asking Nenni to disassociate himself from in July 1953, one could hardly have done better than give the PSI's leader a copy of Sereni's remarks. Or, indeed, the minutes of the meeting in their entirety.

The political crisis that followed the June 1953 elections, therefore, was taking place in a climate of international uncertainty. Neither the PCI nor the PSI had budged an inch from their adhesion to the Soviet side in the wider global conflict (indeed, they had expressed loyalty to Moscow and exhibited revulsion for the United States). One might accordingly have expected the much-depleted parliamentary contingents of the three centrist parties to conclude that their place was at De Gasperi's side. United, they would have provided the premier with a wafer-thin majority in the chamber. Instead, all three opted to stay out of the cabinet and even to deny De Gasperi a positive vote of confidence.

On 15 July, De Gasperi formed a *monocolore*, to use the Italian term (i.e. a government with only DC ministers). De Gasperi was premier and foreign minister; Amintore Fanfani received a big promotion, which reflected his growing party following, and became minister of the interior. Attilio Piccioni was deputy premier and minister without portfolio; Giuseppe Pella remained in charge of the treasury. These were the *papabili* for the premiership if De Gasperi did not win a confidence vote, although the premier had 'no formal succession plan in place'.[73] The major absentee was Mario Scelba, who disapproved of the fact that De Gasperi had held exploratory talks with the PNM with a view to securing their benevolence in parliament towards the government's measures. In the absence of a majority prize, such deals were inevitable, but Scelba, the iron anti-communist, was also the most intransigent republican in the senior ranks of the DC.

The parliamentary arithmetic was against the new government. De Gasperi commanded 263 seats in the 590-seat Chamber of Deputies and 116 seats in the 237-seat Senate. If the centrist parties abstained, it was hoped that a compact vote by the DC plus some Monarchist support, or abstentions, would enable De Gasperi to limp along until the spring of 1954 and see through the ratification of the EDC. In front of packed public galleries waiting to see if the premier would survive, the Chamber voted by 282 votes to 263 against the government on 28 July. Thirty-seven deputies abstained. Eight deputies did not vote. The Monarchists and the MSI had allied with the PCI and PSI to bring De Gasperi's long tenure as premier to a close: the extremes had overcome the centre. No vote was held in the Senate since, constitutionally, a government needed the support of both chambers.

The DC was furious at the failure of the centrist parties to back the government. Party Secretary Guido Gonella grumbled that those who had voted against De Gasperi had rendered a disservice to both the country and to democracy. De Gasperi was the man who had led the 'rebirth of Italy', and had always put country before party. The DC, Gonella added, was 'closer to him than ever' in his hour of defeat.[74] Gonella's declaration read oddly like an obituary, even though, in July 1953, Italy's chattering classes still expected De Gasperi to return, revitalized, to government after a break for rest and recuperation.

De Gasperi acted as caretaker prime minister while his preferred choice as successor, Piccioni, tried and failed to persuade the three centre parties to join a government under his leadership. He was eventually replaced as premier by Pella on 17 August 1953, who won a vote of confidence in the chamber with a majority of 100, thanks to the support of the PNM.[75]

By then, De Gasperi had migrated to the peaceful surroundings of the Val di Sella. He must have been even more ready than usual to leave the murkiness of politics in Rome behind – and to breathe untainted Alpine air.

AFTER DE GASPERI

Giuseppe Pella was only fifty-one and hence represented a generational change. During Fascism, he had 'certainly not been an active opponent of the regime', although, unlike Fanfani, he had not been an enthusiastic supporter of it either.[76] Pella was a professional economist and university professor well versed in macroeconomic theory and public finance. He was dry, well-prepared, cold, somewhat uncharismatic. His principal claim to the premiership was his technical expertise. He would be a safe pair of hands while the budget was being passed.

Pella's government lasted a mere 155 days. It is chiefly remembered for the new premier's unanticipated truculence in foreign affairs. Within days of Pella's government taking office, the Trieste situation flared up. Yugoslavia, irritated by Italy's increasing role in the government of 'Zone A' (i.e. the city and suburbs of Trieste) pronounced that it would 'probably' annex 'Zone B' (northern Istria). The Yugoslav declaration was the starting gun for a two-month stand-off that fanned nationalist sentiment in both countries. In September, the Pella government ostentatiously moved troops nearer to the city of Trieste; Tito held a huge rally of Istrian partisans in Zone B and made an inflammatory anti-Italian speech. Pella replied by proposing a plebiscite throughout both zones under international supervision (which Italy would certainly have won). On 4 November 1953, he spoke to 100,000 people in Piazza San Marco in Venice and made a nationalist speech promising that his government – any Italian government – would 'stand guard' over Italian interests in Trieste. The speech led to nationalist riots in Trieste and to the military police of the city, under British command, firing on a crowd, killing several civilians. Anglo-Italian relations became tense. All the same, Pella's flag-waving over the situation in Trieste pushed the great powers to find a solution: the logical one of giving Italy administrative control over Zone A and Yugoslavia control over Zone B (formal sovereignty over the territories was only accorded by the Treaty of Osimo, in 1974). This was the essence of the agreement reached in London in October 1954 that enabled the city of Trieste to return, de facto, to Italian rule.

Pella's rhetoric was popular with the MSI and conversely unpopular with the powers-that-be within the DC, notably De Gasperi and Scelba. De Gasperi returned to politics on 26 September 1953 when he was elected party secretary by the National Council of the DC by forty-nine votes to zero (but with twenty-two blank ballots). He soon began to refer to Pella's government as a 'friendly' one that the DC *supported*, rather than identify it as an emanation of the party itself.[77] By the first week of 1954, the prime minister was out. He was replaced by Amintore Fanfani, who formed a government on 19 January 1954. Fanfani, however, was denied the confidence of the Chamber of Deputies on 30 January: Nenni, unconvinced that he would orient its policies leftwards, did not lend the PSI's expected support.

The United States regarded the upheaval as disastrous. Ambassador Boothe Luce feared that parliamentary chaos would condemn the country to fall into the hands of communism. Reaching for an easy historical cliché, she regarded Fanfani as 'an Italian Kerensky' out of synch with American goals and values, who might easily sell the pass to the PCI.[78] Accordingly, she envisaged an 'agonizing reappraisal' of US policy towards Italy with the goal of shifting the governmental coalition rightwards and cracking down on the activities of the PCI. News of the plan was deliberately leaked to an eminent American journalist, James 'Scotty' Reston, whose subsequent article 'U.S. to Bid Italy Curb Reds' caused a furore, and not merely for its illiterate headline.[79]

De Gasperi intervened to warn Italy's 'dear friends' in Washington that there was 'no need to exaggerate'. Italy was not about to 'throw itself into the arms of communism', although he acknowledged that the Italian electorate was 'disorientated' in the wake of the election. The United States did not have to deal with multi-party politics and proportional representation. They should judge with more 'serenity' Italian democrats who were 'fighting on a hard terrain'.[80] Subsequently, he denounced an alarmist report by the magazine *Il Borghese* into communist infiltration in Italian institutions as an example of 'international McCarthyism'.[81] Boothe Luce, as De Gasperi was presumably aware, was being influenced by the 'no-holds-barred anti-communism' of aristocratic intellectuals and pundits connected with this Milanese magazine, which acted as a 'constant right-wing goad'.[82]

The next government was headed by a figure the Americans regarded as congenial. On 10 February 1954, Mario Scelba formed a three-party government, with the PSDI and PLI. Saragat re-entered the cabinet as deputy prime minister. Nenni, never averse to a good sound bite, condemned the creation of an 'SS' government.[83] Scelba survived longer than his two predecessors: he was prime minister until July 1955. There were, in short, four governments in the first seven months of the legislature begun by the June 1953 elections that marked De Gasperi's downfall. It was precisely this descent into intrigue that De Gasperi had been striving to avoid with the electoral reform.

The Eisenhower administration continued to flap about the situation in Italy. The National Security Council (NSC) set 'U.S. policy towards Italy' on 15 April 1954 in a document that underlined 'the profound political, psychological and military damage to the free world' that would ensue from the 'loss' of Italy. It emphasized that:

> Italian domestic progress and international cooperation have now been jeopardized as a result of the 1953 election. The previously firm governing majority of pro-Western parties has been replaced by an unstable situation in which it is very difficult for the Christian Democrats to form a viable government. If present conditions continue, there is grave danger that a succession of weak governments will increasingly discredit the Center and strengthen the Right and Left extremes ... Italy's value to the West would be appreciably lessened under rightist or authoritarian regimes. Although a moderate rightist government would probably continue cooperation with the West, its domestic policies might aggravate internal frictions and ultimately strengthen the Communists. An extreme rightist government would be almost certainly authoritarian, probably ultra-nationalist and opposed to European unity, and possibly neutralist. However, even a right-wing authoritarianism would be far less dangerous than a Communist regime.

The document stated that the key objective of the United States was:

An Italy free from Communist domination or serious threat of Communist subversion, having a constitutional, democratic government and a healthy self-sustaining economy, and able and willing to make important political, economic, and military contributions in support of the free world coalition.

To this end, the US should, first and foremost:

Promote strengthened Italian political, economic and military collaboration with the United States and Western Europe through such organizations as NATO, OEEC, CSC and EDC.[84]

The DC's own propaganda had of course contributed to the alarmism that suffused the NSC's statement of strategy. Contrary to fable, if you cry wolf loud enough, you will probably be believed. The NSC's statement oozed American Cold War paranoia, but it also reflected over-heated rhetoric in Rome. Less obviously, it testified to the scale of De Gasperi's achievement in the previous seven years. By April 1954, the Americans' key objectives had already been met. Italy was free of any danger of communist domination or subversion, it had a functioning constitutional democracy, and its economy was on the point of boom. Italy did not need Washington poo-bahs to tell them solemnly that it should work through the Atlantic alliance and the institutions of European cooperation. It had consciously been doing that since 1948. As De Gasperi told the national congress of the DC in Naples on 27 June 1954, the only possible foreign policy for Italy was one of 'progressively weaving' Italy into the 'international fabric', especially that of the nascent European institutions. It was 'useless and dangerous' for Italy to think of acting in isolation. Its decision to join the Atlantic alliance had been 'dictated' by a 'clear understanding of realities' even more than by 'affinity in sentiments' or 'shared perception of threat'. Italy had needed the West and its resources to survive as a democracy. European unity, meanwhile, was 'at the summit of our thoughts and first among our interests'.[85] Rome would also take advantage of the 'thaw' in the Cold War to join the United Nations in 1955: its able diplomats were hard at work to this end, as the NSC pontificated.

By the time he spoke in Naples, De Gasperi was retiring from politics.

(He passed the baton of the party secretaryship to Fanfani, who was elected by a thin margin that reflected the DC's divisions, on 29 June.) He was ill and he had been weakened by a personal matter that had wounded him deeply. In January 1954, Giovanni Guareschi, who was a strident Cold Warrior despite the gentle humour of his Don Camillo stories, and an active monarchist, libelled De Gasperi in his weekly newspaper, *Candido*, by publishing letters that purported to show that De Gasperi had written to the Allies in 1944 urging them to bomb the suburbs of Rome. The letters have since been demonstrated to have been a hoax, though Guareschi seemingly printed them in good faith, but the attack on his *bona fides* caused De Gasperi great personal distress. Guareschi was sentenced to a year in prison. The humorist not unnaturally believed the trial was a farce.

De Gasperi's opening speech to the Naples congress is regarded as his 'testament'. After a brief discussion of the DC's numbers and organization, it concentrated on the principles underpinning his strategy as party and national leader – and counselled the DC to offer more of the same. To begin with it was necessary to work for greater national unity, which meant respecting the republican constitution, even if one were a monarchist or fascist. It also meant delivering social justice and giving the poorest classes 'a tolerable standard of living' and ensuring that everybody had 'a job, a house, an existence worthy of a free man'. There should be unity between all parties that accepted the 'spirit and methods of constitutional democracy'. The PSI had excluded itself from this category by the fact that, of all the Western European socialist parties, it was the 'only one on the other side of the barricade'. The implication was that, were it genuinely to change, the PSI should be welcomed into the fold. Last, but not least, there had to be unity within the DC, which should never be allowed to decay into a mere electoral machine, since that would inevitably 'rust away', or become a mere conglomeration of factions that wasted their energies on internal disputes and struggles for power. De Gasperi wanted a party with a coherent ideological message whose electoral pacts with other parties were a means to a shared end, not mere ways of harvesting votes.[86]

The last of these recommendations would prove to be beyond the DC's powers of restraint. Its factionalism became legendary. Its reliance on clientelism – on using the power of government to buy political support – would become its *modus operandi*. In 1954, the DC administered 4,128 towns out of 7,804 (53 per cent) and 57 out of 92 provinces (62 per cent), which meant that people all over Italy saw the DC as the embodiment of the state. DC politicians, starting with Fanfani, abused this privileged position.[87] Clientelism, and the corruption that accompanied it, would ultimately be one of the defining features of Republican Italy (as it had been of both Fascist and Liberal Italy). The 'republic of the parties' constructed after 1953 was one in which all the principal parties, and factions within them, controlled intricate networks of supporters with jobs in the public administration. Party politics became a de facto tax on society. This was not an exclusively Italian disease – in neighbouring Austria, the practice was at least as widespread – but it was a blight.

Otherwise, De Gasperi's prescriptions were followed. Within two years, the process of realigning the PSI with the parties of the centre was begun. The events of 1956 (Khrushchev's 'secret speech' and the suppression by Soviet troops in November of an attempt by Hungary to leave the Soviet bloc) finally brought the PSI to the point of divorce with the PCI, whose behaviour in 1956 was so embarrassing – so uncritically pro-Moscow – that many important intellectuals and tens of thousands of ordinary members tore up their party cards in disgust.[88] Many of these disaffected communists joined the PSI. The events of Budapest gave Nenni, who had condemned the entire Soviet system, not just the personality cult of Stalin, once the content of the secret speech became known, cover to heal the breach with Saragat and to break decisively with the PCI.[89] Encouraged by the British Labour Party, the PSI found an interlocutor in the person of Amintore Fanfani, who also had the ear of the Americans after 1956, when he visited the United States. The policy of the US slowly became more nuanced in response to Fanfani's patient diplomacy.[90] This eventually led to the 'Opening to the Left' during the Kennedy administration, though, in the meantime, the policy of working with Nenni had caused internal dissent within the DC and exacerbated the party's factionalism.

The task of delivering greater social justice was made the heart of the DC's domestic policy. From 1954 onwards, DC governments followed ambitious policies of domestic economic expansion that Boothe Luce and her advisers regarded as dangerously socialistic but could do nothing to stop. Italy no longer needed America to hold its hand. These policies led to much unchecked development in construction and generated a lot of bribes for politicians. That was the downside. The upside was that the DC's state-led investment boom after 1954, together with the export boom caused by trade, kickstarted the *miracolo economico* that put ten million scooters and a million FIAT mini-cars on the roads and made Italy one of Europe's most dynamic countries within a decade. Almost 25 million Italians changed their home town between 1954 and 1964; 10 million changed region.[91] They were looking for and finding work. Millions of Italians were freed from the abject poverty revealed by the cross-party Commission in 1953. Fanfani, in a book published as propaganda for the 1958 elections, self-effacingly described the years between 1953 and 1958 as 'difficult but not sterile', but he presented the economic expansion launched by the DC with Soviet-style enthusiasm for its scope.[92]

Last, but not least, Italy's centre held. Support for the Monarchists evaporated to nothing as southern Italy achieved more tolerable standards of living. Achille Lauro, ever the pragmatist, struck a deal with the local DC in Naples as early as 1954. The MSI paid only lip service to the constitution but were anyway excluded from power. The one attempt by a DC premier, Fernando Tambroni, to widen the DC's majority to the right, and to cooperate with the neo-fascists, led to rioting across the country in 1960. The greatest scorn of the young rebels of the 1960s would be directed not at the DC, but at the PCI, which was regarded as bureaucratic, square, and unrevolutionary. Perhaps: but in the mid-1950s cities like Bologna were run by communist mayors with exemplary efficiency and scrupulous respect for constitutional norms (and ordinary honesty).

Rosario Forlenza, a thoughtful Italian historian influenced by the theories of cultural anthropology, recently defined the period 1943–8 as a 'liminal' one for Italy. For Forlenza, the 'concept of liminality' captures an 'ambiguous state of trial and uncertainty, betwixt and between: a separation from a previous social and political order, preceding a return to a new, and different, state of normality'.[93] The transition to democracy, for Forlenza, represented the 'emergence of new markers of certainty from conditions of profound uncertainty over the forms and structures of legitimate authority and government'.[94]

In 1940, the 'markers of certainty' that people lived by (whether they agreed with them or not) were fascist ones. They were smashed – discredited for ever, at any rate for decades to come – by the regime's abject *failure* in 1943. The future 'markers of certainty', as we have seen, were decided little by little. The political parties emerged from the resistance and acquired legitimacy by leading the struggle against the Germans. The monarchy, the symbol of pre-fascist Italy, was narrowly defeated in June 1946 and the Republic gradually acquired almost universal public assent; the constitution represented a huge compromise that satisfied almost everyone, even though its core principles were promises for the future, not realities in the present; the conflicts between East and West, America and Russia, capitalism and socialism, left and right, pluralism and totalitarianism, were existential ones but the aftermath of the 7 June 1953 elections settled them permanently. Italy's future was set as a gradually modernizing Western democracy. When looking at Italy (and not just in the 1950s) we need to look beyond the drama of the *teatrino politico*. The obsession of the Italian educated classes with the political show, and its artificial, almost daily crises, is reflected in newspapers around the world, which don't realize, always, that the show will usually go on. One should, instead, focus on the big picture.

By the time De Gasperi spoke at Naples in June 1954, the big picture was clear. Italy had not become a model democracy, but it *was* a democracy, not Fascism in clerical garb, as the PCI's propagandists would have it. It was far from being a just country, but it was more just than it ever had been before and was on the road to becoming juster still. It was an ally of the United States, a self-conscious part of the 'West', but it was not a colony run from the American Embassy in Rome. It still had a lengthy list of unresolved social and political questions capable of causing controversy, but so did many other countries in Europe. Compared to France, say, the challenges facing its democracy were minor. The absence of majoritarian government meant that every dispute between the parties, or within the DC, turned into a government crisis, true, but there was a party of government, with able leaders, and deep roots in civil society, to act as a fulcrum for the political system. Italy was a precarious democracy, one that was frustrating to manage, but it was vital, and its potential was immense.

12

A Realist and a Democrat

When, during the 1953 election campaign, De Gasperi told the crowd in Palermo that it would most likely be the last time that he would see their faces, he was telling the truth. His time was short. In February 1953, he had been diagnosed with azotemia, a kidney disease caused by high levels of nitrogen in the blood, which had brought on heart problems. He fought the arduous battle for the electoral law, and then the election campaign, against his doctors' advice, pushing his heart to the limit. His physical condition worsened after he stepped down as premier in August 1953. The man who led Christian Democracy through the short-lived Pella and Fanfani governments, and who brokered Scelba's accession to power in February 1954, was one for whom every speech, every long meeting, every scribbled article, was deeply debilitating.

De Gasperi gave his farewell address to the Naples Congress of the DC in a state of near prostration. He was given a caffeine injection before he took to the stage and was only able to speak, 'his face covered with cold sweat', while sitting down.[1] Hitherto his medical condition had been kept secret, while his powers of recovery had disguised how weak he had become. When he departed for the Val di Sella on 29 July 1954, his condition became apparent. He was unable to dissimulate further and to his chagrin the crowd of well-wishers who had gathered to see him off saw how much effort the simple task of getting on the train cost him.

De Gasperi insisted on going to the Val di Sella, although spending the summer at over 1,000 metres of altitude was a risky thing to do for a man with a serious heart condition. His family wanted him to go to Sella. They believed the mountains rejuvenated him. It seems clear that De Gasperi silently knew, though his family did not want to accept it, that it was improbable he would survive the summer and had, in his daughter Maria Romana's moving words, 'returned to his own realm to die'.[2]

De Gasperi spent the next three weeks in Sella without the paraphernalia of a head of government. There was no telex machine, no visits from papal envoys, no journalists calling for interviews. He was alone with his family, without even a doctor in attendance. The nearest hospital was in Borgo Valsugana, several miles of twisting road away. It seemed to De Gasperi's family that the valley had 'gone back to a time when Sella did not know the world and when no one cared about it'.[3]

Even now, De Gasperi concerned himself with politics. Although he was only capable of short outings in the woods – the slightest incline made his face pale visibly from the effort of walking – he would have liked to take part in final negotiations over the EDC in Brussels. As the price of ratification, France had asked for amendments to the treaty that weakened the supranational dimension of the defence community. De Gasperi sent anxious letters to Rome and had one telephone conversation with Scelba, in which, with 'unabashed tears rolling down his cheeks' he implored the prime minister to save the treaty: 'It is better to die than not implement the EDC.'[4] De Gasperi thought, correctly, that the French amendments would delay the creation of a European Union for several decades and feared this would be a disaster. Building Europe, however difficult, was better than relapsing into nationalism. A strong letter on the subject to Fanfani, on 14 August 1954, urging the Italian government to avoid compromise with the French and to warn its European partners and the Americans that its commitment to the treaty was absolute, was De Gasperi's last significant political act.[5]

In the face of pressure from its partners, the French government reluctantly agreed to place an unamended EDC treaty before the National Assembly for a vote of ratification on 30 August 1954. It was rejected by an unlikely coalition of communists, Gaullists, socialists, and even some nominal supporters of European unity. Most French politicians could not accept that France should be put on a par with 'three minor and two defeated states', as one prominent deputy pungently expressed the sentiment. Charles de Gaulle's view that the EDC represented a *mélange apatride* won more favour.

The defeat of the EDC would have broken De Gasperi's heart, but by then it was broken anyway. On 18 August he stayed in bed with chest pains, and then had a heart attack towards nine in the evening. His daughter Maria Romana's husband rushed off to fetch the local doctor, Giovanni Toller, a personal friend and companion on innumerable mountain hikes. When he arrived, Toller administered an injection, and promised that they would begin a new cure the following day. It was too late. At 2.30 in the morning on 19 August, De Gasperi suffered a further, fatal, heart attack. According to his daughter, his last word was 'Jesus'.

Three funeral services were held for him. The first was in Borgo Valsugana the next day, 20 August. Despite the presence of President Einaudi, Prime Minister Scelba, and other prominent authorities, it

De Gasperi's funeral, Borgo Valsugana, 20 August 1954.
The front two pallbearers are Oscar Luigi Scalfaro,
President of the Republic, 1992–9, and Giovanni Gronchi,
President of the Republic, 1955–62.

was an emotional, popular occasion, not a stilted ceremony. The coffin was carried through the little town by a succession of pallbearers, including two future presidents of the Republic, Giovanni Gronchi and Oscar Luigi Scalfaro, a Christian Democrat deputy from Piedmont. The many volunteer pallbearers were of different heights, so, in Maria Romana Catti De Gasperi's evocative image, the coffin seemed to bob along an 'uneven roller of human heads'.[6]

A more imposing church service took place in Trento Cathedral the following day. The coffin was then transported to Rome by train. Vast crowds lined the platforms of the stations on the way. After a mass in the Chiesa del Gesù, in the same square as the DC's party headquarters, De Gasperi was laid to rest on 23 August 1954 in the Basilica of San Lorenzo fuori le mura in Rome, a church in whose reconstruction from war damage the DC leader had taken a personal interest.[7] Thousands paid their respects. Some prominent political rivals were among the well-wishers. Long friendship and a warm heart ensured the presence of Pietro Nenni. Giuseppe Di Vittorio also attended. Better than anyone, he knew how much De Gasperi's governments had done for Italy's poorest in Apulia, Lucania, and Calabria.

The DC did not refrain from making political capital out of their leader's death. It was the party, not his family, that wanted De Gasperi to be buried in Rome, rather than Trento, or Borgo. The DC was ensuring that he would be remembered as a *national* leader, rather than as a figure from a province that most Italians regarded as remote, bucolic, and semi-German. The entrance to the basilica was draped on the day of the funeral with a banner describing De Gasperi as the 'rebuilder of the country'.[8]

The central interpretative question surrounding De Gasperi soon became, in fact, whether he was a rebuilder of the Italian nation or a *restorer* of a social order in which both the Vatican and big business had had their interests preserved, or even enhanced, while most Italians languished in poverty. Had De Gasperi's governments created a democracy, or a mere parliamentary regime that contained within it the same failings and injustices that had led to Fascism?

Christian Democrats were obviously proponents of the 'rebuilder' thesis and of equating De Gasperi's name with the establishment of democracy. In the months after De Gasperi's death, the editor of *Il*

Popolo, Igino Giordani, produced a book entitled *De Gasperi: The Rebuilder* as part of an orchestrated campaign to create a myth, or narrative, of De Gasperi as the founding father of the new nation that had emerged from the fall of Fascism.[9]

This campaign took physical form after the steering committee of the DC decided, on 16 February 1955, to construct a monument to De Gasperi in Trento. The work was to celebrate his achievements as the nation's rebuilder, celebrate his faith, and underline his role as one of the founding fathers of European unity. The work was entrusted to a Florentine sculptor called Antonio Berti, who had achieved a high reputation in ecclesiastical circles. Berti was to be the 'inspirer of the monument in its complete architectural form' by being at once its designer, sculptor, and architect.[10]

Whether or not Berti succeeded is a moot point. The monument has been derided as an egregious example of kitsch.[11] This judgement is too harsh, though the monument is undeniably over-freighted with symbolism. It consists of a tall (26-metre) *stele* (obelisk) soaring from a block of granite. At the front, shallow steps run up to a plinth upon which a 4-metre-tall statue of De Gasperi stands: the plinth is decorated with four women in contemporary dress symbolizing faith, reflection, justice, and politics, though it is not immediately obvious what distinguishes one from the other. The back of the monument is decorated with a large statue of *L'Italia turrita*, her hands clasped in piety and with her face fixed in a forbidding frown: no soft touch, she. The base is decorated with bronze representations of children symbolizing 'work', 'love', 'happiness', 'European union', and 'play'. Again, they are all much of a muchness.

The monument is saved, aesthetically, by the statue of De Gasperi himself, which is extremely lifelike, and which fully captures his personal dynamism, and by two bronze high reliefs (the dark areas in the picture) representing (viewer's left) 'Destruction' and (viewer's right) 'Reconstruction'. 'Destruction' is rendered in an almost vorticist style; 'Reconstruction' in a manner that recalls Socialist Realism.

The monument was inaugurated on 14 October 1956 by Scelba's successor as prime minister, Antonio Segni, the former reformist agriculture minister, as a prelude to the 6th Congress of the DC, which

Monument to Alcide De Gasperi, Piazza Venezia, Trento, September 2023.

was held in Trento. The first day of the congress was a celebration of De Gasperi's life and achievements.[12]

The message communicated by the monument, be it kitsch or not, was very clear. Italy moved from destruction to reconstruction thanks, above all, to the wisdom and élan of the man on the plinth. This notion led to two decades of debate: in 1976 a 1,010-page book entitled *De Gasperi On Trial* was published containing over 200 different attempts to confirm or rebut the significance attributed by the DC to the statesman from Trentino.[13] The most important critique of the DC's thesis was produced by his rival, Palmiro Togliatti. The PCI's leader could not let the DC's propaganda effort gain traction. Between October 1955 and June 1956, Togliatti published a series of articles – some 30,000 words in all – in *Rinascita* that told a darker story about De Gasperi's role in recent Italian history. There is no space here fully to depict all the interpretative twists of Togliatti's argument, but his peroration deserves quoting at length:

> His action was ultimately efficacious in two principal directions: in restoring economic power to a closed, selfish capitalist ruling class, one that has no long-term future ahead of it, and in conferring upon the ecclesiastical authorities a new form of political power. He did not block the forward march of us communists. Indeed, he made us all the more aware of our strength, of what we were capable of achieving. Even the two new things that took shape during his government were hardly the result of his deliberate action. He should be seen rather as a devious power-broker and an unscrupulous performer utilized by the former [i.e. the capitalist class] more or less well, and pushed hard by the latter [i.e. the Church] in pursuit of goals that will doubtless unfold over time, but which will certainly not lead to the consolidation of the two principal outcomes of his action.[14]

Togliatti's diagnosis had a definite impact on Italian historiography, which has, in some quarters at least, depicted Italy between April 1948 and June 1953 as a 'democracy at risk'. According to this interpretation, Italian democracy was only saved from an 'irreversible step towards an authoritarian regime' during De Gasperi's term in office by the opposition's tenacious defence of democratic principles during the debate on the Swindle Law; and, more in general, by the wisdom of the parties of the left, which managed to construct an 'alternative and antagonistic' opposition to the DC within 'democratic-bourgeois institutions' that was neither 'mere protest politics' nor yet 'subversive rebellion'.[15]

British authors have been kinder. Denis Mack Smith regarded De Gasperi as the 'most effective parliamentary leader since Giolitti, or indeed, since Cavour', as well as being 'one of the most principled'. Mack Smith emphasized that De Gasperi sought to include democratic socialists and republicans in his governments and to avoid making

Italian politics 'a simple conflict of Right and Left'.[16] Paul Ginsborg, in his landmark history of post-war Italy, pointed out that De Gasperi's 'stern, moralist, and devoutly Catholic character, when combined with his Republicanism and anti-Fascism, were in welcome contrast to what had gone before'. He adds that De Gasperi's 'qualities as a politician were very great'. Where, for Ginsborg, De Gasperi fell short was in not turning the rhetoric of social reform into reality. He argues that under his leadership the DC 'became the party of stagnant centrism and virulent anti-communism'.[17]

More recently, David Gilmour has described De Gasperi as a 'man of wisdom, honesty, and sound judgement', whose break with the left, 'inevitable though it was', polarized the country. Germany was divided by the Cold War, but in Italy 'communism and christian democracy were competing in the same arena'. Nevertheless, De Gasperi knew it would be 'fatal' to 'take his party to the Right or to allow it to be closely identified with the Church'. He was followed, Gilmour emphasizes, by 'lesser men'.[18]

I agree with Gilmour, as the previous chapters must have made clear. There is another dimension to De Gasperi that should be remembered, however. Again and again, he took brave decisions, often against the advice of more cautious followers. Above all, the decision in May 1947 to break with the PCI and the PSI, when the constitution was still not agreed, was a massive risk that probably saved Italy's nascent democracy, which was subsequently able to obtain Marshall Plan aid and take part in the first steps of European integration. One can only dimly imagine the chaos that would have ensued in the autumn of 1947, after Moscow's change of tack, had the PCI still been in government.

Judgement on De Gasperi's stature as a leader ultimately depends on whether one believes that the PCI could could have been trusted with power after the summer of 1947. If one thinks that it could, then De Gasperi was a divisive figure who broke the resistance coalition and retarded the rapid implementation of the constitution's provisions. If one thinks it could not, then De Gasperi was a formidable leader who saved the nation from subversion. There is not much middle ground here.

De Gasperi was certainly not the reactionary that Togliatti depicts. His government joined the ECSC and embraced free trade in the face of resistance from the capitalist cliques of which he was supposedly a pawn. He limited the influence of the Americans and the Vatican over Italian politics, while making overtures to Nenni; it was not his fault that the PSI's leader refused to listen. De Gasperi was influenced by his knowledge of how democracy had collapsed in the German-speaking world, which meant supporting a strong state to check the enemies of representative government, and to keep inflation low. He was a conservative, not certainly an opponent of social progress.

De Gasperi, for all his personal piety, was a man of power with a strong element of self-regard – nothing else can explain his error of trying to form a government in July 1953. He was a politician through and through, not a saint, though there are those in Italy who wish to beatify him (the process was begun by the diocese of Trento in 1993). In De Gasperi, however, Christian principles tempered his love of power. Togliatti, by contrast, was a cynic: that was how he stayed alive in Moscow and that was how he managed to walk the wobbling tightrope of the party line with such aplomb. Yet Togliatti, too, by virtue of his moderation in May–June 1945, again after the attempt on his life in 1948, after his return from Moscow in February 1951, and, above all, during the Constituent Assembly, played a substantial role in consolidating Italian democracy.

Our judgement on De Gasperi's stature also depends on whether one believes that Italy could have regenerated itself from its own resources (for none would have been forthcoming from the Americans had the 'resistance coalition' survived in the summer of 1947). De Gasperi concluded – rightly – that the answer to this question was 'no' and acted accordingly. He grasped that there was no way a country as war-torn as Italy could be transformed democratically without American investment, higher levels of output, and openness towards Europe. The brutality of the modernization taking place in the so-called Peoples' Democracies was very evident to him between April 1948 and June 1953. The PCI was right to say that communist societies were eliminating poverty faster than Italy was, but at what price? De Gasperi was a democrat, as well as a realist.

The historian A. J. P. Taylor once remarked that we tend to 'take the characters of the past too seriously' and 'blow them up beyond their deserts'.[19] The opposite is also true. So much modern historiography concentrates on broad social forces and downplays the role that individual political actors can have on the course of history. It can sometimes seem that political leaders are mere ciphers, swept along by the flow of their times. Whatever our ultimate judgement about De Gasperi, it is hard to deny that he, like his contemporary Charles de Gaulle or his close friend Konrad Adenauer, made a real mark on history. Had he suffered a heart attack in the spring of 1947, rather than the summer of 1954, Italy's subsequent history, and that of contemporary Europe, would have been different.

De Gasperi embodied a central truth of Machiavelli's understanding of politics. By that, I mean not that he was a liar, a cynic, and lover of power for power's sake – which are the attributes we associate with the adjective Machiavellian – but that he was a man of *virtù*. He was devout, a seeker of compromise, and courteous in conduct unless the long-term national interest – reasons of state – meant he could not be. The 1948 election campaign illustrates the point vividly. One reason why the parties of the left regarded him as authoritarian (though to call him 'totalitarian' was absurd) was that they knew he would have ordered repressive measures without a qualm had they overstepped the red line dividing confrontational politics from an attempt to seize power illegally.

De Gasperi eventually over-reached himself with the electoral law. Perhaps if the majority prize had been set at 60 per cent of seats, not 65 per cent, if he had toned down his evocations of a 'strong state', and been less overbearing in his conduct during the passage of the bill, then things might have turned out differently. He was becoming a self-righteous and occasionally irascible figure by the end of his premiership: the cares of office had frayed his nerves. He died concerned that the DC might veer to the right, that Europe might not be rebuilt, that the PCI might yet grow in power, that the PSI would never break free of its subjugation to its brother party. He did not realize himself, perhaps, quite how far his country had advanced along the road to democracy since December 1945, when his first government swore the oath of office in flickering candlelight at the Quirinale Palace.

A Guide to Further Reading

This book has dealt primarily with the decline and fall of Fascism and the construction and consolidation of Italian democracy. Its principal source material has overwhelmingly been primary and contemporary sources in Italian: I wanted to bring the fundamental debates of the time to life by allowing the protagonists of Italy's political struggle to speak for themselves. Nevertheless, since I hope anybody who has read this far will want to know more about Italy and its political development, I thought it was worthwhile to add this short guide to the literature on modern and contemporary Italy, and especially Italian politics, in English. The guide makes no pretence of being exhaustive. It is designed for the general reader, not a specialist.

Two wonderfully readable general histories of Italy from medieval times to the present day are Giuliano Procacci's *History of the Italian People* (tr. 1970) and, more recently, David Gilmour's erudite and elegant *The Pursuit of Italy: A History of a Land, Its Regions, and Their Peoples* (2011). Both authors possess enviable powers of synthesis. Denis Mack Smith's *Modern Italy* (2nd edition 1997) is a famous political history, first published in 1959, from the Risorgimento to the upheavals of the 1990s. Spencer Di Scala's *Italy from Revolution to Republic* (4th edition 2009) is a comprehensive overview of modern Italian history, while Vera Zamagni's *The Economic History of Italy 1860–1990* (1990) remains unsurpassed as a survey of Italy's economic transition from the periphery of Europe to its centre. The *Oxford Handbook of Italian Politics* (2015), edited by Erik Jones and Gianfranco Pasquino, contains useful essays by experts on many of the individuals, political parties, and institutions of the post-war decade, as well as providing an excellent introduction to the politics of the First Republic more generally.

The first book I ever read on Italian history, as a precocious thirteen-year-old, was G. M. Trevelyan's *Garibaldi and the Making of Italy* (1911): romanticized, dated, great-man history, of course, but terribly readable even today. Lucy Riall has written a fascinating study, *Garibaldi: Invention of a Hero* (2007), which presents a more scientific account of the Garibaldi myth. Derek Beales and Eugenio F. Biagini's *The Risorgimento and the Unification of Italy* (2002) is an outstanding introduction to the Risorgimento in English. The period from 1871 to 1922 is covered by Christopher Seton-Watson's magisterial *Italy from Liberalism to Fascism* (1967). It is a pity, to use no stronger term, that there is no more recent single-author general history of Italy in this period, although Christopher Duggan's monumental biography of *Francesco Crispi* (2002) and Alexander De Grand's *The Hunchback's Tailor: Giovanni Giolitti and Liberal Italy from the Challenge of Mass Politics to the Rise of Fascism* (2000) do fill part of the gap. John Davis's *Italy in the Nineteenth Century 1796–1900* (2001) is a *tour de force* that covers a tumultuous century of political and social developments in 300 pages.

Mark Thompson's *The White War: Life and Death on the Italian Front* (2010) vividly illustrates the horrors of the Italian Front during the First World War. Selena Daly engagingly discusses the experience of intellectuals at the front in *Italian Futurism and the First World War* (2016). MacGregor Knox's *To the Threshold of Power, 1922–33: Origins and Dynamics of the Fascist and National Socialist Dictatorships* (2008) emphasizes that the First World War was a decisive experience for the political development of both Italy and Germany.

There is no point listing all the works in English on Fascism: there are hundreds. Philip Morgan's *Italian Fascism 1915–1945* (2003) is an excellent introduction; the same author's excellent *The Fall of Mussolini* (2008) deals with the social consequences of the war in Italy, not just the regime's downfall. F. W. Deakin's *The Brutal Friendship: Mussolini, Hitler and the Fall of Italian Fascism* (1962) remains relevant today: it tells the story of Mussolini's downfall with a wealth of documented detail and a hint of pathos. The military consequences of the regime's disastrous pro-Nazi turn in foreign policy are charted in exemplary fashion in John Gooch's *Mussolini's War: Fascist Italy from Triumph to Collapse, 1935–1943* (2020). R. J. B. Bosworth has written a trilogy of accessible yet scholarly works on Mussolini's Italy: *Mussolini* (2002), *Mussolini's Italy: Life Under the Dictatorship* (2007) and, most recently, *Mussolini and the Eclipse of Italian Fascism: From Dictatorship to Populism* (2021). Relations between the Vatican and the Fascist state are the province of David Kertzer, whose book *The Pope and Mussolini: The Secret History of Pius XI and the Rise of Fascism in Europe* (2014) is a classic of contemporary historical scholarship.

Remarkably little Italian work on Fascism and the Second World War has been translated into English and Italian historians, for whatever reason, tend not to publish in English. Renzo De Felice, author of a seven-volume 'biography' of Mussolini (in reality, a history of Fascism), published thousands, perhaps tens of thousands, of pages of research on the regime but almost none of it has been issued in English. Even De Felice's *Breve storia del Fascismo* (2001), which is written in a pungent, almost journalistic style quite unlike his ponderous major works, has never been translated, though, in my view, it is the best synthesis of Italian Fascism available.

A second important (and equally prolific) scholar of the regime, Emilio Gentile, has published *The Sacralisation of Politics in Fascist Italy* (1996) and *La Grande Italia: The Myth of the Nation in the Twentieth Century* (2009) in English. Unfortunately, most of his very readable books have only been published in Italian. The classic discussion of the place of women in Fascist Italy is by Vittoria De Grazia in *How Fascism Ruled Women: Italy 1922–1945* (1992). The most important book on 8 September 1943 and the surrender and flight of the king and Badoglio is *Una nazione allo sbando* (3rd edition 2007) by Elena Aga Rossi. This classic of modern historiography has been translated into English as *A Nation Collapses: The Italian Surrender of September 1943* (tr. 2000). David W. Ellwood's *Italy 1943–1945* (1985) skilfully shows how the Italy of Badoglio and Bonomi was an *alleato-nemico* (ally-enemy) in the eyes of British policymakers particularly.

The Italian Resistance has a growing literature in English. Claudio Pavone's *A Civil War: A History of the Resistance in Italy* (tr. 2013) is a translation of the author's classic 1991 study in Italian. Caroline Moorehead, *A House in the Mountains: The Women Who Liberated Italy from Fascism* (2020) compellingly tells the story of the resistance from the perspective of a group of Italian women intellectuals. Philip Cooke's *The Legacy of the Italian Resistance* (2011) looks, as its title suggests, at how the resistance was interpreted and used in post-war political and cultural debates. More recently, David Broder, *The Rebirth of Italian Communism, 1943–44* (2021) has given an inside portrayal of the PCI's resistance to the German occupation in Rome.

Giacomo Debenedetti's famous essay *16 October 1943*, depicting the *rastrellamento* of the Rome ghetto, was published in English (2001), along with a separate essay on eight of the Jews killed in the Fosse Ardeatine. Simon Levis Sullam's book *Italy's Executioners: The Genocide of the Jews of Italy* (tr. 2018) is, to my knowledge, the first comprehensive account of the Holocaust in Italy to be published in English.

One major reason why I wrote this book was my conviction that the renewal of Italy as a democracy after the Second World War had attracted relatively little interest from authors writing in English. There are dozens of biographies of Mussolini in English, but none of De Gasperi. Biographies of De Gaulle and Adenauer are numerous, but the Italian statesman remains little known outside Italy. There is also no doubt that the contribution that the democratization of Italy made to the construction of the 'West' has been underestimated because fewer scholars can work in Italian than in French or German.

The literature on Italy's democratization has also suffered from the tendency of scholars to downplay the role of the DC in the construction of Italian democracy. The notion that Italy might have become a progressive democracy, unaligned perhaps in the Cold War, haunts the early chapters of Paul Ginsborg's rich and complex *A History of Contemporary Italy: Society and Politics 1943–1988* (1990), which remains the standard general history of those decades in English. As this book has pointed out, Italy's choice between 1947 and the early 1950s was between De Gasperi's somewhat shaky pro-Western centrism or political chaos, which is why De Gasperi and Scelba were forceful, even authoritarian, in their defence of the political order. Elena Aga Rossi and Victor Zaslavsky's *Stalin and Togliatti: Italy and the Origins of the Cold War* (tr. 2011) is indispensable reading if one wants to understand the character and role of the PCI in the Second World War and immediately after. A meticulously researched and argued monograph, it illustrates, in my opinion definitively, that the PCI was first and foremost part of the international communist movement, rather than a national party, working for national ends. The book's thesis remains an uncomfortable one for many Italian academics.

The PSI's contribution is covered, in exemplary fashion, by Spencer Di Scala, *Renewing Italian Socialism: Nenni to Craxi* (1988), but by nobody else since. There is no critical biography of Nenni in English, though an account of his life would give us a panoramic view of left-wing European politics throughout almost the whole of the twentieth century. The only biographical study of Togliatti in English, Aldo Agosti's *Togliatti: A Biography* (2008), while learned, is unambiguously the work of an admirer.

The birth of the Italian Republic after the Second World War is the subject of Steven F. White's *Modern Italy's Founding Fathers: The Making of a Postwar Republic* (2020). This is a valuable short book that concentrates on the role and interactions of De Gasperi, Togliatti, and Nenni in the period until the April 1948 elections. It does have a skimpy chapter on 'Cold War Stasis', but its focus is emphatically on the immediate post-war period. Rosario Forlenza, *On the Edge of Democracy: Italy 1943–1948* (2018), by contrast, looks at the politics of Italy in the same years, but from the 'bottom up', rather than top down. Forlenza's work is dense and theoretical, but full of rewarding insights. *Italy in the Cold War: Politics, Culture and Society, 1948–1958* (1995), edited by Christopher Duggan and Christopher Wagstaff, is a now dated but still interesting collection of essays.

The role of the United States in the construction of Italian democracy has been discussed by John Lamberton Harper, *America and the Reconstruction of Italy, 1945–1948* (1982), while the US's interference in Italian domestic affairs, especially during the crucial 1948 election, is the subject of Kaeten Mistry, *The United States, Italy, and the Cold War: Waging Political Warfare* (2014). Robert Ventresca, *From Fascism to Democracy: Culture and Politics in the Italian Election of 1948* (2004) deals with the election from the cultural-religious

431

angle. On Italy's role in the construction of 'Europe' in the 1940s and 1950s there is virtually nothing in English.

I regret that I did not have space for a chapter on how Italy *lived* democracy after the 1948 elections. The social history of Italian democracy – the rallies, rituals and pageantry of the political parties, the use of film and literature to communicate political messages, the heated battles of the Italian intelligentsia – is a topic that is worthy of a book of its own. I cannot resist pointing the reader to Stephen Gundle's *Between Hollywood and Moscow: The Italian Communists and the Challenge of Mass Culture, 1943–91* (2000), which is a milestone in the field of film studies in Italy: its chapters on the immediate post-war are outstanding. The best introduction to political ideas and the conflicts that animated Italy's influential intellectuals during Fascism and in the post-war years is Norberto Bobbio's *Ideological Profile of Twentieth-Century Italy* (tr. 1995). It should be read together with his autobiography, *A Political Life* (tr. 2002).

Literature is always a valuable supplement to works of historical scholarship. The most graphic description of the effects of the war on ordinary Italians is arguably *History: A Novel* (tr. 2000), by the writer Elsa Morante. I discussed Carlo Levi's *Christ Stopped at Eboli* (tr. 2000) in Chapter Six. Anybody wanting to know about the social problems that faced Republican Italy cannot do better than read it. Similarly, anyone wishing to get the flavour of the struggle between the PCI and the Church should read Giovanni Guareschi, *The Little World of Don Camillo* (the most recent reprint in English is from 2013) and absorb the author's gently ironic portrait of the early years of Italian democracy. I particularly recommend a June 1947 story called 'The Rally' (*Il comizio*). Leonardo Sciascia's *Candido, or a Dream Dreamed in Sicily* (tr. 1995), a reworking of Voltaire's *Candide* in a post-war Italian setting, is a great satire, one of the greatest in all post-war world literature. Ignazio Silone's memoir 'Emergency Exit' is perhaps the most revealing account of the internal workings of the international communist movement ever published. Stanislao Pugliese's *Bitter Spring* (2009) is an insightful biography of Silone and a valuable introduction to his intellectual legacy. We should all read Silone more.

Notes

INTRODUCTION

1. Jason Horowitz, 'Giorgia Meloni Wins Voting in Italy, in Breakthrough for Europe's Hard Right', *New York Times*, 26 September 2022.
2. My book *The Italian Revolution: The End of Politics, Italian Style* (Boulder, CO: Westview Press, 1995) was an early attempt to interpret the causes of the crisis of the First Republic.
3. Steven Levitsky and Daniel Ziblatt, *How Democracies Die: What History Reveals About Our Future* (New York: Viking, 2018).
4. In that greatest of all dissections of the traditional British character, *How to Be an Alien* (London: André Deutsch, 1946).
5. Norberto Bobbio, *Eravamo ridiventati uomini. Testimonianze e discorsi sulla resistenza in Italia, 1955–99* (Turin: Einaudi, 2015), 63.
6. Umberto Gentiloni Silveri, *Storia dell'Italia contemporanea* (Bologna: Il Mulino, 2019), 51.
7. Richard J. Samuels, *Machiavelli's Children: Leaders and Their Legacies in Italy and Japan* (Ithaca, NY: Cornell University Press, 2003), 224.
8. To use the formula of Pietro Scoppola, *La repubblica dei partiti. Profilo storico della democrazia in Italia* (Bologna: Il Mulino, 1991).

I. UNDEMOCRATIC ITALY

1. The exception was Bettino Ricasoli, prime minister from June 1861 to March 1862, and June 1866 to April 1867.
2. For Bernini's transformation of Rome, see Loyd Grossman, *An Elephant in Rome: Bernini, the Pope and the Making of the Eternal City* (London: Pallas Athena, 2020).
3. David Gilmour, *The Pursuit of Italy: A History of a Land, Its Regions and Their Peoples* (London: Penguin, 2012), 235.

4. For Pius IX's flight, see David Kertzer, *The Pope Who Would Be King: The Exile of Pius IX and the Emergence of Modern Europe* (New York: Random House, 2017).
5. The Latin phrase was *non expedit*.
6. Gilmour, *The Pursuit of Italy*, 258.
7. In 1861, Italy's annual income per head was approximately $2,600 in 2016 figures. To put this in perspective, that would mean that the Italy of Victor Emmanuel II had a standard of living like modern-day Nigeria's. https://clio-infra.eu/Countries/Italy.html
8. Vittorio Daniele and Paolo Malanima, 'Alle origini del divario', in *Nord e Sud a 150 anni dall'Unità d'Italia (Roma: SVIMEZ, 2012)*, 102.
9. Ibid., 96.
10. See Rosa Vaccaro, *Unità politica e dualismo economico in Italia (1861–1993)* (Padua: Cedam, 1995), 207, table 19.
11. Francesco Barbagallo, *Lavoro ed esodo nel sud, 1861–1971* (Naples: Guida, 1973), ch. III, 'Disaggregazione sociale e esodo di massa', 54–141 passim. All statistics, rounded to the nearest thousand, are from this chapter. The *lucani* are the inhabitants of Basilicata.
12. It was founded in Genoa on 15 August 1892 as the Italian Workers' Party. It became the PSI in 1895.
13. The 'Legge Zanardelli' of 1882 extended the suffrage to all literate men over twenty-one. The reform in effect enfranchised those who had completed primary education, which had been extended in 1877. Those who paid just under 20 lire in taxes were also enfranchised, literate or not. This amounted in 1882 to about 7 per cent of the total population; a number that gradually increased as primary education became more widespread.
14. For *trasformismo*, see Giovanni Sabbatucci, *Il trasformismo come sistema* (Rome-Bari: Laterza, 2003).
15. A point made by Michele Pantaleone, *Mafia e politica, 1943–1962* (Turin: Einaudi, 1962), 37.
16. Filippo Tommaso Marinetti, *Manifeste du Futurisme*, in *Le Figaro* (20 February 1909).
17. Antonio Varsori, *Radioso maggio. Come l'Italia entrò in guerra* (Bologna: Il Mulino, 2015), is the best account of Italy's decision to side with the Entente.
18. G. M. Trevelyan, 'Autobiography of An Historian', in Trevelyan, *An Autobiography and Other Essays* (London: Longmans, 1949), 36. 'Povero fante' means 'poor infantryman'.

19. On this topic, see Vanda Wilcox, *Morale and the Italian Army During the First World War* (Cambridge: Cambridge University Press, 2016).

20. *I sacrifici della nazione* (Rome: Ministry of Defence, 2018). https://www.difesa.it

21. Federico Chabod, *Italia contemporanea* (1918–48) (Turin: Einaudi, 1961), 27–35. The English word 'billion' is being used to translate the Italian word *miliardo* (i.e. thousand million).

22. On a scale where 1913 = 1, consumer prices were 0.929 in 1891; 0.882 in 1900; 1.070 in 1915; 2.641 in 1918; 3.523 in 1920; 4.143 in 1922. *Sommario di statistiche dell'Italia* (Roma: Istituto Centrale di Statistica, 1968), 109.

23. See Margaret Macmillan, *Peacemakers: The Paris Peace Conference of 1919 and Its Attempt to End War* (London: John Murray, 2001), ch. 22 passim for the Italian case.

24. See Giordano Bruno Guerri, *Disobbedisco: Cinque cento giorni di rivoluzione. Fiume 1919–20* (Milan: Mondadori, 2019), for D'Annunzio's adventurism.

25. This is a reference to the PPI's first manifesto, 'A tutti gli uomini liberi e forti', adopted on 18 January 1919. The inspiration for the party's economic policy was the *Rerum Novarum*, a papal encyclical issued by Leo XIII in May 1891.

26. Maria Serena Piretti, *Le elezioni politiche in Italia dal 1848 a oggi* (Rome-Bari: Laterza, 1995), 410. No fewer than twelve parties were represented in parliament.

27. The PSI had refused to take a 'patriotic' line during the war. It described its war policy as 'neither adhesion nor sabotage'.

28. Gaetano Salvemini, 'Elezioni', *L'Unità* (27 November 1919).

29. Camillo Prampolini, 'All'inizio della nuova società', *Avanti!* (Milan) (19 November 1919).

30. Quotations from Antonio Gramsci, 'La taglia della storia', in *Scritti politici*, ed. Paolo Spriano (Rome: Riuniti, 1967), 198–207. The original article appeared in *L'Ordine nuovo* on 7 June 1919.

31. Chabod, *Italia contemporanea*, 47.

32. To take a good example: 'Il terrore', *Critica sociale* (1918), 19 (1–15 October). See also Franco Andreucci, 'Il bolscevismo nella mentalità della Sinistra italiana e la nascita del PCI', *Storia e Politica. Annali della Fondazione Ugo La Malfa*, 31 (2016), 196–216.

33. Giorgio Bocca, *Togliatti* (Milan: Feltrinelli, 2014), 74.

34. For a classic case study, in English, of the impact of Fascism at the provincial level, see Paul Corner, *Fascism in Ferrara, 1915–1925* (Oxford: Oxford University Press, 1975).

35. See Davide Lajolo, *Di Vittorio. Il volto umano di un rivoluzionario* (Milan: Bompiani, 1972), 53.
36. Maria Romana Catti De Gasperi, *De Gasperi uomo solo* (Milan: Mondadori, 1964), 88.
37. Curzio Malaparte, *Tecnica del Colpo di Stato* (Florence: Ponte delle Grazie, 1998), 205 (1st edn 1931).
38. P. Milza and S. Bernstein, *Storia del Fascismo. Da Piazza San Sepolcro a Piazzale Loreto* (Milan: Rizzoli, 1995), 145.
39. Gabriele De Rosa, *Il partito popolare italiano* (Roma: Laterza, 1976, 4th edn), 183–9 for Don Sturzo's opposition.
40. Chamber of Deputies (16 November 1922), 8389–95.
41. Steven Levitsky and Lucan A. Way, 'The Rise of Competitive Authoritarianism', *Journal of Democracy*, vol. 13, no. 2 (April 2002), 51–65.
42. Witness Matteotti's last speech in the Chamber of Deputies on 30 May 1924. The speech has been recently reprinted in Giacomo Matteotti, *Il Fascismo tra demagogia e consenso. Scritti 1922–1924* (Rome: Donzelli, 2020), 187–99.
43. Cesare Sobrero, 'Mussolini e la situazione', *La Stampa* (19 June 1924).
44. For an excellent account of the PSU leader's abduction, see Mauro Canali, 'The Matteotti Murder and the Origins of Mussolini's Totalitarian Fascist Regime in Italy', *Journal of Modern Italian Studies*, vol. 14, no. 2 (2009), 143–67.
45. Pietro Nenni, *Taccuino 1942* (Rome: Avanti!, 1955), 8 (entry for 4 January 1942).
46. 'Il discorso di Pio XI', *Civiltà Cattolica* (20 September 1924), 492–4.
47. Chamber of Deputies (3 January 1925), 2028–32, for Mussolini's speech.
48. Pietro Nenni, 'Che cosa vuole il partito socialista?', in *Una battaglia vinta* (Rome: Edizioni Leonardi, 1946), 10.
49. Piero Gobetti, *La Rivoluzione liberale: Saggio sulla lotta politica in Italia* (Turin: Einaudi, 1995), 165. This classic was first published in 1924 by the Bologna publisher Cappelli in a small edition of 1,000 copies. Gobetti was just twenty-five years old when he was murdered.
50. Ibid., 166.
51. Ibid., 29.
52. Cited in Giorgio Tupini, *De Gasperi. Una testimonianza* (Bologna: Il Mulino, 1992), 31.
53. For De Gasperi's early political career, see Paolo Pombeni, *Il primo De Gasperi. La formazione di un leader politico* (Bologna: Il Mulino, 2007).

54. Benito Mussolini, 'The Doctrine of Fascism', in *The Social and Political Doctrines of Contemporary Europe*, ed. Michael Oakeshott (New York: Cambridge University Press, 1950), 176–8. This is the best English translation of Mussolini's essay 'La Dottrina del Fascismo', published in the *Enciclopedia Italiana* in 1931.

55. Giovanni Gentile, 'Beati Possidentes', *Corriere della Sera* (11 March 1931), in *Giovanni Gentile, Scritti per il 'Corriere', 1927–1944*, ed. Gabriele Turi (Milan: Fondazione CDS, 2009), 114.

56. On this subject, see Enrico Pontieri, *Piccole sovversioni quotidiane* (Bologna: Viella, 2022), which is a fascinating piece of social history.

57. For statistics, C. F. Delzell, 'Il fuoriuscitismo italiano dal 1922 al 1943, *Italia contemporanea*, no. 23 (1953), 3.

58. In the so-called 'Ascension Day Speech', 26 May 1928. I first found this citation in Norberto Bobbio, 'Il regime fascista (1)', in *Trent'anni di storia Italiana (1915–1945)* (Turin: Einaudi, 1961), 163.

59. Amintore Fanfani, *Il significato del corporativismo* (Como: Cavalleri, 1941, 5th edn). Quotations from vol. 2, pp. 14, 15, 18, 102.

60. Quotations from Pius XI, *Non abbiamo bisogno*, Rome, from the Vatican (29 June 1931).

61. David Kertzer, *The Pope and Mussolini: The Secret History of Pius XI and the Rise of Fascism in Europe* (New York: Random House, 2014), 405.

62. Ernesto Rossi, *Il Manganello e l'aspersorio* (Bari: Laterza, 1968), 296. A *manganello* was the truncheon used by the Fascist militia. The *aspersorio* is the aspergillum, the metal stick with which the priest sprinkles the faithful with holy water during mass.

63. Quoted in Giovanni Belardelli, *Il Ventennio degli intellettuali. Cultura, politica, ideologia nell'Italia fascista* (Bari-Rome: Laterza, 2005), 66.

64. 'Razzismo italiano', *La Difesa della Razza*, no. 1 (August 1938), 1. For excellent background, see Aaron Gillette, 'The Origins of the "Manifesto of Racial Scientists"', *Journal of Modern Italian Studies*, vol. 6, no. 3 (2001), 306 and 315.

65. Fanfani, *Il significato del corporativismo*, vol. 2, 103. These words were written by a collaborator, Prof. Carlo Marzorati, a teacher at Milan's prestigious Liceo Gonzaga, who 'compiled' Part V of the book.

66. All quotations are from texts collected in Renzo De Felice and Luigi Goglia, *Mussolini Il Mito* (Rome: Laterza, 1983), 93–134. In order of appearance, they are by Torquato Nanni (the Duce's first biographer), the cultural journalist Giuseppe Prezzolini, the futurist essayist Emilio Settimelli, an unnamed parliamentary deputy, the Fascist intellectual

Pietro Gorgolini, Prezzolini again, the futurist poet and painter F. T. Marinetti, Carlo Delacroix, a war hero and writer, and Ugo D'Andrea, a nationalist journalist who became, between 1963 and 1972, a senator of the Italian Republic for the Liberal Party (PLI).

67. Pantaleone, *Mafia e politica*, 42.

68. All quotations from Ignazio Silone, *Fontamara* (London: Penguin, 1938), 7–12. Giovanni Torlonia (1873–1938), the third prince, became a senator in October 1920 and was president of the Bank of Fucino between 1923 and 1938.

69. Ibid., 15–16.

70. Ibid., 191.

71. Marina Cattaruzza, *L'Italia e il confine orientale* (Bologna: Il Mulino, 2007), 162.

72. For a useful contemporary account, see Harry J. Carmen, 'Austria Resents Italianization of Tyrol', *Current History*, vol. 28, no.1 (1928), 136–40.

73. Cattaruzza, *L'Italia e il confine orientale*, 168–81.

74. This expressive term is from Maura Hametz, 'Naming Italians in the Borderland, 1927–43', *Journal of Modern Italian Studies*, vol. 15, no. 3 (2010), 410–30.

75. Piero Melograni, 'The Cult of the Duce in Mussolini's Italy', *Journal of Contemporary History*, 11 (1976), 230.

76. *L'Impero d'Italia* (Rome: La Libreria dello Stato, 1939), 8–9 for the maps, 96 for the quotation, italics added. The author was a geographer called Luigi Filippo de Magistris, though he was not credited on the cover.

77. Angelo Del Boca, *La guerra d'Etiopia: L'ultima impresa del colonialismo* (Milan: Longanesi, 2010), 95.

78. Marcello Staglieno, *Montanelli: Novant'anni controcorrente* (Milan: Mondadori, 2001), 75.

79. See, in English, Ian Campbell, *The Addis Ababa Massacre: Italy's National Shame* (Oxford: Oxford University Press, 2017).

80. Angelo Del Boca, *Italiani brava gente?* (Vicenza: Neri Pozza Editore, 2010), 229.

81. Luigi Arbizzani, *Spagna e Italia: una sola battaglia* (Bologna: Arte Stampa, 1966), 6–7.

82. Piero Calamandrei, *Diario 1939–1945*, vol. 1 (Florence: La Nuova Italia Editore, 1982), 48. Entry for 18 June 1939.

83. Quotations from Galeazzo Ciano, *Diario 1937–1943* (Rome: Castelvecchi, 2014), 188–90. Entries for 6–9 May 1938.

84. *Una giornata particolare* (A Special Day, 1977), directed by Ettore Scola and starring Sophia Loren and Marcello Mastroianni, is the story of a brief love affair between a homosexual anti-fascist journalist and a Roman housewife who is married to an ardent fascist and has a brood of children. As Hitler and Mussolini parade through the streets, what life under Fascism meant for women and non-conformists is deftly revealed.

85. Ciano, *Diario 1937–1943*, 361. Entry for 25 May 1939.

86. For numbers, see the informative website on the question maintained by the province of Bozen/Bolzano: https://www.provinz.bz.it/pariserv ertrag/accordo/antefatti.asp

87. In the immediate post-war period, marriages between the children of the *optanti* and those who had remained were very rare. The stigma of having become Italian was real.

88. Emilio Gentile, 'Fascism as a Political Religion', *Journal of Contemporary History*, 25 (1990), 248.

89. Mussolini, 'Doctrine of Fascism', 170.

2. INTO THE ABYSS

1. Piero Calamandrei, *Il fascismo come regime della menzogna* (Bari-Rome: Laterza, 2014), 64.

2. Piero Calamandrei, *Diario 1939–1945*, vol. 1 (Florence: La Nuova Italia, 1982), 72–73. Entry for 2 September 1939.

3. Ciano, *Diario 1937–1943*, 513.

4. 'GUERRA!', *Tempo* (13 June 1940).

5. Ibid.

6. Ibid.

7. Piero Melograni, *Italia in guerra. 10 giugno 1940* (Venice: Marsilio, 2010), 7.

8. 'Il duplice problema', *Gerarchia*, vol. XIX, no. 7 (July 1940), 344–5.

9. Pietro Nenni, *Vent'anni di fascismo* (Milan: Edizioni *Avanti!*, 1965), 255. Entry for 10 June 1940.

10. Calamandrei, *Diario 1939–1945*, vol. 1, 153. Entry for 27 April 1940.

11. *Come Cartagine* (Rome: Ufficio Propaganda del PNF, 1941), 1–5 for quotations.

12. Giorgio Candeloro, *Storia dell'Italia moderna. Volume decimo* (Milan: Feltrinelli, 1986), 70.

13. Giorgio Rochat, 'Mussolini: Chef de guerre (1940–1943)', *Revue d'histoire de la Deuxième Guerre mondiale*, no. 100 (October 1975), 58.

14. See *Il Fronte greco* (Rome: Ufficio Propaganda del PNF, 1941), 19–23.

15. Benito Mussolini, *Parlo con Bruno* (Roma: Edizione Il Popolo d'Italia, 1941). The front cover featured Bruno with a flying helmet and goggles.

16. R. J. B. Bosworth, *Mussolini* (London: Arnold, 2002), 386.

17. A point made by Rochat, 'Mussolini', 64.

18. *L'Unità* (7 November 1942).

19. Benito Mussolini, speech to the Camere dei Fasci e delle Corporazioni (2 December 1942), 1175.

20. 'Un resoconto di Himmler sulla sua visita a Mussolini dall'11 al 14 ottobre 1942', *Il movimento di liberazione in Italia*, no. 47 (1957), 49–52. Mussolini told Himmler that the 20 million people living in the cities were 'genuinely suffering from hunger'.

21. Umberto Massola, *Gli scioperi del 43. Marzo–Aprile: Le fabbriche contro il fascismo* (Rome: Edizioni Riuniti, 1973), 20.

22. *Sommario di statistiche storiche dell'Italia*, 1861–1965 (Rome: Istituto Centrale di Statistica, 1968), 138.

23. Paolo Spriano, 'Gli scioperi del marzo 1943', *Studi Storici*, vol. 13, no. 4 (1972), 729.

24. Massola, *Gli scioperi*, 30. Massola was editor of the clandestine edition of *l'Unità* in Milan in 1943.

25. *L'Unità* (20 February 1943), 1.

26. 'La crisi del PNF e il Fronte nazionale', *l'Unità* (20 December 1942).

27. 'Belve hitleriane'. I have translated the word 'belve' as 'animals' since it conveys ferocity more than the obvious translation, 'beasts'.

28. 'Evviva il venticinquesimo anniversario della rivoluzione sovietica', *l'Unità* (7 November 1942).

29. 'Una pace separata e immediata', *l'Unità* (31 January 1943). The call for 'armed and disciplined squads' was made in the 27 December 1942 edition.

30. Testimony of Carlo Pelotta, a factory worker from Turin, in Massola, *Gli scioperi*, 74. Strike statistics from ibid., 165–8.

31. David W. Ellwood, *Italy 1943–1945* (Leicester: Leicester University Press, 1985), 13.

32. Oreste Lizzadri, *Il Regno di Badoglio* (Milan: Edizioni *Avanti!*, 1963), 68–9. Entry for 3 April, 1943.

33. Palmiro Togliatti, *Da Radio Milano Libertà* (Rome: Rinascita, 1974), 98–9. Togliatti's original Italian word was 'scalzacane', literally, 'dog-kicker'. It confers an idea of sullenness.

34. Mauro Canali and Clemente Volpini, *Mussolini e i ladri di regime. Gli arricchimenti illeciti del fascismo* (Milan: Mondadori, 2019), 164.

35. Elena Aga Rossi, *Una Nazione allo sbando. L'armistizio italiano del settembre 1943* (Bologna: Il Mulino, 1993, 1st edn), 49.

36. Benito Mussolini, *Il tempo del bastone e della carota. Storia di un anno (ottobre 1942–settembre 1943)* (Milan: Edizioni FPE, 1966), 41, citing *The Times*. This book was originally published in instalments by the *Corriere della Sera* in June–July 1944.

37. *Morti e dispersi per cause belliche negli anni 1940–1945* (Rome: Istituto Centrale di statistica, 1957), 8.

38. F. W. Deakin, *The Brutal Friendship: Mussolini, Hitler and the Fall of Italian Fascism* (New York: Harper & Row, 1962), 407–8.

39. Mussolini, *Il tempo del bastone e della carota*, 47.

40. https://www.archivioluce.com/2018/07/17/19-luglio-1943-bombe-su-roma

41. Mussolini, *Il tempo del bastone e della carota*, 56.

42. Ibid., 58. The most balanced account of the meeting of the Grand Council is Emilio Gentile, *25 luglio 1943* (Rome: Laterza, 2018).

43. Mussolini, *Il tempo del bastone e della carota*, 63.

44. See Deakin, *The Brutal Friendship*, 337–45, for an excellent survey of Victor Emmanuel's conversations.

45. Calamandrei, *Diario 1939–1945*, vol. 2, 156. Entry for 2 August 1943.

46. Sergio Luzzatto, *Il Corpo di Mussolini* (Turin: Einaudi, 2019), 48.

47. Pietro Ingrao, *Volevo la luna* (Turin: Einaudi, 2006), 115.

48. The programme was published in *l'Unità* (27 July 1943).

49. Togliatti, *Radio Milano Libertà* (27 July 1943), 347.

50. Giorgio Bocca, *La repubblica di Mussolini* (Bari-Rome: Laterza, 1977), 3.

51. Aldo Agosti, 'Mauro Scoccimarro', in *Il Movimento operaio italiano. Dizionario biografico*, vol. 3, eds. Franco Andreucci and Tommaso Detti (Roma: Riuniti, 1977), 584.

52. Umberto Terracini, *Intervista sul comunismo difficile* (Bari-Roma: Laterza, 1978), 117.

53. Ibid., 128.

54. See Silvio Pons, *I comunisti italiani e gli altri. Visioni e legami internazionali nel mondo del Novecento* (Turin: Einaudi, 2021), 57–8. The quotation from Stalin is on p. 71.

55. Elena Dundovich, 'Nel Grande Terrore. Togliatti dirigente dell'Internazionale comunista tra le due guerre', in *Togliatti nel suo tempo*, eds. Roberto Gualtieri, Carlo Spagnolo, and Ermanno Taviani (Rome: Carocci, 2007), 141.

56. Togliatti claimed that he arrived in Spain only in July 1937. His (critical) biographer Giorgio Bocca was convinced, by Spanish Republican sources, that Togliatti arrived in Valencia at the end of August 1936. 'Witch-hunt' quotation from Pons, *I comunisti italiani e gli altri*, 72, who dates Togliatti's arrival in Spain to August 1937.

57. Ibid., 76.

58. Text of the Political Declaration in Luciano Guerci, ed., *Il partito socialista italiano dal 1919 al 1946* (Bologna: Cappelli Editore, 1969), 199–204.

59. Pietro Nenni, *Tempo di Guerra Fredda*, 32, for a succinct expression of this dual conviction. Entry for 26 August 1943.

60. C. F. Delzell, 'Il Fuoriuscitismo Italiano dal 1922 al 1943', *Il movimento di liberazione in Italia*, no. 23 (1953), 27.

61. Alexander De Grand, 'To Learn Nothing and to Forget Nothing: Italian Socialism and the Experience of Exile Politics, 1935–45', *Contemporary European History*, vol. 14, no. 4 (2005), 553.

62. See Nenni, *Tempo di Guerra Fredda*, 13–19, for his grim journey to Ponza, after his arrest in France and extradition to Nazi Germany.

63. See Giovanni De Luna, *Il Partito della resistenza. Storia del Partito d'Azione, 1942-47* (Turin: UTET, 2021, 4th edn), 7.

64. *L'Italia Libera*, no. 1 (January 1943), 3–4.

65. Ugo La Malfa, *Scritti 1925–1953* (Milan: Mondadori, 1988), 105–9, quotations from pp. 108 and 109.

66. Piero Craveri, *De Gasperi* (Bologna: Il Mulino, 2006), 125, citing a June 1944 letter from Don Sturzo to Alcide De Gasperi.

67. Candeloro, *Storia dell'Italia moderna*, vol. X, 162.

68. For this period in De Gasperi's life, see Giorgio Tupini, *De Gasperi: Una Testimonianza* (Bologna: Il Mulino, 1992), 25–46; Maria Romana Catti De Gasperi, *De Gasperi: Uomo Solo* (Milan: Mondadori, 1964), ch. VI passim; Alberto Melloni, 'Alcide De Gasperi alla biblioteca vaticana', in *Alcide De Gasperi. Un percorso europeo*, eds. Eckhart Conze, Gustavo Corni, and Paolo Pombeni (Bologna: Il Mulino, 2005), 141–68.

69. 'Demofilo', 'Le idee ricostruttive della Democrazia Cristiana', in *Atti e documenti della Democrazia cristiana* (Rome: Edizioni Cinque Lune, 1959), 12–15.

70. Alcide De Gasperi, letter, 10 September 1943, to Sergio Paronetto, Istituto Luigi Sturzo (henceforth ILS), Fondo Bartolotta, vol. 1 (1943), 40–41.

71. Togliatti, *Da Radio Milano Libertà*, 349–50, broadcasts on 31 July and 3 August 1943.

72. *L'Unità*, 'Pace', (4 August 1943).

73. Elena Aga Rossi, *Una nazione allo sbando*, 69.

74. Lutz Klinkhammer, *L'Occupazione tedesca in Italia, 1943–45* (Turin: Bollati Boringhieri, 1993), 30.

75. Togliatti, *Da Radio Milano Libertà*, 360.

76. 'O Badoglio fa la pace, o Badoglio deve andarsene', *Avanti!* (3 September 1943).

77. Rudolf Rahn, *Ambasciatore di Hitler a Vichy e Salò* (Milan: Res Gestae, 2019), 265.

78. Aga Rossi, *Una nazione allo sbando*, 79–80.

79. Fulvio Cammerano, 'La fuga dei Savoia: una scommessa obbligata', in *Ottosettembre 1943: le storie e le storiografie*, ed. Alberto Melloni (Reggio Emilia: Diabasis, 2005), 20–21.

80. Aga Rossi, *Una nazione allo sbando*, 119–21, for the king's flight.

81. Ibid., 125.

82. *L'Italia Libera*, 'Tradimento' (15 September 1943).

83. The number, long estimated at 9,000, has been reassessed by Elena Aga Rossi, *Cefalonia. La resistenza, l'eccidio, il mito* (Bologna: Il Mulino, 2018), as being between 1,800 and 2,500. It remains the largest single massacre of Italians by Germans during the Second World War. Klinkhammer, *L'Occupazione tedesca*, p. 39, puts the number at 5,170.

84. Klinkhammer, *L'Occupazione tedesca*, 38–9.

85. Nenni, *Tempo di Guerra Fredda*, 37. Entry for 9 September 1943.

86. A Neapolitan word meaning, literally, 'urchins'; more generally, 'street youth'.

87. See Sergio Benvenuti, *La patria incerta: contributi per una biografia di Adolfo De Bertolini* (Trento: Museo Storico, 2013), for a balanced account of this controversial figure.

88. Bocca, *La repubblica di Mussolini*, 19.

89. Ibid., 21.

90. Deakin, *A Brutal Friendship*, 560.

91. 'I tedeschi e i fascisti complottano contro nostro paese', *l'Unità* (7 September 1943).

92. Calamandrei, *Diario 1939–1945*, vol. 2, 207. Entry for 23 September 1943.

3. THE EMERGENCE OF THE PARTIES

1. Max Ascoli, 'Italy: An Experiment in Reconstruction', *Annals of the American Academy of Political and Social Science*, vol. 234 (July 1944), 37.

2. He is usually referred to by the diminutive of his name: 'Meuccio'.

3. *l'Italia Libera*, no. 9 (25 September 1943).

4. *l'Italia Libera*, no. 11 (17 October 1943).

5. 'Strumento di resa dell'Italia', *Documenti diplomatici italiani*, decima serie (1943–48), vol. I (9 settembre 1943–11 dicembre 1944) (henceforth: DDI (10), vol. 1), doc. 20.

6. David W. Ellwood, *Italy 1943–1945* (Leicester: Leicester University Press, 1984), 40.

7. Harold Macmillan, *War Diaries: Politics and War in the Mediterranean*, January 1943–May 1945 (London: Macmillan, 1984), 238–44, for the surrender talks. Macmillan notes, 244, 'After the conference, we had an excellent lunch (Italians excluded!) on H.M.S. Nelson.'

8. For the transcript of Eisenhower's conference with Badoglio, see DDI (10), vol. 1, doc. 21.

9. Pierre Guillen, 'Les Français et la Résistance italienne', *Revue d'histoire de la Deuxième Guerre mondiale et des conflits contemporains*, 36 (Juillet 1986), 82.

10. Ibid., 84.

11. Bob Moore, 'Enforced Diaspora: The Fate of Italian Prisoners of War during the Second World War', *War in History*, vol. 22, no. 2 (2015), 174–90. In September 1943, the British Empire alone held 315,966 prisoners who were mostly at work in the UK itself, in India (over 66,000), the Middle East, and East Africa. Some 4,600 were interned in Australia. Some remained as prisoners until the peace treaty was signed in 1947.

12. Quotations from Macmillan, *War Diaries*, 219 (entry for 16 September 1943) and 399 (entry for 27 March 1944).

13. Ivanoe Bonomi, *Diario di un anno* (Roma: Castelvecchio, 2014; orig. ed., 1947). Entry for 29 September 1943.

14. Rennell of Rodd, 'Allied Military Government in Occupied Territory', *International Affairs*, vol. 20, no. 3 (July 1944), 311–12.

15. Memorandum from Sergio Paronetto to Alcide De Gasperi (18 May 1944), ILS (Rome). Fondo Bartolotta (1944), vol. I, 51.

16. 'Il Partito comunista al popolo italiano', *l'Unità* (21 October 1943).

17. 'Il re fedifrago', *Avanti!* (27 September 1943). 'L'equivoco Badoglio', *Avanti!* (18 October 1943).

18. 'Niente unione nazionale con il re', *Avanti!* (15 October 1943).

19. Full text in Bonomi, *Diario di un anno* (16 October 1943).

20. Ibid. (1 November 1943).

21. DDI (10) vol. 1, docs. 115, 133.

22. Macmillan, *War Diaries*, 364. The British establishment regarded Sforza as an 'old peacock'.

23. DDI (10), vol. 1, doc. 130.

24. Antonio Varsori, 'La politica inglese e il conte Sforza (1941–1943)', *Rivista di Studi Politici Internazionali*, vol. 43, no. 1 (1976), 55–6.

25. Benedetto Croce, 'Risposte ad alcune domande', in Croce, *Per la nuova vita dell'Italia* (Naples: Riccardo Ricciardi Editore, 1944), 58. The questions were posed by a Reuters journalist, Cecil Sprigge, on 4 March 1944.

26. Bonomi, *Diario di un anno* (22 December 1943).

27. ILS (Rome). Text of a communiqué approved by the *direzione nazionale* of the DC (16 December 1943). Fondo Bortolotta (1943), vol. I, 68–9.

28. Giorgio Candeloro, *Storia dell'Italia moderna*, vol. X (Milan: Feltrinelli, 1984), 236.

29. Oreste Lizzadri, *Il Regno di Badoglio* (Milan: Edizioni Avanti! 1963), 140.

30. Carlo Sforza, 'Processo a Vittorio Emanuele', in *Dalla Monarchia alla Repubblica*, ed. Enzo Santarelli (Rome: Riuniti, 1974), 96–8.

31. See De Luna, *Il Partito della resistenza*, 131; Aurelio Lepre, *La svolta di Salerno* (Rome: Riuniti, 1966), 40, prints the motion in full. An executive committee, including Croce and Sforza, was selected by the Congress, but its subsequent role was marginal.

32. For an interesting account of the PdA's position on the constitutional question after the Congress of Bari, see Riccardo Bauer, 'Le attività del CLN in Roma nel maggio 1944', *Il Movimento di Liberazione in Italia*, no. 50 (1957), 57–83.

33. *HC Deb* (22 February 1944), vol. 397, cols. 690–92. It was a metaphor he had originally used in conversation with Macmillan. See Macmillan, *War Diaries*, 361, entry for 13 January 1944.

34. See 'Memorandum by the Executive Junta of the Italian Committee of Liberation to the Chief Commissioner of the Allied Control Committee for Italy (MacFarlane)', 18 February 1944, FRUS 1944, The British Commonwealth and Europe, vol. 3, doc. 948.

35. Elena Aga Rossi, 'La politica degli Stati Uniti verso il governo Badoglio', in Aga Rossi, *L'Italia tra le grandi potenze. Dalla Seconda guerra mondiale alla guerra fredda* (Bologna: Il Mulino, 2019), 91–2.

36. The British prime minister to President Roosevelt, 13 March 1944, FRUS 1944, The British Commonwealth and Europe, vol. 3, doc. 962.
37. Giulio Andreotti, *De Gasperi e il suo tempo* (Milan: Rizzoli, 1956), 141. Nenni good-naturedly turned the music down when asked.
38. Contacts with the USSR were initiated during Vyshinsky's visit in January by Renato Prunas, Secretary General of the Foreign Ministry, DDI 10 (1), docs. 118-19, both 12 January 1944. Prunas suggested that Soviet recognition of Italy would lead to the PCI's current 'violently anti-governmental' line being modified to a less 'sterile' position. Such a change in the PCI's position, Prunas hinted, would 'probably lead' to a 'more widely based' democratic government.
39. The irony is Bonomi's, *Diario di un anno* (7 April 1944).
40. Luigi Cortesi, 'Palmiro Togliatti, la "svolta di Salerno" e l'eredità gramsciana', *Belfagor*, vol. 30, no. 1 (1975), 1-44, quotations pp. 22 and 24.
41. 'Sotto la guida del compagno Ercoli, Il Partito Comunista propone la formazione di un governo appoggiato da tutti i partiti che sono per la guerra contro il nazismo', *l'Unità* (10 April 1944).
42. Giorgio Bocca, *Togliatti* (Milan: Feltrinelli, 2014), 321.
43. See *The Diary of Georgi Dimitrov, 1933-1949*, ed. Ivo Banac (New Haven: Yale University Press, 2003), 303-4; Michail M. Narinskj, 'Togliatti, Stalin e la svolta di Salerno', *Studi storici*, vol. 35, no. 3 (1994), 657-66; Elena Aga Rossi and Victor Zaslavsky, *Togliatti e Stalin. Il PCI e la politica estera staliniana negli archivi di Mosca* (Bologna: Il Mulino, 1997, 2nd edn), 64-74. The publication of these works, especially *Togliatti e Stalin*, led to polemic from scholars historically close to the PCI. There is no space here to discuss this *Historikerstreit*; Gianluca Fantoni, 'After the Fall: Politics, the Public Use of History and the Historiography of the Italian Communist Party, 1991-2011', *Journal of Contemporary History*, vol. 49, no. 4 (2014), 815-36, gives an able overview of this and other controversies regarding recent historiography on the PCI.
44. One scholar of the PCI (and biographer of Togliatti), Giorgio Agosti, insists that Ercoli influenced Stalin's decision: Agosti, 'Togliatti', *Dizionario della Resistenza*, vol. II (Turin: Einaudi, 2002), 654. Paolo Pombeni, *Sinistre. Un secolo di divisioni* (Bologna: Il Mulino, 2021), 57, recently described the Kremlin meeting as an 'interview' in which there was an 'encounter between two positions'. Meetings with Stalin in the Kremlin at three in the morning were less interlocutory than these formulations suggest.
45. Palmiro Togliatti (Ercoli), *La politica di unità nazionale dei comunisti. Rapporto dei quadri della organizzazione comunista napoletana*, 11 aprile 1944 (Federazione Milanese del PCI, 1944), 8.

46. Ibid., 7.

47. Ibid., 3.

48. 'The American Representative on the Advisory Council for Italy (Murphy) to the Secretary of State' (10 April 1944), FRUS 1944, The British Commonwealth and Europe, vol. 3, doc. 1005.

49. Pietro Nenni, *Tempo di Guerra Fredda, Diari 1943–1956* (Milan: SugarCo, 1981), (2 April 1944), 62.

50. Ibid. (21 April 1944), 70.

51. Ibid. (7 April 1944), 64.

52. Meeting of the *Direzione nazionale* of the DC (5 April 1944), ILS, Fondo Bartolotta (1944), vol. I, 25.

53. De Luna, *Il Partito della resistenza*, 158–63. The two *azionisti* were Adolfo Omodeo and Alberto Tarchiani, who became ministers of education and public works, respectively.

54. 'Un esordio falso e pericoloso', *l'Italia Libera* (19 April 1944).

55. Quoted in Guillen, 'Les Français et la Résistance italienne', 86. De Gaulle's original French is 'radicalement débarrassée du fascisme'.

56. Leo Valiani, *Sessant'anni di avventure e di battaglie* (Milan: Rizzoli, 1983), 109–10.

57. See Ellwood, *Italy 1943–1945*, 96, for Mason–MacFarlane's report and Churchill's angry reaction.

58. Macmillan, *War Diaries*, 468.

59. In a speech at Rome's Teatro Brancaccio (23 July 1944). ILS, Fondo Bartolotta (1944), vol. II, 102.

60. Fabrizio Onofri, quoted in Nello Ajello, *Intellettuali e PCI 1944/58* (Roma: Laterza, 2018, 8th ed.), 37. In the 1950s, Onofri would become head of the PCI's propaganda section and a member of the Central Committee. He became Togliatti's most outspoken critic after the PCI applauded the Soviet intervention in Budapest in November 1956. He was subsequently expelled from the party. In 1944, he was a young writer and translator who was an active member of the resistance.

61. Nenni, *Tempo di Guerra Fredda*, 85. Entry for 12 June 1944.

62. Italian troops in French camps were only liberated following a Franco-Italian agreement of 29 October 1945, six months after the war had ended.

63. 'Memorandum by the President of the Italian Council of Ministers (Bonomi) for the Secretary of State', FRUS 1944, vol. III, doc. 1060 (22 July 1944). The Italian original is printed in DDI (10), vol. 1, appendix to doc. 303.

64. Speech at Rome's Teatro Brancaccio (23 July 1944). ILS, Fondo Bartolotta (1944), vol. II, 107.

65. Decreto-legge luogotenenziale 25 June 1944, n. 151. Art. 1. The law came into force on 8 July.

66. Davide Lajolo, *Di Vittorio. Il volto umano di un rivoluzionario* (Milan: Bompiani, 1972), 91.

67. From 3,000 to almost 30,000, including some 5,000 applicants still being vetted. New PCI members became 'candidates' who had to prove their dedication to the cause before being given 'tenure'. Enrico Minio, 'Organizzazione Romana dopo la liberazione della capitale', in *Al lavoro per la conquista della democrazia*, Relazioni della conferenza provinciale della federazione comunista di Roma (Rome: PCI, 1944), 11.

68. Eugenio Reale, 'Comunisti e Cattolici', *Rinascita*, vol. I, no. 1 (June 1944), 18.

69. Luciano Canfora, *La metamorfosi* (Bari-Rome: Laterza, 2021), 31.

70. Palmiro Togliatti (Ercoli), *Per la libertà d'Italia. Per la creazione di un vero regime democratico* (Rome: PCI, 1944), 9. Togliatti caused 'hilarity' by thanking the audience for the demonstration which, he added deadpan, he 'had done nothing to provoke'.

71. Ibid., 11.

72. Ibid., 15.

73. 'E sia'. A freer translation would be 'If they say so'.

74. I am quoting the typescript of the speech in ILS, Fondo Bartolotta (1944), vol. II, 119.

75. For a sophisticated statement of these intellectuals' ideas, see Franco Rodano, 'Democrazia progressiva' *Rinascita*, vol. I, no. 4 (1944), 12–16.

76. De Gasperi, Brancaccio Theatre speech, ILS, Fondo Bartolotta (1944), vol. II, 123–5.

77. See Pietro Scoppola, *La proposta politica di De Gasperi* (Bologna: Il Mulino, 1977), 59–91 passim.

78. De Gasperi, Brancaccio Theatre speech, ILS, Fondo Bartolotta (1944), vol. II, 113.

79. Letter to A. De Gasperi, 9 September 1944, in Palmiro Togliatti, *La guerra di posizione in Italia. Epistolario 1944–1964* (Turin: Einaudi, 2014), ed. Gianluca Fiocco and Maria Luisa Righi, 27.

80. A. De Gasperi to Togliatti (12 September 1944), in ibid., 28–9.

81. *L'Unità* (10 January 1944), 2.

82. The same (June 1944) edition of *Rinascita* that appealed for Catholic–Communist cooperation also featured a five-column, 3,000-word, hagiographic article on the political infallibility of Stalin that has almost liturgical overtones. Mario Montagna, 'Il Maresciallo Stalin', *Rinascita*, vol. I, no. 1 (June 1944), 11–13.

4. RESISTANCE AND LIBERATION

1. Norberto Bobbio, 'Cittadini, torinesi, uomini e donne della Resistenza' (25 April 1957), speech on the 11th anniversary of the liberation of Turin, reprinted in *Eravamo diventati uomini: testimonianze e discorsi sulla Resistenza in Italia, 1955–1999* (Turin: Einaudi, 2015), 21.

2. A point made to me by Elena Aga Rossi in the conversations preparatory to our joint publication, 'Against the Current: An Interview with Elena Aga Rossi', *Journal of Modern Italian Studies*, vol. 27, no. 4 (2022), 485–503.

3. 'Avanti, per la battaglia insurrezionale', *La Nostra Lotta*, vol. 2, no. 10 (June 1944), 4.

4. *Repubblicani* are supporters of a popular republic rather than a monarchy. The 'chini' suffix applied to Mussolini's followers gives an idea of pettiness.

5. See Mimmo Franzinelli, *Storia della Repubblica Sociale Italiana. 1943–1945* (Bari-Rome: Laterza, 2020), 70.

6. 'Le linee maestre del nuovo Stato popolare nel Manifesto del Partito repubblicano fascista', *Corriere della Sera* (17 November 1943). The Manifesto is reproduced as an appendix in Marino Viganò, *Il Congresso di Verona. Un'antologia di documenti e testimonianze* (Rome: Settimo Sigillo, 1994), 211–15.

7. A brief account of Ciano's life that concludes with film clips from the trial and execution can be seen at https://archivio.quirinale.it

8. Angelo Tarchi, *Teste dure* (Milan: Edizioni SELC, 1967), 72. Ambassador Rahn had to dissuade the Duce from writing a posthumous article praising his son-in-law's achievements. Rudolf Rahn, *Ambasciatore a Vichy e Salò* (Milan: Res Gestae, 2019), 295.

9. Tarchi, *Teste dure*, 71. Tarchi has the bad habit for a memorialist of remembering complex conversations word for word.

10. Aurelio Lepre, *La storia della repubblica di Mussolini. Salò: Il tempo dell'odio e della violenza* (Milan: Mondadori, 1999), 125.

11. Point 7 of the Manifesto: 'All those who belong to the Jewish race are foreigners. During this war they belong to an enemy nationality.'

12. These paragraphs are based on Giacomo Debenedetti, *16 ottobre 1943* (Turin: Einaudi, 2015). A classic of Holocaust literature in Italian, the text was originally published in December 1944 in the magazine *Mercurio*.

13. Franzinelli, *Storia della Repubblica Sociale Italiana, 1943–1945*, 417 and 419.

14. Luciano Casali, 'La deportazione dall'Italia. Fossoli di Carpi', in *Spostamenti di popolazioni e deportazioni in Europa 1939–1945*, ed. Rinaldo Falcioni (Bologna: Cappelli, 1987), 382.

15. 'L'arresto di tutti gli ebrei', *Corriere della Sera* (1 December 1943). *La Stampa*'s headline on 1 December was 'Tutti gli ebrei inviati a campi di concentramento'. The paper described Italy's Jews as a cancer.

16. For the estimate of 5,000 deportees, which depends upon a calculation using bread rations, see Casali's excellent chapter, 'La deportazione dall'Italia. Fossoli di Carpi', 391–5.

17. Franzinelli, *Storia della Repubblica Sociale Italiana, 1943–1945*, 412–13.

18. Ibid., 457; Luigi Ganapini, 'The Dark Side of Italian History, 1943–1945', *Modern Italy*, vol. 12, no. 2 (2007), 215.

19. Giovanni Preziosi, 'Gli ebrei hanno voluto la guerra', in *Gli ebrei hanno voluto la guerra* (Florence: Vallecchi, 1942), 45.

20. See Luca Menconi, 'Il complottismo come categoria interpretativa: Giovanni Preziosi e la minaccia pangermanica', *Studi Storici*, vol. 57, no. 1 (2016), 111–36, for both Preziosi's interventionism in 1915 and the notion, borrowing from the American historian Richard Hofstadter, of a 'paranoid style' in Italian politics.

21. Giovanni Guareschi, *Diario clandestino 1943–1945* (Milan: Biblioteca Universale Rizzoli, 2012), 162. Entry for 31 January 1945.

22. See Claudio Sommaruga, 'Quanto dura uno "Schiavo di Hitler"', *Rassegna dell'Associazione nazionale dei reduci della prigionia*, vol. 24, nos. 1–2 (2002), 9.

23. Mauro Cereda, *Storie dei lager. I militari italiani internati dopo l'8 settembre* (Rome: Edizioni Lavoro, 2004), 28.

24. *Uomini e tedeschi. Scritti e disegni dei deportati*, ed. Armando Borrelli and Anacleto Benedetti (Milan: Casa di Arosio, 1947).

25. Mario Ghidini, 'Uomini e tedeschi', in ibid., 256–7.

26. See Giovanni Guareschi, 'Storia della famosa Caterina', *Oggi*, no. 11 (1946).

27. Guareschi, *Diario clandestino 1943–1945*, ix–x.

28. For the IMI prisoners' courage, see, in English, Janet Sanders, 'Debunking the Cliché of Italian Military Cowardice: The Italian Military Internees and Guareschi', *Journal of Modern Italian Studies*, vol. 21, no. 5 (2016), 747–63.

29. The first few houses of Via del Boccaccio, a side street off Via Rasella, are pockmarked with bullet holes to this day. So far as I can see, they are the only memorial to the partisans' action.

30. Quoted in Alessandro Portelli, *L'ordine è già stato eseguito. Roma, le Fosse Ardeatine, la memoria* (Roma: Donzelli, 2019), 192.

31. 'Allegedly', because we know of Hitler's order only from the testimony of the Nazi commanders at post-war trials during which they claimed they were only 'obeying orders'.

32. After consultation with the minister of the interior of the RSI, Buffarini Guidi. Caruso was captured shortly after the liberation of Rome and shot, after a perfunctory trial, on 22 September 1944.

33. For biographical details of all the victims, see the website of the Fosse Ardeatine mausoleum: https://www.mausoleofosseardeatine.it

34. This is the theme of Roberto Rossellini's magnificent film, *Roma Città aperta*, which was made in 1945, when the wounds were still fresh.

35. Quotations from Portelli, *L'ordine è già stato eseguito*, 4 and 206.

36. 'Un appello del CLN', *L'Italia Libera* (19 April 1944).

37. See 'Discorso agli italiani,' in Giovanni Gentile, *Dal discorso agli italiani alla morte* (Rome: Senato della Repubblica, 2004), 72–3.

38. Ibid., 68 and 70.

39. Gian Enrico Rusconi, *Resistenza e postfascismo* (Bologna: Il Mulino, 1995), 58.

40. For Rahn's role, see Lutz Klinkhammer, *L'Occupazione tedesca in Italia, 1943–45* (Turin: Bollati Boringhieri, 1993), 106–9.

41. Mirko Giobbe, 'Gli Ebrei', *La Nazione* (20–21 February 1944), cited in Matteo Mazzoni, 'La Repubblica sociale italiana in Toscana', in *Storia della resistenza in Toscana*, vol. I, ed. Marco Palla (Rome: Carocci, 2006), 159.

42. See Valeria Galimi, 'Persecuzioni antiebraiche a Firenze: dalla guerra alla Shoah', in *Firenze in guerra 1940–1944*, ed. Francesca Cavarocchi and Valeria Galimi (Florence: Firenze University Press, 2014), 85–7.

43. Camilla Brunelli, 'La deportazione politica a Firenze e in Toscana', in ibid., 82.

44. Enrico Minio, 'Organizzazione Romana dopo la liberazione della capitale', in *Al lavoro per la conquista della democrazia*, Relazioni della conferenza provinciale della federazione comunista di Roma (Rome: PCI, 1944), 6.

45. *L'Unità* (21 October 1943), 2.

46. Tristano Codignola, *La Libertà* (20 April 1944). Reprinted in *Il Ponte*, vol. 50, no. 4 (April 1994), 151–3.

47. Piero Calamandrei, *Diario 1939–1945, vol. 2, 1942–1945* (Florence: La Nuova Italia Editrice, 1982), 407. Entry for 17 April 1944.

48. Concetto Marchesi, 'Sentenza di morte', *Rinascita*, vol. I, no. 2 (July 1944), 6.

49. Ibid., 6.

50. Luigi Longo, *Un popolo alla macchia* (Milan: Edizioni Res Gestae, 2013, orig. edn, 1947), 96.

51. See *l'Unità* (10 May 1944).

52. 'Attesismo', *Il Combattente* (Tuscany) (7 December 1943), 2. Italics in the original.

53. 'Partigiane e combattenti dei popoli liberi: donne d'Italia seguiamole', *La nostra lotta* (March 1944), 10.

54. The great, but often controversial, historian Renzo De Felice insisted that temporizing had been the position of most Italians in occupied Italy (hence, presumably, the PCI's campaign against it). The 'overwhelming majority of the Italians . . . not only avoided taking a clear position in favour of the Resistance, but shrewdly avoided taking sides with the RSI, too'. For De Felice, there had been a 'great grey zone composed of all those who managed to survive between two fires'. Renzo De Felice, *Rosso e Nero* (Milan: Baldini & Castoldi, 1995), 58–9. I'm grateful to Tommaso Milani for this reference.

55. For many years, it was politically incorrect to use this term since it implied that the entire Italian people was not unified against Mussolini and the Germans. The taboo was broken by Claudio Pavone, *Una guerra civile. Saggio sulla moralità nella Resistenza* (Turin: Bollati Boringhieri, 1991). Pavone was on the left politically. Had a historian reputed to be conservative done so, it would have caused a civil war among historians (I owe this insight to Elena Aga Rossi).

56. The RSI's main resource was the National Republican Guard, which was mostly composed of the former royal carabinieri. In June 1944, members of the PFR were enrolled in 'Black Brigades', in effect, 1920s-style *squadristi* that launched punitive raids against the rebels and those who harboured them.

57. This paragraph is a synthesis of the hundreds of gruesome accounts presented by Mimmo Franzinelli, *Tortura. Storie dell'occupazione nazista e della guerra civile (1943–45)* (Milan: Mondadori, 2018), chs. 1–5, pp. 9–192.

58. Quoted in ibid., 109.

59. See Fondo Piero Calamandrei, Istituto Storico Toscano della Resistenza e della Storia Contemporanea (ISTR), Busta 7, Fascicolo 4. The stories of Irma Bandiera and the Zebri sisters can also be found in an interesting pamphlet published on the tenth anniversary of the end of the war: Renata Viganò, *Donne della resistenza* (Bologna: STEB, 1955).

60. These statistics come from the website of the *Associazione nazionale dei partigiani* (ANPI). https://www.anpi.it/donne-e-uomini-della-resistenza

61. Longo, *Un popolo alla macchia*, 320.

62. Fondo Piero Calamandrei, op. cit. Iris Versari was awarded the gold medal for valour in April 1976.

63. Enrico Mattei, *L'apporto delle forze demo-cristiane alla guerra di liberazione* (Milan: Democrazia cristiana, 1946), estimates on page 21 the total number of Christian Democrats who fought in the resistance as 65,000, of whom almost 2,000 were killed. All such contemporary accounts tend to inflate numbers, but the contribution of DC formations to the resistance war was greater than many realize.

64. For biographies of fifty partisan priests, see https://www.anpi.it/donne-e-uomini/status/religiosi

65. Gianni Oliva, *La Resistenza. Dall'armistizio alla liberazione* (Florence: Giunti, 2019), 101.

66. There is even a book on the subject: Franco Giannantoni and Ibio Paolucci, *La bicicletta nella resistenza* (Varese: Edizioni Arterigere, 2010).

67. Longo, *Un popolo alla macchia*, 106.

68. *L'Unità* (25 July 1944).

69. Santo Peli, *Storia della resistenza in Italia* (Turin: Einaudi, 2015), 87.

70. Pier Luigi Ballini, 'Qui gli alleati trovarono una nuova Italia', in *Firenze in guerra 1940–1944*, 119–28.

71. 'La nuova nazione', *La Nazione del Popolo* (12 August 1944).

72. 'L'Epurazione', *La Nazione del Popolo* (6–7 September 1944). Notice the repeated use of 'Fascism' and of a contorted sentence structure to emphasize the word 'totally'.

73. 'Sei mesi di attività partigiana nell'Emilia-Romagna', *Il Combattente* (Emilia-Romagna) (16 December 1944).

74. Peli, *Storia della resistenza*, 99.

75. Ibid., 101. For more extended treatment, see Giorgio Bocca, *Una repubblica partigiana. Ossola 10 settembre–23 ottobre 1944* (Rome: Il Saggiatore, 1965).

76. 'Il Proclama Alexander e l'atteggiamento della Resistenza all'inizio dell'inverno 1944–1945', *Il Movimento di Liberazione in Italia*, no. 26 (1953), 25–6.

77. 'Serrare le file e vincere ogni difficoltà per la vittoria dell'insurrezione nazionale,' *l'Unità* (25 November 1944).

78. Elena Aga Rossi, 'La politica anglo-americana verso la resistenza italiana', in Aga Rossi, *L'Italia tra le grandi potenze. Dalla seconda guerra mondiale alla guerra fredda* (Bologna: Il Mulino, 2019), 180.

79. Longo, *Un popolo alla macchia*, 153.
80. M. Elisabetta Tonizzi, 'Nazisti contro i civili: le stragi in Italia', *Storia e memoria*, vol. 9, no. 1 (2000), 147. The figure includes only massacres conducted by German troops and counts those with eight or more deaths. If one includes all murders, plus killings by RSI militia, the number would be far higher. Tonizzi points out that 30,000 people were killed in a few days at Babi Yar near Kiev in 1941.
81. The official figure cited in the Gold Medal for valour that was awarded to the villages in 1949 was 1,830, but this counts all those who fell during the war, including partisans, those who died in bombing raids etc. SS troops had shot approximately 500 people at Sant'Anna di Stazzema in Tuscany on 12 August.
82. A point made in *Marzabotto non dimentica Walter Reder*, ed. Nazario Sauro Onofri (Bologna: Grafica Levino Editore, 1985), 21.
83. 'Sterminare i traditori', *Bollettino di Partito*, special edition (March 1944), 43.
84. 'Discorso al Lirico' (16 December 1944), in *Benito Mussolini. Scritti e discorsi 1904–1945*, ed. David Bidussa (Milan: Feltrinelli, 2022), 625.
85. 'Un ultimo sforzo e sarà la vittoria', *l'Unità* (20 March 1945).
86. See Peli, *Storia della resistenza in Italia*, 170. The proclamation was reprinted by the principal party newspapers.
87. Nazario Sauro Onofri, *Il triangolo rosso, La Guerra di liberazione e la sconfitta del fascismo (1943–47)* (Rome: Sapere 2000, 2007), prints an Interior Ministry memorandum from November 1946 that puts the numbers of those killed after 25 April as 8,197 killed and 1,167 missing, presumed dead. Giorgio Bocca, *La Repubblica di Mussolini* (Bari-Rome: Laterza, 1977), 339, talks of 3,000 in Milan and 10,000–15,000 across the other provinces of the North.
88. An eight-minute silent black-and-white film containing shocking images can be found at https://patrimonio.archivioluce.com.
89. Gianni Oliva, *La resa dei conti. Aprile-maggio 1945: foibe, Piazzale Loreto e giustizia partigiana* (Milan: Mondadori, 1999), 34.

5. THE REPUBLIC

1. Giorgio Tupini, *De Gasperi. Una testimonianza* (Bologna: Il Mulino, 1992), 63.
2. Rosario Forlenza, 'Europe's Forgotten Unfinished Revolution: Peasant Power, Social Mobilization, and Communism in the Southern Italian

Countryside, 1943–45', *American Historical Review*, vol. 126, no. 2 (June 2021), 504–29. Quotation from p. 504.

3. Ibid., 522.
4. Herbert L. Matthews, 'Italian Monarchy Must Move Left, Crown Prince Humbert Declares', *New York Times* (1 November 1944).
5. *Bollettino del Partito*, vol. 1, nos. 4–5 (November–December 1944), 6.
6. See the front-page interview with Togliatti in *l'Unità* (12 December 1944). The interview was made an obligatory topic of discussion for party militants at all levels.
7. Minutes of a meeting of the representatives of the six parties, Rome (7 December 1944). In ILS, Fondo Bortolotta, (1944), vol. III, 240.
8. Decreto legislativo luogotenenziale, no. 23/45. *Gazzetta Ufficiale* (1 February 1945).
9. Palmiro Togliatti, *I comunisti nella lotta per la democrazia* (Milan: Casa Editrice L'Unità, 1945), 15.
10. Pietro Nenni, 'Vento del Nord', *Avanti!* (27 April 1945), 1.
11. Pietro Nenni, 'La Costituente all'ordine del giorno della nazione', in *Una battaglia vinta* (Rome: Leonardo, 1946), 27.
12. Ibid., 32. The Majella (more often spelled Maiella) are the mountains of the Abruzzi.
13. Minutes of a meeting between the CLN and the CLNAI (24 May 1945), ILS, Fondo Bartolotta (1945), vol. II, 116–20.
14. Ibid., 121.
15. Ibid., 123.
16. Letter from Alcide De Gasperi to the steering committee of the PSI (7 June 1945), in ibid., 139.
17. The best account is Elena Aga Rossi and Bradley F. Smith, *Operation Sunrise. La resa tedesca in Italia, 2 maggio 1945* (Milan: Mondadori, 2005). Parri's memoir, *Due mesi con i nazisti* (Rome: Carecas, 1973), is fascinating reading.
18. See the minutes of the *Direzione* of the PSIUP, Istituto storico toscano per la resistenza (ISTR), Foscolo Lombardi Archive (AFL), File b2, fascicolo 4 (12 June 1946).
19. Ibid. (15 June 1946).
20. Pietro Nenni, *Tempo di guerra fredda* (14 June 1945), 124, (24 November 1945), 156.
21. Ibid.
22. Antonio Gambino, *Storia del dopoguerra. Dalla Liberazione al potere DC* (Bari-Rome: Laterza, 1978), 116.
23. Sir Noel Charles, Rome to London, TNA FO 371 / ZM 3754 (30 June 1945).

24. The Acting Secretary of State to Rome (12 September 1945), FRUS, 1945, Europe, vol. 4, doc 932.

25. *I comunisti alla Consulta. Democrazia! Costituente! Unità!* (Rome: L'Unità, 1945), 28.

26. 'Verso la Costituente', *Rinascita*, vol. II, nos. 5–6 (1945), 130. See also 'Socialismo Liberale', *Rinascita*, vol. II, no. 3 (1945), 65–7, which attacked the Justice and Liberty tradition as anti-progressive.

27. Alessandro Natta, 'La resistenza e la formazione del 'partito nuovo', in *Problemi di storia del Partito comunista italiano* (Rome: Edizioni Riuniti/Istituto Gramsci, 1976), 57.

28. Reprinted in Sandro Setta, *L'Uomo Qualunque* (Bari-Rome: Laterza, 1975), 16.

29. For example, 'Domande e risposte', *l'Unità* (7 September 1944).

30. 'Dirigenti e militanti del tipo nuovo', *Bollettino del Partito*, vol. 1, no. 3 (October 1944), 8–9.

31. The publication of Antonio Gramsci's *Prison Notebooks* did not begin until 1947, but they had long been in Togliatti's possession. See Salvatore Vacca, *Il comunismo italiano. Una cultura politica del Novecento* (Roma: Carocci, 2021), 185–232, for a detailed account of how Togliatti obtained the manuscripts that Gramsci had written while incarcerated.

32. Giorgio Amendola, 'Pietà l'è morta', *l'Unità* (29 April 1945).

33. See Nazario Sauro Onofri, *Il triangolo rosso, La Guerra di liberazione e la sconfitta del fascismo* (1943–47) (Roma: Sapere 2000, 2007), 69–84 passim.

34. See Sara Morgan, 'The Schio Killings: A Case Study of Partisan Violence in Post-War Italy', *Modern Italy*, vol. 5, no. 2 (2000), 147–60, for an excellent discussion in English.

35. See Giampaolo Pansa, *Il sangue dei vinti* (Milan: Pickwick, 2013), 218–24, for a balanced account of the events at Schio, although the book has a reputation for sensationalism. The first, 2003, edition sold an astonishing 400,000 copies.

36. Francesca Grandi, 'Why Do the Victors Kill the Vanquished? Explaining Political Violence in Post-World War II Italy', *Journal of Peace Research*, vol. 50, no. 5 (2013), 588.

37. Leone Cattani, letter to the leaders of the CLN (29 May 1945), in ILS, Fondo Bartolotta (1945), vol. II, 127–8.

38. ILS, Fondo Bartolotta (1945), vol. II, 134.

39. All quotations in this paragraph from 'Epurare nell'ordine e nella legalità', *Bollettino del Partito*, vol. 2, nos. 5–6 (May–June 1945), 5–6.

40. Cesare Brunetti, 'Il borghese emiliano vive tra queste paure', *Il Risorgimento Liberale* (16 January 1946).

41. A famous example of such propaganda is *La seconda liberazione dell'Emilia* (Rome: Democrazia Cristiana, 1949).

42. See *Porzûs. Violenza e resistenza sul confine occidentale*, ed. Tommaso Piffer (Bologna: Il Mulino, 2012), especially the overview of the incident, and its historiographical reception, by Elena Aga Rossi. For a brief synthesis, see Raoul Pupo, *Trieste '45* (Bari-Rome: Laterza, 2010), 71–4.

43. Paolo Spriano, *Storia del Partito comunista italiano. La Resistenza. Togliatti e il partito nuovo* (Turin: Einaudi, 1975), 437.

44. Marina Cattaruzza, *L'Italia e il confine orientale* (Bologna: Il Mulino, 2007), 286–7.

45. Cattaruzza, *L'Italia e il confine orientale*, 293.

46. The most notorious *foiba* is that of Basovizza, https://www.foibadibasovizza.it, which is today a national monument.

47. See Raoul Pupo, *Trieste '45*, chapter IX passim.

48. This is an allusion to Alcide De Gasperi, 'Rispondo a Togliatti', *Il Popolo* (10 July 1945), in which De Gasperi uses the same metaphor.

49. Ennio di Nolfo and Maurizio Serra, *La Gabbia infranta. Gli alleati e l'Italia dal 1943 al 1945* (Bari-Rome: Laterza, 2010), ix–x.

50. There were 3,500 civilian deaths and 20,000 injured in accidents involving Allied vehicles between the Liberation and 30 November 1946. See Mario Avagliano and Marco Palmieri, *Dopoguerra. Gli italiani fra speranze e disillusioni (1945–1947)* (Bologna: Il Mulino, 2019), 144.

51. Ibid., 112–13.

52. *Verbali del Consiglio dei ministri. Governo Parri* (Roma: Presidenza del Consiglio dei ministri, 1994–98), ed. Aldo G. Ricci, vol. 1 (26 June 1945) (afternoon session), 12–13. I am applying the modern usage of billion in this book. The ministers said *miliardi*, i.e. 'milliards' (thousand million), a usage that has become uncommon in English.

53. Ibid. (3 August 1945), 202.

54. Ugo La Malfa, 'La rete ferroviaria unificata entro la prossima primavera', *L'Italia Libera* (5 November 1945), in La Malfa, *Scritti 1925–1953* (Milan: Mondadori, 1988), 312.

55. Ferruccio Parri, speech to the plenary session of the *Consulta Nazionale* (Wednesday, 26 September 1945), 6.

56. *Verbali del Consiglio dei ministri. Governo Parri* (9 August 1945), 238.

57. Guido Melis, 'Note sull'epurazione nei ministeri, 1944–1946', *Ventunesimo Secolo*, vol. 2, no. 4 (2003), 21.

58. See Roy Palmer Domenico, *Italian Fascists on Trial, 1943–48* (Chapel Hill, NC: North Carolina University Press, 1991).

59. Ferruccio Parri, speech to the plenary session of the *Consulta Nazionale* (Wednesday, 26 September 1945), 18.

60. I am basing this account of the crisis on a typescript copy of De Gasperi's own handwritten notes. ILS, Fondo Bartolotta (1945), vol. V, 356–72.

61. The meteorological detail is from Giuseppe Romita, *Dalla Monarchia alla Repubblica. Taccuino politico del '45* (Milan: Mursia, 1973), 3.

62. Anybody who has read the diaries of Falcone Lucifero, the minister for the Royal Household, will be struck by the febrile atmosphere during Parri's premiership among upper-class elites. It is easy to understand why Parri thought he had been the victim of a plot: there was plenty of plotting going on. Falcone Lucifero, *L'ultimo Re. I diari del ministro della Real Casa, 1944–46* (Milan: Mondadori, 2002).

63. ILS, Fondo Bartolotta (1945), vol. V, 374–6; see also Piero Cravero, *De Gasperi* (Bologna: Il Mulino, 2006), 201–2.

64. Ibid., 386.

65. Lucifero, *L'ultimo Re*, 457. Entry for 30 November 1945. De Gasperi had an explorative mandate until 3 December, when he began the concrete task of forming a cabinet.

66. Romita, *Dalla Monarchia alla Repubblica*, 6.

67. Ibid., 7.

68. Ibid., 14.

69. Ibid., 18.

70. Nenni, *Tempo di guerra fredda*, 162. Entry for 29 December 1945.

71. *Statuto del Partito Comunista Italiano* (Roma: PCI, 1946), Article 1, p. 5. The only trace of the old 'sectarian' revolutionary approach was Art. 40, which banned factionalism in no uncertain terms.

72. This account of the PCI's programme is a synthesis of 'Sotto la bandiera della democrazia. Il programma del PCI approvato al V congresso', *l'Unità* (January 1946), 1–10.

73. Mauro Scoccimarro, *La Costituente e il rinnovamento nazionale* (Rome: Edizioni *l'Unità*, 1946), 4–5. This pamphlet was the printed text of his speech to the 5th Congress.

74. 'Tutt'il popolo sotto la bandiera della democrazia', *l'Unità* (9 January 1946).

75. The ambassador in Italy (Kirk) to the Secretary of State (7 December 1946), FRUS, 1946, The British Commonwealth, Western and Central Europe, vol. 5, doc. 588.

76. Romita, *Dalla Monarchia alla Repubblica*, 80.

77. Ibid., 36.

78. Norberto Bobbio, 'Autogoverno e libertà politica', in Bobbio, *Tra due repubbliche. Alle origini della democrazia italiana* (Roma: Donzelli Editore, 1996), 105–6. Cited in Rosario Forlenza, 'Beppe, Tonio e le donne vanno a votare. L'educazione al voto per le elezioni amministrative del 46', *Dimensioni e problemi di ricerca storica*, 1/2008 (gennaio–giugno), 126.

79. This paragraph is based on Forlenza's excellent article 'Beppe, Tonio e le donne'.

80. *Noi Donne* (15 March 1946). Foglio speciale, 1–2.

81. Patrizia Gabrielli, *Il 1946, le donne, la Repubblica* (Rome: Donzelli, 2009), 67.

82. Pietro Nenni, 'I socialisti nella lotta per lo stato repubblicano', in *Una battaglia vinta* (Rome: Edizioni Leonardo, 1946), 113.

83. The three motions are reprinted in *Il Partito socialista nei suoi Congressi, vol. 5: 1952–1955*, ed. Franco Pedone (Milan: Edizioni Gallo, 1968), 84–91.

84. Nenni, 'I socialisti nella lotta per lo stato repubblicano', 119.

85. Ibid., 116.

86. Giuseppe Saragat, *Socialismo Democratico e Socialismo Totalitario. Per l'Autonomia del Partito Socialista* (Milan: Critica Sociale, 1946). Quotations, in order, 17, 21, 22.

87. Giovanni De Luna, *Il Partito della Resistenza. Storia del Partito d'Azione* (Turin: UTET, 2021), 325, says the split was only marginally due to divisions over policy and had much to do with 'personal overtones' and a general 'erosion' of the party's 'political patrimony'.

88. See Ugo La Malfa, 'Il problema politico della democrazia', speech to the PdA Conference, Rome (6 February 1946), in La Malfa, *Scritti 1925–1953*, 341–58.

89. The signatories of the MDR's manifesto included several eminent historians, the future Nobel laureate for literature Eugenio Montale, an acclaimed scholar of Islam, Giorgio Levi della Vida, the literary critic Carlo Muscetta, Bruno Pincherle, the editor of *L'Italia Libera*, and Altiero Spinelli, one of the founding fathers of the movement for European Unity.

90. Giuseppe Chiarante, *La Democrazia cristiana* (Rome: Riuniti, 1980), 34.

91. In the provincial assemblies preceding the Congress, 503,000 party members voted for the Republic, 146,000 for the monarchy, 187,000 for an agnostic position. Figures from Attilio Piccioni, 'Repubblica o Monarchia', *I Congressi nazionali della Democrazia cristiana* (Rome: Democrazia Cristiana, 1959), 67.

92. 'Messaggio della Democrazia cristiana agli italiani' (31 May 1946). Reprinted in Maurizio Ridolfi and Nicola Tranfaglia, *1946. La nascita della Repubblica* (Bari-Rome: Laterza, 1996), 103-5.

93. In *De Gasperi. Uomo Solo* (Milan: Mondadori, 1964), 213, De Gasperi's daughter Maria Romano reveals that, though her father certainly voted Republican, his wife and sister were monarchists.

94. All details from 'Organizzazione e forme della propaganda', internal PCI document reprinted in Ridolfi and Tranfaglia, *1946. La nascita della Repubblica*, 151-5.

95. See A. Marrani, *La Propaganda*, which was the first of a successful series of 'guides for propagandists' produced in 1945-6 ahead of the elections. The eighth booklet in the series, Augusto Del Noce's *Il voto obbligatorio*, makes the best case for compulsory voting that I have ever read. The whole set is available in the pamphlet collection of the ILS, *Guide del propagandista*, Cassetto 1, Fasc. 1, Sottofasc. 3.

96. Pius XII, 'Discorso ai partecipanti al convegno indetto dalla presidenza centrale della gioventù italiana di Azione cattolica', The Vatican (20 April 1946). https://www.vatican.va/content/pius-xii/it.html

97. Quoted Guido Crainz, *Storia della Repubblica. L'Italia dalla liberazione ad oggi* (Rome: Donzelli Editore, 2016), 41.

98. HM Vittorio Emanuele III to Umberto II, 9 May 1946, in *Libro azzuro sul 'referendum' 1946*, ed. Niccolò Rodlico e Vittorio Prunas-Tola (Turin: Superga, 1953), 40.

99. In fairness, they were worth 100 million lire.

100. The Istituto Luce newsreel gave a dramatic account of the sequence of events on 9-10 May. See https://www.youtube.com/watch?v=lrCHXt-xh2g

101. Lucifero, *L'ultimo Re*, 538. Entry for 20 May 1946.

102. Data from Ridolfi and Tranfaglia, *1946. La nascita della Repubblica*, 235-6.

103. Dino Messina, *2 giugno 1946. La battaglia per la Repubblica* (Milan: Corriere della Sera, 2016), 125.

104. Felice Platone, 'Panorama politica della Repubblica', *Rinascita*, vol. III, nos. 5-6 (1946), 99-103, blamed clerical interference and conspicuously avoided the topic of the PSIUP's relative victory.

105. Ibid., 101.

106. Romita, *Dalla Monarchia alla Repubblica*, 167.

107. Ibid.

108. Lucifero, *L'ultimo Re*, 545. Entry for 5 June 1946.

109. Letter from Enzo Selvaggi, secretary of the Italian Democratic Party (PDI), to De Gasperi, 8 June 1946. ILS, Fondo Bartolotta (1946), vol. XIV, 1234.

110. The final figure, communicated on 18 June, was Republic 12,718,461, Monarchy 10,718,502. In the end, there were 1,509,735 invalid votes.

111. For Togliatti and Nenni's remarks, see *Verbali del Consiglio dei Ministri*, luglio 1943–maggio 1948, Vol. VI, no. 2, Governo De Gasperi, ed. Aldo G. Ricci (Rome: Presidenza del Consiglio dei Ministri, 1996), 1369.

112. ILS, Fondo Bartolotta (1946), XIV, 1279–80. Lucifero, *L'ultimo Re*, 550 (entry for 10 June 1946) does not report this exchange but describes the discussions as 'snervanti' (fraught).

113. https://patrimonio.archivioluce.com/luce-web/detail/IL5000008865/2/2-giugno-1946-risultati-del-referendum-istituzionale.html?startPage=0

114. Electoral data from Ridolfi and Tranfaglia, *1946*, 241.

115. Indro Montanelli, *L'Italia della Repubblica* (Milan: Rizzoli, 2018), 49.

6. FALTERING STEPS

1. Meeting of the steering committee of the PSIUP, Archivio Foscolo Lombardi (AFL), Istituto Storico Toscano per la Resistenza (ISTR), File b4, fascicolo 20 (22 June 1946).

2. Constituent Assembly (16 July 1946), 68.

3. AFL, File b4, fascicolo 20 (22 June 1946).

4. In the 1951 census, the first for twenty years, Naples' population was 1,024,543 citizens; Milan's was 1,276,521; Rome was the largest city with 1,701,913.

5. Indro Montanelli, *L'Italia della Repubblica. 2 giugno 1946–18 aprile 1948* (Milan: Rizzoli/Corriere della Sera, 2018), 103.

6. Sandro Pertini, in AFL, File b4, fascicolo 20 (22 June 1946).

7. See Decreto presidenziale n. 4 (23 June 1946). https://www.gazzettaufficiale.it/eli/id/1946/06/23/046U0004/sg

8. Giorgio Bocca, *Togliatti* (Milan: Feltrinelli, 2014), 393.

9. Rodolfo Graziani, *Ho difeso la patria* (Milan: Garzanti, 1947). The book had been reprinted six further times by 1949, which is the date of the edition in my possession.

10. Claudio Pavone, 'La continuità dello stato', in Pavone, *Gli uomini e la storia*, ed. David Bidussa (Turin: Bollati Boringhieri, 2020), 141.

11. Constituent Assembly (15 July 1946), 30–36 for De Gasperi's speech.

12. Carlo Levi, *Cristo si è fermato a Eboli* (Turin: Einaudi, 2014), 76.

13. Ibid., 107.

14. See Giorgio Amendola, *La Democrazia nel Mezzogiorno* (Rome: Editori Riuniti, 1957), 244–5, for an account, written in 1950, of the state of Naples.

15. The PCI obtained 748,335 votes in the Mezzogiorno (11 per cent) and the islands, the PSIUP 772,872. The DC secured 2,658,248 votes. By contrast, the UDN, the landlords' party, obtained 1,023,721 votes.

16. Giorgio Amendola, 'Prime considerazioni sulle elezioni nel Mezzogiorno', *Rinascita* vol. III, no. 6 (May–June 1946), 105–9. Reprinted as 'Sulle elezioni del 2 giugno nel Mezzogiorno', in Amendola, *La Democrazia nel Mezzogiorno*, 55–70. Quotations pp. 58, 65, 68.

17. These data are taken from *Sommario di statistiche storiche dell'Italia, 1861–1965* (Rome: Istituto Centrale di Statistica, 1968).

18. 'La spesa della massaia', *Vie nuove* (29 settembre 1946).

19. Giorgio Candeloro, *Storia dell'Italia moderna. La fondazione della Repubblica e la ricostruzione, 1945–50* (Milan: Feltrinelli, 1987), 107.

20. See 'Giornata di tumulti a Roma per il licenziamento di 30 mila operai', *La Nuova Stampa* (10 October 1946). Three of the wounded subsequently died.

21. Pietro Ingrao, 'Colpire a fondo', *l'Unità* (10 October 1946).

22. AFL, File b4, fascicolo 20 (22 June 1946), pp. 11–15 of the minutes.

23. 'Il nuovo corso', *Rinascita*, vol. III, no. 9 (September 1946), 209–11.

24. See Mario Montagna, 'Nell'interesse della nazione', *Rinascita*, vol. III, no. 7 (July 1946), 137–9; Unsigned, 'La politica di Corbino', *Rinascita*, vol. III, no. 8 (August 1946), 177–81, for the PCI's critique of Corbinismo.

25. 'Corbino annuncia alla stampa di aver presentato le dimissioni', *l'Unità* (3 September 1946).

26. Candeloro, *Storia dell'Italia moderna*, 110.

27. James Miller, *The United States and Italy, 1940–1950* (Chapel Hill, NC: North Carolina University Press, 1986), 180.

28. John Lamberton Harper, *America and the Reconstruction of Italy, 1945–1948* (Cambridge: Cambridge University Press, 1986), 108.

29. Michele Pistillo, *Giuseppe Di Vittorio, 1944–57* (Rome: Editori Riuniti, 1977), 108–9.

30. Giuseppe Di Vittorio, quoted in ibid., 107.

31. Emilio Sereni, *Diario (1946–1952)* (Roma: Carocci, 2015), 41. Entry for 14 December 1946. Emphasis in the original.

32. In addition to the 'big four', the conference was attended by Australia, Belgium, Brazil, Canada, Czechoslovakia, Ethiopia, Greece, India, the Netherlands, New Zealand, Poland, South Africa, and Yugoslavia, as well as the two Soviet Republics.

33. David Gilmour, *The Pursuit of Italy: A History of a Land, Its Regions and Their Peoples* (London: Penguin, 2012), 399.

34. Constituent Assembly (Monday, 15 July 1946), 28.

35. Ibid., 29.

36. All quotations from the official English translation in FRUS, 1946, Paris Peace Conference Proceedings, vol. 3.

37. An excellent recent overview, with a substantial documentary appendix, of the question of the South Tyrol/Alto Adige can be found in *L'accordo De Gasperi–Gruber. Una storia internazionale*, ed. Giovanni Bernardini (Trento: Fondo Bruno Kessler, 2016).

38. Armando Vadagnini, 'Partecipazione di popolo e sviluppi diplomatici nell'elaborazione dello Statuto del 1948', in 'Progetti e documenti per lo Statuto speciale di autonomia del 1948', *Annali dell'Istituto storico italo-germanico* (Trento: Fondazione Bruno Kessler, 2010), 35.

39. A useful history of early post-war politics in Trento is Fabio Giacomoni and Renzo Tommasi, *Dall'ASAR al Los von Trient* (Trento: Temi, 1995). The *ladini* are a linguistic minority within the provinces of Bolzano, Trento, and Belluno.

40. *L'accordo di Parigi*, https://www.regione.taa.it/Documenti/Documenti-tecnici-di-supporto/Accordo-Degasperi-Gruber#. The De Gasperi–Gruber accord was included as Appendix 4 of the Peace Treaty in February 1947. It was originally written in English, not German or Italian, and translated into French and Russian, the other two official languages of the conference.

41. 'Una repubblica popolare, democratica, progressiva', *Vie nuove* (17 November 1946).

42. Palmiro Togliatti, 'Per l'Italia e per la pace', *Rinascita*, vol. III, no 10 (October 1946), 249–50. The edition was published in November and a single November–December edition was published in December.

43. *Vie nuove* (1 December 1946).

44. Nenni, *Tempo di guerra fredda*, 296. (Entry for 7 November 1946).

45. Marina Cattaruzza, *L'Italia e il confine orientale* (Bologna: Il Mulino, 2007), 307.

46. Sara Lorenzini, *L'Italia e il trattato di pace del 1947* (Bologna: Il Mulino, 2007), 90.

47. Emilio Sereni, 'Terra ai contadini', *Vie nuove* (22 September 1946).

48. There were several towns where over 20 per cent of the adult population carried a party card: Siena, Modena, Ferrara, Bologna, Ravenna.

49. Statistics from *L'attività del partito in cifre* (Roma: PCI, 1948). This was a document reserved for delegates to the 6th Party Congress in

1948 that gave details of the party's growth since the previous Congress in January 1946.

50. The 'battle of ideas' was the title given to the reviews' pages of *Rinascita*. The most notorious 'excommunication' in the autumn of 1946 was of the magazine *Il Politecnico*, for its excessive independence of thought. See, Palmiro Togliatti, 'Lettere a Elio Vittorini', *Rinascita*, vol. III, no. 10 (October 1946), 284–5.

51. *No alla fame!* (Rome: UEISA, 1946?), 27.

52. Mario Osti, 'Soltanto i poveri pagano le imposte. Gli agenti fiscali non scoprono le grandi fortune', *Vie nuove* (3 November 1946).

53. Alcide De Gasperi, 'Per la libertà democratica e l'autorità dello stato', in De Gasperi, *Discorsi politici* (Roma: Edizioni Cinque Lune 1956), vol. 1, 117. De Gasperi gave his speech on 4 November 1946.

54. Setta, *L'Uomo Qualunque*, 190, reproduces a cartoon showing the people of the South blowing a rasberry at De Gasperi.

55. Figures from Candeloro, *Storia dell'Italia moderna*, 113–14.

56. See Setta, *L'Uomo Qualunque*, 180.

57. Quoted in Elena Aga Rossi and Victor Zaslavsky, *Togliatti e Stalin. Il Pci e la politica estera staliniana negli archivi di Mosca* (Bologna: Il Mulino, 2007), 213.

58. 'Mozione della corrente di sinistra', published in *Avanti!* (7 December 1946). Reprinted in the documentary appendix of *Storia del Socialismo italiano, vol. 5. Il secondo dopoguerra (1943–55)* (Rome: Il Poligono, 1981), 486.

59. Pietro Nenni, *Intervista sul socialismo italiano* (Bari-Rome: Laterza, 1977), 84.

60. This decision was confirmed, after the ratification of the treaty in September 1947, by a referendum among the territory's approximately 5,000 inhabitants.

61. Fabrizio Onofri, *Democrazia progressiva* (Rome: Società Edizioni L'Unità, 1945), 8.

62. See E. H. Carr, *Nationalism and After* (London: Macmillan, 1945), and Carr, *The Soviet Impact on the Western World* (London: Macmillan, 1946).

63. Gaetano Salvemini, 'Le voci del cuore' *Belfagor*, vol. 1, no. 6 (15 November 1946), 746.

64. Pius XII, Discorso ai fedeli, 22 December 1946. https://www.vatican.va/content/pius-xii/it/speeches/1946/documents/hf_p-xii_spe_1946 1222_missione-roma.html

65. Arturo Carlo Jemolo, *Chiesa e Stato in Italia. Dalla unificazione ai giorni nostri* (Turin: Einaudi, 1977), 291.

66. See Paolo Pombeni, *Giuseppe Dossetti. L'avventura politica di un riformatore cristiano* (Bologna: Il Mulino, 2013), 34–6.

7. HINGE YEAR

1. Giulio Andreotti, *1947. L'anno delle grandi svolte nel diario di un protagonista* (Milan: Rizzoli, 2005).
2. This excellent joke is usually credited to the journalist Indro Montanelli. In his biography, Montanelli recounts he received a note from Andreotti saying 'at least the priest replies to me'.
3. Domenico Fracchiolla, *Un ambasciatore della 'nuova Italia' a Washington. Alberto Tarchiani e le relazioni tra Italia e gli Stati Uniti 1945–1947* (Milan: Franco Angeli, 2012), 189.
4. Quoted in Harper, *America and the Reconstruction of Italy, 1945–1948* (Cambridge: Cambridge University Press, 1982), 109.
5. Ibid., 111.
6. Andreotti, *1947*, 16. Entry for 1 January.
7. A voiceless newsreel of the departure, including De Nicola's handshake, can be seen at https://patrimonio.archivioluce.com.
8. *L'Unità* (3 January 1947).
9. Maria Romana Catti De Gasperi, *De Gasperi Uomo Solo* (Milan: Mondadori, 1964), 241.
10. Harper, *America and the Reconstruction of Italy*, 113.
11. The official American account of the meeting, by Ambassador James C. Dunn, FRUS 1947, The British Commonwealth, Europe, vol. III, doc. 543, certainly portrays De Gasperi making detailed requests and receiving only generic replies.
12. ILS, Fondo Bartolotta, (1947), vol. I, 17. Bartolotta reconstructed De Gasperi's visit with the help of a book rushed into print by Tarchiani, *America-Italia. Le dieci giornate di De Gasperi negli Stati Uniti* (Milan: Rizzoli, 1947), and private communications.
13. ILS, Fondo Bartolotta, (1947), vol. II, 135.
14. Ibid. ('un numero infinito').
15. Miller, *The United States and Italy, 1940–1950*, 219.
16. I am quoting from the text of the Cleveland speech recorded by Tarchiani and reprinted in his book and in ibid., 69–81. *Il Popolo* published an edited version on 11 January 1947.
17. Piero Craveri, *De Gasperi* (Bologna: Il Mulino, 2006), 275. De Gasperi emphasized the point in his conversation with Byrnes, for example, on 6 January 1947.

18. ILS, Fondo Bartolotta, (1947), vol. I, 13.
19. 'Mercato orientale a Washington', *Vie nuove* 2 February 1947.
20. The Catholic historian Gianni Baget Bozzo, quoted by Craveri, *De Gasperi*, 278.
21. Pietro Nenni, *Tempo di guerra fredda. Diari 1943–56* (Milan: SugarCo, 1981), 326. Entry for 10 January 1947.
22. She was also Mussolini's lover during his Socialist years.
23. Renato Carli-Ballola, 'Ma perchè se ne vanno?', *Avanti!* (12 January 1947). The facial characterization of Saragat is from the same source.
24. Giuseppe Saragat, 'La democrazia e il suo contrario', *L'Umanità* (4 February 1947).
25. See M. Donno, 'G. Saragat e la socialdemocrazia italiana, 1947–1954', PhD thesis, University of Bologna, XVIII cycle (2007), 135ff for an excellent discussion.
26. Anybody who doubts this statement should read Basso's 'Speech to the 25th Congress', reprinted in *Avanti!* (14 January 1947).
27. Pietro Nenni, 'I problemi interni e esterni', speech to the 25th Congress of the PSI, quoted in Paolo Emiliani, *Dieci anni perduti. Cronache del partito socialista dal 1943 ad oggi* (Pisa: Nistri-Lischi, 1953), 73. 'Paolo Emiliani' was the pseudonym of Valdo Magnani, of whom more later.
28. All quotations from Giuseppe Romita, *Origini, crisi e sviluppo del socialismo italiano* (Rome: Opere nuove, 1951), 30.
29. APC, meeting of the *Direzione* (19 January 1947).
30. Nenni informed De Gasperi that it was necessary to 're-examine the political situation' while the premier was still in the United States.
31. The UQ's leader, Giannini, urged De Gasperi to form a government 'drawn from the democratic parties' on 22 January. ILS, Fondo Bartolotta (1947), vol. III, 160.
32. Ibid., 146–7.
33. Elena Aga Rossi and Victor Zaslavsky, *Togliatti e Stalin. Il PCI e la politica estera staliniana negli archivi di Mosca* (Bologna: Il Mulino, 2007, 2nd edn), 136.
34. Palmiro Togliatti, 'Il tamburino e il tamburo', *l'Unità* (28 January 1947).
35. APC, meeting of the *Direzione* (4 February 1947). The American ambassador, Dunn, was of the same opinion. See, 'The Ambassador in Italy (Dunn) to the Secretary of State' (4 March 1947), FRUS 1947, The British Commonwealth, Europe, vol. III, doc. 565.
36. Togliatti, speech to the Constituent Assembly on 19 February 1947. Published as 'Le manovre di De Gasperi per rompere l'unità democratica', in Palmiro Togliatti, *Discorsi alla Costituente*, ed. Salvatore d'Albergo (Rome: Riuniti, 1973), 142.

37. *L'Unità* published a short piece on 20 January, the day after the elections, and then ignored developments until 5 February 1947 when it reported the inauguration of the new Polish parliament in a factual piece in the bottom right-hand corner of the front-page. *Rinascita* made no mention of the elections at all.

38. In addition to Britain, the USSR, the USA, China, and France, peace was made with Australia, Belgium, Brazil, Canada, Czechoslovakia, Ethiopia, Greece, India, the Netherlands, New Zealand, Poland, South Africa, and Yugoslavia, as well as the Soviet Republics of Belorussia and Ukraine. Strictly speaking, the actual signature took place in an adjacent room.

39. 'Imposto non negoziato. Il trattato è stato firmato ieri', *Il Popolo* (11 February 1947).

40. ILS, Fondo Bartolotta (1947), vol. V, 331.

41. This paragraph is based upon Sara Lorenzini's evocative description of 10 February in *L'Italia e il trattato di pace* (Bologna: Il Mulino, 2007), 107.

42. Its formal name was the Commission for the Constitution. It was composed of 75 members divided into three sub-committees on the rights and duties of citizens, the institutional organization of the state, and economic and social relations. There were 26 DC members, 13 from each of the PSIUP (including Lelio Basso) and PCI (including Togliatti and Terracini). The other parties made up the numbers. There were five women.

43. Commissione per la Costituzione, Adunanza plenaria (28 November 1946). The Sicilian jurist cited was the Christian Democrat Carmelo Caristia.

44. Croce's comparison can be found in Constitution Assembly (11 March 1947), 2,007.

45. Ibid., p. 1,995.

46. Nenni, cited in Arturo Carlo Jemolo, *Chiesa e Stato in Italia. Dalla unificazione ai giorni nostri* (Turin: Einaudi, 1977, 4th edn), 297.

47. For De Gasperi's speech, see the debates of the Constituent Assembly (25 March 1947), 2,453–6.

48. Togliatti, *Discorsi alla Costituente*, 50.

49. Andreotti, *1947*, 52. Entry for 25 March 1947.

50. Franco Rodano, 'L'articolo 7', *Rinascita*, vol. IV, no. 4 (1947), 76. The article rebuked the PCI's critics on the left for accusing the PCI of 'Machiavellianism'. Rodano was a devout Catholic himself.

51. Nenni, *Tempo di guerra fredda*, 348–9.

52. APC, meeting of the *Direzione* (16 April 1947), 1–5.

53. Ibid. (18 April 1947), 62.
54. 'Prestiti americani e garanzie italiane', *Rinascita*, vol. IV, no. 5 (1947), 107–8.
55. Sandro Pertini, 'De Gasperi fugge', *Lavoro nuovo* (14 May 1947), in Pertini, *Anni di guerra fredda. Scritti e discorsi 1947–1949*, ed. Stefano Caretti (Rome: Piero Lacaita Editore, 2010), 50.
56. *Sommario di statische storiche dell'Italia, 1861–1965* (Rome: Ist. Poligrafico, 1968), Table 87, 109. I have rounded to the first decimal point.
57. Text of the broadcast in ILS, Fondo Bartolotta (1947), vol. X, 918 and 922.
58. Guido Formigoni, *Storia d'Italia nella guerra fredda (1943–1978)* (Bologna: Il Mulino, 2016), 103. The text of the letter can be found in ILS, Fondo Bartolotta (1947), vol. X, 899–902.
59. 'The Secretary of State to the Embassy in Italy' (1 May 1947), FRUS 1947, The British Commonwealth, Europe, vol. III, doc. 584.
60. 'The Ambassador in Rome (Dunn) to the Secretary of State' (3 May 1947), ibid., doc. 585.
61. Ibid.
62. See Mario Spinella, 'Mediterraneo americano?', *Vie Nuove* (23 March 1947), for an expression of this suspicion.
63. Andreotti, *1947*, 80. Entry for 12 May 1947.
64. Radio broadcast by De Gasperi (13 May 1947), ILS, Fondo Bartolotta (1947), vol. XI, 1,029–39.
65. Tarchiani to De Gasperi (16 May 1947), ILS, Fondo Bartolotta (1947), vol. XII, 1,052–6.
66. ILS, Fondo Bartolotta (1947), vol. XII, 1,073.
67. Palmiro Togliatti, 'Ma come sono cretini', *l'Unità* (20 May 1947).
68. Victor Zaslavsky, *Lo Stalinismo e la sinistra italiana. Dal mito dell'URSS alla fine del comunismo, 1945–1991* (Milan: Mondadori, 2004), 123.
69. Craveri, *De Gasperi*, 298.
70. ILS, Fondo Bartolotta (1947), vol. XIII, 1,118.
71. Ibid., 1,120–21.
72. Ibid., 1,123–31 for the exchanges. Also, Craveri, *De Gasperi*, 299.
73. Andreotti, *1947*, 88. Entry for 26 May 1947.
74. Even the motion passed by the steering committee merely 'took note' of the 'serious difficulties' De Gasperi had encountered and 'expressed its opinion' that he should 'continue his efforts to achieve the best solution to the crisis'. It did not explicitly say that he should break with the

left-wing parties. *Atti e documenti della Democrazia Cristiana, 1943–67* (Rome: Edizioni Cinque Lune, 1967), 323.

75. Paolo Emilio Taviani, *Politica a memoria d'uomo* (Bologna: Il Mulino, 2002), 124. Taviani was deputy secretary of the party and one of four who voted against.

76. In a letter of 11 July 1947, cited in Craveri, *De Gasperi*, 301.

77. 'No al tripartito', *Il Popolo* (30 May 1947).

78. Tarchiani, personal letter to De Gasperi (4 June 1947), ILS, Fondo Bartolotta (1947), vol. XIII, 1,188.

79. Togliatti, 'La rottura dell'unità democratica', *Discorsi alla Costituente*, 188.

80. Aga Rossi and Zaslavsky, *Togliatti e Stalin*, 218, citing Russian documents.

81. Ibid., 214.

82. ILS, Fondo Bartolotta (30 June 1947), 1,444–7.

83. APC, meeting of the *Direzione* (3–5 June 1947), 3 and 4.

84. Palmiro Togliatti, 'Abbiamo salvato la unità nazionale', *Vie nuove* (27 July 1947).

85. For the distinction between *la guerra di posizione* and *la guerra manovrata*, see Antonio Gramsci, *Pensare la democrazia. Antologia dai 'Quaderni di carcere'*, ed. Marcello Montanari (Turin: Einaudi, 1997), 111–12.

86. Minutes of the Consiglio dei Ministri (9 January 1948), ILS Fondo Bartolotta (1948), vol. I, 26.

87. Indro Montanelli and Mario Cervi, *L'Italia della Repubblica. 2 giugno 1946–18 aprile 1948* (Milan: RCS, 2018), 129.

88. *Sommario di statische storiche dell'Italia, 1861–1965*, Table 87, 109.

89. Silvio Pons, *I comunisti italiani e gli altri. Visioni e legami internazionali nel mondo del 900* (Turin: Einaudi, 2021), 110, quoting Eugenio Reale's memoir *Nascita del Cominform* (Milan: Mondadori, 1958), 17.

90. Pons, *I comunisti italiani e gli altri*, 111. The transcript of the debate is available (in English) in *The Cominform: Minutes of the Three Conferences 1947/1948/1949*, ed. G. Procacci (Milan: Annali della Fondazione Giangiacomo Feltrinelli, 1994), 217–51.

91. All quotations are from APC, meeting of the *Direzione* (7–10 October 1947). Terracini's comments on p. 3.

92. Ibid., 9.

93. 'Come Togliatti difende il nuovo organismo internazionale', *Nuovo Corriere della Sera* (9 October 1947). Asked whether the PCI would 'keep faith' with democratic practices, Togliatti responded with a

question: 'Why should it fail to live up to them?' The interview was included in a dossier for the delegates of the 6th Party Congress in January 1948: *I comunisti per la pace, la democrazia, l'indipendenza dei popoli* (Conferenza di Varsavia) (Rome: CDS, 1947), 57.

94. For an extended discussion of this fascinating episode, see Aldo Agosti, 'Il caso di Terracini', in *Pagine sul PCI*, a special dossier published by *l'Unità* (21 January 1990). Renzo Martinelli, *Storia del Partito Comunista. Il Partito Nuovo dalla Liberazione al 18 aprile* (Turin: Einaudi, 1995), 244–9, gives a useful synthesis.

95. See Emanuele Bernardi, 'L'ordine pubblico nel 1947', *Ventunesimo secolo*, vol. 6, no. 1 (2007), 105–29.

96. See Eugenio Reale, 'Contro Wall Street', in *I comunisti per la pace, la democrazia, l'indipendenza dei popoli* (Conferenza di Varsavia) (Rome: CDS, 1947), 61–2.

97. 'Per un vasto fronte della pace, del lavoro e della indipendenza nazionale', *l'Unità* (16 November 1947).

98. ILS, Fondo Bartolotta (1947), vol. XXVII, 2,339.

99. Gervasio Federici, a former partisan. He was supposedly stabbed by a PCI squad for refusing to shout 'Viva il comunismo!'

100. See 'La Democrazia Cristiana e la guerra fredda: una selezione di documenti inediti', *Ventunesimo secolo*, ed. Emanuele Bernardi, 5 (2006), 119–52.

101. The story is recounted by Miriam Mafai, *L'Uomo che sognava la lotta armata. La storia di Pietro Secchia* (Milan: Rizzoli, 1984), 56.

102. Mario Scelba, speech (untitled) to the Second National Congress of Christian Democracy, Naples (15–20 November 1947), ILS, Fondo Scelba, B. 172. Fasc. 1731. Quotations on p. 5 and p. 10 of the typescript.

103. The description is from Montanelli and Cervi, *L'Italia della Repubblica*, 148. Montanelli was an eyewitness.

104. Togliatti's speech in *Discorsi alla Costituente*, 297–325.

105. The most likely candidate so far, the Radical Emma Bonino, who has been an EU Commissioner and senior UN official, famously quipped that she had 'more chance of becoming pope'.

106. Both chambers must vote on proposed amendments twice, with a three-month gap between votes, by an absolute majority of each chamber for a revision to pass. Even then the proposed changes can be contested by a national referendum (and usually are).

107. Andreotti, *1947*, 181. Entry for 31 December.

8. MOMENT OF TRUTH

1. The law governing elections to the Senate was passed on 6 February 1948.

2. Giulio Andreotti, *1948. L'anno dello scampato pericolo* (Milan: Rizzoli, 2005), 10. Entry for 2 January 1948.

3. Legislation confirming this was passed on 20 January 1948.

4. See Gianfranco Pasquino, 'Il Sistema e il comportamento elettorale', in *La Politica italiana. Dizionario critico 1945–95*, ed. G. Pasquino (Bari-Rome: Laterza, 1995), 135.

5. Renzo Martinelli, *Storia del Partito comunista italiano. Il partito nuovo dalla liberazione al 18 aprile* (Turin: Einaudi, 1995), 335.

6. Dino Del Bo, *Perché la DC vincerà le elezioni* (Milan: SPES, 1948), 2.

7. An 'Alliance for the Defence of Culture' held its inaugural meeting at the Duse Theatre in Rome on 19 February 1948. More than 300 intellectuals, among them distinguished scholars and writers, adhered to the project, including some who had not previously sided with the two Marxist parties. See Nello Ajello, *Intellettuali e PCI 1944/56* (Roma: Laterza, 2018, 8th edn), 155–60.

8. Quotations from *Carta costituiva del Fronte. Appello agli italiani*. The seven-page manifesto was printed in a minuscule version that fitted into one's wallet, as well as in pamphlet form.

9. See 'Salviamo la nostra industria', 'Vuoi continuare a vivere come un asino o vuoi essere un uomo?' 'Una burocrazia moderna democratica imparziale', and 'L'azione dei comunisti era intesa ad alleviare la sofferenza del popolo', all in ISTR, AFL b7 fasc. 63 (Propaganda for 1948 elections).

10. Giorgio Bocca, *Palmiro Togliatti* (Milan: Feltrinelli, 2014), 418.

11. See the summary of the conversation between Secchia and Zhdanov in Silvio Pons, *I comunisti italiani e gli altri. Visioni e legami internazionali nel mondo del Novecento* (Turin: Einaudi, 2021), 115. An Italian translation of the discussion, and a note 'Sulla tattica del Pci nel periodo attuale', which is believed to be the transcript of Secchia's actual comments, can be found in *Dagli archivi di Mosca. L'Urss, il Cominform e il PCI*, ed. Francesca Gori and Silvio Pons (Rome: Carocci, 1998), docs. 18–19, 276–88.

12. Elena Aga-Rossi and Victor Zaslavsky, *Togliatti e Stalin. Il PCI e la politica estera staliniana negli archive di Mosca* (Bologna: Il Mulino, 2nd ed. 2007), 319–23 for the transcript.

13. Pons, *I comunisti e gli altri*, 117.

14. The letters, and a handwritten draft of Togliatti's letter, are an annex to the minutes of the meeting of the *Direzione* of the PCI, 21 January 1948. Some of them are eulogies, others are simply scribbled notes giving assent.

15. See Aga Rossi and Zaslavsky, *Togliatti e Stalin*, 311–18, for the discussion between Stalin and Thorez.

16. Cited in Martinelli, *Storia del Partito comunista italiano*, 324.

17. Ibid., 327.

18. Gianluca Scroccu, 'Pacifismo, frontismo e autonomia. Pertini, il PSI e la fase calda della guerra fredda (1945–1950), *Diacronie*, vol. 9, no. 1 (2012), 5. Scroccu says that the 'integrity of the Socialist house' was Pertini's lodestar. He was suspicious of anybody 'aiming to annex it' (*con mire annessionistiche*).

19. Sandro Pertini, *Anni di guerra fredda. Scritti e discorsi: 1947–1949*, ed. Stefano Caretti (Rome: Lacaita, 2010), 167.

20. Scroccu, 'Pacifismo, frontismo e autonomia', 11.

21. 'Il compagno Pietro Nenni al XXVI Congresso. Impegnare a fondo il socialismo nella lotta per la conquista del potere', *Avanti!* (22 January 1948).

22. Pietro Nenni, *Tempo di guerra fredda*, 399. Entry for 24 November 1947.

23. Victor Zaslavsky, *Lo Stalinismo e la sinistra italiana. Dal mito dell'Urss alla fine del comunismo, 1945–1951* (Milan: Mondadori, 2004), 156–7.

24. Ibid., 161–3.

25. Ibid., 159.

26. Nenni, *Tempo di guerra fredda*, 401. Entry for 29 November 1947.

27. Moscow decided in April 1950 to subsidize the political action of 'left-wing workers' organizations'. The Soviet Union ultimately provided 80 per cent of the cash disbursed, although other Eastern bloc countries also contributed money and offered other sources of assistance. The PCI received $400,000 in 1950, the PSI received $100,000 (money was also provided to the PCI of Trieste). In 1951–2, these figures were significantly increased, while in 1953, an election year, the PCI received $1,500,000 and the PSI $550,000. In 1955, the PCI overtook the French Communist Party as the biggest recipient of Soviet funds ($2,640,000). The PSI received $400,000 in the same year, and $500,000 in 1956 (the PCI took $2,500,000). Funds for the PSI were blocked after Nenni broke with Moscow in February 1957. See Zaslavsky, *Lo Stalinismo e la sinistra italiana*, 129–31. The expression 'Moscow Gold' is a reference to

Gianni Cervetti, *L'Oro di Mosca. La testimonianza di un protagonista* (Milan: Baldini & Castoldi, 1993). Cervetti was given the task of severing the PCI's financial links with Moscow in the 1970s.

28. Thus Paul Ginsborg, *A History of Contemporary Italy: Society and Politics 1943–1988* (London: Penguin, 1990), 115–17.

29. Denis Mack Smith, *History of Modern Italy: A Political History* (New Haven, CT: Yale University Press, 1997), 424, says that the coup in Prague 'started a panic'.

30. Ottavio Pastore, 'Risposta di popolo', *l'Unità* (26 February 1948).

31. Pietro Nenni, 'La conferma di Praga', *Avanti!* (Milan) (26 February 1948).

32. Pietro Ingrao, 'Discutiamo su Praga', *l'Unità* (28 February 1948).

33. Pietro Secchia, untitled, *Vie nuove* (7 March 1948).

34. 'La lezione di Praga', *Il Nuovo Corriere della Sera* (26 January 1948).

35. https://www.vatican.va/content/pius-xii/it/speeches/1947/documents/hf_p-xii_spe_19471224_natale.html

36. Quoted in Avagliano and Palmieri, *1948. Gli italiani nell'anno della svolta*, 48. I have paraphrased, not translated.

37. Robert Ventresca, 'The Virgin and the Bear: Religion, Society, and the Cold War in Italy', *Journal of Social History*, vol. 37, no. 2 (2003), 440 and 441. Ventresca discounts the idea that the Church was manipulating the visions.

38. Luigi Gedda, *18 aprile 1948. Memorie inedite dell'artefice della sconfitta del Fronte Popolare* (Milan: Mondadori, 1998). 119.

39. See Gedda, *18 aprile 1948*, 123 and 133.

40. All the films discussed here (and others for which there was no space) have been made available on Youtube by the Istituto Luigi Sturzo's digitization programme.

41. Guido Formigoni, *Storia d'Italia nella guerra fredda, 1943–1978* (Bologna: Il Mulino, 2016), 128.

42. Kaeten Mistry, 'Re-Thinking American Intervention in the 1948 Italian Election: Beyond a Success-Failure Dichotomy, '*Modern Italy*, vol. 16, no. 2 (2011), 187–8. See also James E. Miller, review of Robert Ventresca, *From Fascism to Democracy: Culture and Politics in the Italian Elections of 1948* (Toronto: Toronto University Press, 2004), in *Journal of Modern History*, vol. 77, no. 4 (2005), 1127–9.

43. Quoted in C. Edda Martinez and Edward A. Suchman, 'Letters from America and the 1948 Elections in Italy', *Public Opinion Quarterly* (Spring 1950), 115.

44. Gedda, *18 aprile 1948*, 137.

45. The office was called SPES, 'Studi Propaganda e Stampa' (Research, Propaganda and Press). It means 'hope' in Latin, which is unlikely to be a coincidence. I'm grateful to Tommaso Milani for pointing this out to me.

46. Rosario Forlenza, 'In Search of Order: Portrayal of Communists in Cold War Italy', *Journal of Cold War Studies*, vol. 22, no. 2 (2020), 101.

47. ILS, Fondo Bartolotta (1948), vol. VI, 495.

48. Ibid., 501.

49. Ibid., 511.

50. Ibid., 515.

51. Ibid., 518.

52. First quotation from an impromptu speech in Cassino in Campania, 29 March. The second, in Trento on 5 April, ILS, Fondo Bartolotta (1948) vol. VIII, 697.

53. James Miller, 'Taking off the Gloves: The United States and the Italian Elections of 1948', *Diplomatic History*, vol. 7, no. 1 (1983), 35–56.

54. Stephen F. White, *Modern Italy's Founding Fathers: The Making of a Post War Republic* (London: Bloomsbury, 2020), 153, quoting the memoirs of the journalist Vittorio Gorresio.

55. Palmiro Togliatti, *La guerra di posizione in Italia. Epistolario 1944–1964* (Turin: Einaudi, 2014), 114–15. Several PCI activists were killed during the campaign in the South by the mafia, presumably at the behest of local elites.

56. 'Il Piave mormorava', *l'Unità* (15 April 1948).

57. The discussion between Togliatti and Kostylev, and Moscow's reply, is reported in Aga Rossi and Zaslavsky, *Togliatti e Stalin*, 237–8.

58. First published by Piero Craveri, 'Prove della guerra civile nella DC', *Ventesimo secolo*, vol. 5, n. 10 (2006), 123. Reprinted in Aga Rossi and Zaslavsky, *Togliatti e Stalin*, 250.

59. Aga Rossi and Zaslavsky, *Togliatti e Stalin*, 251.

60. The rally was reported in exultant terms: 'Il Fronte democratico vince! Evviva la vittoria del popolo!', *l'Unità* (17 April 1948).

61. Andreotti, *1948*, 62. Entry for 19 April 1948.

62. So far as I can tell, the only elections that beat it are the Czechoslovakian elections of May 1946, won by the Communists on a turnout of almost 94 per cent, and the subsequent 1953 elections in Italy itself.

63. This figure, moreover, would not be superseded, albeit in a larger parliament, until 1976. See *Parità vo cercando* (Rome: Senato della Repubblica, 2018), 2.

64. Felice Platone, 'Esame critico dei risultati elettorali', *Rinascita*, vol. V, nos. 4–5 (1948), 144.

65. A point made by Paolo Emiliani (pseud. Valdo Magnani), *10 anni perduti* (Pisa: Nistri-Lischi, 1953), 107.

66. In the Turin-Novara-Vercelli electoral district, the DC obtained 668,730 votes to the Front's 530,083. The DC elected thirteen representatives to the Chamber of Deputies, the FDP elected ten. Negarville was elected to the Senate.

67. 'Un'intervista con De Gasperi', *Il Messaggero* (17 April 1948).

68. *Franchi tiratori.* The Italian term used to refer to those who disobey the party whip.

69. Indro Montanelli and Mario Cervi, *L'Italia della Repubblica. 2 giugno 1946–18 aprile 1948* (Milan: RCS, 2018), 201.

70. Andreotti, *1948*, 73. Entry for 10 May.

71. Montanelli, *L'Italia della Repubblica*, 203.

72. Pietro Secchia, 'Nato nel sangue', *Vie nuove* (30 May 1948).

73. Ibid., 3.

74. Giancarlo Pajetta, APC, meeting of the *Direzione* (26 April 1948), 15.

75. For a wider discussion of this tactic, see Andrea Guiso, 'From Political Enemy to Profane Reality: The "friend–enemy" Relation in the Political Ideology of Italian Communists', *Journal of Modern Italian Studies*, vol. 22, no. 1 (2017), 91.

76. 'Cento trucidati al giorno nella Grecia dei gauleiter di Truman', *Vie nuove* (23 May 1948). The article was accompanied by a photograph of a Greek fascist shooting a man in the head.

77. Quotes from 'Direttive di lavoro per la realizzazione della risoluzione del C.C. del 4/5/6 maggio 1948'.

78. All quotations in these two paragraphs from 'Direttive di lavoro per la realizzazione della risoluzione del C.C. del 4/5/6 maggio 1948', a seven-page document submitted to the party steering committee meeting of 24 and 25 May 1948 by Luigi Longo.

79. I am quoting the intervention of Secondo Pessi, a resistance hero and party secretary in Genoa, during the 26 April 1948 meeting of the PCI's steering committee.

80. Paolo Mattera, 'Dopo il 18 aprile. La crisi e la seconda "rifondazione" del PSI', *Studi Storici*, vol. 43, no. 4 (2002), 1150–54.

81. A point made by Stefano Zurlo, *Quattro colpi per Togliatti. Antonio Pallante e l'attentato che sconvolse l'Italia* (Milan: Baldini & Castoldi, 2019), 59. The book is based upon interviews that Zurlo, a journalist, carried out with the ninety-five-year-old Pallante in 2018.

82. Zurlo, *Quattro colpi per Togliatti*, 78. Pallante was sentenced in 1949 to a thirteen-year prison sentence, reduced in October 1953 to ten years and eight months. As a result of an amnesty, he left prison in December 1953 having served only five years and five months for his crime.

83. Walter Tobagi, *La rivoluzione impossibile. L'attentato a Togliatti: Violenza politica e reazione popolare* (Milan: Il Saggiatore, 1978). This book, which is a compilation of prefects' reports about the events in the provinces under their control, gives a vivid and comprehensive account of the disturbances.

84. Declaration of the CGIL (14 July 1948), quoted in Michele Pistillo, *Giuseppe Di Vittorio 1944–1957* (Rome: Editori Riuniti, 1977), 163.

85. Cartoonists delighted in drawing her with a matrimonial rolling pin in hand to chastize her intimidated husband.

86. See, 'Nostra signora di Montecitorio: Nilde Iotti vista da vicino', interview with Lina Coletti, in *L'Europeo*, vol. XLII, no. 37 (1990), 49–53.

87. *L'Unità* (Rome) (14 July 1948).

88. 'La dichiarazione del Partito socialista', *Avanti!* (14 July 1948).

89. 'Il telegramma di Stalin', *l'Unità* (Rome) (16 July 1948).

90. Umberto Terracini, Senate of the Republic (14 July 1948), 925, 926 and 928.

91. C.A. (Carlo Andreoni), 'Paranoia', *l'Umanità* (13 July 1948).

92. Giorgio Bocca, *Palmiro Togliatti* (Milan: Feltrinelli, 2014), 438, citing personal information given to him by Riccardo Lombardi, the editor of *Avanti!*

93. Togliatti's interview can be seen at https://archivio.quirinale.it/aspr/gianni-bisiach/AV-002-000340/14-luglio-1948-attentato-togliatti

94. Gabriella Fanello Marcucci, *Scelba. Il ministro che si oppose al fascismo e al comunismo in nome della libertà* (Milan: Mondadori, 2006), 143–4.

95. Tom Behan, 'Going Further: The Aborted Italian Insurrection of July 1948', *Left History*, vol. 4, no. 1 (1996), 171, quoting Pietro Di Loreto, *Togliatti e la 'doppiezza'. Il PCI tra democrazia e insurrezione* (Bologna: Il Mulino, 1991), 320.

9 · COLD WAR NATION

1. H. Stuart Hughes, 'Italy under De Gasperi', *American Perspective* (January 1949), 419. The correct spelling is Dollfuss.

2. Total American military and civilian aid to Italy *before* the Marshall Plan was approximately $1.9 billion. See Francesca Fauri, *Il Piano Marshall e l'Italia* (Bologna: Il Mulino, 2010), 127–8.

3. Pietro Quaroni, quoted in ibid., 54.

4. *Relazione sul I e II Trimestre ERP in Italia* (1 aprile–30 settembre 1948) (Rome: CIR-ERP, October 1948), 35–6.

5. Fauri, *Il Piano Marshall*, 170.

6. Ibid., 76.

7. *L'ERP in Italia* (Rome: ERP Mission to Italy, undated but almost certainly 1950), 3–4.

8. Fauri, *Il Piano Marshall*, 80.

9. *Relazione sul I e II Trimestre ERP in Italia*, 48.

10. Alcide De Gasperi, Senate of the Republic (29 November 1949), 12,323. I am grateful to Vera Zamagni for pointing this speech out to me.

11. Fauri, *Il Piano Marshall*, 186.

12. *Guida alla città dell'ERP* (Rome: ERP Mission to Italy, 1951), 7.

13. Ibid., 5.

14. All quotations are from *1945–1950. L'avvenire tuo e dei tuoi figli è nelle tue mani* (Rome: Comitato CISI, 1951?). There are no page numbers and no author is named.

15. Ibid.

16. Ibid.

17. David W. Ellwood, 'The Propaganda of the Marshall Plan in Italy in a Cold War Context', *Intelligence and National Security*, vol. 18, no. 2 (2003), 231.

18. This rare poster is preserved at the Museo Salce in Treviso and in my office (I have a copy hanging on the wall). It is hard to date: it is probably late 1948 since there is a reference to the 'Lire fund'.

19. The United States Information Service, *I gangli vitali degli Stati Uniti*. The pamphlet, p. 3, translated 'life, liberty, and the *pursuit of happiness*' as 'vita, libertà, e il *perseguimento del benessere*'. This cannot have been an error in translation.

20. David W. Ellwood, 'The Force of American Modernity: World War II and the Birth of a Soft Power Superpower', *International Journal for History, Culture and Modernity*, vol. 6, no. 1 (2018), 6.

21. Vera Zamagni, 'La politica economica di De Gasperi: le fondamenta del miracolo economico italiano', in *Lezioni degasperiane, 2004–2018*, ed. Giuseppe Tognon (Trento: Fondazione Bruno Kessler Press, 2018), 135. By gold standard, Zamagni means the parity of $35 for an ounce

of gold agreed at the Bretton Woods conference in 1944 and maintained until August 1971.

22. Antonio Varsori, *La Cenerentola d'Europa. L'Italia e l'integrazione europea dal 1947 a oggi* (Soveria Mannelli: Rubbettino, 2010), 75.

23. Ugo La Malfa, *Senza l'Europa avrete il deserto*, ed. Silvia Di Bartolomei (Soveria Mannelli: Rubettino, 2005).

24. Paolo Acanfora, *Miti e ideologia nella politica estera DC. Nazione, Europa e Comunità atlantica (1943–1954)* (Bologna: Il Mulino, 2013), 77. Piero Craveri, *De Gasperi* (Bologna: Il Mulino, 2006), 493, underlines that the Vatican gave 'strong backing' to European integration.

25. Varsori, *La Cenerentola d'Europa*, 73.

26. This is the classic formulation of Eugenio Colorni, Ernesto Rossi, and Altiero Spinelli, *Il Manifesto di Ventotene*, a wartime study of the case for European political unity.

27. Cited in Craveri, *De Gasperi*, 490.

28. Alcide De Gasperi, 'Agli italiani perché ricerchino le vie dell'Europa', speech in Rome (9 June 1949), cited in Acanfora, *Miti e ideologia*, 92.

29. Ugo La Malfa, 'Germania al di là del nazismo', in *Scritti 1925–1953* (Milan: Mondadori, 1988), 239.

30. See Mark Gilbert, 'Italy: The Astuteness and Anxieties of a Second-Rank Power', in *European Foreign Policies: Does Europe Still Matter?*, ed. R. Tiersky and J. Van Oudenaren (Boulder, CO: Rowman and Littlefield, 2009), 235–59.

31. See, in English, a pamphlet published by the European Movement (a political pressure group whose titular leader was Winston Churchill, who contributed a foreword), *The European Movement and the Council of Europe* (London: Hutchinson, 1949).

32. Guido Carli, *Cinquant'anni di vita italiana* (Bari-Rome: Economica Laterza, 1996), 101–10 for his experience in this post.

33. For La Malfa's actions, see Lorenzo Mechi, *L'Europa di Ugo La Malfa. La via italiana alla modernizzazione* (Milan: Franco Angeli, 2001), 45–78.

34. By the end of 1953, the percentage of Italian imports exempted from quantitative restrictions had reached 99.7 per cent, the best in the OEEC. Only 17.9 per cent of imports into France, by contrast, were exempt. See Fauri, *Il Piano Marshall e l'Italia*, 69.

35. Varsori, *La Cenerentola d'Europa*, 80.

36. Ugo La Malfa, 'Aspects and Problems of Italy's Foreign Trade', *The Statist* (25 October 1952), repr. in La Malfa, *Scritti 1925–1953*, 806–9. All quotations from this latter source.

37. For the negative British reaction to the Schuman Plan, see Edmund Dell, *The British Abdication of Leadership in Europe* (Oxford: Oxford University Press, 1995).

38. Varsori, *La Cenerentola d'Europa*, 87.

39. These paragraphs on the creation of the Coal and Steel Community are based upon Varsori, *La Cenerentola d'Europa*, 81-8, and Ruggero Ranieri, 'L'Italia e i negoziati sul Piano Schuman', in *L'Italia e la politica di potenza in Europa (1945-50)*, ed. E. Di Nolfo, R. H. Rainero, and B. Vigezzi (Milan: Marzorati, 1986), 547-73.

40. Giuseppe Boffa, 'Gli arsenali della Ruhr e della Saar riuniti in un gigantesco cartello', *l'Unità* (10 May 1950).

41. Mauro Scoccimarro, 'Manifestazione di servilismo', *Vie nuove* (11 June 1950).

42. *La Minaccia del Piano Schuman*, ed. Bruno Trentin, no. 1 (Rome: Quaderni di Notizie Economiche, 1952). The identity of the pamphlet's editor is interesting. Trentin, who was then a recent graduate, would go on to become the head of the CGIL – and a convinced supporter of European integration. All quotations pp. 6-17.

43. Geir Lundestad, 'Empire by Invitation? The United States and Western Europe, 1945-52', *Journal of Peace Research*, vol. 23, no. 3 (1986), 263-77.

44. Varsori, *La Cenerentola d'Europa*, 52.

45. Ibid., 63.

46. Acanfora, *Miti e ideologia*, 22.

47. Ibid., 37.

48. Mozione della Commissione di studio della DC per la politica estera (8 March 1949), in *Atti e documenti della Democrazia cristiana, 1943-1967* (Rome: Edizioni Cinque Lune, 1967), 402.

49. Varsori, *La Cenerentola d'Europa*, 62.

50. See Effie Pedalieu, *Britain, Italy and the Origins of the Cold War* (Basingstoke: Palgrave, 2003), 96-127, for Whitehall's efforts to keep Italy out of the North Atlantic Treaty.

51. For the State Department's analysis, see E. Timothy Smith, 'The Fear of Subversion: The United States and the Inclusion of Italy in the North Atlantic Treaty', *Diplomatic History*, vol. 7, no. 2 (1983), 139-56.

52. Varsori, *La Cenerentola d'Europa*, 65.

53. Alcide De Gasperi, 'Una realistica politica di pace', *Il Popolo* (6 March 1949).

54. Pietro Nenni, *Tempo di Guerra Fredda. Diari 1943-1956* (Milan: SugarCo, 1981), 481. Entry for 12 March 1949.

55. *Atti e documenti della Democrazia cristiana, 1943–1967*, 494.

56. Palmiro Togliatti, 'Per la Pace', *l'Unità* (26 October 1948). Reprinted in Togliatti, *Pace o Guerra* (Milan: Milano-sera editrice, 1949), 14–19, all quotations from 17.

57. Ibid., 18.

58. Ibid., 19.

59. Togliatti, 'Salvare la Pace', in *Pace o Guerra*, 117.

60. Ibid., 99.

61. Ibid., 98.

62. Ibid., 97.

63. Ibid., 101.

64. Ibid., 102.

65. Ibid., 95.

66. Ibid., 106.

67. Ibid., 122.

68. Ibid., 124.

69. Chamber of Deputies (16 March 1949), 7006.

70. The Status of Forces Agreement was signed in London on 19 June 1951. https://www.nato.int/docu/basictxt/b510619a.htm. American and British troops had been withdrawn after the ratification of the Treaty of Peace in September 1947.

71. Andrea Guiso, *La Colomba e la spada. Lotta per pace e antiamericanismo nella politica del Partito comunista italiano* (1949–1954) (Saverio Mannelli: Rubettino, 2006), 618–19.

72. Giulio Petrangeli, 'I partigiani della pace in Italia 1948–1953', *Italia Contemporanea*, no. 217 (December 1999), 680.

73. https://www.wpc-in.org/statements/70-years-ago-first-world-congress-peace-partisans-o

74. The word 'noose' is a reference to a collection of Nenni's writings and speeches, *Il cappio delle alleanze* (Milan: Milano Sera Editrice, 1949).

75. Stockholm Appeal of the World Peace Congress (15 March 1950). Available on the World Peace Council website.

76. *Plebiscito della Pace. Contro le armi atomiche*, supplement to the *Bollettino dei partigiani della pace*, nos. 1–3 (July 1950).

77. 'Giù le mani dalla Corea e dalla Cina', *Vie nuove* (9 July 1950).

78. Petrangeli, 'I partigiani della pace in Italia', 682.

79. Giovanni Guareschi, 'The Petition', in *The Don Camillo Omnibus* (London: The Companion Book Club, 1955), 185.

80. Sereni nevertheless denounced the 'scandalous inadequacy of our press' in helping the work of the Partisans of Peace and singled out *l'Unità* for

its lack of commitment. APC, meeting of the *Direzione* (26 September 1951).

81. *Fai firmare tutti contro l'atomica* (Rome: Partigiani della Pace, 1950), 9.

82. Ibid., 13–21. The two quotations are from pp. 19 and 21.

83. *Noi donne*, no. 12 (1949), 3 and 6.

84. See 'Sono tutti angioletti della pace', *Noi donne*, no. 8 (1949), and in subsequent editions of the paper.

85. Ida Tumulini, 'Guerra alla guerra', *Noi donne*, no. 11 (1950).

86. Emilio Sereni, 'La crociata delle donne contro l'atomica', *Noi donne*, no. 28 (1950).

87. See Nina Rothenberg, 'The Catholic and Communist Women's Press in Post-War Italy: An Analysis of *Cronache* and *Noi donne*', *Modern Italy*, vol. 11, no. 3 (2006), 285–304, for a comparison between Catholic and communist perceptions of femininity.

88. Matteo Lodevole, 'The Western Communists and the European military Build-Up, 1949–50: A Preventative Strategy', *Cold War History*, vol. 10, no. 2 (2010), 207.

89. For an able summary of Italian diplomacy, see Varsori, *La Cenerentola d'Europa*, 94–105.

90. On this issue, Linda Risso, 'Against Rearmament or Against Integration? The PCI and PCF's Opposition to the European Defence Community and the Western European Union, 1950–55', *Journal of European Integration History*, vol. 13, no. 2 (2007), 11–31.

91. *No al militarismo tedesco! No al trattato capestro della CED!* (Rome: Comitato Nazionale della Pace, 1953). No author was named, but the text echoes phrases and metaphors used by Emilio Sereni in other publications.

92. This is a personal reflection that I was determined to insert somewhere because I think it is true. It is based, above all, on reading the minutes of the PCI's steering committee from 1944 to 1954. Guiso, *La Colomba e la spada*, talks of the 'organization of enthusiasm', 157. If one substitutes 'indignation' for enthusiasm, this phrase conveys exactly what I want to express.

93. See Koestler's contributions to the Congress of Cultural Freedom held in Berlin in June 1950, reprinted as 'The Right to Say No', in Koestler, *The Trail of the Dinosaur and Other Essays* (London: Collins, 1955), 179–203.

94. Terracini, in *Intervista sul comunismo difficile*, ed. Arturo Gismondi (Rome-Bari: Laterza, 1978), 153.

95. When the Soviet leader Nikita Khrushchev visited Belgrade in May 1955, and thus ended Tito's excommunication from the communist world, Terracini's reaction, during a meeting of the PCI steering committee, was to say, 'at last we can say what we think'.

96. 'Per lo studio della storia del PC (b) della URSS', APC, meeting of the *Direzione* (10 December 1948). Quotes from pp. 3–4.

97. Ibid., 6.

98. A point made by Mauro Boarelli, *La fabbrica del passato. Autobiografie di militanti comunisti (1945–1956)* (Milan: Feltrinelli, 2007), 62. This brilliant book is based upon the experience of the alumni of the party school in Bologna (there were also schools in Rome and Milan).

99. Paolo Robotti, *Nell'Unione sovietica si vive così* (Roma: Edizione di cultura sociale, 1950).

100. Paolo Spriano, 'L'amore per il padre', in *1946–1956. Le passioni di un decennio* (Rome: l'Unità, 1992), 149.

101. 'A Giuseppe Stalin. Doni da tutta l'Italia', *Vie nuove* (1 January 1950).

102. This is a reference to Paul Hollander, *Political Pilgrims: Western Intellectuals in Search of the Good Society* (New York: Oxford University Press, 1981), which is a broad survey of how Western writers and scholars were taken in by communist regimes when they visited Moscow, Beijing, Havana, or Hanoi.

103. Maria Antonietta Macciocchi, 'I bimbi di Mosca inneggiano a papà Stalin sulla Piazza Rossa', *Vie nuove* (1 January 1950).

104. Quotations from Nello Ajello, *Intellettuali e PCI 1944/58* (Rome: Laterza, 2018, 8th imprint), 251–6.

105. Ignazio Silone, 'Emergency Exit', in *The God that Failed: A Confession*, ed. Richard Crossman (New York: Harper and Brothers, 1949). The other five writers were Arthur Koestler, Richard Wright, André Gide, Louis Fischer, and Stephen Spender. See Palmiro Togliatti, 'I sei che sono falliti', *Rinascita*, VII (May 1950). See also Stanislao Pugliese, *Bitter Spring: A Life of Ignazio Silone* (New York: Farrar, Straus and Giroux, 2009), 199–212, for Silone's clashes with Togliatti and his role in the Congress for Cultural Freedom.

106. The distinguished biologist Luigi Silvestri, quoted in Ajello, *Intellettuali e PCI*, 266–7.

107. V. Lazarev, 'Contro la falsificazione della storia della cultura rinascimentale', *Rassegna sovietica*, 3 (June 1952), 8–25. Lazarev, who was not provided with a biography, was presumably Viktor Nickitich Lazarev, then professor of art history at Moscow University. Giuseppe Toffanin was a professor at the University of Naples, and the author,

among many other books, of *Storia dell'Umanesimo*, 3 vols. (Bologna: Zanichelli, 1942), which was the cause of Lazarev's spleen.

108. See, as an illustration, *Il Processo Kostov* (Rome: Edizioni di Cultura Sociale, 1950), *Il Processo Rajk* (Roma: UESISA, 1950), *Il Processo di Tirana* (Rome: Edizioni di Cultura Sociale, 1950).

109. Ottavio Pastore, preface to *Il Processo Kostov*, 25.

110. *Il Processo Rajk*, 4.

111. Ibid., 6.

112. Ibid., 15.

113. Renato Mieli, *Deserto rosso. Un decennio da comunista* (Bologna: Il Mulino, 1996), 73. Mieli was a research scientist turned political journalist. He was the PCI's foremost analyst of foreign affairs in this period. He was also the father of Paolo Mieli, one of contemporary Italy's most prominent intellectuals and editor of the *Corriere della Sera* 1992–7 and 2004–9.

114. This description of Togliatti's journey to Russia draws closely upon Giorgio Bocca, *Togliatti* (Milan: Feltrinelli, 2014), 459–60. It is based on the personal recollections of Iotti and Amadesi.

115. Ibid., 460.

116. Ibid., 461.

117. Ibid., 462.

118. Quotations from: Top secret letter of P. Togliatti to I. V. Stalin (4 January 1951), reprinted in Elena Aga-Rossi and Victor Zaslavsky, *Togliatti e Stalin. Il PCI e la politica estera staliniana negli archivi di Mosca* (Bologna: Il Mulino, 2007, 2nd ed.), 324–7, and elsewhere.

119. Silvio Pons, *I comunisti italiani e gli altri. Visioni e legami internazionali nel mondo del Novecento* (Turin: Einaudi, 2021), 133.

120. Bocca, *Togliatti*, 463, reporting Longo's recollections.

121. Miriam Mafai, *L'uomo che sognava la lotta armata. La storia di Pietro Secchia* (Milan: Rizzoli, 1984), 89.

122. Pons, *I comunisti italiani e gli altri*, 134.

123. Ibid., 135.

124. Mafai, *L'uomo che sognava*, 82 and 84.

125. 'La medaglia d'oro a Aldo Cucchi', *Vie nuove* (21 May 1950). Cucchi was pictured on the front cover with Togliatti and Longo.

126. 'Due traditori', *l'Unità* (30 January 1951); Luigi Longo, 'Rigurgiti di provocazione', *l'Unità* (1 February 1951).

127. 'Dichiarazioni di Togliatti all'*Unità* sul soggiorno in Urss e sulla situazione italiana', *l'Unità* (28 February 1951).

128. Franca Schiavetta, quoted in P. Buchignani, 'Una purga staliniana nell'Italia degli anni 50. La reazione del PCI all'eresia "Magnacucchi"', *Nuova Rivista Storica*, vol. 103, no. 1 (2019), 227. Cucchi and Magnani explained their choice in an article entitled 'Perché entrammo nel PCI e perché ne siamo usciti', *Risorgimento Socialista*, no. 1 (16 June 1951).

129. Elena Aga Rossi in Mark Gilbert, 'Against the Current: An Interview with Elena Aga Rossi', *Journal of Modern Italian Studies*, vol. 27, no. 4 (2022), 499.

130. Bocca, *Togliatti*, 465. The interview with Amendola is in *L'Espresso* (23 March 1970).

131. Ibid., 466–7.

132. Mafai, *L'uomo che sognava*, 91.

133. Aga Rossi and Zaslavsky, *Togliatti e Stalin*, 289.

134. Artur London, *The Confession* (New York: Morrow, 1970), orig. in French, *L'Aveu* (Paris: Gallimard, 1969). Heda Margolius Kovály, *Under A Cruel Star: A Life in Prague 1941–1968* (Cambridge, MA: Plunkett Lake Press, 1986).

135. Pons, *I comunisti italiani e gli altri*, 135.

136. For the reactions of the two left-wing parties, see 'Tutta l'Italia si è levata contro la guerra. Quattro cittadini uccisi dai servi di Eisenhower', *l'Unità* (19 January 1951).

137. Pons, *I comunisti e gli altri*, 136.

138. Ibid., 137.

139. For the distinction between Bolsheviks and Mensheviks, see Orlando Figes, *The Story of Russia* (London: Bloomsbury, 2022), 170.

10. PRECARIOUS CENTRE

1. See Paolo Pombeni, *Giuseppe Dossetti. L'avventura politica di un riformatore cristiano* (Bologna: Il Mulino, 2013), 69.

2. Amintore Fanfani, *Diari*, vol. II (1949–1955) (Soveria Mannelli: Rubbettino/Senato della Repubblica, 2011), 104. Entry for 1 January 1950.

3. Indro Montanelli and Mario Cervi, *L'Italia del Miracolo. 14 luglio 1948–19 agosto 1954* (Milan: Rizzoli, 2020), 61.

4. In all, 350,000 homes were built thanks to Fanfani's plan, the success of which led to the scheme's expansion in 1955. See Fanfani, *Diari*, vol. II, 48–9 (entry 13 January 1949), and 74 (entry for 15 October 1949).

5. Ibid., 177–80 (entry for 10 January 1950) for the meeting with De Gasperi. See also Amintore Fanfani, 'La miseria non è tutta nel Sud', *Oggi* (20 April 1950), for a broader statement of his ideas. Fanfani was brought back into the government as minister of agriculture in July 1951.

6. It is often impossible to reconstruct the rights and wrongs of the many clashes between protesters and the police in Italy in 1949–50, but in the case of Modena it seems clear that the police units came to the factory looking for trouble and that they opened fire without cause.

7. Pietro Nenni, *Tempo di Guerra Fredda. Diari 1943–56* (Milano: SugarCo 1982), 501. Entry for 11 January 1950.

8. Jonathan Dunnage, 'Inhibiting Democracy in Post-War Italy: The Police Forces, 1943–1948', *Italian Studies*, vol. 51, no. 1 (1996), 167–80.

9. Enzo Fimiani, 'Occupying Spaces, Regulating Bodies: A Cultural History of the Celere and Mobilizing Police Units in the Italian Republic', *Journal of Modern Italian Studies*, vol. 27, no. 2 (2022), 207.

10. The statistics are from Giorgio Candeloro, *Storia dell'Italia moderna. Vol. XI. La fondazione della Repubblica e la ricostruzione. 1945–1950* (Milan: Universale Economica Feltrinelli, 2015), 192.

11. This is a synthesis of Basso's essay 'Il colpo di stato di De Gasperi', collected in Basso, *Fascismo e Democrazia cristiana. Due regimi del capitalismo italiano* (Milan: Mazzotta Editore, 1975), 163–70. It was originally published in a pamphlet of the same name in 1953.

12. R. Zangheri, 'Le celere considerate come squadrismo', *Rinascita*, vol. VI, no. 4 (1949), 149–51.

13. Andrea Guiso, *La Colomba e la spada. 'Lotta per pace' e antiamericanismo nella politica del partito comunista italiano (1949–1954)* (Soveria Mannelli: Rubbettino, 2006), 91.

14. Giorgio Napolitano, *Dal PCI al socialismo europeo. Un'autobiografia politica* (Bari-Rome: Laterza, 2006), 33.

15. For the role of perceptions, see Guiso, *La Colomba e la spada*, 92–3.

16. Togliatti, cited in ibid., 96.

17. Ibid., 97.

18. See David Caute, *The Great Fear: The Anti-Communist Purge under Truman and Eisenhower* (New York: Touchstone, 1979), for an exceptional account of these years.

19. SENSAZIONALE! I QUARANTA SPIETATI DEL COMUNISMO ITALIANO! (Rome: PCI, 1949), quotations on pp. 2 and 16.

20. 'De Gasperi a Matera – toccanti episodi della visita del Presidente ai "sassi", orridi tuguri nei quali vive il 60 percento della popolazione', *La Stampa* (24 July 1950).

21. A monument to De Gasperi, designed by Othmar Winkler, an artist from the Trentino, is placed at the entrance to the housing estate.

22. Candeloro, *Storia dell'Italia moderna*, 208–9.

23. This paragraph synthesizes a superb article: Emanuele Bernardi, 'Alcide De Gasperi tra riforma agraria e guerra fredda (1946–1950)', *Ventunesimo Secolo*, vol. 3, no. 5, 71–97.

24. Cited in ibid., 89.

25. Nenni, *Tempo di Guerra Fredda*, 520. Entry for 22 March 1952.

26. Bruno Caprettini, Lorenzo Casaburi, and Miriam Venturini, 'Il clientelismo nato dalla riforma agraria', *lavoce.info* (2 May 2022).

27. Amadeo Lepore, 'Cassa per il Mezzogiorno e politica per lo sviluppo', in *Istituzioni ed Economia*, ed. Andrea Leonardi (Bari: Cacucci, 2011), 117.

28. For the organizational structure of the Cassa, see Leandra D'Antone, 'L'interesse straordinario per il Mezzogiorno (1943–1960)', *Meridiana*, 24 (1995), 17–64.

29. Lepore, 'Cassa per il Mezzogiorno', 122.

30. Christopher Duggan. 'Italy in the Cold War Years and the Legacy of Fascism', in *Italy in the Cold War: Politics, Culture and Society, 1948–58*, ed. Christopher Duggan and Christopher Wagstaff (Oxford: Berg Publishers, 1995), 15.

31. https://archivio.camera.it/inventari/profilo/commissione-sulla-miseria-italia-e-sui-mezzi-combatterla-1951-1954

32. For the composition of the committee, see https://storia.camera.it/organi/commissione-parlamentare-d-inchiesta-sulla-miseria-italia-e-sui-mezzi-combatterla-01#nav

33. All statistics from *Inchiesta sulla miseria in Italia (1951–52). Materiali della Commissione parlamentare*, ed. Paolo Braghin (Turin: Einaudi, 1978), 14–35. This book is a useful compilation of the Commission's findings: the actual documentation, stored in the *Archivio dello Stato* runs to thousands of pages.

34. Ibid., 24–5.

35. Ibid., 43 and 47.

36. Ibid., 67.

37. Ibid., 77–8.

38. Ibid., 109.

39. Giuseppe Parlato, 'Romualdi, Giuseppe Nettuno', in *Dizionario Biografico degli Italiani*. https://www.treccani.it/enciclopedia/giuseppe-nettuno-romualdi_%28Dizionario-Biografico%29

40. See Mair Michelis, 'Mussolini's Unofficial Mouthpiece: Telesio Interlandi – *Il Tevere* and the Evolution of Mussolini's Antisemitism',

Journal of Modern Italian Studies, vol. 3, no. 3 (1998), 217–40, for the milieu in which Almirante cut his journalistic teeth.

41. Sandro Setta, 'De Marsanich, Augusto', in *Dizionario Biografico degli Italiani*. https://www.treccani.it/enciclopedia/augusto-de-marsanich_% 28Dizionario-Biografico%29

42. An interesting introduction to Evola's life and ideas is a collection of writings and interviews, *Autobiografia spirituale*, ed. Andrea Scarabelli (Roma: Edizioni Mediterranee, 2019).

43. Carlo Maria Lomartire, *O Comandante. Vita di Achille Lauro* (Milan: Mondadori, 2009), 32.

44. Montanelli and Cervi, *L'Italia del Miracolo* (Milano: Rizzoli, 2020), 128.

45. This paragraph is a synthesis of Lomartire, *O Comandante*, ch. IV passim, 45–58.

46. Nello Ajello, 'E la Borboni uscì in pigiama', *La Repubblica* (24 July 1993).

47. Lomartire, *O Comandante*, 80.

48. See 'Colloquio con Alcide De Gasperi su mandato di sua eccellenza Tardini a nome del Santo Padre', in Andrea Riccardi, *Pio XII e Alcide De Gasperi. Una storia segreta* (Bari-Rome: Laterza, 2003), 71–9 for quotations.

49. Agostino Giovagnoli, *Il Partito italiano. La Democrazia cristiana dal 1942 al 1994* (Bari-Rome: Laterza, 1996), 59.

50. Amintore Fanfani, *Diari*, vol. II, 286 (entry for 17 April 1952). Gedda, in his turn, regarded De Gasperi as a 'dictator' and had no faith in the DC's ability to resist communism.

51. Montanelli and Cervi, *L'Italia del Miracolo*, 124.

52. Alcide De Gasperi, *Polemiche della campagna per le elezioni amministrative 1952* (Rome: Edizione 'Il Popolo', 1952), 57–8. 'Gun-toting bravos' is an attempt to convey the derision implicit in De Gasperi's word, 'moschettieri'.

53. Ibid., 62.

54. Quotations from ibid., 6–8. The *Oggi* article acted as an introduction to the pamphlet.

55. Lomartire, *O Comandante*, 92.

56. Ibid., 87.

57. Rosario Forlenza, 'Politics, Power, and Soccer in Post-War Italy: The Case of Naples', in *Football and the Boundaries of History*, eds. Brenda Elsey and Stanislao G. Pugliese (New York: Hofstra University/Palgrave, 2017), 255.

58. Ibid., 253.

59. Lomartire, *O Comandante*, 92.
60. Father Lombardi, the 'microphone of God', allegedly used this expression with De Gasperi's wife, Francesca, in a bid to enlist her in the cause of persuading her husband.
61. Gonella's comments at the steering committee of the DC (30 May 1952), ILS, Fondo Bartolotta (1952), vol. VIII, 985–92.
62. *MSI* (Roma: SPES, August 1952?). ILS Pamphlet Collection, Cass. 1., Fasc. 4., sottofasc., 34. Doc. 1.
63. Law 645 of 1952. Article 1. My translation.
64. Davide Conti, *L'anima nera della repubblica. Storia del MSI* (Bari-Rome: Laterza, 2013), 11.
65. All quotations from Movimento Sociale Italiano, *Programma per le elezioni politiche*, 1953.
66. 'Lo stato forte e la libertà. Un colloquio con De Gasperi', *Il Messaggero* (8 July 1952). Also in Alcide De Gasperi, *Scritti e discorsi politici, vol. 4: La stabilizzazione della repubblica 1948–1954*, eds. S. Lorenzini and B. Taverni (Bologna: Il Mulino, 2009), 1,686–91.
67. De Gasperi was elected by a landslide as member of the Vienna parliament for the valleys of north-east Trentino on 20 June 1911, obtaining 3,116 out of 4,275 votes. He also represented the area in the Tyrolean Diet in Innsbruck.
68. ILS, Fondo Bartolotta (1952), vol. VIII, 1,367–8, for Nenni's letter, and 1,381 for De Gasperi's reply.
69. Riccardi, *Pio XII e Alcide De Gasperi*, 81–5.
70. In the process, especially since the 1990s, they have stumbled upon a fair number of Boojums.
71. See a rebuking letter that he wrote to Don Sturzo on 24 August 1952 criticizing him for having attacked the notion of a 'majority prize' in print. The letter defends the majority prize concept with vehemence from Don Sturzo's objections. De Gasperi concludes by apologizing if 'one or two harsh words' had escaped him, but the apology was perfunctory. The letter is in ILS, Fondo Bartolotta (1952), vol. XIII, 1, 399–1,404, and has been reprinted many times.
72. The town's primary school is named after her.
73. Alas, relations between the German-speaking community and the Italian majority soon degenerated, leading in 1956 to the German minority walking out of the regional assembly with the slogan *Los von Trient!* The region, over time, in part to placate ethnic and linguistic divisions, became much laxer in its control of public spending and clientelist practices. *Via mundi.*

74. See Giorgio Tupini, *De Gasperi. Una testimonianza* (Bologna: Il Mulino, 1992), 177–81, for this point.

75. For background to the *Vital Center*, see Arthur M. Schlesinger Jnr., *A Life in the Twentieth Century: Innocent Beginnings, 1917–50* (New York: Houghton Mifflin, 2000), ch. 25 passim, and Richard Aldous, *Schlesinger: The Imperial Historian* (New York: W. W. Norton, 2017), 124–40.

76. The Predazzo speech is collected in many places. It was first published in the DC weekly magazine *Libertas*, no. 30 (18 September 1952), 7–10. It was reprinted as 'Combattiamo per essere liberi', in Alcide De Gasperi, *Discorsi politici* (Rome: Edizioni Cinque Lune, 1956), ed. Tommaso Bozza, 63–85. All quotations are from this latter source.

77. Amintore Fanfani reports De Gasperi saying that it was his 'constant life's work' to detach the PSI from the PCI. Fanfani, *Diari*, vol. II, 330. Entry for 2 January 1953.

78. Pietro Nenni, *Tempo di Guerra Fredda*, 537. Entry for 17 July 1952. 'Smiling beneath his moustaches' is a literal translation of the Italian 'ridere sotto i baffi', which means to 'smirk'. A literal translation seemed appropriate in this case.

11. THE CENTRE HOLDS

1. Minutes of the DC Parliamentary Group in the Chamber of Deputies (9 October 1952), *Atti e documenti della Democrazia Cristiana 1943–1967* (Roma: Edizioni Cinque Lune, 1967), 550.

2. I am following Gonella's argument in ibid., 551.

3. Ibid., 552.

4. Many prominent members of the DC had been ardent defenders of PR in 1923, as the PCI pointed out: *Vie nuove*, 'Come fu varata la legge Acerbo' (21 December 1953).

5. Ibid., 556.

6. 'Dichiarazione dei quattro partiti democratici (DC–PSDI–PLI–PRI) sulla riforma della legge elettorale' (15 November 1952), *Atti e documenti della Democrazia Cristiana 1943–1967*, 557–8. I have summarized rather than translated the three key points of the agreement.

7. De Gasperi briefly contemplated a 'little reform' to the constitution to harmonize the terms of the Senate and Chamber of Deputies, but concluded that there was not enough time before the election. Incidentally, the fact that the law was not extended to the Senate makes nonsense of the claim, common at the time, and still repeated in the historiography,

that the 'Swindle Law' was designed to enable the DC to change the constitution. It was necessary to have a two-thirds majority in *both* chambers to do that.

8. Pietro Nenni, *Tempo di guerra fredda. Diari 1943–1956* (Milano: SugarCo, 1981), 545–7, for Nenni's description of his conversation with De Gasperi.

9. Ibid., 554. Entry for 27 November 1952.

10. Ibid., 568. Entry for 13 March, 1953.

11. Sandro Pertini, Senate of the Republic (10 March 1953), 39,355.

12. Chantal Mouffe, 'Deliberative Democracy or Agonistic Pluralism?', in *Social Research*, vol. 66, no. 3 (Fall 1999), 745–78. Mouffe's point is that deliberative concepts of democracy underestimate how often politics is about irreconcilables, not finding compromise or debating merits.

13. See Giulio Andreotti, *1953. Fu legge truffa?* (Milan: Rizzoli, 2007), 52. Entry for 23 March 1953 for a background account.

14. Cited in Maria Serena Piretti, *Le elezioni politiche in Italia dal 1848 a oggi* (Bari-Rome: Laterza, 1995), 376. See also Andreotti, *1953*, 56. Entry for 25 March 1953.

15. Senate of the Republic (26 March 1953), 40,781.

16. Quotations from Andreotti, *1953*, 57. Entry for 26 March 1953.

17. Attilio Piccioni, who was now deputy prime minister, quoted in minutes of the Consiglio dei Ministri, ILS, Fondo Bartolotta (1953), vol. XIII, 1920–23.

18. His decision set a precedent. In 1958, Giovanni Gronchi, who replaced Einaudi as president in 1955, also dissolved both Chambers simultaneously. The constitution was amended in 1962 to make the two legislatures' terms coincide.

19. Alcide De Gasperi, radio broadcast (7 June 1953), ILS, Fondo Bartolotta (1953), vol. XIV (1939).

20. https://patrimonio.archivioluce.com/luce-web/detail/IL5000025516/2/la-morte-stalin.html

21. Paolo Spriano, *1946–1956. Le passioni di un decennio* (Roma: l'Unità, 1992), 153.

22. 'Il cordoglio unanime del popolo italiano', *Rinascita*, vol. X, no. 2 (February 1953), 69.

23. Giuseppe Petronio, 'Stalin: Un Costruttore', *Mondo Operaio*, vol. VI, no. 6 (21 March 1953).

24. Luigi Longo, 'Gloria a Stalin!', *Rinascita*, vol. X no. 2 (February 1953), 65–9.

25. Renato Mieli, 'La politica di pace dell'Unione Sovietica nella concezione e nell'azione di Stalin', ibid., 78–87, and 'La necessità dell'autocritica dimostrata da Stalin', 87–8.

26. Mieli concluded his article 'La politica di pace . . .' with a discussion of Malenkov's declaration.

27. For Churchill's démarche, see John Young, 'Churchill and East-West Détente', *Transactions of the Royal Historical Society*, 11 (2001), 381–4. See also Anthony Glees, 'Churchill's Last Gambit', *Encounter*, 64 (April 1985), 27–35.

28. I have reconstructed De Gasperi's campaign from the files in ILS, Fondo Bartolotta (1953), vols. XV and XVI.

29. De Gasperi, interview with *Il Tempo* (4 June 1953), in ILS, Fondo Bartolotta (1953), vol. XVII (4 June), 2,264.

30. ILS, Fondo Bartolotta (1953), vol. XVI (30 May), 2,236–7.

31. Andreotti, *1953*, 88.

32. Speech in Trento. See ILS, Fondo Bartolotta (1953), vol. XVI (25 May), 2,188ff.

33. *5 anni di Governo Togliatti.* (DC-SPES, 1953). ILS, collection of pamphlets and leaflets, Cassetto 1, Fasc. 5, Sottofasc. 55. The reason Di Vittorio was cast as an anti-revolutionary saboteur was that he had been rebuked by the PCI for supporting the DC's land reforms and the Cassa per il Mezzogiorno.

34. On antisemitism in the Soviet bloc, see *Il Comunismo contro gli ebrei.* (DC-SPES, 1953). ILS. Cassetto 1, Fasc. 5, Sottofasc. 69, doc. 1. This pamphlet, published just before Stalin's death, was a well-informed account of Soviet policy towards Jews in Russia and the satellite states since the creation of the Cominform.

35. See 'Cosa vogliono', poster collection of the Istituto Gramsci Emilia-Romagna.

36. Fanfani, *Diari*, 355. Entry for 5 June 1953.

37. ILS, Fondo Bartolotta (1953), vol XVI (26 May), for a summary of the meeting with Boothe Luce.

38. Arnaldo Cortesi, 'Mrs Luce Hints Aid to Italy Will Stop If Extremists Win', *New York Times* (29 May 1953), contains extracts from the speech. For Luce's tenure as ambassador see Mario Del Pero, 'American Pressures and their Containment in Italy during the Ambassadorship of Clare Boothe Luce, 1953–1956', *Diplomatic History*, vol. 28, no. 3 (June 2004), 407–39. Del Pero discusses the Milan speech and its reception on pp. 417–18.

39. Ibid. (29 May), 2,219.

40. Togliatti's remarks in APC, meeting of the *Direzione* (12 February 1953), 1–4.
41. The relationship between the PCI and the development of popular culture in Italy deserves a chapter to itself. On 'Miss Vie nuove', see Stephen Gundle, 'Feminine Beauty, National Identity, and Political Conflict in Post-War Italy, 1945–1954', *Contemporary European History*, vol. 8, no. 3 (1999), 359–78. Gundle's classic work *Between Hollywood and Moscow: The Italian Communists and the Challenge of Mass Culture, 1943–1991* (Durham, NC: Duke University Press, 2000), is a must-read for the cultural history of the PCI.
42. Palmiro Togliatti, 'Alpinismo', *Vie nuove* (31 August 1952).
43. The four-party pact was joined by two autonomist parties, the South Tyrol People's Party and the Sardinian Action Party.
44. Pietro Calamandrei, 'La resistenza ha resistito', *Il Ponte*, vol. IX, no. 6 (1953), 733. Cited in Paolo Spriano, *1946–1956. Le passioni di un decennio* (Rome: l'Unità, 1992), 180.
45. Indro Montanelli and Mario Cervi, *L'Italia del miracolo* (Milan: Rizzoli BUR, 2018), 167.
46. Andreotti, *1953*, 92. Entry for 10 June 1953.
47. See Togliatti's remarks in APC, meeting of the *Direzione* (17–18 June 1953). He warned that the DC also had 'tremendous powers of recovery'.
48. The ambassador (Luce) to the Department of State, FRUS, 1952–1954, Western Europe and Canada, vol. VI, Part 2, Doc. 743 (12 June 1953).
49. Togliatti's comments in APC, meeting of the *Direzione* (17–18 June 1953).
50. Andreotti, *1953*, 98. Entry for 16 June 1953. De Gasperi regarded Saragat's silence as a personal discourtesy and told him so to his face.
51. Pietro Nenni, 'Via Libera', *Mondo operaio* (27 June 1953).
52. During the count, political parties opposed to the majority prize insisted on a literal interpretation of the law, even when the voters' intentions were clear. A more flexible approach would have triggered the majority prize. I'm grateful to Tommaso Milani for pointing this out to me.
53. Paolo Pombeni, *L'apertura. L'Italia e il centrosinistra 1953–1963* (Bologna: Il Mulino, 2022), 25.
54. Andreotti, *1953*, 92. Entry for 10 June 1953.
55. Churchill had the debilitating stroke that eventually led to his retirement from office the night after De Gasperi's dinner with the cabinet.

56. Interview with *Il Messaggero* (10 June 1953), in ILS, Fondo Bartolotta (1953), vol. XVII, 2,302–4.

57. Maria Romana Catti De Gasperi, *De Gasperi. Uomo Solo* (Milan: Mondadori, 1964), 360.

58. Nenni, *Tempo di Guerra Fredda*, 584–5. Entry for 6 July 1953.

59. Text of the press conference given by Nenni and Morandi after their meeting with De Gasperi. ILS, Fondo Bartolotta (1953), vol. XVIII (6 July), 2,410.

60. See Catti De Gasperi, *De Gasperi*, 361–2.

61. See Andreotti, *1953*, 127–30, with the quotation about democracy at 129.

62. Sergey Radchenko, *To Run the World: The Kremlin's Cold War Bid for Global Power* (Cambridge University Press, 2024), 148. I am grateful to my colleague for allowing me to read a chapter in manuscript.

63. See, for instance, 'Si moltiplicano a Berlino democratica le dichiarazioni di fiducia nel governo', *Avanti!* (21 June 1953), and 'Paracadutisti e carichi d'armi catturati nella Germania Est. Il Piano "X" dei provocatori', *Avanti!* (23 June 1953). Also, 'Totalmente fallita a Berlino la provocazione americana. Ufficiali degli Stati Uniti in divisa hanno capeggiato i dimostranti', *l'Unità* (19 June 1953), 'Che cosa è accaduto a Berlino', *l'Unità* (19 June 1953), and 'La Provocazione a Berlino Est', *l'Unità* (20 June 1953).

64. See 'I Rosenberg Assassinati!', *Avanti!* (20 June 1951), and 'La paura della pace ha armato la mano al fascismo americano. Hanno assassinato i Rosenberg!', *l'Unità* (20 June 1953).

65. The classic scholarly study of the case is Ronald Radosh and Joyce Milton, *The Rosenberg File: The Search for Truth* (New York: Henry Holt, 1983), which concluded that Julius Rosenberg was indeed a Soviet spy and that his wife knew it and may have helped him.

66. Del Pero, 'American Pressures and their Containment', 438.

67. Leopoldo Nuti, 'The United States, Italy, and the Opening to the Left', *Journal of Cold War Studies*, 3 (Summer 2002), 39.

68. Beria was 'liquidated' without a show trial in December 1953.

69. See the front page of *l'Unità* (12 July 1953), with the giant headline 'Il popolo approva le decisioni del Partito e afferma la forza incrollabile della Democrazia Sovietica', and accompanied by a leading article, 'I guerrafondai si illudano!' *Avanti!*'s headline on the same day was 'Unanime approvazione nell'Urss per le sanzioni prese contro Beria'. It

was accompanied by an article by Nenni, 'La grande occasione', asserting that Soviet foreign policy would be unchanged.

70. Pietro Secchia, 'Insegnamenti del caso Beria', *Rinascita*, vol. X, no. 7 (July 1953), 393–7.

71. All comments from APC, meeting of the *Direzione* (17 July 1953), 1–7.

72. Emilio Sereni, ibid., 8.

73. Pombeni, *L'apertura*, 25.

74. 'Dichiarazione del Segretario Politico della DC. On. Gonella' (28 July 1953), in *Atti e documenti della Democrazia cristiana, 1943–1967*, 603.

75. Nenni (with the support of Togliatti) previously offered to abstain in support of Piccioni if the Italian government proclaimed an amnesty for persons arrested during protests in the previous five years, and the abrogation of the electoral law, but this move provoked a revolt by De Gasperi and others within the DC. See Spencer M. Di Scala, *Renewing Italian Socialism: Nenni to Craxi* (New York: Oxford University Press, 1988), 96.

76. Montanelli and Cervi, *L'Italia del miracolo*, 183.

77. Giorgio Galli, *Fanfani* (Milan: Feltrinelli, 1975), 55. The twenty-two blank ballots were probably cast by party leaders who thought De Gasperi would favour Fanfani.

78. Guido Formigoni, *Storia d'Italia nella guerra fredda (1943–78)* (Bologna: Il Mulino, 2016), 211.

79. James Reston, 'U.S. to Bid Italy Curb Reds', *New York Times* (13 January 1954). For a discussion, see Del Pero, 'American Pressures and Their Containment', 425–6.

80. Alcide De Gasperi, 'Non bisogna esagerare', *Il Popolo* (22 January 1954); reprinted in *La Discussione* (24 January 1954).

81. Alcide De Gasperi, 'Noi e il comunismo in Italia', *Il Popolo* (25 February 1954; reprinted in *La Discussione* (28 February 1954).

82. See Mario Del Pero, 'Anticomunismo d'assalto. Lettere di Indro Montanelli all'ambasciatrice in Italia Clare Boothe Luce', *Italia Contemporanea*, 212 (September 1998), 633–46, and Formigoni, *Storia d'Italia nella guerra fredda*, 177.

83. 'Scelba-Saragat', Di Scala, *Renewing Italian Socialism*, 98.

84. 'US Policy Toward Italy', NSC 5411/2. In FRUS, 1952–1954, Western Europe and Canada, vol. VI, Part 2, doc. 776 (15 April 1954).

85. Alcide De Gasperi, 'Nella Lotta per la Democrazia', in De Gasperi, *Discorsi Politici*, ed. Tommaso Bozza (Rome: Cinque Lune, 1956), 302–3.

86. Quotations are from Alcide De Gasperi, 'Nella Lotta per la Democrazia', in De Gasperi, *Discorsi Politici*, ed. Bozza, 271–316.

87. The classic study in English is Judith Chubb, *Patronage, Power, and Poverty in Southern Italy: A Tale of Two Cities* (Cambridge: Cambridge University Press, 1982). The two cities are Naples and Palermo.

88. For a contrary view on the PCI and 1956, which puts emphasis on domestic developments, see the very interesting article by Alessandro Iandolo, 'Unforgettable 1956? The PCI and the Crisis of Communism in Italy', *Contemporary European History*, vol. 23, no. 2 (2014), 259–82.

89. Di Scala, *Renewing Italian Socialism*, 108.

90. Nuti, 'The United States, Italy, and the Opening to the Left', 42–3. Fanfani's views on international affairs can be found in a collection of speeches, *Autunno 1956. La Democrazia Cristiana e i problemi internazionali* (Rome: Edizioni Cinque Lune, 1956).

91. Umberto Gentiloni Silveri, *Storia dell'Italia contemporanea 1943–2019* (Bologna: Il Mulino, 2019), 67.

92. Amintore Fanfani, *Anni difficili ma non sterili* (Bologna: Cappelli, 1958). Cement, motorways, pictures of high-rise flats and statistics abound.

93. Rosario Forlenza, *On the Edge of Democracy: Italy, 1943–48* (Oxford: Oxford University Press, 2018), 13.

94. Ibid., 9.

12. A REALIST AND A DEMOCRAT

1. Maria Romana Catti De Gasperi, *De Gasperi. Uomo solo* (Milan: Mondadori, 1964), 408.

2. Ibid., 417.

3. Ibid., 410.

4. Ibid., 411.

5. The text is in the digital collection of De Gasperi's extant letters, Fondazione Alcide De Gasperi, Trento: https://epistolariodegasperi.it/#/archivio_digitale/lettera?id=e2d2d53e-6514-4b2e-bd60-19e73fc34273

6. Catti De Gasperi, *De Gasperi*, 418.

7. There was one last problem with Pius XII over the inscription on the tomb, which was carved by the sculptor Giacomo Manzù. De Gasperi had wanted the words 'Ut domine superatis pacis inimicis secura tibi serviat christiana libertas', i.e. 'Now that, O Lord, the enemies of peace

are defeated, without hesitation I shall serve Christian freedom for You.' This obvious reference to the DC in the final words ('libertas' was the party slogan) led Pius to substitute a blander formulation: 'Ei qui pacem patriam quedilexit lux requietis aeternae affulgeat', i.e. 'Upon he who loved peace and country, let eternal light shine.' I owe this information to Marco Odorizzi, the president of the Fondazione Trentina Alcide De Gasperi. The story is backed up by the fact that De Gasperi's choice of words was found in Manzù's papers.

8. For a visual representation of these events, see https://patrimonio. archivioluce.com/luce-web/detail/IL5000033802/2/l-italia-saluta-de-gasperi.html

9. Igino Giordani, *De Gasperi. Il Ricostruttore* (Rome: Edizioni Cinque Lune, 1955).

10. *Il Monumento a De Gasperi dello scultore Antonio Berti* (Rome: Collana di Arte Contemporanea, 1956), 14.

11. The local townsfolk described the monument as the 'biggest suppository in Italy'. Or so my mother-in-law tells me.

12. See *Il Popolo* (14–15 October 1956) for an account of the festivities and speeches.

13. *Processo a De Gasperi*, ed. Giovanni di Capua (Rome: Edizioni EDE, 1976).

14. Palmiro Togliatti, *De Gasperi Il Restauratore*, ed. Fabio Silvestri (Rome: Alberto Gaffi Editore, 2004), 130. This book is a reprint, in book form, of the original articles.

15. Quotations from Mario G. Rossi, 'Una democrazia a rischio. Politica e conflitto sociale negli anni della guerra fredda', in *Storia dell'Italia Repubblicana, vol. 1., La Costruzione della democrazia*, ed. Francesco Barbagallo (Turin: Einaudi, 1994), 917 and 969.

16. Denis Mack Smith, *Modern Italy: A Political History* (New Haven, CT: Yale University Press, 1997), 425.

17. Paul Ginsborg, *A History of Contemporary Italy: Society and Politics, 1943–1988* (London: Penguin, 1990), 143–4.

18. David Gilmour, *The Pursuit of Italy: A History of a Land, Its Regions and Their Peoples* (London: Penguin, 2012), 341–3 for quotations.

19. A. J. P. Taylor, 'Fiction in History', in *Essays in English History* (London: Pelican, 1976), 14. It is not an accusation that can be fairly levelled at Taylor.

Index